The *Revels*
History of Drama
in English

GENERAL EDITORS
Clifford Leech
& T. W. Craik

The *Revels* History of Drama in English

VOLUME III 1576–1613

J. Leeds Barroll, Alexander Leggatt,
Richard Hosley & Alvin Kernan

Methuen & Co Ltd
London

First published 1975 by Methuen & Co Ltd
11 New Fetter Lane, London EC4P 4EE
© 1975 J. Leeds Barroll, Alexander Leggatt,
Richard Hosley, Alvin Kernan
© Richard Hosley 1975 for the drawings in Part III.
Printed in Great Britain by
Richard Clay (The Chaucer Press), Ltd
Bungay, Suffolk

ISBN (hardbound) 0 416 13040 2

ISBN (paperback) 0 416 81380 1

Distributed in the USA by
HARPER AND ROW PUBLISHERS, INC.
BARNES AND NOBLE IMPORT DIVISION

Contents

List of illustrations   *page* ix

Acknowledgements   xi

Chronological table   xiii

I   **The social and literary context**   J. LEEDS BARROLL   1

1   Drama and the court   3

2   The players and their problems   28

3   The question of censorship   41

4   The audience   47

II   **The companies and actors**   ALEXANDER LEGGATT   95

III   **The playhouses**   RICHARD HOSLEY   119

1	Introduction	121
2	The Swan playhouse (1595)	136
3	The First Globe playhouse (1599)	175
4	The Second Blackfriars playhouse (1596)	197
5	Conclusion	227
IV	**The plays and the playwrights** ALVIN KERNAN	237
	Introduction	239
1	'Who would not admire this our chameleon?': the new theatre of the late sixteenth century	241
(i)	Homo ludens	241
(ii)	*'Our thoughts are ours': Marlowe's* Tamburlaine	250
(iii)	*'Ends none of our own':* The Spanish Tragedy	257
2	From ritual to history: the English history play	262
(i)	*The rituals of order*	262
(ii)	*Killing the king: Shakespeare's* Richard III	265
(iii)	*The* Henriad: *Shakespeare's major history plays*	269
3	'Jack shall have Jill': Elizabethan comedy	300
(i)	*Knight and clown: the two comic views*	300
(ii)	*'The cornucopia of the mind': the plays of John Lyly*	304
4	'Ducdame': Shakespearian comedy to *Twelfth Night*	307
(i)	*The songs of the cuckoo and the owl: the first comedies*	307
(ii)	*From the city to the woods:* A Midsummer Night's Dream	311
(iii)	*The return to the city: the later comedies and* Twelfth Night	319
5	Alchemy and acting: the plays of Ben Jonson	326
6	The entrance to hell: the new tragedy	346
(i)	*The shape of fear*	346
(ii)	*The magician's circle: Marlowe's* Doctor Faustus	347
(iii)	*'A wilderness of tigers':* Titus Andronicus	354

7 'I will not go from Troy': the first phase of
    Shakespearian tragedy   361
(i) *The mind is its own place* : Romeo, Caesar *and* Troilus   361
(ii) *The desire is boundless, and the act a slave to limit* :
     Hamlet   372

8 'Banisht!': the dark world of Jacobean tragedy   384
(i) *The Italian palace*   384
(ii) *Virtue in labour with eternal chaos'* : *the plays of
     Chapman, Marston and Tourneur*   387
(iii) *Short sillables must stand for periods'* : *the plays of
      John Webster*   394

9 The sight of the spider: Shakespeare's major tragedies   404
(i) *The tragic formula*   404
(ii) Othello   407
(iii) King Lear   415
(iv) Macbeth   426

10 'The full stream of the world'   434
(i) Timon of Athens *and* Coriolanus   434
(ii) Antony and Cleopatra   436
(iii) *The late romances*   446
(iv) The Winter's Tale   446

11 The great fair of the world and the ocean island:
    Bartholomew Fair and *The Tempest*   456
(i) *Jonson and Shakespeare*   456
(ii) Bartholomew Fair   458
(iii) The Tempest   465

    Bibliography   475
    Index   509

List of Illustrations

1   William Cecil, Lord Burghley (painting attributed to
Marcus Gheeraerts the Younger)   *facing page*   30

2   Thomas Radcliffe, 3rd Earl of Sussex (artist unknown)   31

3   Edward Clinton, 1st Earl of Lincoln (artist unknown)   62

4   Robert Dudley, Earl of Leicester (artist unknown)   63

5   Richard Burbage (self-portrait)   126

6   Edward Alleyn (artist unknown)   127

7   Richard Tarlton (Harleian MS 3885 fol 19)   158

8a William Kempe (title page of *Kemps Nine Days Wonder*
by William Kempe, 1600)   159

8b The Children of the Chapel (from drawings of Queen
Elizabeth's funeral procession, probably by William
Camden)   159

9a Performance of *Titus Andronicus*, 1594 (drawing by Henry
Peacham, from the Harley Papers)   190

9b A Masquer Lord: a star (design by Inigo Jones for
T. Campion, *The Lords' Masque*, 1613)   190

9c A torchbearer: an oceania (design by Inigo Jones for Ben
Jonson, *The Masque of Blackness*, 1608)   190

10 Oberon's Palace (design by Inigo Jones for Scene II of
   Ben Jonson, *The Masque of Oberon*, 1611)   191
11 The interior of the Swan playhouse (drawing by Arend van
   Buchell, after the lost original by Johannes De Witt
   (*c.* 1596)   222
12a Detail from a drawing by Wenzel Hollar, The West Part of
   Southwark towards Westminster (*c.* 1640) showing the
   Second Globe, the Hope and (very faintly) the Blackfriars   223
12b Detail from the engraving by Wenzel Hollar, A Long
   Bird's-Eye View of London (1647), showing the Second
   Globe (erroneously captioned 'Beere bayting h.'), the Hope
   (erroneously captioned 'The Globe') and the Blackfriars   223
13 John Fletcher (artist unknown) and Francis Beaumont   286
14 Christopher Marlowe (artist unknown)   287
15 William Shakespeare (engraving by Martin Droeshout)   318
16 Ben Jonson (painting after A. Blyenberch)   319
17a The hall screen at Hampton Court Palace (*c.* 1535)   414
17b Design by Robert Smythson for the hall screen at
   Worksop Manor (*c.* 1585)   414
18a The hall screen at the Middle Temple, London (1574)   415
18b The hall screen at the Charterhouse, London (1571)   415
19a Detail from 'The Kermess of St George' by Peter Breughel
   the Elder (*c.* 1560) showing a Flemish booth stage   446
19b Copy of a lost drawing by G. Boonen dated 1594 (in
   Edward van Even, *L'Omgang de Louvain*, 1863) showing a
   booth stage in a market square of Louvain   446
20a Detail from an engraving by R. Booms (1618) showing a
   booth stage in Holland   447
20b Detail from a painting attributed to A. F. van der Meulen
   (*c.* 1660) showing a booth stage in a market square   447

Acknowledgements
& Abbreviations

Acknowledgements

The authors and publishers would like to thank the following for permission to reproduce the illustrations appearing in this book:

The Marquess of Bath for No. 9a
The Bibliothèque Nationale for No. 19b
The Bodleian Library for Nos. 19a and 20a
The British Museum for Nos. 7, 8a and 8b
The Governors of Sutton's Hospital, Charterhouse for No. 18b
The Chatsworth Trust for Nos. 9b, 9c and 10
The Courtauld Institute for Nos. 9a, 9b, 9c, 10 and 13
The Master, Fellows and Scholars of Corpus Christi College, Cambridge, for No. 14
The Drottningholm Theatre Museum for No. 20b
The Governors of Dulwich College, London, for Nos. 5 and 6
The Guildhall Library for No. 12b
The National Portrait Gallery for Nos. 1, 2, 3, 4, 13b, 15 and 16
The Royal Institute of British Architects, London, for No. 17b
The Royal Commission on Historical Monuments for No. 17a
The Royal Library, Stockholm, for the endpapers
Lord Sackville for No. 13a

Richard Southern for all the figures in Part III
The Bibliotheek der Rijksuniversiteit, Utrecht, for No. 11
Mrs Iolo A. Williams for No. 12a

Abbreviations

ES	E. K. Chambers, *The Elizabethan Stage*
MSC	*Malone Society Collections*
MSR	*Malone Society Reprints*
SR	Stationers' Register

Chronological Table

This table draws freely on the relevant volumes in the *Oxford History of English Literature* and on S. Schoenbaum's revision of Alfred Harbage's *Annals of English Drama 975–1700*. For plays, the Schoenbaum–Harbage date is given, with one or two exceptions, even where the present editor feels dubious (as in the dating of some of Marlowe's plays).

The editor is largely responsible for columns 2–7, but is indebted to Professor Alexander Leggatt for help on column 3. Column 8 is wholly the work of Professors F. J. and L.-L. Marker, to whom the editor is sincerely grateful.

It will be understood that the table is highly selective: for example, the plays listed under 'notable plays', though including many that are not generally read, are only those that seem of special interest. Titles of both dramatic and non-dramatic writings have been frequently abbreviated.

Non-dramatic writings are listed under the date of publication, unless otherwise indicated, and plays under their approximate date of first performance (or composition in the case of plays not performed).

A question mark before an entry indicates a doubt about the date; a question mark after an author's name indicates a doubt about authorship.

1	2	3	4
Date	Historical events	Theatrical events	Non-dramatic literary events
1575		Children of Paul's begin (or continue) playing	
1576	Grindal Archbishop of Canterbury; Frobisher's voyage begins; priests from Douai arrive in England	The Theatre built; Children of the Chapel Royal begin playing at First Blackfriars	Gascoigne, *Princely Pleasures of . . . Kenilworth*; *Steel Glass*; Pettie, *The Petite Palace of Pettie his Pleasure*
1577	Drake's voyage round the world begins	The Curtain built	Harvey, *Ciceronianus*; Holinshed, the *first* and *last* volumes of the *Chronicle*
1578			Du Bartas, *Sepmaine*; Lyly, *Euphues, the Anatomy of Wit*; Mercator, *Tabulae Geographicae*; *Mirror for Magistrates* (Blennenhasset's *Second Part*)
1579	Jesuit mission to England organized; Simier visits Elizabeth to discuss her possible marriage with the Duke of Anjou		Fenton, tr. of Guicciardini's *History*; Gosson, *School of Abuse*; North, tr. of Plutarch's *Lives*; Spenser, *Shepherd's Calendar*
1580	Campion and Parsons in England		Belleforest, *Histoires tragiques*; G. Harvey, *Three Proper . . . Letters*; *Two other . . . Letters*; Lyly, *Euphues and his England*; Montaigne, *Essais* I–II; Stow, *Chronicles*
1581	Secret recusant press established in Essex (imprint 'Douai'); Campion executed		Hall, tr. of *Iliad* I–X; Rich, *Farewell to Military Profession*; Studley etc., tr. *Seneca his Ten Tragedies*; Tasso, *Jerusalem Delivered* (rev. ed.); Watson, Latin tr. of Sophocles, *Antigone*

5 *Birth and death dates of non-dramatic writers*	6 *Dates of notable plays*	7 *Birth and death dates of playwrights*	8 *Continental theatrical events*
			Henri III grants patents to Confrérie de la Passion
(?) Peacham b.	Anon, *Common Conditions*	Marston b. Sharpham b.	French parliament expels the Gelosi *commedia dell' arte* troupe; Hegelund's *Susanna*, first published Danish school drama; Hans Sachs d.
Burton b. Purchas b.	Anon, *Titus and Gisippus* [lost]		The Gelosi troupe returns to Paris
W. Harvey b.	Sidney, *The Lady of May*; Whetstone, *Promos and Cassandra*	Gascoigne d.	Robert Garnier's *Antigone*; guest performance of Drusiano Martinelli, famous Italian Harlequin, in London; *commedia dell'arte* troupe 'Uniti' founded
		Fletcher b.	Newly built Corral de la Cruz opens in Madrid; Alberto Ganassa's *commedia dell'arte* troupe performs at Corral del Puente in Madrid; Danish king Frederick II engages troupe of English strollers
Camoens b. (?) Holinshed d.	Legge, *Richardus Tertius*	Middleton b. J. Taylor b. Kinwelmershe d.	Palladio begins Teatro Olimpico in Vicenza. Palladio d.
Overbury b. Ussher b. T. Wilson d.	Peele, *The Arraignment of Paris*; Wilson, *The Three Ladies of London*		*Ballet Comique de la Reine* staged in Salle du Petit Bourbon; Brollmann's school drama *Laurentius-Spiel* acted in Cologne; Cervantes' first play, *El trato de Angél*

1	2	3	4
Date	Historical events	Theatrical events	Non-dramatic literary events
1582	University of Edinburgh founded; plague in London		Gosson, *Plays Confuted*; Hakluyt, *Diverse Voyages*; Rheims *New Testament*; Stonyhurst, tr. of *Aeneid* I–IV (Leyden); Watson, *Hecatompathia*; Whetstone, *Heptameron of Civil Discourses*
1583	Whitgift Archbishop of Canterbury; Throckmorton Plot; Court of High Commission organized	Queen's Men founded	Du Bartas, *Seconde Sepmaine*; Gilbert, *True Report of the Newfound Lands*; Stubbs, *Anatomy of Abuses* and *Second Part* . . .
1584	William of Orange assassinated; 'Bond of Association' formed; Ralegh's failure in Virginia	(?) Children of the Chapel Royal cease playing at First Blackfriars	Bruno, *Cena delle Cinere*; *De la Causa*; *De l'infinito*; Greene, *Card of Fancy*; Hakluyt, *Western Discoveries*; Scott, *Discovery of Witchcraft*
1585	Sixtus V Pope; Elizabeth refuses sovereignty of Netherlands; bachelors and undergraduates at Oxford ordered to confine themselves (in Logic) to Aristotle 'and those that defend him'		Bruno, *Eroici Furori*; Greene, *Planetomachia*; Watson, *Amyntas*
1586	Battle of Zutphen; Babington Plot; trial of Mary of Scotland; the Pope promises Philip II a million crowns on his landing in England; Star Chamber decree forbidding all publications without previous ecclesiastical approval		Camden, *Britannia*; Warner, *Albion's England*; Webbe, *Discourse of English Poetry*
1587	Pope proclaims crusade against England; Mary executed; Drake at Cadiz	(?) The Rose built	A. Day, tr. of Longus, *Daphnis and Chloe*; Fraunce, tr. of Watson's *Amyntas*; Greene, *Euphues his Censure*; *Penelope's Web*; Hakluyt, *Voyages into Florida*; Holinshed, *Chronicle*

5 Birth and death dates of non-dramatic writers	6 Dates of notable plays	7 Birth and death dates of playwrights	8 Continental theatrical events
Phineas Fletcher b.	Anon (? Munday), *The Rare Triumphs of Love and Fortune*		Tasso's *Aminta* performed in Ferrara. Rasser's school drama *Drei evangelische Parabelen* staged 'with complex machinery' in marketplace at Dortmund
Herbert of Cherbury b. Sir H. Gilbert d.	Gager, *Dido*	Massinger b.	Lucerne Passion Play directed by Renwart Cysat; Ingegneri's *Danza di Venere* staged in Parma
Selden b.	Gager, *Oedipus*; Lyly, *Campaspe*; *Sappho and Phao*; Anon (? Munday), *Fedele and Fortunio*	(?) Beaumont b. Norton d.	Teatro Olimpico completed by Scamozzi; Cosimo I commissions Bernardo Buontalenti to build theatre in the Uffizi in Florence
(?) Giles Fletcher b.	Lyly, *Gallathea*; Anon (? Tarlton), *Five Plays in One*; *Three Plays in One* [both lost]		Opening of Teatro Olimpico with Giustiniani's version of *Oedipus Rex*; Giovanni de Bardi's *L'Amico fido* performed in Uffizi Theatre with décor by Buontalenti; Guarini's *Il Pastor Fido* completed
Sidney d.	Anon, *The Famous Victories of Henry V*; *Timon*	Ford b.	English strollers, including Will Kempe and Thomas Pope, enter Frederick II's service at Elsinore
Foxe d. (?) Whetstone d.	Greene, *Alphonsus, King of Aragon*; Kyd, *The Spanish Tragedy*; Marlowe *1* and *2 Tamburlaine*; Marlowe and Nashe, *Dido Queen of Carthage*; Peele, *David and Bethsabe*	Field b.	The Spanish church condemns the immorality of the stage

1	2	3	4
Date	Historical events	Theatrical events	Non-dramatic literary events
1588	The Armada		Byrd, *Psalms, Sonnets, and Songs*; Greene, *Pandosto*; *Perimedes the Blacksmith*; 'Martin Marprelate', *O Read over Dr Bridges*; Montaigne, *Essais* III; Stapleton, *Vita Thomae Mori*
1589			Greene, *Menaphon*; Hakluyt, *The Principal Navigations*; Lodge, *Scillaes Metamorphosis*; Lyly, *Pap with a Hatchet*; 'Martin Marprelate', *Ha' ye any Work for a Cooper?*; Puttenham, *Art of English Poesie*; Warner, *Albion's England* I–VI; Anon, *Mar Martin*; *Martin's Month's Mind*
1590	Urban VII Pope; Walsingham d.	Paul's Boys cease playing	Guarini, *Il Pastor Fido*; Lodge, *Rosalynde*; Munday, tr. of *Amadis of Gaul*; Nashe, *Almond for a Parrot*; Peele, *Polyhymnia*; Sidney, *Arcadia* I, II and part of III; Spenser, *The Faerie Queene* I–III; Sylvester, tr. of Du Bartas
1591	Fight of *The Revenge* at Flores; county commissions appointed to examine belief and church attendance		Greene, *Notable Discovery of Cozenage*; *Second Part of Coney-Catching*; Harrinton, tr. of *Orlando Furioso*; Saville, tr. of Tacitus' *Histories*; Sidney, *Astrophel and Stella*; Southwell, *Mary Magdalene's Tears*; Spenser, *Complaints*; *Daphnaida*

5 *Birth and death dates of non-dramatic writers*	6 *Dates of notable plays*	7 *Birth and death dates of playwrights*	8 *Continental theatrical events*
Hobbes b. Wither b.	Hughes etc., *The Misfortunes of Arthur*; Lodge, *The Wounds of Civil War*; Lyly, *Endimion*; Porter, *The Two Angry Women of Abingdon*; Wilson, *The Three Lords and the Three Ladies of London*; Anon, *1* and *2 The Troublesome Reign of King John*	Tarlton d.	Scamozzi builds theatre in Sabbionetta; Gelosi troupe makes guest appearance in Paris
	Greene, *Friar Bacon and Friar Bungay*; Lyly, *Midas*; *Mother Bombie*; Marlowe, *The Jew of Malta*; Munday, *John a Kent and John a Cumber*; Peele, *The Battle of Alcazar*; Anon (? Kyd), *Hamlet* [lost]; *The Taming of a Shrew*		Florentine intermezzi prepared by Giovanni de Bardi and Buontalenti for wedding of Ferdinand I, Grand Duke of Tuscany, to Christine of Lorraine
(?) W. Browne b. Puttenham d.	Greene, *George a Green, The Pinner of Wakefield*; Greene and Lodge, *A Looking Glass for London and England*; Lyly, *Love's Metamorphosis*; Peele, *The Old Wives Tale*; Wilson *The Cobbler's Prophecy*; Anon, *Edward III*; *Fair Em*; *King Leir*; *Mucedorus*		Robert Browne's English troupe arrives in Leyden; Garnier d.; Emilio del Cavaliere's *Il Satiro* and *La dizperazioni di Fileno* performed at Florentine court
Herrick b. (?) W. Webbe d.	Greene, *Orlando Furioso*; Peele, *Edward I*; Shakespeare, *2* and *3 Henry VI*; Anon, *Arden of Faversham*; *Jack Straw*; *Locrine*; *The True Tragedy of Richard III*		Joseph Furttenbach b.

Date	Historical events	Theatrical events	Non-dramatic literary events
1592	Clement VIII Pope; plague in London	Plague; theatres closed for almost two years	Constable, *Diana*; Daniel, *Delia*; Greene, *Philomena*; *Third Part of Coney-Catching*; *Quip for an Upstart Courtier*; *Groatsworth of Wit*; Harvey, *Four Letters*; Nashe, *Pierce Penniless*; Stow, *Annals*; Sylvester, first instalment of Du Bartas tr.; Warner, *Albion's England* I–VIII
1593	Henri IV changes his religion; churchgoing enforced in England on pain of banishment; plague in London		Chettle, *Kind Heart's Dream*; Drayton, *Idea*; Hooker, *Of the Laws of Ecclesiastical Polity* I–IV; Marlowe, tr. of Lucan's *Pharsalia* I (entered); *Hero and Leander* (entered); Morley, *Canzonets*; Nashe, *Christ's Tears over Jerusalem*; Shakespeare, *Venus and Adonis*; Sidney, *Arcadia* I–V
1594	Period of bad harvests begins in England	Consolidation of Admiral's Men (Alleyn leading actor) and of Chamberlain's Men (Burbage leading actor, Shakespeare a sharer); both companies playing in Theatre at Newington Butts	Carew, tr. of Tasso's *Jerusalem Delivered* I–VI; Daniel, *Rosamond Augmented*; *Cleopatra*; Davies, *Orchestra*; Drayton, *Idea's Mirror*; Mercator, *Atlas*; Morley, *Madrigals to Four Voices*; Nashe, *Terrors of Night*; *The Unfortunate Traveller*; Shakespeare, *The Rape of Lucrece*; 'Hen. Willoby', *Willoby his Avisa*
1595	Southwell executed; Ralegh's voyage to Guiana; Drake and Hawkins die on unsuccessful voyage to the West Indies	(?) The Swan built	Beddington, tr. of Machiavelli's *Florentine History*; Chapman, *Ovid's Banquet of Sense*; Daniel, *Civil Wars* I–IV; Drayton, *Endimion and Phoebe*; Edwards, *Narcissus*; *Cephalus and Procris*; Montaigne, *Essais* (final edition); Sidney, *Defence of Poesie*; Spenser, *Colin Clout's Come Home Again*; *Amoretti*; *Epithalamion*

5 *Birth and death dates of non–dramatic writers*	6 *Dates of notable plays*	7 *Birth and death dates of playwrights*	8 *Continental theatrical events*
N. Ferrar b. H. King d. Quarles b. T. Watson d.	Greene (?), *1 Selimus*; Greene (?) and perhaps Chettle, *John of Bordeaux*, or *2 Friar Bacon*; Marlowe, *Doctor Faustus*; *Edward II*; Nashe, *Summer's Last Will and Testament*; Shakespeare, *The Comedy of Errors*; *1 Henry VI*; Warner tr. of Plautus' *Menaechmi*; Anon, *A Knack to Know a Knave*; *Woodstock*	Greene d.	Robert Browne's troupe acts *Gammer Gurton's Needle* in Frankfurt
Hubert b. I. Walton b. W. Harrison d. (?) Stubbs d.	Daniel, *Cleopatra*; Lyly, *The Woman in the Moon*; Marlowe, *The Massacre at Paris*; Shakespeare, *Richard III*; *The Two Gentlemen of Verona*	Marlowe d.	Henry Julius, Duke of Brunswick, engages Thomas Sackville
B. Googe d. Painter d.	Bacon, etc., *Gesta Grayorum*; Kyd, *Cornelia*; Shakespeare, *The Taming of the Shrew*; *Titus Andronicus*; Anon (? Peele), *Alphonsus Emperor of Germany*; Anon, *A Knack to Know an Honest Man*	Kyd d.	The first opera, Jacopo Peri's *Daphne*, with libretto by Ottavio Rinuccini, performed in Florence; Orazio Vecchi's *L'Amfiparnasso* performed; Tasso's *Discourses on the Heroic Poem*
Hawkins d. Southwell d.	Munday etc. (probably including Shakespeare), *Sir Thomas More*; Shakespeare, *Love's Labour's Lost*; *A Midsummer Night's Dream*; *Richard II*; *Romeo and Juliet*		Tasso d.

		3	4

Date	Historical events	Theatrical events	Non-dramatic literary events
1596	Essex storms Cadiz	The Second Blackfriars built in Upper Frater of former Dominican Priory (but performances forbidden by Privy Council); (?) De Witt's drawing of the Swan Playhouse made	Deloney, *Jack of Newbury*; Drayton, *Mortimeriados*; Harrington, *Metamorphosis of Ajax*; Johnson, *The Seven Champions*; Lodge, *A Margarite of America*; *Wit's Misery*; Munday, tr. of *Palmerin of England*; Nashe, *Have with you to Saffron Walden*; Ralegh, *Discovery of Guiana*; Spenser, *The Faerie Queene* IV–VI (with new edition of I–III); *Prothalamion*; *Four Hymns*; Warner, *Albion's England* I–XII
1597	Philip II's second Armada dispersed by bad weather		Bacon, *Essays*; Deloney, *The Gentle Craft*; Dowland, *First Book of Songs*; Drayton, *England's Heroical Epistles*; Hooker, *Of the Laws of Ecclesiastical Polity* V; James VI, *Demonology*
1598	Philip II d.; Edict of Nantes; Burghley d.; unsuccessful appeal to Rome by secular priests and moderate Catholics; threatened with an interdict, they are nevertheless supported by the University of Paris	Trouble caused by *The Isle of Dogs*; all London companies except Admiral's and Chamberlain's suppressed	Bacon, *Essays* (second edition); Chapman, *Achilles' Shield*; *Iliad* I–VII; Chapman–Marlowe, *Hero and Leander*; Hakluyt, *Principal Navigations* (second edition, 3 vols., 1598–1600); Hall, *Virgidemiarum*, IV–VI; Marston, *Pygmalion and Certain Satires*; *Scourge of Villainy*; Meres, *Palladis Tamia*; Speght, edition of Chaucer; Stow, *Survey of London*; Yonge, tr. of Montemayor's *Diana*
1599	Essex the queen's general in Ireland; his return and imprisonment	The Globe built; Paul's Boys resume playing	Daniel, *Poetical Essays* (including *Civil Wars* I–V); Hayward, *Life of Henry IV*; Jaggard (ed.), *The Passionate Pilgrim*; James VI, *Basilikon Doron*; Marston, *Scourge of Villainy corrected with New Satires*

5 *Birth and death dates of non-dramatic writers*	6 *Dates of notable plays*	7 *Birth and death dates of playwrights*	8 *Continental theatrical events*
	Chapman, *The Blind Beggar of Alexandria*; Greville, *Mustapha*; Jonson, *A Tale of a Tub*; Shakespeare, *King John*; *The Merchant of Venice*; Anon, *Captain Thomas Stukely*	Shirley b. Peele d.	
	Chapman, *An Humorous Day's Mirth*; Jonson, *The Case is Altered*; Nashe (? and others), *The Isle of Dogs* [lost]; Shakespeare, *1* and *2 Henry IV*		Peri's *Daphne* revived in Rome
Burghley d.	Bernard, tr. of six plays by Terence; Chettle and Munday, *The Downfall and Death of Robert, Earl of Huntingdon* (*1* and *2 Robin Hood*); Dekker and Drayton, *1*, *2* and *3*, *The Civil Wars of France* [lost]; Haughton, *Englishmen for my Money*; Jonson, *Every Man in his Humour*; Shakespeare, *Much Ado about Nothing*	J. Heywood d.	Ingegneri's *Della poesia rappresentativa e del modo di rappresentare le favole sceniche*
Cromwell b. R. Scott d. Spenser d.	Dekker, *The First Introduction to the Civil Wars of France* [lost]; *Old Fortunatus*; *The Shoemakers' Holiday*; Drayton, etc., *1 Sir John Oldcastle*; Heywood (?), *1* and *2 Edward IV*; Jonson, *Every Man out of his Humour*; Marston, *Antonio and Mellida*; *Histriomastix*	H. Porter d.	Valleran le Conte and his troupe play before French court and subsequently before a wide audience at the Hôtel de Bourgogne; Guarini's *The Compendium of Tragicomic Poetry*

1	2	3	4
Date	Historical events	Theatrical events	Non-dramatic literary events
1599			
1600	Giordano Bruno burned at Rome; East India Company founded; Prince Charles (later Charles I) b.	Chapel Boys begin playing at Second Blackfriars; the Fortune built	Dowland, *Second Book of Songs*; *England's Helicon*; *England's Parnassus*; Fairfax, tr. of Tasso's *Jerusalem Delivered*; Holland, tr. of Livy's *History*; Kempe, *Nine Days' Wonder*; Marlowe, *All Ovid's Elegies* (with Davies's *Epigrams*); *Lucan's First Book* (published); Tourneur *Transformed Metamorphosis*; W. Vaughan, *Golden Grove*
1601	Rising and execution of Essex; Parliament attacks monopolies		J. Chamber, *Treatise against Judicial Astrology*; Daniel, *Works* (enlarged); Dolman, tr. of La Primaudaye's *French Academy* III; Holland, tr. of Pliny's *History of the World*; Rosseter and Campion's *Book of Airs*
1602	Bodleian Library founded	Worcester's Men established in London; playing recorded at the Boar's Head	Brereton, *Discovery of the North Part of Virginia*; Campion, *Observations in the Art of English Poesy*; Davison (ed.), *Poetical Rhapsody*; Lodge, tr. of Josephus; Patericke, tr. of Gentillet's *Means of Well Governing against N. Machiavel*
1603	Elizabeth d.; James VI of Scotland accedes as James I; monopolies revoked; plague	Chamberlain's Men become King's Men; Admiral's Men Prince Henry's Men, Worcester's Men, Queen Anne's Men; Children of the Chapel Royal; Children of the Queen's Revels	Daniel, *Defence of Rhyme*; Dekker, *Wonderful Year*; Dowland, *Third Book of Songs*; Drayton, *Barons' Wars*; Florio, tr. of Montaigne; Holland, tr. of Plutarch's *Morals*; Perkins, *Treatise of the Vocations*

5 Birth and death dates of non-dramatic writers	6 Dates of notable plays	7 Birth and death dates of playwrights	8 Continental theatrical events
	Shakespeare, *As You Like It*; *Henry V*; *Julius Caesar*; Anon, *Look About You*; *The Pilgrimage to Parnassus*		
(?) Earle b. (?) Prynne b. (?) Deloney d. Hooker d.	Chettle, etc., *Patient Grissil*; Heywood, *The Four Prentices of London*; Marston, *Antonio's Revenge*; *Jack Drum's Entertainment*; Shakespeare, *The Merry Wives of Windsor*; *Twelfth Night*; Anon, *1 The Return from Parnassus*; *Thomas Lord Cromwell*		Rinuccini and Peri's *Euridice* performed in Palazzo Pitti, Florence, for wedding of Maria Medici to Henri IV of France; English itinerant troupes in Germany begin to act in German; Calderon de la Barca b.
Nashe d. (?) Sir Thomas North d.	Dekker (? with Marston), *Satiromastix*; Dymock (?), tr. of Guarini's *Il Pastor Fido*; Greville, *Antony and Cleopatra* [lost]; Jonson, *Cynthia's Revels*; *Poetaster*; Marston, *What You Will*; Shakespeare, *Hamlet*; Anon (? Middleton), *Blurt Master Constable*	(?) Carlell b. Nashe d.	*Commedia dell'arte* troupe 'Fedeli' founded; the famous Harlequin Tristano Martinelli publishes *Compositions de rhetorique de M. Dom Arlequin*
(?) Felltham b. Perkins d.	Chapman, *The Gentleman Usher*; *May-Day*; *Sir Giles Goosecap*; Chettle, *Hoffman*; Middleton (? and Dekker), *The Family of Love*; Shakespeare, *All's Well*; *Troilus and Cressida*; Anon, *The Merry Devil of Edmonton*; *Wily Beguiled*	Mildmay Fane b.	Piêter Cornelisz Hooft's tragedy *Theseus und Ariadne* performed in the Riderijkekammer; Francesco Cavalli b.
Sir K. Digby b. W. Gilbert d.	Alexander, *Darius*; Heywood, *A Woman Killed with Kindness*; Jonson, *Sejanus*; Anon, *2 The Return from Parnassus*	Marmion b. (?) W. Montague b.	Ingegneri d.

1	2	3	4

Date	Historical events	Theatrical events	Non-dramatic literary events
1604	Hampton Court Conference; Bancroft Archbishop of Canterbury; peace with Spain	(?) Alleyn's final retirement; children of the Queen's Revels replace Chapel Boys at Second Blackfriars	James I, *Counterblast to Tobacco*; Middleton, *Black Book*
1605	Gunpowder Plot	(?) The Red Bull built	Bacon, *Advancement of Learning*; Camden, *Remains concerning Britain*; Daniel, *Certain small Poems, with Philotas*; Drayton, *Poems* (collected); Sylvester, *Divine Weeks and Works*, tr. from Du Bartas
1606	Penal legislation against recusants, with new oath of allegiance; Coke Chief Justice of Common Pleas; charter for Virginia	(?) The Whitefriars built in the Great Hall of former Carmelite Priory	Dekker, *The Seven Deadly Sins of London*; Warner, *Albion's England* (XIV–XVI added)

5 *Birth and death dates of non-dramatic writers*	6 *Dates of notable plays*	7 *Birth and death dates of playwrights*	8 *Continental theatrical events*
Sir T. Browne b. Churchyard d.	Alexander, *Croesus*; Chapman, *All Fools*; *Bussy d'Ambois*; *Monsieur d'Olive*; Daniel, *Philotas*; Dekker and Middleton, *The Honest Whore*; Dekker and Webster (? and others), *Sir Thomas Wyatt*; *Westward Ho*; Heywood, *1 If You Know Not Me, You Know Nobody*; *The Wise Woman of Hogsdon*; Marston, *The Dutch Courtesan*; *The Malcontent*; Middleton, *The Phoenix*; Rowley, *When You See Me, You Know Me*; Shakespeare, *Measure for Measure*; *Othello*; Anon, tr. of Guarini's *Il Pastor Fido*		Isabella Andreini dies and the Gelosi troupe is disbanded by her grieving husband
Randolph b. Stow d.	(?) Chapman, *Caesar and Pompey*; *The Widow's Tears*; Chapman, Jonson, Marston, *Eastward Ho*; Daniel, *The Queen's Arcadia*; Dekker, *2 The Honest Whore*; Dekker and Webster, *Northward Ho*; Heywood, *2 If You Know Not Me, You Know Nobody*; Jonson, *The Masque of Blackness*; Marston, *Parasitaster*; *Sophonisba*; Middleton, *A Trick to Catch the Old One*; *Your Five Gallants*; Munday, *The Triumphs of Reunited Britannia*; Shakespeare, *King Lear*	(?) Hobbes b. Randolph b. Haughton d.	Moritz of Hessen erects his Ottonium, the first permanent playhouse in Germany, in Kassel
Waller b. Golding d.	Beaumont (? and Fletcher), *The Woman Hater*; Day, *The Isle of Gulls*; Dekker, *The Whore of Babylon*; Jonson, *Hymenaei*; *Volpone*;	Davenant b. Lyly d.	Giovanni Batista Aleotti experiments with side-wings in his Teatro dei Intrepidi in Ferrara; Ranch's Plautus imitation, *Karrig Niding*, acted in

1	2	3	4
Date	Historical events	Theatrical events	Non-dramatic literary events
1606			
1607		(?) Paul's Boys cease playing	Anon, *Dobson's Dry Bobs*
1608	Separatist congregation moves to Holland	Children of the Queen's Revels cease playing at Second Blackfriars	Dekker, *Bellman of London*; Hall, *Characters of Virtues and Vices*; Perkins, *Damned Art of Witchcraft*; J. Smith, *True Relation of Virginia*; Sylvester, tr. of Du Bartas (first complete edition)

5 Birth and death dates of non-dramatic writers	6 Dates of notable plays	7 Birth and death dates of playwrights	8 Continental theatrical events
	Middleton, *A Mad World my Masters*; *Michaelmas Term*; Shakespeare, *Macbeth*; Sharpham, *The Fleer*, Wilkins, *The Miseries of Enforced Marriage*; Anon (? Tourneur), *The Revenger's Tragedy*; Anon, *The Puritan*; *A Yorkshire Tragedy*		Randers, Denmark; P. Corneille b.
	Alexander, *The Alexandrean Tragedy*; *Julius Caesar*; Barnes, *The Devil's Charter*; Beaumont (? and Fletcher), *The Knight of the Burning Pestle*; Day, Rowley, Wilkins, *The Travels of the Three English Brothers*; Heywood, *The Rape of Lucrece*; Machin (?), *Every Woman in her Humour*; Shakespeare, *Antony and Cleopatra*; *Timon of Athens*; Sharpham, *Cupid's Whirligig*; Tomkis, *Lingua*; Anon, *Claudius Tiberius Nero*	Chettle d. Legge d.	Monteverdi's *Orfeo* performed in Mantua; Buffcquin bccomes machinist for the Comédiens du roi and experiments with perspective scenery at the Hôtel de Bourgogne
Fanshawe b. Fuller b. Milton b. Sackville d.	Armin, *The Two Maids of More-Clacke*; Barry, *Ram Alley*; Chapman, *The Conspiracy and Tragedy of Charles Duke of Byron*; Day, *Humour out of Breath*; Dekker and Middleton, *The Roaring Girl*; Fletcher, *The Faithful Shepherdess*; Jonson, *The Hue and Cry after Cupid*; *The Masque of Beauty*; Rowley (? and another), *The Birth of Merlin*; Shakespeare, *Coriolanus*; *Pericles*	Cokain b. Sharpham d.	*Arianna*, by Rinuccini and Monteverdi, performed in Mantua; Monteverdi's ballet-opera *Ballo dell' Ingrata* lavishly staged in Mantua; Buontalenti d.; Giacomo Torelli b.; Tiberio Fiorelli, the famous Scaramouche, b.

I	2	3	4
Date	Historical events	Theatrical events	Non-dramatic literary events
1609	New charter for Virginia; Virginian commissioners wrecked at Bermuda	(?) King's Men begin playing at Second Blackfriars; the Cockpit (or Phoenix) built as a cockpit (used as a theatre from 1617)	Chapman, *Tears of Peace*; (?) tr. of *Iliad* I–XII; Daniel, *Civil Wars* (eight books); Dekker, *Gull's Hornbook*; Roman Catholic version of Old Testament (completed 1610); Spenser, *Faerie Queene* (first edition with 'Mutability' cantos)
1610	Petition of Right; plantation of Ulster; Hudson's last voyage		Donne, *Pseudo-Martyr*; Healey, tr. of Augustine's *City of God*; Jourdain, *Discovery of the Bermudas*; Strachey, *True Reportory of the Wreck upon the Bermudas*
1611	Abbot Archbishop of Canterbury; sale of baronetcies		Byrd, *Psalms, Songs and Sonnets*; Coryate, *Coryate's Crudities*; Cotgrave, *Dictionary of the French and English Tongues*; Donne, *Anatomy of the World*; *Ignatius his Conclave*; King James Bible; Speed, *Theatre* and *History of Great Britain*; Spenser, first Folio of collected works

5 Birth and death dates of non-dramatic writers	6 Dates of notable plays	7 Birth and death dates of playwrights	8 Continental theatrical events
Suckling b. Winstanley b. Warner d.	Beaumont and Fletcher, *Philaster*; Fletcher (with Beaumont), *The Coxcomb*; Fletcher (?), Middleton (?), Rowley (?), *Wit at Several Weapons*; Field, *A Woman is a Weathercock*; Heywood and Rowley, *Fortune by Land and Sea*; Jonson, *Epicene*; *The Masque of Queens*; Shakespeare, *Cymbeline*; Tourneur, *The Atheist's Tragedy*	B. Barnes d.	Lope de Vega's *The New Art of Writing Plays* published; Neues Auditorium built in Strasburg
(?) Falkland b.	Beaumont and Fletcher, *The Maid's Tragedy*; Chapman, *The Revenge of Bussy d'Ambois*; Daniel, *Tethys' Festival*; Heywood, *The Fair Maid of the West*; *The Golden Age*; Jonson, *The Alchemist*; Marston and Barksteed, *The Insatiate Countess*; Shakespeare, *The Winter's Tale*	Glapthorne b.	Hieronymo Giacobbi's opera *Orpheo* performed in Bologna
G. Fletcher, sr., d.	Beaumont and Fletcher, *A King and No King*; Cooke, *Greene's Tu Quoque*; Dekker, *Match Me in London*; Dekker (? with Daborne), *If It Be Not Good, The Devil is in It*; Field, *Amends for Ladies*; Fletcher, *The Night Walker*; *The Woman's Prize*; Heywood, *The Brazen Age*; *The Silver Age*; Jonson, *Catiline*; *Love Freed from Ignorance and Folly*; *Oberon*; Middleton, *A Chaste Maid in Cheapside*; Shakespeare, *The Tempest*; Anon (? Middleton), *The Second Maiden's Tragedy*	Cartwright b.	Flaminio Scala's *Il teatro delle favole*, containing forty-eight *commedia dell' arte* scenarios, published; Messenius' *Disa*, Sweden's first national history play, acted in Uppsala; first English translations of Sebastiano Serlio's *Second Book of Architecture* (1545); Jean de la Taille d.

Date	Historical events	Theatrical events	Non-dramatic literary events
1612	Lancashire witches hanged; Prince Henry d.; improved charter for Virginia		Bacon, *Essays* (enlarged); (?) Chapman, *Iliad*, I–XXIV; Donne, *Second Anniversary*; Drayton, *Poly-Olbion* I–XVIII; Gibbons, *First Set of Madrigals and Motets*; Heywood, *Apology for Actors*; Shelton, tr. of *Don Quixote* I; J. Smith, *Map of Virginia*
1613	Princess Elizabeth marries the Elector Palatine; Coke Chief Justice of King's Bench; Countess of Essex divorced and marries Somerset; Sarmiento (later Gondomar) Spanish ambassador	Amalgamation of Children of the Revels and the Lady Elizabeth's Men; the Globe burned; (?) Shakespeare retires	Browne, *Britannia's Pastorals* I; (?) Campion, *Two Books of Airs*; Purchas, *Purchas his Pilgrimage*; Whitaker, *Good News from Virginia*; Wither, *Abuses Stript and Whipt*; many elegies (in this and the following year) on Prince Henry
1614		The Hope built; the Second Globe built	
1615			

5 *Birth and death dates of non-dramatic writers*	6 *Dates of notable plays*	7 *Birth and death dates of playwrights*	8 *Continental theatrical events*
(?) Crashaw b. Harrington d.	Dekker, *Troia Nova Triumphans*; Fletcher (? and Beaumont), *The Captain*; Fletcher (? with Beaumont or Field), *Four Plays in One*; Heywood, *1* and *2 The Iron Age*; Jonson, *Love Restored*; Webster, *The White Devil*	T. Killigrew b.	
J. Taylor b. Sir Thomas Bodley d. Constable d. Overbury d.	Beaumont, *Masque of the Inner Temple and Gray's Inn*; Beaumont and Fletcher, *The Scornful Lady*; Campion, *The Lords' Masque*; Chapman, *Masque of the Middle Temple and Lincoln's Inn*; Fletcher, *Bonduca*; Fletcher (? with others), *The Honest Man's Fortune*; Jonson, *A Challenge at Tilt*; *The Irish Masque*; Middleton, *No Wit, No Help, Like a Woman's*; Shakespeare, (? and Fletcher), *Henry VIII*; Shakespeare and Fletcher, *Cardenio* [lost]; *The Two Noble Kinsmen*; Tailor, *The Hog hath lost his Pearl*		
H. More b. Cornwallis d.	Fletcher, *Valentinian*; *Wit without Money*; Jonson, *Bartholomew Fair*; Webster, *The Duchess of Malfi*		
R. Baxter b. Denham b. (?) Lilburne b.			

I The social and literary context

J. Leeds Barroll

1 Drama and the court

The crown, and the court which surrounded the monarch, played an important role in the evolution of Elizabethan drama. Therefore any account of the sociological factors affecting the profession of the player from 1576 onwards must first consider the crucial influence exerted by activity at court. Although records of specific performances are sparse, we do have knowledge of other happenings which can complement and illuminate the few records we do possess. These happenings have a bearing upon any notion of the kind of 'history' which drama indeed did experience between 1576 and the first known references to the plays of Marlowe, Greene, Kyd and Shakespeare.

To review the disposition of the royal household in 1576, at least as it concerned drama, it is important to note what had happened about four years prior to this date. Lord William Howard, younger son of the 2nd Duke of Norfolk, created Lord Howard of Effingham even before Elizabeth's accession, had become the queen's first Lord Chamberlain by 20 November 1558. As such, he was the incumbent of one of the most powerful offices in the land, an office which, among other things, exercised supervision over the Office of the Revels. Between July and August of 1572, however, the ageing Howard had begun relinquishing his post. He was, in fact, appointed Lord Privy Seal on 13 July although he did not actually give up the Chamberlainship until

5 August.[1] Howard's successor in this office was Thomas Radcliffe, 3rd Earl of Sussex, who was referred to as Lord Chamberlain on 28 October 1572.[2]

A significant incident occurs several months later, as far as the drama is concerned. The Earl of Sussex had a company of actors who were playing in the provinces between 1569 and 1572, but on 7 February 1573, 'Therle of Sussex players' are recorded as having been paid for a performance at court, the first payment to them that is known. The event is especially interesting because records do not show them as being paid again for a court performance until three years later, at Shrovetide. Although subsequently Sussex's Men would enjoy a longish career of court performances, they emerge for the first time in coincidence with the first holiday season in which their patron is Lord Chamberlain. And if the reason for their appearance was the new and relevant status of the noble whose name they bore, this appearance may be considered even more interesting because of the three-year gap thereafter. For if the new Lord Chamberlain felt it incumbent on his status to provide the queen with entertainment by his own 'servants', it may be that they proved to lack the requisite 'polish'. They were 'perused', for instance, on 14 December 1574, when they exhibited two plays for the approval of the Office of the Revels which would then allow them to perform before the queen, but they did not, in fact, act at court in this season.[3] Since the old Lord Chamberlain had never, so far as is known, patronized a company of players, the action of Sussex suggests not only that his accession had some influence on the fortunes of 'Sussex's Men' but also that they may have been forced to improve the quality of their presentations. In any event, they began appearing regularly at court after 1576.

The Earl of Leicester's Men suggest a parallel which would tend to reinforce the notion that the careers of the nobility exercised some direct influence on the development of the acting companies of the time. The players of Robert Dudley, Earl of Leicester, had not performed at court since the Christmas season of 1562–3, some months prior to the creation of Dudley as Earl of Leicester on 29 September 1564. The company was to be found in the provinces during the intervening ten years, but they did not appear at court again until the winter of 1572–3, during the same season as the new Lord Chamberlain's company first performed there. Why they began performing again can only be speculated upon, but several events are not irrelevant. A

1 See *MSC*, I, 32 n 1, and *Calendar of the Patent Rolls* (Elizabeth I), V, No. 2937.
2 See *Patent Rolls*, No. 3087.
3 See Albert Feuillerat, 'Documents relating to the Office of the Revels in the time of Queen Elizabeth' in W. Bang, *Materialien*, XLIV, 238.

year prior to their resumption of performances at court, the queen promulgated the following document:

The Queen's Majesty understanding, as well by her own careful observation of her policy as by the report of such as have the administration of justice in her realm, how universally the unlawful retaining of multitude[s] of unordinary servants by liveries, badges, and other signs and tokens (contrary to the good and ancient statutes and laws of this realm) both manifestly withdraw from Her Majesty's crown the due services of her officers, tenants, and subjects, and both also plainly hinder justice and disorder the good policy of the realm by maintenance of unlawful suits and titles and by stirring up and nourishing of factions, riots, and unlawful assemblies (the mothers of rebellion) besides such other great inconveniences that already are seen and more likely daily to follow if speedy remedy be not provided, is moved with a most earnest intention to procure a speedy reformation thereof. And because Her Majesty's intent is rather to have generally her laws duly observed and the defaults quietly reformed than [to have] the great forfeitures to be levied which are due to Her Majesty and might greatly by justice enrich her treasure (especially in the straight execution of the said laws as well by the persons that have and do unlawfully retain others, as also by them that are so unlawfully retained against the laws), therefore Her Majesty, of her special grace, doth by this her proclamation notify to all persons (of what estate or degree so ever the same be) who shall, after the 20th day of February next following, unlawfully retain or be retained in any service by livery, badges, or other token, contrary to the statutes and laws of this realm therefore provided, the same shall not have any manner of favour or grace of Her Majesty for any such offence committed against the said laws before nor after the same 20th day. And, contrariwise, whoever shall, upon his admonition, forbear to offend herein, from and after the said 20th day of February next, shall not be in any wise impeached at Her Majesty's suit nor shall forfeit anything to Her Majesty for the same. And so Her Majesty's pleasure is that all her justices and officers, before whom any suit is or shall be commenced for any offence committed or to be committed before the said 20th of February, [are] to have regard to this Her Majesty's gracious dispensation. And for the better execution of the laws and statutes remaining in force against any such unlawful retainers, Her Majesty chargeth all manner [of] her justices and officers, to whom the execution of the same is prescribed, to cause inquisition or examination accordingly to the said laws to be made in all places of the realm immediately, or as soon as conveniently they may after the said 20th day of February. And [Her Majesty chargeth] that all justices of assize and jail deliveries, as well in towns corporate and franchises as in any counties, shall at their next sessions have due regard by good examination and trial that no person be impanelled in any jury before them that is unlawfully retained without due reformation and punishing of the same, for the better example thereof, in their open sessions. And further, they shall cause a sufficient new jury to be charged apart at the same sessions diligently for that only purpose to inquire of the points and articles of all the statutes being in force, *and especially of the statute made in the third year [1487–8] of Her Majesty's noble grandfather, King Henry the Seventh, against unlawful retainers*, and give also some order that, as the truth may be therein understood, some good evidence may be given to the said jury in that behalf. And [Her Majesty chargeth] that all other things, by the care of the said justices, may be done at their next sessions, and at all other [of] their sessions following whereby the inconveniences above mentioned may be the more speedily reformed and the laws hereafter in this behalf better kept. And to the intent [that] Her Majesty may be better satisfied in her earnest desire to see the effect of her desire in this behalf, Her Majesty willeth that her said justices of assize shall, after their next sessions, at some convenient time, make report to Her Majesty of their doings and of their opinions for the better execution hereof, as cause shall require. *And further, Her Majesty chargeth all manner of persons that have any servants unlawfully retained, by liveries, badges, or by any other compact, who shall require to be discharged for any offence punishable before the said 20th day of February, that they shall, before the said 20th day, discharge their said servants, so unlawfully retained, of their services in respect of the danger of the laws. And thereupon the said servants shall accept the said discharge, and shall cease to wear the badges or other tokens whereby they were accustomed to be retained*, upon pain that if the said servants shall continue to be retained unlawfully in the said service or in wearing of the same badges or tokens after the said 20th of February, they shall not be in any wise forborne from punishment for their defaults committed against the laws before the said 20th of February. And forasmuch as by the said statute made in the third year of Her Majesty's noble grand-father, King Henry the Seventh, provision is specially made, upon weighty considerations, by great penalties of forfeitures, against sundry

officers [such] as stewards, auditors, receivers, and bailiffs of the Queen's
Majesty's honours, manors, and lands, and against constables or keepers
of Her Majesty's castles, wardens, masters of game, parkers, keepers, or
any other officer of Her Majesty's forests, chases, parks, or warrens, for
being themselves unlawfully retained or for their unlawful retaining, or
for suffering to be retained, any manner of person dwelling within their
said offices or rules without informing Her Majesty thereof within forty
days, [and by great penalties of forfeitures] against all Her Majesty's
farmers, or tenants of any of her lands, that are or shall be unlawfully
retained by any others upon pain of forfeiture of their farms, Her
Majesty hath thought good specially and particularly, for better information and to avoid ignorance, to give warning hereof to all persons
having any such offices and to all other[s] being her farmers and tenants
whom the said statute may touch, that they also do speedily reform
themselves in the offences therein particularly specified before the said
20th of February upon pain that if they shall not do so, Her Majesty
assureth them that she will not in any wise remit the said penalties and
forfeitures which, by execution of the said statutes and other laws, may
duly and justly grow to her for the offences that are, or shall be committed before the said 20th day of February against the said laws and
statutes.

The document is dated 3 January 1572.

This document has been quoted *in toto* (with italics added) not only because it suggests how actors might become involved in statutes not specifically
directed against the theatre, but also because it comprises the broad rationale
for the association of acting companies with individual members of the
nobility up to the year 1603 when King James would put the leading companies under the theoretical control of members of the royal household. The
logic underlying the law may be gathered from the Henrician statute referred
to in the proclamation itself. As Chambers has observed, the statute of 1487
was itself promulgated to strengthen such earlier statutes as that of Henry VI
in 1429 and of Edward IV in 1468, all of which forbade knights or those of
lesser rank to enrol in the liveries of their personal households anyone but
menials and specific kinds of officers. The spirit of such acts against unlawful 'retaining', as one may gather from the wording of the document,
seems to have been a desire of the crown to discourage conflicts of interest.
Clearly if a knight or any member of the nobility were unilaterally to appoint
certain minor officials as his liveried retainers, local adjudications would

obviously be affected. And when an act of 1406 even directed that 'all those that shall take any such liveries . . . of any Lord, spiritual or temporal, or of any great Lady in or of England, against the form of the said statutes' would also be punished, it is fairly clear what Elizabeth had in mind. Not only was conflict of interest a possible problem but also the danger of certain members of the nobility amassing for themselves private armies of liveried 'retainers' who, immune from arrest by civil authorities, could be sources of potential civil disturbance in case of feuds such as one witnesses in Shakespeare's *Romeo and Juliet*.

What the Elizabethan statute meant to actors may immediately be gathered from the reaction to it by that same company of players, the Earl of Leicester's Men, who have previously been alluded to:

> To the right honourable Earl of Leicester, their good lord and master. May it please your honour to understand that forasmuch as there is a certain Proclamation out for the reviving of a statute as touching retainers, as your Lordship knoweth better than we can inform you thereof, we, therefore, your humble servants and daily orators your players, for avoiding all inconvenience that may grow by reason of the said statute, are bold to trouble your Lordship with this our suit, humbly desiring your honour that, as you have always been our good lord and master, you will now vouchsafe to retain us at this present as your household servants and daily waiters – not that we mean to crave any further stipend or benefit at your Lordship's hands but our liveries, as we have had, and also your honour's licence to certify that we are your household servants when we shall have occasion to travel amongst our friends as we do usually once a year, and as other noblemen's players do and have done in times past – whereby we may enjoy our faculty in your Lordship's name as we have done heretofore.[1]

To go further afield for the moment, it is important to indicate the reasons for the concern shown by Leicester's Men about the new statute, because this item is also crucial to an understanding of the total legal context. The old so-called 'mystery plays' and craft cycles such as the Coventry group had theoretically been the products of recognized craft guilds operating as discrete and recognized mercantile bodies of honest and stable workmen incidentally mounting plays for the greater glory of God. To travel in Henrician, Marian, Edwardian or Elizabethan England simply as an independent troupe of 'players', however, was something else again. There was,

[1] For these several documents, see *MSC*, I, 348 ff. and Feuillerat.

after all, no recognized 'Players' Guild' and therefore, when travelling, such companies of actors as call upon Hamlet in Denmark, for example, were simply a group of adults in an uncertainly defined socio-economic position. More importantly, such a group, either as individuals or as a company, constantly incurred the risk when travelling of being apprehended under the statute promulgated by Henry VIII in 1530–1 and strengthened under all succeeding monarchs. This act concerned the punishment of beggars and vagabonds, and, as becomes clear from the definitions, it was directed against persons who neither owned land nor participated in the guild system and therefore were without 'masters' to whom they were apprentices. In a re-affirmation of this act, promulgated on 29 June 1572, shortly after the crown's deadline for the enforcement of the act against retainers, 'rogues', 'vagabonds' and 'sturdy beggars' were redefined as those persons above the age of four-teen who were

> whole and mighty in body and able to labour, having not land or master, nor using any lawful merchandise, craft, or mystery whereby he or she might get his or her living, and can give no reckoning how he or she doth lawfully get his or her living. And all fencers, bear-wards, common players in interludes, and minstrels not belonging to any baron of this realm or towards any other honourable personage of greater degree.

Such persons, among whom were also included 'jugglers, pedlars, tinkers, and petty chapmen', if they were apprehended and defined as 'rogues' or 'vaga-bonds', would be immediately condemned to be 'grievously whipped and burned through the gristle of the right ear with a hot iron of the compass of an inch about' unless some respectable person indicated his willingness to take the offender into his service for a calendar year. A second conviction required service to some respectable person for two years while a third conviction would result in the offender being adjudged and deemed a 'felon' and suffering pains of death and loss of lands and goods as a felon without allowance or benefit of clergy or sanctuary.[1]

Clearly, a professional 'vagabond' could evade such punishment by the exercise of ingenuity, but actors were obviously putting themselves under scrutiny at any time when it was known that they were mounting a play, of necessity, in a specified parish and locality. It is not surprising therefore to observe that even before 'players' were specifically included in the various reaffirmations of this ancient act, they were making efforts to have some kind of 'master'. Although such activity must have been earlier, one need merely

[1] See E. K. Chambers, *The Elizabethan Stage* (Oxford, 1923), IV, 269–70.

note a 1544 entry in the records of the town of Canterbury, paying actors who are described as servants of the Earl of Bridgewater and other actors described as servants to the Earl of Leicester.[1] One need only imagine, then, the plight of the actor in 1572 when caught between the Scylla of the old act against vagabonds and the Charybdis of the old act against retainers, especially when both acts were vigorously renewed in this year. And it may, therefore, have been to demonstrate to the queen that his retainers were indeed servant-actors that Leicester, powerful enough in his own right, had his company performing three times at court during the Christmas holiday season of 1572–3 which also witnessed, as heretofore noted, the appearance of the new Lord Chamberlain's company (Sussex's Men). In short, it may have been prudent both for Sussex and for Leicester, either for reasons of their own, or because of the importunities of their acting 'servants', to re-affirm the relevance of their 'retainers' as a group of household servant-actors, and this circumstance may itself, concomitantly, have provided an impulse for the actors themselves further to professionalize in order to maintain the precarious status they enjoyed. The reader of a history of the drama may have his own specialized orientation in favour of actors, but, from the standpoint of the prudent sixteenth-century player, any close and compelling interest in his case by a vaguely benevolent Leicester or Sussex busy with his own political career at court must have seemed a tenuous thread indeed whereby one remained attached to legality, a thread to be woven into more sturdy bonds, perhaps, by constant application of effort and ingenuity. As for the nobility itself, display of their acting 'servants' may have been only one among a number of displays of different groups of liveried adults to demonstrate the legality of their status as 'retainers'. If so, the players would hardly have suffered, since exhibition is obviously the *raison d'être* of dramatic endeavour.

The appearance of Leicester's Men at court in 1572–3 may, however, have occurred for other reasons, from Leicester's point of view. In June 1572 a party representing the king of France made a formal visit to England. They were sumptuously entertained. This entertainment would be executed under the direct supervision of the Office of the Revels which, as has been noted, would have been under the general jurisdiction of the Lord Chamberlain. No doubt because the old Lord Chamberlain was then failing in health, others were appointed to supervise the Office of the Revels for this occasion: not only Sussex, as seems natural enough since he was shortly to become Lord Chamberlain, but also the Earl of Leicester – 'or either of them' as the

[1] See *MSC*, VII, 11.

warrant for issue dated 17 June indicates.[1] What this notation also suggests, however, is that Leicester himself may have been an active candidate for the office of Lord Chamberlain. He thus may have responded favourably to the petition of his acting company that previous winter so that he would have retainers to pay honour to the queen should the old Lord Chamberlain survive (as he did) into the New Year of 1573. Furthermore, matters may have been complicated, with this complicated earl, by the fact that he had in 1571 contracted to marry Douglas Lady Sheffield, the daughter of the old Lord Chamberlain. When the old Lord Chamberlain died on 12 January, however, Douglas Lady Sheffield was no longer important as the daughter of the old Lord Chamberlain but as the sister of Charles Howard who, becoming 2nd Baron Howard of Effingham upon their father's death, was also married to the First Lady of the Privy Chamber, the daughter of Henry Carey, 1st Lord Hunsdon, Warden of the East Marches and first cousin to the queen. Leicester was to marry Howard's sister in May of 1573, a child being born to them in the same year. How those problems and prospects affected Leicester's sense of paying honour to the queen during the Christmas season of 1572–3 and whether his power and connections enabled him to surmount any remaining animosity between himself and Sussex, with whom he had openly quarrelled in 1566,[2] can only be a matter for conjecture. However, given the background of these various events, and given the possible relevance of the two acts under recent discussion, it may not be surprising that not only did the servants of Leicester and of Sussex perform at court in the holiday season of 1572–3, but that Lawrence Dutton's company also did, under the patronage of the Earl of Lincoln. In this particular season, in fact, for the first time in existing records, more adult acting companies performed at court than did companies of boy actors who had hitherto dominated holiday proceedings.

As the years unfold in this decade, one continues to be struck by the way in which certain changing relationships at court continue to throw light on some facets in the development of the adult dramatic companies. The players of the powerful Leicester, after that first court appearance in so many years, continued to be invited to perform at least twice in each holiday season up to 1578. On the other hand, Christmas appearances by any other particular adult companies varied. Or, again: a group of actors for whom no noble patron was designated in the first subsequent payment began to appear at court under the leadership of Lawrence Dutton on 27 December 1571. They

[1] Feuillerat, *Documents*, p. 153 n.
[2] See *Dictionary of National Biography*: Dudley, Robert.

acted again on Shrove Sunday, 1572, the warrant for payment naming Sir Robert Lane as their patron. However, Lord Clinton is later this spring (May 1572) created 1st Earl of Lincoln. Then, in the next holiday season of Christmas and New Year (1572–3), an instance which we alluded to above, Dutton's company performed, but Dutton, in the warrant for payment, is described as 'servant to the Earl of Lincoln'. One would also assume that Dutton was really (Clinton's) Lincoln's 'servant' in 1571; otherwise, Robert Lane, named in that warrant, would have been the only patron of actors not possessing an earldom. Possibly, the appearances of Dutton's company under ambiguous auspices in 1571–2 were connected with Clinton's anticipated move upwards, Sir Robert Lane being a convenient 'patron' for the record. Though this is speculation, it is not speculation when we state that the Earl of Lincoln's Men subsequently appeared at least once in every holiday season until the season of 1575–6 when Lawrence Dutton and his company are described in the record of payment as the Earl of Warwick's Men. Chambers has observed, in this connection, that the Duttons were 'evidently a restless folk'[1] because of such changes, but this may be an unrealistic appraisal. With the resurrection of the old Henrician statute in 1572, it is difficult to imagine any group of players risking their livery, or more, by arbitrarily departing from the 'household' of an earl who would thus be left without what had become one of his usual means of complimenting the queen at Christmas: at this point skilful dramatic companies probably did not grow on trees. All this may therefore be reason enough to consider an alternative explanation which would not assume Dutton and company as desiring to risk a situation in which the Earl of Lincoln would either be irritated or, worse, insulted.

The Earl of Leicester's brother, Ambrose Dudley, a childhood friend of Elizabeth, had after her accession been re-created Earl of Warwick in 1561. From 1562 to 1565 he allowed a group of players to use his name, and they

[1] Chambers, *ES*, II, 98. The patronage of the company in 1571–2 is at least obscure. It is questionable whether even Sir Robert Lane was connected with it. 'Dutton and his fellowes' are designated as the payees for 5 January 1572 in the accounts of the Treasurer of the Chamber (*MSC*, VI, 5) and they are identically so referred to in the Privy Council Register less than a month later, 29 February, in payment for the Shrove Sunday performance. But this Shrove Sunday performance, or another one on the same day, receives a payment warrant not only in the Privy Council Register but also in the Chamber accounts. In this latter record, payment is warranted to 'John Greaves and Thomas Goughe servantes to Sir Robert Lane knighte'. Nothing is known about the actors Greaves and Goughe beyond this reference. The question is thus whether they were in Dutton's company or were a separate group. If so, Sir Robert Lane would have nothing to do with the subject of Dutton's activities.

not only appear in provincial records but they also performed twice at court in the Christmas season of 1564–5. Then for ten years no trace can be found of them, even though they may have existed. In the meantime Warwick became Chief Butler of England on 4 May 1571, and on 5 September 1573 he was admitted to the Privy Council. In the holiday season of 1574–5, a company described as the Earl of Warwick's made its appearance at court for the first time in ten years, giving one performance, probably on Shrove Sunday, for which they were paid at Richmond. This same year was also the last in which an 'Earl of Lincoln's' company appeared before the queen, the warrant for the last payment to them being dated 11 January 1575, to recompense them for acting on 2 January. The warrant for the first payment to 'The Earl of Warwick's Players' is dated 16 February 1574–5, recompensing them for the Shrove Sunday or Shrove Monday performance of 13 or 14 February. It was in the following season that the 'Earl of Warwick's Players' were identified in the warrant for payment as Dutton and company. If Dutton's company was a talented one – and Dutton himself seems to have been since he eventually became a member of the famous Queen's company which dominated the 1580s – it may be curious that, as the Earl of Lincoln's Men, they appeared only once at court in the 1571–2 season, once in the 1572–3 season, once in the 1573–4 season, twice in the 1574–5 season in which Warwick's new company appears once, and then in the following season appeared thrice as 'The Earl of Warwick's Players', for the next three years in a row appearing twice each Christmas. One must ask whether there was a sudden upsurge of talent in the company, inspired by the prospect of being Warwick's players, or whether Warwick's standing at court may have made its own contribution to their frequency of performance. Reverting to the problem of the Duttons as 'restless', one might, without too much implausibility, wonder whether some agreement may not have been worked out between a privy councillor (Warwick) and the ambassador to France (Lincoln), for since one hears no more of the Earl of Lincoln's Players at court (although a group bearing this name is found in Southampton and Coventry in 1576 and 1577), clearly the Earl of Lincoln is not represented at those times when Christmas season compliments would be paid to the queen. Perhaps Lincoln's absences in his ambassadorship, together with the revival of the Henrician statutes, made it convenient for the Duttons to have a patron close at hand, while Warwick's own increased importance may have required some show of concern on his part for the queen's recreation at Christmas. In this general context, for one earl to put himself in the position of insulting another by nonchalantly taking a group of his liveried servants away seems a little improbable, and one may, rather, imagine a little friendly persuasion from the privy councillor whose brother was Earl of Leicester. In any event, it cannot be completely without significance that during the 1575–6 Christmas season, the adult companies which performed before the queen were those who served the Earl of Warwick, the Earl of Leicester, also of the Privy Council, and the Earl of Sussex, Lord Chamberlain. This pattern of interdependence between power at court and the development of acting companies continued with the advent of a group of players serving Charles Howard, 2nd Baron Howard of Effingham, son of the deceased Lord Chamberlain. In the seasons of 1576–7 and 1577–8, Howard's men gave a total of three plays before they disappeared into the provinces, from which they did not emerge until 1585 when Howard was made Lord High Admiral. Then his company once more appeared at court to begin their career as the group with which Shakespeare and his fellows were to compete throughout the 1590s.

Primarily, between 1575 and 1580, the companies which performed at court were Leicester's, Warwick's and Sussex's men, and it was not until the Earl of Sussex died on 9 June 1583 that the configuration of performances at court began to undergo a change. To understand the quality of this change, it is necessary to consider more closely those areas of responsibility at court which were directly concerned with plays. The nobility, of course, were hardly conscious of helping to mould a Renaissance drama, and, considering the responsibilities of such men as Sussex, Leicester and Warwick, their contact with their companies must have been so fugitive that their players only came to mind when it was a question of entertainment, ceremony or prestige. In these moments, to be sure, symbolic status would have been extremely important, but the day-to-day details would not have concerned them. If a Lawrence Dutton could not have ready access to an earl and a member of the Privy Council, however, the student of the drama of this period must necessarily consider who was accessible to a Dutton when it was a question of everyday details regarding performances.

To clarify this situation, it will now be convenient to review what is known of the Office of the Revels, as it may pertain to the parameters of control exercised by the court upon the performances of plays and thus, by implication, upon the development of the drama. One point of departure is a document among the Additional MSS. 19256 in the British Museum. The author is anonymous, but is obviously connected with the office, and the document itself can be dated from chronological references within it as being written, significantly, between 17 November 1572 and 16 November 1573, since reference is made to the fifteenth year of Elizabeth's reign. A paraphrase of certain portions most conveniently marshals the relevant considerations. The Office of the Revels, the document begins, derives its existence from the fact that 'the Prince being disposed to pastime' would appoint one person or another whose qualifications in 'witte' and 'learnynge' would make him a suitable Master of the Revels who could supervise such 'devices' as might be most agreeable to the prince's expectation. At this time, also, there seem to have been various minor officials with specific tasks appointed for the physical and financial arrangements of this particular office. Eventually Sir Thomas Cawarden, himself a member of the king's Privy Chamber, was preferred to the office, but because he disliked the inferior rank assigned to the task ('Sergeant Yeoman'), Cawarden was successful in changing the title of the position to 'Master of the Revels', and it was he who began to organize the office into constituent functions supervised by officials.

After his death in 1559, almost coincident with the accession of Elizabeth I, one gathers from the document, the queen allowed the office to become decentralized, not appointing a Master, but allowing three officials to operate. Sir Thomas Benger was appointed as Master of the Revels on 18 January 1560. During his term of office, the document would seem to suggest, Elizabeth had allowed decentralization to take place, and the queen's majesty 'divided the said Office into diverse offices'. The Revels were under the charge of Benger, the Master of the Revels, but the Office of the Tents and the Office of the Toils were administered by separate officials, both members of the Privy Chamber. Some idea of the general responsibilities of the whole office may be derived from this subdivision if it is recalled that 'Toils' would refer to the supervision of the various paraphernalia connected with hunting, while 'Tents' referred to the erection and maintenance of pavilions – an important consideration during a royal progress through the land – and also, until 1559, to the supervision of banquets and banquet houses.

'Revels' themselves were, of course, the subdivision of greatest importance to the student of the drama because 'revelry' included plays, masques and other modes of artistic performance. There would have been special occasions, receptions of ambassadors or of visiting monarchs, marriages and so forth, but stated periods of 'revelry' at court were largely concentrated into the weeks between Christmas and Ash Wednesday. Throughout the years 1576–1613, the pattern for dramatic entertainment in this period of revelry was as follows, the exceptions being noted in Table 1. 26, 27 and 28 December, St Stephen's Day, St John the Evangelist's Day and Innocents' Day

(Childermas) respectively, almost always saw the presentation of a play at court. In January, New Year's Day and Twelfth Night were occasions for plays, while an extra day, 2, 3 or 4 January, frequently appears in records of payment for plays at court. In February, Candlemas (the feast of the Purification of the Virgin Mary) occurred on the 2nd and was often the occasion for a play, although between 1585 and 1600 only one play is paid for on this date, while between 1573 and 1581 a play on this date was an annual occurrence. The period of Lent, of course, would be variable as to date, but there were usually plays on the Sunday, Monday and Tuesday preceding Ash Wednesday: Shrove Sunday, Shrove Monday and Shrove Tuesday.

The document under consideration, after alluding to the partition of the Office of the Revels, goes on to suggest that, though the official in charge of the Revels may have been responsible in certain ways, other functionaries in the office seem to have reported directly to the crown also, because the writer is rather forceful on the subject of establishing an administrative system within which subordinates report to superiors, not circumvent them. It is also clear that the office itself was a large financial responsibility and problem, for the recommendations in the document suggest that the workmen serving in the Office of the Revels might very well serve in the other offices (i.e., Tents and Toils). Apparently the officers of Revels, Tents and Toils of the time must have been expending more than was allowed by the monarch 'in fee or wages' and, the writer avers, he cannot see how anyone serving in this office at an arbitrarily fixed salary can ultimately be efficient financially, because the individual is naturally going to want to gain by his salary, not lose by it. Therefore the only logical course of action is either to inflate the bills or to contribute to the deficits out of one's own income, especially since it is the monarch's whim that will decide, not what can be spent, but what entertainment must be offered. For example, the writer continues, it is impossible to estimate an annual sum to be expended on the banqueting houses for 'the charges will growe according to the Princes pleasure in the number of theym in the length, bredth, fasshion, and forme of theym, and in the costlye or sleight deckinge or tryminge of theym'.

It is not the number of officials which constitutes the financial problem, the writer avers, but the fact that none of them individually can really afford to put out the kind of financing required for the varied jobs. For example, hiring men simply to keep workmen from their tendency to 'spoyle, filche, or steale' requires more than the fee and the wages, for one has 'to attende and watche both daye and night'. Then there is the problem of airing the garments and other materials used for the plays and masques. It may be argued that too much money is being spent here, but the material simply must be aired periodically, and, accordingly, officials are needed to guard it from being stolen, to determine whether certain materials may be re-used, and for what. 'It is not possible for the officers to carye in memorye the forme of thinges, they be so manye and of such diversitye whiche manye tymes maye serve aswell to purpose as if the Quenes Maiestye shoulde be at charge to make newe.'

Therefore, the writer recommends, let there be an organization which would consist of a *Master* of the Revels (presumably as in Cawarden's time) who would be seconded by a Sergeant of the Revels who would be responsible for seeing that a 'platte' or 'devise' (presumably the specific plan for an entertainment such as a particular play, a decorative motif at a banquet and so forth) be followed through after the Master of the Revels has worked it out in his own planning. The Master, after all, cannot very well wait around for the queen to give him ideas, and such planning as he must do cannot spare him the time to oversee the workmen and the physical execution. Furthermore, this 'Sergeant' should join the Master and other officers 'at the rehersall of playes'. He should solicit the Master's opinion 'to correcte and chaunge the matter after the Masters mynde' while the rest of the officers should see to 'the provision of the stuffe and for makinge of the garmentes and other thinges accordingelye'.

The Master and his Sergeant should also confer with the 'Comptroller Clerke' and others to see how the entertainment plan can be executed at the least cost 'and that the devise growe not more chargeable then well satisfyinge the Prince's expectacion as of necessitye it ought'. Meanwhile, the Clerk Comptroller should keep a strict cost-accounting constantly available to the Master and his Sergeant, and in no case should this Comptroller expend funds without the permission of the Master, the Sergeant and the other pertinent officials. There should also be a 'Clerke' whose duty would comprehend the keeping of 'perfect bookes' on workmen, noting their hours worked, their absences and the like, by having among other things a roll call in the morning and in the afternoon so that the Comptroller can dock their wages accordingly. This Clerk would also check out the mathematics of all transactions to determine 'whither the Prince be abused in the service or noe'.

The writer then goes on to make two more points. He realizes that in the past certain officials (presumably in this whole complex of Tents-Toils-Revels) were appointed by and are directly responsible to the Privy Council, and he can see reasons for this, but he would urge, for the sake of coherence and for the affixing of responsibility, that nevertheless these officials report to the Master, who would thus have no one to blame but himself should the work be performed unsatisfactorily. It is the Master's signature on all documents, financial or otherwise, which should be definitive and binding on other officials concerned in this area. However, his second point is: if the queen or the Privy Council will not accept this concept, then let there be *specific* allocation of responsibilities, through ordinances which, presumably, would fix the blame where it belongs. He then suggests the following ordinances (along with a simple draft of an order so that the queen and her Privy Council can simply sign on the dotted line, so to speak).

When 'Hollantide' (All Hallows' Eve and All Saints' Day: another popular entertainment period), Christmas, Candlemas and Shrovetide are impending, as well as other times decreed by the order of the queen, the Lord Chamberlain, the Vice-Chamberlain or others so authorized, the Master and the other officers should meet together to consider the following matters.

They should peruse the remains of all existing material on hand to determine whether any of it is re-usable. They should then determine their financial plan: whether to secure an advance from the Treasury, whether to pay cash, and thus reduce the rate of interest, for new materials, or whether to procure the materials on 'trust' with the resultant interest rate. They should determine 'whiche Platt devised to be drawen and sett fourth in payntinge by some connynge Artificer in that Arte and to be considered of by all the officers'. The best 'devise' that is also the least expensive, relatively, should then be chosen, with the approval of the Master.

There should be 'servitours' appointed to have authority to bargain for prices and wages, and to dismiss workmen.

The chief business of the office rests especially in three points: 'In makinge of garmentes, in making of hedpeces, and in payntinge.' By this we may take it the writer means the chief *financial* business, for he then goes on to observe that the 'Connynge' or cunning of the office 'resteth in skill of devise, in understanding of historyes [stories], in judgement of comedies, tragedyes and shewes, in sight of perspective and architecture'. Some smack of 'geometrye and other thinges' is also useful, and the officers might avail themselves, in this respect, of a 'good choyce of cunnynge artificers severally according to their best qualitie'. If there are to be various officers responsible, they must be sure to obtain a good grasp of the monarch's tastes and not attempt to put forward their own ideas over those of others unless they are honestly motivated by their loyalty to the sovereign.

It would be tedious to follow the details too closely, but several are illustrative. Those men paid by day-wages must work ten hours per day; those paid by night-wages must work six hours in the evening. Receipts should be signed for all garments and materials brought from the queen's great wardrobe. Because this material is so expensive, an elaborate set of safeguards should protect it from being stolen, embezzled, cut too generously when garments are being made and the like. Painters too must be closely supervised so that they do not keep the paint they do not use.

When all has been prepared under these elaborate cost-control measures and all things are ready, the officers should meet again to perfect the balance sheets, to make out the bills and also, 'at that syttinge', to give order for a 'connynge paynter' to enter into a fair large ledger book, by sketching, all the masques and shows set forth in this particular operation so that 'varyetye may be used from tyme to tyme'.

Finally, if any of this property is afterwards to be lent out to others for money, let the responsibility be strictly established with one officer so that he and only he will be to blame for any abuses.

This maze of 'officers' suggested by the writer of this document should not obscure the forest of which all these trees are composed. Clearly, the author of this 1572–3 treatise is either one of the leading altruists of the period or is a candidate for the Mastership of the Revels. The points which he is making, however, still offer a clear picture of the relationship of the Office of the Revels both to the court and to the drama of the time. In the first place, there seem to have been Privy Council appointments, presumably of favourites, to some of the subordinate but possibly key positions in the Revels, and this is useful to remember when one considers that Leicester, Sussex and later Warwick were members of this body. It also seems clear that among the peers of the Privy Council the writer assumes the Lord Chamberlain to be the individual in control, although he is, of course, wise enough to leave himself an 'out' should any of the council take umbrage at this assumption. It is also possible that Sir Thomas Benger, as opposed to those who ran 'Tents' and 'Toils', may have had less influence with the Lord Chamberlain than did his opposite numbers: this may have accounted for the temporary trifurcation of the total office which handled all of the sovereign's entertainments. Beyond noting these political valencies, however, one does gather what the writer regarded as a reasonable description of the nature of the office. Ultimately he is asserting that one individual should be unquestionable Master of the Revels, and, if not, then if the situation is to avoid administrative anarchy, responsibilities should be affixed officially to specific persons. The document may, of course, be exaggerating the number of officials needed, possibly in the hope that whatever earls were reading the exposition would turn pale at the prospect of so many salaries, but there are several consistent notes which ring throughout. Clearly the whole situation presents many financial problems and may, in retrospect, suggest why there were to be so many time lags in payments to actors in the records which we possess. But the talk about finances also suggests something about performances. Clearly the actors could expect gorgeous costumes, and perhaps elaborate scenery as well, without any outlay of their own money. In fact, it is interesting to speculate on the possibility that these conditions may have influenced the writing of plays to be offered for court performances, their authors consciously making them amenable to lavish costume and settings.

In this connection, if there are merely overtones of a subtle and perhaps unknowing fiscal influence on aesthetics by the crown, then as regards other matters 'subtlety' is hardly the appropriate word. The Master of the Revels is definitely conceived of, in this document, as an aesthetician (with a flair for managing money) who decides what will entertain the queen, what the order of plays will be, what constitutes appropriate variety in one holiday season and perhaps even what the scenery will be. And if there is an implicit complaint in this document, it is not that the crown does not use these powers, but that they are distributed among too many individuals. Here is a plea not for power over actors, but for the consolidation of various powers already exercised and taken for granted.

It is important to grasp this latter point because the situation which was the object of complaint seems to have persisted. There was no Master of the Revels, in our writer's sense, after the death of Sir Thomas Benger at approximately this time (between 12 July 1572 and 7 June 1573). Rather, one finds that by 20 December 1573 Thomas Blagrave (appointed clerk both of the Tents and Revels on 25 March 1560) has moved 'into the execucon of the Masters office' with some implication that the Lord Chamberlain made this appointment.[1] The matter comes up again at the end of February 1575 in another Revels account: 'Thomas Blagrave esquier being appoynted Master of the same [Revels Office] (as by sundry letters from the Lorde Chamberlaine maye appeare).' This latter notation is worth considering. All the appointments to the Mastership of the Revels which we possess, that of Sir Thomas Cawarden in 1545, that of Sir Thomas Benger in 1560 and that of Edmund Tilney in 1579, were royal appointments coming from the 'office'

[1] See Feuillerat, *Documents*, p. 191, and for the previously cited documents, see ibid., *passim*.

either of Henry VIII or Elizabeth I. Blagrave's entries, on the other hand, seem simply to indicate a temporary authority given to him by the Lord Chamberlain. It is interesting that this was so, because the accession of Sussex as Lord Chamberlain in 1572 almost coincided with the death of the former Master of the Revels, Benger, yet it is quite clear that within the period 1573–83, as the acting companies of various earls began to make their holiday appearances at court, Sussex and others were allowing a decentralized situation to exist in the Office of the Revels. Chambers believes that the accession of Burghley as Lord Treasurer may have had something to do with the uncertainty here,[1] because Burghley may have wanted to effect economies and 'do an audit' so to speak. Whatever the case, the situation persisted until December 1579 when Edmund Tilney received a patent from the queen as Master of the Revels, the first such patent issued since Benger's appointment in 1560.

Since the wording of the Latin patent, given in July 1579, was in all crucial matters the same as that of Benger's, it is difficult to determine whether Tents and Toils reverted to Tilney or not, but much information can be garnered from the commission (in English) of 24 December 1581. And since Tilney was to be the definitive official for the control of the drama in its 'working' aspects until the end of the sixteenth century and since his duties therefore are crucial to our familiarity with modes of governmental control over the drama, this information warrants attention. Following the order of subjects raised in the patent itself, one observes first that Tilney is authorized to hire, in the queen's name, all or any artisans and artificers necessary and requisite to any 'peece of service' pertaining to the Office of the Revels. He is also authorized to buy any materials and pay for their carriage either by land or water. Tilney is further authorized in his own person, or through his subordinates, to imprison without bail any party refusing to participate in whatever pertinent work may be in hand. Such parties will remain in prison until Tilney decides that they have been sufficiently punished, and when the parties are released they are to have no recourse to suits against the Master of the Revels for their treatment. On the other hand, any person who happens to be imprisoned by other authorities while engaged in work for the Office of the Revels can be set free by order of the Master of the Revels. Tilney may also command actors 'either belonginge to any noble man or otherwise' to appear at any time to exhibit their repertoire. A parenthetical clause follows, more important than the foregoing (itself interesting because of the remark about noblemen) because this parenthesis indicates that Tilney, as Master of the

[1] See Chambers, *ES*, I, 80.

Revels, is authorized 'to order and reforme' and 'to aucthorize and put down' all such shows, 'plaies, plaiers and playmakers, together with their playing places', as shall be thought appropriate by him. Through these few but significant words, then, specific authority suddenly moved from the area of the court to comprehend the actors' environment in the world outside. And, the patent continues, if any commandments in this regard are ignored, Tilney has the right to imprison individuals in the queen's name, again without fear of suit against himself, any act, statute, ordinance or provision heretofore existing to the contrary notwithstanding.

It is interesting to follow the record of events in the next few years. Feuillerat notes that Tilney seems responsible to several members of the Privy Council other than the Lord Chamberlain (Sussex), for the Master of Revels is seen reporting to the Lord Treasurer in several instances and, at one time in 1581, it seems that he must deal with both Sussex and the Earl of Leicester, who was, as we know, powerful at court.[1] As others have observed, there must have been some interest on the part of certain court officials in auditing the Office of the Revels, hence the Lord Treasurer is named, but what happens in the next few years seems to transcend the financial. In the Christmas season following Tilney's official appointment (1580–1), there is no substantial change in the companies performing at court. The Earl of Derby's company had begun appearing in Tilney's first year (1579–80), and they appeared again in 1581–2; however, there is no record at all of an adult company performing at court in 1580–1. Children's companies appear to carry the burden of entertainment in this season. It is possible that performances may have been offered as gifts to the crown by the sponsoring nobles, such a circumstance precluding any record of payment by the crown, but if this is so, it was a unique event, as a glance at Table 1 will indicate. It may be that the plague in the autumn of 1581 was to blame. The players had been prohibited from acting since 10 July 1581. Michaelmas Term had been deferred on 21 September because of the plague, and finally minutes of the Privy Council on 3 December 1581 show a petition from the actors stating that, since they all have wives and children to support and since they have had no other trade from childhood but music and acting, they beg to be allowed to resume their profession now that plague deaths are down. The Privy Council itself, considering these matters, and also considering that the players were to present certain plays before the queen's majesty for her solace in the Christmas time, acquiesced in the request.[2] But it is possible – and

[1] See Feuillerat, *Documents*, pp. 330, 341, 342, 360.
[2] See J. R. Dasent, *Acts of the Privy Council of England* (London, 1895), XIII, 269.

here one speculates – that a new Master of the Revels may have been rather particular about the standard of performance and that none of the adult companies had either a suitable repertoire or polished performances owing to the long period of enforced idleness. The extraordinary powers given to Tilney in this season, on 24 December 1581, may well have been a move to ensure the availability of Christmas entertainment for the future, plague or no plague, by establishing some official in the court bureaucracy whose responsibility would extend to powers over actors away from court. Thus plague in the following autumn was severe enough to dictate the deferring of Michaelmas Term and then the removal of this law term to Hertford, but there were no petitions from the actors and the 1582–3 Christmas season saw court plays by four adult companies.

One of these companies, we note, was that of Henry Carey, Lord Hunsdon, whose players were making their first appearance at court, although they are to be noted in the provinces in 1581 and again in 1582.[1] The significance of their first appearance at court would seem to be an anticipatory one, ushering in the next phase in the process of court control of the drama, for the Lord Chamberlain, Sussex, may have been ailing. He would die the following spring and Hunsdon may have been beginning to structure a bid for the office. However, matters were to go otherwise, and from the tissue of possibilities may be derived some reason for the formation of the Queen's Men on 9 June 1583 after the death of the Lord Chamberlain. On 19 April 1583 Sussex, Lord Chamberlain, died, but he was not immediately replaced. Rather, it would seem that some temporizing was to go on about this subject for several years. Looking forward a moment, Charles Howard of Effingham would be mentioned as being Lord Chamberlain on 5 March 1584.[2] On 18 June 1584, a Lord Chamberlain and a Vice-Chamberlain would be alluded to when Fleetwood wrote to Lord Burghley concerning a disturbance at the Theatre. Apparently the Lord Chamberlain and the Vice-Chamberlain did not agree with the consensus of the other nobles to suppress the Theatre and the Curtain, but a letter was obtained 'to suppresse theym all'. James Burbage, owner of the Theatre, refused to come to be bound, because he said he was one of Hunsdon's Men. When he did appear, he was refractory until he was shown Hunsdon's hand, presumably on the document mentioned.[3] This suggests that Hunsdon was acting either as Vice-Chamberlain or Chamberlain. Moving ahead again, in June 1585 Charles Howard of

[1] See Chambers, *ES*, II, 192.
[2] See *Calendar of State Papers: Domestic Series* (1581–90), p. 163.
[3] *MSC*, I, 163.

Effingham would be appointed Lord Admiral, acquiring the title with which students of Elizabethan drama usually associate him, and it would be in the following month that Henry Carey, Lord Hunsdon, officially became Lord Chamberlain. To return to the subject of Sussex's death, then, it would seem that, after his demise, the queen or some of her advisers wished to keep the matter of his successor to the Chamberlainship in a fluid state for a while.

It would seem that there were precautions against plague this summer of 1583,[1] while the collapse of Paris Garden on Sunday 13 January 1583 had already resulted in virtuous letters from the lord mayor of London to Burghley, Lord Treasurer, suggesting that there be no plays on Sunday after this evidence of God's wrath. Lord Burghley agreed, and recommended this action.[2] From all this it is possible to infer a growing, if temporary, atmosphere of restrictiveness at court concerning the matter of players. They were clearly becoming a bone of contention with the aldermen of London, honours going presumably to the aldermen with the collapse of Paris Garden on a Sunday. The evident disturbance, somewhere in ruling circles, over unlawful retainers, the granting of extraordinary powers to Tilney and the hesitation at naming a successor to Sussex as Lord Chamberlain all seem of a pattern, although one can hardly suppose that the affairs of the realm revolved around acting. Players may, however, have been a symbol of whatever ailed the royal household. In any event, the facts are that as early as 10 March 1583, two months after the Paris Garden incident, and one month prior to the new proclamation against retainers, Edmund Tilney was sent for to 'choose out a companie of players for her maiestie'.[3] This company is first recorded in the following summer, acting at the Red Lion in Norwich on 15 June.[4] Throughout, Walsingham seems to have been involved, whether through his personal power or his role as principal secretary to the queen, and in the absence of any Lord Chamberlain. In any event, on 26 November 1583, the Privy Council requested the lord mayor of London to allow 'hir maiesties playeres' to play within the city, especially since they were shortly to present plays before the queen. Among those who signed the Privy Council letter were Hunsdon, Walsingham and Burghley.

This important new company was made up of players from other groups, at least three of the actors (Wilson, Laneham and Johnson) coming from Leicester's Men. The formation of the Queen's Men has been regarded as a

---

[1] Chambers, *ES*, IV, 347.
[2] See *MSC*, I, 58–60.
[3] See Feuillerat, *Documents*, p. 359.
[4] See J. O. Halliwell, *Affray at Norwich in 1583* (London, 1864).

great step forward, at least socially, for acting in the sixteenth century, and this must be true. On the other hand, it cannot be denied that, once chosen, the resultant group implied a possibly restrictive monopoly, both as regards court performances and as regards available pools of talent, which may in the end have retarded the development of the drama in England. The mayor and his aldermen, for example, used the formation of the group as a reason to allow only the Queen's Men and none else to play in London,[1] and one can see the beauty of their rationale. If the justification for plays was the solace of the sovereign during established periods of revelry, and if to forbid players such public performances as would allow them to rehearse their offerings elsewhere to ensure better royal entertainment was to show disloyalty to the crown, the creation of the Queen's Men was a way out. Only one company, rather than several, needed to be deferred to, and concomitantly other companies could be forbidden without the City being guilty of indifference towards the recreation of the sovereign. Thus the Queen's Men might be allowed to play within the City, at the Bull and the Bell inns, but other companies had to make do in the liberties north or south of the town.

However one may speculate, the facts, as gathered from court records of payments to players, are that the Queen's Men dominated holiday season performances until 1590–1 – a period of about seven years. There were exceptions, but they were logical enough, in terms of court politics. In the holidays of 1585–6, Charles Howard's Men were at court twice, once together with Hunsdon's Men. But in the previous summer Howard had been made Lord Admiral and Hunsdon had been made Lord Chamberlain. In the holidays of 1586–7 the Earl of Leicester's Men appear at court. But in the previous January, when he was in the Low Countries, Leicester had been created Absolute Governor of the United Provinces. Again, in the holidays of 1588–9, the Lord Admiral's Men appeared twice. But this was the first holiday season following the defeat of the Spanish Armada in the summer of 1588. This favour in which Howard was held seems to have continued into the next year, for one notes his servants not only offering 'feats of activity' on Innocents' Day of 1589, but also offering a play on Shrove Tuesday several months later. The absence of Leicester's Men, however, is impressive because that prime mover in the development of dramatic companies, although losing at least three of his actors to the Queen's Men, could yet number in his own company by 1585 such talents as Will Kempe, George Bryan and Thomas Pope, all of whom would become members of the group with which Shakespeare would work.

[1] See *MSC*, II, 314: the licence for the Queen's Men to play in the City.

The new system of a queen's company must have been a satisfactory solution, but it could not have lasted for ever, given the fact that the new Lord Chamberlain had his own company which, as early as 1584, numbered in it James Burbage, builder of the Theatre and thus one of the innovative dramatic impresarios of his age. And speaking here, as always, from the point of view of the court and the problem of control, a curious kind of 'anarchy' seems to have begun with the season of 1591–2. In the previous year the Queen's Men had acted in five court performances, while for the first time the players of Lord Strange (Ferdinando Stanley, son of the 4th Earl of Derby, who was still living) made an appearance. In the next year (1591–2), the Queen's Men only appeared at court once, while Lord Strange's Men appeared *six* times – thus, in effect, monopolizing the holiday season – the Earl of Hertford's Men once and Sussex's Men once. Chambers opines that the elaborate entertainment offered Elizabeth on 20–24 September 1591 by Hertford in his attempt to ingratiate himself after the disgrace in which he had lived owing to his first marriage to Lady Catherine Grey, heiress under Henry VIII's will to Elizabeth's throne, may have been a factor working for Hertford's Men. Elizabeth said that the entertainment was so honourable that Hertford hereafter 'should find the rewarde thereof in her especiall favour'.[1] It is difficult, however, to explain the presence of the servants of the 4th Earl of Sussex, son of the deceased Lord Chamberlain, and even more difficult to explain the overwhelming onslaught of Lord Strange's Men. Chambers attributes their success to the presence of Edward Alleyn, adducing evidence to suggest that Strange's Men had begun combining with the Lord Admiral's Men to whom Alleyn owed his allegiance. But this is to speak of results, not of causes. The fact remains that whatever plan had been instituted for regulating court performance and performers seems to have been breaking down, and in the next two years there was equivalent variety until the plague of 1592 seems to have dispersed the companies.

The Revels Accounts break off after 1589 until 1604 so that one can only speculate about the progress and development of modes of control at court itself during that interval. However, one can detect a thread of consistency in the crown's approach to the matter of revelry as it applied to acting. In the Christmas season of 1594–5, after plague had receded, two companies performed all the court plays. One company was made up of the servants to the Lord Chamberlain, Henry Carey, Lord Hunsdon, and the other was attached to Charles Howard of Effingham, Lord Admiral. These two, and Burghley, had been made Earls Marshal in 1590 and were surely among the most

[1] See Chambers, *ES*, II, 116.

powerful barons at court. From 1594 until the death of Elizabeth in 1603 there were only these two companies, with rare exception, which performed at court, although this decade witnessed the flourishing of many companies and many playhouses in and about London itself. This duality may be viewed as an alternative to a system of 'queen's players', especially since the system continued even after the death of Hunsdon when William Brooke, Lord Cobham, became Chamberlain for a brief time (8 August 1596 to 5 March 1597). The payment for that holiday season of 1596–7 was, in fact, exclusively to the 2nd Lord Hunsdon's Men, and when George Carey, Lord Hunsdon, became Lord Chamberlain, probably on 17 March 1597,[1] his acting 'servants' continued, with those of the Lord Admiral who had become Earl of Nottingham on 22 October 1596, to dominate the holiday performances. The situation prevailed until the accession of James when the new king, in effect, continued the system by giving patents to three companies, including Hunsdon's and Howard's, and they bore the names of the king, of Prince Henry and of the queen, a situation which would persist until the closing of the theatres in 1642. As for the Office of the Revels, Sir Edmund Tilney remained in it for about thirty years and, upon his death in 1609, his nephew, Sir George Buc, succeeded to the post.

[1] See *MSC*, I, 39.

2 The players and their problems

This survey has reviewed extra-theatrical forces which may have influenced the development of the drama from 1576 to 1613. It is understandable that at the beginning of this period such considerations focused upon the court, for in many ways the area of the court seems to have served as an intellectual and certainly as a legal caretaker of the emerging genre until the concept of the city playhouse was sufficiently established in the city and in the suburbs to achieve a momentum of its own and to furnish the actors with a plausible livelihood. It will be convenient now, however, to consider the drama of the period not from the viewpoint of the court, which ultimately would only be interested in plays as the material for royal entertainment and ceremonial expression, but from the viewpoint of the actors who were trying to bring a number of people – an audience – together in specific places to pay money to see dramatic entertainment.

The basic difficulty for the actors was with the City of London as represented by the lord mayor and his aldermen who were the governing 'committee'. London was an obvious market for remunerative entertainment, but London's governing group did not approve of drama. Before consequently dismissing the city fathers as hopelessly philistine Puritans, however, a sense of cultural relativity may permit some empathy with how governing circles may have seen the nature of the problem. In the final analysis, a structured mode of social entertainment was, in the 1570s and 1580s, altering locale from its longstanding environment of palaces and noble households, in which drama was ultimately only one of many forms of celebration activity, to the city and its environs. One need hardly be surprised then if this gradual alteration was to exert an impact of confusion upon bourgeois tenets of urban economics and the civil order which contributed to it. When any form of entertainment evolved for and subsidized by a court aristocracy super-imposes itself upon commercially interlocked configurations of city economics and regulations designed to insure health, order and domestic tranquillity, then confusion and conflict are at least likely. The tension between those who promoted commercial popular entertainment and those responsible for the stability of society in the sixteenth century may, in fact, be parallel to a situation in the 1970s wherein a mode of musical entertainment, formerly accessible only to a moneyed class in the confines of expensive night clubs and hotel resorts, began to move out of these confines into public areas, taking the form of the 'rock festival' highly disturbing to the authorities who feared for the corruption of youth by reason of the many people gathered there together, and for the many inconveniences arising from the great number of vehicles, sellers of drugs, lewd and unchaste behaviour and the offence to other people, not necessarily God-fearing, who proudly have old-fashioned ideas.

The frequency of the craft cycles, previously alluded to, would not necessarily have disturbed the fabric of social peace in the urban areas, for those who entertained in this manner did so, as it were, in the spirit of en-acting a pastime distinct from the basic manner in which they made their livings. It was the new phenomenon itself, occurring during working hours, and promulgated by groups which had no identity in a structured quasi-guild system, which caused disturbance. And, ultimately, it may be useful to observe that for the more conservative London burghers the question of their resistance to dramatic entertainment was a function merely of their sense of time and place. One has, after all, only to consider events accompanying the traditional date for the installation of the new lord mayor of London which fell on St Simon and St Jude's Day (28 October). On the following morning the new lord mayor would proceed by water to Westminster Hall to be re-ceived by the barons of the Exchequer, and on his return he would be met by the members of his guild, escorted to dinner in the guildhall, to a service at St Paul's and then back to his own house. His return from Westminster would be celebrated by a pageant. The fact that such pageants had been temporarily forbidden as long ago as 1481 attests to the strength of the tradition, and when these shows made their appearance again in the late 1530s their continuity is an ample refutation of any notion of specifically anti-dramatic prudery in the conservative guilds from whose ranks the lord mayor arose. Thus, to cite an example within our period, John Allot of the Worshipful Company of Fishmongers was given a pageant by his guild to celebrate his installation in 1590, and there were speeches by such characters as Fame, the Peace of England, Wisdom, Jack Straw, Science and Labour, and Richard II, as well as by those who rode the 'Merman' and the 'Unicorn'. This pageant was printed in the same year as written (or reported) by Thomas Nelson, and perusing it may suggest that the guilds, the lord mayor and the aldermen were not necessarily against show in what they considered its proper time or place. It was the definition of proper time or place that was the issue.

Whether the mayors and their aldermen were motivated by a feeling of sincere godliness, whether they were reacting against a phenomenon which did not fit the socio-economic structure as they knew it, or whether the presence of playhouses or of plays performed for the public in some inn was a clear and present danger is, however, something which finally cannot be fully determined. At one end of the spectrum, of course, hindsight can recognize that, when the Puritans actually did gain power, playhouses and commercial acting were certainly suppressed in 1642, so that the objection against playing may well have been from religious scruple. Certainly the Patristic tradition, so often cited by such a writer as Stephen Gosson in 1582 or Phillip Stubbes in 1583, was anti-histrionic in its comments on the Roman *ludi* and other forms of *spectacula* and this tradition probably defined the religious viewpoint. On the other hand, since the lord mayor was elected by and from the guilds, the real motivation may have been a sense that the guild system was threatened by a group of professionals who could not be controlled by that system. Whatever the reasons, the English actor of the 1570s and 1580s did have to be adept at running a maze of obstacles put in his way by the city fathers, and if he survived at all, it was because he seems to have mastered the art of invoking a noble patron to the point where it became a matter of that patron's prestige and 'face'. To cite a random example, in 1582 Ambrose Dudley, Earl of Warwick, and brother to the Earl of Leicester, wrote to the lord mayor on behalf of one John David, asking the mayor and aldermen to allow David to perform an exhibition of swordsmanship. Twenty-two days later, one finds Dudley writing again, saying: 'My Lord Mayor, I cannot think myself friendly dealt with to have my servant put to such public disgrace . . . to repulse him and to forbid the place appointed after allowance

1 William Cecil, Lord Burghley

and publication of his bills (wherein my name was also used) and my servant hereby greatly charged, wanteth some part of that good and friendly consideration which in courtesy and common humanity I might look for.' The tone is instructive, as is the answer wherein the lord mayor protests that he did indeed give David a licence, 'albeit the law in case of fencers have some hard exposition in some men's judgement', but that the man was indeed restrained from playing at a particular inn because of the danger from infection. The fencer was given licence therefore to play in an open place, but he apparently did not use this licence. Yet because the lord mayor has no wish to offend Warwick and also his brother, both of whom he respects dearly, he has gone to the trouble to get David a licence to play in the Theatre, or any other open place, and David has permission to pass openly through the city with trumpet, drums and with his company, as long as this does not take place on Sunday, 'which is as much as I may justify in this season'.[1]

The foregoing also indicates that there were indeed prerogatives of the City which the nobility were unwilling (or perhaps unable) to circumvent, for the tone of these letters is always as courteous as it is careful. One may, in response, cite the concept of *noblesse oblige*, but there may have been more to it than this, for the lord mayor, frequently equating acting with disorderly behaviour and the danger of spreading the plague, could always adopt the rhetorical position that he was only trying to obey previous commandments of the Privy Council and of the queen regarding disorders and plague.[2] Therefore whose commands was he to obey? In effect, one observes a 'perilous balance' between the two forces, a balance which became upset in times of political trouble, when there was too much religious pressure, or when plague became epidemic. In fact, to glance at these matters is to derive some idea of what the actor had to face in the way of restrictions throughout the period 1576–1613.

At the outset, it is useful to note the jurisdictional difference between the 'City' and the 'suburbs', for it is this distinction which was definitive not only regarding the seasons in which the actors were allowed to play but also in determining where playhouses were eventually to be erected. The jurisdiction of the lord mayor did not extend to the suburbs outside the City. Thus in the sixteenth century that part of the county of Middlesex north of the old city limits, and that part of the county of Surrey just across the Thames, were areas which did not come directly under the lord mayor's control, but the actors would naturally wish to perform in the City itself, especially in the

[1] See *MSC*, I, 54–7.
[2] Cf., e.g., the lord mayor to Walsingham, 3 May 1583, in *MSC*, I, 63.

2 Thomas Radcliffe, 3rd Earl of Sussex

winter, and it is here that the primary friction arose between the City authorities and the players. Ultimately, however, it must have seemed wiser to the actors that they should concentrate their activities in the suburbs if they were to count upon any notion of a fixed income and playing schedule free from the kinds of harassment which the lord mayor certainly could exert. The suburbs were more loosely organized for administration, and this allowed the actors more leeway, which would compensate for the comparative distance of their playing places from the centre of the City. Thus it is not surprising to observe that the first playhouses were built north of the City and that later, in the 1590s, the 'Bankside', the southern (Surrey) side of the Thames opposite the City, would become the centre of theatrical activity with such houses as Henslowe's Rose and Shakespeare's Globe being erected in the borough of Southwark. Nevertheless, at the beginning of the period here under examination, players tended to try to act at inns in the City, and it is in this general context that one follows some of the more significant efforts by the City to control the drama.

The lords mayor had prohibited playing in the City several times before 1576, but perhaps the most detailed order pertaining to this period was that of 6 December 1574, when Sir James Hawes was lord mayor of London. An act of Common Council of the City of London was then brought forth. It begins by observing that great disorders and inconvenience have come to the City because of the crowds of people, especially youths, who attend the plays. Plays and playing places have been the occasion of quarrels and even open battles. Furthermore young girls are being led into trouble because of the 'chambers and secrete places' which adjoin the open stages and galleries of the inns where the plays are being presented. The playing areas abound in pickpockets and other criminals, and also increase the danger of plague. In addition the plays themselves frequently exhibit either seditious or prurient matter. Finally, because plays occur especially on holy days and on Sundays, those who are inclined to plays are being diverted from divine worship. Therefore the following measures will be taken. (1) Any persons showing plays containing unchaste or seditious material will be imprisoned for fourteen days and fined £5. (2) No one may show a play that has not first been 'perused and allowed' by such persons as the lord mayor and the court of aldermen may appoint for the purpose. (3) No owners of buildings may allow public plays on their premises except those owners permitted by the lord mayor and the court of aldermen. (4) These owners will deposit a bond with the lord mayor to cover any public disorder or inconveniences resulting from the showing of plays. (5) These owners will not show plays during time of plague, on holy days or on Sundays, at least during the time of divine service. (6) At the risk of losing the licence to show plays if they violate this condition, owners shall pay or cause to be paid a certain sum for the use of the poor in London, such a sum being defined by the lord mayor and the court of aldermen. (7) This whole act will not apply to those who are showing plays in their houses for private entertainment at weddings, banquets and the like; however, the lord mayor and the court of aldermen reserve the right to determine what constitutes such a private showing.[1] It is not surprising that such an act should have caused the players to move from the City to the suburbs, and in fact the first known playhouse, the Theatre, was operant in the northern 'suburbs' by 1577.[2]

A situation analogous to that of the 'suburbs' was the presence of 'liberties' which offered certain opportunities to alert players. A 'liberty' was, in essence, an area within the City itself not subject to the jurisdiction of the lord mayor, being, because of certain historical circumstances, directly administered by the crown, at least in theory. Especially relevant to the drama of the time was such an area called 'the Blackfriars', the site of the former Dominican monastery which had existed there until 1538. When Henry VIII confiscated this and other monastic properties, the area gradually became a residential district, still under crown jurisdiction, one upon which the City often and naturally attempted to impinge but without great success at first. It is not surprising that one of the structures in this area was often used for different types of acting performances, the precincts being dominated by boys' companies during the sixteenth century. In the early seventeenth century, however, part of the area was taken over by Shakespeare's company, the King's Men, as a second, indoor facility for the winter playing which was otherwise closed to them by the City's denial of the inns. That one could carry on acting in the Blackfriars despite the lord mayor may be observed in 1601 when plays were performed there in Lent. The lord mayor did not intervene until he was requested to by the crown.[3] In any event, the purchase of property in the area and the framing of an adult theatre in one of the buildings in about 1608–9 brought the locale into great prominence as the site of what became the principal playhouse of the King's Men until the closing of the theatres in 1642. Since Blackfriars, and Whitefriars, another liberty which was the former precinct of the Carmelites, both passed into the jurisdiction of the City on 20 September 1608, the details of the relationship

[1] See Chambers, *ES*, IV, 273–6.
[2] See *MSC*, I, 152.
[3] See Chambers, *ES*, II, 480.

of these areas to the London authorities is a matter best left to the next volume of this history.

If moving from the City avoided the control of the lord mayor, this change in area could not, however, solve certain other basic problems inherent in the times. One of the greatest for the players was the bubonic plague, endemic in England, but often expanding to epidemic proportions especially in the summer and autumn. Both the City and the crown were obviously concerned about this matter, and one would certainly expect the City to seize the slightest excuse to enforce what had become recognized precautionary measures against the plague. The most pertinent and certainly, from a modern viewpoint, one of the most effective of such measures was a ban on public gatherings. The effect on acting of such prohibitions may quickly be gathered from the listing below which indicates those periods of time when playing was explicitly or implicitly forbidden by the Privy Council of England which, of course, could enforce a staying of plays not only in the City but in Middlesex and in Surrey as well. In this list, one may assume that plays were implicitly forbidden when the beginning of the autumn law term, Michaelmas Term, which started on the 'octave' of the saint's day (eight days after 29 September), 7 October, would be postponed because of plague. In this case, plague was probably serious in July or August, and the authorities probably waited until the last moment to decide whether to postpone the necessary business of the law courts. One might therefore speculate that a delay of Michaelmas Term implies some prohibition of public gatherings from August until the end of October. Sometimes the records only show the beginning of a play restraint, but not the end, or vice-versa: cases are listed as recorded:

1576 Michaelmas Term postponed on 29 September.
1577 Plays forbidden from 1 August until Michaelmas (29 September). Michaelmas Term deferred twice: 16 September; 15 October.
1578 Michaelmas Term deferred three times: 22 September; 20 October; 14 November. 10 November: Privy Council restrains plays in Southwark. 23 December: certain companies are allowed to play again.
1580 Playing restrained on 17 April until Michaelmas.
1581 Playing restrained from 10 July to 18 November.
1582 Michaelmas Term postponed twice: 18 September; 8 October, when it is announced that the term will be kept at Hertford.
1583 A restraint on playing ends on 26 November.

1586 Playing is restrained on 11 May 'in respect of the heat of the year now drawing on'.

1587 Playing is restrained on 7 May until 24 August because the season of the year is growing 'hotter and hotter'.

1592 Playing is restrained on 23 June until Michaelmas because of civil disorders and danger of plague. Michaelmas Term in deferred twice: 18 September; 21 October, when it is transferred to Hertford; the term is adjourned there on 22 November.

1593 Playing is restrained on 18 January and is not resumed until 30 December.

1594 Playing is restrained on 3 February, and resumes in April.

1596 Playing is restrained on 22 July. It resumes on 27 October.

1603 Playing is restrained because of the queen's impending death: 19 March. Plague begins to be recognized by 9 May and dominates until Christmas.

1604 There is probably a summer interval to guard against recurrence of plague.

1605 Plays are restrained on 5 October until 15 December.

1606 There is plague from March to December.

1607 There is plague from July to November.

1608 There is plague from July to December.

1609 There is plague from April to December.

1610 There is plague from September to November.

1611–13 Plague is not a serious problem.[1]

There were other problems faced by the players, when it came to the matter of permission to show plays. The lord mayor and the court of aldermen had always been negative about allowing plays to be shown during Lent, but in 1579, on 13 March, the Privy Council itself commanded not only the mayor but also the justices of the peace in Middlesex to prohibit all playing during Lent until the end of Easter week; furthermore, this order was to be observed hereafter every year. The City licence requested by the Privy Council for the Queen's Men in 1583 also stipulates that there will be no playing during Shrovetide.[2] So one must add the Lenten interval to whatever plague times applied to given years if one wishes to compute the ordinary shape of the playing 'season'.

Lacking plague, one might expect a precautionary restraint of playing

[1] See for all the above, Chambers, *ES*, IV, 346–51, and Barroll, 'Shakespeare's Jacobean chronology', in G. R. Smith (ed.), *Essays on Shakespeare* (University Park, 1965).
[2] See Barroll, op. cit., pp. 122 ff. and n 6.

towards May, lasting until the beginning of Michaelmas Term. In the autumn, playing would be resumed until Ash Wednesday, when the Lenten restraint would be in force. In sum, again excepting the time of plague, one might expect a full autumn, one or two months after New Year's Day, depending on when Lent began, and then a short spring schedule until probably the end of the Easter law term. At this time the companies would begin travelling in the provinces. The exception to all of these stipulations, however, was the matter of performance at court. Whether or not there was plague, and, in James's time, whether or not Lent had already begun, performances at court occurred regularly during Christmas and in Shrovetide, sometimes in the latter case continuing to occur as long as several weeks after Ash Wednesday. It would seem that the theories regarding plague contamination did not apply to court activities, while there Lent was observed only after it had been in progress for several weeks. The cavalier attitude towards plague may, however, have been fortunate for the history of the drama, for the record of the plague years shows that very often court performance could have been the only dramatic outlet.

Another exception to the restraints upon acting is to be found in the emerging role of Edmund Tilney, Master of the Revels. His influence is early attested to by an extract from the records of the court of the Guild of Merchant Taylors concerning a meeting on 22 March 1592. On 18 March the lord mayor had sent Sir Richard Martin and William Horn to treat with Edmund Tilney regarding the restraining of plays within the city. Apparently the result of this conversation translated itself into a message from the lord mayor to most of the guilds, for the Merchant Taylors, after their dinner, met to discuss the mayor's request that the Merchant Taylors yield to the payment of one annuity to Mr Tilney, Master of the Revels of the Queen's House, in whose hands the redress of this inconveniency of playing and playhouses rests. The assembly of Merchant Taylors concluded, however, that 'albeit the Company think it a very good service to be performed, yet, weighing the damage of the precedent and innovation of raising annuities upon the companies of London [considering] what further occasions it may be drawn unto', they wish that 'some other ways were taken in hand to expell out of our city so general a contagion of manners and other inconveniency, wherein if any endeavour or travail of this company might further the matter' the company stood ready to 'use their service therein'.[1] There is no way of telling whether the bribe was Tilney's or the mayor's idea, but clearly there was little support for it, just as, in the previous March, an entreaty by the

[1] See Chambers, *ES*, IV, 309.

mayor to the Archbishop of Canterbury to intercede with Tilney, although favourably received by the archbishop himself, apparently came to nothing.[1]

Given this influence, it is interesting to follow the dealings of the playhouse owner, Philip Henslowe, with the Master of the Revels between 1592 and 1598 when detailed record-keeping regarding plays finally begins to falter in Henslowe's *Diary*. The matter has been discussed from various[2] viewpoints, but one need not enter into much greater detail than to observe the configuration of the monthly payments which Henslowe seems to have been required to make to Sir Edmund Tilney in the winter and spring seasons of 1592. A week of playing commenced ten days after Ash Wednesday despite the order of 1579. At the end of this week, on 26 February, Henslowe paid Tilney 5s. This happened again on the following Saturday, 4 March, on the Friday after that, 10 March, and on the Fridays, 17 and 24 March, Easter finally occurring on the 26th. These payments were made not only in Lent, but during the time when the lord mayor had been in touch with the archbishop to intercede with Tilney and with the Merchant Taylors' Guild to raise money for the 'annuity' (6, 18, 22 March).

During each week after Easter, Henslowe paid Tilney 5s. on one or another day of the week throughout April and into the first week of May and on Wednesday 10 May. Then, two days later, on Saturday, Henslowe paid Tilney not 5s. but 12s. On the following Saturday, 20 May, Tilney was paid 6s. 8d. instead of the usual 5s. and was not paid again for about three weeks until Friday 9 June when the payment was again 6s. 8d. It was 6s. 8d. again on the following Wednesday, 14 June. Seven more plays were performed between this time and the Privy Council restraint of 23 June. Discounting the three payments of 6s. 8d. which add up to the equivalent of one extra payment of 5s., and noting that Tilney is not paid for the week of 21–27 May, matters seem normal enough given the pattern of previous bribery, but Henslowe had also paid out an extra 12s. on 13 May. During May Henslowe himself received play payments on the last Sunday of April (the 30th), on three Sundays in May and on one Sunday in June preceding the last day of playing. Although conclusions cannot be certain, one could connect this information with the escalation of his payments to the Master of the Revels. Playing on the Sabbath, after all, was forbidden, and playing through May and June had also become a somewhat difficult matter with the tradition of playing restraint in the summer owing to plague.

[1] See *MSC*, I, 68–70.
[2] See *Henslowe's Diary*, eds. R. A. Foakes and R. T. Rickert (Cambridge, 1961), p. xxviii and n 5.

When payments to Tilney are next directly ascertainable in Henslowe's *Diary*, one notes Tilney's man receiving for him on 2 January 1595, 'in full payment of a bond of one hundred pounds', the sum of £10. This is also, says the notation by Tilney's man, 'full payment of whatsoever is due from the day above written until Ash Wednesday next ensuing'. In the spring of 1597 Henslowe paid Tilney 20s. for two weeks, however, and this sum seems to have become the established rate. Henslowe did not receive payments for plays in Lent this year, but in the following year, in February, Lent began on the 9th and Henslowe was still noting receipts from plays up to the Saturday after Ash Wednesday. He paid Tilney for the month (40s.) on 23 February, and on 3 March, still in Lent, Henslowe began receiving money from performances again, making twelve entries before Easter actually arrived, and paying Tilney his 40s. on 31 March.[1]

Speculation only can draw definite conclusions about Tilney's extortions, but if the manner in which licences for plays were handled by him is at all relevant, there are analogies. In January 1598 Henslowe loaned an individual money to pay the Master of the Revels for licensing two playbooks: the sum was 14s., or 7s. per book, an amount verified often in other Henslowe entries as on 24 July 1598, when Henslowe paid Tilney 21s. for the licensing of three plays.[2] Since nothing in the various acts of the Privy Council stipulated such payments, one can only conclude that Tilney was indulging in a practice not unusual for the times, one which, however, may have enabled the players to circumvent certain restraints, or, if not, at least required them to figure Tilney in their financial projections. Some indication of the value of what Tilney realized from these activities may be gathered from the fact that in 1592 Henslowe paid a workman 3s. 6d. for three days' work on his playhouse, and he could pasture his horse at someone's farm for 20d. or 1s. 8d. a week.

Finally, notice should be taken of the kinds of occasional problems to which the players were subject in their relationship both to City and crown. By at least 1583, for example, no acting was allowed on Sunday. Such a day was so potentially profitable, however, that new orders frequently had to be given to enforce this prohibition.[3] There was also the matter of holy days. The lord mayor insisted that there should be no plays given during service time and that the players should not take in people during service time to see a play given at the end of service time. This meant that the short interval of daylight remaining after evening prayer in the winter greatly incon-

[1] See *Diary*, pp. 45, 57, 75.
[2] See *Diary*, pp. 86, 94.
[3] See *MSC*, I, 66, 187, and Dasent, op. cit., XV, 271.

venienced the actors if they were playing in the suburbs. In fact they sent a petition to the Privy Council on the subject. The Privy Council sent it to the lord mayor, who answered it in detail but remained adamant.[1] Winter must have been a problem for the actors, who had to make their money then if there was going to be some kind of summer restraint anyhow.

If it was not a question of the holy days, there was the problem of the suburbs themselves. Given the locations, which were general recreation grounds, there was always the danger of riots which would result in the closing of the playhouses themselves by a Privy Council which tended to lose its sense of humour when it was a matter, not of the theoretical question of the morality of histrionics, but of disorder and possibly sedition. For example, during the week of 7 June 1584, on Monday night, an apprentice had been lying upon the grass in the near vicinity of the Theatre and the Curtain playhouses. Another individual appears to have jumped on his stomach, but the apprentice, not sharing this sense of humour, began fighting with the joker, and gradually the number of people on both sides grew. The original attacker and others remarked that they were gentlemen and that apprentices were 'the scum of the world'. On the next day, Tuesday, a number of apprentices began assembling with the purpose of freeing the fighting apprentices, who had evidently been jailed the day before, and also to take revenge upon the attackers. This was nipped in the bud by alert police intelligence, however, and the four or five ringleaders were themselves jailed before anything could happen. The next day 'a serving man in a blue coat' who fancied himself a wit decided to pick a quarrel at the door of the Theatre with some handicraft apprentices, striking some of them and actually wounding one of the boys on the left hand. At that point about 1,000 people gathered, but Brown, the wit, managed to get lost. Being caught by chance, he was dismissed because of lack of witnesses, and, when charged again by another official, he managed to talk himself out of trouble. The narrator of this incident then indicated to Lord Burghley, who was the recipient of this account, that he sent a warrant for this Brown, and that the constables found him at the Bell inn where he had locked himself in a room and finally managed to slip away with the help of the host of the inn. Fleetwood, the writer, then indicated that he sent for this host and had him committed to jail until he would produce his erstwhile 'guest'. He did so the next day, and Brown was arrested. All this used up Wednesday, Thursday, Friday and Saturday. On Sunday the lord mayor sent two aldermen to 'the Court' with a petition 'for the suppressing and pulling down' of the Theatre and the Curtain. 'All the

[1] See *MSC*, I, 168.

Lords', presumably on the Privy Council, agreed except the Lord Chamberlain and the Vice-Chamberlain, but the aldermen were able to obtain the appropriate writ. Two playing companies were then informed of the action and obeyed it. Upon the advice of some of the Queen's Men, the owner of the Theatre, James Burbage, was sent for to be bound, but Burbage irritatedly resisted until he himself was shown the writ.[1] Clearly these playhouses were not pulled down, and the immediate sequel is unknown. But happenings such as this, in which no players were involved, must have been a source of constant apprehension, for, at the very least, the resultant pressure would inhibit acting for a certain amount of time. One can perhaps sympathize with the irritation of a Burbage in such a situation.

[1] See *MSC*, I, 163; cf., e.g., Dasent, op. cit., XXII, 549.

3 The question of censorship

When reviewing the role of the authorities in their relation to Elizabethan and Jacobean drama, it is, finally, important to consider the matter of control of content. The drama was a social phenomenon, after all, and the authorities would naturally be concerned with those possible derogations of established ideologies and mores which might take place in front of an assembled group of people. One has only to recall the well-known suspicion centering around a performance of Shakespeare's *Richard II* in connection with the Essex plot, a matter which need not be re-examined here. Rather, it will be more useful to indicate what rulings were in effect by 1576, and how these rulings concerning play content may have changed or modified through the years to 1613.

Shortly after Elizabeth came to the throne, the act for the uniformity of common prayer was promulgated, and one of its provisions, to take effect after 24 June 1559, was that if any person or persons should speak anything in derogation, depraving or despising of the Book of Common Prayer in any interludes, plays, songs or rhymes, the offenders would forfeit to the crown 100 marks for the first offence. Such a ruling can, of course, hardly be regarded as organically related to the development of the drama, the subject matter being so constricted; rather the act is more revelatory of the social conditions of 1559 in which such activity seemed to be at least feared as taking place in some of the polemically oriented drama of the times. More pertinent, then, is the proclamation of 16 May 1559, wherein the chief officers of the various cities in England were charged to permit no plays to be performed which handled matters of religion or of the governance of the 'estate of the common weale'. The penalty was fourteen days' imprisonment. The proclamation also specifically addressed itself to any of the nobility who might be keeping players as their servants.

About fifteen years later, the matter was reaffirmed by an act of the Common Council of London, one section of which empowered the City to ban plays which contained not only seditious matter but also 'words, examples, or doings of unchastity'. This act would, of course, have applied only in the City, but if the players felt the necessity of coming into the City during the winter when potential customers might be reluctant to travel to Finsbury Fields or to the Bankside, then they were putting their repertoire at the mercy of whatever criteria the city fathers used in their assessment of 'unchastity'. As we have seen (above, p. 33), the other provisions of this act stimulated the players to concentrate their activities in the suburbs so that it is difficult to determine the general effect of the act on playing within the City. One can infer its effect on playing in general, however, for in 1589 the Privy Council on 12 November reinforced the commission which the crown had given to Edmund Tilney as Master of the Revels in 1581. Then Tilney had been given general authority over all companies 'to order and reform, authorize and put down, as shall be thought meet or unmeet' not only players and playmakers, but shows and plays, and it seems reasonable to assume that, as a successful courtier, Tilney had already assured himself concerning the content of plays presented at court. The Privy Council order of 1589, however, suggests that Tilney may have enlarged his industry to see that his powers specifically applied to playing in general, for the 1589 order directed the Archbishop of Canterbury, the lord mayor of London and Sir Edmund Tilney to join together, the two former personages appointing representatives, to look over the repertoire of the players. Specifically, the Master of the Revels was charged to join with the aforementioned persons to require the players, no matter whom they might officially serve,

> to deliver unto them their books [prompt books] that they [the 'com-
> mittee'] may consider of the matters of their comedies and tragedies, and
> thereupon to strike out such parts and matters as they shall find unfit and
> undecent to be handled in plays, both for divinity and state, commanding

the said company of players in Her Majesty's name that they forbear to present and play publicly any comedy or tragedy other than such as they three shall have seen and allowed, which if they [the players] shall not observe, they shall then know from their Lordships that they shall be not only severely punished, but made incapable of the exercise of their profession forever hereafter.[1]

It is significant that Tilney was made a part of this group, because his inclusion greatly strengthened his office and made him virtual dictator not only in the realm of acting and theatres, but of subject matter also. In this respect, the act to restrain abuses of players promulgated under James on 27 May 1606 is perhaps even more aesthetically relevant. It was the next in the sequence of regulatory acts and it ruled that 'if at any time or times after the end of the present session of Parliament any person or persons do or shall, in any stage-play, interlude, show, May-game, or pageant, jestingly or profanely speak or use the holy name of God, or of Christ Jesus, or of the Holy Ghost, or of the Trinity (which are not to be spoken but with fear and reverence)'[2] such persons shall forfeit for every such offence £10. Presumably the act was not exclusively objecting to ridicule of Christianity, but perhaps more specifically to such language put into the mouth of a character as might invoke the name of the Deity in the emotional stress of the dramatic moment. 'Swearing' is our modern term. Whether or not this ruling applied to printed books, an illustrative example may be drawn from comparing the 1604 Quarto of *Hamlet* with the Folio version, for the latter exhibits an almost enthusiastic 'cleaning up' of such language, going beyond the letter to observe the spirit of this edict. Consequently, some of the speeches lose the kind of vehemence which characterizes them in Quarto, 'before God!', for example, being changed to 'before Heaven!'.

Finally, at least for the period under our attention here, there was the order promulgated at the General Session of the Peace for Middlesex, an order which, from the wording, seems to have applied to the Fortune theatre, but which may be usefully illustrative in general. This order suppressed jigs at the end of plays (see p. 107 in Part II). Jigs were combinations of song and dance with broadly lewd connotations, and Hamlet, we recall, accused Polonius of falling asleep in all plays unless he was watching this kind of performance. From the wording of the order it would seem that 'divers cut-purses and other lewd and ill-disposed persons in great multitudes' came in

[1] See Dasent, op. cit., XVIII, 214.
[2] W. C. Hazlitt, *The English Drama and Stage* (London, 1869), p. 42, reprints this statute (3 *Jac.* I, c. 21).

at the end of the play for the jig, and by their presence caused 'tumults and outrages'.[1] Therefore all actors in all theatres in Middlesex were expressly forbidden to perform 'jigs, rhymes, and dances' at the ends of their plays. Very few jigs survive, in the printed books, at any rate, so it is difficult to determine the aesthetic result of such a ruling.

That all these various rulings were enforced may be gathered from random incidents on record. On 16 August 1597 the Privy Council ordered the arrest of the players of a drama given on the Bankside, as well as of the author, Ben Jonson, who was released on 8 October along with Gabriel Spencer and Robert Shaw, who were members of Pembroke's company.[2] On 10 May 1601 the Privy Council ordered that certain players at the Curtain in Middlesex be forbidden to continue showing a particular play which seemed to be impersonating 'some gentlemen of good desert and quality'.[3]

If such orders controlled the enacted plays themselves, it is of interest to determine whether the printed books, almost our sole source of knowledge concerning Elizabethan and Jacobean drama itself, were subject to the same restrictions. By association, one might opine, any printed book purporting to be a play acted by such and such a company might be a matter of concern to Tilney on general principles, for if the matter contained therein were unsatisfactory, here would be prima facie evidence that Tilney or his subordinates had not maintained a requisite alertness. On the other hand the Privy Council may have been, in its rulings, primarily concerned with the effect of the spoken word and accompanying pageantry on a volatile group of people gathered in one place. Therefore a glance at the mechanism for the control of book content may not be irrelevant. One notes that in 1559, the same year as the legislation against seditious or anti-religious material in plays, the injunctions of the crown were promulgated concerning the clergy and the laity of the realm. One section had to do with the printers of books. The injunction simply states that no book was to be printed unless licensed by the crown, or by the Archbishops of Canterbury and York, the Bishop of London, the Chancellors of Oxford and Cambridge, and various religious officials. The names of these or, presumably, their deputies who 'allowed' any book also had to be added to the end of every work. There follows in the injunctions a special emphasis on 'pamphlets, plays, and ballads', and the general ruling also applies to sellers of such books, while the attention of the whole Company of Stationers, the guild of the book trade, was called to this

---

[1] See Chambers, *ES*, IV, 340.
[2] See Dasent, op. cit., XXVII, 338; XXVIII, 33.
[3] See Dasent, op. cit., XXXI, 346.

order.[1] This law was reaffirmed by the new decrees of the Star Chamber on 23 June 1586, where punishment was specified as the defacing and destruction of all presses concerned in the printing of the offending book, the prohibition of the printer from practising his trade, and six months' imprisonment.

What were the criteria for offence in this connection? One gathers from the injunctions that, as far as plays were concerned, the crown would censor matter 'heretical, seditious, or unseemly for Christian ears'. This would seem both to cover a great deal of territory and also to allow great latitude at the same time. Certainly an unlooked-for aesthetic result is that such laws may have saved posterity from a great deal of topical satire of interest only to social historians. At the same time, if one takes the viewpoint that such a play as *King Lear* is religiously nihilistic, as well as politically sceptical about the divinity of kings, one may note that the fact that the play was indeed printed as well as acted attests to a sensible kind of tolerance in these matters, at least in the Jacobean era. As for the period of Elizabeth, we are not wholly subject to the process of guesswork, for we are fortunate in possessing the manuscript of parts of *Sir Thomas More* along with the marginal commentaries of Sir Edmund Tilney.[2] Most interesting is that commentary (on folio 3A) on the so-called Ill May Day scene in which a conspiracy and rebellion are planned by the commoners. In the margin Tilney has written 'Leave out the insurrection wholly and the cause thereof and begin with Sir Thomas More at the mayor's sessions [a succeeding scene] with a report afterwards of his good service done being shrieve of London upon a mutiny against the Lombards only by a short report and not otherwise at your own perils.' Again, in Scene iii, lines 1–8 have been crossed out by Tilney with the admonition 'mend this'. The last six lines of this particular section may be worth quoting as illustrative. The Earl of Shrewsbury is the speaker, 'vulgar brow' presumably referring to the aspect of the common people:

> I tell ye true, that in these dangerous times
> I do not like this frowning vulgar brow.
> My searching eye did never entertain
> A more distracted countenance of grief
> Than I have late observ'd
> In the displeased commons of the city.

[1] See Chambers, *ES*, IV, 264–5.
[2] See A. W. Pollard *et al.*, *Shakespeare's Hand in the Play of Sir Thomas More* (Cambridge, 1923).

Clearly the censoring emphasis is indeed on sedition throughout. If so, however, the Office of the Revels must have mellowed during the Jacobean era if we recall the opening scene of *Coriolanus* and the many episodes in it which treat the complainings of the commons.

4 The audience

A survey of social aspects of the drama from 1576 to 1613 cannot be complete without some inquiry into the nature of those for whom the plays were meant to be performed. In certain cases, of course, the situation of the audience would be self-defining: performances at court would hardly have been open to the public and the concept that plays were performed for the solace and recreation of the sovereign argued that, in theory, the monarch was the sole intended audience. It was upon this theory, after all, that the whole concept of an Office of the Revels rested in the first place. And if the nobility happened to share the sovereign's recreation, it was nevertheless an incidental participation, depending, in the last analysis, upon whom the sovereign permitted to be present. Since all this is sufficiently uncomplicated, the more interesting object of inquiry would therefore be the public audience which, after all, furnished the players with their means of livelihood.

Assessing this audience is difficult for the early years of the sixteenth century when public playing was occasional and when, therefore, records are sparse. For this reason it is important to consult the provenance of any given play when this provenance may be determined. The schools, such as Eton or the Merchant Taylors' School, were theoretically perfecting their pupils in the arts of elocution, rhetoric and literary appreciation of the classics, and one might assume that plays performed by them were for the school, the masters therein and, when fortunate enough, for the sovereign who might invite such an acting group of the boys to perform during the holidays at court. Much the same may be said for the choir schools attached to the various royal chapels and to St Paul's cathedral, except that in the late 1590s and increasingly into the next century such groups attained an entity (whether legal or not) in themselves which eventually resulted in the establishment of a kind of coterie drama performed in private theatres before an audience which could afford a larger price of admission than could those who frequented the public theatres. It is these public theatres, however, which are the most appropriate areas of concern if it is a question of inquiring into the nature of those audiences for whom a Marlowe, a Shakespeare or a Jonson fashioned their plays, no matter how often these plays may, in turn, have finally been performed by their companies at court before the sovereign.

It has been calculated that the population of London of the sixteenth and seventeenth centuries (London with its suburbs both north and south) was, in 1605, about 160,000.[1] Naturally one becomes interested in determining just what degree of support or enthusiasm was generated by such a number, for obviously there could have been no Elizabethan or Jacobean drama without spectators. Unfortunately, the detailed book-keeping of only one individual, Philip Henslowe, is known, but his *Diary*, in which he recorded payments to him made by companies of actors who played in the theatres which he owned, is sufficiently detailed for 1594 and 1595 to allow some idea of what proportion of the population actually came to plays. About 21,000 in a six-day week probably attended all the theatres in 1605, and if the estimate of about 15,000 a week for 1595 is anywhere near accurate, based as it is on payments recorded by Henslowe, the resultant figure emerges as 13 per cent of the accessible population in and around London. Such a number, about three out of every twenty-five people, is obviously not excessive, but, since London companies obviously stayed in business, it is clear that the audience was a faithful one.

The audience itself would seem to have been composed of just about every class, with the possible exception of the highest nobility, and one may perhaps derive some notion of what kind of people might have found playgoing financially feasible by observing the most inexpensive rate for admission: 1d. Since currency values are obviously relative, the figure of a 'penny' is not extremely useful in comparison with other factors. Thus one should observe that a workman received 7s. a week, so that the cheapest ticket for a play

[1] See Alfred Harbage, *Shakespeare's Audience* (New York, 1961: reprint), pp. 38–41.

could be purchased for one eighty-fourth of the workman's weekly salary. Since such a figure is still not very meaningful, it is worth noting that ale could be purchased for 4d. a quart. It is useful to concentrate upon ale because the prices of what we may regard as common materials may have been notably higher before the industrial revolution made mass production possible – Henslowe, for example, paid 6s. for 'four long pieces of timber'. A quart of ale, it is easy enough to see, however, cost four times as much as the cheapest admission to a theatre; but a quart of the most inferior beer, however, cost 1d. Translating this into modern terms which can never be absolute because of changing prices, one could formulate the following rough equations. To wish to spend an afternoon drinking a quart of decent ale was to spend 4d. out of the total of 84d. which one, as an average workman, received per week; this was one twenty-first of one's weekly salary, because one twenty-first of 84d. equals 4d., the price of a quart of ale. Play admissions appear quite reasonable in one sense, but not cheap. If one speculates upon viable alternatives, and if every penny counted, one might easily drink a quart of cheap beer for 1d. and go to the theatre for another 1d., still not having spent as much as for a quart of ale which, in retrospect, strikes one as really rather an expensive item, even if consumed by the pint every other day. Finally, when speaking of entertainment, going out to dinner would cost, by gradation from cheapest to most expensive class of place: 3d.; 6d.; 8d.; 12d.; 18d. Clearly, ale was in the price category which, in the 1970s, might be associated with 'hard liquor', and theatres were much less expensive than either a quart of ale or the cheapest dinner to be bought. The fact that there were also 2d. and 3d. classes of admission to the theatres will sufficiently suggest the possible variety in classes of audience.

Table 1: court performances

This table indicates which companies acted on the various holidays at Christmas and in Lent. The information for such activity between 1570 and 1600 is probably more useful than that for the period after 1600. Before 1600 fewer plays were paid for, and they can thus be traced with more exactitude. However, after the accession of James I in 1603, so many more plays were presented that those who noted the payments began to lump them together without specifying dates, especially between 1604 and 1614. In these, and in other such years, plays were usually given at odd times in December or January close to but not on the dates of the traditional holidays around which the table is organized to offer the reader a representative sampling. Such instances are designated by the term *other*. Because any such table is at the mercy of what records survive, we should not assume that after 1604–5, for instance, no play was offered, say, on Shrove Sunday: it is simply that a payment

Table 1

Year	Stephen's	John's	Innocents'	New Year's	Twelfth Night	Candlemas
1571-2		Lane	St Paul's	Chapel (W)	Chapel (W)	
1572-3	?Leicester	?Leicester	?Leicester	Chapel (W)	Eton	?St Paul's
1573-4	Leicester	St Paul's	Leicester	Westminster	Chapel (W)	Merchant Taylors'
1574-5	Leicester	Lincoln		Leicester	Chapel (W)	St Paul's
1575-6	Warwick	Chapel (W)	Leicester	Warwick	St Paul's	Sussex
1576-7	Warwick	Howard	?Leicester	St Paul's	Chapel (W) + Chapel	Sussex
1577-8	Leicester	Chapel	Warwick	Howard	Warwick	Sussex
1578-9	Warwick	?Chapel	Sussex	St Paul's	Sussex	[Warwick]
1579-80	Sussex	Chapel	[Leicester]	Warwick	Leicester	Sussex
1580-1	Leicester	Sussex		Derby	St Paul's	Sussex
1581-2	St Paul's		Strange [A]			
1582-3	Chapel	Hunsdon		Strange [A]	Sussex	
1583-4	Queen's			Oxford	Chapel	Chapel
1584-5	Queen's	Oxford (boys)		Oxford [A]	Queen's	
1585-6	Queen's	Howard		Queen's	Hunsdon + Howard	
1586-7	Queen's	Leicester		Queen's	Queen's	
1587-8	Queen's		?Queens [A]	St Paul's	Queen's	St Paul's
1588-9	Queen's	St Paul's		St Paul's		
1589-90	Queen's		Howard + St Paul's [A]	St Paul's	St Paul's	
1590-1	Queen's	Strange + Howard		Queen's	Queen's	
1591-2	Queen's	Strange	Strange	Strange	Hertford	
1592-3	Pembroke	Strange		Strange	Pembroke	
1593-4					Queen's	
1594-5	Hunsdon	?Hunsdon	?Howard	Howard	Howard	
1595-6	Hunsdon	Hunsdon	Hunsdon	Howard	Hunsdon	
1596-7	Hunsdon	Hunsdon		Hunsdon	Hunsdon	
1597-8	Hunsdon	Howard		Hunsdon	Hunsdon	
1598-9	Hunsdon	Howard		Hunsdon	Howard	
1599-1600	Hunsdon	Howard		Howard	Hunsdon	
1600-1	Hunsdon		Howard	Derby / St Paul's	Chapel / Hunsdon / Howard / Derby	Howard
1601-2	Hunsdon	Hunsdon / Howard		Hunsdon	Chapel	
1602-3	Hunsdon	Howard		St Paul's	Hertford	Hunsdon
1603-4	King's	King's	King's	King's / King's		King's
1604-5	King's		King's	Revels		King's
1605-6		Queen's		Prince's		
1606-7	King's		Prince's		King's	King's
1607-8	King's	King's	King's		King's: 2	King's
1608-9				Blackfriars		
1609-10	Prince's	Queen's	Prince's			
1610-11		Queen's	Prince's			
1611-12	King's	Queen's	Prince's	King's		Queen's
1612-13				Queen's Revels		
1613-14		King's		King's		King's

Shrove Sunday	Shrove Tuesday	Other	Other	Other	Other	Other
Lane	Westminster					
?Sussex	Merchant Taylors'	Lincoln				
Leicester	Merchant Taylors'	Lincoln				
?Warwick	?Merchant Taylors'	Chapel	Lincoln			
Leicester	Merchant Taylors'	Warwick	Italian players			
Howard	St Paul's	Warwick				
Warwick	Lady Essex	St Paul's				
Warwick	Sussex	Chapel	Leicester			
Derby	Sussex	St Paul's				
Chapel	?Leicester					
	Chapel	Chapel	Five plays and two masques			
Leicester	Merchant Taylors'	Derby				
	Oxford + Chapel Queen's	Queen's				
Queen's	Queen's	Queen's				
Queen's		Strange boys [A]				
St Paul's	Queen's	St Paul's				
Queen's	Evelyn	Gray's Inn				
Queen's	Howard	Howard	St Paul's			
Queen's	Howard					
Queen's	Strange + Howard [A]	Queen's				
Strange	Strange	Sussex	Strange			
		Strange				
Hunsdon	Howard	Howard				
Howard						
Hunsdon	Hunsdon					
Hunsdon	Howard					
Howard	Hunsdon					
Hunsdon	Derby					
Chapel	Hunsdon					
Hunsdon		Chapel	Worcester			
Chapel						
Howard	Howard					
King's	Revels	King's: 2	Prince's: 5	Queen's: 2	St Paul's: 1	
King's	King's	King's: 7	Prince's: 8		Queen's: 1	Revels: 1
	Prince's	King's: 13	Prince's: 4			St Paul's: 3
King's		King's: 5	Prince's: 5			
King's: 2		King's: 6	Prince's: 4			
		King's: 12	Prince's: 3		Queen's: 5	Blackfriars: 3
		King's: 13	Prince's: 2	York's: 1		Whitefriars: 5
King's		King's: 15	Prince's: 3	York's: 3	Queen's: 3	
King's	Elizabeth's	King's: 21	Prince's: 4	York's: 4	Queen's: 4	Whitefriars: 1
						Elizabeth's: 3
	King's	King's: 21	Prince's: 2	Revels: 3		Elizabeth's: 3
King's	King's	King's: 11			Queen's: 2	Elizabeth's: 2

for that date may not have been specified. In James's reign too, November, beginning with All Saints' Day on the first of the month, became a popular time, while various plays were also given during the first week of Lent as well as in December and January.

It should be noted that no playing instance has been mentioned twice in the tables. If, in 1584–5, the Queen's Men played on some specified or unspecified date (see under *other*), this playing date was in addition to those instances already mentioned for that year. The number sometimes appearing after the name of a company indicates the number of performances recorded. Thus in 1607–8 'Kings: 2' means that there are two performances on record.

When question marks precede the name of a company, the indication refers to the fact that although the company is recorded as the payee, and although no specific date is given, other information, or, in some cases, reasonable assumption, would suggest the day indicated as the date of performance. After 1604 there is little point in making specific chronological assumptions without evidence, because playing times were so widely scattered.

We construct the dramatic year as beginning on 1 September. Thus '1607–8' comprehends 1 September 1607 to 31 August 1608.

Name abbreviations are, for the most part, obvious. 'St Paul's' does of course refer to the boys' groups derived from the choir schools attached to the great cathedral. 'Chapel' refers to the boys' group at the choir school of the Chapel Royal while 'Chapel (W)' refers to the boys' group at the choir school of the Chapel Royal at Windsor. The names of various schools in the 1570s indicate groups of boy actors who were brought from these schools to perform at court by invitation. In the seventeenth century 'Blackfriars', 'Whitefriars', and 'Revels' (The Children of the Queen's Revels) refer to boys' acting groups whose history is discussed at greater length in Part II of this volume. Howard, who became Lord Admiral, and then Earl of Nottingham, is always termed 'Howard' while 'Hudson' is always used to refer to father and then son, both of whom became Lords Chamberlain. Other names can be clarified by consulting other sections of this volume. The Queen's Men, formed in the reign of Elizabeth I, should not be confused with the acting group brought together under the name of the consort of James I after his accession.

[A] after the notation of a company indicates the fact that these companies performed various 'feats of activity', not plays, on the day indicated. It is interesting that Innocents' Day seems to have been associated with such activity.

Since many more plays were given at court in James's reign, and since they were often lumped together in bulk payments, a year such as 1607–8 might yield a good picture of how matters were going. We note that the King's Men were given most of the important holiday playing dates and that, in addition, they were paid for six other playing times. It is clear that the company itself was a favourite.

Table 2: a calendar of plays 1576–1613

This calendar of plays includes not only those which are available because they were printed during the period, but also those for which we have only titles. This former category may be illustrative of the popularity of a given play; in many cases, however, the reverse may be true. A very popular play may not have been printed for a long time simply because it could not be protected by copyright laws as we now understand them. The nearest approach to a 'copyright' benefited only the printer or the publisher of any book, not the author or the dramatic company owning it. Ownership of the printing rights to a manuscript was established by a printer entering it into the Stationers' Register, a record book located in the guild-hall of the Company of Stationers, the organization for all printers and publishers in England. The hearings which the Company of Stationers held from time to time constituted the final arbitration in adjudicating disputes between members of the *company* regarding the ownership of any material.

If the Company of Stationers, however, only recognized 'ownership' as it might pertain to the publisher or printer, then an Elizabethan or Jacobean acting company might very well have wished to withhold a play manuscript from print, for printing would simply make a popular play available to rival acting companies who could then perform it with impunity.

The register itself was kept by the clerk of the company and it is this document which provides us with the greater part of our knowledge concerning the probable chronology of Elizabethan and Jacobean drama. Therefore it is customary, in the dating of a published play, to offer, when available, two dates. One is the date on which the title was entered by the printer 'SR 10 March 1592', this indicating that there is an entry for this title in the Stationers' Register on 10 March 1592. The other date is, of course, that which was printed on the title page of the published book itself. Often, publication did not immediately follow entry into SR: and there might even be a lapse of years. In such cases, the SR entry, of course, provides valuable information for dating the play. All this being so, neither SR nor publication dates necessarily define dates of performance or of composition unless such information is used in combination with other factors. Since we must be concerned, however, with the Elizabethan and Jacobean reading public as another dimension of 'dramatic audience', so to speak, we therefore indicate data available from the previously indicated source, and we also note whether or not, in any given year, a play has been reprinted. Thus '*Jocasta* (1573; 1575)' when entered under the heading of 1587 means that the play *Jocasta* was reprinted in 1587 but had been printed before once in 1573 and once in 1575.

The sources of information concerning plays that were performed are usually the Revels Accounts, for court, and for public playhouses, the record of payments in Henslowe's *Diary*. Sometimes title pages furnish such information also. What emerges therefore can hardly be regarded as a typical profile of performances, because we are limited by the nature of our source materials which can indicate only what indeed is known at present. The dates affixed to the Henslowe plays may be debatable because scholars are in some disagreement as to whether an entry of receipts in the *Diary* really refers to the day of performance. A typical entry would run '25 of September 1595 Rd at the Worldes Tragedy . . . xxxviij s' or, as it were, 'received on 25 September 1595, 38s. for *The World's Tragedy*'. There is, however, evidence to support the view that the dates may refer to performance on that day or on a day extremely close to the one indicated. (For example, in 1595, Lent ends with Easter on 20 April and, on 21 April, Henslowe is noting receipts for a play again. In July 1597 the Privy Council orders on the 28th that there be no play until All Hallows, and there is no entry by Henslowe after 28 July. On 23 June 1592, as we have seen, the Privy Council restrained playing until Michaelmas because of disorders at the Theatre and Curtain. Henslowe's last entry is the day before, on the 22nd. That autumn, on 7 September, well before Michaelmas, there is an order to stop playing because of the plague and we see no further Henslowe entries until 29 December, a plausible date for the resumption of playing. There are receipts for 29, 30, 31 December. In January plays are entered every day except on the 2nd, 7th, 21st, 27th, 28th and 29th, including three Sundays. When, on 28 January, the Privy Council prohibits playing within seven miles of London, the City making the proclamation on the 31st, Henslowe notes his last payment on 1 February. Henslowe's entries then resumed on 27 December, and he continues to note payments daily throughout January except on five different days. On 3 February the Privy Council restrains plays again, and two days later we witness another final entry of receipts by Henslowe.)

Henslowe's *Diary* begins alluding to performances of plays in 1592 and breaks off in 1597. Therefore, although the information from that document is listed in the table, the reader must constantly bear in mind that the material can only be illustrative of the practices of one form of management within a period for which there is this information: 1592–7. With these qualifications in mind, however, some idea may be derived of the variety of plays, and their frequency. The shape of the theatre season for all companies may also be derived from a glance at the Henslowe titles, for it seems safe enough to assume that when one company was presenting plays, all companies were. In any event, the listing even of titles for which we lack printings will be useful as it indicates both the frequency of performances and the system of rotation. Fortunately, some of the most popular plays do survive in print. The titles are chronologically arranged: although there may be controversy as to whether the payment date was the playing date, the dating itself establishes for us with a high degree of certainty the sequence of presentation. The popularity of some of the plays is indicated by the numerals following a title. Under 1595, for example, '2 *Tamburlaine* (4)' means that this is the fourth known performance of Marlowe's *Tamburlaine*, Part II.

The sources for information regarding the titles of plays presented at court offer problems. There are two primary and slightly parallel records, the Chamber Accounts which record the payments of moneys for court entertainments, and the Revels Accounts which were made out by the Office of the Revels and presented for payment to the Treasurer of the Chamber. The Chamber Accounts, listing payments to companies, and only occasionally alluding to play titles, are relatively complete for the period 1576–1613, but the Revels Accounts exist only for the periods 1571–89, 1604–5 and 1611–12. There will thus seem to be gaps in the following list of plays performed, but these gaps should be understood as due to lack of information, not as indicating an absence of dramatic activity. Often one play was presented two or more times in one month. In such instances the titles are repeated. See 'Muly Mollocco' for February 1592.

Dates of performance are only alluded to when a specific day is known, or when the play falls within a very brief time period. Other performances are known by contemporary references, but there is no need to cover this material which has been fully dealt with elsewhere. The value of this listing to the reader is to gain some sense of the dramatic 'flavour' of each given year as reflected in known performances, printings and reprintings, and the listing of titles to plays which do not survive will be useful because of the subject matter they seem to indicate.

Plays which survive either in printings or in manuscript are always italicized. The reader should consult E. K. Chambers, *The Elizabethan Stage*, W. W. Greg, *A Bibliography of the English Printed Drama to the Restoration* and *Dramatic Documents from the Elizabethan Playhouses*, and Alfred Harbage (revised S. Schoenbaum), *Annals of English Drama 975–1700* for full information on all such titles italicized. Occasional entertainments and 'welcomes', even though published, are not listed here. Their titles may be found in the above-named works.

Authors of plays are never listed because, in many cases, authorship is open to conjecture. Henslowe's *Diary*, for example, rarely alludes to authorship and the printings of the time seldom list the name of the playwright on the title page. Should the reader wish to find the real or conjectured author, he should consult the index to this volume, where he will be directed to further information about any given play title.

Table 2

1576 PERFORMANCES
        At court: 'The Painter's Daughter' (26 December)
                'Toolie' (27 December)
                'The Historie of the Collier' (30 December)
     Elsewhere: 'The Red Knight' (25 July–5 August): Bristol.

PRINTINGS
Common Conditions. SR 26 July 1576.
The Tide Tarrieth No Man. SR 22 October 1576. Two editions.

REPRINTINGS
None known.

Table 2 – *continued*

1577   PERFORMANCES

> *At court:* 'The History of Error' (1 January)
> 'The History of Mutius Scaevola' (6 January)
> 'The History of the Cynocephali' (2 February)
> 'The History of the Solitary Knight' (17 February)
> 'The Irish Knight' (18 February)
> 'The History of Titus and Gisippus' (19 February)
> 'The Play of Cutwell' (not performed but referred to:
> 17–20 February)
> *Elsewhere:* 'Mingo' (13–19 October): Bristol.

PRINTINGS
All for Money. SR 25 November 1577.
Abraham's Sacrifice. Title page indicates that the translator of Theodore
Beza's French play finished on 11 August 1575.

REPRINTINGS
The Chief Promises of God (?1547)
Darius (1565)

1578   PERFORMANCES

> *At court:* 'The Three Sisters of Mantua' (26 December)
> 'An History of the Cruelty of a Stepmother' (26 December)
> *Elsewhere:* 'What Mischief Worketh in the Mind of Man'
> (6–12 July): Bristol.

PRINTINGS
Promos and Cassandra. SR 31 July 1578: 'divided into twoe Comicall
discourses'.
The Most Virtuous and Godly Susanna. SR April/May 1569.

REPRINTINGS
None known.

1579   PERFORMANCES

> *At court:* 'The Marriage of Mind and Measure' (1 January)
> 'A Pastorall or History of a Greek Maid' (4 January)
> 'The Rape of the Second Helen' (6 January)
> 'The Knight in the Burning Rock' (1 March)
> 'Loyalty and Beauty' (2 March)
> 'The History of Murderous Michael' (3 March)
> 'A History of the Duke of Milan and the Marquess of
> Mantua' (26 December)
> 'Alucius' (27 December)
> *Elsewhere:* Hymenaeus (March): Cambridge.

PRINTINGS
None known.

REPRINTINGS
None known.

1580 PERFORMANCES
>   *At court:* 'The Four Sons of Fabius' (1 January)
>   'Scipio Africanus' (3 January)
>   'Portio and Demorantes' (2 February)
>   'The Sultan and the Duke of ——' (14 February)
>   'Sarpedon' (16 February)
>   'A Comedy Called Delight' (26 December)
>   *Elsewhere:* Not known.

PRINTINGS
None known.

REPRINTINGS
None known.

1581 PERFORMANCES
>   *At court:* 'Pompey' (6 January)
>   *Elsewhere:* Not known.

PRINTINGS
Seneca his Ten Tragedies. SR 4–9 July 1581: *Thebais, Hippolytus, Hercules Oetaeus* are new. For the others, see *Reprintings* below.
Sophocles, *Antigone*, tr. Thomas Watson. SR 31 July 1581.
The Conflict of Conscience. Two issues.

REPRINTINGS
Seneca, *Troas*, tr. J. Heywood (1559; 1559; n.d.)
>   *Thyestes*, tr. J. Heywood (1560)
>   *Hercules Furens*, tr. J. Heywood (1561)
>   *Oedipus*, tr. A. Neville (1563)
>   *Agamemnon*, tr. J. Studley (1566)
>   *Medea*, tr. J. Studley (1566)
>   *Octavia*, tr. T. Nuce (?1566). Ascribed to Seneca.

1582 PERFORMANCES
>   *At court:* 'A Comedy or Moral devised on a Game of the Cards'
>   (26 December)
>   'A Comedy of Beauty and Housewifery' (27 December)
>   *Love and Fortune* (30 December). See 1589.
>   *Elsewhere:* Not known.

Table 2 – *continued*

PRINTINGS
None known.

REPRINTINGS
None known.

1583 PERFORMANCES
       At court : 'Ferrar' (6 January)
               'Telomo' (10 February)
               'Ariodante and Genevora' (12 February)
    Elsewhere : *Rivales* (11 June): Oxford.
               Dido (12 June): Oxford.

PRINTINGS
None known.

REPRINTINGS
None known.

1584 PERFORMANCES
       At court : 'A Pastoral of Phillyda and Choryn' (26 December)
               'Agamemnon and Ulysses' (27 December)
               Campaspe (6 January)
               Sappho and Phao (3 March)
    Elsewhere : *Philomathes' Dream* (11 February): St Paul's School.

PRINTINGS
Sappho and Phao. SR 6 April 1584. Two editions.
Campaspe. Three editions.
The Arraignment of Paris
The Three Ladies of London

REPRINTINGS
None known.

1585 PERFORMANCES
       At court : 'Felix and Philiomena' (3 January)
               'Five Plays in One' (6 January)
               'Three Plays in One' (21 February). Prepared but not
                performed.
               Fedele and Fortunio (date not known)
    Elsewhere : Not known.

PRINTINGS
Fedele and Fortunio. SR 12 November 1584. (A tr. of Pasqualigo's
Il Fidele.)

REPRINTINGS
None known.

1586   PERFORMANCES
  At court : Dates known; titles not known.
  Elsewhere : Philomathes' Second Dream (February): St Paul's School.

PRINTINGS
None known.

REPRINTINGS
None known.

1587   PERFORMANCES
  At court : Dates known; titles not known.
  Elsewhere : Not known.

PRINTINGS
None known.

REPRINTINGS
Like Will to Like (1568; n.d.)
Supposes (1573; 1575)
Jocasta (1573; 1575)
Masque for Lord Montacute (1573; 1575). These last three titles are
always in Gascoigne's collected works published at the dates indicated.

1588   PERFORMANCES
  At court : Galathea (1 January)
    Endymion (2 February)
  Elsewhere : The Misfortunes of Arthur (28 February): actually shown
    at Greenwich but performed by the gentlemen of Gray's
    Inn.
    'Sylla Dictator' (16 January): Gray's Inn.

PRINTINGS
The Misfortunes of Arthur. Dated '1587' Old Style (i.e. 1588).

REPRINTINGS
None known.

1589   PERFORMANCES
  At court : Dates known; titles not known.
  Elsewhere : Not known.

Table 2 – *continued*

PRINTINGS
The Rare Triumphs of Love and Fortune.

REPRINTINGS
None known.

1590   PERFORMANCES
        At court: Midas (6 January)
        Elsewhere: Not known.

PRINTINGS
The Three Lords and Three Ladies of London. SR 31 July 1590.
Tamburlaine the Great [*1* and *2 Tamburlaine*]. SR 14 August 1590.

REPRINTINGS
Gorboduc: (1565; ?1570). This time collected in Lydgate's *Serpent of Division.*

1591   PERFORMANCES
        At court: Dates known; titles not known.
        Elsewhere: Not known.

PRINTINGS
Amynta's Pastoral (closet pastoral?) in *The Countess of Pembroke's Ivychurch* by Abraham Fraunce. SR 9 February 1591.
The Hunting of Cupid. SR 26 July. Lost, but fragments remain: see *Malone Society Collections,* I, 307–14.
Endymion. SR 4 October 1591.
The Troublesome Reign of King John (Parts I and II)
Tancred and Gismund. A variant copy of the title page indicates '1592'.

REPRINTINGS
Sappho and Phao (1584; 1584)
Campaspe (1584; 1584; 1584)

1592   PERFORMANCES
        At court: Dates known; titles not known.
        Elsewhere: Ulysses Redux (6 February): Oxford.
                     Hippolytus (5 February): Oxford.
                     At the Rose playhouse on the Bankside:
        19–29 February: Friar Bacon   (1)
                          Muly Mollocco   (1)
                          Orlando Furioso   (1)
                          The Spanish Comedy   (1)
                          Sir John Mandeville   (1)

19–29 February: Harry of Cornwall   (1)
The Jew of Malta   (1)
Chloris and Orgasto   (1)
Muly Mollocco   (2)
1–31 March: Pope Joan   (1)
Machiavelli   (1)
Henry VI   (1)
Bindo and Ricardo   (1)
Four Plays in One   (1)
Henry VI   (2)
A Looking Glass for London and England   (1)
Zenobia   (1)
The Jew of Malta   (2)
Henry VI   (3)
The Spanish Comedy   (2)
The Spanish Tragedy   (1)
Henry VI   (4)
Muly Mollocco   (3)
The Jew of Malta   (3)
The Spanish Tragedy   (2)
Constantine   (1)
Jerusalem   (1)
Harry of Cornwall   (2)
Friar Bacon   (2)
A Looking Glass for London and England   (2)
Henry VI   (5)
Muly Mollocco   (4)
The Spanish Comedy   (3)
The Spanish Tragedy   (3)
1–30 April: Sir John Mandeville   (2)
Machiavelli   (2)
The Jew of Malta   (4)
Henry VI   (6)
Brandimer   (1)
The Spanish Tragedy   (4)
Muly Mollocco   (5)
The Spanish Comedy   (4)
Titus and Vespasian   (1)
Bindo and Ricardo   (2)
Henry VI   (7)
The Spanish Tragedy   (5)
Sir John Mandeville   (3)
Muly Mollocco   (6)
The Jew of Malta   (5)

Table 2 – *continued*

1–30 April : *A Looking Glass for London and England* (3)
Titus and Vespasian (2)
Henry VI (8)
The Spanish Comedy (5)
The Spanish Tragedy (6)
Jerusalem (2)
Friar Bacon (3)
Muly Mollocco (7)
2 Tamar Cam (1)
Harry of Cornwall (3)
Muly Mollocco (8)

1–31 May : *The Spanish Tragedy* (7)
Titus and Vespasian (3)
Henry VI (9)
The Jew of Malta (6)
Friar Bacon (4)
Brandimer (2)
Henry VI (10)
Titus and Vespasian (4)
The Spanish Tragedy (8)
2 Tamar Cam (2)
The Jew of Malta (7)
The Spanish Tragedy (9)
Henry VI (11)
Titus and Vespasian (5)
Sir John Mandeville (4)
Muly Mollocco (9)
Harry of Cornwall (4)
Henry VI (12)
The Jew of Malta (8)
The Spanish Comedy (6)
The Spanish Tragedy (10)
The Tanner of Denmark (1)
Titus and Vespasian (6)
Henry VI (13)
2 Tamar Cam (3)
The Spanish Tragedy (11)
Machiavelli (3)
The Jew of Malta (9)
Muly Mollocco (10)

1–21 June : Bindo and Ricardo (3)
Titus and Vespasian (7)
A Looking Glass for London and England (4)

3 Edward Clinton, 1st Earl of Lincoln

1–21 June: [2] Tamar Cam (4)
               The Spanish Tragedy (12)
               A Knack to Know a Knave (1)
               Henry VI (14)
               Muly Mollocco (11)
               The Jew of Malta (10)
               A Knack to Know a Knave (2)
               Sir John Mandeville (5)
               The Spanish Tragedy (13)
               Henry VI (15)
               The Spanish Comedy (7)
               [2] Tamar Cam (5)
               A Knack to Know a Knave (3)
29–31 December: Muly Mollocco (12)
               The Spanish Tragedy (14)
               A Knack to Know a Knave (4)

PRINTINGS

Galathea. SR 4 October 1591.
Midas. SR 4 October 1591.
Arden of Faversham. SR 3 April 1592.
Garnier, *Antonius*, tr. the Countess of Pembroke. SR 3 May 1592.
The Spanish Tragedy. SR 6 October 1592. No date on title page but an entry of 18 December regarding controversy over the ownership refers to the play as having been printed.
Soliman and Perseda. SR 20 November 1592. No date on title page.

REPRINTINGS

Three Ladies of London (1584)

1593 PERFORMANCES

      At court: Dates known; titles not known.
      Elsewhere: At the Rose playhouse on the Bankside:
1–31 January: *The Jew of Malta* (11)
               A Knack to Know a Knave (5)
               Sir John Mandeville (6)
               The Jealous Comedy (1)
               Titus [and Vespasian?] (8)
               The Spanish Tragedy (15)
               Muly Mollocco (13)
               Friar Bacon (5)
               The Comedy of Cosmo (1)
               Sir John Mandeville (7)
               A Knack to Know a Knave (6)
               Titus [and Vespasian?] (9)
               Henry VI (16)

4 Robert Dudley, Earl of Leicester

Table 2 – *continued*

1–31 January: Friar Bacon   (6)
               The Jew of Malta   (12)
               [2] Tamar Cam   (6)
               Muly Mollocco   (14)
               The Spanish Tragedy   (16)
               The Comedy of Cosmo   (2)
               A Knack to Know a Knave   (7)
               Titus [and Vespasian?]   (10)
               The Tragedy of the Guise (The 'Duke of Guise' and
               thus *The Massacre at Paris?*)   (1)
               Sir John Mandeville   (8)
               Friar Bacon   (7)
               Henry VI   (17)
               The Jew of Malta   (13)
27–31 December: (by a different company):
               God Speed the Plough   (1)
               Huon of Bordeaux   (1)
               George a Green   (1)
               Buckingham   (1)
               Richard the Confessor   (1)

PRINTINGS

Edward II. SR 6 July 1593. Possible fragment only (see *Malone Society Reprints* of *Edward II*, pp. vii, x).
Edward I. SR 8 October 1593.
Fair Em. Not dated. Advertised as acted by 'Lord Strange his Servants'. Lord Strange became Earl of Derby after the death of his father in September 1593. Since 'Lord Strange' had a company from at least 1590, the play could be listed in any of the three years prior to this.
Jack Straw. SR 23 October 1593. Title page indicates this year, but colophon reads '1594'.

REPRINTINGS

1 and *2 Tamburlaine* (1590)

1594   PERFORMANCES
      At court: Dates known; titles not known.
       Elsewhere: At the Rose playhouse on the Bankside:
  1–31 January: Buckingham   (2)
               George a Green   (2)
               Huon of Bordeaux   (2)
               William the Conqueror   (1)
               God Speed the Plough   (2)
               Friar Francis   (1)

1–31 January : *George a Green* (3)
               Abraham and Lot (1)
               Buckingham (3)
               Huon of Bordeaux (3)
               The Fair Maid of Italy (1)
               Friar Francis (2)
               George a Green (4)
               Richard the Confessor (2)
               Abraham and Lot (2)
               King Lud (1)
               Friar Francis (3)
               The Fair Maid of Italy (2)
               George a Green (5)
               Titus Andronicus (1)
               Buckingham (4)
               Titus Andronicus (2)
               Abraham and Lot (3)
1–6 February : *The Jew of Malta* (14)
               Titus Andronicus (3)
1–8 April : *Friar Bacon* (8)
               The Ranger's Comedy (1)
               The Jew of Malta (15)
               The Fair Maid of Italy (3)
               Friar Bacon (9)
               King Leir (1)
               The Jew of Malta (16)
               King Leir (2)
14–16 May : *The Jew of Malta* (17)
               The Ranger's Comedy (2)
               Cutlack (1)
3–27 June : Hester and Ahasuerus (1)
               The Jew of Malta (18)
               Titus Andronicus (4)
               Cutlack (2)
               Belin Dun (1)
               Hamlet (probably the so-called 'ur-Hamlet') (1)
               Hester and Ahasuerus (2)
               The Taming of a Shrew (1)
               Titus Andronicus (5)
               The Jew of Malta (19)
               Belin Dun (2)
               Cutlack (3)
               The Ranger's Comedy (3)
               The Tragedy of the Guise (2)

Table 2 – *continued*

3–27 June :	Belin Dun	(3)
	The Ranger's Comedy	(4)
	The Jew of Malta	(20)
	Cutlack	(4)
	The Massacre at Paris	(3)
	Galioso	(1)
	Cutlack	(5)
	The Jew of Malta	(21)
1–31 July :	Belin Dun	(4)
	The Massacre at Paris	(4)
	Cutlack	(6)
	The Ranger's Comedy	(5)
	Belin Dun	(5)
	The Massacre at Paris	(5)
	Phillipo and Hippolito	(1)
	The Jew of Malta	(22)
	Belin Dun	(6)
	Galioso	(2)
	Phillipo and Hippolito	(2)
	Cutlack	(7)
	The Massacre at Paris	(6)
	The Ranger's Comedy	(6)
	Phillipo and Hippolito	(3)
	2 Godfrey of Bulloigne	(1)
	Belin Dun	(7)
	The Jew of Malta	(23)
	Galioso	(3)
	Phillipo and Hippolito	(4)
	Belin Dun	(8)
	[?2] Godfrey of Bulloigne	(2)
	The Massacre at Paris	(7)
	Cutlack	(8)
	The Merchant of Emden	(1)
	Belin Dun	(9)
1–31 August :	The Ranger's Comedy	(7)
	Phillipo and Hippolito	(5)
	Galioso	(4)
	The Jew of Malta	(24)
	2 Godfrey of Bulloigne	(3)
	Phillipo and Hippolito	(6)
	The Jew of Malta	(25)
	The Massacre at Paris	(8)
	Cutlack	(9)

1–31 August : Belin Dun   (10)
Tasso's Melancholy   (1)
Galioso   (5)
[?2] Godfrey of Bulloigne   (4)
Mahommed   (1)
Phillipo and Hippolito   (7)
The Massacre at Paris   (9)
Tasso's Melancholy   (2)
Belin Dun   (11)
The Ranger's Comedy   (8)
Galioso   (6)
Cutlack   (10)
Phillipo and Hippolito   (8)
The Venetian Comedy   (1)
[?2] Godfrey of Bulloigne   (5)
Mahommed   (2)
Tamburlaine   (1)
Belin Dun   (12)

1–30 September : *The Jew of Malta*   (26)
Tasso's Melancholy   (3)
Phillipo and Hippolito   (9)
The Venetian Comedy   (2)
Cutlack   (11)
The Massacre at Paris   (10)
[?2] Godfrey of Bulloigne   (6)
Mahommed   (3)
Galioso   (7)
Belin Dun   (13)
Tamburlaine   (2)
Phillipo and Hippolito   (10)
The Venetian Comedy   (3)
The Ranger's Comedy   (9)
Palamon and Arcite   (1)
Tasso's Melancholy   (4)
Phillipo and Hippolito   (11)
[?2] Godfrey of Bulloigne   (7)
Mahommed   (4)
The Venetian Comedy   (4)
Belin Dun   (14)
The Venetian Comedy   (5)
The Love of an English Lady   (1)
The Massacre at Paris   (11)
Cutlack   (12)
Tamburlaine   (3)

Table 2 – *continued*

    1–30 September: Galioso   (8)
                    Doctor Faustus   (1)
      1–30 October: The Ranger's Comedy   (10)
                    The Venetian Comedy   (6)
                    The Love of a Grecian Lady   (1)
                    [?2] Godfrey of Bulloigne   (8)
                    Phillipo and Hippolito   (12)
                    Tasso's Melancholy   (5)
                    Doctor Faustus   (2)
                    The Venetian Comedy   (7)
                    Belin Dun   (15)
                    Mahommed   (5)
                    Tamburlaine   (4)
                    Palamon and Arcite   (2)
                    Tamburlaine   (5)
                    The French Doctor   (1)
                    The Jew of Malta   (27)
                    Doctor Faustus   (3)
                    A Knack to Know an Honest Man   (1)
                    Tasso's Melancholy   (6)
                    The Love of an English Lady   (2)
                    Galioso   (9)
                    Palamon and Arcite   (3)
                    The French Doctor   (2)
                    A Knack to Know an Honest Man   (2)
                    2 Godfrey of Bulloigne? ('Bullen')   (9)
    1–30 November: *A Knack to Know an Honest Man*   (3)
                    Belin Dun   (16)
                    Tamburlaine   (6)
                    Doctor Faustus   (4)
                    Mahommed   (6)
                    A Knack [to Know an Honest Man?]   (4)
                    Caesar and Pompey   (1)
                    Palamon and Arcite   (4)
                    The Venetian Comedy   (8)
                    Tasso's Melancholy   (7)
                    The Love of a Grecian Lady   (2)
                    Caesar and Pompey   (2)
                    Belin Dun   (17)
                    Diocletian   (1)
                    The French Doctor   (3)
                    Doctor Faustus   (5)
                    A Knack to Know an Honest Man   (5)

1–30 November: Diocletian   (2)
       The Grecian Comedy   (1)
       Caesar and Pompey   (3)
       The Venetian Comedy   (9)
       Tamburlaine   (7)
       Warlamchester   (1)
       A Knack to Know an Honest Man   (6)
       Warlamchester   (2)
1–30 December: The Grecian Comedy   (2)
       The Wiseman of Westchester   (1)
       Tasso's Melancholy   (8)
       Mahommed   (7)
       The Wiseman of Westchester   (2)
       Doctor Faustus   (6)
       The Jew of Malta   (28)
       Caesar and Pompey   (4)
       Warlamchester   (3)
       A Knack to Know an Honest Man   (7)
       A Set at Mawe   (1)
       Tamburlaine   (8)
       2 Tamburlaine   (1)
       Doctor Faustus   (7)
       The Grecian Comedy   (3)
       The Siege of London   (1)
       Doctor Faustus   (8)
       The Wiseman of Westchester   (3)
       Tamburlaine   (9)

PRINTINGS
A Knack to Know a Knave. SR 7 January 1594.
Garnier, *Cornelia*, tr. Thomas Kyd. SR 25 January 1594.
Titus Andronicus. SR 6 February 1594.
A Looking-Glass for London and England. SR 5 March 1594
The First Part of the Contention of the Two Famous Houses of York and Lancaster. SR 12 March 1594.
The Taming of a Shrew. SR 2 May 1594. (Not to be confused with the play in Shakespeare's First Folio.)
Friar Bacon and Friar Bungay. SR 14 May 1594.
The Wounds of Civil War. SR 24 May 1594.
Orlando Furioso. SR 7 December 1593, and transferred to another printer 28 May 1594.
The Cobbler's Prophecy. SR 8 June 1594.
Mother Bombie. SR 18 June 1594.
The True Tragedy of Richard the Third. SR 19 June 1594.

Table 2 – *continued*

The Tragedy of Cleopatra. SR 19 October 1593.
The Tragedy of Dido
The First Part of the Tragical Reign of Selimus
The Wars of Cyrus
The Massacre at Paris. Conjectured as published this year. *Terminus ad quem* might be 1597–8 since title page reads 'plaide by the right honourable the Lord high Admirall his Servants'. Charles Howard was created Earl of Nottingham in 1597 and all plays printed after this date and bearing some indication of acting-provenance refer to the latter title if they refer to his company as having acted the play.

Six other plays were entered in SR, only one of which is known to have survived:

The Jew of Malta. SR 17 May 1594. Earliest surviving copy: 1633.
'The Famous History of John of Gaunt'. SR 14 May 1594.
'The Pleasant Comedy of Robin Hood and Little John'. SR 14 May 1594.
'The Famous Chronicle of Henry the First'. SR 17 May 1594. (See below, 1595.)
'Godfrey of Bulloigne'. SR 19 June 1594 (Part II?).
'The Life and Death of Heliogabalus'. SR 19 June 1594.

REPRINTINGS
The Spanish Tragedy (?1592)

1595   PERFORMANCES
       At court: Dates known; titles not known.
    Elsewhere: *Laelia* (1 March): Cambridge.
           At the Rose playhouse on the Bankside:
1–31 January: *2 Tamburlaine*   (2)
           A Set at Mawe   (2)
           The French Doctor   (4)
           Antony and Vallia   (1)
           A Knack to Know an Honest Man   (8)
           Doctor Faustus   (9)
           The Grecian Comedy   (4)
           Tasso's Melancholy   (9)
           A Knack to Know an Honest Man   (9)
           The Siege of London   (2)
           The Wiseman of Westchester   (4)
           A Set at Mawe   (3)
           Caesar and Pompey   (5)
           The Ranger's Comedy   (11)
           Tasso's Melancholy   (10)
           The Siege of London   (3)

1–31 January : The Wiseman of Westchester   (5)
　　　　　　　Doctor Faustus   (10)
　　　　　　　The Grecian Comedy   (5)
　　　　　　　Tamburlaine   (10)
　　　　　　　A Set at Mawe   (4)
　　　　　　　2 Tamburlaine   (3)
　　　　　　　The French Doctor   (5)
　　　　　　　The Grecian Comedy   (6)
1–28 February : Caesar and Pompey   (6)
　　　　　　　The Siege of London   (4)
　　　　　　　The Wiseman of Westchester   (6)
　　　　　　　Mahommed   (8)
　　　　　　　A Knack to Know an Honest Man   (10)
　　　　　　　The French Doctor   (6)
　　　　　　　Doctor Faustus   (11)
　　　　　　　The Venetian Comedy   (10)
　　　　　　　The French Comedy   (1)
　　　　　　　The Wiseman of Westchester   (7)
　　　　　　　The Siege of London   (5)
　　　　　　　Long Meg of Westminster   (1)
　　　　　　　Tasso's Melancholy   (11)
　　　　　　　Tamburlaine   (11)
　　　　　　　2 Tamburlaine   (4)
　　　　　　　The Wiseman of Westchester   (8)
　　　　　　　Long Meg of Westminster   (2)
　　　　　　　The Mack   (1)
　　　　　　　The Grecian Comedy   (7)
　　　　　　　The French Doctor   (7)
　　　　　　　The Venetian Comedy   (11)
　　　　　　　A Knack to Know an Honest Man   (11)
　　　　　　　The French Comedy   (2)
　　　　　　　The Wiseman of Westchester   (9)
1–14 March : Long Meg of Westminster   (3)
　　　　　　　The Siege of London   (6)
　　　　　　　Long Meg of Westminster   (4)
　　　　　　　Olympio and Eugenio   (1)
　　　　　　　Caesar and Pompey   (7)
　　　　　　　A Knack to Know an Honest Man (12)
　　　　　　　Tamburlaine   (12)
　　　　　　　2 Tamburlaine   (5)
　　　　　　　Long Meg of Westminster   (5)
　　　　　　　The Siege of London   (7)
21–30 April : The French Doctor   (8)
　　　　　　　A Knack to Know an Honest Man   (13)

Table 2 – *continued*

21–30 April : The Grecian Comedy   (8)
The Wiseman of Westchester   (10)
The Wiseman of Westchester   (11)
[2 ?] Godfrey of Bulloigne   (10)
Warlamchester   (4)
Long Meg of Westminster   (6)
Doctor Faustus   (12)

1–31 May : Long Meg of Westminster   (7)
Olympio and Eugenio   (2)
The French Doctor   (9)
A Knack to Know an Honest Man   (14)
The Wiseman of Westchester   (12)
1 Hercules   (1)
The Venetian Comedy   (12)
Olympio and Eugenio   (3)
Warlamchester   (5)
The French Comedy   (3)
Long Meg of Westminster   (8)
Tasso's Melancholy   (12)
The Wiseman of Westchester   (13)
The Grecian Comedy   (9)
[2 ?] Godfrey of Bulloigne   (11)
Olympio and Eugenio   (4)
1 Hercules   (2)
Tamburlaine   (13)
2 Tamburlaine   (6)
2 Hercules   (1)
The French Doctor   (10)
The Wiseman of Westchester   (14)
1 Hercules   (3)
2 Hercules   (2)
Olympio and Eugenio   (5)
Warlamchester   (6)
The French Comedy   (4)

3–26 June : Seven Days of the Week   (1)
The Wiseman of Westchester   (15)
Doctor Faustus   (13)
Seven Days of the Week   (2)
Olympio and Eugenio   (6)
A Knack to Know an Honest Man   (15)
Seven Days of the Week   (3)
The Wiseman of Westchester   (16)
1 Hercules   (4)

3–26 June: 2 Hercules (3)
             Seven Days of the Week (4)
             Warlamchester (7)
             The French Comedy (5)
             2 Caesar and Pompey (1)
             Long Meg of Westminster (9)
             Antony and Vallia (2)
             A Knack to Know an Honest Man (16)
             Seven Days of the Week (5)
             The French Comedy (6)
             1 Caesar and Pompey (8)
             2 Caesar and Pompey (2)
25–30 August: A Knack to Know an Honest Man (17)
             The Wiseman of Westchester (17)
             Seven Days of the Week (6)
             Long Meg of Westminster (10)
             Longshanks (1)
             The Siege of London (8)
1–30 September: 1 Hercules (5)
             2 Hercules (4)
             Seven Days of the Week (7)
             Olympio and Eugenio (7)
             Crack me this Nut (1)
             Antony and Vallia (3)
             The Wiseman of Westchester (18)
             Longshanks (2)
             Doctor Faustus (14)
             Crack me this Nut (2)
             Seven Days of the Week (8)
             Long Meg of Westminster (11)
             1 Tamburlaine (14)
             [2?] Godfrey of Bulloigne (12)
             The New World's Tragedy (1)
             A Knack to Know an Honest Man (18)
             The French Doctor (11)
             The Siege of London (9)
             Seven Days of the Week (9)
             1 Hercules (6)
             2 Hercules (5)
             Crack me this Nut (3)
             The New World's Tragedy (2)
             Doctor Faustus (15)
             Crack me this Nut (4)
             The Wiseman of Westchester (19)

Table 2 – *continued*

1–30 September:	Longshanks (3)
2–30 October:	Disguises (1)
	Olympio and Eugenio (8)
	Long Meg of Westminster (12)
	Seven Days of the Week (10)
	The Wiseman of Westchester (20)
	The New World's Tragedy (3)
	Crack me this Nut (5)
	The Grecian Comedy (10)
	Disguises (2)
	1 Hercules (7)
	2 Hercules (6)
	Seven Days of the Week (11)
	A Wonder of a Woman (1)
	Disguises (3)
	Seven Days of the Week (12)
	The Wiseman of Westchester (21)
	Crack me this Nut (6)
	Longshanks (4)
	The New World's Tragedy (4)
	A Wonder of a Woman (2)
	Crack me this Nut (7)
	1 Hercules (8)
	Antony and Vallia (4)
	Disguises (4)
	Bernardo and Fiammetta (1)
	Seven Days of the Week (13)
	Disguises (5)
2–29 November:	2 Hercules (7)
	The New World's Tragedy (5)
	A Wonder of a Woman (3)
	Crack me this Nut (8)
	Bernardo and Fiametta (2)
	The Wiseman of Westchester (22)
	Longshanks (5)
	Disguises (6)
	1 Tamburlaine (15)
	2 Tamburlaine (7)
	A Toy to Please Chaste Ladies (1)
	Seven Days of the Week (14)
	Crack me this Nut (9)
	Bernardo and Fiammetta (3)
	A Wonder of a Woman (4)

2–29 November : A Toy to Please Chaste Ladies   (2)
                    Olympio and Eugenio   (9)
                    1 Hercules   (9)
                    2 Hercules   (8)
                    Longshanks   (6)
                    The New World's Tragedy   (6)
                    Harry the Fifth   (1)
                    The Welshman   (1)
1–30 December : A Toy to Please Chaste Ladies   (3)
                    Harry the Fifth   (2)
                    Bernardo and Fiammetta   (4)
                    A Wonder of a Woman   (5)
                    Crack me this Nut   (10)
                    Harry the Fifth   (3)
                    Longshanks   (7)
                    The New World's Tragedy   (7)
                    Seven Days of the Week   (15)
                    Harry the Fifth   (4)
                    1 Hercules   (10)
                    The New World's Tragedy   (8)
                    A Wonder of a Woman   (6)
                    Bernardo and Fiametta   (5)
                    Harry the Fifth   (5)
                    Longshanks   (8)
                    The Wiseman of Westchester   (23)

PRINTINGS

The Peddler's Prophecy. SR 13 May 1594.
Plautus, *Menaechmi*, tr. William Warner. SR 10 June 1594.
Locrine. SR 20 July 1594.
The Old Wives Tale. SR 16 April 1595.
The True Tragedy of Richard Duke of York. Thought by most scholars to be an early version of Shakespeare's *3 Henry VI*.
Three other plays were entered in SR but no copies are known:
'The Tragedie of Ninus and Semiramis, the First Monarchs of the World'. SR 10 May 1595.
'An Interlude of Valentyne and Orsson'. SR 23 May 1595.
'The True Tragicall Historie of Kinge Rufus the First with the Life and Death of Belyn Dun'. SR 24 November 1595. Entered by the printer William Blackwell. Thomas Gosson entered a 'book' about Henry I (Rufus) in the previous year (see above, 1594). There is no record of transfer of such a play from one printer to the other; therefore, two separate plays may have existed (unless Gosson's was a prose work: see Chambers, *ES*, IV, 403).

Table 2 – *continued*

REPRINTINGS

Antonius (1594)
Cornelia (1594)
Cleopatra (1594)

1596   PERFORMANCES

   At court: Dates known; titles not known.
   Elsewhere: At the Rose playhouse on the Bankside:
 1–31 January: Seven Days of the Week   (16)
     Crack me this Nut   (11)
     Chinon of England   (1)
     Harry the Fifth   (6)
     1 Hercules   (11)
     A Knack to Know an Honest Man   (19)
     The New World's Tragedy   (9)
     The Jew of Malta   (29)
     A Toy to Please Chaste Ladies   (4)
     Chinon of England   (2)
     The Siege of London   (10)
     Crack me this Nut   (12)
     A Wonder of a Woman   (7)
     Pythagoras   (1)
     The Wiseman of Westchester   (24)
     The Jew of Malta   (30)
     Harry the Fifth   (7)
     Bernardo and Fiammetta   (6)
     Chinon of England   (3)
     ? 2 Seven Days of the Week ('Rd. at the 2 wecke')   (1)
     Pythagoras   (2)
     The New World's Tragedy   (10)
     ? 2 Seven Days of the Week   (2)
     Chinon of England   (4)
     Pythagoras   (3)
     The Jew of Malta   (31)
     A Wonder of a Woman   (8)
 1–28 February: The Jew of Malta   (32)
     1 Fortunatus   (1)
     The Wiseman of Westchester   (25)
     Longshanks   (9)
     Harry the Fifth   (8)
     Crack me this Nut   (13)
     Pythagoras   (4)
     1 Fortunatus   (2)

1–28 February: Chinon of England   (5)
     The Blind Beggar of Alexandria   (1)
     Doctor Faustus   (16)
     Pythagoras   (5)
     The Blind Beggar of Alexandria   (2)
     The Jew of Malta   (33)
     Olympio and Eugenio   (10)
     The Blind Beggar of Alexandria   (3)
     1 Fortunatus   (3)
     The Blind Beggar of Alexandria   (4)
     Pythagoras   (6)
     Chinon of England   (6)
     ? 2 Seven Days of the Week   (3)
     The Blind Beggar of Alexandria   (5)
     Longshanks   (10)
12–30 April: Bernardo and Fiametta   (7)
     A Toy to Please Chaste Ladies   (5)
     1 Fortunatus   (4)
     The Blind Beggar of Alexandria   (6)
     A Knack [*to Know an Honest Man?*]   (20)
     The Wiseman of Westchester   (26)
     Doctor Faustus   (17)
     The Jew of Malta   (34)
     Longshanks   (11)
     Pythagoras   (7)
     Chinon of England   (7)
     Harry the Fifth   (9)
     The Blind Beggar of Alexandria   (7)
     The New World's Tragedy   (11)
     Longshanks   (12)
     Julian the Apostate   (1)
     The Wiseman of Westchester   (27)
1–31 May: A Wonder of a Woman   (9)
     Chinon of England   (8)
     The Blind Beggar of Alexandria   (8)
     Pythagoras   (8)
     Doctor Faustus   (18)
     *Tamar Cam   (1)
     Crack me this Nut   (14)
     Julian the Apostate   (2)
     1 Fortunatus   (5)
     Tamar Cam   (2)
     The Blind Beggar of Alexandria   (9)
    * The 'platte' or outline of this play survives.

Table 2 – *continued*

   1–31 May: The Jew of Malta   (35)
         Chinon of England   (9)
         Tamar Cam   (3)
         The Blind Beggar of Alexandria   (10)
         The Tragedy of Phocas   (1)
         Julian the Apostate   (3)
         Pythagoras   (9)
         The Tragedy of Phocas   (2)
         1 Fortunatus   (6)
         Tamar Cam   (4)
         Harry the Fifth   (10)
         Chinon of England   (10)
         Pythagoras   (10)
  1–27 June: Chinon of England   (11)
         Longshanks   (13)
         The Blind Beggar of Alexandria   (11)
         The Tragedy of Phocas   (3)
         Tamar Cam   (5)
         Crack me this Nut   (15)
         The Wiseman of Westchester   (28)
         A Toy to Please Chaste Ladies   (6)
         Tamar Cam   (6)
         2 Tamar Cam   (7)
         Doctor Faustus   (19)
         The Siege of London   (11)
         Pythagoras   (11)
         The Tragedy of Phocas   (4)
         Harry the Fifth   (11)
         Tamar Cam   (7)
         2 Tamar Cam   (8)
         The Jew of Malta   (36)
         The Tragedy of Phocas   (5)
         Troy   (1)
         Crack me this Nut   (16)
         The Blind Beggar of Alexandria   (12)
         Tamar Cam   (8)
         2 Tamar Cam   (9)
  1–18 July: The Paradox   (1)
         Troy   (2)
         Doctor Faustus   (20)
         The French Doctor   (12)
         The Tragedy of Phocas   (6)
         The Blind Beggar of Alexandria   (13)

1–18 July : The Siege of London   (12)
The Wiseman of Westchester   (29)
Troy   (3)
Tamar Cam   (9)
2 Tamar Cam   (10)
Longshanks   (14)
Harry the Fifth   (12)
Belin Dun   (18)
A Toy to Please Chaste Ladies   (7)
Pythagoras   (12)
Harry the Fifth   (13)
Troy   (4)
The Tragedy of Phocas   (7)
The Tinker of Totnes   (1)
27 October–27 November : Chinon of England   (12)
Doctor Faustus   (21)
The French Doctor   (13)
Long Meg of Westminster   (13)
Chinon of England   (13)
A Knack [*to Know an Honest Man ?*]   (21)
Doctor Faustus   (22)
Long Meg of Westminster   (14)
The Blind Beggar of Alexandria   (14)
A Toy to Please Chaste Ladies   (8)
The French Doctor   (14)
Chinon of England   (14)
Seven Days of the Week   (17)
The Blind Beggar of Alexandria   (15)
Tamar Cam   (10)
Seven Days of the Week   (18)
Long Meg of Westminster   (15)
Seven Days of the Week   (19)
A Toy to Please Chaste Ladies   (9)
2–31 December : *The Blind Beggar of Alexandria*   (16)
Vortigern   (1)
Vortigern   (2)
The Blind Beggar of Alexandria   (17)
Captain Thomas Stukeley   (1)
Seven Days of the Week   (20)
Captain Thomas Stukeley   (2)
Vortigern   (3)
Doctor Faustus   (23)
Nebuchadnezzar   (1)
Vortigern   (4)

Table 2 – *continued*

2–31 December : Nebuchadnezzar   (2)
The Blind Beggar of Alexandria   (18)
Vortigern   (5)
Nebuchadnezzar   (3)
Captain Thomas Stukeley   (3)
Vortigern   (6)
That will be shall be   (1)
Seven Days of the Week   (21)

PRINTINGS
A Knack to Know an Honest Man. SR 26 November 1595.
Edward III. SR 1 December 1595.
One other play was entered in SR but no copy is known:
'The First Part of the Famous History of Chinon of England'. SR
20 January 1596.

REPRINTINGS
The Taming of A Shrew (1594)

1597   PERFORMANCES
At court : *Love's Labour's Lost* ('Christmas')
Machiavellus (9 December): Cambridge.
Elsewhere : *At the Rose playhouse on the Bankside :*
1–31 January : Vortigern   (7)
That will be shall be   (2)
Nebuchadnezzar   (4)
Doctor Faustus   (24)
That will be shall be   (3)
The Spanish Tragedy   (17)
Vortigern   (8)
Captain Thomas Stukeley   (4)
The Spanish Tragedy   (18)
Nebuchadnezzar   (5)
That will be shall be   (4)
Alexander and Lodowick   (1)
The Blind Beggar of Alexandria   (19)
The Spanish Tragedy   (19)
That will be shall be   (5)
Nebuchadnezzar   (6)
Captain Thomas Stukeley   (5)
Vortigern   (9)
The Spanish Tragedy   (20)
That will be shall be   (6)
The Blind Beggar of Alexandria   (20)
Nebuchadnezzar   (7)

1–31 January: A Woman Hard to Please   (1)
Long Meg of Westminster   (16)
A Woman Hard to Please   (2)
The Spanish Tragedy   (21)
1–12 February: A Woman Hard to Please   (3)
That will be shall be   (7)
Marshal Osric   (1)
A Woman Hard to Please   (4)
Vortigern   (10)
Marshal Osric   (2)
A Woman Hard to Please   (5)
The Spanish Tragedy   (22)
Captain Thomas Stukeley   (6)
Alexander and Lodowick   (2)
Alexander and Lodowick   (3)
1–31 March: That will be shall be   (8)
Alexander and Lodowick   (4)
A Woman Hard to Please   (6)
The Spanish Tragedy   (23)
Alexander and Lodowick   (5)
Vortigern   (11)
The Blind Beggar of Alexandria   (21)
Captain Thomas Stukeley   (7)
Guido   (1)
Alexander and Lodowick   (6)
Nebuchadnezzar   (8)
Guido   (2)
A Woman Hard to Please   (7)
Alexander and Lodowick   (7)
Guido   (3)
Belin Dun   (19)
1–30 April: *The Blind Beggar of Alexandria*   (22)
Vortigern   (12)
Guido   (4)
Alexander and Lodowick   (8)
That will be shall be   (9)
Five Plays in One   (1)
A Woman Hard to Please   (8)
Belin Dun   (20)
Alexander and Lodowick   (9)
Time's Triumph and Fortune   (1)
Captain Thomas Stukeley   (8)
Five Plays in One   (2)
A Woman Hard to Please   (9)

Table 2 – *continued*

1–30 *April:* The French Doctor   (7)
Belin Dun   (21)
Five Plays in One   (3)
The Spanish Tragedy   (24)
The French Comedy   (8)
Guido   (5)
Five Plays in One   (4)
The French Comedy   (9)
Alexander and Lodowick   (10)
Belin Dun   (22)
Uther Pendragon   (1)
That will be shall be   (10)

1–31 *May:* The French Comedy   (10)
Uther Pendragon   (2)
The Spanish Tragedy   (25)
The French Comedy   (11)
Five Plays in One   (5)
Uther Pendragon   (3)
Alexander and Lodowick   (11)
A Woman Hard to Please   (10)
An Humorous Day's Mirth   (1)
Uther Pendragon   (4)
Five Plays in One   (6)
Uther Pendragon   (5)
Alexander and Lodowick   (12)
Captain Thomas Stukeley   (9)
An Humorous Day's Mirth   (2)
Belin Dun   (23)
The French Comedy   (12)
Five Plays in One   (7)
An Humorous Day's Mirth   (3)
The Spanish Tragedy   (26)
Henry I   (1)
A Woman Hard to Please   (11)
Alexander and Lodowick   (13)
Henry I   (2)
An Humorous Day's Mirth   (4)

1–30 *June:* The French Comedy   (13)
Uther Pendragon   (6)
*Frederick and Basilea   (1)
An Humorous Day's Mirth   (5)
That will be shall be   (11)

* The 'platte' or outline of this play survives.

1–30 June: An Humorous Day's Mirth   (6)
Henry I   (3)
*Frederick and Basilea   (2)
Five Plays in One   (8)
An Humorous Day's Mirth   (7)
Uther Pendragon   (7)
Henry I   (4)
Belin Dun   (24)
The French Comedy   (14)
An Humorous Day's Mirth   (8)
*Frederick and Basilea   (3)
The Spanish Tragedy   (27)
An Humorous Day's Mirth   (9)
Hengist   (1)
The French Comedy   (15)
Henry I   (5)
Belin Dun   (25)
Captain Thomas Stukeley   (10)
Five Plays in One   (9)
Alexander and Lodowick   (14)
Martin Swarte   (1)
1–28 July: Henry I   (6)
The French Comedy   (16)
*Frederick and Basilea   (4)
That will be shall be   (12)
Martin Swarte   (2)
An Humorous Day's Mirth   (10)
The Wiseman of Westchester   (30)
Martin Swarte   (3)
The Wiseman of Westchester   (31)
An Humorous Day's Mirth   (11)
The Witch of Islington   (1)
Alexander and Lodowick   (15)
The French Comedy   (17)
The Wiseman of Westchester   (32)
The Spanish Tragedy   (28)
Five Plays in One   (10)
The Witch of Islington   (2)
11–31 October: *The Spanish Tragedy*   (29)
An Humorous Day's Mirth   (12)
Doctor Faustus   (25)
Hardicanute   (1)
Friar Spendleton   (1)
* The 'platte' or outline of this play survives.

Table 2 – *continued*

PRINTINGS

Richard II. SR 29 August 1597.
Richard III. SR 20 October 1597.
The Woman in the Moon. SR 22 September 1595.
Romeo and Juliet. First Quarto.

REPRINTINGS

1 and *2 Tamburlaine* (1590; 1593)

1598   PERFORMANCES

   At court : Date known; titles not known.
   Elsewhere : Not known.

PRINTINGS

1 Henry IV. SR 25 February 1598. Two editions, the first surviving only
in a fragment.
The Blind Beggar of Alexandria. SR 15 August 1598.
The Virtuous Octavia. SR 5 October 1598. Two issues.
The Famous Victories of Henry V. SR 14 May 1594.
James IV. SR 14 May 1594.
Love's Labour's Lost. Title page reads: 'Newly corrected and augmented'
but no previous printing is known.
Mucedorus
Entered in SR but no surviving copy known: 'The Tragick Comedy of
Celestina'. SR 5 October 1598.

REPRINTINGS

A Looking-Glass for London and England (1594)
Mother Bombie (1594)
Edward II (1594)
Cleopatra (1594; 1595)
Richard II (1597)
Richard III (1597)

1599   PERFORMANCES

   At court : Old Fortunatus (27 December)
   Elsewhere : Not known.

PRINTINGS

1 and *2 Edward IV*. SR 28 August 1599.
A Warning for Fair Women. SR 17 November 1599.
George a Green. SR 1 April 1595.
The Love of King David and Fair Bathsheba. SR 14 May 1594.

Clyomon and Clamydes
An Humorous Day's Mirth
The Two Angry Women of Abingdon
Romeo and Juliet. Second Quarto.

REPRINTINGS
Arden of Faversham (1592)
Soliman and Perseda (?1593)
The Spanish Tragedy (?1592; 1594)
Edward I (1593)
Orlando Furioso (1594)
Cleopatra (1594; 1595; 1598)
Edward III (1596)
1 Henry IV (?1598; 1598)

1600 PERFORMANCES
At court: *The Shoemaker's Holiday* (1 January)
Elsewhere: Not known.

PRINTINGS
Old Fortunatus. SR 20 February 1600.
Every Man out of his Humour. SR 8 April 1600. Two editions.
The Maid's Metamorphosis. SR 24 July 1600.
Henry V. The 'bad' Quarto of Shakespeare's play. Possible entry SR
4 August 1600: 'Henry the Fift, a booke . . . to be staied'.
The First Part . . . of Sir John Oldcastle. SR 11 August 1600.
2 Henry IV. SR 23 August 1600. Two issues.
Much Ado about Nothing. SR 23 August 1600.
The Wisdom of Doctor Dodypoll. SR 7 October 1600.
A Midsummer Night's Dream. SR 8 October 1600.
The Weakest Goeth to the Wall. SR 23 October 1600.
The Merchant of Venice. SR 22 July 1598 'subject to licence from the
Lord Chamberlain' and again SR 28 October 1600.
Summer's Last Will and Testament. SR 28 October 1600.
Look About You
The Shoemakers' Holiday
Five other plays were entered in SR, but no copies are known:
SR 31 March 1600: 'A famous history called Valentine and Orsson'
SR 27 May 1600: 'A Morall of Clothe Breeches and velvet hose'
SR 24 July 1600: 'Gyve a man luck and throwe him into the Sea'
SR 11 August 1600: 'the second and last parte' of the 'History of Sir John
Oldcastle'
SR 14 August 1600: 'The Tartarian Crippell Emperor of Constantinople'

Table 2 – *continued*

REPRINTINGS

Titus Andronicus (1594)
The First Part of the Contention etc. (1594)
The True Tragedy of Richard Duke of York (1595)
1 and *2 Edward IV* (1599)

1601   PERFORMANCES

At court : *The Contention between Liberality and Prodigality*
                    (22 February)
Elsewhere : Not known.

PRINTINGS

Every Man in his Humour. SR 14 August 1600.
Jack Drum's Entertainment. SR 23 October 1600.
Love's Metamorphosis. SR 25 November 1600.
The Downfall of Robert, Earl of Huntingdon. SR 1 December 1600.
The Death of Robert, Earl of Huntingdon. SR 1 December 1600.
The Fountain of Self-Love (Cynthia's Revels). SR 23 May 1601.
Two Lamentable Tragedies.
Three other plays were entered in SR, but only the copy of the last is
known:
SR 1 March 1601: 'God spede the ploughe'
SR 3 July 1601: 'The true historye of George Scanderbarge'
SR 3 August 1601: 'A Woman will have her Will'. In 1616 appears
*Englishmen for my Money, or a Pleasant Comedy called a Woman will have
her Will*, the first known copy.

REPRINTINGS

Cleopatra (in collection: 1594; 1595; 1598; 1599)

1602   PERFORMANCES

At court : Dates known; titles not known.
Elsewhere : Not known.

PRINTINGS

Guarini, *Il Pastor Fido*, tr. anonymous. SR 16 September 1601.
Antonio and Mellida
Antonio's Revenge. Both: SR 24 October 1601: 'the fyrst and second partes
of the play called Anthonio and Melida'.
The Merry Wives of Windsor. SR 18 January 1602.
Blurt Master-Constable. SR 7 June 1602.
Thomas Lord Cromwell. SR 11 August 1602.
A Larum for London. SR 29 May 1600.
Satiromastix. SR 11 November 1601.

The Contention between Liberality and Prodigality
How a Man may Choose a Good Wife from a Bad
A Satire of the Three Estates

REPRINTINGS
The Spanish Tragedy (?1592; 1594; 1599)
A Looking Glass for London and England (1594; 1598)
Richard III (1597; 1598)
Henry V (1600)

1603 PERFORMANCES
      At court: Dates known; titles not known.
      Elsewhere: Not known.

PRINTINGS
Hamlet (First Quarto). SR 26 July 1602.
Nero (in Latin). SR 23 February 1603.
Patient Grissel. SR 28 March 1600.
The Tragedy of Darius
Philotus [not Daniel's *Philotas*]

REPRINTINGS
The Spanish Tragedy (?1592; 1594; 1599; 1602)

1604 PERFORMANCES
      At court: *The Vision of the Twelve Goddesses* (8 January)
                Othello (1 November)
                The Merry Wives of Windsor (4 November)
                Measure for Measure (26 December)
                The Comedy of Errors (28 December)
                'How to Learn of a Woman to Woo' (30 December)
      Elsewhere: Not known.

PRINTINGS
Doctor Faustus. SR 7 January 1601.
The Malcontent. SR 5 July 1604. Three editions.
1 Honest Whore. SR 9 November 1604. A second issue with additions
entitled *The Converted Courtesan.*
The Monarchic Tragedies. SR 30 April 1604. Contains *Croesus*, a new play,
and *Darius*, see 1603.
Hamlet (Second Quarto)
The Wit of a Woman
The Vision of the Twelve Goddesses
Entered in SR but no surviving copy known: 'A Booke called the Owle'.
SR 8 February 1604. This may not have been a play.

Table 2 – *continued*

REPRINTINGS

Jack Straw (1594)
1 Henry IV (?1598; 1598; 1599)
A Satire of the Three Estates (1602)
Darius (1603)

1605   PERFORMANCES

At court : *All Fools* (1 January)
The Masque of Blackness (6 January)
Love's Labour's Lost (between 9 and 14 January)
Every Man in His Humour (2 February)
The Merchant of Venice (10 February)
'The Spanish Maze' (11 February)
The Merchant of Venice (12 February)

Elsewhere : 'Alba or Vertumnus' (27 August): Oxford.
'Ajax' (28 August): Oxford.
Vertumnus sive Annus Recurrens (29 August): Oxford.

PRINTINGS

King Leir (not *King Lear*). SR 14 May 1594 and 8 May 1605.
Sejanus. SR 2 November 1604 and 6 August 1605.
Captain Thomas Stukeley. SR 11 August 1600.
Philotas. SR 29 November 1604.
The Trial of Chivalry. SR 4 December 1605.
The Fair Maid of Bristow. SR 8 February 1605.
When You See Me You Know Me. SR 12 February 1605.
The Dutch Courtesan. 26 June 1605.
1 If You Know Not Me You Know Nobody. SR 5 July 1605.
Eastward Ho. SR 4 September 1605. One edition with two issues and two subsequent editions.
All Fools
The First Part of Jeronimo
The London Prodigal
Entered in SR but no surviving copy known: 'Richard Whittington'. SR 8 February 1605.

REPRINTINGS

1 and *2 Tamburlaine* (1590; 1593; 1597). Parts 1 and 2 published separately.
Cleopatra (in collection 1594; 1595; 1598; 1599; 1601)
Richard III (1597; 1598; 1602)
1 and *2 Edward IV* (1599; 1600)
How a Man May Choose a Good Wife from a Bad (1602)
1 Honest Whore (1604; 1604)

1606   PERFORMANCES
            At court: *Hymenaei* (5 January)
                        King Lear (26 December)
                        'Abuses' (30 July)
            Elsewhere: Not known.

PRINTINGS
2 If You Know Not Me You Know Nobody. SR 14 September 1605. A
second issue can probably be assigned to this year also.
The Return from Parnassus. SR 16 October 1605. (This play is often
referred to as '2 Return from Parnassus' because the first two titles in the
trilogy are *Pilgrimage to Parnassus* and *The Return from Parnassus,* but
were not printed in the Renaissance, surviving only in manuscript.) Two
editions.
The Gentleman Usher. SR 26 November 1605.
The Queen's Arcadia. SR 26 November 1605.
Sir Gyles Goosecap. SR 10 January 1606.
Nobody and Somebody. SR 12 March 1606. No date on title page.
The Fawn. SR 12 March 1606. Two editions.
Sophonisba. SR 17 March 1606. Two issues.
Wiley Beguiled. SR 12 November 1606.
The Isle of Gulls
Monsieur D'Olive
Hymenaei

REPRINTINGS
Mucedorus (1598)
1 If You Know Not Me You Know Nobody (1605)

1607   PERFORMANCES
            At court: *Masque at Lord Hay's Marriage* (6 January)
                        The Devil's Charter (2 February)
            Elsewhere: *Saturnalia* (25 December): Oxford.
                        Philomela (29 December): Oxford.
                        'Aeneas and Dido' (25 May): Earl of Arundel's Banquet.

PRINTINGS
Westward Ho. SR 2 March 1605.
Caesar's Revenge. SR 5 June 1606. Two issues: one bearing no date.
The Fleer. SR 21 November 1606.
Masque at Lord Hay's Marriage. SR 26 January 1607.
Lingua. SR 23 February 1607.
Claudius Tiberius Nero. SR 10 April 1607.
The Whore of Babylon. SR 20 April 1607.

Table 2 – *continued*

The Fair Maid of the Exchange. SR 24 April 1607.
The Phoenix. SR 9 May 1607.
Michaelmas Term. SR 15 May 1607.
The Woman-Hater. SR 20 May 1607.
Bussy d'Ambois. SR 3 June 1607.
Cupid's Whirligig. SR 29 June 1607.
The Travels of the Three English Brothers. SR 29 June 1607. Two issues.
The Miseries of Enforced Marriage. SR 31 July 1607.
Northward Ho. SR 6 August 1607.
The Puritan. SR 6 August 1607.
What You Will. SR 6 August 1607.
The Revenger's Tragedy. SR 7 October 1607.
The Devil's Charter. SR 16 October 1607. Two issues.
The Monarchic Tragedies. Adds to *Darius* and *Croesus* (see 1603 and 1604): *The Alexandrian Tragedy* and *Julius Caesar.*
Sir Thomas Wyatt
A Woman Killed with Kindness
Volpone. Two issues.

REPRINTINGS
The Taming of a Shrew (1594; 1596)
Cleopatra. Two issues (in collection: 1594, 1595, 1598, 1599, 1601, 1605).
Philotas. Issued in two different collections of the author, Daniel (1605).
The Queen's Arcadia (1606)

1608   PERFORMANCES
At court: *The Masque of Beauty* (10 January)
Elsewhere: *Periander* (13 February): Oxford.
Philomathes (15 January): Oxford.

PRINTINGS
A Trick to Catch the Old One. SR 7 October 1607.
The Family of Love. SR 7 October 1607.
The Merry Devil of Edmonton. SR 22 October 1607.
King Lear. SR 26 November 1607.
Your Five Gallants. SR 22 March 1608. No date on title page.
Law Tricks. SR 28 March 1608.
Humour out of Breath. SR 12 April 1608.
The Masque of Blackness
The Masque of Beauty
The Masque at Lord Haddington's Marriage. SR 21 April 1608: 'two Royall Maskes' but these appear in one volume which has no date. The next editions of these last two masques will appear in the Jonson Folio of 1616.

The dating is thus conjectural. The printer, Thomas Thorpe, who made the entry, died in 1635.
A Yorkshire Tragedy. SR 2 May 1608.
The Rape of Lucrece. SR 3 June 1608.
The Conspiracy and Tragedy of Charles Duke of Byron. SR 5 June 1608.
A Mad World My Masters. SR 4 October 1608.
The Dumb Knight. SR 6 October 1608.
SR 29 April 1608: 'the second parte of the converted Courtisan or honest Whore'. Not published, so far as is known, until 1630.

REPRINTINGS
Richard II (1597; 1598; 1598)
1 Henry IV (?1598; 1598; 1599; 1604)
How a Man May Choose a Good Wife from a Bad (1602; 1605)
1 If You Know Not Me You Know Nobody (1605; 1606)

1609 PERFORMANCES
      At court: *A Trick to Catch the Old One* (1 January)
               The Masque of Queens (2 February)
      Elsewhere: Not known.

PRINTINGS
Pericles Prince of Tyre. SR 20 May 1608. Two editions.
Mustapha. SR 25 November 1608.
Troilus and Cressida. SR 7 February 1603. Two issues.
The Masque of Queens. SR 22 February 1609.
The Case is Altered. SR 20 July 1609.
Every Woman in her Humour
Two Maids of Moreclacke
SR 27 January 1609: 'An Enterlude called Bonos Nochios' and 'An Enterlude called, Craft uppon Subtiltyes backe'. No publications are known.

REPRINTINGS
Romeo and Juliet (1597 [First Quarto]; 1599)
Doctor Faustus (1604)
2 If You Know Not Me You Know Nobody (1606; 1606)
A Trick to Catch the Old One (1608)
The Rape of Lucrece (1608)

1610 PERFORMANCES
      At court: *Tethys' Festival* (5 June)
      Elsewhere: Not known.

Table 2 – *continued*

PRINTINGS

The Turk. SR 10 March 1609.
Histriomastix. SR 31 October 1610.
The Faithful Shepherdess. No SR entry and no date on title page, but
Bonian and Walley, the joint publishers, were only associated between
December 1608 and January 1610.
Tethys' Festival

REPRINTINGS

Mucedorus (1598; 1606)
The Shoemakers' Holiday (1600)
1 If You Know Not Me You Know Nobody (1605; 1606; 1608)
The Fleer (1607)

1611   PERFORMANCES

At court : *The Masque of Oberon* (1 January)
Love Freed from Ignorance and Folly (2 February)
Mucedorus (3 February)
The Tempest (1 November)
The Winter's Tale (5 November)
A King and No King (26 December)
Greene's Tu Quoque (27 December)
'The Almanac' (29 December)
At the Globe : 'Richard II' (30 April): not Shakespeare's.
The Winter's Tale (15 May)

PRINTINGS

Ram Alley. SR 9 November 1610.
The Atheist's Tragedy. SR 14 September 1611.
The Golden Age. SR 14 October 1611.
Catiline
May Day
The Roaring Girl

REPRINTINGS

1 and 2 Troublesome Reign of King John (1591)
The Spanish Tragedy (?1592; 1594; 1599; 1602; 1603)
Titus Andronicus (1594; 1600)
Cleopatra (in collection: 1594; 1595; 1598; 1599; 1602; 1605; 1607
twice)
Mucedorus (1598; 1606; 1610)
Hamlet (1603 [First Quarto]; 1604)
Doctor Faustus (1604; 1609)
Philotas. Two issues. (1605; 1607; 1607)
The Queen's Arcadia (1606; 1607)

Cupid's Whirligig (1607)
The Miseries of Enforced Marriage (1607)
Pericles Prince of Tyre (1609; 1609)

1612   PERFORMANCES

        At court: 'The Twins' Tragedy' (1 January)
                Cupid's Revenge (5 January)
                The Silver Age (12 January)
                The Rape of Lucrece (13 January)
                Greene's Tu Quoque (2 February)
                'The Nobleman' (23 February)
                'Hymen's Holiday' (24 February)
                'The Proud Maid's Tragedy' (25 February)
                ?The Coxcomb (2 or 3 November)
                1 Henry IV
                Julius Caesar
                Much Ado About Nothing (twice)
                Othello
                The Winter's Tale
                The Tempest
                The Alchemist
                Philaster (twice)
                The Maid's Tragedy
                A King and No King
                The Captain
                'The Nobleman'
                'The Twins' Tragedy'
                'A Bad Beginning Makes a Good Ending'
                'Cardenio'
                The Merry Devil of Edmonton
                'A Knot of Fools'
                (All the above during the Christmas season)
      Elsewhere: Not known.

PRINTINGS

A Woman is a Weathercock. SR 23 November 1611.
The Alchemist. SR 3 October 1610.
A Christian Turned Turk. SR 1 February 1612.
The Widow's Tears. SR 17 April 1612.
If It Be Not Good the Devil is in It
The White Devil
Entered in SR but no surviving copy known:
    SR 15 February 1612: 'a play booke beinge a Tragecomedye called,
    The Noble man'
    SR 15 February 1612: 'The Twynnes tragedye'

Table 2 – *continued*
REPRINTINGS
Edward II (1594; 1598)
Richard III (1597; 1598; 1602; 1605)
Philotus (1603)
Sir Thomas Wyatt (1607)
The Merry Devil of Edmonton (1608)

1613 PERFORMANCES
At court : *Cupid's Revenge* (1 January)
Cupid's Revenge (9 January)
The Masque of the Middle Temple and Lincoln's Inn
(15 February)
The Masque of the Inner Temple and Gray's Inn
(20 February)
The Dutch Courtesan (25 February)
The Widow's Tears (27 February)
'Raymond Duke of Lyons' (1 March)
'1 The Knaves' (2 March)
Adelphe (2 March)
Scyros (3 March)
'2 The Knaves' (10 March)
'Cardenio' (8 June)
The Dutch Courtesan (12 December)
The Irish Masque (29 December)
Elsewhere : *The Hog Hath Lost his Pearl* (21 February): Whitefriars.

PRINTINGS
The Revenge of Bussy d'Ambois. SR 17 April 1612.
The Tragedy of Mariam. SR 17 December 1612.
The Masque of the Inner Temple and Gray's Inn. SR 27 February 1613.
Possibly two editions (one undated).
The Brazen Age
Cynthia's Revenge
The Insatiate Countess
The Knight of the Burning Pestle
The Silver Age
The Lords' Masque

REPRINTINGS
1 Henry IV (?1598; 1598; 1599; 1604; 1608)
Mucedorus (1598; 1606; 1610; 1611)
1 and 2 Edward IV (1599; 1600; 1605)
Thomas Lord Cromwell (1602)
When You See Me You Know Me (1605)
1 If You Know Not Me You Know Nobody (1605; 1606; 1608; 1610)

II The companies
and actors
Alexander Leggatt

The companies
and actors

When an Englishman of Shakespeare's time went to the theatre, he went to see not only a play but a company of actors – perhaps even a particular, favourite actor. In many cases, then as now, the spectator would be more interested in the performers than in the play. What were Elizabethan actors like? How would they have interpreted the plays of Shakespeare and his contemporaries? How would the nature of a play in performance have been affected by the special abilities of a particular company? These are questions to which we should very much like the answers, but the evidence has mostly disappeared, leaving only a few teasing echoes.

Theatre criticism as we know it hardly existed. It is possible for someone who never saw Henry Irving to get a reasonable impression of his acting from the detailed accounts of contemporary spectators. But the contemporaries of Burbage and Alleyn describe them (if at all) in terms so generalized and conventional that we are left little wiser than we were. It is possible to get some sense of their peculiarities as actors from the parts we know they played; but even here there are obstacles. For one thing, parts can be assigned with confidence to particular actors only in comparatively few instances. T. W. Baldwin has laboured heroically to establish particular 'lines' for the actors of Shakespeare's company, and to assign parts to them on this basis: John Heminges playing 'the irascible and "humorous" old nobleman', William Sly the 'young gallant, either princely or comic', and so on.[1] But the versatility demanded by constant doubling must have meant that no actor could stick to one 'line' too rigidly, and Baldwin's arguments, resting as they do on a number of dubious assumptions – such as the belief that descriptions of characters in Elizabethan plays are descriptions of the actors who played them[2] – have not won general acceptance. Moreover, even if we knew every part Burbage played, we could not assume he was equally successful in all of them. We know his repertoire included parts as different as Richard III and King Lear; what we should really like to know is which aspects of these two characters he was most successful at conveying.

However, a few inferences may reasonably be drawn from the evidence we have. *Tamburlaine* and *Hamlet* would not have been as popular as they clearly were if Alleyn and Burbage had been quite inadequate in the leading roles. We may fairly imagine Alleyn as an actor of some majesty, with more than ordinary physical and vocal stamina, and Burbage as capable of quick passion and sardonic wit. And with some of the clowns we are on safer ground still, for the clown, more than the 'straight' actor, trades on his own personality, and that personality can often be detected in the parts written for him. Kempe is going to be Kempe no matter what lines he is given, and we can see Shakespeare accommodating himself to that fact; though even here the identification of role with actor is not absolute, for we have reason to believe that Robert Armin later played Dogberry, originally Kempe's part.[3] In the theatre, such adjustments must always be allowed for.

Another question is whether the companies, or at least the long-established and stable ones, had 'lines' of their own. Alfred Harbage, in his *Shakespeare and the Rival Traditions*,[4] has argued that the adult companies in the public theatres offered healthy, moral, good-tempered plays, while the boys' companies specialized in mocking and salacious satire, much of it directed against the middle class. But, here again, exceptions must constantly be allowed for. A spectator at the Globe would be as likely to see *Volpone* or *The Malcontent* as *The London Prodigal*. If he went to Paul's, he might see citizens duped in the comedies of Middleton; but he would be as likely to see *Westward Ho* or *Northward Ho*, comedies of class warfare in which middle-class figures have the last laugh. And the idea that there were two

[1] *The Organization and Personnel of the Shakespearean Company* (New York, reprinted 1961), pp. 249, 252.
[2] Ibid., p. 227.
[3] E. K. Chambers, *The Elizabethan Stage* (Oxford, reprinted 1961), II, 300.
[4] (Bloomington, reprinted 1970.) See especially pp. 72–8, 274–7.

rival traditions is too simple: from extant plays, and from contemporary references, we can detect differences between one public theatre and another, or one private theatre and another, that are at least as important as the differences between each group seen *en bloc*. Each major company seems to have had a particular tradition, and to have fostered certain expectations in its audience; the failure of Webster's *The White Devil* at the Red Bull suggests the dangers of selling a play to the wrong company. But none of these traditions can have been monolithic. For one thing, it was not possible for a company to tie up the performing rights to a play as securely as a modern theatre management can. Robert Greene was accused of selling *Orlando Furioso* to two different companies, and when the King's Men produced *The Malcontent*, it was probably tit for tat; the new induction they used suggests that the boys had produced an old favourite of the adult companies, *The Spanish Tragedy*.

In recovering some idea of what the companies and actors of Shakespeare's time were like, one must always remember that no human enterprise, certainly no theatrical one, follows a totally logical or consistent pattern. Moreover, the full picture can never be recovered: many of the actors are names only, many of the companies little more. But from the evidence we have, a few reasonable inferences may be drawn, and the theatrical life of the time can be sketched in rough outline.

One begins inauspiciously, for the history of dramatic companies in the 1580s and early 1590s is obscure and confused. Beset with official suppressions and outbreaks of plague, companies were unstable, and spent much of their time touring. There was no sign yet of the firm traditions that would develop after 1594. One group, however, claims our attention. In 1583 Sir Francis Walsingham picked out from the companies of the time a collection of actors to form an élite troupe entitled to wear the royal livery, and known as the Queen's Men. This group enjoyed considerable prestige during the 1580s, though they may not have been a company of sharers like the great companies of ten years later, held together by a mutual business interest in the enterprise,[1] and they do not appear to have had a firm foothold in a London theatre: they played at a variety of different houses.[2] Their repertoire reflected the fashions of the time: it included comedies by Greene and Peele, and a number of plays on English history.

Their chief claim to distinction was that they had gained the services of

[1] M. C. Bradbrook, *The Rise of the Common Player* (Cambridge, Mass., 1962), p. 193.
[2] Chambers, *Elizabethan Stage*, II, 108–9.

Richard Tarlton, the leading clown of his day, and the first English actor to win a national reputation. It is part of a clown's business to be instantly recognizable, and Tarlton has left a sharper visual impression than his successors Kempe and Armin; this may be one reason why they never achieved quite the same popularity. The squinting eyes, flat nose and curly hair were as much a part of his equipment as the drum that seems to have been his chief prop (Plate 7). His picture was posted up as a sign for taverns, and as a means of identifying privies – suggesting, perhaps, the clown's connection with the ancient tradition of scatological humour. And the drum was remembered after his death: we are told of a fighting-cock who was named Tarlton because of the drumming noise of his wings.[1] Tarlton's repertoire seems to have included a drunk act and a comic fight with a dog, though probably neither was unique to him;[2] the ghost of the dog act can be seen in *The Two Gentlemen of Verona*. He was renowned for extemporizing verses on themes thrown at him by the audience; and the jig – a comic, musical afterpiece to the main play – may have been developed to its full potential by Tarlton.[3]

He was also a playwright, author of a play on the Seven Deadly Sins, of which only the 'plot' to Part 2 (a summary of entrances and other information useful for a prompter) has survived. But our main impression of him is of a performer out on his own, winning the audience in his own way, and not bound by the confines of a particular play. When we hear of him as an actor, it is a story of how at short notice he took the part of the judge struck by Prince Hal in a play of Henry V; reappearing in his usual role of the clown, he claimed to be so terrified by the report of the blow 'that me thinkes the blow remaines still on my cheeke, that it burnes againe'.[4] This and other stories about Tarlton were collected after his death in a volume called *Tarlton's Jests*. Most of the jests have a very ancient and fish-like smell, and probably attached themselves to Tarlton from other sources; but one can detect at several points throughout the collection a distinctive personality: excitable, quick to anger, and hard to stop when roused. This impression, if authentic, would put him at the head of the line of comics that includes Dan Leno and Frankie Howerd. One of the anecdotes in *Tarlton's Jests* has an authentic ring and bears out the impression of an edgy, aggressive performer: once when Tarlton appeared on stage, a man in the

[1] Chambers, *Elizabethan Stage*, II, 345.
[2] Charles Read Baskervill, *The Elizabethan Jig and Related Song Drama* (Chicago, 1929), pp. 98–9.
[3] Ibid., p. 105.
[4] *Tarlton's Jests and News out of Purgatory*, ed. J. O. Halliwell (London, 1844), p. 25.

audience, for the benefit of a friend who had never seen the great clown, pointed at him. Tarlton responded by extending two fingers in the sign of the cuckold's horns.[1]

There are more allusions to Tarlton than to any other player of his time; Burbage may have been the greatest actor of his age, but Tarlton was the most popular. The standing of Kempe and Armin was assured when they were hailed as his successors; and a generation after his death the stage-keeper in Jonson's *Bartholomew Fair* proclaims his connection with the good old days of the theatre by telling us, 'I kept the *Stage* in Master *Tarletons* time . . .'[2] When Marlowe, in the Prologue to *1 Tamburlaine*, set his face against the prevailing fashion by promising his audience a change '*From iygging vaines of riming motherwits, And such conceits as clownage keepes in pay*',[3] he may have had particularly in mind the jigs and extempore rhymes of Tarlton. The Queen's Men had other notable players, particularly the playwright and comedian Robert Wilson, but Tarlton was unquestionably their star, and after he died in 1588 the company languished. Their court performances declined, and through the 1590s they died a slow death in the provinces.

Since the 1574 Order of the City Council had threatened to punish as vagabonds any players not protected by a nobleman's livery, it was normal for a theatrical company to be under the patronage of a peer of the realm; the Queen's Men, enjoying royal patronage, were exceptional. But, apart from the prestige of the queen's name, royal patronage conferred no special privilege or protection. It did not save the Queen's Men when they lost their most popular actor, and lack of it did not prevent another company, the Admiral's Men, from rising as they fell. The records of court performances in 1590–1 show four plays given by the Queen's Men, two by the Admiral's company; in 1591–2 the balance is sharply reversed, with the Admiral's company giving six plays, to one by the other troupe. The Admiral's company was led by Edward Alleyn, and included plays by Marlowe in its repertoire. These two remarkable talents placed it ahead of its rivals in the early 1590s.

From 1588 to 1594 the Admiral's Men operated in an amalgamation, the exact nature of which is unclear, with Lord Strange's Men.[4] But the grim period of plague that closed the theatres in 1592–4, besides being a testing

[1] Ibid., pp. 14–15.
[2] Induction, 36–7. *Ben Jonson*, ed. C. H. Herford and Percy and Evelyn Simpson (Oxford, 1938), VI.
[3] Prologue, 1–2. *The Works of Christopher Marlowe*, ed. C. F. Tucker Brooke (Oxford, reprinted 1929).
[4] Chambers, *Elizabethan Stage*, II, 119–21, 138–9.

time during which many lesser companies failed, was a period of reorganization for the Admiral's Men. When the theatres reopened in 1594, the Admiral's Men were an independent company, and many of their late fellows had joined the newly consolidated Lord Chamberlain's company. The Admiral's and the Chamberlain's Men briefly shared the same theatre (Philip Henslowe's playhouse at Newington Butts) early in 1594, but by mid-June the Admiral's Men had transferred to the Rose, where they operated to the end of the decade. In 1598 the Earl of Pembroke's Men came to grief when their satiric play *The Isle of Dogs* brought down the wrath of the Privy Council, and the result was an order that allowed only two men's companies to play in London: the Chamberlain's and the Admiral's.[1] This joint monopoly, however, merely confirmed the pre-eminence the two companies had already won in their own right.

The Admiral's Men are chiefly remembered as the company that performed Marlowe, and certainly the entries in the diary of Philip Henslowe (their landlord and financial manager) show the continuing popularity of *Tamburlaine* and *Doctor Faustus*. But their contemporaries would have seen the company in a more varied light. Their repertoire included Kyd's *The Spanish Tragedy* and Greene's *Friar Bacon and Friar Bungay* (the latter acquired from the Queen's Men); they introduced George Chapman as a playwright; and with the appearance in 1598 of William Haughton's *Englishmen for my Money* they played the first known London comedy. G. B. Harrison's analysis of the entries in Henslowe's *Diary* from 1594 to 1597 shows their most frequently produced play in this period to have been *The Wiseman of West Chester*, which Harrison identifies as Munday's *John a Kent and John a Cumber*.[2] The Admiral's Men thus had in their repertoire a vein of native comedy to balance the exotic heroics of Marlowe. The comic nature of many scenes in *Doctor Faustus* (some of which may be later additions) suggests that this vein was popular with their audiences, and that exploiting it was the obvious way to keep an old play, even a popular one, fresh.

Their chief drawing card, however, seems to have been Edward Alleyn, whose prestige was such that his name 'was able to make an ill matter good'. The title page of the 1594 edition of *A Knack to Know a Knave* announces

[1] Bernard Beckerman, *Shakespeare at the Globe 1599–1609* (New York, 1962), p. 3.
[2] *Elizabethan Plays and Players* (Ann Arbor, reprinted 1958), pp. 139–44. The identification with Munday's play is not certain.
[3] Thomas Nashe, *Strange News out of Purgatory*, quoted from Chambers, *Elizabethan Stage*, II, 297.

that the play was performed by 'Ed. ALLEN and his Companie'. This identification of the leading actor is unusual, and suggests the degree of Alleyn's popularity. He seems to have had an imposing presence: the portrait in Dulwich College (Plate 6) shows commanding eyes, and a nose that might have belonged to the Duke of Wellington. He was, by one account, nearly 7 feet tall.[1] These details, and the knowledge that he played the leading parts in *Tamburlaine*, *Doctor Faustus* and Greene's *Orlando Furioso*, add up to an actor in the heroic mould – perhaps with an added gift for grotesque comedy, since he also played Barabas in *The Jew of Malta*. We are told that he acted the part of Faustus in a surplice, with a cross on his breast,[2] presumably to ward off the evil spirits who reputedly appeared during performances of this play.[3] This touch may suggest the piety that was part of Alleyn's private character; but in its emphasis on the danger to the performer, it is not without an element of pure showmanship as well.

Alleyn's reputation has suffered with posterity by the assumption of G. B. Harrison (widely echoed) that he is reincarnated in Ancient Pistol;[4] in other words, that his style was a matter of strutting and bellowing, laughably outmoded by the end of the century when the new, 'natural' style of Burbage and the Chamberlain's Men was setting the fashion. William A. Armstrong has argued against this view, pointing out, among other things, that Alleyn and Burbage were not contrasted by their contemporaries, but praised in similar terms.[5] However, theatre criticism was in such a primitive state at this period that the lack of a detailed contrast between the two actors does not preclude the possibility that their styles were quite different. While there is every reason to believe that Alleyn was no mere barnstormer, but an excellent actor in his vein, that vein was probably looking old-fashioned by the turn of the century. No one was writing plays like *Tamburlaine* any more, and you could raise a laugh by quoting it. Whatever the reason, Alleyn retired from acting in 1597. He was lured back for a while, but by 1604 his retirement was permanent.[6]

Without Alleyn, the Admiral's Men moved into the new century with a handsome new theatre, the Fortune, and a repertoire increasingly dominated

[1] Ashley H. Thorndike, *Shakespeare's Theater* (New York, reprinted 1960), pp. 383–4. Thorndike does not give a reference for this.
[2] Samuel Rowlands, *The Knave of Clubs*, quoted in C. F. Tucker Brooke and Nathaniel Burton Paradise (eds.), *English Drama 1580–1642* (Boston, 1933), p. 168.
[3] Chambers, *Elizabethan Stage*, III, 423–4.
[4] Harrison, *Elizabethan Plays*, p. 173.
[5] 'Shakespeare and the acting of Edward Alleyn', *Shakespeare Survey 7* (1954), pp. 82–9.
[6] Chambers, *Elizabethan Stage*, II, 297–8.

by native comedy. As the century advanced their interest in London life was sometimes taken to the point of documentary. The two-part Middleton–Dekker collaboration, *The Honest Whore*, ostensibly set in Italy, includes scenes in Bedlam and Bridewell; and *The Roaring Girl*, by the same authors, brings Moll Frith, an actual London character, to the stage. The company continued to prosper, but in the late 1590s artistic pre-eminence had passed to the Chamberlain's Men, and so it remained. The position of the Admiral's Men as England's second acting company was confirmed in 1603, when at the start of the new reign the Chamberlain's Men became the King's Men and the Admiral's were assigned to Prince Henry.

There was a Chamberlain's company in the dark and confused period of the 1580s, traceable mostly in the provinces; but the great company of Shakespeare and Burbage was virtually a creation of the reorganization that followed the easing of the plague in 1594. Through the rest of the decade they gradually supplanted the Admiral's Men as England's leading company. This can be traced in the record of court performances; and while the shift was not so sudden or dramatic as the transfer of favour from the Queen's Men to the Admiral's, it was steady, and by the Christmas and Shrovetide seasons of 1596–7 the Chamberlain's Men were playing regularly at court, the Admiral's not at all. The plays of Shakespeare, the acting of Burbage, and – it is generally supposed – a more restrained and natural style, as recommended in Hamlet's advice to the players, may all have contributed to this growing popularity. More remarkable, however, was the tenacity with which the company maintained its leading position, even after the deaths of Shakespeare and Burbage and up to the closing of the theatres. It was an unusually stable company, losing few of its members to other groups, and recruiting largely from its own apprentices; when it took players from outside, it could pick the best.[1] The company was also unique in that, from the building of the Globe in 1599, they owned the theatre they played in; this gave them a security no other group enjoyed.

Of all the companies of the period, they had the most catholic repertoire. The universality of Shakespeare's appeal is unquestionable; but his works were simply the centre of a repertoire that reached out in all directions. The company played cheerful, undemanding entertainments like *Mucedorus* and *The Merry Devil of Edmonton*; moralizing social plays like *The London Prodigal* and *The Miseries of Enforced Marriage*; and the clever, sophisticated work of Beaumont and Fletcher. From other companies they took works as

[1] Baldwin, *Organization and Personnel*, pp. 87, 279–80.

old-fashioned as *The Spanish Tragedy*[1] and as contemporary as *The Malcontent*. They were willing to pioneer, and to take risks: they performed Jonson's *Every Man in his Humour*, and thus helped to set a new fashion in comedy; they were willing also to try the same author's *Every Man out of his Humour* and *Sejanus*. They appear to have insisted on cuts in one case, and rewriting by a second author in the other;[2] but the fact that they tackled such difficult, experimental works at all suggests an admirable spirit of enterprise.

One of their experiments had more far-reaching effects than they could have imagined. In 1608 Burbage was able to take over the Blackfriars theatre for the King's Men. While they retained the large outdoor playhouse of the Globe, they now had, as a second theatre, a smaller, indoor house where they would play by artificial light. Gradually the Blackfriars came to be regarded as their main playhouse.[3] Famous though the Globe is in legend, its heyday seems to have been brief, barely a decade, and the future lay with the Blackfriars. For good or ill, the decision of England's leading company to move indoors, and play for a smaller, more select audience, was a decisive point in the shift from the popular theatre of the middle ages to the minority theatre we know today.

If the company was versatile, so, it would appear, was its leading actor, Richard Burbage. He was, we are told, 'a delightful Proteus, so wholly transforming himself into his Part, and putting off himself with his Cloathes, as he never (not so much as in the Tyring-house) assum'd himself again until the *Play* was done . . .'.[4] This is late evidence, from the Restoration, but a contemporary elegy on his death praises him in similar terms, for his identification with his parts, and for the emotional conviction of his acting:

> Oft haue I seene him, leap into the Graue
> Suiting the person, which he seem'd to haue
> Of a sadd Louer, with so true an Eye
> That theer I would haue sworne, he meant to dye . . .[5]

---

[1] Or so contemporary evidence suggests. This has been disputed by Philip Edwards in his Revels edition of *The Spanish Tragedy* (London, 1959), pp. 146–7.

[2] See the title page of the 1600 Quarto of *Every Man out of his Humour*, and the Epistle 'To the Reader' in *Sejanus*. Herford and Simpson, III (1927), p. 418 ff.; and IV (1932), p. 351.

[3] Gerald Eades Bentley, *Shakespeare and his Theatre* (Lincoln, Nebraska, 1964), p. 109.

[4] Richard Flecknoe, *A Short Discourse of the English Stage*, quoted from Chambers, *Elizabethan Stage*, IV, 370.

[5] 'A Funerall Elegye on ye Death of the famous Actor Richard Burbedg . . .', quoted from Edwin Nungezer, *A Dictionary of Actors* (New York, reprinted 1968), p. 74.

One of Sir Thomas Overbury's *Characters*, 'An Excellent Actor', is often taken as referring to Burbage, for the actor described is 'much affected to painting', as Burbage was. This sketch emphasizes the naturalness and decorum of the performer: 'He doth not striue to make nature monstrous, she is often seene in the same Scaene with him, but neither on Stilts nor Crutches; and for his voice tis not lower than the prompter, nor lowder than the Foile and Target.'[1] It would appear that Hamlet's advice to the players, to be neither too bombastic nor too tame, was put into the mouth of a performer who himself exemplified the ideal middle way. He is remembered chiefly as a tragic actor: the elegy on his death lists among his parts Hamlet, Lear, Othello and Hieronimo, and we know that he played Ferdinand in *The Duchess of Malfi*. But he cannot have been without some comic gift, for he played in some of Jonson's major comedies, and a vein of macabre wit runs through even his serious roles. Like Tarlton, though in a very different way, Burbage became a national figure: when in 1619 he died after a long career, there were complaints that London mourned more for him than for Queen Anne, who had died a few days earlier.[2]

But this was not a one-man company. Its most famous performer apart from Burbage was the clown Will Kempe, who came to the company from Strange's Men in the reorganization of 1594. In the 1580s Kempe had toured the Low Countries with Leicester's Men, and he is also heard of in Denmark. His contemporaries may be recalling his continental wanderings in jocular references to 'Don Guilhelmo' and 'Monsieur du Kempe'.[3] In *The Travels of the Three English Brothers*, by Day, Rowley and Wilkins, Kempe is seen improvising a part at short notice with a troupe of Italian players. The 1594 title page of *A Knack to Know a Knave* advertises 'KEMPS *applauded Merrimentes* of the men of Gotheam'. In print, the scene is short and uninteresting, and contains no obvious leading comic role; probably Kempe expanded it in performance, by speaking more than was set down for him. If he had a special 'line', it was that indicated in *Part II* of *The Return from Parnassus*, where Kempe auditions a prospective actor in the role of a foolish, pompous minor official, and shows him how the part should be played. One notices, besides the pomposity, a distinctive trick of language: 'Now therefore I am determined not onely to teach but also to instruct, not onely the ignorant, but also the simple, not onely what is their duty towards their

---

[1] Quoted from Chambers, *Elizabethan Stage*, IV, 258. The 'Character' has been attributed to John Webster.
[2] Thorndike, *Shakespeare's Theatre*, p. 387.
[3] Nungezer, *Dictionary*, p. 216.

betters, but also what is their dutye towards their superiors . . .'[1] The trick is different from the malapropisms of Dogberry or the transpositions of Bottom, but the comic approach to language is similar. Such effects would not have been peculiar to Kempe, of course, but evidently he was good at them, and Shakespeare seems to have kept this in mind when writing parts for him. And while the image of pompous officialdom is clearest in the role of Dogberry (which we know to be Kempe's) it can be seen in other roles we may reasonably assume to be his: Bottom, in particular, moves among the fairies with the aplomb and condescension of a visiting dignitary.

Kempe left the Chamberlain's Men in 1599. The reasons are not known, but he seems to have coveted, and in large measure achieved, the kind of independent stardom that Tarlton enjoyed. Like Tarlton, he was famous for his jigs (a chance for the individual clown to shine), and his Morris dance from London to Norwich (Plate 8a), followed by the more grandiose project of dancing across the Alps, argues a hunger for publicity. Quite simply, he may have chafed under company discipline. He was succeeded by Robert Armin, who, according to legend, had been discovered by Tarlton and who, in addition to his performing ability, was a prolific writer, taking a serious interest in the business of foolery and in the various kinds of 'natural' fools. Armin's play *The Two Maids of Moreclacke* includes an actual 'natural', 'John o' th' Hospital', designed for Armin himself to play. It is commonly supposed that Armin's arrival brought to the company a 'more delicate, introspective, and sophisticated style of fooling',[2] exemplified in Feste and in Lear's Fool. But as the company's clown, he would not only have succeeded to Kempe's old parts; he would presumably have been asked to play Thersites in *Troilus and Cressida* and Pompey in *Measure for Measure*. And the shrewdness of Shakespeare's fools is something very different from the pathetic simplicity of John o' th' Hospital. It may be that the change from Kempe to Armin was not so much from a robust, coarse-grained performer to a lyrical, introspective one, as from an old-fashioned clown trading on a single personality to a sophisticated and versatile character actor.

Other notable members of the company included John Heminges and Henry Cundall, to whose piety we owe the First Folio of Shakespeare; and John Lowin, the original Bosola in *The Duchess of Malfi*, a remarkable veteran who was still alive after the Restoration, and who reputedly passed on Shakespeare's instructions for playing Henry VIII to Davenant, who passed

---

[1] *The Three Parnassus Plays*, ed. J. B. Leishman (London, 1949), IV. iv. 1825–9. The later reference, given in the text, is to this edition.

[2] William A. Armstrong, 'Actors and theatres', *Shakespeare Survey 17* (1964), p. 195.

them on to Betterton.[1] Shakespeare himself was an actor in his own company, but what little evidence we have about his acting is late and unreliable; had he been as remarkable a performer as he was a playwright, his contemporaries would surely have commented on the fact. Most frustrating is our almost complete ignorance of the boys who played the great female roles that have since tested, and often defeated, the abilities of famous actresses. Several critics have traced, through Shakespeare's comedies of the 1590s, a team of women, one tall and one short, the former being the leader: Rosalind and Celia, Portia and Nerissa.[2] This is taken to indicate a particular, talented pair of boy actors; but boys grow up, and it may suggest nothing more than the custom of giving the leading role to the oldest and most experienced apprentice. The general quality of the boy actors is suggested by the reaction of an English traveller who saw in Venice women playing the parts of women; he remarked, in pleased surprise, that they were as good as the boys.[3]

There were also, of course, companies consisting entirely of boy actors at this period; but before we turn to them, something should be said about another adult group. The Earl of Worcester had maintained a provincial company throughout the 1590s, and in 1602 he succeeded in breaking the Chamberlain's–Admiral's monopoly and establishing his company in London. They became Queen Anne's Men in 1603, and around 1606 moved to the theatre most associated with them, the Red Bull. Thomas Heywood was their leading playwright, and one of their actors; and they specialized in domestic comedy, domestic drama, history plays and swashbuckling plays of adventure. A contemporary ballad comments:

> The players of the Banke side,
>   the round Globe and the Swan,
> Will teach you idle tricks of loue,
>   but the Bull will play the man.[4]

Kempe joined them briefly, but is not heard of after 1603. Their leading actor was Thomas Greene, 'the leane foole of the Bull',[5] a clown in the old

---

[1] Chambers, *Elizabethan Stage*, II, 329.

[2] Michael Jamieson, 'Shakespeare's celibate stage', in Gerald Eades Bentley (ed.), *The Seventeenth Century Stage* (Toronto, 1968), p. 84. Reprinted from G. I. Duthie (ed.), *Papers Mainly Shakespearian* (Edinburgh, 1964), pp. 21–39. See also Bentley, *Shakespeare and his Theatre*, p. 45.

[3] Jamieson, 'Celibate stage', p. 76.

[4] 'Turner's Dish of Lenten Stuff', in Hyder E. Rollins (ed.), *A Pepysian Garland* (Cambridge, 1922), p. 35.

[5] Ibid.

manner whose popularity was such that a play, Cooke's *Greene's Tu Quoque*, was named for one of his catch-phrases. His part in this play, Bubble, a foolish servant who has come into money, is (in print) unremarkable; but there is one significant exchange:

SCATTERGOOD: . . . let's go see a play at the Globe.

BUBBLE: I care not; any whither, so the clown have a part; for, i'faith, I am nobody without a fool.

GERALDINE: Why, then, we'll go to the Red Bull: they say Green's a good clown.

BUBBLE: Green! Green's an ass.

SCATTERGOOD: Wherefore do you say so?

BUBBLE: Indeed, I ha' no reason; for they say he is as like me as ever he can look.[1]

If one wanted old-fashioned entertainment, with a fat part for the clown, who could break out of the dramatic frame as in Master Tarlton's time,[2] the Red Bull was the place to go.

We have been discussing adult, professional performers. But throughout the sixteenth century companies of boy players made a significant contribution to the theatrical scene. Until around 1570 the grammar schools were dominant, but after that the lead was taken by the choristers of St Paul's cathedral and of the Chapel Royal.[3] Their tradition was, initially, one of private, amateur and occasional performances, a tradition that survives in schools today. But in 1576, when Richard Farrant took over the Chapel children, they began to give public performances in a theatre in the Blackfriars (perhaps because they were forbidden to play in the Chapel itself),[4] and in the early 1580s the Paul's Boys, in a theatre whose location remains a mystery,[5] followed their example of growing professionalism. Admission was charged, and the aim was to make a profit; there was even, in 1583–4, a temporary amalgamation at the Blackfriars of a number of children's companies, including the Paul's and Chapel Boys, apparently under the patronage of the Earl of Oxford.[6] The nature and purpose of this amalgamation remain murky, but the fact that it took place at all suggests the degree to

[1] *A Select Collection of Old English Plays* . . ., ed. Robert Dodsley (fourth edition, revised by W. Carew Hazlitt, London, 1875), XI, 240.
[2] See above, p. 100.
[3] Harold Newcomb Hillebrand, *The Child Actors* (New York, reprinted 1964), p. 22.
[4] Ibid., p. 96.
[5] Ibid., pp. 112–14.
[6] Chambers, *Elizabethan Stage*, II, 40.

which the choristers' companies were becoming independent of the institutions to which they nominally belonged. There was, however, some danger in the companies' being on their own, for they were unprotected in a crisis. When the Blackfriars theatre was closed around 1584, the Chapel Boys had to stop playing; and the Paul's Boys were dissolved in 1590, apparently because of their involvement in the religious pamphlet warfare of the Marprelate controversy.[1]

The leading playwright for the boys' companies at this period was John Lyly, whose plays were generally performed by the children of Paul's, initially during their period at Blackfriars, mentioned above.[2] It is commonly believed that his emphasis on verbal cleverness rather than deep feeling reflects the abilities, and the limits, of the children. Their repertoire was, however, a varied one, and included plays on classical subjects (titles like *Pompey* and *Scipio Africanus* survive) which may indicate a wider range of style than Lyly alone would require. We know less about the Chapel repertoire, though we know they played Peele's *The Arraignment of Paris*. Both companies, however, made their most notable impact on English drama with the new century.

For most of the 1590s the children's companies lay dormant. A new Paul's company appears to have begun acting in 1599, initially with a repertoire of old plays. One of their earliest original works, Marston's *Jack Drum's Entertainment*, includes a passage praising the charm of the actors – 'the Apes in time will do it hansomely' – and the select nature of the audience –

> A man shall not be choakte
> With the stench of Garlicke, nor be pasted
> To the barmy Iacket of a Beer-brewer.

– but deploring the staleness of the repertoire, 'mustie fopperies of antiquitie'.[3] The musty fopperies, however, were soon replaced by Marston's own early plays, colourful and extravagant, and by the London comedies of Middleton, with their emphasis on social satire and financial intrigue. The lighter side of the repertoire included Dekker and Webster's *Westward Ho* and *Northward Ho*, which exploit the unchanging formulae of bedroom farce. In a very different vein, the company performed Chapman's tragedy *Bussy d'Ambois*. While satiric comedy was their forte, the Paul's Boys seem to have avoided the sort of direct contemporary references that embroiled the other children's company in frequent controversy; and they appear to

[1] Hillebrand, *Child Actors*, pp. 97, 143.
[2] Chambers, *Elizabethan Stage*, II, 39.
[3] Tudor Facsimile Texts (1912), sig. H3v.

have been wound up, quietly enough, around 1607 – why, we do not know.[1]

The Chapel Boys, on the other hand, resumed at the Blackfriars in 1600 with a flurry of impressments, resulting in at least one complaint to the Privy Council by an aggrieved father. For the rest of its existence, the company was torn with dissension among its own managers and threatened by the wrath of the authorities. Their connection with the Chapel Royal was now entirely nominal, and while they were renamed the Children of the Queen's Revels in 1603, even this degree of royal favour was made insecure by their own actions. Daniel's *Philotas* (1604) brought its author before the Privy Council, through its alleged reference to the career of the Earl of Essex. Chapman, Jonson, and Marston's *Eastward Ho* (1605) contained sardonic jokes about the Scots; Chapman and Jonson were imprisoned, Marston fled, and 'the Children of the Queen's Revels' became simply 'the Children of the Revels' or 'the Children at Blackfriars'. In 1606 Day's *Isle of Gulls*, with its veiled references to the court, resulted in a number of unspecified persons, perhaps even some of the children themselves, being committed to Bridewell. As the scale of the official punishments increased, so, remarkably, did the scale of the offences. In 1608 the French ambassador complained that the Blackfriars company had performed a play (probably one of Chapman's *Biron* plays) which showed the French queen in an undignified light, adding for good measure that in the same week King James himself had been depicted on the Blackfriars stage, drunken, violent and blaspheming. One would have expected the company to be suppressed outright; but their appearance at court in the Christmas season 1608–9 shows that they were allowed to continue, though only under a new manager.[2] In 1609 they moved to the Whitefriars theatre, and in 1613 they were amalgamated with an adult company, Lady Elizabeth's Men.[3]

Their spectacular record of indiscretion should not blind us to their artistic achievements: like the Paul's Boys, they pioneered a new vein of satiric comedy whose influence could still be felt after the Restoration. Many of Chapman's comedies were written for them, as were two of Jonson's experimental 'comicall satyres' and his *Epicœne*. Marston became one of their managers in 1604, and they performed his major plays. The company included two of the most notable child actors of the period – Salomon Pavey, described in Ben Jonson's famous epitaph as a specialist in old men,[4] and

---

[1] Hillebrand, *Child Actors*, pp. 213, 216.
[2] Ibid., pp. 192–201.
[3] Ibid., p. 239.
[4] Herford and Simpson, VIII (1947), p. 77.

Nathan Field, a protégé of Jonson and later a dramatist in his own right and a member of the King's Men. Field's career suggests that acting in the boys' companies was not always a matter of the childish imitation of adult behaviour: when in 1609 Field played for the Revels company in *Epicœne*, he was twenty-two. Indeed, in its later years this company may have looked more and more like a normal adult troupe, and eventually the boys themselves, like the best of their plays, were absorbed into the regular public theatre.[1] By the same token, their practice of indoor performances in a small house by artificial light did not die with them, but was continued, as we have seen, by Burbage and the King's Men. The heyday of the boys' companies in the seventeenth century was brief, but their influence was lasting.

If we had the blueprints of the Globe theatre, and could build an exact replica, we would still have only the shell of the theatre Shakespeare knew. The organization of the companies, their methods of rehearsal and performance, their relations with their audience – all these would still elude us. Their repertory system made demands that would seem harrowing to a modern actor. Bernard Beckerman has calculated that an actor might have to master a new role every second week, while keeping thirty or forty other roles in his head, and that an actor such as Alleyn, in a three-year period, would have to learn over fifty new parts, as well as retaining around twenty old ones.[2] Obviously, there was no time for the prolonged and detailed rehearsals we now take for granted. And there was, of course, no director in the modern sense to conduct such rehearsals. The adult companies consisted of shareholders who – in the stable major companies at least – would be used to working with each other, boys who were apprenticed to the shareholders, and hired men for the smaller parts. This structure is reflected in the plays themselves: according to William A. Ringler Jr, none of Shakespeare's early plays has more than six major roles (that is, roles with over 200 lines).[3] In other words, a comparatively small number of actors regularly carried the main burden. Their instincts and experience would be the main shaping factor in the performance, and their responsibilities would include instructing the boy actors who were apprenticed to them.

However, a foreign visitor, early in the seventeenth century, reports that

---

[1] R. A. Foakes, 'Tragedy at the children's theatres after 1600: a challenge to the adult stage', in David Galloway (ed.), *The Elizabethan Theatre II* (Toronto, 1970), p. 58.
[2] *Shakespeare at the Globe*, pp. 9, 130.
[3] 'The number of actors in Shakespeare's early plays', in Bentley (ed.), *Seventeenth Century Stage*, p. 120.

in England actors 'are daily instructed, as it were in a school, so that even the most eminent actors have to allow themselves to be taught their places by the dramatists . . .'.[1] It is hard to imagine Burbage taking daily acting lessons from Shakespeare, and one wonders if the visitor really understood what was happening. But this report may mean that the author was present at rehearsals, perhaps to do some rough blocking and to give guidance on points of interpretation. In the children's theatres the author's responsibility may have been greater. The boys were apprenticed, not to adult actors, but to the manager of the company, who was generally more businessman than artist. In Edward Sharpham's *Cupid's Whirligig*, a play written for the Children of the King's Revels (a minor boys' company with a brief existence), the schoolmaster, Master Correction, says of his pupils, 'I haue taken as much paines with them, as any poet whatsoeuer cold haue don, to make them answere vppon their Q. with good action, distinction, and deliberation . . .'[2] The playwright as director may have had to work harder at the private theatres than at the public ones.

In actual performance the actors, then as now, were largely on their own. A 'plot' hung up backstage would give an outline of entrances, property requirements and cues for sound effects, and the bookholder would act as prompter and callboy. One thing they could not count on was a quiet, polite audience whose members, if bored, would merely yawn. Particularly at a first performance, the judgement of the audience (which would be expressed on the spot, often in a devastating way) could decide the play's life or death. Playwrights regularly complained about how easy it was for a play to be damned for the wrong reasons: ' 'tis growne into a custome at playes if anyone rise (especially of any fashionable sort) about what serious busines soeuer, the rest thinking it in dislike of the play, tho he neuer thinks it, cry "Mew! by Jesus, vilde!" and leaue the poore hartlesse children to speake their Epilogue to the emptie seates.'[3] The agreement drawn up between playwright and spectators in the Induction to Jonson's *Bartholomew Fair*, with its jocular attempt to regularize the touchy relations between stage and audience, is a jest that must be more than half in earnest. And the conventional appeal for applause that ends so many plays must have been, at the first performance of an untried work, more than a routine gesture.

[1] Johannes Rhenamus, preface to *Speculum Aistheticum*, quoted from David Klein, 'Did Shakespeare produce his own plays?', *Modern Language Review*, LVII (October 1962), p. 556; Klein's translation.
[2] London, 1607, sig. K3r.
[3] John Day, *The Ile of Gulls*, *The Works of John Day*, ed. A. H. Bullen (London, reprinted 1963), p. 214.

The Elizabethan actor, performing for a volatile crowd, speaking a part he had had little chance to practise (plays of the period are full of references, joking and not so joking, to actors forgetting their lines), dependent on his own nerve and judgement and those of his fellows, must have needed a temperament like that of a competitive athlete. Certainly he could not sink too comfortably into a planned routine. Improvisation, of the sort that earlier drama regularly called for – 'Here entereth with some jest ILL WILL'[1] – is still required in some plays of Shakespeare's age: 'He playes and sings any odde toy ...',[2] 'Here they two talk and rail what they list ...'.[3] And one may imagine that the players (especially the clowns, judging by Hamlet's complaint about them) would add to the performance in ways we cannot now recover. One contemporary reference indicates a piece of comic business in A Midsummer Night's Dream that does not appear in any text: 'Faith like Thisbe in the play, a has almost kil'd himselfe with the scabberd ...'[4] For every detail like this, preserved by accident, countless must have been lost.

But more has been lost than the details. The general nature of Elizabethan acting style has been, in our time, a matter of hot dispute. The contemporary pronouncements on the subject are reducible to a few commonsense principles that do not take us very far. According to Thomas Heywood, one of the pleasures of the theatre is 'to see a souldier shap'd like a souldier, walke, speake, act like a souldier'. Accordingly, 'Actors should be men pick'd out personable, according to the parts they present ...'.[5] We have noted already how Burbage was praised for sinking himself into the parts he played, and making them convincing. A bad actor, by the same token, was felt to be one who let the audience see the actor behind the character by overplaying, underplaying or neglecting the business of his part: 'When he doth hold conference upon the stage; and should looke directly into his fellows face; hee turnes about his voice into the assembly for applause-sake, like a Trumpeter in the fields, that shifts places to get an eccho.'[6] In Part II of

---

[1] Wealth and Health, in Early English Dramatists: Recently Discovered 'Lost' Tudor Plays with Some Others, ed. John S. Farmer (London, 1907), p. 283.

[2] Robert Greene, Orlando Furioso, IV. ii. 1112. The Plays and Poems of Robert Greene, ed. J. Churton Collins (Oxford, 1905), I.

[3] Cooke, Greene's Tu Quoque (see n 1, p. 109), p. 255. There is a full discussion of the question of improvisation in John Alan Beaufort Somerset, 'The comic turn in English drama 1470–1616' (unpublished PhD dissertation, University of Birmingham, 1966), pp. 434–84, 801–11.

[4] Edward Sharpham, The Fleire (London, 1607), sig. E1v.

[5] An Apology for Actors (Scholars' Facsimiles and Reprints, New York, 1941), sigs. B3v, E3r.

[6] J. Cocke, 'A common player', quoted from Chambers, Elizabethan Stage, IV, 256.

The Return from Parnassus, Will Kempe is shown criticizing the university amateurs for not being able to speak and walk simultaneously; in other words, for not making the performance look natural (IV. iii. 1757-61). The Lord's praise of one of the players in *The Taming of the Shrew* is as concise and representative a statement as we are likely to get of what the Elizabethans admired in acting: 'that part Was aptly fitted and naturally perform'd.'[1] The most elaborate modern attempt to reproduce Elizabethan acting has been made by B. L. Joseph, with the aid of rhetorical theory and stock gestures recorded in 1644 by a teacher for the deaf and dumb; when in 1952 he produced *Macbeth* on these principles, some newspaper critics remarked that the results looked simply like normal acting.[2] One concludes – though Joseph does not take the point – that he might as well have stuck with Hamlet's familiar advice to the players, or even left his performers to their own untutored common sense.

But where would the common sense of an Elizabethan actor have led him? There has been much debate over whether Elizabethan acting was 'formal' or 'naturalistic', or some combination of the two, or whether indeed these terms have any meaning at all.[3] The safest guide is probably a study of the plays themselves, holding in our minds the principle of decorum the Elizabethans valued so highly.[4] Burbage would have needed to modulate his style from the patterned laments of Richard II to the jagged outbursts of Leontes; and it seems fair to assume that in the period as a whole the acting would have reflected the move from a declamatory, stylized drama, such as that of Marlowe and the early Shakespeare, to the more natural, open style we associate with the mature Shakespeare and such contemporaries as Webster and Middleton – where, for all the rhetorical cunning, we hear the sound of a natural speaking voice. To state the extremes, it is a change from 'with that S. bent his browes and fetcht his stations up and downe the rome, with such furious Iesture as if he had beene playing Tamberlane on a stage'[5] to '*Enter* FRANKFORD, *as it were brushing the crumbs from his clothes with a napkin, as newly risen from supper.*'[6] In each case, the manner is

[1] Induction, i. 84-5. William Shakespeare, *The Complete Works*, ed. Peter Alexander (London, reprinted 1968).
[2] See B. L. Joseph, *Elizabethan Acting* (2nd edition, Oxford, 1964), p. 55, where the reviews in question are quoted.
[3] The major combatants, with their positions, are listed in the bibliography.
[4] See Lise-Lone Marker, 'Nature and decorum in the theory of Elizabethan Acting', in Galloway (ed.), *Elizabethan Theatre II*, pp. 87-107.
[5] E.S., *The Discouerie of the Knights of the Poste* (London, 1597), sig. C2v.
[6] Thomas Heywood, *A Woman Killed with Kindness*, ed. R. W. van Fossen (London, 1961), viii. 21. 1-2.

appropriate to the play and the character, and the naturalistic touch is as pointed and artistically controlled as the heightened, heroic manner of the tyrant. Plays written for the children's companies generally do not require much emotional depth, and playwrights sometimes exploited the childishness of the actors for ironic effect; but within these limits even the children were required to display a wide stylistic range, from the declamatory to the colloquial.[1] And the theatre itself could be as much a factor as the play: there is evidence that, once the adult troupes had the experience of playing in small private houses as well as large public ones, they developed a quieter style for the former.[2]

We may imagine the degree of stylization in their acting, then, as dependent on the requirements of the play and the auditorium, and not on some elaborate pre-existing theory. There would be no attempt at reproducing the details of life merely for their own sake. Indeed, a passage from Nashe's *Summer's Last Will and Testament* reads like an attack on the 'method' acting of the 1950s: 'And this I bar, over and besides: that none of you stroke your beards to make action; play with your codpiece points, or stand fumbling on your buttons, when you know not how to bestow your fingers. Serve God, and act cleanly.'[3] If Shakespeare's sour references to strutting, ranting players are to be trusted, actors were more inclined to go to the other extreme, to indulge in overblown passion, larger than life. In both cases, the fault is one that calls attention to the actor; he is working either too hard, or not hard enough. In all acting, a degree of stylization must be achieved, but not exceeded. The exact point at which the balance is struck so that the audience is convinced by the performance will vary from one age to another, and we cannot be sure where the Elizabethans placed it; probably it shifted during the period. We do know, however, that they recognized its importance, and censured actors who went too far one way or the other.

Whatever faults the Elizabethan actors committed, their belief in decorum makes it unlikely that they would seek self-consciously for novel ways of interpreting familiar roles. Much of the theorizing in favour of 'formal' Elizabethan acting really comes down to a dislike of 'interpretation', as practised by actors (and directors) who twist a play to their own ends. In the theories of Alfred Harbage and S. L. Bethell there is an implicit irritation at the gimmickry that has afflicted some Shakespeare productions in the

[1] Michael Shapiro, 'Children's troupes: dramatic illusion and acting style', *Comparative Drama*, III (spring, 1969), pp. 42–53.
[2] Armstrong, 'Actors and theatres', p. 198.
[3] *Thomas Nashe*, ed. Stanley Wells (London, 1964), p. 93.

twentieth century, and a desire to return to a simple respect for the author's intentions.[1] Now it seems likely that, even with Shakespeare keeping an eye on him, Burbage could have found more than one way of playing Hamlet, and his performance probably did undergo subtle changes as he himself developed. Even so, he was spared the disconcerting experience of having his performance compared with a line of Hamlets stretching out behind him, of hearing old playgoers muttering that he was not so good as X, or that Y had done something quite different in the play scene. He would not have been driven to seek novelty in an attempt to create a Hamlet that was his own and no one else's. Not only were Burbage and his fellows given, as their raw material, some of the most exciting dramatic texts in the English language; they could approach them fresh, as no players have been able to do since. Novelty would come unbidden, for the plays themselves were new. In our endless and often fruitless speculations as to what they did with those plays, we might take a moment simply to envy them.

[1] Alfred Harbage, 'Elizabethan acting', *Publications of the Modern Language Association of America*, LIV (September 1939), pp. 705–6; and S. L. Bethell, 'Shakespeare's actors', *Review of English Studies*, new series, I (July 1950), p. 205.

III The playhouses

Richard Hosley

1 Introduction

Playhouses in England during the Renaissance fall into two major classes, outdoor and indoor. Outdoor playhouses were of two chief kinds: inn yard playhouses such as the Boar's Head in Whitechapel Street, London, and 'public' playhouses such as the Swan or Globe. The inn yard playhouses were more or less permanent adaptations of existing structures, and they were rectangular in ground plan. The public playhouses were permanent buildings whose design was adapted from existing structures (bear- or bull-baiting houses) but which were constructed explicitly for the purpose of exhibiting plays; they were, in general, 'round' (that is, polygonal) in ground plan. Both kinds of outdoor playhouse were used exclusively by professional players for commercial purposes. Indoor playhouses were of four chief kinds: (1) academic playhouses set up in halls like that of St John's College, Cambridge, or the Middle Temple, London; (2) non-scenic court playhouses set up in halls like the great Hall of Hampton Court Palace (a rather different, later example, adapted from a cockpit, was the Cockpit-in-Court at Whitehall); (3) 'private' playhouses such as the First or Second Black-friars; and (4) scenic court playhouses set up in halls like the Great Hall of Whitehall Palace or the First Jacobean Banqueting House at Whitehall. Academic and non-scenic court playhouses were alike in being (for the most part) temporary adaptations of domestic halls but different in that the one kind was used generally by amateur players whereas the other was used generally by professional players – although not for commercial purposes. Private playhouses were, in general, permanent adaptations of domestic halls, and they were used exclusively by professional players for commercial purposes. And scenic court playhouses were, in general, temporary adaptations of domestic halls; they were used by both amateur and professional players – but, again, not for commercial purposes.

All of the enumerated kinds of playhouse were in use in or around London during the period from 1576 to 1613. Since it is not practical, however, to treat all of them in a work of limited length which seeks to give fairly full details, I shall, in the present essay, deal only with the two most important kinds, the public playhouse and the private playhouse, illustrating the one by studies of the Swan and the First Globe, the other by a study of the Second Blackfriars.

(i)

During the period 1576–1613 there were, at various times, eleven permanent playhouses within or immediately outside the City of London in which professional actors put on plays for commercial purposes. Seven of these were 'public' playhouses operating immediately outside the City:

> The Theatre (1576–98)
> The Curtain (1577–c. 1627)
> The Rose (c. 1587–1605)
> The Swan (1595–c. 1637)
> The First Globe (1599–1613)
> The First Fortune (1600–21)
> The Red Bull (1605–c. 1663)[1]

And four were 'private' playhouses, three operating within the City and one immediately outside:

> The Paul's Boys' Playhouse (1575, 1588–90, c. 1600–c. 1608)
> The First Blackfriars (1576–84)
> The Second Blackfriars (1596, 1600–55?)
> The Whitefriars (1606?–29)

[1] In this essay dates are generally taken from E. K. Chambers, *The Elizabethan Stage* (1923), or Alfred Harbage, *Annals of English Drama*, revised S. Schoenbaum (1964). Quotations from primary sources are generally taken, as appropriate, from Chambers and from G. E. Bentley, *The Jacobean and Caroline Stage* (1941–68).

Despite an awkward ambiguity in the Elizabethan terms *public* and *private*, the very real differences between the two kinds of playhouse are sufficiently clear. In general, the public playhouses were large, 'round' (that is, polygonal), outdoor theatres, whereas the private playhouses were smaller, rectangular, indoor theatres. (The First Fortune, a square playhouse, was an exception among public playhouses in this respect.) The maximum capacity of a typical public playhouse like the Swan was about 3,000 spectators; that of a typical private playhouse like the Second Blackfriars, about 700 spectators. At the public playhouses a majority of spectators stood in the yard for 1d., the remainder sitting in galleries or boxes for 2d. or more; whereas at the private playhouses all spectators were seated (in pit, galleries or boxes) and paid 6d. or more. Originally the private playhouses were used exclusively by boys' companies, but this distinction disappeared about 1609 when the King's Men began using the Blackfriars in winter as well as the Globe in summer. Originally also the private playhouses were found only within the City of London (the Paul's playhouse, the First and Second Blackfriars), the public playhouses only in the suburbs (the Theatre, the Curtain, the Rose, the Swan, the Globe, the Fortune, the Red Bull); but this distinction disappeared about 1606 with the opening of the White-friars to the west of Ludgate. Public-theatre audiences, though socially heterogeneous, were drawn mainly from the lower classes – a situation that has caused modern scholars to refer to the public-theatre audiences as 'popular'; whereas private-theatre audiences tended to be better educated and of higher social rank – 'select' is one of the words commonly opposed to 'popular' in this respect. Thus the taste of the audience varied considerably in the two kinds of playhouse, and so accordingly, to some degree, did the kind of play presented.[1]

The terms *public* and *private* need not be discussed in detail. It is probable that the word *private*, as used by publishers on the title pages of plays, was designed 'to increase their sales by advertising the fact that the play was of the sophisticated kind written for the indoor theatres', the term merely connoting 'a degree of exclusiveness and superiority'.[2] Thus the opposed term *public* was applied to playhouses of the outdoor variety which lacked the 'exclusiveness and superiority' of the indoor playhouses. These are the specific senses used in the preceding paragraph. It is also clear, however, that both terms could bear such general meanings in relation to payment by the audience as we might expect. The term *public* was sometimes used in reference to

[1] Alfred Harbage, *Shakespeare and the Rival Traditions* (1952).
[2] William A. Armstrong, *The Elizabethan Private Theatres* (1958).

performance at a playhouse, whether public or private in the specific sense, that anyone could attend by virtue of paying the price of admission; whereas the term *private* was sometimes used in reference to performance at a playhouse, whether at court or at one of the universities or at an inn of court, which one might attend only by invitation.[1] Thus we find references both to 'public' performances (paid for by the audience) at 'private' playhouses like the Blackfriars, and to 'private' performances (before an invited audience) at academic or court playhouses which were not 'private' in the specific sense appropriate to the Blackfriars. Such performances could be described as 'private' regardless of whether the actors were amateur or professional; in the latter case the actors would, of course, be paid, but by the host rather than by the audience.

(ii)

Discussion of representative public and private playhouses may appropriately be prefaced by a brief inquiry into the kinds of temporary playhouse and stage that existed in England on the eve of construction of the first permanent English playhouse – that is, about 1575. By that date the two major forms of production of the fifteenth century, both of which continued well into the sixteenth, had fallen into disuse: the round theatre of Place and scaffolds (the Place or *platea* defined by a surrounding earthwork hill or some manner of fence), and the stop-to-stop theatre of the pageant wagons (however its puzzling 'processional' technique was managed). The kind of temporary stage that was most common in England about 1575 was the booth stage of the marketplace or village green – a small rectangular stage mounted on barrels or trestles and 'open' in the sense of being surrounded by spectators on three sides; see Plates 19a–20b and the drawing by Richard Southern reproduced as Figure 1.[2]

The stage proper of the booth stage generally measured from 15 to 25 feet in width and from 10 to 15 feet in depth; its height above the ground averaged about 5 feet 6 inches, with extremes ranging as low as 4 feet and as high as 8 feet; and it was backed by a cloth-covered booth, usually open at

---

[1] Richard Hosley, 'The playhouses and the stage', in Kenneth Muir and S. Schoenbaum (eds.), *A New Companion to Shakespeare Studies* (1971). Parts of the present chapter are based on this essay.

[2] I wish to thank Dr Southern for making the drawings which illustrate this essay, for suggesting helpful criticism of its arguments and for generously putting at my disposal, in more than one instance, the fruit of his own unpublished research.

the top, which served as a tiring-house (that is, an 'attiring' house). In typical small examples the booth proper employed four upright posts joined at the top by horizontal poles or timbers, so that the whole booth was constructed as a single bay and the booth front, accordingly, consisted of a single opening in which curtains were hung. In larger examples six or eight or even ten uprights were used, so that the booth was constructed in two or three or even

Figure 1 A booth stage

four bays and the booth front, accordingly, consisted of two or three or even four openings in which curtains were hung. The booth stage did not usually employ a 'containing' barrier or playhouse. But growth in the size of audiences and the experience of having performed in rounds enclosed by a fence or an earthwork hill apparently led the players to investigate ways of controlling access to the performance and thus of more efficiently collecting charges for viewing the show. About 1575 there were two kinds of building in England, both designed for functions other than the acting of plays, which were adapted by the players as temporary outdoor playhouses.

One was the animal-baiting ring or 'game house' (bear garden or bullring), examples of which are recorded in both pictorial and verbal records as standing on the south bank of the Thames opposite the City of London in the 1560s. The early Bankside baiting-houses were round wooden amphitheatres consisting of (probably) two galleries superimposed one upon the other and defining a circular 'pit' some 60 or more feet in diameter (Figures 2–3). We have no record of the use of a baiting-house for the performance

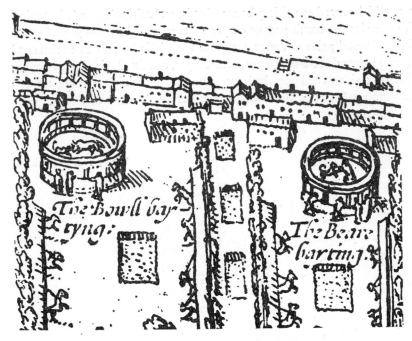

Figure 2 Detail from the Hogenberg Map of London (in Braun and Hogenberg's *Civitates Orbis Terrarum*, 1572) showing animal-baiting houses on Bankside. *Folger Shakespeare Library*

of plays, but the close physical resemblance between the baiting-houses and later 'public' playhouses makes the hypothesis of such use a defensible one. Presumably a booth stage was set up against the baiting-house frame, an audience standing in the pit collected around the three 'open' sides of the stage, and an additional audience, corresponding to spectators in balconies or upper storey windows of houses in the marketplace situation, viewed the performance from seats in the galleries (Figure 4). Both pit and gallery spectators would, of course, upon entrance to the 'house', have paid fees for the privilege of watching the performance.

The other kind of building was the inn – or, more precisely, that particular kind of 'great inn' which consisted of a group of adjoining buildings arranged usually in a rectangular plan so as to define an enclosed 'yard'.[1] Use of inn yards for the performance of plays is indicated by (among other records) the Act of Common Council of the City of London in 1574 restraining

[1] See W. J. Lawrence, 'The inn-yard playing places', in *Pre-Restoration Stage Studies* (1927).

5 Richard Burbage

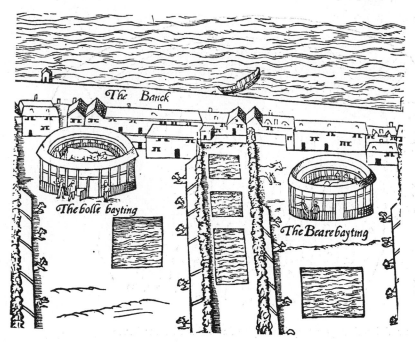

The Banck

The bolle bayting

The Beare bayting

Figure 3 Detail from the *Civitas Londinum* Map formerly attributed to Ralph Agas (c. 1633) showing animal-baiting houses on Bankside. *Guildhall Library*

innkeepers and others from permitting plays to be performed 'within the hous, yarde or anie other place within the Liberties of this Cyttie'. Like the animal-baiting house, the inn yard constituted a 'natural' playhouse: presumably a booth stage was set up against a wall at one side of the yard (usually one of the 'long' sides), an audience standing in the yard surrounded the stage on three sides, an additional audience observed the performance from seats in windows and galleries overlooking the yard, and, most important, a charge for admission was 'gathered' at the moment of each spectator's entrance to the 'house' (Figure 5).

In one respect the inn yard may have constituted a better playhouse than the animal-baiting house: if paved, a given yard, unlike the necessarily unpaved pit of a baiting-house, would have afforded protection against the miring of standing spectators during or following wet weather. But it seems clear that in at least three respects the baiting-house must have been superior to the inn yard as a playhouse: usually its pit was considerably greater in area than the yard of an inn, it was 'round' instead of rectangular in ground plan (hence more efficient in the accommodation of both pit and gallery

6 Edward Alleyn

Figure 4 A booth stage set up in the pit of an animal-baiting house

spectators) and it had galleries that entirely surrounded the pit as opposed to a gallery here and there and occasional windows overlooking the yard of the normal inn. In this respect it is significant that in the permanent playhouse constructed in 'the great yard' of the Boar's Head inn in London in 1598 galleries were apparently built around the four sides of the yard.[1]

The booth stage was essentially an outdoor stage, and the temporary playhouse that accommodated it in baiting-house or inn yard was, despite the location of part of the audience in roofed galleries or upper storey rooms of an inn, essentially an outdoor playhouse. What was the situation when, during the century ending about 1575, the players performed indoors – in guildhalls, schools or colleges, inns of court, manor houses, palaces, churches, inns and elsewhere? In most cases what the players did was to convert a domestic (or public) hall into a temporary indoor playhouse. There is some reason to believe that they occasionally set up a booth stage against one wall of the hall in question, and such practice is recorded pictorially in France or Italy in the *Andria* illustrations of the Lyons Terence of 1493 – most notably in the

[1] Herbert Berry, 'The playhouse in the Boar's Head inn, Whitechapel', in David Galloway (ed.), *The Elizabethan Theatre I* (1969); C. J. Sisson, *The Boar's Head Theatre*, ed. Stanley Wells (1972).

Figure 5 A booth stage set up in an inn yard

frontispiece and the illustrations of the opening scene of that play.[1] It also seems probable, however, that English players performing in a hall would generally have preferred to use the already existing 'screens' passage as a tiring-house (Plates 17a–18b). In part because of the customary placement of the high table on the dais at the 'upper' end of a hall, plays were for the most part performed at the 'lower' end – either upon the hall floor or upon a low stage set up against the hall screen or upon both. At this period the domestic hall screen was normally equipped with two doorways, and these, being without doors, were covered with hangings in order to exclude draughts from the hall. Thus the players, in most situations in which they

[1] Convenient reproductions may be found in *Shakespeare Quarterly*, XIII (1962), plate facing p. 451; XIV (1963), cuts on pp. 114, 120.

Figure 6 A performance on the floor of a theatrically unmodified domestic hall

might undertake to perform a play indoors, found ready at hand, without the necessity of special preparation, that indispensable convenience of booth stage production, a pair of curtained entranceways to the playing area (in this case the hall floor or a low stage set up against the hall screen or both). In a majority of halls, furthermore, use of the screens passage as a tiring-house afforded the players the secondary convenience of a musicians' gallery directly over the passage which could, at need, be put to use as an 'upper station' for the performance of action at an upper storey window or upon the walls of a town or castle (Figure 6).[1]

(iii)

Although both the baiting-house and the inn yard were used as temporary playhouses before the construction of the first permanent Elizabethan playhouse, it seems likely that the physical form of the public playhouse

[1] More detailed discussion of the hall screen, together with illustrations, may be found in my article, 'Three Renaissance English indoor playhouses', *English Literary Renaissance*, III (1973); and in Richard Southern, *The Staging of Plays before Shakespeare* (1973).

originated mainly in the animal-baiting house. (It is possible, however, that the rectangular shape of the inn yard may have been an influence upon the square Fortune.) In accordance with this theory we may suppose that James Burbage, when he built the Theatre in 1576, merely adapted the form of the baiting-house to theatrical needs. To do so he built a large round structure very much like a baiting-house but with five major innovations in the received form. First, he paved the ring with brick or stone, thus trans-forming what had been an unpaved 'pit' into a paved 'yard'. In doing this his chief purpose would have been to make possible an efficient system of drainage to carry off rainwater falling into the yard. Here his model, both for the thing itself and for its name, may have been the yard of a great inn or the courtyard of a great house or palace. Second, Burbage erected a stage in the yard. Here his model was the booth stage of the marketplace, built rather larger than any recorded example and, since a permanent structure, suppor-ted by posts rather than by trestles or barrels. Third, Burbage erected a permanent tiring-house in place of the booth which had been set up in front of a few bays of the frame in the earlier temporary arrangement in an animal-baiting ring. Here his chief model was the screens passage of the Tudor domestic hall, modified to withstand the weather by the insertion of large (hence double-hung) doors in the doorways. Presumably the tiring-house, as a permanent structure, was inset into the frame of the playhouse rather than, as in the older temporary situation involving a booth stage, set up against the frame of a baiting-house. Thus Burbage produced a structure which, when the leaves of the doors had been opened outward through an arc of 180° and hangings placed within or in front of the open doorways, reproduced that indispensable convenience of the booth stage, a pair of curtained entranceways to the stage; and the gallery over the tiring-house (presumably divided into boxes) was capable of serving variously as a 'Lords' room' for privileged or high-paying spectators, as a music room and as a station for the occasional performance of action above. Fourth, Burbage built a 'cover' or 'heavens' over the rear part of the stage, supported in part by posts rising from the yard and surmounted by a 'hut'. The precise origin of such a 'stage superstructure' is difficult to identify, but it must have been designed primarily to house suspension gear for flying effects. And, fifth, Burbage added a third gallery to the frame, for the original Bankside bait-ing-houses (as recorded in the 'Civitas Londinum' View attributed to Ralph Agas, Figure 3)[1] appear to have been two-storey buildings. Here Burbage

[1] This view, dated c. 1633 by modern scholars, represents the City as it was in 1553–9; see Ida Darlington and James Howgego, *Printed Maps of London circa 1553–1850* (1964), p. 13.

may have been influenced only by normal business acumen, but any of a number of three-storeyed architectural forms might have served as his model. In the matter of one other important element of the public playhouses, exterior stair-towers, we cannot be certain whether Burbage accepted a tradition or introduced an innovation. It is possible that the early baiting-houses had exterior stairs but in rudimentary form – open at the sides, unroofed and only two storeys high. In this case Burbage would have accepted the exterior location of the stairs but developed their design by enclosing them with walls and a roof and extending them to a height of three storeys.

There is insufficient evidence on which to base a reconstruction of the Curtain (1577) or the Rose (c. 1587). It may be assumed that these two play-houses generally imitated the design of the Theatre and that the three play-houses had a collective influence upon the design of the Swan in 1595.

It seems likely that the physical form of the private playhouse originated mainly in the Elizabethan great hall. In accordance with this theory we may suppose that Sebastian Westcott, when he built the unnamed playhouse of the Paul's Boys in or shortly before 1575,[1] merely adapted a small hall connected with St Paul's church to theatrical needs. To do so he may have made only one major innovation, the construction of a low stage (perhaps 4 feet high) running across the hall from one wall to the other immediately in front of the hall screen. The stage, if the containing hall were (let us suppose) 26 feet wide, would have been 26 feet in width and therefore, it may be assumed, about 16 feet 6 inches in depth (dimensions in a ratio of about 8:5). The screens passage could have served without adaptation as a tiring-house, hangings being fitted up within or in front of the two doorways, and the musicians' gallery over the passage could have served as an upper station for the performance of occasional action above (or a gallery, if lacking, could readily have been added to an original one-storey screen). Three tiring-house doors, if desired, could have been provided by the expedient of converting the central panel of the screen into a middle doorway. Westcott might then have completed his theatrical arrangements by running benches across the remainder of the hall floor from wall to wall, or by setting up low ground degrees around a narrow section of floor containing benches (Figure 7), or by constructing shallow galleries around a narrow 'pit' containing benches.

Nothing is known about the dimensions of the hall (or even the very identity of the hall) in which the Paul's Boys' playhouse was presumably

[1] That the Paul's Boys' playhouse was in commercial use in 1575 is clear from a record printed by H. N. Hillebrand, *The Child Actors* (1926), p. 123.

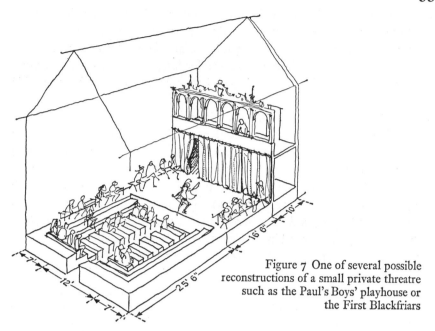

Figure 7 One of several possible
reconstructions of a small private threatre
such as the Paul's Boys' playhouse or
the First Blackfriars

housed. In the case, however, of the First Blackfriars playhouse, constructed by Richard Farrant in 1576, we are on firmer ground, since we know that
the hall in question, an upper storey room of the Old Buttery of the Dominican Priory of London (see Figure 41 below), was 26 feet wide (internal
measure). (The building was 95 feet long, but presumably only about half
that length was used for the playhouse.) Thus the general arrangement of the
First Blackfriars would have been, presumably, much the same as that
suggested for the Paul's playhouse (Figure 7). Because of the absence of a
continuous tradition it seems doubtful that either of the early private playhouses could have had much influence upon the design of the Second Blackfriars in 1596.

(iv)

Evidence for stage and tiring-house is of two kinds. 'External' evidence, un-
connected with the staging requirements of particular play texts, includes
allusions, descriptions, dictionary definitions, statutes, records of litigation,
contracts, plans, pictures and surviving architectural forms. External evidence of the verbal variety can be extremely useful, especially when it provides dimensions, but usually verbal evidence occurs in such generalized

language as to afford little in the way of concrete detail about the physical arrangements of a given playhouse. External evidence of the architectural variety, consisting usually of analogues, can also be problematical in that a given example will sometimes seem more (or less) relevant to one investigator than to another. External evidence of the pictorial variety is by all odds the most useful, but even here there are difficulties since it is possible to disagree on the interpretation of a given pictorial source because of different assumptions brought to bear on the interpretation by investigators working in different scholarly traditions. 'Internal' evidence, consisting of the staging requirements of particular play texts, is also for the most part ambiguous since all dialogue and some stage directions (such as *on the walls* or *in his study*) may confuse the stage element in question with the fictional locale to be represented by it, and since most other stage directions (such as *above* or *is discovered*) are couched in such generalized language as to give no clue to the specific physical nature of the stage element referred to.

Unfortunately, the proper uses of external and internal evidence have not always, in studies of the Renaissance English stage, been distinguished with sufficient care. External evidence (usually of the pictorial sort) is the only kind that will establish anything concrete about the nature of a particular stage and tiring-house, whereas in most cases internal evidence will establish anything or everything and hence nothing. It follows that internal evidence should properly be used not as a source of specific theories about stage or tiring-house but only as a means of testing particular theories which, properly, should be based as solidly as may be upon external evidence.

Accordingly, in each of the three parts of this essay the method of investigation will be to establish a theory of theatrical form (a 'reconstruction') on the basis of such external evidence as is available and then to test that theory, in respect of stage and tiring-house, by reference to pertinent internal evidence. The method works well enough in the case of the Second Blackfriars, where there is a good deal of external evidence and also a good deal of internal evidence – twenty extant plays belonging to the period from 1600 to 1608.[1] The Swan and the First Globe, however, pose special problems. A full

---

[1] This is the period during which the Blackfriars was used successively by the Children of the Queen's Chapel and the Children of the Queen's Revels; from 1609 to 1613 the playhouse was used by the King's Men. I have not extended the later limit of the present study to 1613 because the two extant plays probably written for performance at the Blackfriars during the period 1609–13 (*The Maid's Tragedy* and *The Two Noble Kinsmen*) constitute too small a sample of evidence on which to base inferences about possible changes in stage and tiring-house made by the King's Men upon their taking over the playhouse in 1609.

reconstruction of the Swan is possible because of the abundance of external evidence, yet a theory based on that evidence cannot be adequately tested because of the paucity of internal evidence, there being only one extant play (1613) probably written for performance at the Swan. Conversely, only a very limited reconstruction of the Globe is possible because of the dearth of external evidence, whereas for this playhouse there is considerable internal evidence – twenty-nine extant plays belonging to the period from 1599 to 1608.[1] I suggest that the two problems may profitably be treated as complementary. Thus if we suppose that the stage and tiring-house of the two playhouses were essentially similar, we can test a theory based on the external evidence for the Swan by reference to the internal evidence for the Globe. This is the argument of the next two chapters.

[1] I have used a later limit of 1608 rather than 1613 because there are no extant plays probably written for performance at the Globe during the period 1609–13.

2 The Swan
playhouse (1595)

The Swan playhouse was constructed by Francis Langley in 1595. It was situated on Bankside, about three-quarters of a mile to the west of London Bridge and somewhat over 100 yards to the south of Paris Garden Stairs. For this playhouse we have exceptionally full evidence in Arend van Buchell's copy (preserved in the Bibliotheek der Rijksuniversiteit at Utrecht) of a lost drawing by Johannes De Witt dating from around 1596.[1] Van Buchell's drawing is reproduced as Plate 11.

The Swan drawing contains some errors and distortions, and it is also a compound of unusual artistic conventions whose interpretation almost inevitably generates controversy. Nevertheless, as the only extant representation of the interior of an Elizabethan public playhouse, the drawing deserves our most careful consideration. It is, I believe, generally reliable. There is also useful, though less detailed and less reliable, evidence for the Swan playhouse in a map of Paris Garden Manor and in various panoramic views of London. Further, these sources relating specifically to the Swan can be supplemented by three extremely valuable sources of information about other public playhouses: the Fortune Contract (1599), the Hope Contract

[1] The Swan Drawing was discovered by Karl T. Gaedertz and first published (by him) in *Zur Kenntnis der altenglischen Bühne* (1888).

(1613) and Wenzel Hollar's Long Bird's-Eye View of London (1647), which provides detailed and generally reliable views of the Second Globe and the Hope (both 1614; see Plate 12b). (Hollar's general reliability in the Long View is strengthened by the existence of his preliminary sketch, *c.* 1640, entitled The West Part of Southwark toward Westminster, which also shows the Second Globe and the Hope; see Plate 12a.)[1] In the present chapter I shall propose a reconstruction which, closely based on a reconstruction of 1963,[2] is much indebted to the research on Elizabethan public playhouses published by G. Topham Forrest, C. Walter Hodges and Richard Southern.[3] First I shall deal with a number of problems connected with the 'frame' of the Swan playhouse (its shape, size, number of sides, galleries, entrances and staircases), the tiring-house and the stage superstructure; and then I shall test the proposed reconstruction of stage and tiring-house by reference to the staging of Middleton's *Chaste Maid in Cheapside* (1613), the only extant play that we have reason to believe was designed for performance at the Swan.

(i)

In pictorial sources which seem to record independent information on the subject, the shape of the Swan is represented in five different ways: as round in the Swan drawing, the Second Norden Map (1600) (Figure 8) and the Inigo Jones sketch of London from the south-west (*c.* 1637) (Figure 9); as a round building constructed in fifteen bays (hence presumably having fifteen sides) in the Paris Garden Manor Map (1627) (Figure 10); as a twelve-sided building in the Visscher View (1616) (Figure 11); as an eight-sided building in the Merian View (1638) (Figure 12); and as a six-sided building in the *Civitas Londini* Panorama (1600) (see Figure 13 and endpapers).[4] At first glance the evidence seems hopelessly contradictory, yet a very simple

[1] See I. A. Shapiro, 'An original drawing of the Globe Theatre', *Shakespeare Survey 2* (1949).

[2] Richard Hosley, 'Reconstitution du théâtre du Swan', in Jean Jacquot (ed.), *Le Lieu théâtral à la Renaissance* (1964); a paper presented at the international conference sponsored by the Centre National de la Recherche Scientifique on Le Lieu Théâtral à la Renaissance at Royaumont, March 1963.

[3] Forrest, 'The architecture of the First Globe Theatre', appendix to W. W. Braines, *The Site of the Globe Playhouse* (1921); Hodges, *The Globe Restored* (1953; rev. ed., 1968); Southern, 'On reconstructing a practicable Elizabethan public playhouse', *Shakespeare Survey 12* (1959). Forrest's reconstruction is largely the work of his colleague J. H. Farrar.

[4] Much useful information on these and other pictorial sources is provided by I. A. Shapiro in 'The Bankside theatres: early engravings', *Shakespeare Survey 1* (1948).

Figure 8 *(left)* Detail from the Second Norden Map of London (1600) showing the Swan Playhouse. *Royal Library, Stockholm*

Figure 9 *(right)* Detail from a scenic design by Inigo Jones for Davenant's *Britannia Triumphans* (1638) showing the Swan Playhouse. *Devonshire Collection, Chatsworth*

Figure 10 *(below)* Detail from a map of Paris Garden Manor (1627) showing the Swan Playhouse. *Christ Church Parochial School, London*

Figure 11 *(below)* Detail from the Visscher View of London (1616) showing
the Swan Playhouse. *Guildhall Library*

Figure 12 Detail from the Merian View of London (in Gottfried's *Neuwe Archontologia Cosmica*, 1638) showing the Swan Playhouse. *Folger Shakespeare Library*

theory, while not establishing the particular number of sides in the Swan frame, will account for the evidence in general. The theory was accepted both by William Poel in his model of an Elizabethan playhouse (1897) and by J. H. Farrar in the reconstruction published by G. Topham Forrest (1921). Forrest makes a convenient statement of the theory. As we should expect in a timbered building, each of the 'round' playhouses was built to a ground plan in the shape of a polygon, 'the straight pieces comprising the framework being simply joined together at the angles' and the structure having so many sides as from a distance to give the effect of a fully round building (p. 37). As a consequence, it may be added, the draughtsman who depicted a given playhouse had to choose between three modes of representation. He could give the general effect from a great distance (a round building), a

Figure 13 Detail from the *Civitas Londini* Panorama (1600) showing the Swan Playhouse. *Royal Library, Stockholm*

specific effect from nearby (a polygonal building with a particular number of sides) or a compromise effect embracing both roundness and polygonality (a 'round' building divided into a particular number of bays, hence having a particular number of 'sides'). One draughtsman, Hondius, apparently divided his allegiance between the first two modes, for in a single illustration, his panoramic View of London (1610), he depicted both an eight-sided Beargarden and a round Globe (Figure 38).

Without yet inquiring into the particular number of sides in the Swan frame, let us inquire into the size of ground plan, or the diameter, of the Swan. A hypothetical diameter can be inferred from dimensions for the stage given in the builder's contract for the Fortune playhouse (1599). The Fortune Contract calls for a square frame 80 feet on a side, with a square yard 55 feet on a side. (Hence the frame was 12 feet 6 inches wide at ground level; such a width of frame is assumed in the present discussion.) The stage was to be 43 feet wide and presumably, since it was to extend 'to

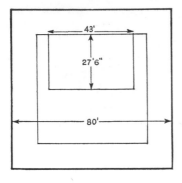

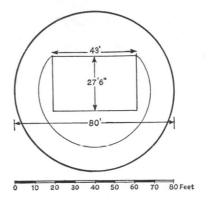

Figure 14 The Fortune: a square playhouse with a 'large' stage (capacity about 2,340 spectators)

Figure 15 A 'small' round playhouse with a large stage (capacity about 1,600 spectators)

the middle of the yarde', 27 feet 6 inches deep. (The area of such a stage is 1,183 square feet.) The situation is shown in Figure 14. The total capacity of such a playhouse has been estimated by Alfred Harbage as about 2,340 spectators.[1]

If we apply the dimensions cited from the Fortune Contract to a round playhouse, it quickly becomes apparent either that a frame 80 feet in diameter is not large enough to contain a stage measuring 43 feet by 27 feet 6 inches or that such a stage is too large for such a frame: the stage extends so far beyond the middle of the yard as to cut its audience capacity by about half that of the Fortune (Figure 15). Using Harbage's assumptions, we may estimate the total capacity of such a playhouse as about 1,600 spectators.

Two immediate courses are open. Following the lead of Hodges and Southern, we can accept a round frame 80 feet in diameter and place within it a stage having the same proportions as the Fortune stage and extending to the middle of the yard. Such a stage measures 34 feet by 21 feet 6 inches (Figure 16). (The area of such a stage is 723 square feet.) This is approximately the size of stage adopted by Southern in his model of an Elizabethan playhouse built for the British Council (1954). (In actuality, because of the distribution of angles in a sixteen-sided frame, Southern's stage – compare Figure 20 below – is of slightly different proportions from those of the

[1] *Shakespeare's Audience* (1941), p. 23. Harbage assumes an area of 2·25 square feet for each spectator standing in the yard, subtracts 20 per cent from the total area of the galleries as probably unavailable for seating, and assumes an area of 3·75 square feet for each spectator sitting in the galleries. He does not consider the Lords' rooms, and he omits overhang from his computation of the areas of the middle and top galleries.

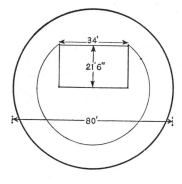

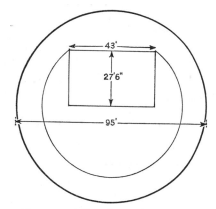

Figure 16 A small round playhouse with a 'small' stage (capacity about 2,020 spectators)

Figure 17 A 'large' round playhouse with a large stage (capacity about 2,730 spectators)

Fortune stage and slightly smaller than the stage suggested in Figure 16: 31 feet by 23 feet, or 713 square feet.) The total capacity of such a playhouse may be estimated (again on Harbage's assumptions) as about 2,020 spectators.

Or, as seems to me preferable, we can accept a stage measuring 43 feet by 27 feet 6 inches and place it within a round frame large enough to permit the stage to extend to the middle of the yard. Such a frame measures 95 feet in diameter (Figure 17), though in practice this dimension must be increased to 96 feet if we are to allow for overhang in the upper storeys of the frame – the 10-inch 'juttey forwardes' of the Fortune Contract. (In this case the depth of the stage will be a bit more or less than 27 feet, depending on how much, if at all, the tiring-house projects from the inner circle of the first gallery.) The total capacity of such a playhouse may be estimated (on the basis of Harbage's assumptions in calculating the capacity of the Fortune) as about 2,730 spectators – a figure that begins to accord with De Witt's statement that the Swan had a capacity of 3,000. De Witt's figure has occasionally been questioned as too large, but it is confirmed by the independent testimony of the Spanish ambassador in 1624, apropos of Middleton's *Game at Chess*, that the Second Globe had a capacity of over 3,000.[1] (The figures cited may be compared with Harbage's estimate, p. 30, based on Philip Henslowe's record of daily receipts in 1595, of the total capacity of the Rose as about 2,490.) Still another consideration is that Hollar, in his Long Bird's-Eye View of London (Plate 12b), evidently depicted the Second Globe, and apparently depicted the Hope, as having a diameter about three

[1] Bentley, *The Jacobean and Caroline Stage*, IV, 871–2.

times as great as their height to the eaves. If the height to the eaves of these playhouses was about the same as that of the Fortune (some 33 feet according to vertical dimensions given in the Fortune Contract), a diameter of about 100 feet would thus be indicated for the Second Globe and the Hope, and hence also for the Swan since the Hope, as its builder's contract informs us, was to be 'of suche large compasse, fforme, widenes, and height as the Plaie house called the Swan'.

The precise number of sides in the frame of the Swan is difficult to determine, for those draughtsmen who chose to depict the exterior of the Swan as polygonal evidently drew the frame with differing numbers of sides or bays: fifteen, twelve, eight and six. Forrest, assuming a polygonal frame with the surprisingly small outer diameter of 65 feet, suggested that the Globe had '16 sides of suitable lengths for single straight timbers, and giving convenient bays for division into boxes' (p. 40). The length of such horizontal timbers (or 'bressumers') would be 12 feet 8 inches: certainly a length easy to procure and convenient to manage in construction. Moreover, the bressumers running round the inner face of the frame would be 7 feet 10 inches long: again an eminently practicable length since 'prick-posts' would not have been necessary as secondary central supports between the 'principal posts', each bay being left with an unobstructed opening almost 8 feet wide through which to view the stage (see Figure 18-A). If, however, we postulate a sixteen-sided building with a diameter of 80 feet, as Southern does in his British Council model and as Hodges does in some of his reconstruction drawings in *The Globe Restored*, the length of bressumer in the inner face of each bay increases to 10 feet 9 inches and in the outer face to 15 feet 7 inches (Figure 18-B). These lengths may not be impracticable, but they are a good deal less convenient than the approximately 8- and 13-foot lengths of bressumer in Forrest's reconstruction. Correspondingly, if we postulated a sixteen-sided building with a diameter of 96 feet, the length of inner bressumer would increase to 13 feet 10 inches, of outer to 18 feet 9 inches (Figure 18-C). These dimensions seem impracticable. Fourteen-foot bressumers (measuring 9 by 7 inches in the first storey and 8 by 6 inches in the middle, as specified in the Hope Contract) would certainly have required prick-posts between principal posts, so that the 14-foot opening of each bay would have been obstructed by a centrepost. On balance, it seems likely that such an arrangement would have been avoided in favour of one that placed fewer posts, at greater intervals, in the spectators' line of vision. Moreover, outer bressumers almost 19 feet long would have posed considerable difficulties both of procurement and of management in

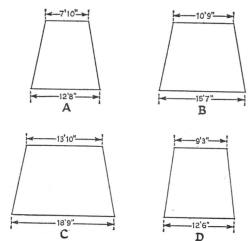

Figure 18 Various possible sizes of playhouse bay: (A) sixteen-sided frame 65 ft in diameter; (B) sixteen-sided frame 80 ft in diameter; (C) sixteen-sided frame 96 ft in diameter; (D) twenty-four-sided frame 96 ft in diameter. In each case the short side is part of the inner circle of the playhouse frame (cf. Figure 19)

construction. (We need not consider the possibility that outer faces about 19 feet long were produced by using two bressumers each about 9 feet 6 inches long, for in this case the frame would presumably have been built with sixteen additional angles at the sixteen additional principal posts, so that a thirty-two-sided building would have resulted.) Hence we may infer that a round Swan with a diameter of 96 feet must have had more than sixteen sides if only in order to avoid in part supporting the inner bressumers with prick-posts and to reduce the outer bressumers to a readily manageable size.

How many sides may we suppose in a 'round' Swan 96 feet in diameter? A hypothetical answer to this question can be arrived at by considering likely lengths of bressumer in the outer and inner faces of each bay – assuming for present purposes that the sides of the bay measure 12 feet 6 inches, as suggested by the depth of frame specified in the Fortune Contract. For the outer bressumers let us postulate a length of 13 feet, a round figure based on the dimension 12 feet 8 inches of Forrest's reconstruction of a sixteen-sided Globe 65 feet in diameter. A round frame 96 feet in diameter (or 300 feet in circumference) would require twenty-three bays with outer bressumers 13 feet long. (In such a frame the inner bressumers would measure 9 feet 6 inches.) Alternatively, for the inner bressumers let us postulate a length of 8 feet, a round figure based on the dimension 7 feet 10 inches of Forrest's reconstruction. A playhouse frame 96 feet in diameter would require twenty-eight bays with inner bressumers 8 feet long. (In such a frame the outer bressumers would measure 10 feet 6 inches.) The difference in number of bays between the two estimates results, of course, from the different arcs involved in the bay of a 65-foot frame (for which the postulated lengths of outer and inner bressumers are appropriate) and in the bay of a 96-foot frame (for which they are not): obviously the outer and inner bressumers approach equality of length both as the diameter of the frame increases and as the number of bays increases. Hence, by shortening our theoretical outer bressumer and lengthening the inner, we can arrive at those dimensions which will be as close as possible to the postulated dimensions of 13 and 8 feet but which will also produce the same number of faces in the outer as in the inner circle of a frame 96 feet in diameter. By experiment with diagrams we arrive at 12 feet 6 inches for the outer bressumer and 9 feet 3 inches for the inner (see Figure 18-D). The first dimension produces twenty-four outer faces in a frame 96 feet in diameter, the second twenty-four inner faces. We may conclude that the most convenient number of sides for a playhouse 96 feet in diameter is 24 – assuming, of course, that we wish to keep as close as possible to the desiderata of 13- and 8-foot bressumers in the outer and inner faces of the frame respectively. It may be added that the inner angles of a twenty-four-sided frame 96 feet in diameter fall so as readily to accommodate a stage 43 feet wide by about 27 feet deep (the precise value of the latter dimension depending upon how much, if at all, the tiring-house projects from the inner circle of the first gallery) and extending to the middle of the playhouse yard. That is to say, the chord defined by the rear edge of such a stage would run between points located six angles apart in the inner circle of the frame. Hence the stage would occupy an arc of the circle exactly equivalent to that occupied by five bays (75°). These points can be clarified by a glance at Figure 19 below.

Let us now test the hypothesis of a twenty-four-sided Swan by reconsidering the evidence of the Swan Drawing. Richard Southern, in a penetrating analysis of the gallery posts shown in the drawing, has suggested an explanation of the curious fact that there are more posts shown in the voids above the gallery fronts than in the gallery fronts themselves: the additional posts in the gallery openings are not (as Van Buchell, in copying the original drawing by De Witt, apparently understood them to be) supports set in the inner 'wall' of the playhouse frame, but studs set midway between the outer and inner walls of the frame: 'De Witt saw two rows of posts, one on the façade, and one within under the binding joists' (p. 25). The theory finds confirmation in the fact that a post is left dangling in mid-air in each *ingressus*. Since these two posts are obviously not based on the gallery front, they must be based within the frame, presumably at points intermediate between the outer and inner walls of the frame.

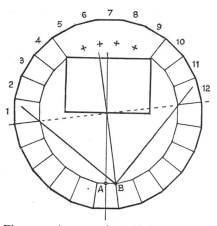

Figure 19 A twenty-four-sided playhouse frame 96 ft in diameter: seven bays fall within the half circle opposite De Witt's secondary point of view (B)

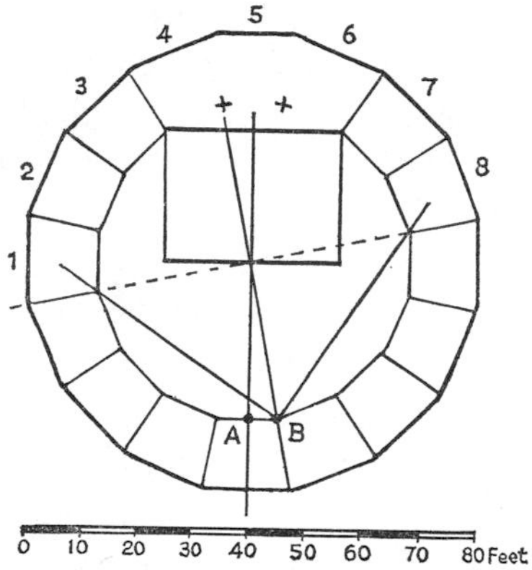

Figure 20 A sixteen-sided playhouse frame 80 ft in diameter: five bays fall within the half circle opposite De Witt's secondary point of view (B)

Southern's interpretation of the gallery posts enables us to determine the number of bays in the half circle of the playhouse frame shown in the Swan Drawing – assuming that a full half circle is intended, as seems likely from the depiction of the full round of the yard. Apparently De Witt drew four bays to the left of the stage (indicated by three principal posts in the gallery fronts) and three to the right (indicated by two such posts). The disparity in number may be only an inadvertent inconsistency: in a half circle we should expect to be shown an equal number of bays on either side of the stage since the total number of bays in the frame was presumably even and since De Witt's point of view for the stage and tiring-house seems to be on the centreline of the frame. But the disparity may be intentional and thus carry a special significance. In a twenty-four-sided playhouse frame each bay would occupy an arc of 15°, the tiring-house (defined by the width of the stage) an arc of 75° (the equivalent of five bays). Hence if the Swan frame was composed of twenty-four bays, the tiring-house (75°) and the seven bays shown in the drawing (105°) would occupy exactly 180°, or a full half circle. So perhaps De Witt, when he came to sketch the galleries, shifted his point of view about 4 feet to the right of the centreline so as to be able to draw a half of the frame composed of complete bays. From this secondary point of view he drew four bays to the left of the stage and three to the right, instead of the three and a half bays he would have had to show on either side of the stage if he had maintained his point of view for stage and tiring-house on the centreline of the frame. The situation is illustrated in Figure 19, where A indicates De Witt's centreline point of view for stage and tiring-house, B his postulated secondary point of view for the tiring-house and seven bays, and a broken line the half of the frame presumably depicted in the Swan Drawing. For the sake of comparison, a similar diagram of a sixteen-sided frame is presented in Figure 20. Here, from a point of view on the centreline of the frame (A), De Witt could have depicted only two and a half bays on either side of the stage or, from a point of view displaced about 5 feet to the right of the centreline (B), only three bays to the left of the stage and two to the right.

In sum, there is reason to believe that De Witt portrayed a twenty-four-sided playhouse frame. Hence we find support for the hypothesis, based on the assumption of convenient lengths of bressumer in the outer and inner walls of each bay, that the Swan was a twenty-four-sided building.

(ii)

Reconstruction of the horizontal dimensions of the frame of the Swan playhouse is controlled by two basic assumptions. The first is that the ground plan of the frame was in the shape of a twenty-four-sided polygon having a diameter of 96 feet (measuring from the middle of one side of the polygon to the middle of the side directly opposite). The other is that the first storey of the frame measured 12 feet 6 inches from inner to outer face of each bay, as called for in the requirement of the Fortune Contract that the frame of that playhouse 'shall conteine Twelve foote and a halfe of lawfull assize in breadth'. (This figure, since half the difference, 25 feet, between the additionally specified outer and inner dimensions of the Fortune frame, 80 and 55 feet, evidently includes the thickness of timbers in the outer and inner walls of the frame.) Thus the width of the inner face of each first-storey bay is 9 feet 4 inches, the width of the outer face of each bay 12 feet 7 inches, and the length of the sides of each bay 12 feet 7 inches (see Figure 21-A). The dimensions of upper storeys from inner to outer face of each bay will be slightly greater if we assume that, as also required in the Fortune Contract, there was a 10-inch 'juttey forwardes' in 'either' of the two upper storeys of the frame. If we interpret *either* in the sense of 'each of the two', the requirement indicates an overhang in both of the upper storeys of the frame (as in the various reconstructions by Hodges); or, if we interpret *either* in the sense of 'one or other of the two', the requirement indicates an overhang in one only of the upper storeys (as in the reconstructions by Forrest and Southern, both of whom suppose overhang only

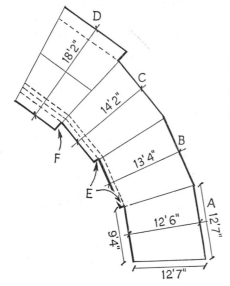

Figure 21 Plan of bays of the Swan frame:
(A) first storey; (B) second storey; (C) third
storey; (D) roof; (E) 10-inch overhang of
second and third storeys; (F) 2-foot overhang
of roof

in the middle storey). Here a relevant consideration is the structural function of an overhang, namely to strengthen the frame of a building by allowing the weight of the upper storey to create a stress on the joists outside the
supporting wall opposite to the stress on the same joists inside the wall.[1]
Since such strengthening would be as desirable in the one upper storey as
the other, we may read the Fortune Contract as calling for an overhang in
both of the upper storeys (E in Figure 21). Thus the second storey of our
reconstruction will measure 13 feet 4 inches from inner to outer face of
each bay (B), the third storey 14 feet 2 inches (C). And if we suppose that the
eaves of the roof overhang the frame by 2 feet (F), the roof will measure
18 feet 2 inches in plan from inner to outer eaves (D).

In reconstructing the vertical dimensions of the Swan frame, we may again
draw on the Fortune Contract, which specifies that the first storey of the
frame of that playhouse is 'to conteine Twelve foote of lawfull assize in
heighth', the second 'Eleaven', the third 'Nyne'. Since, as we have seen, the
specified width of frame evidently includes construction, these dimensions
are presumably 'from floor to floor', the builder having been expected to

[1] Fred H. Crossley, *Timber Building in England* (1951), p. 117. Compare Hugh Braun,
The Story of the English House (1940), pp. 45–6. Other explanations of the overhang are
that it served as a drip-course and that it was a device to secure additional space on upper
floors.

make appropriate allowance for such difficult-to-predict variables of construction as length of posts, depth of floor-joists, and thickness of floorboards. The Fortune Contract also requires the brick foundation of that playhouse 'to be wroughte one foote of assize at the lieste above the grounde'. And we may assume (as in the reconstructions by Forrest and Southern) that the combined height of ground-sill, floor-joists and floorboards was 1 foot. (This dimension is based on the assumption that floor-joists were fully inset into ground-sills; if, alternatively, floor-joists were only partly or not at all inset into ground-sills, the dimension would have been greater, perhaps as high as 1 foot 6 inches.) Accepting these several vertical dimensions, we arrive (as in Southern's reconstruction) at a height of playhouse frame of 34 feet above ground ($1 + 1 + 12 + 11 + 9 = 34$). (Because of slightly different interpretations of the Fortune Contract, the height of frame is 35 feet in the reconstructions by Forrest and Hodges.) A 34-foot height of frame was apparently typical of house construction during the period, for, if we again assume a foundation rising 1 foot above ground, it is exactly the same as the height of frame of a three-storey timbered house given as an example by Joseph Moxon in his treatise on housebuilding published in 1679 – although the heights of Moxon's individual storeys are slightly different from the heights of storey specified in the Fortune Contract ($1 + 1 + 11 + 11\frac{1}{2} + 9\frac{1}{2} = 34$).[1] Thus the eaves of the Swan frame, if they extended 6 inches below the top of the frame, would have been 33 feet 6 inches above ground. Finally, we may assume a roof angle of 45° and thus a roof height of 9 feet 1 inch above the eaves. Accordingly, the ridge of the frame would have been 42 feet 7 inches above ground. A section of the frame is shown in Figure 25 below.

The De Witt Drawing suggests that the Swan had a tiled roof, and this interpretation is confirmed by the Hope Contract, which calls for a tiled roof and specifies that the tiles are to be as at the Swan.

In reconstructing the frame of the Swan playhouse we are much aided by the Hope Contract, which names four different kinds of structural member: (1) 'brest sommers' (Figures 22-A, B): horizontal timbers lying in the outer and inner walls of the frame and joined into the ends of principal posts and binding-joists; (2) 'byndinge jostes' (Figure 22-C): horizontal timbers running transversely through the frame and 'binding' outer to inner wall through being joined into the ends of principal posts and bressumers or ground-sills; (3) 'Principall postes' (Figures 22-D, E): major vertical timbers

---

[1] *Mechanick Exercises, or The Doctrine of Handiworks Applied to the Art of House Carpentry* (1679), Plate 11.

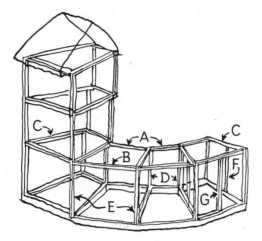

Figure 22 Structural members
of the Swan frame: (A) inner
bressumer; (B) outer bressumer;
(C) binding-joist; (D) inner
principal post; (E) outer
principal post; (F) stud; (G)
prick-post

standing at the angles of the outer and inner walls of the frame and joined
into the ends of binding-joists and bressumers or ground-sills; and (4)
'prick postes' (Figure 22-G): secondary vertical timbers standing in the
outer wall of the frame and joined into the mid-sections of bressumers or
ground-sills. A fifth kind of structural member, studs or 'quarters' (Figure
22-F), is indicated by the stipulation that the 'particions betwne the Rommes'
at the Hope must be as at the Swan: secondary vertical timbers standing in
partitions between 'rooms' and joined into the mid-sections of binding-
joists. Ground-sills, not mentioned in either contract, may be assumed:
horizontal timbers lying on and attached to the foundations of the outer and
inner walls of the frame and joined into the ends of principal posts and
binding-joists. And floor-joists, not specified in either contract, are implied
by mention in the Fortune Contract of 'all the flowers of the saide Galleries,
Stories, and Stadge': horizontal timbers running transversely through the
frame and supported at their ends either by resting on or by being inset into
bressumers or ground-sills.

The Hope Contract gives dimensions for the four kinds of structural member mentioned. The principal posts are required to be 10 inches square in
the 'first' storey, 8 inches square in the 'midell' storey and 7 inches square in
the 'upper' storey. The prick-posts are required to be 8 inches square in the
'first' storey, 7 inches square in the 'seconde' storey and 6 inches square in
the 'upper most' storey. The location of these vertical members of the frame
is clear. However, the location of horizontal members of the frame is not clear
since in referring to a given storey the author of the contract does not specify

whether he intends the level at the top or bottom of that storey. We can, of course, correct his oversight by making a series of related assumptions. The binding-joists are required to be 9 inches high by 8 inches thick in the 'firste' storey (presumably at the second level of the frame), and 8 inches high by 7 inches thick in the 'midell' storey (presumably at the third level). Again, the bressumers are required to be 9 inches high by 7 inches thick in the 'lower moste' storey (presumably at the second level of the frame), and 8 inches high by 6 inches thick in the 'midell' storey (presumably at the third level). These ten sets of dimensions are set out in the accompanying table, together with the conjectured dimensions (enclosed in square brackets) of binding-joists and bressumers or ground-sills at the first and fourth levels of the frame.

Table 1 *Dimensions of structural members of the frame*
(*as given or implied in the Hope Contract*) (in inches)

	Principal posts	Binding-joists	Bressumers or ground-sills	Prick-posts
4th level		[7 × 8]	[8 × 6]	
3rd storey	7 × 7			6 × 6
3rd level		7 × 8 ⟷	8 × 6	
2nd storey	8 × 8			7 × 7
2nd level		8 × 9 ⟷	9 × 7	
1st storey	10 × 10			8 × 8
1st level		[10 × 11]	[11 × 9]	

Arrows in the table call attention to correspondences among the dimensions of structural members of the frame given in the Hope Contract. Principal posts have the same width as the binding-joists on which they stand (7 inches in the third storey and at the third level of the frame, 8 inches

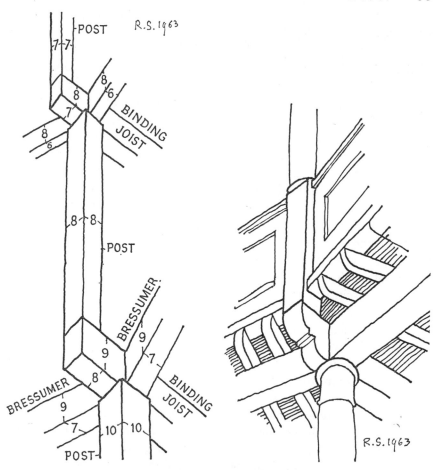

Figure 23 Correspondence of dimension among inner principal posts, bressumers, and binding joists at the second and third levels of the Swan frame

Figure 24 A reconstruction of inner principal posts, bressumers, binding-joist, and floor-joists at the second or third level of the Swan frame

in the second storey and at the second level of the frame). (For this reason we may suppose that binding-joists at the first level were 10 inches wide; hence they would probably have been 11 inches high.) Binding-joists have the same height as the bressumers which they adjoin (8 inches at the third level, 9 inches at the second). (For this reason we may suppose that the ground-sills were 11 inches high; hence they would probably have been 9 inches deep.) And bressumers have the same thickness as the prick-posts which stand on them (6 inches at the third level of the frame and in the third storey, 7 inches at the second level of the frame and in the second storey). (For this reason we might suppose that the ground-sills were 8 inches thick; I have, however, preferred the thickness of 9 inches suggested by the pattern of dimensions given for bressumers.) The dimensions of structural members called for in the Hope Contract are thus seen to correspond in a manner making possible, wherever practicable, joints between timbers that are flush in plane. Figure 23 illustrates the stated correspondences of dimension among inner principal posts, bressumers and binding-joists at the third and second levels of the frame. (In this diagram, which is not to scale, the upper parts of the posts are represented as square rather than turned.) Figure 24, in which the assumption of floor-joists resting on bressumers is accepted, shows a possible reconstruction of the finished carpentry at the second or third level of the Swan frame.

The Fortune Contract requires 'ffower convenient divisions for gentlemens roomes', the word *divisions* probably being used in the sense of 'compartments' rather than 'partitions'. Presumably the gentlemen's rooms at the Fortune were situated on both sides of the stage, in the two bays of the first gallery nearest the tiring-house on each side. They were to be 'seeled with Lathe, lyme and haire'. The Hope Contract also calls for gentlemen's rooms, specifically for 'two Boxes in the lowermost storie fitt and decent for gentlemen to sitt in'. Presumably these boxes were situated on both sides of the stage, in the bay of the first gallery nearest the tiring-house on each side. De Witt indicates two gentlemen's rooms at the Swan by the label *orchestra* (in the sense, recorded in Cotgrave's *Dictionary*, 1611, of seats for high-ranking persons) applied to the two left-hand bays of the first gallery nearest the tiring-house. Thus there were probably four gentlemen's rooms at the Swan, two on each side of the stage in the first-gallery bays nearest the tiring-house. Southern assumes that spectators reached the gentlemen's rooms by passing through the tiring-house, but it seems to me more likely, for reasons given in the following section, that access to the gentlemen's rooms was by way of the first-gallery passageway.

After mentioning 'divisions' for the gentlemen's rooms, the Fortune Contract specifies 'other sufficient and convenient divisions for Twoe pennie roomes', the word *divisions* again probably being used in the sense of 'compartments'. These also are to be 'seeled with Lathe, lyme and haire'. And after mentioning two 'Boxes' for gentlemen, the Hope Contract requires that 'the particions betwne the Rommes' must be as at the Swan. Presumably the 'rooms' of the Hope Contract correspond to the 'twopenny rooms' of the Fortune Contract. The twopenny rooms, as Southern suggests, would be

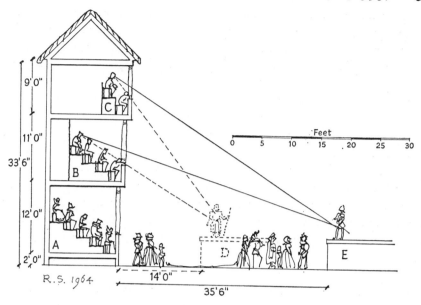

Figure 25 Transverse section of galleries of the Swan frame showing sightlines and a possible reconstruction of the seating: (A) first gallery; (B) middle gallery; (C) top gallery. The stage is represented in solid line (E) in relation to the three bays directly opposite the stage; and in broken line (D) in relation to the three bays directly to the side of one of the front corners of the stage

the compartments of the first and middle galleries, each consisting of one bay of the frame and separated from adjacent rooms by low 'partitions'. (Presumably there were no partitions in the top gallery.) De Witt refers to the twopenny rooms by the label *sedilia* ('seats') applied to the middle gallery.

In reconstructing the seating of the Swan galleries I have closely followed Southern's hypothesis of benches on degrees (pp. 26–7), though with some slight variation in dimensions.

In the first gallery, if the front railing was 6 inches thick and the outer wall of the frame 10 inches thick, a depth of 11 feet 2 inches is available for seating. I have assumed five rows of seats, one on the floor and four on degrees rising by steps of 1 foot 3 inches to an elevation of 5 feet above the floor (see Figure 25-A). On the top degree there is headroom of about 6 feet under the second-level binding-joists. I have assumed a depth of 2 feet 2 inches for the first row of seating on the floor and for each of the first three degrees; and a depth of 2 feet 6 inches for the top degree, which serves both

for seating and as a passageway running round the rear of the first gallery at
an elevation of 7 feet above ground. As will be made clear in the following
section, I suppose that entrance to the first gallery was at this level through
doors in the outer wall of the frame giving access to the exterior stair-
towers.

In the middle gallery, if the front railing was 6 inches thick and the outer
wall of the frame 8 inches thick, a depth of 12 feet 2 inches is available for
seating. Here, because of poorer sightlines and somewhat less headroom than
in the first gallery, I have assumed four rows of seats, one on the floor and
three on degrees rising by steps of 1 foot 5 inches to an elevation of 4 feet
3 inches above the floor (Figure 25-B). On the top degree there is headroom
of about 5 feet 9 inches under the third-level binding-joists. I have assumed
a depth of 2 feet 2 inches for the first row of seating on the floor and for each
of the three degrees. Thus a space 3 feet 6 inches wide is available to serve
as a floor-level passageway running round the middle gallery behind the
degrees.

In the top gallery, if the front railing was 6 inches thick and the outer wall
of the frame 7 inches thick, a depth of 13 feet 1 inch is available for seating.
Here, because of much poorer sightlines and considerably less headroom
than in the first gallery, I have assumed two rows of seats, one on the floor
and one on a degree rising 2 feet 6 inches above the floor (Figure 25-C).
On the degree there is headroom of about 5 feet 6 inches under the fourth-
level binding-joists. I have assumed a depth of 2 feet 2 inches for the row
of seating on the floor and also for the single degree. Thus a space 8 feet
9 inches wide is available for use as a floor-level passageway running round
the top gallery behind the degree. Presumably it is this passageway to which
De Witt refers by the word *porticus* ('gallery' in the architectural rather
than the theatrical sense) applied to the top storey of the frame in the Swan
Drawing.

Sightlines from the galleries are illustrated in Figure 25, which shows, in
solid line (E), the stage placed in relation to the three bays of the frame
directly opposite the front of the stage; and, in broken line (D), the stage
placed in relation to the three bays of the frame directly to the side of one of
the front corners of the stage.[1]

[1] Other seating arrangements are of course possible. Six and five (rather than five and
four) rows of seats might have been squeezed into the first and middle galleries respectively. Benches might have been dispensed with in favour of sitting on degrees. And the
degree here suggested in the top gallery might have been omitted in favour of a single
row of spectators seated on benches with standing spectators behind, as suggested in
Figure 36 below.

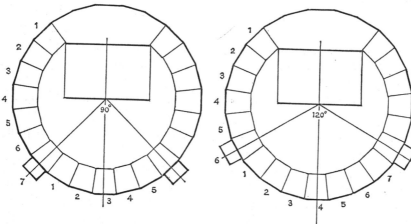

Figure 26 Siting of the stair-towers in a twenty-four-sided Second Globe (90° apart): five bays fall between the towers

Figure 27 Siting of the stair-towers in a twenty-four-sided Hope or Swan (120° apart): seven bays fall between the towers

(iii)

Two related problems of some complexity may be considered together: the gallery stairs, and entrances to the playhouse.

The Fortune Contract calls for 'suchelike steares, conveyances, and divisions withoute and within' as are to be found at the Globe, and the Hope Contract requires 'two stearecasses without and adjoyninge to the saide Playe house in suche convenient places as shalbe moste fitt and convenient for the same to stande uppon, and of such largenes and height as the stearcasses of the saide playehouse called the Swan nowe are or bee'. The contracts tell us nothing specific about the staircases except that they were outside the frame, and of course for that reason they are not shown in the Swan Drawing. However, Hollar's Long Bird's-Eye View of London provides us with considerable information (see Plate 12b). Hollar shows the staircases as narrow rectangular towers attached to the outer faces of the Second Globe and the Hope. Each tower is as tall as the frame, having a gable whose ridge connects with the ridge of the frame. And each tower, since depicted one-ninth as wide as a playhouse frame that may be assumed to be 96 feet in diameter, may be estimated as 10 feet 6 inches wide.

In the Second Globe, as seems clear from the relative position of the stage superstructure in Hollar, the stair-towers are situated opposite the stage at points about 90° apart; in the Hope, as again seems clear from the position of the stage superstructure in Hollar, they are opposite the stage at points

about 120° apart. Thus, in a twenty-four-sided reconstruction of the
Second Globe, the stair-towers would butt up against the seventh bay on
either side of the stage, five bays falling between the towers; and in such a
reconstruction of the Hope or Swan the towers would butt up against the
sixth bay on either side of the stage, seven bays falling between the towers.
The first arrangement (stair-towers 90° apart) is illustrated in Figure 26;
the second (stair-towers 120° apart), in Figure 27. Further reconstruction
of the stair-towers will be presented after discussion of the related problem of entrances to the playhouse.

General entrances to the Elizabethan public playhouse pose an especially
delicate problem in the interpretation of evidence. There is unanimous
agreement on the theory of a door at the rear of the tiring-house for the use
of players and favoured members of the audience, and such a door at the
Rose is apparently referred to in Henslowe's record of a payment, in 1592,
for 'makeinge the penthowsse shed at the tyeringe-howsse doore'. But there
is disagreement on whether there were one or two general entrances to the
playhouse. The older view, held by Forrest, Hodges and Southern, is that
there was only one, in the bay directly opposite the stage. A more recent view,
proposed by R. C. Bald,[1] is that there were two, one in the foot of each stair-
tower.

We may begin the inquiry with the observation that there is no evidence
for a single entrance to the yard opposite the stage. (Southern's statement is
fairly qualified by a 'possibly'.) Further, certain interpretations are forced
upon us as soon as we accept the assumption of a single entrance. Perhaps
our most important evidence is Van Buchell's picturing of two openings in
the façade of the first gallery at the Swan, one on either side of the stage.
The opening on the left is labelled *ingressus*, and this term (on the basis of
our initial assumption) can be interpreted only in the special sense of
'entrance to the galleries from the yard', for if we interpreted it in the special
sense of 'entrance to the yard from outside the playhouse' we should in
effect be led to a theory of three such entrances, which (if we assume a
similarity of the Globe and the Swan in this respect) seems forbidden by
John Chamberlain's statement that the audience evacuating the burning
Globe in 1613 had 'but two narrow doors to get out'. From this interpretation it follows that the 'horizontal' lines drawn in each *ingressus* must be

---

1 'The entrance to the Elizabethan theater', *Shakespeare Quarterly*, III (1952). The two-
entrance theory is accepted also by David Knight in his unpublished reconstruction of
the First Globe. I am indebted to Professor Knight for helpful criticism of my own
theory.

7 Richard Tarlton

8a William Kempe, 1600

8b The Children of the Chapel (from drawings of Queen Elizabeth's funeral procession)

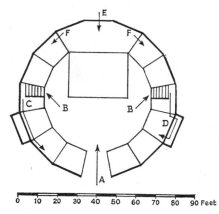

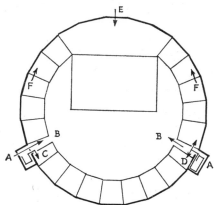

Figure 28 A single-entrance system (sixteen-sided playhouse frame 80 ft in diameter): (A) entrance to playhouse and yard; (B) entrance to galleries (*ingressus*); (C) to first gallery (by way of *ingressus* stairs); (D) to middle (or top) gallery (by way of stair-tower); (E) tiring-house door; (F) to gentlemen's rooms (by way of tiring-house)

Figure 29 A two-entrance system (twenty-four-sided playhouse frame 96 ft in diameter): (A) entrance to playhouse; (B) entrance to yard (*ingressus*); (C) to first gallery (by way of stair-tower); (D) to middle (or top) gallery (by way of stair-tower); (E) tiring-house door; (F) to gentlemen's rooms (by way of first gallery)

steps leading up into the first gallery. This is the theory proposed by W. J. Lawrence[1] and accepted by Forrest, Hodges and Southern. Thus, as in Southern's reconstruction (Figure 28), all spectators would enter the yard from outside the playhouse by the single entrance opposite the stage. A spectator intending to sit in the galleries would then traverse part of the yard to right or left, enter the frame by mounting the steps of an *ingressus* and either take a seat in the first gallery or ascend further to the middle gallery by way of the stair-tower outside the frame; or he might, if he wished, ascend even further to the top gallery, again by way of the stair-tower.

But such a system is complicated and inefficient. As Lawrence himself observed, 'No arrangement could have been clumsier.' A spectator bound for the galleries must pass through the frame, traverse part of the yard and then re-enter the frame; and after the performance, instead of descending directly to ground level and leaving the playhouse by an exit in the foot of the stair-tower, he must, after descending to the level of the first gallery, re-enter the frame only to leave it for the yard, traverse part of the yard and then, after waiting upon the yard spectators who would be ahead of him,

[1] 'Early systems of admission', in *The Elizabethan Playhouse*, 2nd ser. (1913).

re-enter the frame in order to leave the playhouse by its single exit. The system involves so much unnecessary traffic, and would give rise to so much congestion in evacuating a full house (since some 3,000 spectators might be crowding to pass through the single exit from the yard), that the theory would never (one supposes) have been entertained for long were it not for the apparent steps of De Witt's *ingressus* leading up into the first gallery from the yard.[1]

In view of the shortcomings of the single-entrance system, let us postulate two general entrances to the playhouse, one in the foot of each stair-tower (Figure 29). On the basis of this assumption we naturally interpret Van Buchell's openings in the façade of the first gallery as entrances to the yard, the term *ingressus* being used in the special sense of 'entrance to the yard from outside the playhouse'. Each of these openings would lead, by a ground-level passage running through the playhouse frame, to a stair-tower and thus to a presumptive exterior door in the foot of the tower. Thus the two doors of the stair-towers would correspond to the 'two narrow doors' mentioned by Chamberlain in his account of the burning of the Globe. A stair-tower door at the Second Globe and the Hope is not depicted by Hollar because of intervening trees and houses, but such a door at the Theatre or Curtain may be depicted in the View of the Cittye of London from the North towards the Sowth (*c.* 1600, reproduction in Hodges, revised ed., Plate 7). The Theatre or Curtain door, to judge from the relative position of the stage superstructure, is apparently sited about 45° round the frame from its centreline – that is, about 90° apart (as at the Second Globe) from a presumptive second door on the other side of the frame.

What then of Van Buchell's 'horizontal' lines drawn in each *ingressus*? Bald suggests (p. 19) that they represent steps down from the ground level of the passageway to the slightly lower level of the yard, but this theory requires the dubious assumption of a sunken yard and in any case it would have been easier to accommodate the postulated drop by sloping the floor of the passageway. I suggest that the lines drawn in each *ingressus* represent (or derive from an attempt to represent) the lowermost degrees of the first

---

[1] Southern's reconstruction of a single-entrance system was additionally complicated by reliance on William Lambarde's description of an admission system in *The Perambulation of Kent*. The description was supposed by Chambers (II, 359) to originate with Lambarde's second edition of 1596, where (if we credit the text) it relates to Paris Garden, the Bel Savage and the Theatre. However, the description originates with Lambarde's first edition of 1576, where (according to the text) it relates only to the Bel Savage inn. See F. P. Wilson, 'Lambarde, the Bel Savage, and the Theatre', *Notes and Queries*, CCVIII (1963).

gallery, which cannot be seen elsewhere because they are below the top of the gallery front (see Plate 11). If De Witt had represented the ends of the lowermost degrees as visible through each *ingressus*, it would have been an easy error for Van Buchell, perhaps not fully comprehending the significance of what he was copying, to have drawn the degrees as though they extended across each *ingressus*; or he might even have misunderstood the original drawing as indicating steps.

There is a further problem. In the Swan Drawing the *ingressūs* are situated at the sides of the stage (see Plate 11). In Hollar, on the other hand, the stair-towers, which were presumably attached to the same bays of the frame as contained the entrances to the yard, are situated in front of the stage (see Plate 12b). Presumably Hollar is right in this respect and De Witt is 'wrong', for one would expect the stair-towers to be sited at points on the circumference of the frame where each could accommodate an approximately equal number of departing spectators from the gallery areas lying on either side of the stair-tower. I believe, however, that De Witt's placement of the *ingressūs* is not, strictly speaking, an error but the exercise of a convention that enabled him to record them, for his chosen point of view directly opposite the stage would have made it impossible to represent the *ingressūs* if, as at the Second Globe and the Hope, they fell within the half circle of the frame nearer his point of view. I assume therefore that De Witt 'moved' each *ingressus* round the frame towards the tiring-house about 45° in order to include it in his picture. He employed comparable artistic licence in depicting the hut over the stage from two different points of view about 45° apart: thus he was able, Picasso-style, to include in his picture what his chosen point of view technically forbade – a side view as well as a front view of the hut.[1]

On the basis of the suggested interpretation of the *ingressūs* of the Swan Drawing, we may visualize the two-entrance system as operating in the following manner. (Compare Figure 29.) Whether his destination was the yard, a gallery or one of the gentlemen's rooms, a spectator would enter the playhouse by the exterior door in the foot of one of the stair-towers, paying 1d. to a gatherer stationed at that point. Having entered that door, the spectator could continue directly along the passage running through the playhouse frame and, without further payment, emerge into the yard through

[1] At first glance Hollar's small shed leaning against the outer shell of the Hope frame appears to confirm De Witt's location of the left-hand *ingressus*. But this shed (sited too far around the frame to serve the tiring-house door) probably sheltered a special door, not required in other playhouses, for the purpose of bringing animals into the yard.

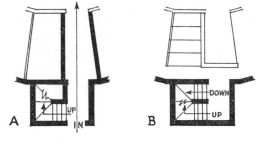

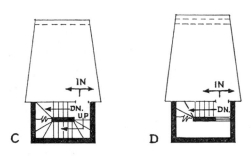

Figure 30 Reconstruction of a stair-tower at the Swan (plans): (A) ground level (entrance to yard); (B) first landing (entrance to first gallery); (C) second landing (entrance to middle gallery); (D) third landing (entrance to top gallery)

one of the openings designated *ingressus* in the Swan Drawing. Or, if he were willing to pay additionally for a seat in one of the galleries or one of the gentlemen's rooms, he could, immediately after having entered the stair-tower, turn at right angles and pass through an interior door giving access to the tower stairs. At this door he would pay a second 1d. to a second gatherer. His second 1d. would entitle the spectator to a place in any of the three galleries. Thus he would ascend the stairs to the landing at the top of the first flight, from which he could enter the first gallery at the level of the top degree. Or, if he preferred, the spectator could, without further payment, continue up the stairs to the middle gallery. In either gallery he would sit in what the Fortune Contract calls a 'Twoe pennie roome'. Or, if the two lower galleries were filled, the spectator would have no choice but to continue up the stairs to the top gallery. This would presumably be less desirable than either of the lower galleries, but no further payment would be required, and sitting (or standing) in the top gallery might well be preferable to standing in the yard. Thus the top gallery would be a sort of overflow area, in general use only when the house enjoyed full or nearly full capacity. Further, if the spectator were willing to pay for even greater comfort than

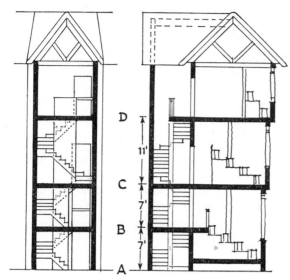

Figure 31 Reconstruction of a stair-tower at the Swan (longitudinal and transverse sections): (A) ground level; (B) first landing; (C) second landing; (D) third landing

that afforded by the 2d. rooms, he could pass round the frame along the top degree of the first gallery to the gentlemen's rooms (lying adjacent to the tiring-house), which he could then enter through a pass door after paying a third 1d. to a third gatherer.[1] It will be seen that the system conforms to Thomas Platter's description of the progressive gathering of admission fees at a Bankside playhouse (presumably the Globe) in 1599: 'For he who remains standing below pays only one English penny, but if he wants to sit he is let in at another door, where he gives a further penny; but if he desires to sit on cushions in the pleasantest place, where he not only sees everything well but can also be seen, then he pays at a further door another English penny.'[2] I assume that Platter's phrase 'the pleasantest place' refers to the gentlemen's rooms, since they, unlike the lords' rooms over the stage, could readily be reached by way of doors at the postulated paying stations in stair-tower and first gallery. Presumably spectators sitting in the lords' rooms entered the playhouse through the players' door at the rear of the tiring-house after paying at one shot the full fee (could it have been as high as 6d.?) to a gatherer stationed at that point. Thus the system requires a total of seven gatherers.

[1] Thus a gentleman's room could be described as a threepenny room, as perhaps by Wye Saltonstall in *Picturae Loquentes* (1631): 'at a new play he'll be sure to be seen in the threepenny room' (cited by Lawrence, 'Early systems of admission').
[2] Translation by Ernest Schanzer, 'Thomas Platter's observations on the Elizabethan stage', *Notes and Queries*, CCI (1956).

We are now in a position to take a closer look at the stair-towers. A width of 10 feet 6 inches has already been suggested, for the reason that Hollar depicted the stair-towers of both the Second Globe and the Hope as one-ninth the width of playhouse frames that may be estimated as 96 feet in diameter. This is an external dimension: by subtracting 9 inches for timbers of the tower frame at one side and 9 inches for timbers of the tower frame at the other side, we arrive at an internal dimension of 9 feet. Since this is not sufficiently great to accommodate a straight flight of stairs rising 11 feet (the difference of elevation between floors of the middle and top galleries), we may suppose that the stairs are of the 'winding' variety, fully contained within the tower (Figure 29), instead of, as in the reconstructions by Forrest, Hodges and Southern, straight flights running in one direction only and utilizing the middle gallery for the 'turnaround' (Figure 28). Hence the depth of tower (internal measure) would be about 6 feet – that is, about 3 feet for the length of treads rising in one direction and 3 feet more for that of treads rising in the opposite direction, after the turnaround. Accordingly the area available for one full flight of stairs would be 54 square feet (9 × 6 feet). This would allow for a landing with an area of 9 square feet and for seventeen treads each having an average area of 2·65 square feet. (Seventeen treads are the concomitant of eighteen risers, which, at a height of about 7½ inches each, would be necessary for the 11-foot rise in elevation between the floors of the middle and top gallery.) The proposed figure of 6 feet for the depth of the tower is an internal dimension: by adding 9 inches for timbers in the face of the tower frame, we arrive at an external dimension of 6 feet 9 inches. Assuming, then, a stair-tower 10 feet 6 inches wide and 6 feet 9 inches deep (external measure), we may represent the interior arrangement of a stair-tower as in Figures 30 and 31. Various other interior arrangements are of course possible. This particular one is advanced in order to suggest the general practicability of the stair-towers as depicted by Hollar.

(iv)

In proceeding to a discussion of the Swan tiring-house and stage super-structure we must keep in mind two basic considerations. The mode of construction of the tiring-house and stage superstructure (laid out for the most part in rectangular ground plan) differed radically from that of the playhouse frame (laid out in radial, or twenty-four-sided, ground plan). And the several floors of the tiring-house seem to have been at different levels from the corresponding floors of the frame.

The Swan Drawing implies that the tiring-house ran the full length of the stage. The proposition is not certain since in the drawing the corners of the tiring-house and the rear corners of the stage are obscured by the posts of the stage cover. But we must consider the architectural problem of joining the tiring-house façade to the faces of the playhouse frame. The tiring-house façade is in a single plane, yet the inner faces of the three galleries are in three separate planes, because of a 10-inch 'juttey forwardes' in each of the upper galleries (as suggested by the Fortune Contract). (See Figure 32.) With which face of the frame did the tiring-house façade meet? Presumably with the face of the top gallery (since otherwise the tiring-house would have been slightly recessed within the frame at the levels of the middle and first galleries), thus causing the tiring-house to project about 1 foot from the face of the middle gallery and about 2 feet from the face of the first gallery. (The problem is differently solved in Southern's reconstruction: he assumes only one overhang, in the middle gallery, and also a corresponding overhang in the tiring-house façade – a solution made possible by the assumption that the second floor of the tiring-house was on the same level as the floor of the middle gallery; thus the overhang of the middle gallery lines up with that of the tiring-house.) Such a slight projection, if we assume a frame diameter of 96 feet, has the effect of decreasing the depth of the stage by 9 inches and the length of the tiring-house façade by 12 inches at either end. Thus the stage, in extending to the middle of the yard, would have been 26 feet 9 inches deep instead of the 27 feet 6 inches implied in the Fortune Contract; the tiring-house would have been 41 feet long; and the 43-foot stage would have 'overlapped' the tiring-house by 1 foot at either end. (The area of the Swan stage would thus have been 1,150 square feet – 32 square feet less than the area of the stage implied in the Fortune Contract.) These assumptions (illustrated in Figure 33) have been adopted in the present reconstruction. It may be added that the height of the Swan stage (Figure 34) has here been taken to be 5 feet 6 inches, as generally in the reconstructions by Hodges; in Southern's reconstruction the height of the stage is 6 feet. I assume a single trap door set in the middle of the stage.

The Swan Drawing shows two storeys in the tiring-house beneath the stage cover. (See Figures 34 and 35.) Since the underside of the stage cover (as estimated below) is 28 feet above the yard, and since the first-storey floor of the tiring-house (like the stage) is 5 feet 6 inches above the yard, the height of the tiring-house façade from the stage to the underside of the stage cover (that is, the painted 'heavens' over the stage) is 22 feet 6 inches. If, then, in order to provide what would appear to be the minimal height

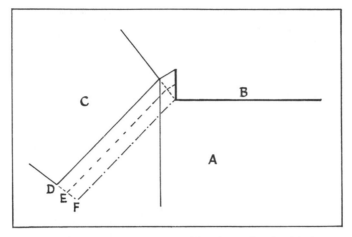

Figure 32 Meeting of the stage and tiring-house façade with three
faces of a twenty-four-sided playhouse frame 96 ft in diameter:
(A) stage; (B) tiring-house façade; (C) bay nearest the stage;
(D) face of first gallery; (E) face of middle gallery; (F) face of top gallery

of 7 feet for the third storey of the tiring-house, we set the third-storey floor
of the tiring-house 27 feet above the yard (1 foot below the underside of the
stage cover), we have 21 feet 6 inches available for the first two storeys of
the tiring-house. At what elevation may we put the second-storey floor?
In his reconstruction Southern follows dominant tradition by putting the
second-storey floor (but not the first- and third-storey floors) of the tiring-
house on a level with the corresponding floor of the frame (that of the middle
gallery). As we have seen, this theory, combined with the assumption of an
overhang in the tiring-house façade, facilitates joining the tiring-house
façade with the (two) faces of the frame in Southern's reconstruction. But
this consideration does not seem to be a compelling reason for avoiding a
differential in elevation between the second-storey floor of the tiring-house
and the floor of the middle gallery, especially since there is already a differential in elevation (3 feet 6 inches) between the first-storey floor of the tiring-
house (5 feet 6 inches above the yard) and the floor of the first gallery (2 feet
above the yard). (There will also be a differential in elevation between the
third-storey floor of the tiring-house and the floor of the top gallery.) Moreover, to put the second-storey floor of the tiring-house on a level with the
floor of the middle gallery would result in tiring-house storeys of disproportionate height. If such an arrangement were adopted in the present reconstruction, for example, the first storey would be 8 feet 6 inches high, the

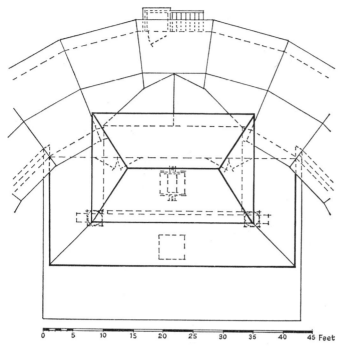

Figure 33 Reconstruction of the Swan tiring-house and stage
superstructure (plan)

second 13 feet high. And quite aside from the disproportion, 8 feet 6 inches
(as in Southern's reconstruction and in several reconstructions by Hodges)
does not seem sufficient for the height of the first storey of a tiring-house.
(Compare the Fortune Contract, which requires the first storey of the playhouse frame to be 12 feet high, the second 11, the third 9.) I have therefore
divided the available height approximately in half, making the first storey
11 feet high, the second 10 feet 6 inches high. Thus the second-storey floor
of the tiring-house is 16 feet 6 inches above the yard, or 2 feet 6 inches
higher than the floor of the middle gallery of the frame (14 feet above the
yard). A generally similar arrangement is postulated by Hodges in his reconstruction based on the Swan Drawing (revised ed., p. 150).

The Swan Drawing shows two large, round-headed, double-hung doors
set in the tiring-house façade. Their width may be estimated as about 7 or
8 feet, for the right-hand door is pictured about one-fifth as wide as the
length of the tiring-house (here estimated as 41 feet), the left-hand door
slightly narrower. The height of the doors, since each is drawn as high as

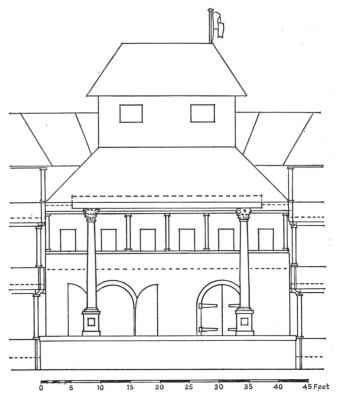

Figure 34 Reconstruction of the Swan tiring-house and stage
superstructure (elevation)

wide, appears also to be about 7 or 8 feet, but presumably the height of the
doors was actually somewhat greater than their width. In the present reconstruction the doors have been made 7 feet 6 inches wide and 8 feet 6 inches
tall. Since hinges are shown on the outside of the Swan doors, we may suppose that the doors opened out upon the stage.

In the second storey of the tiring-house the Swan Drawing shows six
windows, defined by pillars. Each window (on the assumption of a tiring-
house 41 feet long) is about 6 feet wide and 6 feet high. The windows are
not captioned in the drawing, but because of the spectators sitting in them
(and other considerations) we may interpret the area within the windows as
a gallery for audience. A generally similar gallery over the stage (with
two windows) is shown in the *Roxana* Vignette (1632), and both galleries
may be associated with 'the Lords roome' alluded to as 'over the stage' by
Jonson in *Every Man out of his Humour* (1599) – that is to say, a special

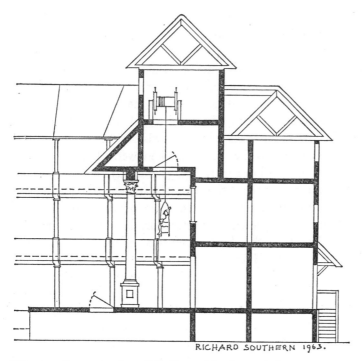

RICHARD SOUTHERN 1963.

Figure 35 Reconstruction of the Swan tiring-house and stage
superstructure (transverse section)

area, comparable to the gentlemen's rooms on either side of the stage, for the
accommodation of high-paying spectators.[1] Presumably the gallery is
divided into boxes, each pillar corresponding to a partition, for Dekker in
Satiromastix uses the plural expression 'Lords roomes' (1602) and in *The
Gull's Hornbook* alludes to 'those boxes' of the lords' room (1609). In the
present reconstruction the gallery windows have been made 6 feet 1 inch
wide (between 8-inch-thick pillars) and 6 feet high. The interior width of
the individual boxes would thus be 6 feet 3 inches (between 6-inch-thick
partitions); the depth of the boxes may be conjectured as 8 feet. The gallery
railing has been set 3 feet above the gallery floor.

The Fortune Contract requires 'convenient windowes and lightes glazed'
to the tiring-house, the reference apparently being to windows in the outer
shell of the playhouse frame designed to light the interior of the tiring-house.
We may suppose such windows in the Swan tiring-house. Presumably there

[1] A fuller discussion of the lords' room may be found in my article, 'The gallery over the
stage in the public playhouse of Shakespeare's time', *Shakespeare Quarterly*, VIII (1957).

was a door at the rear of the tiring-house for the use of players and of spectators occupying the lords' rooms. Such a door at the Rose is apparently referred to in Henslowe's record of a payment, in 1592, for 'makeinge the penthowsse shed at the tyeringe-howsse doore'. And, finally, we may suppose a system of stairs within the tiring-house connecting its three floors, the understage area, the interior of the stage cover and the hut.

The stage superstructure of the Swan consisted of three elements: the stage 'cover' or 'shadow' (sometimes referred to also as 'the heavens'), the posts supporting the cover, and the 'hut' over the cover. (The reconstruction here proposed is illustrated in Figures 33, 34 and 35.) I assume that the floor of the stage cover was at about the same elevation as the third-storey floor of the tiring-house. In Southern's reconstruction the two floors are exactly on a level, but in the present reconstruction the cover floor is a bit higher (1 foot 9 inches) than the third-storey floor of the tiring-house. I assume also that the hut lay mainly over the stage, its weight being carried both by the structure of the tiring-house and by the cover posts. Most of the dimensions of the stage superstructure are reciprocally related to other dimensions within the complex. However, two dimensions are determined by elements outside the superstructure, and it is therefore convenient to begin the reconstruction with these controlling dimensions.

The first is the height of the underside of the stage cover. This I assume (with Southern and Hodges) to have been approximately on a level with the top-gallery railing. In the present reconstruction the underside of the stage cover is 6 inches higher than the top-gallery railing, but since the roof of the cover descends 6 inches below its underside, the eaves of the cover are exactly on a level with the gallery railing (see Figure 35). Thus, on the assumption that the railing extends 2 feet 6 inches above the floor of the top gallery, the underside of the stage cover is 28 feet above the yard, or 22 feet 6 inches above the stage (the figure used above for the height of the tiring-house façade from stage to stage cover).

The second controlling dimension is the length of the stage cover. This is here assumed to be the same as the length of the tiring-house (41 feet). Thus, as would not be the case if the cover were as wide as the stage (43 feet), the side-eaves of the cover join the frame at a point on a vertical line defined by the meeting of the tiring-house façade with the face of the adjoining top gallery (see Figure 34).

Three additional assumptions also control the proposed reconstruction of the Swan stage superstructure. The first is that the slopes of the roof of the stage cover were at an angle of 45°. The second is that the hut was some-

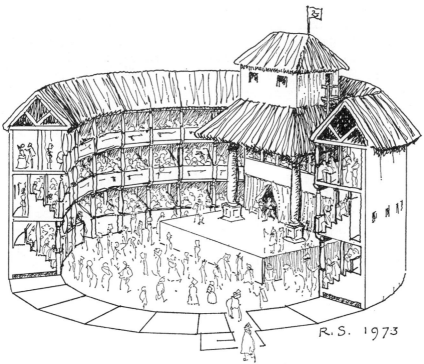

Figure 36 An impression of the Swan playhouse

what over 20 feet long, specifically 23 feet. And the third is that the eaves of the hut were some two or three feet higher than the ridge of the frame. This last arrangement is implied by the Swan Drawing, and it is confirmed by the View of the City of London from the North towards the South (*c.* 1600), which depicts a hut at the Theatre or Curtain generally similar to the hut at the Swan. Alternatively, Southern assumes the eaves of the hut to be exactly on a level with the ridge of the frame, an arrangement which is supported by Visscher's depiction of the Swan hut. (Hodges makes the same assumption in several of his reconstruction drawings.) In the present reconstruction the eaves of the hut have been put at an elevation of 2 feet 8 inches above the ridge of the frame.

Other suggested dimensions of the stage superstructure are more or less arbitrary assumptions arising as much from the need for conforming to one another and to the controlling factors mentioned as from an appeal to whether, when projected into three dimensions, they produce an architectural form having a generally satisfying appearance. In the present reconstruction the height of the cover posts (columns with capitals in the Corinthian mode) is 21 feet (from stage to beam of the stage cover). The posts are placed 10 feet (on centres) away from the tiring-house façade and as far apart as seems necessary to support a 41-foot stage cover while remaining consistent with a practicable span: 26 feet on centres. The cover beam is 32 feet long, 1 foot 6 inches thick and 2 feet deep (the upper 6 inches of the beam being recessed within the cover). The stage cover is assumed to be 9 feet high and to extend 17 feet 9 inches over the stage; the side-roofs are 9 feet in plan. The hut (23 feet long) is assumed to be 14 feet 2 inches wide (the same dimension as the width of the top gallery of the frame) and 9 feet high. The ridge of the hut is 15 feet long. The hut extends 8 feet 9 inches over the stage. Its roof is 8 feet 9 inches high, the main roofs being set at a slope of 45°, the hip-roofs at a slope of 56°. Thus the eaves of the hut (descending 6 inches below the top of the hut frame) are at a height of 45 feet above ground (2 feet 5 inches higher than the ridge of the frame), and the ridge of the hut is 53 feet 9 inches above ground.

The chief function of the stage superstructure would have been to house suspension gear for flying effects. I follow Southern and Hodges in supposing (see Figure 35) that the hut contained a winch to control the suspension line and that the interior of the stage cover functioned as a 'loading room' for players preparing to 'fly' down to the stage.

In Figure 36 Richard Southern has given a general impression of the proposed reconstruction of the Swan playhouse.

(v)

Middleton's *Chaste Maid in Cheapside*, dated by Chambers 1611 but convincingly redated 1613 by R. B. Parker,[1] is said on the title page of the first edition (1630) to have been 'often acted at the Swan on the Banke-side, by the Lady Elizabeth her Servants'. Parker warns that the text may conceivably refer to the stage of a private playhouse (p. lxi), and the late date of the print makes it possible that the text refers to stage practice later than 1613. However, these negative considerations involve only possibilities. There is no evidence against the assumption (which is made in the following discussion) that our text of *A Chaste Maid* relates to the stage of the Swan as it was in 1613. *A Chaste Maid* is the only extant play that may be assigned to the Swan.

The staging of *A Chaste Maid* confirms two salient features of the proposed reconstruction of the Swan. (1) Two tiring-house doors: '*Enter at one*

[1] *A Chaste Maid in Cheapside*, ed. R. B. Parker (Revels Plays, 1969).

Dore the Coffin of the Gentleman . . . At the other Doore, the Coffin of the Virgin' (sig. K2). Presumably the doors of the text refer to the two large double-hung tiring-house doors depicted in the Swan Drawing. (2) A gallery over the stage: '*while all the Company seeme to weepe and mourne, there is a sad Song in the Musicke-Roome*' (sig. K2v). Presumably the music room of the text was one of the boxes of the gallery over the stage shown in the Swan Drawing. Thus the music room would have been 6 feet 3 inches wide and perhaps 8 feet deep. Probably the window of the music room was fitted up with curtains, as in the *Messalina* Vignette (1640) and the *Wits* Frontispiece (1662).

Moreover, at two points the staging of the play is significantly consistent with the proposed reconstruction. The text requires a small discovery-space in which two players can be suddenly revealed to the audience: '*Enter Maudline and Moll, a Shop being discovered*' (sig. B1). Presumably the 'shop' of the text was represented by one of the tiring-house doors depicted in the Swan Drawing. Thus the discovery-space would have been 7 feet 6 inches wide. Its depth is indeterminable, depending on the depth at which a cloth or canvas backing might have been fitted up within the tiring-house – if, indeed, such a backing was used. For practical purposes the depth of the discovery-space need not have been greater than 2 feet – not much more than the thickness of the tiring-house wall if we imagine hangings fitted up some 6 inches in front of that wall. The discovery might have been effected simply by opening the leaves of the door in question (that is, without benefit of curtains); or by opening curtains that had been fitted up within the open doorway (the leaves of the door having been opened out through 180° so as to lie flat against the tiring-house façade); or by opening hangings that had been fitted up along the tiring-house façade in front of the open doorways (see Figure 36). The door or curtains or hangings could have been manipulated by the discovered players or, if the players were discovered seated, by 'servants' or stagekeepers. It should be noted that this discovery is the only one called for in the text. Moreover, the text avoids the use of a large discovery-space in which a bed might have been revealed: '*A Bed thrust out upon the Stage, Allwits Wife in it*' (sig. E4). The open-stage technique called for in this action harmonizes with the failure of the Swan Drawing to record either an 'inner stage' or a curtained booth set up against the tiring-house façade. Presumably the bed (a small curtained four-poster) was 'thrust out' of the tiring-house by 'servants' or stagekeepers through one of the doors to the stage depicted in the drawing. Such open-stage technique is reflected also in the carrying on stage of properties in a later scene:

'*Enter at one Dore the Coffin of the Gentleman . . . At the other Doore, the Coffin of the Virgin . . . Then set them downe one right over-against the other*' (sig. K2).

The staging of *A Chaste Maid* fails to confirm two important features of the proposed reconstruction of the Swan stage and tiring-house: a trap door and suspension gear. But the failure does not deny that those features existed at the Swan: as it happens, the text of the play does not call for trapwork or a flying effect. Neither does it require action above. At no point does the text of the play deny any feature of the proposed reconstruction.

3 The First Globe playhouse (1599)

The First Globe playhouse was built by the Lord Chamberlain's Men in the spring of 1599. It was situated on Bankside, a little over a quarter of a mile to the west of London Bridge and about 150 yards to the south of the Thames. The site, immediately to the south of Maid Lane, is clearly indicated in John Norden's Second Map of London (1600, Figure 37).[1] The playhouse was constructed of the materials of the Theatre, which was dismantled in December or January of 1598–9 by its owners Richard and Cuthbert Burbage and their carpenter Peter Street, who thereupon transported 'all the wood and timber' of the old playhouse across London from Shoreditch 'unto the Banckside in the parishe of St. Marye Overyes, and there erected a newe playehowse with the sayd timber and woode'.[2] The work of construction was apparently completed by 16 May 1599, since the playhouse is described as 'de novo edificata' in a legal document of that date. In June of 1613 the Globe burned to the ground during a performance of Shakespeare's *Henry*

---

[1] Fuller reproductions in Shapiro, 'The Bankside theatres', Plate VII, and Hodges, *The Globe Restored*, Plate 2. The site had earlier, before Shapiro called attention to the evidence of the Second Norden Map, been established by W. W. Braines in *The Site of the Globe Playhouse* (1921).

[2] Quotations of primary sources are from Chambers, *The Elizabethan Stage*.

VIII; and the following year the Second Globe was constructed upon the site of the First.

Very little is known about the physical features of the First Globe.[1] Its exterior is depicted in four panoramic views of London of independent tradition, its shape is alluded to in various sources, its system of admission is described by the Swiss traveller Thomas Platter in 1599, it is referred to several times in the Fortune Contract (1599) and it is mentioned in various contemporary documents apropos of the disastrous fire of 1613. In the present chapter I shall review the external and internal evidence for the First Globe, suggest the hypothesis that its stage and tiring-house were generally similar to the stage and tiring-house of the Swan and test that hypothesis by reference to the staging of the twenty-nine plays that may be supposed probably to have been designed for original performance at the Globe by the Chamberlain's-King's Men during the period 1599–1608.[2]

(i)

We possess firm information on some half-dozen characteristics of the design of the First Globe.

(1) The ground plan of the First Globe was of the same size and shape as that of the Second, as we may infer from the fact that the later playhouse was built upon the foundation of the earlier. This is clear from a draft for a return of new and divided houses made for the Earl Marshal in 1634: 'The Globe playhouse nere Maid Lane built by the company of players, with the dwelling house thereto adjoyninge, built with timber, about 20 yeares past, upon an old foundation.' This fact, when combined with Hollar's depiction of the Second Globe in his Long Bird's-Eye View of London (1647; see Plate 12b), suggests that the First Globe, like the Second, was a 'round' (that is, polygonal) building about 100 feet in diameter, since Hollar draws the Second Globe three times as wide as

---

[1] A fact which perhaps in part accounts for the general dissatisfaction with the detailed reconstruction proposed by John Cranford Adams in *The Globe Playhouse* (1942).

[2] Parts of this chapter are based on my articles, 'The discovery-space in Shakespeare's Globe', *Shakespeare Survey 12* (1959), and 'Was there a music-room in Shakespeare's Globe?', *Shakespeare Survey 13* (1960). These essays (and the present chapter) may be compared with the study by Bernard Beckerman, based on substantially the same internal evidence, in *Shakespeare at the Globe* (1962); and with the study by T. J. King, based on the internal evidence of 276 plays first performed by professional players between the opening of the First Globe and the closing of the theatres, in *Shakespearean Staging 1599–1642* (1971).

its height to the eaves, and that height, as at the Fortune, was presumably about 33 feet. The round shape of the First Globe is confirmed by such references as 'this Woodden O' in the Prologue to *Henry V* (F, 1623), 'this thronged round' in the Prologue to *Every Man out of His Humour* (Q, 1600), 'the Globe's faire Ring' in one of the commendatory verses to *Sejanus* (Q, 1605), 'this round' in the Prologue to *The Merry Devil of Edmonton* (Q, 1608), and 'As round as taylors clewe [= ball]' in the anonymous 'Sonnett upon the pittiful burneing of the Globe playhowse in London' (1613). Its round shape is confirmed also by depiction of the Globe as round in the Second Norden Map (1600, Figure 37) and the Hondius View of London (1610, Figure 38).[1] Presumably the Visscher View of London (1616, Figure 39) and the *Civitas Londini* Panorama (1600, Figure 40 and endpapers) are generally correct in depicting the Globe as polygonal, although specifically erroneous in attributing to it, respectively, eight and six sides. A convenient number of sides for the First Globe, since it had a diameter of about 100 feet, would have been twenty-four, the number that may be supposed for both the Second Globe and the Swan.

(2) The First Globe had exterior staircases, as we know from the requirement of the Fortune Contract that the 'stairs' at that playhouse, which are referred to as 'without', be constructed as at the Globe: 'with suchelike steares, conveyances and divisions withoute and within, as are made and contrived in and to the late erected Plaiehowse on the Bancke in the saide parishe of Ste Saviours called the Globe'. Presumably there were two staircases at the First Globe, generally similar to the stair-towers depicted by Hollar at the Second Globe and the Hope.

(3) The general entrances to the First Globe consisted of 'two narrow doors', as may be inferred from John Chamberlain's account of the burning down of the playhouse in 1613: 'it was a great marvaile and fair grace of God, that the people had so little harm, having but two narrow doors to get out.' (I am rejecting the possible alternative interpretation that Chamberlain's two doors were a single general entrance and a tiring-house entrance.) Presumably each of the two general entrances to the Globe was in the foot of a stair-tower. Presumably also there was a third, special entrance at the rear of the tiring-house for use of the players and of spectators sitting in the lords' rooms over the stage.

---

[1] The Hondius View shows a puzzling 'hip' running round the Globe as high as (apparently) the top of the first gallery. Most investigators disregard this evidence, though William Poel accepted it.

Figure 37 Detail from the Second Norden Map of London (1600) showing the First Globe Playhouse. *Royal Library, Stockholm*

Figure 39 (*below left*) Detail from the Visscher View of London (1616) showing the First Globe Playhouse. *Guildhall Library*

Figure 40 (*below right*) Detail from the *Civitas Londini* Panorama (1600) showing the First Globe. *Royal Library, Stockholm*

Figure 38 Detail from
the Hondius View of
London (in Speed's *Theatre
of the Empire of Great Britain*,
1611) showing the First Globe
Playhouse. *Folger Shakespeare
Library*

(4) The roof of the First Globe was covered with thatch, as is indicated in various accounts of the fire of 1613 and by Ben Jonson's compliment to the King's Men, in 'An Execration upon Vulcan' (*c.* 1623), on having had the wit to roof the rebuilt playhouse of 1614 with tile.

(5) The First Globe had a stage superstructure consisting in part of a hut, as we know from the depictions in the Second Norden Map (1600, Figure 37) and the Visscher View (1616, Figure 39). (The Hondius View, 1610, Figure 38, does not record a hut, and the *Civitas Londini* Panorama, 1600, Figure 40 and endpapers, records a low hut whose ridge connects with the ridge of the frame.) The Visscher View (which is quite detailed in the matter) records a hut consisting of a main block running parallel to the tiring-house façade (as at the Swan) and a 'wing' projecting a few feet from the middle of the main block so as to give the whole hut the plan of a squat T. The projection (stem of the T) ends in a gable whose ridge connects with the ridge of the main block of the hut. One aspect of the design is that the projection extends several feet further forward (relative to the stage) than the front of the Swan hut, and another is that full headroom is available inside the stage cover as far forward as the gable of the projection. Thus at the Globe it may have been possible to bring suspension gear further forward over the stage than at the Swan; or the main block of the Globe hut may have lain further to the rear (relative to the stage) than did the Swan hut.

(6) The posts supporting the gallery fronts of the First Globe playhouse frame were apparently turned columns, as at the Swan, for the Fortune Contract requires that the general style of that playhouse be like that of the Globe, 'saveinge only that the princypall and maine postes of the saide fframe and Stadge forwarde shalbe square and wrought palasterwise, with carved proportions called Satiers to be placed and sett on the topp of every of the same postes'.

(7) Thomas Platter's description (1599) of the progressive gathering of admission fees at a Bankside playhouse (presumably the Globe) has been discussed in the preceding chapter, apropos of the Swan. Unfortunately, the description provides no significant information about physical features of the playhouse except that spectators passed through two separate doors in proceeding to the 2d. and 3d. audience areas.

Thus we may suppose that the First Globe was a 'round' building constructed to a ground plan in the shape of a polygon having perhaps twenty-four sides and a diameter of about 100 feet. We know that the Globe had exterior staircases, presumably two. Probably the general entrances to the playhouse were two doors, each presumably located in the foot of a stair-tower. The playhouse had also a thatched roof, a stage superstructure consisting in part of a hut, and turned columns supporting the gallery fronts. We know nothing, however, about the Globe stage and tiring-house. In view of this lack of information, I suggest the hypothesis that the stage and tiring-house of the First Globe were generally similar to the stage and tiring-house of the Swan. Thus the Globe would have had a large rectangular stage, a trap door set in the middle of the stage, a tiring-house with two doors opening on the stage, a gallery over the stage divided into boxes, and suspension gear housed within a stage superstructure consisting partly of the hut that we know of from pictorial sources and partly of a stage cover that may be postulated immediately beneath the hut, the front of the super-structure being supported by posts rising through the stage from the yard below.

(ii)

Twenty-nine plays may be supposed to have been designed for original performance by the Chamberlain's-King's Men at the First Globe during the period 1599–1608:

1 Shakespeare, *As You Like It*, F (1623)
2 Jonson, *Every Man out of His humour*, Q (1600); F (1616)
3 Shakespeare, *Henry V*, Q (1600); F (1623)
4 Shakespeare, *Julius Caesar*, F (1623)
5 Anon., *A Larum for London*, Q (1602)
6 Shakespeare, *Hamlet*, Q1 (1603); Q2 (1604–5); F (1623)
7 Shakespeare, *Twelfth Night*, F (1623)
8 Shakespeare, *The Merry Wives of Windsor*, Q (1602); F (1623)
9 Dekker, *Satiromastix*, Q (1602)
10 Anon., *Thomas Lord Cromwell*, Q (1602)
11 Shakespeare, *Troilus and Cressida*, Q (1609); F (1623)
12 Shakespeare, *All's Well That Ends Well*, F (1623)
13 Jonson, *Sejanus*, Q (1605); F (1616)
14 Anon., *The Merry Devil of Edmonton*, Q (1608)
15 Anon., *The London Prodigal*, Q (1605)
16 Anon., *The Fair Maid of Bristol*, Q (1605)
17 Shakespeare, *Measure for Measure*, F (1623)

18 Shakespeare, *Othello*, Q (1622); F (1623)
19 Shakespeare, *King Lear*, Q (1608); F (1623)
20 Jonson, *Volpone*, Q (1607); F (1616)
21 Shakespeare, *Macbeth*, F (1623)
22 Anon., *A Yorkshire Tragedy*, Q (1608)
23 Tourneur (?), *The Revenger's Tragedy*, Q (1607–8)
24 Barnes, *The Devil's Charter*, Q (1607)
25 Shakespeare, *Antony and Cleopatra*, F (1623)
26 Wilkins, *The Miseries of Enforced Marriage*, Q (1607)
27 Shakespeare, *Coriolanus*, F (1623)
28 Shakespeare, *Timon of Athens*, F (1623)
29 Shakespeare, *Pericles*, Q (1609)

Twelve of the twenty-nine Globe plays refer in stage directions to two doors: *Henry V*, *Twelfth Night*, *Satiromastix*, *Troilus and Cressida*, *The Fair Maid of Bristol*, *Measure for Measure*, *King Lear*, *The Devil's Charter*, *Antony and Cleopatra*, *Coriolanus*, *Timon of Athens* and *Pericles*. In a few instances, as in *The Devil's Charter* and *Pericles*, three doors would have been useful in staging a given action, but in no case would three doors have been unequivocally necessary and in no case are three doors explicitly called for.

Twenty of the twenty-nine Globe plays do not require a discovery: *As You Like It*, *Every Man out of His Humour*, *Henry V*, *Julius Caesar*, *A Larum for London*, *Hamlet*, *Twelfth Night*, *All's Well That Ends Well*, *Sejanus*, *The London Prodigal*, *The Fair Maid of Bristol*, *Measure for Measure*, *Othello*, *King Lear*, *Macbeth*, *A Yorkshire Tragedy*, *Antony and Cleopatra*, *The Miseries of Enforced Marriage*, *Coriolanus* and *Timon of Athens*.

Of these twenty plays, moreover, ten explicitly avoid the device of discovery by calling for the carrying on stage of properties or players.

(1) *Julius Caesar*: 'Enter Mark Antony, with Caesars body. Heere comes his Body' (sig. 2l1). The 'Pulpit' of III, ii is presumably a property brought on and off stage.

(2) *A Larum for London*: 'enter two with mourning penons: a Drum sounding a dead march: Dalva carried upon a horse [= hearse = coffin] covered with blacke' (sig. B1v.)

(3) *Hamlet*.
(a) 'Enter a King and a Queene ... he lyes him downe uppon a bancke of flowers ... the dead body is carried away' (Q2, sig. H1v). Since the Dumbshow King's body must be carried off stage, the 'bancke of flowers' was apparently carried on earlier.

(b) '*A table prepar'd, Trumpets, Drums and officers with Cushions*' (Q2, sig. N3v).

(4) *Othello*: '*Enter Lodovico, Montano, Iago, and Officers, Cassio in a Chaire*' (Q, sig. N1). The bed of V, ii is presumably brought on stage, the 'Curtaines' referred to in the dialogue being bedcurtains: '*Enter Othello, and Desdemona in her bed*' (F, sig. 2v4).[1] Presumably the '*Table*' of I, iii is also carried on stage.

(5) *King Lear*.
 (a) '*Stocks brought out*' (F, sig. 2q6v).
 (b) '*Enter Lear in a chaire carried by Servants*' (sig. 2s1).
 (c) '*Gonerill and Regans bodies brought out*' (sig. 2s2v).

(6) *Macbeth*: '*Banquet prepar'd*' (sig. 2m5).

(7) *A Yorkshire Tragedy*.
 (a) '*Enter his wife brought in a chaire*' (sig. D2).
 (b) '*Children laid out*' (sig. D2v). Presumably the sleeping Wife is earlier carried on stage in a chair (sig. C3).

(8) *Antony and Cleopatra*.
 (a) '*Enter two or three Servants with a Banket*' (sig. 2x5v).
 (b) '*Enter Ventidius . . . the dead body of Pacorus borne before him*' (sig. 2x6).
 (c) '*Diom[ed]* . . . His Guard have brought him thither. *Enter Anthony, and the Guard*' (sig. 2y6).
 (d) '*Caesar*. . . . Take up her bed, And beare her Women from the Monument' (sig. 2z2v). Since Cleopatra's 'bed' (presumably a day bed) must be carried off stage, it was presumably carried on earlier.

(9) *Coriolanus*.
 (a) '*Enter Volumnia and Virgilia . . . They set them downe on two lowe stooles and sowe*' (sig. 2a2v). Since the players must enter and sit, presumably the stools were carried on stage.
 (b) '*Enter two Officers, to lay Cushions, as it were, in the Capitoll*' (sig. 2a5v).

(10) *Timon of Athens*.
 (a) '*A great Banquet serv'd in*' (sig. 2g2v).
 (b) '*The Banket brought in*' (sig. 2h1).
 Presumably Timon's '*Cave*' in V, i is a tiring-house door, the 'tomb' of V, iii either a door or the tiring-house façade.

---

[1] A fuller discussion may be found in my article, 'The staging of Desdemona's Bed', *Shakespeare Quarterly*, XIV (1963).

Further, in three plays not requiring a discovery there are nevertheless allusions to 'hangings', an 'Arras', a 'Curtin' and a 'seeling' (in the sense of 'curtain').

(1) *Every Man out of his Humour*: '*Fung[oso].* Is this the way? good truth here be fine hangings. *Exeunt Puntarvolo, Briske, Fungoso*' (Q, sig. N4).

(2) *Hamlet*: '*Pol.* . . . Behinde the Arras Ile convey my selfe To heare the Processe. . . . *Exit Hamlet tugging in Polonius*' (F, sigs. 2p1v–2v). Polonius, having been stabbed through the arras, apparently falls forward upon the stage, for Hamlet at the end of the scene drags his body off stage.

(3) *Sejanus*.

(a) '*Ar[runtius].* The Curtin's drawing. [*Enter Afer.*] Afer advanceth' (Q, sig. F2).

(b) '*Lat[iaris to Rufus and Opsius].* Here place your selves, betweene the Roofe, and Seeling, And when I bring him to his words of daunger, Reveale your selves, and take him. . . . *Ops.* Shift to our Holes, with silence. . . . *Ruf.* Lay hands upon the Traytor' (Q, sigs. H3–I1). Presumably, as Robert E. Knoll suggests,[1] the word 'Seeling' (modern 'ceiling') is here used in the sense of 'curtain' or 'hangings' (*OED* 3), the spies hiding behind the curtain and later coming forward to arrest Sabinus.

From these examples it is clear that the primary function of the hangings, arras, curtain or 'ceiling' was something other than to effect discoveries.

Nine of the twenty-nine Globe plays require one or more discoveries.

(1) *The Merry Wives of Windsor*: '*Qu[ickly to Simple].* . . . goe into this Closset . . . *Ca[ius].* . . . vat is in my Closset? Villanie, La-roone' (F, sig. D3v). One player (Simple) goes into the discovery-space, where he is then discovered by another (Caius), as in a 'closet'. (At the point in F where Simple enters the 'closet', Q has '*He steps into the Counting-house*', sig. B3v). The discovering agency is presumably the 'Arras' later referred to: '*Fal.* . . . I will ensconce mee behinde the Arras' (F, sig. E1v; Q has '*Falstaffe stands behind the aras*', sig. E1).

(2) *Satiromastix*: '*Horrace sitting in a study behinde a Curtaine, a candle by him burning, bookes lying confusedly*' (sig. B4). One seated player and a table are discovered by a 'curtain', as in a 'study'.

---

[1] 'The "Seeling" in *Sejanus*', appendix to *Ben Jonson's Plays* (1964).

(3) *Thomas Lord Cromwell:* three discoveries.

(a) '*Cromwell in his study with bagges of money before him casting of account*' (sig. B1v). One seated player and a table are discovered, as in a 'study'.

(b) 'Go take thy place Hodge . . . *Hodge sits in the study, and Cromwell calles in the States.* . . . Goe draw the curtaines, let us see the Earle, O he is writing' (sig. D1). One player goes into the discovery-space, where he is then discovered, seated at a small table as in a 'study', by the drawing of 'curtains'.

(c) '*Enter Gardiner in his studie, and his man*' (sig. E4v). One or two players are probably discovered, as in a 'study'.

(4) *Troilus and Cressida:* '*Enter Achilles and Patroclus in their Tent. Ulis.* Achilles stands i'th entrance of his Tent' (F, sig. ¶6v). Two players are discovered standing, as in the entrance to a 'tent'.

(5) *The Merry Devil of Edmonton:* '*Draw the curtaines.* . . . Behold him heere laide on his restless couch . . . And by him stands that Necromanticke chaire . . . And in meane time repose thee in that chayre. . . . *Sit downe.* . . . Enough, come out' (sigs. A3v–4v). One player (Peter Fable) is discovered reclining on a day bed, together with a chair, by the drawing of 'curtains'. Another player (Coreb) goes and sits in the discovery-space and then 'comes out'.

Presumably the 'Church porch' in which Banks the Miller sits and from which he later '*comes out*' is one of the tiring-house doors (sig E3v).

(6) *Volpone:* '*Volpone* . . . Good morning to the day; and, next, my gold: Open the shrine, that I may see my saint. Haile the worlds soule, and mine' (F, sig. 2P3v). A property (Volpone's gold) is discovered, presumably upon a table. The discovering agency is presumably the 'curtain' or 'traverse' later referred to: 'I'le get up, Behind the cortine, on a stoole, and harken; Sometime, peepe over . . . I'le to my place . . . *Volpone peepes from behinde a traverse*' (F, sig. 2V3v).

(7) *The Revenger's Tragedy:* '*Enter the discontented Lord Antonio, whose wife the Duchesses yongest Sonne ravisht; he Discovering the body of her dead to certaine Lords* . . . A prayer Booke the pillow to her cheeke' (sig. C1v). One player is discovered, recumbent on a coffin or some other convenient property.

It is possible that the entrance of the Junior Brother '*in prison*' (sig. E3v) also involves a discovery.

(8) *The Devil's Charter:* eight discoveries.

(a, b) '*Enter, At one doore betwixt two other Cardinals, Roderigo in his purple habit close in conference with them, one of which hee guideth to a Tent, where a Table is furnished with divers bagges of money, which that Cardinall beareth away ; and to another Tent the other Cardinall, where hee delivereth him a great quantity of rich Plate'* (sig. A2). (a) Properties (bags of money) are discovered, upon a table, as in a 'tent'. (b) Properties (rich plate) are discovered, presumably upon a table, as in a 'tent'. This is one of the actions in the Globe plays for which three doors would have been convenient but which in my view falls short of demonstrating the existence of three doors.

(c) *'Alexander in his study with bookes, coffers, his triple Crowne upon a cushion before him'* (sig. B2v). One seated player is discovered, as in a 'study', together with coffers and (presumably) a small table.

(d) *'Alexander in his studie beholding a Magicall glasse with other observations. . . . Let me looke forth. Alexander commeth upon the Stage out of his study with a booke in his hand. . . . Exit Alexander into the studie'* (sigs. F4v–G2v). One seated player is discovered, presumably at a small table, as in a 'study'. Since he subsequently comes 'upon the stage', the discovery-space appears to be off stage.

(e) *'Barbarossa bringeth from Caesars Tent hir two boyes. . . . Exeunt with the boyes. . . . Behold thy children living in my Tent. He discovereth his Tent where her two sonnes were at Cardes'* (sigs. H3–i2v). Two players are discovered seated at a table, as in a 'tent'.

(f) *'Enter Alexander out of his studie. . . . Exit Alexander into his study. . . . Bernardo knocketh at the study. Alex. What newes man? . . . Alexander upon the stage in his cassock and nightcap with a box under each arme'* (sigs. i2–3v). One player is discovered. Since he subsequently comes 'upon' the stage, the discovery-space appears to be off stage.

(g) *'Alexander unbraced betwixt two Cardinalls in his study looking upon a booke, whilst a groome draweth the Curtaine. . . . They place him in a chayre upon the stage, a groome setteth a Table before him'* (sig. L3). Three players, one seated in a chair, are discovered by the drawing of a 'curtain'. The seated player is then carried on stage in his chair. Again the discovery-space appears to be off stage.

(h) *'Alexander draweth the Curtaine of his studie where hee discovereth the divill sitting in his pontificals'* (sig. L3v). One seated player is discovered by the drawing of a 'curtain'. This and the preceding discovery occur during the same sequence of action and apparently in the same discovery-space.

(9) *Pericles: 'Li[simachus]. May wee not see him? . . . Lys. [= Hellicanus]*

Behold him' (sigs. H2v–3). One seated or recumbent player (Pericles) is probably discovered; he is then presumably carried on stage.

Of the nine plays requiring discoveries, moreover, seven explicitly avoid the device of discovery by calling for the carrying on stage of properties or players.

(1) *The Merry Wives of Windsor* : '*Enter Mistresse Ford, with two of her men, and a great buck busket* [= *basket*]' (Q, sig. D4).
(2) *Satiromastix.*
   (a) '*A banquet set out*' (sig. G1v).
   (b) '*Enter an arm'd Sewer, after him the service of a Banquet*' (sig. K3v).
   (c) '*chaire* [*for the King*] *it* [= *is*] *set under a Canopie*. . . . *Caelestine* [*is brought on stage*] *in a chaire*' (sigs. K4–4v). Presumably the '*Canopie*' is that of a chair of state.
(3) *Thomas Lord Cromwell* : '*they bring out the banquet*' (sig. D2).
(4) *Volpone* : '*Volpone is brought in, as impotent*' (F, sig. 2T6v). A player (Volpone) is carried on and off stage, presumably in a chair or day bed. In Act II the 'banke' (a bench or small scaffold) which Volpone 'mounts' is evidently brought on stage and set up beneath a 'windore' of the upper station. In Acts I and III it may be assumed that Volpone's '*couch*' (a day bed) is brought on and off stage.
(5) *The Revenger's Tragedy* : '*A furnisht Table is brought forth : then enters the Duke and his Nobles to the banquet*' (sig. I2v).
   A bed may be brought on stage in II, ii or imagined as just off stage.
(6) *The Devil's Charter.*
   (a) '*Enter Lucretia* . . . *bringing in a chaire, which she planteth upon the Stage*' (sig. C1).
   (b) '*Luc.* . . . . Bring me some mixtures and my dressing boxes . . . *Enter two Pages with a Table, two looking glasses, a box with Combes and instruments, a rich bowle*' (sig. H1).
   (c) '*a cuppord of plate brought in* . . . *enter a table spread, Viandes brought in*' (sig. L1).
   The bed required in IV, v is apparently brought on stage, since at the end of the action the Cardinal orders that the bodies of Astor and Philippo lying upon the bed be borne in.
(7) *Pericles* : '*Enter two or three with a Chist*. . . . *They carry her away*' (sigs. E3v–4v).
   The '*tombe*' of IV, i may be a property, the tiring-house façade, or a

tiring-house door (conceivably the middle door of three). This is another of the actions in the Globe plays for which three doors would have been convenient but which in my judgement falls short of demonstrating the existence of three doors.

The discovery-space is equipped with an 'arras', 'curtains', a 'curtain' or a 'traverse', and in three instances it is referred to as off stage. It is used relatively infrequently: once in each of seven plays, thrice in an eighth and eight times in the last. Moreover, in seventeen of the twenty-nine Globe plays (including seven that require discoveries) the device of discovery is explicitly avoided by the carrying on stage of properties or players; and in three plays not requiring discoveries 'hangings', an 'arras', a 'curtain' or a 'ceiling' (curtain) are called for. The discovery-space is variously referred to as a 'closet' (or 'countinghouse'), a 'study', the entrance to a 'tent', and a 'tent'. Since it can contain a recumbent player or a day bed and a chair, the discovery-space requires an area of at least 14 square feet. A width of 7 feet and a depth of 2 feet would be convenient dimensions.

Eighteen of the twenty-nine Globe plays do not require action above: *As You Like It, Hamlet, Twelfth Night, The Merry Wives of Windsor, Satiromastix, Thomas Lord Cromwell, Troilus and Cressida, All's Well That Ends Well, Sejanus, The Merry Devil of Edmonton, The London Prodigal, The Fair Maid of Bristol, Measure for Measure, King Lear, Macbeth, A Yorkshire Tragedy, The Revenger's Tragedy* and *Pericles*.

Eleven of the twenty-nine Globe plays require one or more actions above.

(1) *Every Man out of his Humour :* two actions above.
   (a) '*The waiting Gentlewoman appeares at the window*' (Q, sig. E3). One player appears above, as at the window of a house.
   (b) '*Enter Gent[lewoman] above . . . meane time the Ladie is come to the window*' (Q, sigs. E4v–F1). Two players appear above, as at the window of a house; presently they descend to the stage (exit above and re-entrance below noted).

(2) *Henry V :* '*Enter the King and all his Traine before the Gates. . . . Enter Governour [above]*' (F, sigs. h5v–6). One or more players appear above, as on the walls of a town.

(3) *Julius Caesar :* '*Cassi.* Go Pindarus, get higher on that hill . . . *Pind. Above*' (sig. 2l4v). One player appears above, as on a 'hill'; he has ascended from the stage and presently descends to the stage (re-entrance below noted).

(4) *A Larum for London :* '*Enter [above] Danila and the Gunner. . . . Alv[a]*.

Whose that above? Lord Sancto Danila?' (sigs. A4v–B2v). Two players appear above, as on the walls of a castle.

(5) *Othello*: '*Brabantio at a window*' (Q, sig. B2; F has '*Bra. Above*', sig. 2s3v). One player appears above, as at the window of a house; presently he descends to the stage (exit above and re-entrance below noted).

(6) *Volpone*: '*Celia at the windo' throwes downe her handkerchiefe*' (F, sig. 2R2). One player appears above, as at the window of a house. A hand property (handkerchief) is thrown down to the stage.

(7) *The Devil's Charter*: five actions above.

(a) '*Enter Piccolomini upon the walls*' (sig. D1v). One player appears above, as on the walls of a castle.

(b) '*Alexander upon the walls . . . betwixt Caesar Borgia and Caraffa Cardinalls, before him the Duke of Candie bearing a sword, after them Piccolomini[,] Gasperdefois . . . Alexander with his companie of* [= off] *the walles*' (sigs. D2–3v). Six players appear above, as on the walls of a castle.

(c) '*Enter Alexander upon the walls as before. . . . He throwes his keies*' (sigs. D3v–4). Six players appear above, as on the walls of a castle; presently they descend to the stage (re-entrance below noted). A hand property (keys) is thrown down to the stage.

(d) '*Alexander out of a Casement*' (sig. E2). One player appears above, as looking out of a 'chamber' window.

(e) '*Enter upon the walles Countesse Katherine, Julio Sforza, Ensigne, souldiers, Drummes, Trumpets. . . . Caesar the third time repulsed, at length entreth* [*the upper station from the stage*] *by scalado, surpriseth her, bringeth her downe with some prisoners*' (sigs. H3–I1v). Some nine players appear above, as on the walls of a town. Players below climb to the upper station by scaling-ladders, and then descend to the stage with some of the players above.

(8) *Antony and Cleopatra*: '*Enter Cleopatra, and her Maides aloft,* [*namely*] *with Charmian and Iras. . . . Enter* [*below*] *Anthony, and the Guard. . . . They heave Anthony aloft to Cleopatra. . . . Exeunt, bearing of* [= off] *Anthonies body*' (sigs. 2y6–6v). Three players appear above, as at the window (or on the walls) of a 'monument' (a fortified building). They are joined by a fourth player, who is 'heaved aloft' from below and then sits in the upper station before being carried off at the end of the scene. The action of 'heaving Antony aloft' is discussed below as an example of the use of suspension gear.

(9) *The Miseries of Enforced Marriage*: '*Enter Butler and Ilford above. But.*'

. . . stay you heere in this upper chamber . . . *Exit [Butler]*. . . . *Enter Scarborrowes Sister [above]*. . . . *Enter Wentloe, and Bartley beneath. Bart*. Here about is the house sure. . . . *Enter Butler above [to Ilford and the Sister]*' (sig. G3v–4). Three players appear above, as at a 'chamber' window; two of them (Ilford and the Sister) presently descend to the stage (re-entrance below noted).

(10) *Coriolanus*: '*Enter two Senators with others on the Walles of Corialus*' (sig. 2a3). Four or more players appear above, as on the walls of a city.

(11) *Timon of Athens*: '*The Senators appeare upon the wals*. . . . 2 *[Senator]*. Throw thy Glove, Or any Token of thine Honour else . . . *Alc[ibiades]*. Then there's my Glove' (sigs. 2h5–5v). Several players appear above, as on the walls of a city; presently they descend to the stage. A hand property (glove) is thrown to the upper station by a player on the stage.

In the eleven plays requiring action above, the upper station is used relatively infrequently: once in each of nine plays, twice in a tenth play and five times in the eleventh. It is variously referred to as the 'window' of a house, a 'hill', the 'walls' of a town or castle, the 'casement' of a 'chamber', the window or walls of a 'monument', and a 'chamber' window. Since it can contain as many as nine standing players, the upper station requires an area of at least 14 square feet. A width of 6 feet and a depth of 2 feet 4 inches would be convenient dimensions. The stairway used in descents from upper station to stage is evidently out of sight of the audience, for in several instances descending players are directed to exit above and re-enter below. There is no evidence to suggest that the upper station was equipped with curtains.

Seven of the Globe plays refer to the location of a music station.

(1) *Julius Caesar*: '*Low March within*' (sig. 2l2v).

(2) *Troilus and Cressida*: '*Musicke sounds within*' (F, sig. ¶5).

(3) *All's Well That Ends Well*.
    (a) '*Alarum within*' (sig. X3).
    (b) '*A short Alarum within*' (ibid.).

(4) *Othello*: '*Trumpets within*' (Q, sig. E1).

(5) *King Lear*.
    (a) '*Hornes within*' (F, sig. 2q4).
    (b) '*Tucket within*' (sig. 2q6).
    (c) '*Tucket within*' (sig. 2r1v).
    (d) '*Alarum within*' (sig. 2s1v).

9a Performance of *Titus Andronicus*, 1594

9b A Masquer Lord: a star (design
by Inigo Jones for T. Campion, *The
Lord's Masque*, 1613)

9c A torchbearer: an oceania (design by
Inigo Jones for Ben Jonson, *The Masque
of Blackness*, 1608)

10 Oberon's Palace (design by Inigo Jones for Scene II of Ben Jonson,
The Masque of Oberon, 1611)

(e) '*Alarum and Retreat within*' (ibid.).
(f) '*Trumpet answers within*' (sig. 2s2).
(6) *Macbeth.*
   (a) '*Alarum within*' (sig. 2l6).
   (b) '*Drum within*' (sig. 2l6v).
   (c) '*Musicke, and a Song. . . . Sing within*' (sig. 2m6).
(7) *The Devils' Charter :* '*Sound a Horne within*' (sig. M2).

The term *within* might conceivably designate the music room in a tiring-house gallery over the stage, but in that case it seems likely that some at least of the seven plays specifying the location of offstage music would refer to it as 'above'. Since none does, we may conclude that the music station was probably 'within' the tiring-house at stage level.

In *Antony and Cleopatra* music is required 'under the stage' as a special effect when the god Hercules is said to be leaving Antony: '*Musicke of the Hoboyes is under the Stage*' (sig. 2y4).

Inter-act music is referred to in one play, *Sejanus*, which has the direction '*Chorus – of Musicians*' at the end of each of the first four acts (F; Q has '*Mu. Chorus*'). These references to inter-act music in *Sejanus* cannot, however, relate to original performance at the Globe since the play is dated by Jonson 1603 and we know from the Induction to Marston's *Malcontent* that the custom of inter-act music was 'not-received' at the Globe as late as 1604. (The references in *Sejanus* may relate to a performance at court, or Jonson may have added them at the time of publication in order to give his text a proper neoclassical style.) We may conclude that the Globe plays were originally performed without inter-act music.

This conclusion is confirmed, moreover, by the absence of act divisions from some three-quarters of the texts of Globe plays printed before 1609, the year in which the King's Men began using the Blackfriars as well as the Globe. Eighteen of the thirty-nine substantive texts of our twenty-nine Globe plays were printed in 1608 or earlier. Of these, only five, or about one-quarter, are divided into acts.[1] (By contrast, all eighteen of the pre-1609 substantive texts of the twenty plays designed for original performance at the Blackfriars between 1600 and 1608 are divided into acts.) We may

[1] Act divisions in three of these five texts (*Every Man out* Q 1600, *Sejanus* Q 1605, *Volpone* Q 1607) are probably due not to theatrical influence but to Ben Jonson's predilection for neoclassical trappings. Act divisions in Barnes's *The Devil's Charter* Q 1607 may be due to influence of the court production advertised on the title page or to neoclassical taste. The fifth text divided into acts is *The Revenger's Tragedy* Q 1607.

conclude that before 1609 the Globe plays were probably performed without act intervals, hence probably without inter-act music.

Two plays require suspension gear.

(1) *A Larum for London:* two uses, in both of which the English Factor in Antwerp is being tortured by the strappado.

(a) '*Dan[ila]*. Give him the strippado . . . *Hoise him up and let him downe againe*' (sigs. D4–4v).

(b) '*Alv[a]*. That will we try, if roape and Gibbet holde . . . So, let him downe, stand off and give him ayre . . . *Ver[dugo]*. Hang him out-right . . . *Hang him*' (sigs. E4–4v).

Suspension gear may have been used also in hanging the Factor, presumably in combination with a ladder set up against the tiring-house wall, as apparently in *Every Man out of His Humour* where Sordido's unsuccessful attempt to hang himself is accompanied by the direction '*Falls off*' (Q, sig. K2).

(2) *Antony and Cleopatra:* '*Enter Cleopatra, and her Maides aloft,* [*namely*] *with Charmian and Iras. . . . Enter Diomed* [*below*]. . . . *Diom.* . . . Looke out o' th other side your Monument, His Guard have brought him thither. *Enter Anthony, and the Guard. Cleo.* . . . Helpe Charmian, helpe Iras helpe; helpe Friends Below, let's draw him hither. . . . come Anthony, Helpe me my women, we must draw thee up: Assist good Friends. . . . Heere's sport indeede: How heavy weighes my Lord? . . . Yet come a little . . . Oh come, come, come, *They heave Anthony aloft to Cleopatra*' (sig. 2y6). Here, since Cleopatra 'dare not' open the gates of her 'monument' because of fear of capture by the Romans, the dying Antony is 'heaved aloft' to Cleopatra in an upper station representing the window or walls of a fortified building. The heaving aloft is not always recognized as involving a use of suspension gear, chiefly I believe because of the assumption that Antony is carried on stage in a litter (in which he cannot easily be imagined as being hoisted up to a gallery over the stage). (The usual modern practice is to provide a property 'monument' some 6 or 7 feet high, so that the soldiers can lift Antony up at arm's length in his litter and slide him on to the top of the monument.) But if we suppose that Antony is carried on stage in a chair rather than a litter, it becomes possible to imagine the heaving aloft as accomplished by suspension gear; and such a means of lifting Antony harmonizes with the dialogue, which clearly requires that the hoisting be done by Cleopatra and her maids from within the upper station. Antony's chair can be attached by an

appropriate harness to one end of a line descending from the stage cover a few feet in front of the upper station, the other end of the line being 'returned' from the point of suspension (whether this is the drum of a winch within the stage superstructure or a ring or hook or pulley within or on the underside of the stage cover) to the players in the upper station. Thus Cleopatra and her Maids can 'heave Antony aloft', swinging him and the chair into the upper station when they have hoisted him to the necessary height. Antony can then sit in his chair at the front of the upper station until carried off at the end of the action.[1]

Suspension gear may have been used for a flying effect in *Pericles*, the goddess Diana being lowered from stage cover to stage and then raised again after her speech to the sleeping Pericles. Alternatively, Diana can enter and exit by a tiring-house door. The text, which has only the laconic stage direction '*Diana*' (sig. I1v), is non-committal.

In two plays there is reference to a post on the stage.

(1) *A Larum for London:* '*1 Sol[dier]*. . . . Wee'll tye him [the Fat Burgher] by the thumbes unto this poast, And tickle him untill he doe confesse' (sig. F3v).

(2) *The Devil's Charter:* '*Fris[cobaldi]*. . . . Here will I stand close till tha'llarum call, *he stands behind the post*' (sig. F3v).

In each case the post is presumably one of those supporting the stage cover. Such a post could have been used also as the 'tree' which Butler climbs to elude searchers in *The Miseries of Enforced Marriage* (sig. F2v), or as the 'Bulke' (= baulk = beam of wood) behind which Roderigo is ordered to conceal himself in *Othello* (Q, sig. L3).

Four plays require a trap door.

(1) *A Larum for London:* '*wife*. Within that vault lyes all my wretched wealth . . . *Van [End]*. . . . Which is the way? *She pushes him downe.* . . . *Enter Stumpe*. . . . Ile stone the Jew to death . . . *Throw stones*' (sigs. E4v–F1). One player is pushed down into the trap by another, as into a 'vault', and a third player then throws stones into the trap.

(2) *Hamlet:* '*Enter King, Queene, Laertes, and a Coffin* . . . *Laer.* Lay her in'th' earth . . . *Leaps in the grave*' (F, sig. 2p5v; Q1 has '*Leartes leapes into the grave*. . . . *Hamlet leapes in after Leartes*', sig. I1v). A coffin is laid into the trap, as into a 'grave', and two players then descend into

[1] A fuller discussion may be found in my article, 'The staging of the monument scenes in *Antony and Cleopatra*', *Library Chronicle*, XXX (1964).

the trap, the upper parts of their bodies apparently remaining within view of the audience; presumably they are standing upon the coffin which in turn rests upon the ground beneath the stage. If the trap were about 6 feet long, the coffin could have been laid into the trap without tilting; but if the trap were only about 4 feet long, the coffin would have had to be tilted as it entered the trap.

(3) *Macbeth*: '*1. Apparation, an Armed Head* [*rises*]. . . . *He descends*. . . . *2 Apparition, a Bloody Childe* [*rises*]. . . . *Descends*. . . . *3 Apparition, A Childe Crowned,* [*rises*] *with a Tree in his hand*. . . . *Descend*. . . . *Macb.* . . . Why sinkes that Caldron?' (sig. 2m6v). Three 'apparitions' successively rise and descend through the trap, as through the ground. The 'cauldron' of the dialogue may be fictional colouring. Or, if the cauldron is staged, there are two possibilities. The cauldron may have a false bottom and itself rise and descend through the trap, the apparitions in turn rising and descending through the cauldron held in the open trap. Or the cauldron may rise and descend through a second trap.

(4) *The Devil's Charter*: three examples.

(a) '*To whome* [*Roderigo*] *from an other place* [*comes*] *a Moncke with a magical booke and rod, in private whispering with Roderick, whome the Monke draweth to a chaire on midst of the Stage which hee circleth, and before it an other Circle, into which* . . . *appeare exhalations of lightning and sulphurous smoke in midst whereof* [*rises*] *a divill in most ugly shape* . . . *hee beeing conjured downe after more thunder and fire, ascends another divill.* . . . *Hee discendeth: after more thunder and fearefull fire, ascend* [*the same devil*] . . . *a divill him ensuing* . . . *the divills discend*' (sig. A2v). Two or three 'devils' successively rise and descend through the trap, as through the ground. The trap appears to be just forward of the 'midst of the stage'.

(b) '*Caesar and Frescobaldi stab him* [*Candy*]. . . . *Caes.* . . . Helpe Frescobaldi let us heave him over, That he may fall into the river Tiber, Come to the bridge with him. . . . Stretch thee, stret[c]h out thine armes feare that he Fall not upon the arches. . . . The divell goe with you both for company. *Caesar casteth Frescobaldi after*' (sig. F4). Two players are successively dropped or thrown into the trap, as over the edge of a bridge into the river.

(c) '*Fiery exhalations lightning thunder ascend a King* . . . *riding upon a Lyon, or dragon.* . . . *The divell* [= *the King*] *descendeth with thunder and ligh*[*t*]*ning and after more exhalations ascends another all in armor.* . . . *Devill descendeth with thunder, etc.*' (sigs. G1v–2). Two players, one mounted upon a property beast, successively rise and descend through the trap, as through the ground.

A single trap is required, in one instance described as just forward of the 'midst of the stage'. (In one play there is inconclusive evidence suggestive of a second trap.) The trap is variously referred to as the ground, a 'vault', a 'grave' and a 'river'. And it must be large enough for a coffin to be laid in it. A trap 4 feet square would suffice if the coffin were tipped as it is lowered into the trap; otherwise, a width of 4 feet and a length of some 6 feet would be necessary.

In two plays the understage area is employed without a use of the trap.

(1) *Hamlet* : '*Ghost cries under the Stage*' (Q2, sig. D4v).
(2) *Antony and Cleopatra* : '*Musicke of the Hoboyes is under the Stage*' (sig. 2y4).

We may conclude that the staging requirements of the Globe plays in some instances confirm, in others at least do not deny, the proposed reconstruction of the Globe stage and tiring-house. The demands for doors in the plays would generally have been satisfied by the two doors of the tiring-house. (It is possible that there were three tiring-house doors at the First Globe, but the evidence, while suggestive, is not conclusive.) Discoveries could have been accommodated within one of the tiring-house doorways, which would have provided a discovery-space 7 feet 6 inches wide and some 2 or 3 feet deep if we suppose that curtains or hangings had been fitted up within or in front of the doorways, the leaves of each of the doors having first been opened out upon the stage through an arc of 180° and permitted to lie flat against the tiring-house façade. (In this case the discovery-space would have been, as implied in some of the plays, 'off' stage.) Action above could have been accommodated at the front of one of the boxes of the tiring-house gallery over the stage, which would have provided an upper station about 6 feet wide and some 2 or 3 feet deep. (If desirable, two or more boxes could have been used simultaneously as upper stations.) The stairs used in descents from upper station to stage were evidently, since out of sight of the audience, within the tiring-house. Curtains would not have been needed in the upper station. Music 'within' could have been performed within the tiring-house at stage level, although any of the boxes of the gallery over the stage would have had the potential of being curtained off and used as an upper-storey music room (as apparently at the Swan in 1613). Hoisting or flying effects would have been accommodated by suspension gear descending from the stage cover and the hut over the stage cover. (It should be noted that the suspension line would have passed within 3 or 4 feet of the tiring-house façade, so that an ascending player, as called for in *Antony and Cleopatra*, would have been within easy reach of players standing at the front of one of the boxes of the gallery over the stage.) The occasional demand of the plays for 'posts' would have been satisfied by the two posts supporting the stage cover. And trapwork called for in the plays would have been accommodated by the single trap door set in the middle of the stage.

4 The Second Blackfriars playhouse (1596)

The Second Blackfriars playhouse was constructed by James Burbage in 1596 in a hall of the building known as the Upper Frater of the dissolved Dominican Priory of London. The Upper Frater was situated about 100 yards to the north of Blackfriars Stairs on the north bank of the Thames and just to the east of Fleet Ditch and Water Lane (modern Blackfriars Lane). At its northern end the Upper Frater was joined to a building known as the Old Buttery which had contained the First Blackfriars playhouse during the period 1576–84. And the Old Buttery was in turn joined at its northern end to a building known as the Porter's Lodge. The relationship of the three buildings to one another and to some other buildings of the Blackfriars complex is illustrated in Figure 41. The Blackfriars church was apparently torn down sometime during the middle years of the sixteenth century.

Early in the twentieth century numerous verbal records of the two playhouses and their containing buildings were brought to light by C. W. Wallace and Albert Feuillerat.[1] These are extremely useful but pose a difficulty in that, relating for the most part to legal agreements or lawsuits, they are

---

[1] Wallace, *The Children of the Chapel at Blackfriars* (1908); Feuillerat, *Blackfriars Records*, in *Malone Society Collections*, II (1) (1913). Quotations from primary sources are generally taken from Feuillerat.

concerned chiefly with delimiting the boundaries of ownership or rental. Thus the verbal records tell us a great deal about horizontal dimensions, something about both horizontal and vertical relationships of individual buildings or parts of buildings to one another, but very little about design and nothing about vertical dimensions. Fortunately, there are two other sources of information. One, providing information on design, consists of the pictorial evidence afforded by various of Wenzel Hollar's topographical views of London. The other, providing information both on design and on vertical measurements, consists of architectural tradition. In the present chapter I shall discuss problems posed by the evidence for various of the Blackfriars buildings connected with the two playhouses, propose a reconstruction of the Second Blackfriars closely based on a reconstruction of 1968,[1] and test the proposed reconstruction of stage and tiring-house by reference to the staging of the twenty extant plays that may be assigned to the Second Blackfriars during the period from 1600 to 1608.

(i)

Pictorial evidence for the Second Blackfriars was first identified in 1968, when C. Walter Hodges suggested[2] that the playhouse is depicted as the long building with a gabled roof lying just to the left of Baynard's Castle in Hollar's Long Bird's-Eye View of London (1647; see Plate 12b). The identification is verified by (among other considerations) the fact that St Bride's church, shown directly above the southern end of the building in question in Hollar's engraving, lines up on a modern ordnance survey map with the known site of the Upper Frater and the church of St Mary Overy's (modern Southwark cathedral), the tower of which Hollar presumably used as his point of view. It may be pointed out further that the playhouse building is shown also in a number of Hollar's topographical views connected with the Long View: the pen-and-pencil sketch for that view entitled The West Part of Southwark towards Westminster (c. 1640, see Plate 12a) and two engravings derivative from the Long View – the Parallel Prospects of London before and after the Great Fire (1666) and the Prospect of London in the Fire Time (1669).[3] In the three engravings we are shown the eastern side of the Upper

---

[1] Richard Hosley, 'A reconstruction of the Second Blackfriars', in David Galloway (ed.), *The Elizabethan Theatre I*; a paper presented at the (first) International Conference on Elizabethan Theatre at the University of Waterloo (Ontario), July 1968.

[2] *The Globe Restored*, revised ed., p. 109.

[3] Reproductions in Arthur M. Hind, *Wenceslaus Hollar and His Views of London* (1922), Plates XXVI and XII.

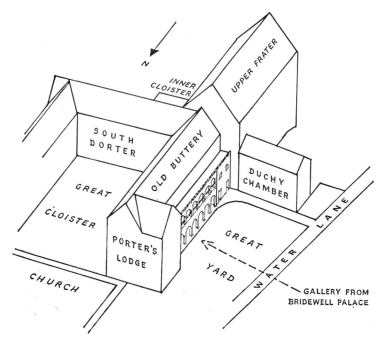

Figure 41 The Blackfriars complex of buildings

Frater, the Old Buttery and the Porter's Lodge; in the sketch, the eastern
side of the Upper Frater only. In 1971 Hodges further suggested (privately)
that the Upper Frater is depicted in Hollar's View of London from the Top
of Arundel House (Hind, Plate XLVIII) – an identification which is confirmed
by the fact that the church of St Andrew's-by-the-Wardrobe, depicted immediately above the building in question, lines up on the map with the site
of the Upper Frater and the site of Arundel House, Hollar's point of view
for the etching. Hodges suggests also that the Upper Frater is represented
in Hollar's View of London by Milford Stairs (Hind, loc. cit.) and in his
preliminary sketch for that etching (Plate X). In this second set of illustrations we are shown the western side of the Upper Frater only.

   The pictorial evidence provides us with two significant pieces of information about the Upper Frater. The first is that the roof of that building was
gabled, as cogently argued by Irwin Smith, and not flat, as supposed by
Wallace and Chambers on the evidence of the roof's being covered with
lead.[1] (Flat roofs were covered with lead, but not all lead roofs were flat.)

[1] Smith, *Shakespeare's Blackfriars Playhouse* (1964), pp. 104–5; Wallace, op. cit., p. 37;
  Chambers, *ES*, II, 489.

The fact of a gabled roof (recorded in all the pictorial sources) is significant. since it enables us to explain (as Chambers, assuming a flat roof, could not satisfactorily do) the verbal record of rooms over the hall[1] by the assumption that a ceiling was inserted over the Parliament Chamber (probably at the time this was partitioned into apartments around the middle of the sixteenth century), an attic thus being created over a hall which had hitherto been open to the rafters.

The other piece of information is that the roof of the Upper Frater probably had dormer windows in it. That it did (at least on the western side) is suggested by the representation of that building in Hollar's View of London from the Top of Arundel House and also in his sketch for a View of London by Milford Stairs. The proposition is confirmed by the record of rooms over the hall, since such rooms would have been denied light from the main windows of the hall below by the floor which created the attic and thus made the rooms possible. Hence most of the rooms not lying at either end of the attic would have had to be lighted by dormer windows. (Rooms lying at either end of the attic would, of course, have been lighted by gable windows.) The proposition is apparently denied, however, by Hollar's representation of the Upper Frater in the Long Bird's-Eye View of London and derivative views, which fail (at least on the eastern side) to record dormers. The discrepancy between the two pictorial traditions can be resolved in various ways.

We can suppose that the tradition represented by the Long View is correct whereas that represented by the Arundel House view is erroneous. This explanation requires the assumption that Hollar, through some aberration, attributed non-existent dormer windows to the Upper Frater in two engravings made while he was resident in London and in fact living at Arundel House in the general area depicted. The explanation seems dubious, and it is further weakened by the apparent representation of dormer windows in the preliminary sketch, presumably done on the spot, for the View of London by Milford Stairs (Hind, Plate X). Or we can suppose, alternatively, that the Arundel House tradition is correct and the Long View tradition erroneous. This explanation requires the assumption that Hollar simply forgot the dormer windows in the Upper Frater roof when he etched the Long View in Antwerp in 1647 – and that he might have done so is made understandable by his evident reliance upon the preliminary sketch of the West Part of Southwark, which omits dormer windows from its rudimentary

[1] 'All that great Hall or Rome wth the roomes over the same' (Wallace, op. cit., p. 41, n 8).

representation of the Upper Frater. The explanation seems defensible, since Hollar was not above making minor factual errors. There is, however, a third possibility. We can suppose that both traditions are correct, there having been dormer windows in the western slope of the Upper Frater roof (as in the Arundel House tradition) but none in the eastern (as in the Long View tradition). This explanation also seems defensible, since rooms on the eastern side of the attic would have been adequately (though poorly) lighted by dormers in the western roof if, as seems likely, the attic rooms did not have ceilings. It is difficult to choose between the second and third explanation. On balance, the third is perhaps preferable.

The pictorial evidence for the Second Blackfriars poses two additional, extremely difficult, problems. The first is that Hollar's depiction in the Long Bird's-Eye View of London implies that the Upper Frater and the Old Buttery were of the same width and height, whereas verbal records give their widths as differing some 16 feet or more, the heights of the two buildings presumably differing also, in accordance with their widths. The other problem is that Hollar's views of London before and after the Great Fire imply that the Upper Frater stood until 1666 when it was destroyed by the Fire, whereas a well-known verbal record states that the playhouse was 'pulled downe to the ground' in 1655.[1] Fortunately, the resolution of these two problems does not affect any of the data on which a reconstruction of the Second Blackfriars must be based.

(ii)

Verbal records afford us no vertical dimensions of the Upper Frater, and some of the horizontal dimensions that we do possess require rationalization. It therefore becomes desirable to cite an architectural analogue, and for this purpose I suggest a hall of comparable size belonging to the same general period, the Great Hall of Kenilworth Castle built by John of Gaunt in the 1390s.[2] This hall is 45 feet wide by 89 feet long (both dimensions internal measure), and the walls are 6 feet thick. The hall is constructed in six bays, and the vaulted understorey is 17 feet high from floor to floor. The walls are 32 feet high measuring from the floor of the hall, hence some 49 feet high measuring from ground level. Since the hall is in ruins, the design of the roof is not known.

[1] Bentley, *The Jacobean and Caroline Stage*, VI, 42.
[2] Longitudinal section and plan of the hall in Augustus Pugin, *Examples of Gothic Architecture*, II (1895 ed.), Plate III.

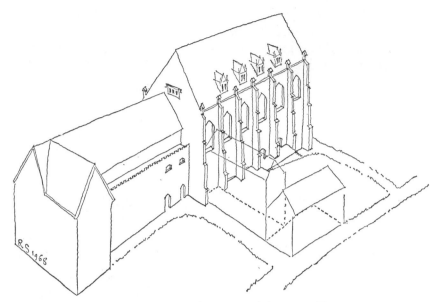

Figure 42 The Porter's Lodge, the Old Buttery and the Upper Frater

Two different records indicate that the Upper Frater was 110 feet long (presumably external measure) and 46 feet wide (presumably internal measure). How thick may we suppose the walls to have been? A thickness of 3 feet would be suggested if the width just given (46 feet) is a correct internal measurement and if another recorded width (52 feet) is a correct external measurement. Walls only 3 feet thick, however, do not seem practicable in a fourteenth-century building of such great height as the Upper Frater (see below). I have therefore assumed a wall thickness of 5 feet, which may be compared with the corresponding dimension of 5 feet in the Blackfriars Old Buttery or of 6 feet in the Great Hall of Kenilworth Castle. Thus, holding with the two dimensions given at the start of this paragraph, we may suppose the dimensions of the Upper Frater to have been 110 by 56 feet (external measure) or 100 by 46 feet (internal measure). Further, there is reason to believe that the Upper Frater, like the Great Hall at Kenilworth, was constructed in six bays. The understorey was probably vaulted, as at Kenilworth, although it might conceivably have been posted, as in the Great Hall of Hampton Court Palace. At Kenilworth the height of the understorey is 17 feet from floor to floor, at Hampton Court 15 feet. In part because the fall of the land towards the Thames had the effect of increasing the height of the Upper Frater at its southern end, I have conjectured the height of its

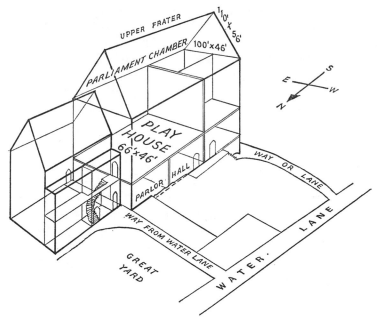

Figure 43 The Parliament Chamber, the playhouse, the understorey (Parlour and Lower Hall) and the Great Winding Stairs

understorey to be relatively low, namely 15 feet from floor to floor. And I have set the height of the walls, as at Kenilworth, at 32 feet above the hall floor. Thus if we assume (for simplicity of calculation) that the understorey floor was at ground level at the northern end of the building (though probably it was 3 or 4 feet below ground level), the walls of the Upper Frater, because of a drop in ground elevation that may be estimated as about 12 feet from northern to southern end of the building, would have had a height of some 59 feet above ground at the southern end (12 + 15 + 32 = 59). (Compare the wall height of 49 feet above ground at Kenilworth.) When one reflects that a gabled roof with a pitch of more than 45° (hence a height of more than 28 feet) must be added to this last dimension in order to arrive at the full height of the building at its southern end (over 87 feet), it becomes clear that the Upper Frater (even though the suggested full height above ground is probably too great by 3 or 4 feet) was a very large building indeed (Figure 42). It seems improbable that such a large building, with a mean height of about 80 feet above ground and a roof-span of 46 feet, could have had walls, even though heavily buttressed, measuring only 3 feet in thickness.

Most of the Upper Frater was purchased by Burbage in February of 1596.

The purchase included the following major parts of the building (see Figure 43): (1) the whole of the upper or 'great hall' storey, called the Parliament Chamber, still divided at the time of the purchase into 'Seaven greate upper Romes'; (2) various rooms lying 'above' or 'over' the Parliament Chamber together with the roof 'over' the Parliament Chamber; (3) two large under-storey rooms called the Parlour and the (lower) Hall, both lying 'under' the northern two-thirds of the Parliament Chamber; (4) the 'Vaultes or Cellers' lying 'under' the Parlour and the Lower Hall; and (5) a staircase at the northern end of the Upper Frater leading from the Great Yard up to the Parliament Chamber – 'that great paire of wyndinge staires with the staire case thereunto belonginge'. Excluded from the purchase was a three-storey block lying under the southern third of the Parliament Chamber and consisting of a hospital or Firmary (on a level with the vaults or cellars to the north), a room 'above' the Firmary (on a level with the Parlour and Lower Hall to the north), and a room 'beneath' the Firmary (presumably an additional cellar made possible by the slope of the land to the south).[1]

Burbage proceeded immediately to convert his new property into a playhouse, as we know from a statement by his son Cuthbert and other Burbages in 1635: 'Now for the Blackfriers that is our inheritance, our father purchased it at extreame rates and made it into a play house with great charge and trouble.' The work of conversion was apparently completed by February of 1597, for in that month James Burbage died; probably it was completed by the autumn of 1596, for it seems likely that the Chamberlain's Men intended to begin using the Blackfriars during the winter season of 1596–7. However, Burbage was restrained from opening the playhouse by an order of the Privy Council in response to a petition of November 1596 by residents of the Blackfriars precinct who objected to having a 'comon playhouse' in their midst. Upon Burbage's death the property passed to his son Richard, who in 1600 leased the playhouse to Henry Evans for use by the Children of the Queen's Chapel, 'under the name of a private house'. After several years of use, first by the Chapel Boys and then (beginning in 1604) by the Children of the Queen's Revels, the playhouse, on surrender of the lease in 1608, was returned to Richard Burbage. Thereupon the King's Men proceeded to operate the playhouse, beginning probably in the winter season of 1609–10 (since a recurrence of the plague would have prevented them from playing in London during the winter of 1608–9) and continuing, during successive winters, until the closing of all playhouses by act of parliament in 1642.

Authorities have disagreed on whether the Second Blackfriars occupied

[1] The word 'Firmary', of course, is here being used in the sense of 'infirmary'.

the upper storey of the Upper Frater (the Parliament Chamber), the under-storey (the Parlour and the Lower Hall), or both (Figure 43). In 1917 Joseph Quincy Adams suggested that space for the playhouse was provided by removing partitions in the understorey.[1] This theory is untenable, however, since only about 13 feet of headroom (at the most) would have been available beneath the ceiling of the understorey. In 1908 Wallace had suggested that space for the playhouse was provided by removing partitions from both storeys and the floor between them (p. 40). This theory is likewise untenable, since the walls of the building would have been excessively weakened as a result of removing their principal internal brace – the floor of the upper storey and its supporting posts. There is now no doubt that, as J. H. Farrar suggested in the reconstruction published by G. Topham Forrest in 1921,[2] space for the playhouse was provided by removing partitions dividing the Parliament Chamber. The theory was accepted by Chambers in 1923: 'a chamber which had held parliaments and a legatine trial [that of Queen Katherine in 1529] could amply suffice to hold a theatre' (II, 513). And the theory was accepted by Irwin Smith in 1964. Thus we may suppose that in 1596 James Burbage merely restored the room (up to two-thirds of its length) which had served originally as the Great Hall of the Dominican Friars of London and, from the fourteenth century onward, as an occasional meeting place for parliament.

(iii)

It is convenient to begin the reconstruction of the playhouse proper with discussion of the Great Winding Stairs at the northern end of the Upper Frater. A reconstruction of the stairs must conform to numerous considerations: (1) at their lower end the stairs led to the Great Yard lying immediately to the west of the Old Buttery and to the north of the Duchy Chamber (see Figure 43); (2) at their upper end the stairs led to the Parliament Chamber; (3) within the staircase at the upper end of the stairs was a 'hall place' which apparently served as a landing; (4) since the stairs are described as 'winding', they must have made a turn of at least 90° in the one-storey flight from the Great Yard to the level of the Parliament Chamber; (5) the stairs are de-scribed also as 'great', but this adjective may be taken as meaning 'principal' (*OED* 6.f) rather than 'large': I assume that the principal stairs leading to a hall as large as the Parliament Chamber would have been wide enough to

[1] 'The conventual buildings of Blackfriars, London, and the playhouses constructed therein', *Studies in Philology*, XIV (1917), 86.
[2] 'Blackfriars theatre: conjectural reconstruction', *The Times*, 21 November 1921.

permit the passage of at least two persons abreast – that is, at least 4 feet wide; (6) the stairs leading up to the Parliament Chamber would have had to clear the ground-level passage lying between the Upper Frater and the Old Buttery which afforded east–west communication between the Great Yard and the Great Cloister (Figure 43); (7) the stairs would not have blocked the gallery running along the western side of the Old Buttery (Figure 43), since presumably a major purpose of that gallery was to afford north–south communication at an upper-storey level (without passing through the Old Buttery) between the Parliament Chamber and both the Porter's Lodge (where the Emperor Charles V was housed during his visit to England of 1522) and that other gallery, constructed for the comfort of the emperor's retinue, which at one time ran in an east–west direction across the Fleet between Bridewell Palace (where the Spanish train was quartered in 1522) and the Old Buttery (Figure 41); and (8) the stairs would probably not have encroached upon the basic structure of the walls of the Old Buttery, for the reasons that the stairs were presumably built to serve the Parliament Chamber in the Upper Frater and that the Upper Frater was presumably constructed at a later date than the Old Buttery. I am assuming that, of the two halls, the one which adjoined the priory church was constructed at the earlier date.

In accordance with these several considerations I suggest that the Great Winding Stairs were located a short distance to the north of the Upper Frater and fully contained within the gallery structure running along the western side of the Old Buttery (Figure 43). Thus the stairs would not have encroached upon the walls of the Old Buttery, they would have cleared the ground-level passage between the Great Yard and the Great Cloister, they would not have obstructed a presumptive upper-storey passageway between the Parliament Chamber and the Old Buttery gallery and there would have been a landing at the top of the stairs that could be described as a 'hall place'. One entered the staircase from the Great Yard, turned 90° to the right in rising one flight of steps to the hall place, and thus arrived at the entry to the Parliament Chamber.

The playhouse proper was constructed within a 'great Hall or Rome' (*magne Aule vel loci*) apparently created by Burbage's removal of partitions from the northern two-thirds of the Parliament Chamber. The hall measured 46 feet from east to west and 66 feet from north to south (both dimensions presumably internal measure). It contained a 'stage' (*Theatro*), and this, since its eastern end is mentioned (*orientalem finem*), apparently ran from east to west. There were 'galleries' (*porticibus*), the floor of the hall was paved, the entrance was at the northern end of the hall and there were 'rooms' (*locis*) 'over' (*supra*) the hall. Thus we know of the existence of a stage, galleries and rooms over the hall; and to these elements may be added boxes and a pit on the authority of contemporary references such as that by Leonard Digges, in the Shakespeare Second Folio (1632), to the 'cockpit, galleries, boxes' of the Blackfriars. Finally, we may suppose the existence of a tiring-house.

A number of assumptions must be made about the Blackfriars tiring-house. I assume (1) that the tiring-house was inside the hall (Figure 44). (By the term 'hall' is meant that part of the Parliament Chamber, measuring 46 feet in width by 66 feet in length, which had been cleared of partitions and contained the playhouse proper.) Location of the tiring-house inside the hall would have made possible the construction of a given number of stage entrances having the requisite shape, height and width; and it would have provided a gallery over the stage in which musicians, players and spectators could be stationed. Both advantages would have been sacrificed if the tiring-house had been located outside the hall, with access to the stage by way of doors cut in one of the end walls of the hall. I assume also (2) that the Blackfriars tiring-house was not adapted from an existing hall screen, since the original screen of the Parliament Chamber (if there was one) could hardly have survived the compartmentation of that room some time during the middle of the sixteenth century. Thus the Blackfriars tiring-house was built 'new' by James Burbage in 1596, on the expectation of immediate use by the Lord Chamberlain's Men. I assume also (3) that the Blackfriars tiring-house was designed after the hall screen or after a tiring-house itself modelled on the hall screen. Burbage appears to have used the hall screen as a model when he built the tiring-house of the Theatre in 1576, for otherwise it is difficult to account for the striking resemblance between the Swan tiring-house, built in 1595, and the hall screen in general – unless we are to suppose that the Swan tiring-house was influenced not by the architectural tradition of antecedent public playhouses (the Theatre, the Curtain, the Rose) but directly by the hall screen. It should be emphasized that this assumption does not depend on the interesting coincidence that the Blackfriars tiring-house was built by the very man who twenty years earlier had built the Theatre tiring-house. Anyone designing a tiring-house in 1596 would, I believe, have taken as his model either the hall screen or a tiring-house based on the hall screen. Francis Langley had done one or the other only the year before when he built the Swan. And I assume (4) that the Blackfriars tiring-house, which ran across the hall (since the stage ran from east to west), was located at the south end of the hall. Thus the tiring-house would have been opposite the principal entrance to the Parliament Chamber – that entrance being framed in the northern wall of the Upper Frater and giving access to the Great Winding Stairs which led down to the Great Yard and Water Lane (Figure 43).

In seeking to arrive at defensible dimensions for the Blackfriars tiring-house we are aided by the analogue of the Fortune tiring-house, which is relevant not only because its dimensions are known or inferable but also because its ground plan was (like the Blackfriars tiring-house but unlike the tiring-house of a 'round' public playhouse) in the shape of a rectangle. For present purposes we may estimate the internal dimensions of the Fortune tiring-house as 11 feet deep (12 feet 6 inches, the width of the playhouse frame as given in the builder's contract, less 1 foot 6 inches for the thickness of two walls) and 41 feet 6 inches long (43 feet, the length of the stage as given in the contract, less 1 foot 6 inches for the thickness of two walls). The internal dimensions 11 feet by 41 feet 6 inches provide a practicable area of 457 square feet. For the Blackfriars tiring-house we may assume a depth substantially the same as at the Fortune, 11 feet 3 inches in the clear (12 feet external measure, less 9 inches for the thickness of the front wall), and a length somewhat greater than at the Fortune, 46 feet (the full width of the hall). The internal dimensions 11 feet 3 inches by 46 feet give the Blackfriars tiring-house a practicable area of 518 square feet, or some 60 square feet greater than that of the Fortune tiring-house. With these dimensions may be compared those of screens passages presumably used as tiring-houses in large halls such as those of the Middle Temple (9 feet by 40 feet, or 360 square feet), the Great Hall of Hampton Court Palace (11 feet 6 inches by 40 feet, or 460 square feet) and the Great Hall of Whitehall Palace (10 feet by 39 feet 6 inches, or 395 square feet).

The height of the Blackfriars stage may be set at 4 feet 6 inches on the analogy of the stage at the Cockpit-in-Court (1630), which was 4 feet 6 inches high, or of the stage in the Great Hall at Whitehall in 1635, which, although raked to a height of 5 feet 6 inches towards the rear, was 4 feet 6 inches high at the front. A single trap door may be assumed, set in the middle of the stage.

Before discussing the horizontal dimensions of the Blackfriars stage, we may return to the tiring-house for consideration of its vertical dimensions. The height of the tiring-house floor above the hall floor is determined by the height of the stage: 4 feet 6 inches. The height of the first and second storeys of the tiring-house may be taken as 12 and 11 feet respectively (floor to floor), on the analogy of the heights of the first and second storeys of the playhouse frame specified in the Fortune Contract. Thus the second-storey floor of the tiring-house would have been 16 feet 6 inches above the hall floor, and the top of the second storey 27 feet 6 inches above the hall floor – reaching to a level 4 feet 6 inches below the ceiling of the hall if we assume this to have been 32 feet above the floor (Figure 50 and Figure 51, right-hand side).

The Blackfriars tiring-house, if designed on the analogy of a hall screen or of a tiring-house itself so designed, would have been constructed in five bays, each about 9 feet wide, the bays being defined by six principal posts set at intervals across the hall at a distance of 12 feet from its end wall. Since the first and fifth bays of the five-bay structure were presumably joined to the ends of the gallery structure running along the sides of the stage, the façade proper of the tiring-house would have consisted of the three middle (that is, the second, third and fourth) bays of the tiring-house structure (Figure 46). Such a three-bay tiring-house façade could have been fitted out with two doors (comparable to those of the normal hall screen and of the tiring-house depicted in the Swan Drawing) by use of the first and third bays of the façade as doorways to the stage (Figure 48), or it could have been fitted out with three doors (comparable to those of the hall screen at the Charterhouse, London, see Plate 18b) by use of all three bays of the façade as stage doorways (Figure 49). In the reconstruction here proposed I have arbitrarily preferred a theory of three doors (Figure 51). The second storey of the Blackfriars tiring-house would presumably have been compartmented into three boxes occupying the three bays of the tiring-house façade (the middle three bays of the five-bay tiring-house structure). For reasons of design it seems likely that the opening of each of the tiring-house boxes over the stage would have been subdivided into two windows, the subdivision resulting in a row of six windows over the stage.

Horizontal dimensions of the Blackfriars stage are more difficult to arrive at. One thing at least is certain: a stage the size of the Fortune stage (43 feet wide by 27 feet 6 inches deep) would have been much too large for accommodation within the Blackfriars hall (46 feet wide by 66 feet long). How large then may we suppose the Blackfriars stage to have been? Much depends, of course, on whether the stage extended the full width of the hall or not. Let us consider first an example of the case in which the stage does not extend the full width of the hall. Such a stage would have had floor-level audience areas on either side of it, and these areas would have had to be sufficiently deep to contain a significant number of spectators – 7 feet perhaps, or 8 feet, or perhaps even 9 feet. If, anticipating the ultimate addition of 8-foot 6-inch-deep galleries to our reconstruction, we suppose a space 8 feet

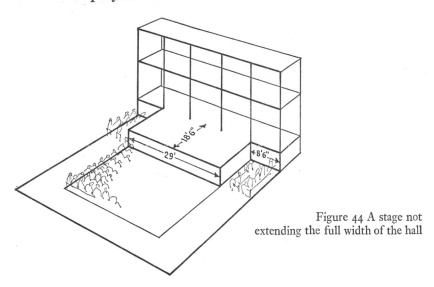

Figure 44 A stage not
extending the full width of the hall

6 inches deep on either side of the stage, the width of our stage becomes 29
feet. The depth of this stage, if we preserve the general ratio of width to
depth of the Fortune stage (about 8:5), becomes 18 feet 6 inches. Figure 44
shows a stage 29 feet wide by 18 feet 6 inches deep, set up against a tiring-
house 12 feet deep (thickness of tiring-house wall included); the area of
such a stage is 537 square feet. This is admittedly a small stage in comparison
with the Fortune stage (1,183 square feet), but it is fairly large in comparison
with twentieth-century stages. (The questioning reader without access to a
stage of comparable size is invited to compare – by performing the experiment of standing in it – a room of about the same dimensions.) In any case,
the suggested stage area of 537 square feet compares favourably with the
area of the Cockpit-in-Court stage (about 427 square feet) and with that of
the scenic stage in the Great Hall at Whitehall in 1635 (about 585 square
feet, excluding space to the sides of the wings and behind the backshutters).

It should be observed that the stage shown in Figure 44 is rather like that
recorded in the well-known *Wits* Frontispiece of 1662, in which spectators
are shown sitting around three sides of a stage set up against a tiring-house
or hall screen that runs the full width of the playhouse or hall.[1] Such an
arrangement might well have been satisfactory in a hall without galleries,
but the addition of galleries to the situation depicted in Figure 44 would
presumably have encouraged extending the stage to the full width of the

[1] A reconstruction of the playhouse depicted in the *Wits* Frontispiece is proposed in my
'Three Renaissance English indoor playhouses', *English Literary Renaissance*, III (1973).

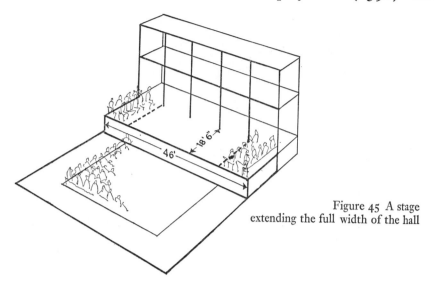

Figure 45 A stage
extending the full width of the hall

hall. Figure 45 shows this second case, in which the depth of stage has been kept at 18 feet 6 inches but the width of stage increased to 46 feet. In effect what has happened in Figure 45 is that the floor-level audience areas at the sides of the stage (as in Figure 44 and the *Wits* Frontispiece) have been raised to stage level and converted into side-stage audience areas which leave the middle 29 feet of the stage clear for production. (Thus we shall be able to account for the many references to the custom of spectators sitting on the stage at the Blackfriars.) I am not suggesting that any such development actually took place at the Second Blackfriars, although something very much like it probably occurred in other halls used as playhouses during the sixteenth century. Figure 44 is designed merely to illustrate, in a hall not yet fitted up with galleries, a stage of defensible proportions with sufficient floor space at the sides to accommodate a significant number of spectators. Such a stage might have been used for the production of an interlude during the 1550s and evidently was used, as the *Wits* Frontispiece informs us, for the production of 'drolls' during the 1650s. Figure 45, on the other hand, suggests diagrammatically what I believe the Blackfriars stage and tiring-house might actually have looked like, during construction, if the stage and tiring-house were built first and construction had not yet proceeded to the point of adding galleries to the hall.

A depth for the Blackfriars galleries can be conjectured on the basis of the analogue available in Inigo Jones's plan of the scenic stage in the Great

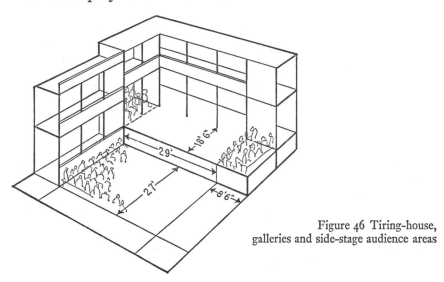

Figure 46 Tiring-house,
galleries and side-stage audience areas

Hall at Whitehall in 1635.¹ The plan calls for galleries with a depth of 8 feet in a hall 39 feet 6 inches wide. Since slightly deeper galleries seem appropriate in a hall 46 feet wide, I have adopted a gallery depth of 8 feet 6 inches in the present reconstruction (Figure 46). Probable heights of the Blackfriars galleries are suggested by the Fortune Contract, which requires 12 feet for the first gallery of that playhouse, 11 feet for the second and 9 feet for the third (all dimensions presumably from floor to floor). Allowing, then, 1 foot 6 inches for the height of ground-sill, floor joists and floor of the first gallery, we may suppose the Blackfriars first-gallery floor to have been at an elevation of 1 foot 6 inches above the hall floor, the second-storey gallery floor at an elevation of 13 feet 6 inches above the hall floor, and the floor of a possible third gallery at an elevation of 24 feet 6 inches above the hall floor (Figure 51, left-hand side). Such a third gallery ('open', since it would not, as in a public playhouse, have needed to support a roof) would therefore have had head-room of 7 feet 6 inches beneath the ceiling of the hall if this was 32 feet above the floor.

It should be noted that the 3-foot differential between the first-gallery floor and the first-storey floor of the tiring-house (caused by the same differential between the first-gallery floor and the height of the stage) is repeated in a 3-foot differential between the second-gallery floor and the

¹ British Museum Lansdowne MS. 1171; reproduction in Richard Southern, *Changeable Scenery* (1952), Plate 4.

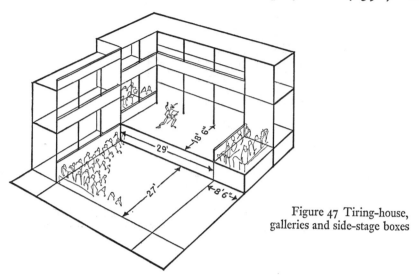

Figure 47 Tiring-house,
galleries and side-stage boxes

second-storey floor of the tiring-house (Figure 50). Architecturally convenient though it undoubtedly would have been to set the corresponding floors
of the galleries and the tiring-house at the same height, the first-gallery floor
and the first-storey floor of the tiring-house clearly could not have been so
set unless we suppose that the first-gallery floor was at a height of 4 feet 6
inches above the hall floor; and if it were, and the two lower galleries were
12 feet and 11 feet high respectively and the walls of the hall 32 feet high,
the headroom on the top gallery would have been reduced to 4 feet 6 inches
beneath the ceiling. This dimension is of course insufficient. Further, if the
first-gallery floor and the first-storey floor of the tiring-house were not set
at the same height, it seems unlikely that the second-gallery floor and the
second-storey floor of the tiring-house would have been so set, for the latter
desideratum could have been accomplished only by departing substantially
from the 12-foot height of the first gallery or from the 12-foot height of the
tiring-house first storey or from both – for example, by increasing the height
of the first gallery from 12 to 15 feet, or by reducing the height of the tiring-
house first storey from 12 to 9 feet, or by simultaneously increasing the
height of the first gallery to (say) 13 feet 6 inches, while reducing that of the
tiring-house first storey to 10 feet 6 inches. From an architectural point of
view the first two propositions seem improbable, the third unlikely.

   The pit in our reconstruction of the Second Blackfriars takes its dimensions from the dimensions of the containing hall and its several elements –
tiring-house, stage and galleries (Figure 46). Thus the pit is 29 feet wide

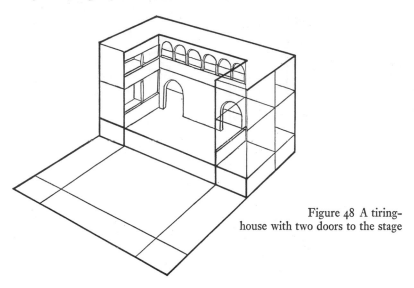

Figure 48 A tiring-
house with two doors to the stage

(46 feet for the width of the hall, less 17 feet for the depth of the two side-galleries) and 27 feet deep (66 feet for the length of the hall, less the sum of 12 feet for the depth of the tiring-house, 18 feet 6 inches for the depth of the stage, and 8 feet 6 inches for the depth of the gallery opposite the stage).

An important question about the second gallery (and, of course, the gallery above it) is whether its 'arms' terminated at the edge of the stage (thus forming a rectangular U in plan, like the galleries in the Great Hall at Whitehall in 1635) or whether they continued (in the form of upper side-boxes) across the stage to butt up against the first and fifth bays of the tiring-house gallery over the stage (thus, as it were, elongating the U and converting it into a closed rectangle). The latter arrangement seems the more likely, partly because it would have provided upper side-boxes for audience where otherwise there would have been only empty air, unproductive of revenue, and partly because it would have strengthened the whole structure of the playhouse by permitting the tiring-house and each arm of the galleries to brace one another reciprocally through the medium of the upper side-boxes. (Thus longitudinal stresses on the gallery structures would have been transmitted to the walls at either end of the Upper Frater). Accordingly, the side-stage audience areas lying between tiring-house and galleries would have been partly enclosed through being roofed over (Figure 46), and this being the case it would have been possible more fully to enclose them by inserting

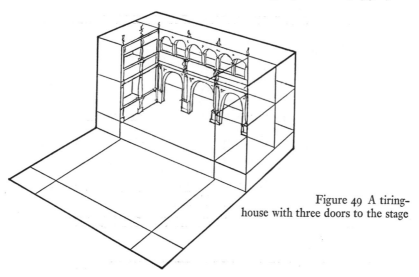

Figure 49 A tiring-
house with three doors to the stage

railings or barriers between them and the stage proper (access to the side-
stage areas presumably being by way of pass doors in the fronts of the first
and fifth bays of the tiring-house). Thus the side-stage audience areas would
have been transformed into side-stage boxes or gentlemen's rooms (Figure
47), and we should have an explanation of the evidence cited by Herbert
Berry to the effect that a spectator standing on the stage at the Blackfriars
in 1632 could hinder the view of a lady sitting in a stage box.[1]

Two theories are possible. The first is that spectators sat at the sides of a
Blackfriars stage running the full width of the hall from the time the playhouse opened in 1600. The reference in the Induction to Marston's *Malcontent* firmly dates the custom as early as 1604. Another reference, by Francis
Lenton in *The Young Gallant's Whirligig*, suggests that the custom was still
observed in 1629. At some time after that date but before 1632, however,
we may suppose that both players and stage-sitting spectators were more
conveniently accommodated by the conversion into stage boxes of the side-
stage audience areas directly beneath the upper side-boxes. Even so, a
spectator might still occasionally stand at the side of the stage, in front of
one of the stage boxes. The other theory is that there were side-stage boxes
at the Blackfriars from the date of its opening in 1600, it being supposed
either that spectators were permitted to sit upon the stage in front of the

[1] 'The stage and boxes at Blackfriars', *Studies in Philology*, LXIII (1966).

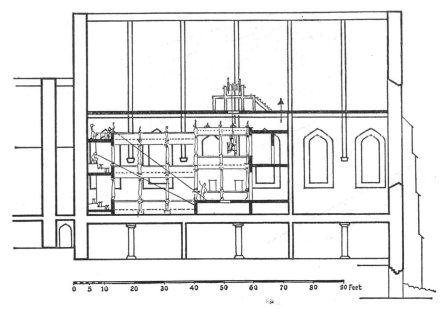

Figure 50 A longitudinal section of the Upper Frater

side-stage boxes or that the custom of sitting in such boxes was itself referred to as sitting upon the stage – since structurally the floors of the boxes
would have been only extensions of the stage.

We come finally to the problem of suspension gear for flying effects. To
be most effective, suspension gear requires a station directly over the stage,
and at the Blackfriars the requirement is met by the record of 'roomes' over
the 'great Hall or Rome'. We need only suppose that, some time during the
sixteenth century, a ceiling was inserted over the Parliament Chamber at
the level of the tops of the side walls of the Upper Frater (these walls
extending presumably some 32 feet above the floor of the hall). The purpose
of such a ceiling (supported by the side walls of the building and the roof
truss) would have been twofold: to make private and more comfortable the
large rooms or 'apartments' into which the Parliament Chamber was divided
around the middle of the sixteenth century, and to provide additional living
and storage space above them. The theory is illustrated in Figures 50 and
51, which show the winch for controlling the suspension line and the
necessary trap door cut in the ceiling, but do not attempt to show either the
precise means of access to the attic from the tiring-house or the partitions
that divided the Blackfriars attic into rooms.

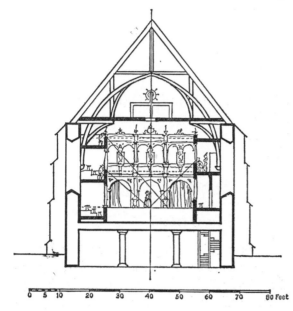

Figure 51 A transverse
section of the Upper Frater
showing (at left) galleries
and (at right) side-stage
boxes

In Figure 52 Richard Southern has given an impression of the Second
Blackfriars, as here reconstructed, during a performance.[1]

(iv)

Twenty plays may be supposed to have been designed for original performance at the Second Blackfriars during the period 1600–8, by either the Children of the Queen's Chapel (1600–3) or the Children of the Queen's Revels
(1604–8):

1 Jonson, *Cynthia's Revels*, Q(1601); F (1616)
2 Jonson, *Poetaster*, Q(1602); F (1616)
3 Chapman, *Sir Giles Goosecap*, Q(1606)
4 Chapman, *The Gentleman Usher*, Q(1606)
5 Marston, *The Dutch Courtesan*, Q(1605)
6 Chapman, *The Widow's Tears*, Q(1612)
7 Day, *Law Tricks*, Q(1608)

[1] The proposed reconstruction of the Second Blackfriars may be compared with the unidentified early seventeenth-century private playhouse for which a set of four drawings
in the hand of Inigo Jones survives in the library of Worcester College, Oxford; see
D. F. Rowan, 'A neglected Jones/Webb theatre project', *New Theatre Magazine*, IX
(1969); reproductions also in *Shakespeare Survey 23* (1970).

8 Marston, *The Malcontent*, Q1 (1604)
9 Chapman, *Monsieur D'Olive*, Q (1606)
10 Daniel, *Philotas*, Q (1605)
11 Chapman, *All Fools*, Q (1605)
12 Marston, *The Fawn*, Q (1606)
13 Chapman, Jonson and Marston, *Eastward Ho*, Q (1605)
14 Sharpham, *The Fleer*, Q (1607)
15 Day, *The Isle of Gulls*, Q (1606)
16 Marston, *Sophonisba*, Q (1606)
17 Beaumont, *The Knight of the Burning Pestle*, Q (1613)
18 Middleton, *Your Five Gallants*, Q (n.d., SR 1608)
19 Chapman, *1 Charles Duke of Byron*, Q (1608)
20 Chapman, *2 Charles Duke of Byron*, Q (1608)

Seven of the twenty Blackfriars plays refer in stage directions to two doors: *Sir Giles Goosecap*, *The Dutch Courtesan*, *The Malcontent*, *The Fleer*, *Sophonisba*, *Your Five Gallants* and *1 Charles Duke of Byron*. And an eighth play, *Eastward Ho*, refers to three doors: '*Enter Maister Touch-stone, and Quicksilver at severall dores ... At the middle dore, Enter Golding discovering a Gold-smiths shoppe, and walking short turns before it*' (sig. A2). This evidence suggests that the Blackfriars tiring-house had three doors.

Fourteen of the twenty Blackfriars plays do not require a discovery: *Cynthia's Revels*, *Poetaster*, *The Gentleman Usher*, *The Dutch Courtesan*, *The Malcontent*, *Monsieur D'Olive*, *Philotas*, *All Fools*, *The Fawn*, *The Isle of Gulls*, *Sophonisba*, *Your Five Gallants*, *1 Charles Duke of Byron* and *2 Charles Duke of Byron*.

Of these fourteen plays, moreover, seven explicitly avoid discoveries by calling for the carrying on stage of properties or players.

(1) *The Gentleman Usher*: '*Enter Strozza; brought in a Chaire*' (sig. G1).
(2) *The Dutch Courtesan*: '*Enter Mrs. Mulligrub, with servants and furniture for the Table*' (sig. E3v).
(3) *All Fools*: '*A Drawer or two, setting a Table*' (sig. H4).
(4) *The Fawn*: '*Herod and Nymphadoro with napkins in their hands, followed by Pages with stooles and meat*' (sig. C1).
(5) *Sophonisba*: '*Enter ... the mournful solemnity of Massinissas presenting Sophon[isba's] body*' (sig. G3).
(6) *Your Five Gallants*: '*Enter his man bringing a trunke*' (sig. A2v).
(7) *1 Charles Duke of Byron*: '*Enter Picoté, with two other spreading a Carpet*' (sig. B4).

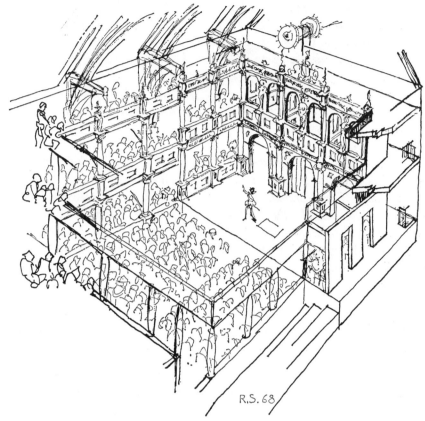

Figure 52 An impression of the Second Blackfriars

In one play not requiring a discovery, *Sophonisba*, a bed is called for in three different scenes, and there is considerable evidence for curtains and discoveries. Since, however, this evidence appears to refer to bedcurtains, there is no reason to suppose that the bed was revealed in a discovery-space. Presumably a small, curtained fourposter bed was brought on and off stage in each scene. Bracketed insertions have been made in the following stage directions in order to illustrate the theory that the curtains referred to are bedcurtains.

(1) '*The Ladies lay the Princes in a faire bed, and close the curtaines [of the bed] . . . the boyes draw [= open] the Curtaines [of the bed] discovering Sophonisba. . . . The Ladies draw [= close] the curtaines [of the bed] about Sophonisba, the rest accompany Massinissa forth*' (sigs. B1v–4v).

(2) '*They lay Vangue in Syphax bed and draw* [= *close*] *the curtaines* [*of the bed*] . . . *Enter Syphax ready for bedd*. . . . *Offering to leape into bed, he discovers Vangue* [*by opening the bed-curtains*]' (sigs. D4v–E1).

(3) '*Enter Erichtho in the shape of Sophonisba, her face vailed and hasteth in the bed of Syphax*. . . . *Syphax hasteneth within the Canopy* [= *bed-curtaines*] *as to Sophonisbas bed*. . . . *Syphax drawes* [= *opens*] *the curtaines* [*of the bed*] *and discovers Erichtho lying with him*. . . . *They leape out of the bed*' (sigs. F1v–2).

And in another play not requiring a discovery, *The Dutch Courtesan*, a 'curtain' is nevertheless required behind which eavesdropping players may hide: '*Enter Franchischina, sir Lyonel, Tissefeu, with Officers*. . . . *She conceales them behinde the curtaine*. . . . *Enter Malhereux*. . . . *Those in ambush rusheth forth and takes him*' (sigs. G3–3v). Apparently the curtain consisted of hangings whose primary function was something other than to effect discoveries.

Six of the twenty Blackfriars plays require one or more discoveries.

(1) *Sir Giles Goosecap*: '*He* [*Clarence*] *drawes the Curtaines and sits within them*. . . . *Eug*[*enia*]. . . . Where is this sickly gentleman at his booke? [*He is discovered*]' (sigs. I2v–3v). One seated player is discovered by means of 'curtains', as in a 'chamber'. Earlier he enters the discovery-space from the stage and conceals himself in preparation for the discovery.

(2) *The Widow's Tears*: six discoveries.

(a) '*Enter Lysander*. . . . Who's in the Tombe there? . . . ope or Ile force it open. [*Ero opens the tomb, discovering herself and Cynthia.*] . . . *Shee shuts up the Tomb*' (sigs. H1v–4). Two players are discovered, the one recumbent, the other effecting the discovery.

(b) '*Cynthia, Ero, the Tomb opening*. . . . *She shuts the tomb*' (sigs. H4–I1v). Two players are discovered.

(c) '*The Tomb opens, Lysander, Cynthia, Ero*' (sig. I2v). Three players are discovered.

(d) '*Tomb opens, and Lysander within lies along, Cynthia and Ero*. . . . *Shut the Tomb*' (sigs. I3v–4v). Three players are discovered, one of them recumbent.

(e) '*Ero opens, and hee sees her* [*Cynthia's*] *head layd on the coffin, etc.* . . . *Shut the Tomb*' (sigs. K1v–2). Two players are discovered, one recumbent on a coffin, the other effecting the discovery.

(f) '*she [Ero] opens [discovering herself and Cynthia] and he enters [the tomb]*' (sig. K2v). Two players are discovered.

In all instances the discovery-space represents a 'tomb'.

(3) *Law Tricks:* four discoveries.

(a) '*discover Lurdo behinde the Arras*' (sig. E1). One player is discovered by means of an 'arras'.

(b) '*Discover Polymetes in his study*' (sig. G1v). One seated player is discovered, as in a 'study'.

(c) '*Polimetes in his study*' (sig. H3). One player is discovered, as in a 'study'.

(d) '*Countesse in the Tombe*' (sig. I3v). One player is discovered, as in a 'tomb'.

(4) *Eastward Ho:* two discoveries.

(a) '*At the middle dore, Enter Golding discovering a Gold-smiths shoppe*' (sig. A2). One player and perhaps some properties suggestive of a 'shop' are discovered in the middle door of three.

(b) '*Goulding and Mildred, sitting on eyther side of the stall. . . . Enter Goulding*' (sigs. B2v–3). Two seated players are discovered, as in a 'shop'. (The first stage direction is anticipatory, the players actually appearing at the second direction.)

(5) *The Fleer:* two discoveries.

(a) '*Enter Signior Alunio the Apothecarie in his shop with wares about him*' (sig. G2v). One player and some properties suggestive of a 'shop' are discovered.

(b) '*Enter Lord Piso with a Torch, a Night-cap, and his Doublet open: In prison*' (sig. H1). One player is discovered, as in 'prison'.

(6) *The Knight of the Burning Pestle:* '*Enter Rafe like a Grocer in's shop, with two Prentices Reading Palmerin of England. . . . Rafe. . . . now shut up shoppe*' (sigs. C1v–2v). Three players are discovered, as in a 'shop'. The discovering agency may be the hangings later alluded to in the dialogue: '*Wife. . . . what story is that painted upon the cloth?*' (sig. E4).

Of the six plays requiring discoveries, moreover, three explicitly avoid discoveries by calling for the carrying on stage of properties or players.

(1) *The Widow's Tears:* '*Enter two or three with cushions*' (sig. G1v).

(2) *Law Tricks:* '*the Herse [= coffin] borne over the stage*' (sig. G3).

(3) *The Knight of the Burning Pestle:* '*Enter two, bearing a Coffin, Jasper in it*' (sig. H4).

The discovery-space is equipped with 'curtains' or an 'arras', and in one instance it is referred to as 'the middle door'. It is used relatively infrequently: once in each of two plays, twice in each of two plays, four times in one play and six times in the last. Moreover, in ten of the twenty Blackfriars plays (including three that require discoveries) the device of discovery is explicitly avoided by the carrying on stage of properties or players; and in one play not requiring a discovery a 'curtain' is used in eavesdropping, evidence which suggests that the curtain in question was not designed primarily for the purpose of effecting discoveries. The discovery-space is variously referred to as a 'tomb', a 'study', a 'shop', a 'stall' and a 'prison'. Since it can contain four seated players or three players together with a coffin, the discovery-space must have had an area of at least 21 square feet. A width of 7 feet and a depth of 3 feet would be convenient dimensions.

Twelve of the twenty Blackfriars plays do not require action above: *Cynthia's Revels*, *Sir Giles Goosecap*, *The Widow's Tears*, *Law Tricks*, *Philotas*, *All Fools*, *The Fleer*, *The Isle of Gulls*, *Sophonisba*, *Your Five Gallants*, *1 Charles Duke of Byron* and *2 Charles Duke of Byron*.

Eight of the twenty Blackfriars plays require one or more actions above.

(1) *Poetaster*: '*Shee* [*Julia*] *appeareth above, as at her chamber window*' (sig. 2E2). One player appears above, as at a 'chamber' window.

(2) *The Gentleman Usher*: two actions above.
   (a) '*Enter Alphonso, Medice, Lasso, Cortezza above*' (sig. H1v). Four players appear above, one of them seated; presently they descend to the stage (exit above and re-entrance below noted). The upper station is an unlocalized point of observation (conceivably a gallery or window overlooking a courtyard).
   (b) '*Enter Corteza, and Margaret above*' (sig. I1). Two players appear above, as at a 'tower' window.

(3) *The Dutch Courtesan*: '*Enter Beatrice above . . . throweth downe a ring to him*' (sigs. B3v–4). One player appears above, as at a 'chamber' window. A hand property (ring) is thrown down from upper station to stage.

(4) *The Malcontent*: '*Male*[*vole*] *out of his Chamber. . . . Pietro* [*below*]. *Come downe*' (sig. B1). One player appears above, as at a 'chamber' window; presently he descends to the stage (re-entrance below noted).

(5) *Monsieur D'Olive*: '*He* [*Digue*] *looks out* [*above*] *with a light. . . .* [*Then enter, successively, Eurione and Marcellina above*]' (sig. G3). First one and

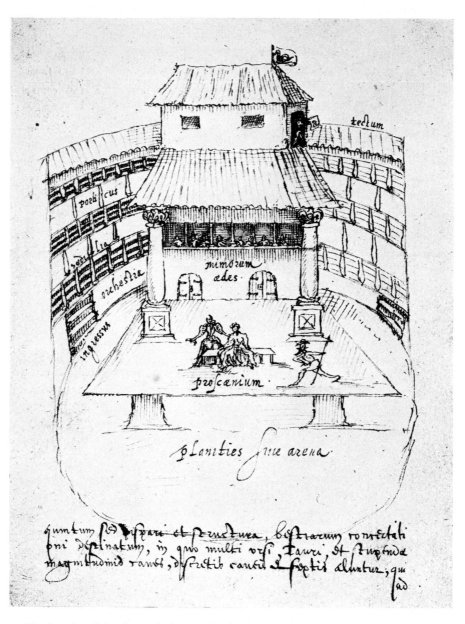

11 The interior of the Swan playhouse (drawing by Arend van Buchell, after the lost original by Johannes De Witt (*c.* 1596))

12a Detail from a drawing by Wenzel Hollar, The West Part of Southwark towards Westminster (c. 1640) showing the Second Globe, the Hope and (very faintly) the Blackfriars

12b Detail from the engraving by Wenzel Hollar, A Long Bird's-Eye View of London (1647). Showing the Second Globe (erroneously captioned 'Beere baything h.'), the Hope (erroneously captioned 'The Globe') and the Blackfriars

then two players appear above, as at a house window; presently the two players descend to the stage. The term *looks out* suggests that the upper station is within a structure.

(6) *The Fawn:* two actions above.

(a) '*Whilest the Act is a playing, Hercules and Tiberio enters, Tiberio climes the tree, and is received above by Dulcimel, Philocalia and a Priest: Hercules stayes beneath*' (sig. H3). Three players appear above, as at a house window; they are joined by a fourth, who climbs from stage to upper station by means of a 'tree' – either a property tree set up against the tiring-house façade or one of the columns of the tiring-house façade. (Compare the 'tree' that Slitgut climbs in *Eastward Ho.*)

(b) '*Tiberio and Dulcimel above are discovered, hand in hand*' (sig. I4v). Two players are discovered above, presumably by the opening of curtains. The upper station is unlocalized.

(7) *Eastward Ho:* two actions above.

(a) '*Enter Winnifride above*' (Q, sig. C3). One player appears above, as at a house window.

(b) '*Enter Slitgut [below], with a paire of Oxe hornes, discovering* [= catching sight of] *Cuckolds-Haven above. Slit.* All haile, faire Haven of married men onely . . . For my part, I presume not to arrive here, but in my Maisters behalfe . . . who sends me to set up . . . these necessarie Ensignes of his homage: And up I got this morning, thus early, to get up to the toppe of this famous Tree . . . to advance this Crest of my Maisters occupation. Up then, Heaven and Saint Luke blesse me, that I be not blowne into the Thames as I clime, with this furious Tempest; Slight, I thinke the Devill be abroade, in likenesse of a storme, to rob me of my Hornes. . . . So, so, I thinke I have made it looke the right way, it runnes against London-Bridge (as it were) even full butt. And now, let me discover [= espy] from this loftie prospect, what pranckes the rude Thames playes in her desperate lunacie. . . . Nowe will I descend my honourable Prospect. . . . Farewell thou Horne Tree that bearest nothing but Stone fruite *Exit*' (sigs. F2–G1v). I have quoted copiously from the dialogue in order to make clear that Slitgut enters on the stage, climbs a 'tree', fastens the pair of horns above and climbs back down to the stage. What he climbs may have been a property tree set up against the tiring-house façade, or it may have been one of the columns of the tiring-house façade. (Compare the 'tree' that Tiberio climbs in *The Fawn.*) Whether 'Cuckold's Haven' is represented by anything (perhaps designated by a signboard) is not clear. In any case, Slitgut, having climbed up, apparently attaches the horns to the gallery front or to one of the columns of the gallery over the stage.

(8) *The Knight of the Burning Pestle:* 'Old merri[thought]. within' (sig. G3). One player appears above, as at a house window. Merrythought, since visible to the locked-out Mistress Merrythought on the stage, is apparently in an upper station. Thus the term *within* is apparently here used in the sense of 'within an upper station'.

The upper station is curtained (or at least curtainable at need), since in one instance two players are discovered in it; and in another instance it is referred to as 'within'. It is used, in the eight plays requiring action above, relatively infrequently: once in each of five plays and twice in each of three plays. It is variously referred to as a 'chamber window', a 'chamber' and a 'tower window'. Since it can contain as many as four standing players, the upper station must have an area of at least 9 square feet. A width of 6 feet and a depth of 1 foot 6 inches would be convenient dimensions. The stairway used in descents from upper station to stage is evidently out of sight of the audience, since in one instance descending players are directed to exit above and re-enter below.

Two of the Blackfriars plays refer to the location of a music station.

(1) *Sophonisba:* 'A treble Violl and a base Lute play *softlyd* [= *softlye*] within the Canopy [= curtain]. . . . A short song to soft Musique above' (sig. F1v). Since the two directions refer to the same music, it is clear that the music station is both 'above' and curtained with a 'canopy'.

(2) *2 Charles Duke of Byron:* 'Musique and a Song, above' (sig. K4). Again the music station is 'above'.

We may conclude that the music station is both on an upper level and curtained.

Inter-act music is referred to in five plays.

(1) *The Gentleman Usher:* 'medice after the song . . .' (after Act II).
(2) *The Malcontent:* '. . . whilst the Act [= act-music] is playing . . .' (after Act I).
(3) *The Fawn:* 'Whilest the Act is a playing . . .' (after Act IV).
(4) *Sophonisba.*
  (a) '. . . the Cornets and Organs playing loud full Musicke for the Act [= act interval]' (after Act I).
  (b) 'Organ mixt with Recorders for this Act' (after Act II).

(c) '*Organs Violls and Voices play for this Act*' (after Act III).

(d) '*A Base Lute and a Treble Violl play for the Act*' (after Act IV).

(5) *The Knight of the Burning Pestle.*

(a) '*Boy danceth, Musick*' (after Act I).

(b) '*Musick*' (after Act II).

(c) '*Musick. . . . Boy danceth*' (after Act III).

Inter-act music is apparently reflected also in the division of the substantive texts of all twenty Blackfriars plays into acts (two imperfectly).

One play, *The Widow's Tears*, requires suspension gear for a flying effect: '*Musique: Hymen descends: and sixe Sylvanes enter beneath, with Torches*' (sig. G2v). One player descends. Presumably he also rises at the end of the action.

Three plays require trapwork.

(1) *Cynthia's Revels*: '*Eccho . . . Ascendit*' (Q, sig. B3). One player rises, as though from under the earth.

(2) *Poetaster*: '*Envie. Arising in the midst of the stage*' (F, sig. Z6). One player rises, trap unlocalized.

(3) *Sophonisba.*

(a) '*So[phonisba]. . . . Deer Zanthia close the vault when I am sunk. . . . She descends. . . . She [Zanthia] descends after Sophonisba. . . . [Syphax] Descends through the vault*' (sigs. D4v–E1v). Several players descend, as through a 'vault'. Since a player on stage can easily close it, the trap door apparently opens upward.

(b) '*Enter Sophonisba and Zanthia as out of a caves mouth. . . . Through the vautes mouth in his night gowne, torch in his hand, Syphax enters just behind Sophon[isba]*' (sigs. E2v–3). Several players ascend, as though from a 'cave's mouth' (referred to also as the 'vault's mouth').

(c) '*Erichtho slips into the ground as Syphax offers his sword to hir*' (sig. E2). One player descends, as though into the 'ground'.

A single trap is required, in one instance described as 'in the midst of the stage'. In another instance there is a suggestion that the trap door opens upward, since a player remaining on stage is asked by a descending player to close it. The trap is variously referred to as a hole in 'the earth', a 'vault' and a 'cave's mouth'. Presumably a trap 4 feet square would be sufficiently large.

We may conclude that the staging requirements of the Blackfriars plays in some instances confirm, in others at least do not deny, the proposed reconstruction of the Blackfriars stage and tiring-house. The demand for three doors in one of the plays would have been satisfied by the three doors of the tiring-house. Discoveries could have been accommodated within the middle tiring-house doorway, which would have provided a discovery-space 7 feet wide and some 2 or 3 feet deep if we suppose that curtains or hangings had been fitted up within or in front of the doorway in question. (Or all three doorways might have been covered with curtains or hangings.) Action above could have been accommodated at the front of one of the boxes of the tiring-house gallery over the stage, which would have provided an upper station about 8 feet wide and some 2 or 3 feet deep. The stairs used in descents from upper station to stage were evidently, since out of sight of the audience, within the tiring-house. Music 'above' could also have been accommodated in one of the boxes of the gallery over the stage, which, if its windows were curtained, would have constituted an upper-storey music room some 9 feet wide and 7 feet deep. Presumably the chief function of the music room curtains was to permit the musicians to remain hidden from view during the performance of dramatic action but to be readily made visible during the performance of inter-act music. Presumably also a secondary function of the music room curtains was to effect discoveries above, and in this case the demand for a discovery above in one of the plays would have been satisfied. The flying effect called for in another of the plays would have been accommodated by suspension gear housed in one of the rooms over the ceilinged hall in which the playhouse was contained; presumably the suspension line descended to the stage through a trap door cut in the floor of the room in question. And the demand of the plays for trapwork would have been satisfied by the single trap door set in the middle of the stage; apparently the trap opened upwards.

5 Conclusion

In this essay I have devoted fairly full attention to representative examples
of the so-called public and private playhouses during the period 1576–1613.
In the cases of the Swan (1595) and the Second Blackfriars (1596) it has been
possible to formulate reconstructions because of the abundance of external
evidence. In the case of the First Globe (1599) it has not been possible, because of the paucity of external evidence, to formulate a reconstruction, but
I have, in view of this deficiency, hypothesized a general similarity of the
Globe to the Swan, partly in response to perennial interest in the playhouse
of Shakespeare, partly in order to make use of the wealth of internal evidence
surviving for the Globe where almost no internal evidence survives for the
Swan. In the case of a fourth playhouse, the First Fortune (1600), it would
have been possible, because of the existence of considerable external evidence, to formulate a reconstruction, but I have not ventured upon such a
reconstruction since it would in part have duplicated the proposed reconstruction of the Swan and since it would also have inordinately increased the
length of the present essay. In the case of a fifth playhouse, the Red Bull
(1605), there is no external evidence on which to base a reconstruction, but
we do have an excellent study by the late George Fullmer Reynolds,[1] which

[1] *The Staging of Elizabethan Plays at the Red Bull Theater 1605–1625* (1940).

establishes, on the basis of internal evidence (hence in general terms and not always without ambiguity), the physical features of the stage and tiring-house of that playhouse. For other playhouses of the period, the Paul's Boys' playhouse (*c.* 1575), the Theatre (1576), the First Blackfriars (1576), the Curtain (1577), the Rose (*c.* 1587) and the Whitefriars (1606?), there is insufficient external evidence to support a reconstruction.

(i)

From the argument of preceding chapters we may conclude that the stage and tiring-house of the Swan differed physically from the stage and tiring-house of the Second Blackfriars in three respects.

First, the Swan stage (area 1,150 square feet) was rather more than twice as large as the Blackfriars stage (area 537 square feet). Moreover, evidence that other public playhouses were approximately the same size as the Swan, together with the unlikelihood that any other private playhouse could have been larger than the Blackfriars (some private playhouses were evidently smaller), suggests that the two playhouses were, in this respect, typical of their respective kinds. Thus we may suppose that public-theatre stages were, in general, about twice as large as private-theatre stages. Size of stage seems not, however, to have been a matter of much concern in production, for certain plays, such as *The Malcontent* (1604) and *Philaster* (*c.* 1611), were performed both on the 'small' stage of the Second Blackfriars and on the 'large' stage of the First Globe. Although each kind of stage presumably had its advantages and disadvantages, a given play could, apparently, be performed equally effectively on either.

Second, the tiring-house of the Swan had two doors, whereas that of the Second Blackfriars had three. The three-door tiring-house of the Black-friars was apparently characteristic of the private playhouses of the period, for there is good internal evidence to suggest three such doors at the Paul's playhouse and the Whitefriars; however, the two-door tiring-house of the Swan was probably *not* characteristic of the public playhouses of the period, for there is internal evidence (admittedly less strong than one could wish) suggestive of three tiring-house doors at the First Fortune and the Red Bull. The First Globe may have had a three-door tiring-house, but the internal evidence does not clearly so indicate; it seems appropriate, therefore, to suppose that the First Globe probably had a two-door tiring-house. Conceivably the two-door arrangement at the Swan and the First Globe represents an older, more conservative style, closer than the three-door arrangement to the normal form of the Tudor hall screen which presumably was the architectural model for the Elizabethan tiring-house. In any case, a third, central doorway in the tiring-house façade would have been a great convenience in the management of discoveries, eavesdroppings and the putting forth from the tiring-house of large stage properties such as tables or beds, since during the preparation for and execution of such pieces of staging the use of a middle door would have left the two side doors free for regular entrances and exits by the players. Again the evidence of particular plays performed both at the Second Blackfriars and at the First Globe suggests that a play designed for performance in a playhouse with a three-door tiring-house could readily be adapted for performance in a playhouse with a two-door tiring-house.

Third, the sides of the Swan stage were separated from galleries on either side of the stage by a yard area (the upper half of a half moon in ground plan) where spectators stood some 5 feet 6 inches below stage level, whereas the sides of the Second Blackfriars stage were contiguous with side-stage boxes where spectators sat at stage level. The difference in arrangement is not, perhaps, very significant (in each case we are dealing with an 'open' stage in the sense that the stage was surrounded by audience on three sides), but the location of spectators at stage level and immediately adjacent to the stage at the Second Blackfriars (together with the smaller size of the theatre) must have made for considerably greater intimacy of acting style at that playhouse; and the arrangement is interesting in its clear prefiguration of the stage boxes that we find in playhouses of the Restoration and eighteenth century. The one arrangement, resulting from the existence of a yard surrounding the stage on three sides in a 'round' public playhouse like the Swan (or, for that matter, in a square public playhouse like the First Fortune), was presumably typical of its kind; the other arrangement, resulting from the absence of a yard or pit that surrounded the stage on three sides in a private playhouse like the Second Blackfriars, was probably typical only of 'large' private playhouses – that is, of playhouses constructed in halls having a width of about 36 feet or more (internal measure). In smaller private playhouses the arrangement probably differed from that of the Second Blackfriars. For example, in a private playhouse about 32 feet wide, such as the playhouse depicted in the *Wits* Frontispiece, the stage might well have been surrounded by pit on three sides in much the same manner as the public-theatre stage was surrounded by yard on three sides (the essential situation is depicted in Figure 44 above); and in a playhouse about 26 feet wide, such as perhaps the Paul's playhouse or the First Blackfriars, the stage might well have extended all the way across the playhouse from wall to wall (see Figure 7 above).

In a fourth respect, use of one of the boxes of the tiring-house gallery over the stage as a music room, the Second Blackfriars seems to have differed radically from the First Globe – at least down to 1608, the terminal date of both ranges of internal evidence. The Blackfriars plays, when they specify the location of off-stage music, invariably call for music 'above' and never 'within'; the natural inference is that at the Blackfriars one of the boxes of the gallery over the stage served as a music room. Conversely, the Globe plays, when they specify the location of off-stage music, invariably call for music 'within' and never 'above'; again the natural inference is that at the Globe (at least down to 1608) music was not performed in a box of the gallery over the stage but within the tiring-house at stage level. The reason for the difference presumably lies in the private-theatre custom of interrupting play performances at the end of each of the first four acts in order to perform music unrelated to the action of the play, as opposed to the public-theatre custom (prevailing at least down to around 1608) of performing the play from start to finish without interruption for the performance of interact music. The differences in theatre technique are alluded to in the Induction to *The Malcontent* (1604), where Burbage, on stage at the Globe, informs the 'spectator' Sly that the public-theatre 'additions' to their borrowed private-theatre play are 'to entertaine a little more time, and to abridge the not-received custome of musicke in our Theater'. The differences are also clearly reflected in the texts of public- and private-theatre plays. Wilfred T. Jewkes has shown that some 90 per cent of the substantive texts of private-theatre plays are divided into acts, whereas some 80 per cent of the substantive texts of public-theatre plays (at least down to around 1608) are not divided into acts.[1] Needless to say, ignorance of these facts has led to much unnecessary controversy over whether performances were, in general, continuous or interrupted by act intervals; and also to some misunderstanding of the neoclassical concept of five-act structure, which has upon occasion been confused by critics with the entirely separate phenomenon of division of a text into five acts.

Jewkes's evidence leads also to an inference of general theatrical significance. He notes that after about 1607 the substantive texts of public-theatre plays tend increasingly to be divided into acts until, by about 1616, the substantive texts of practically all plays, whether designed for public or for private playhouses, are divided into acts. The inference we may draw

[1] *Act Division in Elizabethan and Jacobean Plays 1583–1616* (1958).

is that the custom of inter-act music has spread from the private to the public playhouses. Presumably it did so as a result of the King's Men's accommodating themselves to the private-theatre custom of inter-act music when they began to use the Blackfriars in 1609, together with their consequent introduction of the custom at the Globe when they returned to that playhouse after their first winter at the Blackfriars. Thus we have an explanation of the stage direction in *A Chaste Maid in Cheapside* calling for '*a sad Song in the Musicke-Roome*' at the Swan in 1613: apparently by that date one of the boxes of the tiring-house gallery over the stage at that playhouse had been pressed into service as a music room. A similar explanation will account for directions in other public-theatre plays after 1608 calling for music 'above' (none occurs earlier).

In one other respect the presence or absence of a music room appears to have contributed to a major difference in staging technique between the private playhouses and the public playhouses. Presumably the purpose of a music room was to give musicians a permanent station where, before the play began and during act intervals when they would be performing music unrelated to the action, they could be seen and heard by the audience; but where, also, during performance of the several acts of the play, they could be concealed from the view of the audience. The means by which the musicians were alternately made visible to and hidden from the audience appears to have been curtains or hangings fitted up in the window of the particular tiring-house box chosen to serve as music room. (Such curtains are apparently depicted in the *Messalina* Vignette, 1640, and the *Wits* Frontispiece, 1662.) Thus there would have been music room curtains above in the private playhouses from the beginning and in the public playhouses from about 1609 when inter-act music apparently became a public-theatre as well as a private-theatre custom. (One of the Blackfriars plays considered in the present essay, *Sophonisba*, refers to curtained music above.) And the existence of curtains above would have made it possible for the players to stage discoveries above. (Another of the Blackfriars plays considered in the present essay, *The Fawn*, requires a discovery above.) Thus we have an explanation of discoveries above called for in private-theatre plays throughout the life of the private playhouses and in public-theatre plays after 1609. The hypothesis is confirmed by the fact that there are no discoveries above in public-theatre plays before 1609, by the existence of internal evidence for the use of music room curtains in the discovery of action above and by Jasper Mayne's praise of Ben Jonson, in *Jonsonus Virbius* (1638), for having avoided the sort of spectacular staging for which the Red Bull was famous – 'Thou laidst no sieges to the Musique-Roome.' Again we can see the private playhouses influencing the technique of the public playhouses, and again the avenue of influence appears to have been the King's Men through their alternate occupation of the Globe and the Blackfriars.

(ii)

From the argument of preceding chapters we may conclude also that the stage and tiring-house of the Swan and the Second Blackfriars were physically similar in four respects. Further, study of the full range of extant public- and private-theatre plays suggests that the two playhouses were, in these respects, typical of their kinds.

First, both the Swan and the Blackfriars had a single trap door, perhaps 4 feet square and set presumably in the middle of the stage. At the Blackfriars the trap probably opened upwards.

Second, both playhouses had suspension gear for flying effects or hoisting. Since the winch, located in the hut over the stage cover at the Swan and in one of the 'rooms over the hall' at the Blackfriars, was presumably stationary, descents and ascents were of the bucket-in-a-well variety, the descending or ascending player alighting or taking off from a central point on the stage a few feet in front of the tiring-house façade.

Third, both the Swan and the Blackfriars had an 'upper station' for the performance of action above, in each case presumably a shallow area some 6 or 7 feet wide at the front of one of the boxes of the tiring-house gallery over the stage. (At the Blackfriars, as pointed out in the preceding section, there was also a music room equipped with curtains that permitted discoveries above.) The concept depends on our understanding three characteristics of action above in the public and private playhouses. First, action above was relatively infrequent, demonstrably occurring in only nineteen of the fifty plays considered in this essay and, more important, in fourteen of those nineteen plays only once. Second, action above consisted essentially of the 'appearance' of one character in an elevated place 'to' another character in a scenically related place below. The usual situations are the upper-storey window of a house overlooking the street and the walls of a town or castle overlooking the space below the walls. And, third, action above did not involve movement in depth within the upper station, for in most instances the player above remains standing in the upper station (specifically, framed in the window of the tiring-house box in question) while in dialogue with the player below, sometimes, at the conclusion of that dialogue, descending by way of the tiring-house stairs and re-entering 'to' the player below.

And, fourth, both the Swan and the Blackfriars had a 'discovery-space', in each case presumably a shallow area within an open tiring-house doorway some 7 feet wide within or in front of which curtains or hangings had been fitted up. (In some of the discoveries at the Globe the discovery-space is referred to as though off stage.) The concept depends on our understanding three characteristics of the device of discovery in the public and private play-houses. First, the device of discovery was relatively infrequent, demon-strably occurring in only sixteen of the fifty plays considered in this essay and, more important, in ten of those sixteen plays only once. Second, the device of discovery was essentially a 'show' (usually for the benefit of characters on stage) of a character or object invested with some special interest or significance. (Compare Hieronimo's 'language of sight' when he discovers the body of Horatio to the assembled Court in *The Spanish Tragedy*: '*Beholde* the reason urging me to this, *See* heere my *shew*, *look* on this *spectacle*.') Thus the discovery-space curtains were not used, as curtains commonly are in the proscenium arch theatre, as a device to permit the arrangement of stage properties out of sight of the audience, for in the Renaissance English theatre large properties such as beds or chairs (some-times containing 'sick' or 'sleeping' characters) were simply drawn or carried on and off stage at need, within full view of the audience, by stagekeepers or attendant players. And, third, the device of discovery did not involve movement in depth within the discovery-space, for the discovered player (initially framed for a moment or two in the open doorway) usually leaves the discovery-space and comes forward upon the stage immediately or shortly after being discovered.

A further point of some significance may be made about the upper station and the discovery-space. The upper station was not designed for the purpose of accommodating action above but was an occasional adaptation to that purpose of one of the boxes for spectators or musicians in the second storey of the tiring-house. Correspondingly, the discovery-space was not designed for the purpose of effecting discoveries but was an occasional adaptation to that purpose of a tiring-house doorway together with the curtains or hangings which, fitted up within or in front of the doorway, masked the interior of the tiring-house while at the same time affording the players a convenient means of easy passage between tiring-house and stage. (That the discovery-space was not designed for the purpose of effecting discoveries is clear from the many plays, including *Hamlet*, which do not require or deliberately avoid the device of discovery yet which do require hangings for eavesdropping or as a means of entrance to the stage.) It is the parasitic nature (so to speak) of both the upper station and the discovery-space which explains the relative infrequency of their use: in each case the structural element in question, when not serving its secondary and occasional function as an upper station or as a discovery-space, was not 'going to waste' since it was serving its primary and continuing function as a box for spectators or musicians or as an entranceway from tiring-house to stage. The point can be clarified by comparison of the upper station and the discovery-space (as here defined) with the twentieth-century 'upper stage' and 'inner stage' designed respectively for the sole purposes of accommodating action above and of effecting discoveries. 'Upper' and 'inner stages' are indeed 'wasted' during the performance of plays like *Twelfth Night* or *King Lear* or *Measure for Measure*, which require neither action above nor a discovery, with the result that twentieth-century directors working with 'upper' and 'inner stages' have tended, in order to avoid the charge of constructing such elaborate and expensive stage elements to no purpose, to invent non-documentable uses for them such as the representation of domestic interiors that 'in real life' would have been found, respectively, on upper storeys and on the ground floor of Elizabethan buildings.

(iii)

It remains finally to say a word about the now generally discarded concept of the Elizabethan 'inner stage'.[1] The concept, originating in the nineteenth century, was extensively developed by scholars working early in the twentieth century – Poel, Archer, Thorndike, Lawrence, Granville Barker and others. These men recognized the need to explain references in Elizabethan stage directions to 'curtains' and 'discoveries', yet they were, I believe, so accustomed to realistic conventions of the contemporary proscenium arch stage that they could hardly conceive of Renaissance production without a stage element roughly corresponding to the proscenium arch curtain. As a practical solution to the problem posed by the evidence of the plays they therefore favoured the theory of an 'inner stage' – essentially a small proscenium arch stage at the rear of an 'outer stage' which could be used for the setting of stage properties out of sight of the audience. Moreover, they tended to rely

[1] Other stage elements associated with the 'inner stage' – obliquely set tiring-house doors, multiple traps, the 'upper stage' and the third-storey music room – are discussed in my article, 'The origins of the so-called Elizabethan multiple stage', *The Drama Review*, XII (1967–8).

(whether consciously or unconsciously) upon the conventions of the Restoration stage. Like its predecessor the playhouse of the Renaissance court masque, the Restoration playhouse did have, towards the rear of its changeable-scenery stage, an 'alcove' which was used somewhat in the manner claimed by proponents of the 'inner stage' theory; and the use of such an alcove is occasionally reflected in the stage directions of Restoration plays. Thus it seems to have been casually assumed that an Elizabethan open-stage discovery was the same thing as a scenic-stage discovery, hence that the open-stage discovery-space was the same thing as the scenic-stage alcove (itself probably imperfectly understood). But neither proposition will withstand scrutiny. The Elizabethan discovery-space is not to be understood in terms of the scenic-stage alcove of the Restoration playhouse, nor can its origin be found in the scenic-stage alcove of the Renaissance court playhouse; rather, its nature must be understood in terms of, and its origin is to be sought in, the curtained scaffold of the medieval Place or *platea*, the essence of whose technique of discovery was transmitted to the Renaissance English stage of public and private playhouses through, presumably, the booth stage and the domestic hall screen.

IV The plays and the playwrights

Alvin Kernan

Introduction

The vast amount of critical writing on Elizabethan and Jacobean drama, particularly on Shakespeare, tends to discourage the scholar attempting to keep up in his speciality and trying to see this drama as a coherent whole. But after several years of working with this body of criticism, I can happily report that it does sort itself out in time and that the best work stands out ever more clearly as time passes. Furthermore, the mass and charge of this criticism have laid down over the years a solid foundation of sophisticated readings of all of the major and many of the minor dramatic works. A writer of a history of this period begins not only with excellent bibliography and superb texts but also with at least some awareness of the complex verbal and dramatic styles of the plays and some understanding of the intricate philosophical and psychological issues they dramatize. Most readers of this volume will be aware of the extent of my indebtedness to this body of critical writing and will, I hope, understand that lack of space alone has prevented full acknowledgement in footnotes of that indebtedness. Even in the bibliographies I have been forced to limit myself to providing references only to those fundamental works which will provide the necessary basic information for an understanding of the drama between 1576 and 1613.

This body of criticism, with its close focus on text, poetry and dramaturgy, makes it clear that any true history, as opposed to a chronicle history, of the drama of this period must attempt to follow the pattern traced by the central issues raised in the drama itself. That there is a close relationship between the subject matter and style of the drama and the political and cultural events of the age I have no doubt, and I have speculated on that relationship in a number of brief asides. But the drama is, I would argue, itself a primary historical document of the period, and by approaching it directly we are most likely to come close to the essential concerns, both psychic and social, of Renaissance England. But the drama is within itself extraordinarily various and comprehensive, and its history might be written in any number of related terms: art and nature, the individual and society, freedom and authority, tradition and existence, subjectivity and objectivity, unity and multiplicity, order and chaos, thought and feeling, the process of time and the single moment or, even, hope and despair. While not abandoning any of these traditional philosophical and psychological categories, and while maintaining for the sake of clarity a loose chronological framework and pattern of genre theory (comedy, history, tragedy, romance), I have chosen to centre this history on what is at once the most obvious and the most essential fact: the extraordinary increase in the quality and quantity of theatrical activity in the late sixteenth century, and the concomitant emphasis *within* the plays on the meaning of playing and the validity of treating the world as a stage. Man as actor and world as theatre: these terms both literally describe the medium and figuratively describe the contents of the plays, whose history we will now try to trace.

The texts quoted are in every case those given in the bibliography as the standard text of the works of particular playwrights, with the exception of Shakespeare. For his works the edition of Peter Alexander, *William Shakespeare, The Complete Works* (London, 1951; New York, 1952), is used for quotations, while the lineation is supplied from the *Globe Edition* (1864) of Clark and Wright, in order to facilitate reference to the Bartlett *Concordance to Shakespeare*.

This contribution to the *Revels History* was written over many years at Yale University, which generously supported a leave given by the National Endowment for the Humanities in 1968–9, making possible the writing of the final manuscript. Last corrections were made at Princeton in 1973.

1 'Who would not admire this our chameleon?': the new theatre of the late sixteenth century

(i) *Homo Ludens*

The ability to pretend is a part of man's basic biological and psychological equipment, assumed and used by any system of education, government, character formation or social life. Since this power of pretending to be, and ultimately becoming, what we are not is so fundamental a part of human life, the theatre, the histrionic potential raised to its absolute self-conscious expression in art, is always with us in some form, if only juggling, circuses, ritual games or minstrelsy. In the Western world, theatrical activity, if constant, has remained for the most part at a fairly low level; but at wide intervals there have been a few sudden upsurges of both quantity and quality. One of these occurred in England in the last quarter of the sixteenth and the first quarter of the seventeenth centuries. The first building in England designed exclusively for theatrical performances was built in 1576, to be followed in the next fifty years or so by a large number of elaborate playhouses. About the same time the great professional playing companies began to form and take up residence in London. Talented and famous actors appeared – Tarlton, Kempe, Burbage, Alleyn – a large and various audience began to attend the theatre, and a group of professional playwrights emerged, the first group of Englishmen to attempt to earn their living by writing. We have the titles of over 800 plays[1] from the years 1576–1613, from the building of the first theatre to Shakespeare's retirement to Stratford, of which over 400 have survived; and, while it seems unlikely that we have lost any master-pieces, these are probably only a fraction of the number actually written to supply the enormous needs of the repertory companies. The increase in quantity is not, however, as striking as the increase in quality in a theatre which in 1576 produced George Wapull's moral play, *The Tide Tarrieth No Man*, and in 1601 offered William Shakespeare's *Hamlet*.

Traditional literary history, employing the usual evolutionary model, has treated this new theatre as the culmination of a continuous process of development which began in the sacred drama of the oak groves and the church aisles, moved out into the town squares and the halls of great houses, and at last arrived at the fully secular public and private theatres of late sixteenth-century London. The change in playing locale is paralleled in this historical view by a gradual increase of realism, both social and psychological, as the mystery cycles give way to miracle plays and moralities, and these in turn lead to homiletic drama on historical subjects. Style is gradually shaped by such events as the use of blank verse in *Gorboduc*, and a sense of dramatic form is acquired by imitation of the classics, particularly the comedies of Plautus and Terence and the tragedies of Seneca. No doubt these and the many other elements which have been discerned as factors in the growth of English drama between the eleventh and seventeenth centuries contributed greatly to the form of the new drama, but I would suggest that the proposed causes are not, even in the aggregate, of sufficient power to account for the supposed effects, that a reading of this drama does not provide any sense of a long process of development leading *inevitably* to the plays of Marlowe, Jonson, Shakespeare and Webster. Furthermore, this evolutionary history does not explain the sudden sharp increase in both the quantity and quality of theatrical activity in the late sixteenth century.

We need not, I believe, look in the first instance for explanations of the new drama in events lying prior to and outside that drama, for it in large part explains itself. We can say with certainty that in the last quarter of the sixteenth century writing of plays, playing in plays and seeing plays provided some gratification for playwrights, actors and audiences which was worth considerable effort to satisfy. This fascination with playing extended beyond

[1] These figures are gathered from Alfred Harbage, *Annals of the English Drama 975–1700*, revised S. Schoenbaum (London, Philadelphia, 1964). This volume is the source of the majority of dates used in the present work.

the real world on into the plays themselves, where the characters also delight in playing parts and staging pretences, and the nature of their enthusiasm for theatrical activity provides the needed clue for understanding what gratifications writing, acting in and seeing plays provided Englishmen of the late Renaissance. Shakespeare's Richard, Duke of Gloucester, suddenly apprehends that this ability to pretend and play roles is an enormous power that can lead him to the crown and free him of the agony of helplessness imposed on him by a nature that has disproportioned his body in every part and by a society that has so limited his will that he feels 'like one lost in a thorny wood That rents the thorns and is rent with the thorns':

> Why, I can smile, and murder whiles I smile,
> And cry 'Content!' to that which grieves my heart,
> And wet my cheeks with artificial tears,
> And frame my face to all occasions.
> I'll drown more sailors than the mermaid shall;
> I'll slay more gazers than the basilisk;
> I'll play the orator as well as Nestor,
> Deceive more slily than Ulysses could,
> And, like a Sinon, take another Troy.
> I can add colours to the chameleon,
> Change shapes with Protheus for advantages,
> And set the murderous Machiavel to school.
> Can I do this, and cannot get a crown?
> Tut, were it farther off, I'll pluck it down.
>
> (*3 Henry VI*, III. 2. 182–95)

It is not surprising that the delight in role-playing should be expressed by a villain and a murderer, for the power of acting and playing was, for both the citizens of London and the characters in the plays, a revolutionary power which was a source of both pleasure and fear. To make a villain of the spokesman for the magic of playing, protected audience and playwright from the full consequences of a power offering both player king and audience escape from limitations imposed by a harsh nature and an authoritarian government, offering a way of seizing the crown and shaping the self and the world in the image of human desire rather than accepting it as given. Within the theatre the London citizen escaped into the free world of the imagination created by playwright and actors, and within the play the characters found in their ability to act a freedom from all limits whatsoever, a suppleness approaching godhead,

> that can rise,
> And stoope (almost together) like an arrow;
> Shoot through the aire, as nimbly as a starre;
> Turne short, as doth a swallow; and be here,
> And there, and here, and yonder, all at once;
> Present to any humour, all occasion;
> And change a visor, swifter, then a thought!
>
> *(Volpone*, III. i. 23–9)

The playwrights were extremely self-conscious of the fact that their 'out-stretched heroes', to use Hamlet's term, shared the methods and aims of the theatre with them, and comparisons of the characters to actors playing roles and of their dramatic worlds to theatres are one of the commonplaces of this drama. But even when theatrical metaphor is not present, the characters are struggling to achieve the freedom of shape and control of destiny which are so regularly and naturally imaged as actor and theatre. 'Why', says Sir Giles Overreach in Massinger's *A New Way to Pay Old Debts*, 'is not the whole world Included in my self?' (V. i. 355–6), and the fierce line sums up the desire of magicians and alchemists like Doctor Faustus and Subtle, warriors like Hotspur and Coriolanus, lovers like Romeo and Juliet and Vittoria Corombona, revengers like Hieronimo and Vindici, sensualists like Falstaff and Sir Epicure Mammon, politicians like Henry IV and Octavius Caesar, and philosophers like Brutus and Hamlet to be free to define themselves and re-create worlds as they would like them to be.

It is this delight in freedom, this pleasure in metamorphosis, this desire to break up and change what had been thought fixed, which the new drama enacted, both in production and in subject matter. Theatre is the inevitable ultimate expression of the histrionic sensibility, for here alone can the appetite for transmutation and movement through a variety of shapes have unlimited play uninhibited by any restraints which reality imposes on the chameleon instinct. Only in the theatre can man fully realize that 'flexibility of self'[1]

---

[1] This term is taken from Thomas Greene, 'The flexibility of the self in Renaissance literature', in Demetz, Greene and Nelson (eds.), *The Disciplines of Criticism: essays in literary theory, interpretation, and history honoring René Wellek* (New Haven and London, 1968), pp. 241–64, which analyses the new concept of the self which emerged in the Renaissance.

which, frequently figured as Proteus,[1] was so characteristic of the Renaissance. Montaigne muses over the variety of selves within himself, Castiglione and the numerous handbooks on 'self-improvement' assume an almost limitless potential for change, Machiavelli defines politics as the ability to play the proper role, Vives in his *Fabula de homine* uses the theatrical metaphor to celebrate man's Protean ability to evolve into a civilized being, and Pico in his *Oration on the Dignity of Man* finds the essence of *humanitas* and the source of all human greatness in the ability to change shape. All other created things, God tells Adam, are fixed in their appointed place in the scheme of being, but man alone is free to change:

> 'Neither a fixed abode, nor a form that is thine alone, nor any function peculiar to thyself have We given thee, Adam, to the end that according to thy longing and according to thy judgment thou mayest have and possess what abode, what form, and what functions thou thyself shalt desire. The nature of all other beings is limited and constrained within the bounds of laws prescribed by Us. Thou, constrained by no limits, in accordance with thine own free will, in whose hand We have placed thee, shalt ordain for thyself the limits of thy nature. We have set thee at the world's centre that thou mayest from thence more easily observe what is in the world. We have made thee neither of heaven nor of earth, neither mortal nor immortal, so that with freedom of choice and with honor, as though the maker and molder of thyself in whatever shape thou shalt prefer. Thou shalt have the power to degenerate into the lower forms of life, which are brutish. Thou shalt have the power, out of thy soul's judgment, to be reborn into the higher forms, which are divine . . .' Who would not admire this our chameleon?[2]

The theatre not only provided men with an enactment of this desire for personal freedom and the ability to change the self but also gave by the creation of imaginary worlds

> some shadow of satisfaction to the mind of man in those points wherein the nature of things doth deny it, the world being in proportion inferior to the soul; by reason whereof, there is agreeable to the spirit of man,

[1] The use of the figure of Proteus to image man's ability to change is traced in A. Bartlett Giamatti, 'Proteus unbound: some versions of the sea god in the Renaissance', *The Disciplines of Criticism*, pp. 437–75.

[2] Trans. E. L. Forbes, in Cassirer, Kristeller and Randall (eds.), *The Renaissance Philosophy of Man* (Chicago, 1948), pp. 224–6.

a more ample greatness, a more exact goodness, and a more absolute variety than can be found in the nature of things.[1]

The 'second worlds'[2] which the playwrights created had all the amplitude and variety, if not always the 'exact goodness', that the mind could desire. The scene ranges from the heights of heaven to the depths of hell, from the plains of Asia to the Boar's Head tavern, from magical islands in the ocean sea to the Italian ducal palace, and from the heights of the Caucasus to the Warwickshire woods. The time scale is as vast as the sense of space, and the action, much to the distress of the neoclassical critics, extends from Eden to Elizabethan London, from Creation to Judgement, from Troy to Agincourt, and from the wars of Rome to those of the Roses. This heterocosm is not only extraordinarily vast, but it is also plenteous, varied, dense and full. Yeats catches this quality perfectly in his term 'the image of multitude', which he sees growing out of that characteristic device of the Elizabethan and Jacobean playwrights,

> the sub plot which copies the main plot, much as a shadow upon the wall copies one's body in the firelight. We think of *King Lear* less as the history of one man and his sorrows than as the history of a whole evil time. Lear's shadow is in Gloster, who also has ungrateful children, and the mind goes on imagining other shadows, shadow beyond shadow till it has pictured the world. In *Hamlet*, one hardly notices, so subtly is the web woven, that the murder of Hamlet's father and the sorrow of Hamlet are shadowed in the lives of Fortinbras and Ophelia and Laertes, whose fathers, too, have been killed. It is so in all the plays, or in all but all, and very commonly the sub plot is the main plot working itself out in more ordinary men and women, and so doubly calling up before us the image of multitude.[3]

Most of the dramaturgic devices characteristic of the Elizabethan and Jacobean drama contribute to the image of multitude: the large number and

[1] Francis Bacon, *Advancement of Learning*, Book II.
[2] This term is developed and applied to the drama by Harry Berger, Jr, 'The Renaissance imagination: second world and green world', *Centennial Review*, IX (Winter, 1965), 36–78; and 'Theater, drama, and the second world: a prologue to Shakespeare', *Centennial Review*, XII (Summer, 1968), 3–19.
[3] 'Emotion of multitude', in *Ideas of Good and Evil* (London, 1903; New York, 1903), pp. 340–1.

varied nature of the *dramatis personae*, the great variety of scene – now Rome, now Egypt; now the palace, now the heath – the intermixture of tragic and comic scenes, the presence on the same stage of kings and clowns and the dramatization of long periods of time and the changes which time works. But it is the poetry which above all creates and keeps constantly before us the plenitude and variety of a vast, full creation. The dense, precise and burgeoning imagery furnishes the immediate world of the action with a full setting and links whatever is present with similar or dissimilar things and events drawn from the vast range of space and time. To use another of Yeats's phrasings, nothing in this dramatic world is ever 'separated . . . from all but itself', but always exists in and relates to a dense continuum extending from the farthest reaches of time to the present, from the highest and most noble of things to the lowest and most humble.

Here again, the heroes of the drama imitate their creators and seek to construct within the plays other worlds more golden than those in which their authors placed them. At times this world within a world is openly identified as a theatre – Hamlet's plays within a play which evoke a more honest and more heroic world than that of Elsinore, or Prospero's staging of the masque of Ceres to show the young lovers the potential generosity of the world they are entering – but at other times the second or third world will be created within some other enclosed 'theatrical' space such as the magic circle from which Faustus calls his devils, Barabas's counting-house in *The Jew of Malta* into which the riches of the world flow, the Capulet garden where love creates a new heaven and new earth, Volpone's curtained bed in which the great pretender acts out his sickness, or even the round of Antony's arms enclosing Cleopatra and the desired reality – 'Let Rome in Tiber melt, and the wide arch Of the rang'd empire fall! Here is my space' (I. i. 33–4). Most often the true magical space, the ultimate theatre, is within man himself, inside the eyes of Tamburlaine, 'Whose fiery circles bear encompassed A heaven of heavenly bodies in their spheres' (II. i. 15–16), inside the minds of those great idealistic heroes like Brutus or Hamlet who can imagine a world more permanent, a love more enduring, a justice more perfect, a truth more absolute and a space much larger than what is bounded within the 'nutshells' of the theatre itself, where 'with imagin'd wing our swift scene flies, In motion of no less celerity Than that of thought' (*Henry V*, Prologue 1–3).

But if playing and theatre expressed man's greatest hopes for freedom and change, they also expressed paradoxically the exact opposite: a sense of human helplessness and the transience of life and world. Indeed, this was

the traditional meaning of the metaphor of the theatre,[1] and Sir Walter
Ralegh in his 'On the Life of Man' interprets in a more usual way the conceit of life as play:

> What is our life? a play of passion,
> Our mirth the musicke of division,
> Our mothers wombes the tyring houses be,
> Where we are drest for this short Comedy,
> Heaven the Iudicious sharpe spectator is,
> That sits and markes still who doth act amisse,
> Our graves that hide us from the searching Sun,
> Are like drawne curtaynes when the play is done,
> Thus march we playing to our latest rest,
> Onely we dye in earnest, that's no Iest.

The dramatists, half afraid like Faustus of the spirits they invoked within the magic circle of the theatre, were acutely aware of this sombre
meaning of the theatrical metaphor, and most often when they compare man
to a player and life to a play the first emphasis falls not on man's potential
but on his limitations. Macbeth's absolute despair can find expression only
in an image of life as playing: 'Life's but a walking shadow, a poor player,
That struts and frets his hour upon the stage, And then is heard no more'
(V. v. 24–6). The physical theatre itself seems to have carried this sense of
limitation in its architectural arrangements, which reflected the conservative
world view of the late middle ages and the Renaissance. The gorgeously
painted 'heavens' above, the 'hell' below; the small discovery-space at the
rear for the few scenes of private life opening out onto the great platform
stage where the actor spends most of his life in public view; the upper stage
serving as balcony, battlement or pulpit, overlooking the main stage below;
the onlookers from the pit and surrounding galleries watching the great
actors moving to their destinies; the containing round of the exterior walls
or 'frame', with only a small circle of sky showing above: all this is a *mappa
mundi*. Whether we agree or not with George Kernodle that the parts of the
theatre represented the chief symbols of social order and hierarchy – the

---

[1] The history of the growth and meaning of this metaphor is traced in Anne Righter,
Shakespeare and the Idea of the Play (London, 1962), chapter 3. The history and the
nature of the two opposing views of theatre and playing are traced, with special reference
to Renaissance drama, by Jonas Barish, 'The anti-theatrical prejudice', *Critical
Quarterly*, VIII (Winter 1966), 329–48, and 'Exhibitionism and the antitheatrical prejudice', *ELH*, XXXVI (Spring 1969), 1–29.

throne, the altar, the city gates[1] – the theatre was still an image in plaster and timber of an ordered, well-defined universe with close boundaries. Through its continuing undisguised presence during performances, often intensified by direct references to it, this theatre must constantly have said that the world is not as the men within it would like it to be but the way the theatre represents it.

Bosola in *The Duchess of Malfi* perhaps gives us a sense of how an actor longing for infinity felt within the 'wooden O':

> didst thou ever see a Larke in a cage? such is the soule in the body: this world is like her little turfe of grasse, and the Heaven ore our heades, like her looking glasse, onely gives us a miserable knowledge of the small compasse of our prison. (IV. ii. 127–31)

Hamlet can find no better image for his disillusionment than to compare men to actors, the earth to a theatre, the heavens to the 'shadow':

> this goodly frame, the earth, seems to me a sterile promontory; this most excellent canopy the air, look you, this brave o'erhanging firmament, this majestical roof fretted with golden fire – why, it appeareth no other thing to me than a foul and pestilent congregation of vapours. (II. ii. 310–16)

But it is in the words of the Player King in *Hamlet,* spoken from the theatrical depths of a play within a play, that we get the most authentic dark view of what it means to be an actor in a theatre. Men change, the Player King tells his protesting Queen, and 'what we do determine oft we break'. We propose absolute courses of action, and the very violence with which we swear our vows destroys our purpose – 'Their own enactures with themselves destroy'. We are no more stable than actors in a play, and our fortunes change from one instant to the next. What we think we are and will be lies not in our own hands, any more than an actor controls the plot of his play:

> Our wills and fates do so contrary run
> That our devices still are overthrown;
> Our thoughts are ours, their ends none of our own. (III. ii. 221–3)

The Player King's contrast between 'thoughts' and 'ends' breaks out the two components, the hope and the fear, that exist in tension within the metaphor of the theatre and are latent in the art of playing. In the greatest

[1] George Kernodle, 'The open stage: Elizabethan or existentialist', *Shakespeare Survey 12* (1959), p. 3.

plays of the period the two possibilities are simultaneously present, but at the entryway to the drama we are fortunate in having two plays which isolate in unusually pure form the theatrical sense of freedom and the sense of helplessness.

(ii) 'Our thoughts are ours': Marlowe's *Tamburlaine*

In 1587 and 1588 the great rulers of Europe, after many years of compromise and hesitation, committed their nations to courses of action from which there was no turning back. Elizabeth I at long last sent Mary Stuart with her pale face, scarlet petticoat and auburn wig to the executioner's block; Philip II, from his dark study in the Escurial, ordered the invincible Armada to sail against England; and in France Henry of Navarre won his decisive victory over the royal army, and Henry of Valois ended many years of indecision and ordered the assassination of Henry of Guise.[1] But no king turned his back on the past and committed himself more completely to an unknown future than did the Prologue, speaking for Christopher Marlowe, who stepped onto a London stage in 1587 or 1588 and began:

> From jigging veins of riming mother wits,
> And such conceits as clownage keeps in pay,
> We'll lead you to the stately tent of war,
> Where you shall hear the Scythian Tamburlaine
> Threatening the world with high astounding terms
> And scourging kingdoms with his conquering sword.
> View but his picture in this tragic glass,
> And then applaud his fortunes as you please.

The prophet of this dramatic *Novo Orbe* was a shoemaker's son from Canterbury, Christopher Marlowe (1564–93) (see Plate 14), who between 1587 and 1593 in seven plays – *Dido Queen of Carthage* (*c.* 1587), with Thomas Nashe; the two parts of *Tamburlaine* (*c.* 1587–8); *Doctor Faustus* (*c.* 1588–93); *The Jew of Malta* (*c.* 1589); *Edward II* (*c.* 1592); *The Massacre at Paris* (*c.* 1593) – and a long amorous poem, *Hero and Leander*, dramatized the principal ways in which the Renaissance sought outside the theatre the same power and self-fulfilment that it magically created on the stage: war, words, science, learning, politics, pleasure and love. Marlowe appears to have been as tough, intelligent, bold, individualistic and adventuresome in

[1] The remarkable events of 1587–8 are discussed by Garrett Mattingly, *The Spanish Armada* (Boston, 1959).

thought and action as any of his heroes. He was educated at Canterbury and at Cambridge, and while still an undergraduate seems to have become a spy for the head of the queen's secret service, Sir Francis Walsingham. In London, writing for the theatre and perhaps still engaged in intrigue, he was known as an atheist, a blasphemer and a man of sudden and terrible temper. There is considerable evidence that he was at least interested in homosexuality, and he was involved with a free-thinking group of intellectuals. He was in more or less constant trouble with the authorities, and in early 1593 he was stabbed in the eye in a tavern brawl over paying the bill. His murderer claimed self-defence successfully, but there are good reasons to suspect darker motives.

Marlowe was proudly self-conscious of himself as the destroyer of the old and the creator of a new drama, a new style and new dramatic values. From the moment the Prologue in *Tamburlaine* speaks, the doggerel rhythms and clinking rhymes of the old uneducated authors – the 'mother wits' – the crude comedy and farce of 'clownage', are the dramaturgy of the past. Discredited too is the old style: the flat metaphors, sententious tags, jigging metres, hesitations and repetitive verbiage used merely to fill up a line, all the manifestations of lack of invention and imaginative pressure which Marlowe parodied in the speech of Mycetes, hereditary king of Persia, 'defying' Tamburlaine:

> Full true thou speakst, and like thyself, my lord,
> Whom I may term a Damon for thy love:
> Therefore 'tis best, if so it like you all,
> To send my thousand horse incontinent
> To apprehend that paltry Scythian.
> How like you this, my honourable lords?
> Is it not a kingly resolution? (I. i. 49–55)

This is not only the style of the old drama, but it is in Marlowe's view also the voice of legitimacy, of the establishment, of an exhausted social and moral order, silly, futile and lost deep in a sense of life as unreal and man as helpless. When threatened, Mycetes tries to hide the symbol of authority and power, the crown, and when faced with the need for action he moralizes on the transitoriness of life: 'time passeth swift away, Our life is frail, and we may die to-day' (I. i. 67–8).

From the dreary scene and flat verse of the old drama, Marlowe takes his auditors 'to the stately tent of war', where the verse threatens 'the world with high astounding terms', where the action is the scourging of kingdoms

and the conquest of the universe. The moral earnestness and the orthodox
didacticism of the old drama are replaced by a new objectivity and a new
relativism, which invite us not to regard a sad object lesson but rather to
view the 'picture' reflected in the 'tragic glass', and 'applaud' the fortunes
of the conqueror 'as you please'.

In place of the weak Mycetes stands the conqueror Tamburlaine, the
mighty man of words who claims all earth and the heavens themselves as
his domain, whose will is destiny, whose thoughts are reality:

> I hold the Fates bound fast in iron chains,
> And with my hand turn Fortune's wheel about,
> And sooner shall the sun fall from his sphere
> Then Tamburlaine be slain or overcome. (I. ii. 173–6)

Instead of a colourless world in which life passes in an instant, Tamburlaine's
eye perceives as vast a realm of rich, strange lands, as did the imagination of
the dramatists of the new theatre:

> So from the East unto the furthest West
> Shall Tamburlaine extend his puissant arm.
> The galleys and those pilling brigandines,
> That yearly sail to the Venetian gulf,
> And hover in the straits for Christians' wreck,
> Shall lie at anchor in the Isle Asant,
> Until the Persian fleet and men-of-war,
> Sailing along the oriental sea,
> Have fetched about the Indian continent,
> Even from Persepolis to Mexico,
> And thence unto the Straits of Jubalter,
> Where they shall meet and join their force in one,
> Keeping in awe the Bay of Portingale,
> And all the ocean by the British shore;
> And by this means I'll win the world at last. (III. iii. 246–60)

Within ten years of the appearance of *Tamburlaine*, it already sounded all
huff and rant to the Elizabethans, who considered Marlowe, along with Kyd,
one of the primitives of their theatre. But at least one writer understood that
such a poet had some advantages over his more sophisticated successors:

> Neat *Marlow*, bathed in the *Thespian* springs
> Had in him those brave translunary things,
> That the first Poets had, his raptures were,

All ayre, and fire, which made his verses cleere,
For that fine madnes still he did retaine,
Which rightly should possesse a Poets braine.[1]

In speaking of 'those brave translunary things' and comparing Marlowe to the first poets, Drayton is pointing to a quality in Marlowe's writing which we should now call archetypal or mythic. Instead of presenting life in realistic terms, Marlowe creates symbolic images of Renaissance man's sense of his powers, abilities and force. If they were naïve and crude, so was the new man's dream of what he could make of himself; if over-optimistic, then the power and intelligence and beauty of man seemed great enough to achieve any goal:

Of stature tall, and straightly fashioned,
Like his desire, lift upwards and divine,
So large of limbs, his joints so strongly knit,
Such breadth of shoulders as might mainly bear
Old Atlas' burthen; 'twixt his manly pitch,
A pearl more worth than all the world is placed,
Wherein by curious sovereignty of art
Are fixed his piercing instruments of sight,
Whose fiery circles bear encompassed
A heaven of heavenly bodies in their spheres,
That guides his steps and actions to the throne
Where honour sits invested royally:
Pale of complexion, wrought in him with passion,
Thirsting with sovereignty and love of arms,
His lofty brows in folds do figure death,
And in their smoothness amity and life:
About them hangs a knot of amber hair,
Wrapped in curls, as fierce Achilles' was,
On which the breath of heaven delights to play,
Making it dance with wanton majesty:
His arms and fingers long and sinewy,
Betokening valour and excess of strength:
In every part proportioned like the man
Should make the world subdued to Tamburlaine. (II. i. 7–30)

---

[1] Michael Drayton, 'To My Most Dearely-Loved Friend Henery Reynolds Esquire, Of Poets and Poesie', ll. 105–10, *The Works of Michael Drayton*, III, ed. J. E. Hebel (Oxford, 1932).

The 'long and sinewy' arms and hands of the figure suggest, like those of Michelangelo's David, enormous power and a delight in the physical world, the things that can be touched; they also, because they reveal 'excess of strength', hint at a tragic disproportion of desire and possibility. But limits are only hinted at, and the thrust of the figure is upwards and outwards, as if man, even while in repose, were threatening to fill the entire universe. This expansiveness of man is matched with a simultaneous contraction of the universe into the self. Tamburlaine's eyes are 'fiery circles' which 'bear encompassed' – i.e. surrounded – 'a heaven of heavenly bodies in their spheres', and while the words literally mean no more than that Tamburlaine's eyes shine brightly, taken at full metaphoric value they suggest that the fullness of the world no longer lies outside man but is inside his head. In other words, the model of reality is no longer located in nature and the whirling spheres of the universe, but in the human mind. And within that mind there is no rest or stable order, but a dynamic energy, always struggling, warring and striving for absolute sovereignty:

> Our souls, whose faculties can comprehend
> The wondrous architecture of the world,
> And measure every wandering planet's course,
> Still climbing after knowledge infinite,
> And always moving as the restless spheres,
> Wills us to wear ourselves and never rest,
> Until we reach the ripest fruit of all,
> That perfect bliss and sole felicity,
> The sweet fruition of an earthly crown. (II. vii. 21–9)

This lust for freedom and sovereignty, the *libido dominandi*,[1] the desire 'to be a king', is, in the Marlovian world, the basic motive of human nature, the drive which expresses man's humanity. Tamburlaine has just helped the noble Cosroe achieve the throne of Persia from his weak brother Mycetes, and as he departs to be crowned in the capital, one of his attendants tell us that Cosroe goes to 'ride in triumph through Persepolis'. The new king's entourage passes over the stage, leaving Tamburlaine and his generals behind. Picking up the words of the previous speaker, Tamburlaine muses:

> And ride in triumph through Persepolis!
> Is it not brave to be a king, Techelles?
> Usumcasane and Theridamas,

[1] This term, as well as parts of the analysis of Marlowe's style, is taken from Harry Levin, *The Overreacher: A Study of Christopher Marlowe* (Cambridge, Mass., 1952).

Is it not passing brave to be king,
And ride in triumph through Persepolis?
TECHELLES: O, my lord, 'tis sweet and full of pomp!
USUMCASANE: To be a king, is half to be a god.
THERIDAMAS: A god is not so glorious as a king:
I think the pleasure they enjoy in heaven,
Cannot compare with kingly joys in earth;
To wear a crown enchas'd with pearl and gold,
Whose virtues carry with it life and death;
To ask and have, command and be obeyed;
When looks breed love, with looks to gain the prize,
Such power attractive shines in princes' eyes. (II. v. 50–64)

This sense of life as continuous war for sovereignty shapes the plot of the play. Tamburlaine is born a poor Scythian shepherd but rises by his own courage and superiority to be the ruler of the world. Working both with words and with force of arms he easily overthrows the weak legitimate king of Persia, Mycetes, marries Zenocrate, the daughter of the Sultan of Egypt and the most beautiful woman in the world, and overcomes one established ruler after another, making them his servants, using them as footstools, caging them like beasts for his amusement, and even harnessing them to his chariot. His unrelenting sense of himself as destiny and his will as reality appears most clearly at the siege of Damascus when the virgins of that city with 'blubbered cheeks and hearty humble moans' come to plead with him in the name of all the traditional virtues – pity, love, humanity, family – to spare the town. But Tamburlaine, though he has no particular hatred for Damascus, has sworn that all will die if they resist beyond a certain point. That point has been passed, the black flag hoisted, and now the virgins must die and the city be sacked, because he has sworn that it will be so.

Tamburlaine is as great a poet and orator as he is a warrior. To speak poorly in this play, as the weak Mycetes does, is to show inadequacy in all other areas; while to speak magnificently reflects and instruments all other kinds of power. Indeed, here, as throughout the Elizabethan and Jacobean drama, great poetry is not the secondary but the primary means by which both playwrights and heroes instrument their wills and construct a world in the image of human desire. Marlowe's poetry manifests clearly and openly this use of 'working words'. The chief characteristics of the Marlovian heroic style are (1) the steady, heavy beat of 'Marlowe's mighty line', carrying authority, determination and steady onward movement; (2) the consistent use of present participles for adjectives – 'shining' for 'bright', 'rising' for 'high' – expressing a mind always in movement and always aspiring; (3) frequent appearance of such 'rising' words as 'soar', 'mount' and 'climb'; (4) persistence of the rhetorical figure Hyperbole, conveying a constant striving for a condition beyond any known in this world – 'lovelier than the love of Jove', 'fairer than the whitest snow on Scythian hills' and 'swifter than Pegasus'; (5) parataxis, the joining of several phrases and clauses by 'and' – and . . . and . . . and – to create a sense of endless ongoing, of constant reaching; (6) the use of the privative suffix in words which state limits – 'topless', 'quenchless', 'endless'; (7) frequent use of ringing proper names and exotic geographical places to realize the sensed wideness, brightness and richness of the world.

But the stylistic device which summarizes all the other elements of the Marlovian style is what we might call 'the pathetic fallacy in the imperative mood'. In the 'pathetic fallacy', a form of anthropomorphism frequently used in English poetry and particularly common in Renaissance drama, man assumes that nature feels what he feels, that the earth *sorrows* and trees *sigh* in the wind. Using this trope in the imperative, man commands nature and the gods to share his feelings and obey his wishes. This is Tamburlaine's regular mode of address to the world. He praises Zenocrate and confidently asserts that her beauty will 'clear the darkened sky And calm the rage of thundering Jupiter'. He decrees that the loveliness of humankind will 'scale the icy mountains' lofty tops' and melt the eternal snows with its radiance. In moments of the highest passion, the gods themselves are commanded to 'rain down murdering shot from heaven' on enemies, and the heavens and the earth are commanded to be desolate and bare in sympathy with the sorrow of man. As usual, words issue into action, and after Zenocrate's death in Part II Tamburlaine lays waste to the country in which she dies to bring the landscape into correspondence with his feelings.

Taken together, the elements of Marlowe's style add up to a perfect instance of language as action. In his use of words, Tamburlaine is not merely talking, he is doing; and what he is doing is reaching for 'the sweet fruition of an earthly crown'. His words and sentences constantly strive upwards and outwards, remake the world to fit the grandeur of his own imagination, and reshape nature to his own will. Tamburlaine thirsts not merely for political power or for kingship; kingship itself, with its thrones, sceptres and crowns, is merely the symbolic representation of a transcendent appetite for no less than the power of re-creation. The actual, existent world has a shape and direction of its own, but man has in his head, in his imagination, a new idea of reality which he attempts to impose on nature: 'A heaven of heavenly bodies in their spheres, That guides his steps and actions to the throne.' In its extreme form this is no less than the desire to be a god, and this is the characteristic motive of the heroes of Elizabethan drama, who seek to be gods in love, in honour, in politics, in learning, in pleasure, in morality, in reason. It is also the characteristic motive of the new theatre of sixteenth-century England, where by means of 'working words' the dramatists seek to effect through art the same desires that Tamburlaine tries to fulfil more directly through rhetoric and war. All of Marlowe's heroes are dramatizations of the heroic impulses which lie behind the theatre in which they are but characters.

In his attempt at domination, Tamburlaine is fairly successful, though there are ominous notes. But Marlowe wrote a sequel to *Tamburlaine*, and in Part II, while Tamburlaine remains a conqueror, outer reality forces itself on him in a painful way. He continues in conquest after conquest, but there is no end in sight; a son turns out to be cowardly and effeminate; the beautiful Zenocrate dies; other wills refuse to be broken to Tamburlaine's; and finally he too dies, still determined to storm the heavens themselves and set his black battle flags in the firmament. Marlowe draws no easy conclusion from all this, no sad, subservient moral that says that, since man is mortal and life is short, even heroes should submit and prepare for death. Rather, he sets up an unalterable opposition: on one side an external reality which always eludes and destroys man; on the other the human imagination and will which refuse to settle for any less than a complete conquest of reality.

(iii) 'Ends none of our own': *The Spanish Tragedy*

The son of a scrivener, Thomas Kyd (1558–94) was a Londoner who attended the Merchant Taylors' School but probably did not go on to a university. He began writing for the theatre in the early 1580s and apparently did a good deal of hack work. Some atheistical and seditious pamphlets were found in a search of his papers by the authorities in the early 1590s, and in 1593 he was imprisoned and possibly racked. His personal reputation has been somewhat clouded by the fact that he blamed a greater playwright, Christopher Marlowe, with whom he had once shared working quarters, for the presence of the damning pamphlets and accused Marlowe, in two shrill letters seeking to exonerate himself, of various blasphemies and general viciousness. Kyd died in 1594, perhaps as a result of torture and loss of livelihood. The majority of his work is lost – including the so-called *ur-Hamlet* – and his reputation is based on a poor translation of a tragedy of Garnier, *Cornelia* (1593–4), and the remarkable *Spanish Tragedy* (c. 1587), which, to judge by the frequent references to it, was one of the most popular plays of the age.

Kyd's style is pronouncedly rhetorical, and his subject matter is a sensational blend of ghosts, revenge, murders, madness, executions, Machiavellianism and bitten-out tongues. But despite these crudities Kyd traces and develops in considerable depth a moral question of the greatest importance: the relation of revenge to justice, the conflict of the individual with the laws of God and the state. Hieronimo, who as Marshal of Spain is entrusted with the enforcement of the law, seeks justice for the murder of his only son, Horatio, but is, because of the influence of the murderers, denied in all high places. Raging in madness from his frustrated need for absolute justice, he turns and trudges down the bloody path of revenge to a conclusion which involves his own death and that of most of the major characters of the play.

Below this drama of the self in conflict with society and tradition, another more fundamental issue – the question of freedom and fate – gradually takes shape, largely through the reiterated use of a theatrical perspective. Again and again the action becomes 'playing' and the scene becomes a theatre. In I. iv Hieronimo presents a dumb show of three knights taking the crowns from three kings; Balthazar and Lorenzo, the villains of the piece, watch from above like spectators while Horatio and Bel-imperia play out their love below and plan a future which is never to be; thinking that his pardon is in a black box held by a page, the murderer Pedringano stands on the scaffold joking with the executioner, until 'he turns him off'; there is a nuptial masque in which the torches are extinguished in blood; and finally Hieronimo stages the play within the play of *Soliman and Perseda* to provide an occasion to kill his enemies. Each of these 'plays' exists in turn within still another dramatic framework provided by the constant presence on stage of two spectators, Don Andrea and Revenge, who sit and watch, with occasional comments, the entire play working towards its predestined conclusion, the revenge of Don Andrea's death.

It is this last device that provides the key to the meaning of the insistent theatrical metaphor. Having been killed, apparently in fair fight, in a war between Spain and Portugal, Don Andrea descends for judgement to a pagan underworld where he is promised, seemingly without asking, that he shall have absolute justice, that the man who killed him, Don Balthazar, the Prince of Portugal, shall render up an eye for an eye and a tooth for a tooth. Led by Revenge, Don Andrea returns to the great stage of the world and proceeds to seat himself as a spectator to watch *The Spanish Tragedy*. This supernatural machinery, which suggests that revenge for all deaths is the law of nature, is expressed in the play proper as a chain of psychologically probable desires for revenge following the death of Don Andrea. Andrea's beloved, Bel-imperia, gives her love to Horatio because he was Andrea's friend and because she wishes to revenge herself on Andrea's killer, Balthazar, who now woos her. Balthazar, in turn, seeks revenge for this slight to his pride and joins with Lorenzo, who wishes to revenge himself for an insult to his honour, to kill Horatio. Hieronimo, Horatio's father, then seeks his revenge by killing Balthazar and Lorenzo, as well as Lorenzo's father. In the general destruction with which the play ends, Bel-imperia also dies, and Hieronimo kills himself.

Each of the characters thinks that he is simply pursuing some self-determined goal such as love, honour or justice; but, as G. K. Hunter points out, 'the characters of the play, scheming, complaining, and hoping – are not to be taken . . . as the independent and self-willed individuals they suppose themselves to be, but in fact only as the puppets of a predetermined and omnicompetent justice that they . . . cannot see and never really understand'.[1] Their helplessness and the meaninglessness of human concepts of justice are intensified by the peculiarly inefficient and wasteful way in which revenge works. Like the machines of Rube Goldberg, which go through an infinite number of elaborate steps to perform some simple function, the 'justice machine', as Hunter calls it, grinds up Lorenzo, Horatio, Serberine, Pedringano, Isabella, Hieronimo, Castile and Bel-imperia before Don Andrea is at last revenged on Balthazar. Andrea is himself bewildered by the eccentric way in which this mill of the gods turns, and complains to Revenge:

> Broughtst thou me hether to encrease my paine?
> I lookt that *Balthazar* should have beene slaine:
> But tis my freend *Horatio* that is slaine,
> And they abuse fair *Bel-imperia*,
> On whom I doted more then all the world,
> Because she lov'd me more then all the world. (II. vi. 1–6)

Though Kyd's apparent subject is the relation of revenge to justice, the true centre of *The Spanish Tragedy* is man's helplessness in the great under-tow of fate and history, the way in which life uses him, all unknowing, to work out the slovenly instrumentation of its law that a life must pay for a

[1] 'Ironies of justice in *The Spanish Tragedy*', *Renaissance Drama*, VIII (1965), 100.

life. Such a profound sense of human helplessness as this underlies both the older medieval pessimism about the transitoriness and misery of human life – the dance of death, the turn of Fortune's wheel, and the fall of princes – and the newer Renaissance pessimism of Machiavelli about the nature of power and politics, of Calvin about man's innate sinfulness and inability to act virtuously, and of Hobbes about the possibility of community. Despite their brave hopes for man and their belief in the beauty of his world, the greater Elizabethan and Jacobean dramatists never shook off this fear, and Hamlet will see it plain in the skull of Yorick in the graveyard outside Elsinore, Lear will look at it in the figure of Poor Tom on the heath, and the Duchess of Malfi will both see it and hear it in the dance and song of the madmen of the world as she prepares to die. Fear of helplessness and ignorance will take many shapes in the drama, but will recur frequently and powerfully in the form it takes in *The Spanish Tragedy*: the world imaged as theatre and life as play.

As if to insist that the world is no more real than the pretence of the theatre, life no more durable than the two hours' traffic of the stage, character no more than the role of a player, and history no more in human control than the plot is in the actors', *The Spanish Tragedy* keeps sloughing off the pretence of reality and becoming openly a play. This movement culminates in one of the most intricate theatrical perspectives imaginable. The audience watches Revenge and Don Andrea watching the kings of Spain and Portugal watching Lorenzo, Balthazar, Bel-imperia and Hieronimo playing in the brief play, *Soliman and Perseda*. This long view through theatres within theatres makes the characters seem immensely distant, small and unreal. Their reality and importance are further diminished by the reduction, the bounding in a nutshell, of all their human hopes and sufferings to the brief fifty or so lines and the melodramatic gestures of *Soliman and Perseda*. The effect is very similar to that of Pirandello's *Six Characters*, where the Characters' sense of the complexity of their motives and the uniqueness of their experiences is reduced to meaninglessness in order to get it down to a size and form which can be staged. But where the Characters never cease protesting, Hieronimo accepts his status as player by locking the door of the theatre when he enters to enact his final revenge, and by biting out his tongue in a fit of rage and Iago-like refusal to explain what he has done and why – despite his having told all already.

If the theatre expresses man's greatest hopes, it also expresses his greatest fears, and *homo ludens* appears in the bleakest possible form in the figure of Hieronimo standing locked in a play within a play within a play, reduced beyond actor to a puppet in a dumb show, his tongue gone, and mute, as if in obedience to the iron law of drama that man is what he does, not what he feels and says. History, Jan Kott remarks, 'can do without psychology and without rhetoric. It is just action.'[1] Drama too can exist at its starkest without the human voice and the poetry by which that voice attempts to shape the world to conform to the human imagination.

[1] *Shakespeare Our Contemporary*, trans. Boleslaw Taborski (New York, 1966), p. 153.

2 From ritual to history: the English history play

(i) The rituals of order

Just as the Renaissance *libido dominandi* enacted itself inevitably in the form of drama, so too did a new sense of history seem to demand dramatic form in order to express itself fully. As C. L. Barber says,

> The Renaissance ... was a moment when educated men were modifying a ceremonial conception of human life to create a historical conception. The ceremonial view, which assumed that names and meanings are fixed and final, expressed experience as pageant and ritual – pageant where the right names could march in proper order, or ritual where names could be changed in the right, the proper way. The historical view expresses life as drama. People in drama are not identical with their names, for they gain and lose their names, their status and meaning – and not by settled ritual: the gaining and losing of names, of meaning, is beyond the control of any set ritual sequence.[1]

The English, like the other great nations who discovered and fixed their national identities in the Renaissance, became fascinated during the sixteenth

[1] C. L. Barber, *Shakespeare's Festive Comedy, A Study of Dramatic Form and Its Relation to Social Custom* (Princeton, 1959), p. 193.

century with the concept of the nation and its past, and in chronicle, pamphlet, poem and play they constructed a history of England. But that history was shaped not so much by objective study of the available facts as by a great myth of order, known to us in its different manifestations as 'the great chain of being', 'the Elizabethan world picture', and 'the Tudor political myth' – all variants of what has been called 'the myth of the eternal return'.[1] This world view imaged the whole of creation, from God through the angels and man down to the meanest pebble, as hierarchically organized, like the rungs of a ladder or the links of a chain, in descending order of power, knowledge, purity, responsibility and authority. Each link in the chain, or each category of being, in turn mirrored in its internal organization the hierarchical structure of the whole. The result was an elaborate series of correspondences, very useful for poets, embracing the whole of creation. As God is to man, for example, or the sun to the universe, so is the king to his subjects, the father to his family, the reason to the appetites, the lion to the beasts, the oak to the trees and the diamond to the stones. To act 'naturally' and live in accordance with things as they properly are, was to accept the assigned place in this scheme, justly controlled by the powers above and justly controlling those below entrusted to your care and authority. Life properly lived was thus harmonious and mutually supportive, music or a dance being the images most frequently used to express the ideal. This was recognized, however, as an ideal state only, and disorders and rebellions against duly constituted authority were accepted as inevitable; but when a disturbance occurred in one of the 'little worlds' or microcosms all other parts of the universe trembled sympathetically, and the great equilibrating powers of nature began to react to restore order.

While this myth had its roots in the past, going back at least as far as Aristotle and receiving its most systematic formulation by the scholastic philosophers, it should not, I believe, be thought of as an essentially medieval view of life, conservative, pessimistic and authoritarian, fighting a losing battle with new optimistic Renaissance views about the freedom of man and the possibility of change and evolution. There is a conflict between the two views, and it lies at the centre of the drama of the age, but the great myth of order is as optimistic about life and as characteristic of the Renaissance as is the Promethean myth of freedom, struggle and change. Ulysses's speech on degree in *Troilus and Cressida* (I. iii), the finest statement of the myth in the literature of the time, expresses as much hope in the possible grandeur of man and the goodness of life as does Tamburlaine's surety that

[1] Mircea Eliade, *The Myth of the Eternal Return* (New York, 1954).

he holds the fates bound fast and turns Fortune's wheel about. The methods by which human fulfilment is to be realized are, however, opposite in nature, and while the myth of order seeks the realization of the good in the submission of the part to the whole and in the repetition, with only slight variation, of the traditional patterns of natural, social and individual life, the Promethean myth sees the good resulting from individual effort, rebellion and search for the new and different. Where the myth of order expresses itself as ritual and pageant, the new sense of an open-ended history seeks out the new kind of drama.

Since both the ethic and the dynamic of the myth of order were based on the acceptance and repetition of what had been before, it naturally expressed itself in ritual and pageant, the literary forms where what has been dramatically done before is done once again and the present is made to conform to the ancient patterns. History was discovered by Tudor historians to have the sameness of ritual: a weak or saintly king makes political mistakes and is overthrown by rebellious and arrogant subjects; the kingdom becomes a wasteland and society a chaos in which every man's hand is set against his fellow; after a period of great suffering, reaction against the forces of evil occurs, and a strong and good king restores order. This pattern – so similar to the Eden pattern of disobedience, fall and redemption – governed not only the writing of chronicle history but became through repetition a ritual pattern in the numerous history plays extending from the earlier *Gorboduc* and *Cambyses* through such works as *The Life and Death of Jack Straw* (*c.* 1588), *The Misfortunes of Arthur* (*c.* 1588), and *The Troublesome Raigne of John King of England* (*c.* 1589), to Thomas Lodge's *The Wounds of Civil War* (*c.* 1594), *Leir* (1594) and Shakespeare's earliest plays, the three parts of *Henry VI* (*c.* 1588–92). Even when this ritual view of history is being profoundly questioned, as in Marlowe's *Edward II* and Shakespeare's later plays on English and Roman history, the myth of order continues to control the manifest plot, so that it is possible to read all, or nearly all, of the history plays of this period as rituals of the conservative view of history and the ethic of order, counselling obedience and submission to the old ways and showing the dreadful consequences of rebellion and usurpation.

But at the same time this drama is filled with the murder of kings, the seizure of crowns and the defiance of such figures of authority as prince, judge, father, priest and teacher. 'Killing the king' is the motive force of much of the drama of this period, and in an age in which the major political and social question was the power of authority in all areas, particularly the authority of the crown, it is surprising that these plays generally escaped censorship, as surprising as the frequently repeated view of later critics that this drama had very little to do directly with the political issues of the time. Looking backwards it now seems almost inevitable that the people who created this drama ultimately did actually kill a real king, for, half concealed by the continued skeletal presence of the myth of order in the plots, an exciting and disturbing idea was being constantly enacted. As usual, it is Marlowe who presents it undisguised: after Tamburlaine defeats Bajazeth, the brutal but legitimate ruler of the Turks, by force of arms, Theridamas enters, takes the crown from the head of Bajazeth's empress, Zabina, and places it on the head of Tamburlaine's queen, Zenocrate, saying simply, 'Here, madam, you are empress, she is none' (III. iii. 227). No Miltonic effects follow this disturbance of ancient order – no thunder cracks, no lightning flashes, the world does not incline on its axis – and with this discovery that what was thought to be unalterable can be altered by those who dare, the great age of the history play is under way. Killing the king, defying the authority figure and fleeing the city are the specific dramatic forms taken by the more general impulse to freedom symbolized by the power to act and to create imaginative worlds, and it is noteworthy how often in the plays to come the histrionic power and the ability to see the world as drama are associated with the new sense of history and with political and social rebellion. Killing the king was not, as Shakespeare saw better than anyone else, simply a political act, but was the objective correlative of a new attitude towards established authority and order in all areas: social and family organization, individual psychology, art, and even grammar and geography.

(ii) Killing the king: Shakespeare's *Richard III*

It was in the late 1580s and early 1590s that William Shakespeare (1564–1616) (see Plate 15) began his work as playwright. We know a good deal about Shakespeare, but there is a gap in our knowledge of a crucial period of his life. After his marriage in 1582 to Ann Hathaway and the birth of Susanna in 1583, we hear nothing of him – except indirectly through the birth of twins, Judith and Hamnet, in 1585 – until 1592, when Robert Greene's attack on him in his *Groatsworth of Wit* advises us that Shakespeare was already a notorious, if not a famous, playwright and actor in the London theatre. The dates of and even the extent of his authorship in his earliest plays are in doubt, but if the bits and pieces of knowledge about the man and his works are assembled, they yield an unsurprising pattern. In the late 1580s and the early 1590s, Shakespeare, who apparently entered the theatre as an actor and continued to act until the early 1600s, was at work writing and adapting plays. In general, his earliest plays were elaborations of themes and forms already popular in the London theatre: *Titus Andronicus* in the style of Kyd and Senecan blood-revenge tragedy; *The Two Gentlemen of Verona* expanding on the fashionable theme of love versus honour in the style of Lyly; *The Comedy of Errors* in the manner of Plautine comedy; and three history plays dealing in a fairly conventional way with the reign of King Henry VI.

Shakespeare, Patrick Crutwell remarks, 'was no revolutionary – indeed, if one had to label his political "position", it would be as that of a natural conservative whom the stress of events, internal and external, had driven to the edge of anarchism'.[1] In the early 1590s the 'stress' was not so great as it was later to become, but an extremely complex attitude, containing considerable tension, is already apparent in *Richard III*. Richard, the representative of the new politics, is no godlike Titan like Tamburlaine, but a twisted hunchback with a withered arm, born with teeth in his head to bite the world, devoid of all sense of community – 'I am myself alone' (*3 Henry VI*, V. vi. 83) – and determined to find his way to power by means of treachery, deceit and murder. This is the new politics seen from the conservative point of view, and, in accordance with the Tudor myth, Richard is imaged as the devil raised by the horrors of civil war, the hog who roots in and fouls all the sacred places of life, the shadow which blots out the sun and casts the earth in darkness, the cold wind that blasts all living things. In action, he is the destroyer of pageants and rituals. He interrupts the funeral procession of his victim, Henry VI, to woo the Lady Anne; turns a council of state into a trap for one of the councillors; makes a grotesque joke of a civic petition from the citizens of London; and when in IV. iv the bereaved women gather to form a chorus, to lament in ritual language their losses and to cry out for relief from the adversary, he arrives at the head of an army and orders the trumpets blown to prevent heaven from hearing their curses. Again and again the sufferers are driven together in their fear, only to have Richard burst in and destroy or pervert the attempted rites of concord.

Just as Richard prevents rituals from moving to their fore-ordained end, so he refuses to play the devilish role he is cast for in the pageant of England's crisis and restoration. Morally he is abominable, but dramatically he is attractive, alert, vital. His audacious political manoeuvres, his sure skill in contriving events, his lively wit and sense of the ridiculous, his energy, his

[1] Patrick Crutwell, *The Shakespearean Moment* (London, 1954; New York, 1955), p. 30.

style and his self-awareness command attention and respect. All of these qualities are displayed in the scene in which he stops the Lady Anne, who is following the funeral procession of her father-in-law, Henry VI. Richard has killed both that king and Anne's husband, Prince Edward, and now, having decided that a marriage with Anne would be useful politically, he interrupts the funeral procession and, fully aware of his own physical grotesqueness, tells her that it was her beauty which drove him to murder her husband and her father-in-law. When she spits on him, he gambles and, handing her his sword, bares his breast, and asks her to kill him if she hates him. When she drops the sword, he takes the risk a bit further and agrees to kill himself if she will only command him to do so. She does not, and in a few moments more he is talking familiarly about bedchambers and the pleasures of love. Richard's success is gaspingly incredible, and he himself can scarcely believe that he has brought it off:

> Was ever woman in this humour woo'd?
> Was ever woman in this humour won?
> I'll have her; but I will not keep her long. (I. ii. 228–30)

The same audacious ways of working appear when Richard learns that Hastings will not support him in his bid for the crown while the two young princes, the rightful heirs, are alive. He summons him to a council of state, where Hastings, puffed up with idiocy and vanity, boasts of his closeness to Richard, the Lord Protector. Richard enters, and after some political chitchat casually asks the Bishop of Ely for some of those fine strawberries that the bishop grows in his garden. He then exits with Buckingham, only to return shortly and, holding up the withered arm which has been deformed since his birth, accuses Queen Elizabeth and Dame Shore of having blasted the arm by witchcraft. He then asks Hastings what they deserve who have so plotted against him, and Hastings, presumably with his mouth hanging open, fumbles for a moment: 'If they have done this deed, my noble lord –', and this one slip is all that Richard needs:

> If! – thou protector of this damned strumpet,
> Talk'st thou to me of if's? Thou art a traitor.
> Off with his head! (III. iv. 76–8)

A short time later a scrivener reveals that he has been busy all the preceding night on a fair copy of a warrant for Hastings's death.

In these scenes and many others, Richard turns ritual into drama and pageant into politics and history. What was supposed to have a familiar, foreknown end becomes an open-ended opportunity for the man who plays many parts – the jolly thriving lover, the humble peacemaker, the plain blunt man who cannot conceal the truth, the jocular uncle, the pious recluse, the frightened victim of many plots – to use his histrionic skill to make himself king. As he becomes more confident of his skill at playing, more certain of his own freedom from predetermined roles and patterns, he begins openly to rewrite and stage the ceremonies of state to achieve his own purposes. Desiring a pretext of legitimacy for his seizure of the crown, he has his henchman Buckingham gather together a reluctant mayor of London and a few frightened citizens to exercise their ancient right to petition; and when this stage crowd comes to the courtyard to ask him to be their king, Richard appears in humble dress, flanked by two bishops and reading scripture. After a few pious protestations of his unworthiness and his desire for a life of religious dedication, Richard at last reluctantly agrees to accept the mandate of the people, abandon his privacy and become king.

But the discovery that 'I am myself alone' and the realization that the unique individual is free of traditional moral and social imperatives, while they release tremendous powers, also carry with them, in Shakespeare's view, new dangers. In the end Richard is unable to escape the old ritual view of history, for the forces of outraged good at last gather head under the leadership of Henry Tudor and force Richard to play his assigned role as villain and scapegoat. But while the outlines of the Tudor myth are preserved, the forces which bring about the expected conclusion are not so much the traditional workings of a moral universe as they are psychic forces at work within those depths of self to which George, Duke of Clarence, who has murdered and betrayed so often, plunges in his dream:

> O Lord, methought what pain it was to drown,
> What dreadful noise of waters in my ears,
> What sights of ugly death within my eyes!
> Methoughts I saw a thousand fearful wrecks,
> A thousand men that fishes gnaw'd upon,
> Wedges of gold, great anchors, heaps of pearl,
> Inestimable stones, unvalued jewels,
> All scatt'red in the bottom of the sea;
> Some lay in dead men's skulls, and in the holes
> Where eyes did once inhabit there were crept,
> As 'twere in scorn of eyes, reflecting gems,
> That woo'd the slimy bottom of the deep
> And mock'd the dead bones that lay scatt'red by. (I. iv. 21–33)

Richard comes to these same depths on the eve of his death, when the ghosts of those he has killed come to him in a dream and tell him to 'Despair and die'. He wakes out of being himself 'alone' to the full complexity of his own being:

> What do I fear? Myself? There's none else by.
> Richard loves Richard; that is, I am I.
> Is there a murderer here? No – yes, I am.
> Then fly. What, from myself? Great reason why –
> Lest I revenge. What, myself upon myself!
> Alack, I love myself. Wherefore? For any good
> That I myself have done unto myself?
> O, no! Alas, I rather hate myself
> For hateful deeds committed by myself! (V. iii. 182–90)

Here in the depths of self to which Shakespeare's realism led, Clarence and Richard discover that their actions have violated their own most fundamental selves. In the Shakespearian psychology the human mind is not a *tabula rasa* and man is therefore not Proteus, free to act any part and to make his role into his reality. Instead, man is a mixed creature whose nature is in part at least to cherish and sympathize rather than to kill, and a denial of this life-nourishing force sets one part of the self at war with other parts. And so, in a characteristically Shakespearian way, after rationalism and scepticism seem to have discredited the older, traditional views as nothing more than the hopes of the timid and conventional, these views are re-established on the realistic basis of human psychology. Shakespeare's history is not the Marlovian impact on events of an impossibly pure drive to power, but is rather a slow unfolding in time of the complex totality of man and men, which usually ultimately takes something like the same outward shape as the orthodox views of morality and history. At least it was so when he wrote *Richard III*, but matters became far less simple when he began to explore in greater depth and at greater length the interaction of the events of history and the thoughts of men.

(iii) The *Henriad*: Shakespeare's major history plays

Taken together, Shakespeare's four major history plays, *Richard II*, *1 Henry IV*, *2 Henry IV* and *Henry V* constitute an epic, the *Henriad*.[1] While

[1] Moody Prior, *The Drama of Power, Studies in Shakespeare's History Plays* (Evanston, 1973), p. 346, notes Pater's remark in *Appreciations*, 'It is no *Henriade*, but the sad fortunes of some English kings.' This material was originally printed in somewhat different form as an article in the *Yale Review* (Autumn 1969), pp. 3–32. Permission to reprint is gratefully acknowledged.

there is no evidence that Shakespeare planned the plays as a unit, they do have remarkable coherence and they possess that quality which in our time we take to be the chief characteristic of epic: a large-scale, heroic action, involving many men and many activities, tracing the movement of a nation or people through violent change from one condition to another. In the *Iliad* the action is the wrath of Achilles and the misfortunes which it brought to the Achaeans before Troy; in the *Aeneid*, the transferral of the empire of Troy to Latium; and in *Paradise Lost*, man's first disobedience and the fruit of that forbidden tree. In the *Henriad*, the action is the passage from the England of Richard II to the England of Henry V. This dynastic shift serves as the supporting framework for a great many cultural and psychological transitions which run parallel to the main action, giving it body and meaning. In historical terms the movement is the passage from the middle ages to the Renaissance and the modern world. In political and social terms it is a movement from feudalism and hierarchy to the national state and individualism. In psychological terms it is a passage from a situation in which man knows with certainty who he is to an existential condition in which identity is only a temporary role. In spatial and temporal terms it is a movement from a closed world to an infinite universe. In mythical terms the passage is from a garden world to a fallen world. In the most summary terms it is a movement from ceremony and ritual to history.

It is through ceremony and ritual that the old kingdom expresses itself at the beginning of the *Henriad*. *Richard II* opens on a scene in which two furious peers, Mowbray and Hereford, confront and accuse one another of treason before their king. The place of judgement is the royal court with all its forms and symbols: crowns, trumpets, thrones, ranked retainers, robes of state and heraldic arms. When this ceremonial attempt to absorb and re-order the disorderly elements in man and society fails, an even more solemn ritual is ordered, trial by combat. The combatant knights enter in the required manner and take their assigned places in the lists. They make the expected speeches, and the marshal of the lists puts the traditional questions to them:

> *The trumpets sound. Enter* BOLINGBROKE, DUKE OF HEREFORD,
> *appellant, in armour, and a* Herald.

KING RICHARD: Marshal, ask yonder knight in arms,
   Both who he is and why he cometh hither
   Thus plated in habiliments of war;
   And formally, according to our law,
   Depose him in the justice of his cause.

MARSHAL: What is thy name? and wherefore com'st thou hither
  Before King Richard in his royal lists?
  Against whom comest thou? and what's thy quarrel?
  Speak like a true knight, so defend thee heaven!
BOLINGBROKE: Harry of Hereford, Lancaster, and Derby,
  Am I; who ready here do stand in arms
  To prove, by God's grace and my body's valour,
  In lists on Thomas Mowbray, Duke of Norfolk,
  That he is a traitor, foul and dangerous,
  To God of heaven, King Richard, and to me.
  And as I truly fight, defend me heaven! (I. iii. 26–41)

Here, and throughout the early acts of the play, traditional values – the law, the sanctity of a knight's oath, established duty to God and king – reflected in the ritual gestures, the formulaic phrases and the orderly rhythms, control violent passions and submerge the individual within the role imposed upon him by prescribed ways of thinking, acting and speaking.

But even as we admire, this old world breaks up. The patriarchs of England – the seven sons of Edward III – are, like the patriarchs of *Genesis*, passing from the land, and with them their world passes. The sense of an ancient, more perfect world, fading from existence into memory, is focused in John of Gaunt's comparison of England, as it was only yesterday, to another Eden:

  This royal throne of kings, this scept'red isle,
  This earth of majesty, this seat of Mars,
  This other Eden, demi-paradise,
  This fortress built by Nature for herself
  Against infection and the hand of war,
  This happy breed of men, this little world,
  This precious stone set in the silver sea,
  Which serves it in the office of a wall,
  Or as a moat defensive to a house,
  Against the envy of less happier lands;
  This blessed plot, this earth, this realm, this England. . . . (II. i. 40–50)

By III. iv when the 'sea-walled garden' appears again, presided over by a gardener in 'old Adam's likeness', it is full of weeds, the flowers choked, the trees unpruned, the hedges in ruin, the herbs eaten by caterpillars and the great tree in its centre dead. What is passing is innocence, a sense of living in an immutable golden world, and no one is more innocent than

Richard himself. When Bolingbroke begins his rebellion, Richard confidently expects that God himself will send down soldiers to defend him and destroy the usurper. The order of nature and the laws of men, he believes, guarantee his kingship:

> Not all the water in the rough rude sea
> Can wash the balm off from an anointed king;
> The breath of worldly men cannot depose
> The deputy elected by the Lord.
> For every man that Bolingbroke hath press'd
> To lift shrewd steel against our golden crown,
> God for his Richard hath in heavenly pay
> A glorious angel. Then, if angels fight,
> Weak men must fall; for heaven still guards the right. (III. ii. 54–62)

Richard takes the great myth of order for absolute fact, mistakes metaphor for science, and so believes that God will directly intervene in the coming battle and that the king's appearance in England will cause rebellion to disappear just as the rising of the sun (the 'king' of the cosmos) banishes darkness. But, beneath the surface of ritual and order, powerful political and personal energies are at work in Richard's England which threaten the existence of this idealized world. Mowbray has been involved in graft and assassination for political purposes. Henry Hereford has been courting popularity with the common people, and he accuses Mowbray of treason knowing that he is innocent. His motive may be to embarrass Richard, who is himself deeply implicated in the murder of his uncle, the Duke of Gloucester, the crime of which Mowbray is accused. Richard, violently jealous of his cousin Hereford, stops the trial by combat and under the guise of mercy banishes both his rival, Hereford, and his now embarrassing agent, Mowbray. Pressed by the perpetual need for money, Richard sells his right to gather taxes to profiteers. He neglects affairs of state to spend his time revelling with male favourites. Each of these acts indirectly undermines the order which Richard thinks immutable, and when upon John of Gaunt's death he seizes the banished Hereford's lands, he strikes a direct blow, as the Duke of York points out, against the great law of orderly succession on which his kingship rests:

> Take Hereford's rights away, and take from Time
> His charters and his customary rights;
> Let not to-morrow then ensue to-day;

Be not thyself – for how art thou a king
But by fair sequence and succession? (II. i. 195–9)

The play realizes Richard's implication in his own destruction explicitly in the scene in which he uncrowns himself, names Bolingbroke his successor and confesses the sins which brought him down.

Richard's disorders immediately release a variety of other disorders on all levels of life. Richard having broken the order which made and kept him king, Henry Bolingbroke immediately rebels against Richard. By the end of the play there is already another group of plotters planning to overthrow Henry, and throughout the three succeeding plays political scheming, plotting, raids on the commonwealth and civil wars never cease. As one group of rebels dies, another group is already forming to take its place, each more desperate and violent than the last. Henry IV lives out his days facing endless revolt, and even Henry V, who restores political order, is still forced to deal with treasons which are 'like Another fall of man' (*Henry V*, II. ii. 141–2). Social life becomes chaotic. York's son, the Duke of Aumerle, intrigues against the new king, and the Duchess of York tells her husband that his primary duty lies not to the king but to his own son. But the anguished York goes to the king to accuse his own son of treason, while the Duchess pleads against her husband and for her son. The disorder in York's family expands to the family of Henry, and by the end of the play we learn that Hal, the Prince of Wales, is already roistering in a tavern, defying his father and using his power to break the law with impunity.

As the old order breaks up, a profound psychological confusion parallels the political and social confusion. In that Edenic world which Gaunt describes and Richard destroys, every man knew who he was. His religion, his family, his position in society, his assigned place in processions large and small, his coat of arms and his traditional duties told him who he was, what he should do and even gave him the formal language in which to express this socially assigned self. But once, under the pressures of political necessity and personal desires, the old system is destroyed, the old identities go with it. Man then finds himself in the situation which Richard acts out in IV. i, the deposition scene. Richard is speaking, and when Northumberland attempts to break in with the exclamation 'My lord', he responds with words which reveal how thoroughly shattered is his sense of the power of his name and his identity as Richard Plantagenet, king of England:

No lord of thine, thou haught insulting man,
Nor no man's lord; I have no name, no title –

No, not that name was given me at the font –
But 'tis usurp'd. Alack the heavy day,
That I have worn so many winters out,
And know not now what name to call myself! (IV. i. 254–9)

Like the great actor he is, Richard cannot pass the opportunity to demonstrate visually the lesson he has learned. He calls for a looking glass, and holding it before his face he muses:

No deeper wrinkles yet? Hath sorrow struck
So many blows upon this face of mine
And made no deeper wounds? O flatt'ring glass,
Like to my followers in prosperity,
Thou dost beguile me! Was this face the face
That every day under his household roof
Did keep ten thousand men? Was this the face
That like the sun did make beholders wink?
Is this the face which fac'd so many follies
That was at last out-fac'd by Bolingbroke?
A brittle glory shineth in this face;
As brittle as the glory is the face;
        [*He breaks the mirror.*] (IV. i. 277–88)

The fragments of the mirror are the fragments of an identity, once whole, but now broken into many contradictory parts: Richard as he once was, as he now is; as he feels himself to be inwardly, and as he appears outwardly.

Richard is not the first man in this play to discover that he no longer knows who he is. He has already forced the question of identity on Bolingbroke by banishing him from England and robbing him of his succession as Duke of Lancaster. Bolingbroke – whose names change rapidly: Hereford, Bolingbroke, Lancaster and Henry IV – has understood the lesson well. Speaking to Bushy and Green, two of Richard's favourites, the man who had once confidently answered the question 'What is thy name?' with the proud words 'Harry of Hereford, Lancaster, and Derby, Am I' now tells of the bitterness of banishment and the pain that comes from loss of those possessions and symbols which had heretofore guaranteed identity:

Myself – a prince by fortune of my birth,
Near to the King in blood, and near in love
Till you did make him misinterpret me –
Have stoop'd my neck under your injuries

And sigh'd my English breath in foreign clouds,
Eating the bitter bread of banishment,
Whilst you have fed upon my signories,
Dispark'd my parks and fell'd my forest woods,
From my own windows torn my household coat,
Raz'd out my imprese, leaving me no sign
Save men's opinions and my living blood
To show the world I am a gentleman. (III. i. 16–27)

Man has not merely lost his true identity for a time; he has, once he abandoned the old hierarchies and rituals, broken into a strange, new existence where identity constantly changes and names are secured only by 'men's opinions' and by 'living blood'. John of Gaunt's awkward punning on his name as he lies dying suggests the pervasiveness of the feeling that names are no longer real and permanent but only the roles of the moment. This fluctuation in identity is the basic rhythm of the play, present everywhere, in Richard's everchanging moods, in Bolingbroke's rising fortunes and changing names, in Richard's decline from king of England to his last appearance on stage, a body borne in by his murderer. The pattern of up–down, of restless change in the self, appears in its most complete and concentrated form in Richard's great final speech, sitting in the dungeon of Pomfret Castle (V. v), about to die, and trying desperately to understand himself and this strange world into which he has fallen. Richard began as a great and secure king, seated on a throne, sure of himself, surrounded by pomp, confirmed by ceremony, looking out over a world of light where everything in the universe seemed related and ordered. At the end of the play he is the isolated individual, solitary, sitting in a small circle of candlelight, surrounded by darkness and by a flinty prison wall, uncertain of any reality or truth. Isolated in a mysterious and limited world, Richard takes the confusing and conflicting evidence which his mind offers him and attempts, by means of reason and poetic power, to construct analogies, to 'hammer it out', to give experience some form, to create some new coherence. The results are not comforting. As hard as he hammers, he can discover only endless mutability in the life of man and endless restlessness in his soul. All evidence is now ambiguous: where the Bible promises Innocence an easy salvation in one passage, 'come little ones', turn the page and it speaks in tragic tones of the passage to the kingdom of heaven being as difficult as a camel's threading the eye of a needle. Man's powers at one moment seem infinite and he feels that he can 'tear a passage through the flinty ribs Of this hard world', but at the next moment he is the most helpless of creatures and can only comfort himself that many others have endured like misery. Fate forces new identities on him, and since even in his own mind man can find no stable identity, life becomes theatrical, a playing of many roles in a constantly changing play. To be in history is to be in drama.

> Thus play I in one person many people,
> And none contented. Sometimes am I king;
> Then treasons make me wish myself a beggar,
> And so I am. Then crushing penury
> Persuades me I was better when a king;
> Then am I king'd again; and by and by
> Think that I am unking'd by Bolingbroke,
> And straight am nothing. But whate'er I be,
> Nor I, nor any man that but man is,
> With nothing shall be pleas'd till he be eas'd
> With being nothing. (V. v. 31–41)

To accommodate this shifting reality and unsettled imagination Richard changes from the formal conventional style of the beginning of the play to a metaphysical style capable of handling irony and a reality in which the parts no longer mesh, capable of carrying intense agitation and the passionate effort of thought.

The world continues to speak ambiguously to Richard in the form of two visitors. The first is a poor groom from his stables who, only having seen the king before from a distance, now risks his life to come to speak of duty which alters not when it alteration finds. The second visitor is the murderer Exton who has come to kill Richard in hope of reward from Henry. Richard, having tried to define himself by means of poetry and failed, now takes the way of drama, and acts. He seizes a sword from one of Exton's thugs and strikes two of them down before being killed himself. And so he defines himself in a dramatic or historic, not a philosophical way. He has never solved the question of whether he is king or beggar, never found the meaning he hoped to have; but he has stumbled through experience to quite a different answer. He, like the rest of men, has no stable identity certified by the order of things immutable. He is instead tragic man, whose identity fluctuates between hero and victim, king and corpse; whose values are not guaranteed by anything but his own willingness to enact them; whose life is a painful and continuing process of change. Richard traces the way that all other characters in this historical world must follow in their turn.

Looking back on the lost past, the men of Henry IV's England see the 'fall' occurring at that fatal moment when Richard threw down his warder, the symbol of his office and his duty, to stop for political reasons the ritual trial by combat between Bolingbroke and Mowbray. In *Richard II* the effects of that act are focused in the person of Richard and his passage into tragic existence. In the two parts of *Henry IV*, however, the effects are exploded to create an entire dramatic world and the many various characters who inhabit it. Richard's internal disorders and conflicting values grow into the increasingly bitter political and social disorders of a world racked by rebellion, strife, ambition, self-seeking, squabbling and desperate attempts to hold things together. Richard's growing awareness and fear of the inevitable movement of time into an unknown future expands to its extremities: a complete rejection of time (Falstaff) on one hand, and on the other an obsession with the limited amount of time available to man (Hotspur), which leads ultimately to a fearful vision of infinity. Richard's loss of certainty and his increasing inability to reconcile the contrary evidence of his own feelings and experiences enlarge into the murky confusion of history, the world of rumour, suspicion and half truth, where men must make decisions of the utmost importance without knowledge of the necessary facts. There may even be no definite answer to such crucial questions as: 'Is the king's planned crusade genuine piety or political strategy?', 'Is Hal really a riotous youth or is he only pretending to be a wastrel?', 'Did Mortimer treasonably surrender his army to Glendower, and does Henry refuse to ransom him because he is a traitor or because he has a legal claim to the throne?' The kind of suspicion raised on suspicion, on which men must risk their lives in this world where truth is impossible to come by, is perfectly conveyed in the Earl of Worcester's lines in which he sketches out the reasoning which leads him to rebellion: he helped the king, the king can never forget this and will always fear that his former friends will think themselves not fully rewarded, and therefore they must always fear the king who may fear them:

> For, bear ourselves as even as we can,
> The King will always think him in our debt,
> And think we think ourselves unsatisfied,
> Till he hath found a time to pay us home. (I. iii. 285–8)

As Richard's identity crumbles, he begins with increasing frequency to use images of the theatre, of acting and role-playing, to reflect his instability of character. In the later plays the sense of life as play and man as actor is pervasive. Playing becomes not only an instrument of deceit – Prince John's pretence that he will pardon the rebels if they lay down their arms – but also a means to truth – Hal's parodies of Hotspur's excessive energy and violence. Men in the world of *Henry IV* no longer take their identities as settled but assume that life is a succession of roles, played with skill and style to achieve a desired end. Hal plays the part of the prodigal son and the wastrel in order to appear better when he is settled as king, the Protean Falstaff plays a succession of roles for pleasure and profit, and the one man who will not pretend, Hotspur, soon dies.

Richard's discovery that man is a creature of infinite possibilities ranging all the way from dust to god, beggar to king, is projected in the Henry plays into the wide and varied cast of characters, each of whom seems to be not a whole man but a fragment, some singular power inherent in human nature isolated and carried to its extreme. 'Homo' may be, as Gadshill says, 'a common name to all men' (II. i. 104–5), but the correct adjective is a constant question. To realize his humanity does man properly seek power? pleasure? learning? love? order? glory? Is the truly human setting the place of pleasure and fellowship, the Boar's Head tavern in Eastcheap? the council table in the palace at Westminster? the desperate battlefields far to the north and west along the Scottish and the Welsh marches? Glendower's castle where old songs of love are played and the mysteries of the vast universe are discussed? These are the principal symbolic places in the Henry plays, the places in which man now pursues, in a sudden surge of freedom and released energy, his destiny and his nature. Each of these symbolic places has a resident deity, a genius of the place, whose speeches and actions provide the best understanding of its attitudes and values.

The Glendower world which embodies the values of magic, philosophy, poetry and love remains strangely peripheral, as if, despite the high value Shakespeare elsewhere places on these powers, they were not of fundamental importance in this great conflict. There is perhaps even a disqualifying sensitivity here, a tendency to withdraw from the power struggle, for when Hotspur – who finds love and poetry equally trivial – offends Glendower by laughing at his magic, the Welshman quietly withdraws from the rebellion against order and does not appear again.

Falstaff presides over the tavern world, and when first seen this latter-day Bacchus is waking from a nap on a bench. Sitting up, stretching, he asks the prince, 'What time of day is it, lad?' The prince, who has a supreme sense of the new time, the relentless sequence of irrecoverable moments, understands that Falstaff apprehends time only as instants of pleasure:

What a devil has thou to do with the time of the day? Unless hours were cups of sack, and minutes capons, and clocks the tongues of bawds, and dials the signs of leaping-houses, and the blessed sun himself a fair hot wench in flame-coloured taffeta, I see no reason why thou shouldst be so superfluous to demand the time of the day.

(I. ii. 6–13)

The old knight is enormously fat, a walking version of the roast beef of old England, given over entirely to epicurean pleasures. He never pays his debts; he is a liar, a thief, a drunkard, the very energy of disorder and lawlessness. For him a true man follows the pleasures of the belly and the bed, avoiding pain and labour whenever possible. He takes what he wants without worrying about property rights or morality. Such abstracts as honour, truth, duty and honesty, those hard, painful virtues which he is always being exhorted to practise, seem to him patently ridiculous and self-defeating, and he is an adept at sliding around and under such claims. When trapped in some obvious lie or charged with some gross weakness, he will, without regard for the restraints of logic, gaily change the subject, take up another pose or make some such comment as 'all's one for that'. He is a master at staying alive and comfortable in an extremely dangerous and painful world.

To the moralist, Falstaff is a vice, a demi-devil, a tempter, a mere caterpillar of the commonwealth. Viewed from a more tolerant perspective, Falstaff is only an amusing and cunning old rogue, but still a merely quick-witted glutton and braggart, a victim of his own appetites and a figure of fun. But Falstaff meets such challenges to his value more than halfway, by asking continually the eternal comic questions: 'What is so important about a well-run state? Why all this strange passion for "grinning honour", this order and honesty which cost so much pain and suffering?' These questions are usually asked indirectly, by means of parody and wit, and the shrewdness of mind and style is exquisite at points. For example, when he is urging Hal to join the robbery at Gadshill, and Hal protests that the Prince of Wales cannot become a common thief, Falstaff remarks quickly 'thou cam'st not of the blood royal, if thou darest not stand for ten shillings' (I. ii. 156–8). On the face of it he seems merely to be punning on the meaning of 'royal', a type of coin. But there is an edge to this remark, which Hal apparently misses, for it recalls the fact that the royal blood of England achieved its present eminence by means of robbery, not a little robbery, such as the thieves are planning on Gadshill, but a big robbery in which all of England was taken.

While Falstaff is efficient in the use of the rapier thrust of wit, his most masterful attacks are delivered by means of parody. For example, when Hal seems to have bested him in a wit combat, Falstaff shifts ground and plays the misled youth, the penitent determined to return to the paths of righteousness:

> Thou hast done much harm upon me, Hal – God forgive thee for it! Before I knew thee, Hal, I knew nothing; and now am I, if a man should speak truly, little better than one of the wicked. I must give over this life, and I will give it over. By the Lord, an I do not I am a villain! I'll be damn'd for never a king's son in Christendom.
>
> (I. ii. 102–9)

To his appreciative audience this is no more than another of Monsieur Remorse's self-beguilements or posturings. But several features of the speech – its style, its artistic exaggeration and its sly suggestion that true wickedness comes from the palace, not the tavern – combine to create behind the lines an eye-twinkling self-consciousness, aware at once of how ridiculous is this pretence and yet how good a game it is. The speech is then self-parody, but it goes even further, for Falstaff is also acting out the sanctimonious pretences of the rest of the world to holiness. Behind each of his pretences – the royal king, the brave captain, the innocent child, the loyal knight, the penitent sinner – stands Falstaff himself, the old Adam, fat, red-nosed, slothful and lecherous, a living low burlesque of the establishment.

Each of Falstaff's parodies thus contains the pretence of virtue – the part he acts – and what he takes to be human reality – himself – and as the play progresses he stages ever more pointed demonstrations of the gap between this appearance and that reality. On the eve of the great battle at Shrewsbury, Sir John, acting as draftmaster, has allowed all the healthy and prosperous to buy out and has collected instead the poor, the battered and the inept into a remarkable regiment, 'slaves as ragged as Lazarus in the painted cloth, where the Glutton's dogs licked his sores' (IV. ii. 27–9). As he marches this strange rout toward the battle, he encounters Hal and Westmoreland, banners flying, armour shining, horses snorting, filled with confidence and chivalry. Hal exclaims: 'I did never see such pitiful rascals.' Falstaff's reply contains a grimly realistic view of war and the function of the common soldier:

> Tut, tut; good enough to toss; food for powder, food for powder; they'll fill a pit as well as better: tush, man, mortal men, mortal men.
>
> (IV. ii. 71–4)

War's reality has been paraded before war's pretences. Falstaff's view that since the soldier's function is to be blown to pieces and to fill a ditch one man will do as well as another is proven by the events of the battle in which only three of his men survive, and they so badly wounded that the rest of their lives will be spent begging. Falstaff's most famous use of this parody technique is, of course, his catechism in which he compares the abstraction, honour, with the reality, the body of the honourable but dead Blunt, and draws some very commonsense conclusions about the durability of honour and its ability to set a leg or take away the pain of a wound. Falstaff, and the tavern world which he personifies, is a most dangerous antagonist to any moral point of view, to any set of abstractions such as honour, duty or country. He is always acting out some penetrating truth about the establishment, and each time he asserts such a truth, he strengthens his own case for leading a pleasant, harmless life asleep behind the arras after lunch, drinking a bottle of sack and laughing and joking with a few witty friends about the foolishness of life as most sober-sided citizens lead it.

Henry Percy, Hotspur, is the exact opposite of Falstaff. Where Falstaff is all flesh and fat and body, Hotspur is all spirit. Falstaff longs for a horse but is always forced to walk – Hal steals his horse and later procures for him 'a charge of foot' – Hotspur is fully alive only on the back of his horse. Where Falstaff refuses to have anything to do with time, Hotspur is always rushing forward to meet and outrun it. Falstaff's natural habitat is in the tavern before the fire, but Percy fully lives only on the battlefield. Falstaff always seeks pleasure, Hotspur always seeks fame, honour, *gloire*. Scarcely aware of other people, never aware of their feelings – with the odd exception of his informal but warm relationship with his wife Kate – Hotspur is aimed like an arrow towards that mystical place where absolute honour is to be won. The further away it is and the more difficult to arrive at, the more honour for the man who achieves it:

> By heaven, methinks it were an easy leap
> To pluck bright honour from the pale-fac'd moon;
> Or dive into the bottom of the deep,
> Where fathom-line could never touch the ground,
> And pluck up drowned honour by the locks;
> So he that doth redeem her thence might wear
> Without corrival all her dignities. (I. iii. 201–7)

Honour, as Hotspur understands it, is no longer the honour of the medieval knight, of Roland or Galahad, achieved by humbling one's self and performing the difficult tasks imposed by one's God, one's feudal lord or one's lady. It is instead the Renaissance thirst for individual fame, for immortality of reputation in a world where all else dies and is forgotten in the never-returning movement of time. It possesses Hotspur utterly, and even his sleep is a restless impatient dream of battle which culminates in a breath-taking vision of Fame:

> And in thy face strange motions have appear'd,
> Such as we see when men restrain their breath
> On some great sudden hest. (II. iii. 63–5)

Hotspur's life is a surging rush onward which endures no obstacles. He has no time for love or poetry or song, for grace or manners or political manoeuvring. He prides himself on being honest, direct and bluntly straight-forward. What his heart feels his lips speak. In a world of actors, he alone refuses to pretend, and his virtues lead him to greatness and to death. His bluntness alerts his enemies, his honesty offends his allies, his impetuousness and courage lead him to charge a superior army. The thirst for fame is death-marked even before it dies on Shrewsbury Field, for its demand for liberty cries also for blood, 'If we live, we live to tread on kings' (V. ii. 86). It tastes the pleasure of the battle, feels the charge like a thunderbolt, is all on fire to hear that victims are coming to be offered to its god, 'the fire-ey'd maid of smoky war'. Honour covers a sensual delight in the nearness of death, death for the self and death for all others. 'Doomsday is near; die all, die merrily' (IV. i. 134). A life and values which have so much death in them cannot endure for long, and Hotspur shortly dies at the hands of a more efficient and more durable force, embodied in the greatest of the Lancastrian kings, Prince Hal, later to be Henry V. As Hotspur dies, he glimpses, as Richard did earlier, the vast, infinite reaches of the linear time of history, in which men briefly live, die and are forgotten, until in some distant future even time itself gives way to some unthinkable emptiness:

> But thoughts, the slaves of life, and life, time's fool,
> And time, that takes survey of all the world,
> Must have a stop. O, I could prophesy,
> But that the earthy and cold hand of death
> Lies on my tongue. No, Percy, thou art dust
> And food for – [Dies.] (V. iv. 81–6)

Hal's completion of Percy's thought, 'for worms', suggests the extent to which he too understands and shares this modern vision of time.

It is the work of the politician to control and adjust such extremes as Hotspur's idealism and Falstaff's sensuality, which threaten civil order in the pursuit of what they take as the good. Superb politician though he may be, it is Henry IV's fate to spend his lifetime trying to order such contraries as these, and it is equally his fate never to succeed in doing so. In seizing the throne from the weak and politically inept Richard, Henry sought his own advancement and perhaps even the good of the state (his motivation is never clear, even to himself), but all his skill and canniness cannot restrain the freedom, the individuality and the energies he unleashed by usurping the throne and destroying the traditional order that once kept such powers in bounds. At the end of *Richard II*, the new king, Henry IV, sits on the throne at Windsor Castle with a sense of security bred of his own efficiency and power. Exton enters and offers the body of Richard as Henry's ultimate victory:

> Great King, within this coffin I present
> Thy buried fear. Herein all breathless lies
> The mightiest of thy greatest enemies,
> Richard of Bordeaux, by me hither brought. (V. vi. 30–3)

Without the slightest intention of doing so, Exton defines perfectly the problem which the body of Richard is going to constitute when he offers it to the king as 'Thy buried fear'. Buried the body is in the ground; but the fear of it is also buried deep in the heart of Henry IV. Neither he nor his son will ever forget that their throne was secured by the murder of a king, and throughout their lives, even to the eve of the battle of Agincourt, they continue to make promises of expiation. The ghost of Richard will haunt them in another way as well, for the Lancastrian kings will always remember, and will always be reminded by rebellious subjects, that what they have shown as possible, the murder of a king to seize a throne, abides as a dreadful example for others. The politically necessary act of king-killing is at once a success and a failure.

At what should have been the highest moment of Henry's triumph, this practical, efficient man begins to discover the tragic complexities of his being and his political situation. What are only hints in the closing scene of *Richard II* become obvious facts in the beginning of the first part of *Henry IV*. As the play opens, the king still longs to undertake the crusade to the Holy Land to atone for the murder of Richard, but 'dear expedience' has forced him to postpone this journey earlier and now is forcing him to delay it once more. Although he hopes that peace has come to England at last, even as he hopes, word is brought of new disorders and barbarism on the far edges of the kingdom. The Welsh under Glendower have defeated Henry's army, and after the battle the Welsh women mutilated the bodies of the defeated in unspeakable ways. In the north, where Hotspur commands, the battle has been won against the Scots and Douglas, but the bodies were piled in high windrows oozing blood. The winning general, young Harry Hotspur, has now refused to surrender his prisoners to the king whom he earlier helped to power. While the kingdom trembles and totters, Hal, the Prince of Wales, spends his time drinking in the tavern and rioting in the streets.

Throughout Part I, rebellion and disorder intensify, culminating in the battle at Shrewsbury, but even as the sounds of that battle die away, new rebels spring up and new armies march. As these internal disorders continue in Part II they become more savage and fierce until Northumberland, raging for the death of his son Hotspur, calls for chaos and universal death:

> Let heaven kiss earth! Now let not Nature's hand
> Keep the wild flood confin'd! Let order die!
> And let this world no longer be a stage
> To feed contention in a ling'ring act;
> But let one spirit of the first-born Cain
> Reign in all bosoms, that, each heart being set
> On bloody courses, the rude scene may end
> And darkness be the burier of the dead! (I. i. 153–60)

As rebellion becomes more savage, so do the forces trying to maintain the precarious new order. In Part I the political manoeuvring is adroit and skilful, but in Part II politics becomes a very dirty game indeed, and its full viciousness arrives when Henry's younger son, Prince John, tricks the rebels into dismissing their army by promising them an honest hearing and redress of grievances. But, as soon as the rebel army has been disbanded, John orders all the rebellious lords off to execution. His explanation is the Machiavellian one that there is no need to keep faith with traitors, and after his 'victory' he remarks piously, in the style recommended in *The Prince*, 'God, and not we, hath safely fought to-day' (IV. ii. 121). As their leaders become more savage and more cynical, the ordinary Englishmen become revolting animals, 'beastly feeders', never satisfied with any ruler they have, always restlessly seeking change, willing to embark on any adventure. Having cheered Bolingbroke and rejoiced in the death of Richard, they are now dissatisfied with Henry and, howling like dogs to find and eat their vomit, go crying to the grave of Richard, which has become a shrine (I. ii. 97–102).

Struggling with endless rebellions and increasing savagery, Henry IV comes at last to the place where Richard and Hotspur have already stood – where Adam stands in Books 11 and 12 of *Paradise Lost* – looking out on that vast span of time and change which swallows hope and obliterates the individual life, the place to which his actions have committed him:

> O God! that one might read the book of fate,
> And see the revolution of the times
> Make mountains level, and the continent,
> Weary of solid firmness, melt itself
> Into the sea; and other times to see
> The beachy girdle of the ocean
> Too wide for Neptune's hips; how chances mock,
> And changes fill the cup of alteration
> With divers liquors! O, if this were seen,
> The happiest youth, viewing his progress through,
> What perils past, what crosses to ensue,
> Would shut the book and sit him down and die. (III. i. 45–56)

At the same time that he breaks into the vastness of time and space, the endlessness of change, Henry also discovers the iron law of historical necessity. Having rejected the old social restrictions of obedience, submission to tradition and ritual, and maintenance of assigned station and rank, having chosen freedom, men now begin to discover that freedom leads, ironically, to another kind of necessity, the tragic necessity of history which forces man to endure the unsuspected consequences of what he is and what he has done. 'The main chance of things' to come 'in their seeds And weak beginning lie intreasured' (III. i. 83–5), and just as Richard found that throwing the warder down led to imprisonment within the stone walls of Pomfret dungeon, just as Hotspur followed fame to the point where he became food for worms, so Henry finds that rebellion follows endlessly from rebellion. The only possible virtue is dogged courage: 'Are these things then necessities? Then let us meet them like necessities' (III i. 92–3). In the tragic world the past is never done with, and even as Henry lies dying, having suffered a stroke upon hearing of the defeat of the last rebel army, Hal enters and, thinking his father dead, carries the crown, the 'polished perturbation', away. The act is innocent, perhaps, but it re-enacts the older crime in which the wish was also father to the deed and the crown was taken from another king before he was dead.

Henry's experience is the experience of his world. If at first men felt an exhilarating release from the restraints of the old traditional order and realized in themselves newly discovered potentialities of self, they now begin to discover that freedom and the individual life have their terrifying as well as their grander sides. The continuing turmoil and suffering of the new world are intensified by the will to power and the incompatibility of its dominant energies. The sensualist, the idealist and the politician, each seeks to be king, refuses to recognize the authority of the others. Each wants to be the whole world and scorns all other ways of life. Hotspur must have pre-eminent honour, 'without co-rival', and he is contemptuous of the 'sword and buckler' Prince of Wales. Hal and Falstaff mock Percy's blood-thirstiness, his reckless impatience and his preference of his horse to his wife. Falstaff laughs at and burlesques the pretences to virtue of the great world.

Out of these anatagonisms rises the plot of the plays. The politician seeks social order and stability but runs athwart idealism's headlong pursuit of honour and sensuality's rejection of any restraint of pleasure. Sensuality and idealism in turn find that the social need for order imposes upon them limits which they cannot endure. At first the conflict is managed in terms of word combats, such as Hotspur's angry argument with the king about the return of prisoners, and Falstaff's various parodies of the world of honour or of politics. Words issue into actions as the underworld disturbs the peace and ventures into the kingdom to rob and cheat. The desire for fame and honour finds no satisfaction in peaceful life and flares into open rebellion. The conflict intensifies as the play proceeds, and there is an inevitable move-ment towards the north, where the king marches to encounter the opposing manifestations of will assembled under the banner of Hotspur. Politics and sensuality mix better than either does with idealism and its death-directedness, and Falstaff marches uneasily with the forces of order. Ideal-ism, honour and raw courage lack the sense and control needed for a world where only the fittest survive, and Hotspur's body, with the strange wound in the thigh, is borne off on Falstaff's back. Falstaff's quick opportun-ism, raw common sense and cat-footed sense of survival; the politician's hard, clear objectivity, practicality and ability to control passions: these are the virtues which survive longer.

Despite all the disorders of *1 Henry IV*, life there has a saving vitality, exuberance and even joy – so much so that it is impossible really to regret the loss of the stability and ceremonial order of the older, more peaceful world which lies behind. The vast possibilities of human nature and the

13a John Fletcher   13b Francis Beaumont

mind of man come into view, and men begin to discover what they and their world are really like. As in *Paradise Lost*, the first experience of disobeying God, satisfying appetite and eating of the tree of knowledge is hot and pleasurable. But as in Milton, so in *2 Henry IV* men learn that knowledge is knowledge of good *and* evil. The first joy of freedom soon passes and its previously hidden side begins to turn into view. Justice Shallow and his cousin Silence sitting talking of the old days that are gone and agreeing that 'Death is certain' set the tone of this darkening world. The Boar's Head tavern, formerly the centre of wit and pleasure, now has an ugly quality about it. It is openly a brothel, run by Mistress Quickly, whose name takes on a new significance; and we learn that Pistol and Doll Tearsheet have killed one of the customers. The jokes have lost their cutting edge, and the characters seem to be wearily imitating their successes at wit in Part I. True honour and military virtue seem to have died with Hotspur, existing now only in their grotesque forms: in Prince John who finds it unnecessary for a man of honour to be honourable with rebels, and in the crazed pimp and bully, Pistol, raving about glory and conquest in a jumble of fantastic language picked up from listening in the theatre to the heroic rant of such figures as Marlowe's Tamburlaine.

The pleasure principle and common sense may have more survival value than Hotspur's idealism, but Falstaff also has his fatal necessities, which begin to appear distinctly in Part II. He first appears reeling drunk, just having voided, and throughout the play his flesh reacts with illnesses and pain, gout and pox, to the excesses of pleasure, food, drink, sex. There are flashes here and there of the old Falstaff, but even his wit is blunted by a growing sense of self-satisfaction and sentimentality. As the old king sickens and Hal nears the throne, Falstaff begins to taste power, and his imperial ambitions take open shape. His will to power has always been implicit in such actions as robbing the crown tax money, playing the king, and joking about the offices he will hold when Hal assumes the throne; but now he displays an unconcerned insolence towards authority, mocks the Chief Justice in the streets, and cheats openly. As he begins to take himself more and more seriously, Falstaff turns philosopher, carrying his previously unexamined, amoral sense of life as pleasure to its inevitable and unpleasant extreme, a universal rule of dog-eat-dog: 'If the young dace be a bait for the old pike, I see no reason in the law of nature but I may snap at [Justice Shallow]' (III. ii. 356–9).

His moment comes, as it does to all the others. Upon hearing of the death of King Henry, Falstaff pauses only long enough to borrow £1,000 from

Justice Shallow before riding hard towards London and his king, shouting the ominous words: 'the laws of England are at my commandment. Blessed are they that have been my friends; and woe to my Lord Chief Justice!' (V. iii. 143–5). In most matters Falstaff is a sceptic, but there remains a fatal innocence in this fascinating old man, who now expects that his old companion, Hal, will greet him with open arms, and the tavern and the palace will at last become one. As Falstaff steps out from the crowd towards the coronation train, with all its symbols of the power of England, he opens his arms and cries: 'God save thy Grace, King Hal; my royal Hal! . . . God save thee, my sweet boy!' The mistake of identity is surprising for a man so adept at playing roles and changing masks to suit the need of the moment. It is not Hal who replies but King Henry V, the mirror of all Christian kings:

> I know thee not, old man. Fall to thy prayers.
> How ill white hairs become a fool and jester!
> I have long dreamt of such a kind of man,
> So surfeit-swell'd, so old, and so profane;
> But, being awak'd, I do despise my dream. . . .
> Presume not that I am the thing I was. . . . (V. v. 51–60)

And so Falstaff, who long ago had been page to Thomas Mowbray when he confronted Hereford in King Richard's court, is also banished and comes at last to that place looking over the edge of the world and time into the nothingness of the future where so many have preceded him. His acknowledgement that he is at last trapped is a simple, faintly witty acceptance of the necessity of paying at least one of the many debts he has so often refused to acknowledge: 'Master Shallow, I owe you a thousand pound.' We never see the knight again. He retires to the Boar's Head to die early in *Henry V* with a broken heart, calling for sack, babbling of green fields and swearing still that women are devils incarnate. Ambition should be made of sterner stuff, as another Shakespearian character says; but while pleasure, wit and good-natured common sense may lack the restraint and calculation needed in the long struggle for survival and power, their absence impoverishes. The England which is made by killing Richard, Hotspur and Falstaff is a more efficient but a less vital and less honest realm. And yet their deaths were certain, guaranteed by the very excess of their virtues and by their narrow interpretations of reality. The banishment of Falstaff and the destruction of wit and pleasure does not teach a moral lesson but presents a tragic necessity. Henry V is not here making a wrong choice but simply instrument-

ing the inevitable triumph of politics over pleasure. If he is Falstaff's executioner, as he was Hotspur's, then both Falstaff and Hotspur made that
execution inevitable. If the gain in order achieved by their deaths is at the
same time a loss in energy, pleasure, common sense and selfless dedication
to the ideal, that is the nature of existence east of Eden where every gain is
loss and every good an evil.

Politics and statecraft, the passion for order, ultimately triumph in the
competition for rule. The genius of the palace and council table is finally
not Henry IV but his son Hal, Henry V, and he alone seems to escape the
decline into despair and death. As others sicken he grows stronger, and as
others make fatal mistakes he becomes ever more sure in his actions. Critics
have seen Hal as the ideal prince undergoing a process of education.[1] Not
a cold and careful schemer like his father, Hal – we are told – moves easily
between the world of the flesh in the tavern and the world of honour on the
battlefield. He excels in both ways of life and has in addition the ability to
act with the temperance, prudence and good sense necessary to the politician.
His position on Shrewsbury Field, standing between the body of Hotspur,
whom he has killed, and the supposed body of Falstaff, playing dead in order
to live, is thus an emblematic presentation of his situation in the *Henriad*.
In other words, passing through a series of trials, Hal comes to be not only
the ideal king but also the ideal man, the only total man in a world where
all the rest of the characters are possessed by a single great energy or virtue.
As such he becomes the hero king restoring life to a dying land, removing
the curse of Richard's murder from the kingdom.

There is much evidence to support these ethical and mythic readings, but
Shakespeare complicates the situation enormously by his realistic portrayal
of character. There is from the beginning something cold, withdrawn and
impersonal, even icily calculating, about Hal. He jokes, drinks and joins in
the fun of the tavern world, holds long conversations with the hostess and
her servants, but he seems to be *in*, not *of*, this lower world. Though he may
enjoy the company of Falstaff and his gang, he has a very practical political
reason for being in the tavern, and he regards his boon companions with a
hard awareness of their worth:

> I know you all, and will awhile uphold
> The unyok'd humour of your idleness;
> Yet herein will I imitate the sun,

[1] The most comprehensive presentation of this view is E. M. W. Tillyard, *Shakespeare's
History Plays* (London, 1944; New York, 1946).

Who doth permit the base contagious clouds
To smother up his beauty from the world,
That, when he please again to be himself,
Being wanted, he may be more wond'red at
By breaking through the foul and ugly mists
Of vapours that did seem to strangle him.
If all the year were playing holidays,
To sport would be as tedious as to work;
By when they seldom come, they wish'd-for come,
And nothing pleaseth but rare accidents.
So, when this loose behaviour I throw off
And pay the debt I never promised,
By how much better than my word I am,
By so much shall I falsify men's hopes;
And, like bright metal on a sullen ground,
My reformation, glitt'ring o'er my fault,
Shall show more goodly and attract more eyes
Than that which hath no foil to set it off.
I'll so offend to make offence a skill,
Redeeming time when men think least I will. (*1 Henry IV*, I. ii. 218–40)

There is something grim about 'I know you all', and something even grimmer about the adjective 'unyok'd', suggesting an ethic in which only those things harnessed and made to draw are worthwhile. Everything 'works' for the man who understands so precisely the people's love of change, the value of a political image and the mechanics of constructing one. Henry IV created his political image by appearing only rarely before the people but always acting with the utmost affability and kindness to all, but Hal knows that a new image is now needed and appears like a wastrel in order that expectations will be low and even the most modest achievements will seem magnificent by comparison. His strategy works perfectly, and in *Henry V* the archbishop expresses wonder at the king's unexpected knowledge and ability (I. i. 24–69). Hal never seems to lose sight of the fact that he is preparing to be king of England, and each of his schemes works, each of his predictions is fulfilled. After Falstaff has played the king, Hal surveys him critically and finds that this is no king, and so Falstaff stands down and Hal plays the role with all the sternness, the rhetoric, the authority of true majesty. Falstaff, innocently thinking this is only a merry jape, takes the part of the penitent prince and uses the occasion to put in a good word for himself: 'No, my good

lord: banish Peto, banish Bardolph, banish Poins; but, for sweet Jack Falstaff, kind Jack Falstaff, true Jack Falstaff, valiant Jack Falstaff – and therefore more valiant, being, as he is, old Jack Falstaff – banish not him thy
Harry's company, banish not him thy Harry's company. Banish plump
Jack, and banish all the world. *Prince:* I do, I will' (Part I, II. iv. 521–9).
In that 'I do, I will', we hear the voice of the inevitable future and see the
coronation at Westminster, where a great king proves his ability to rule
himself and others by the words addressed to an old rogue standing with
open arms: 'I know thee not, old man.'

Hal's view of honour is equally detached and his calculations for achieving
it are as precise as his management of the world of pleasure. He can be the
chivalric knight, the man of honour, as well as he can be the tavern roisterer,
but his parodies of the kind of honour which kills a dozen Scots before
breakfast and complains of this quiet life suggest an objective view. Hal
values honour, however, knows that a king must have it, and he has a plan
for acquiring it. When Henry IV berates his son for a wasted life, contrasting
him unfavourably with Hotspur, Hal replies that he intends to become the
very chief of honour on some battlefield where his features will be covered
all in blood – a sign which will, he says, mark him as his father's true son –
and where he will tear honour from Hotspur's heart:

> Percy is but my factor, good my lord,
> To engross up glorious deeds on my behalf;
> And I will call him to so strict account
> That he shall render every glory up,
> Yea, even the slightest worship of his time,
> Or I will tear the reckoning from his heart. (Part I, III. ii. 147–52)

The book-keeping imagery – factor, engross, account – suggests a view of
honour as a negotiable commodity, not the insubstantial ideal of Chaucer's
'verray parfit gentil knight', nor even Hotspur's fame that must be sought
steadfastly in hard and difficult places through a lifetime of honesty and
courage and dedication. But Percy is wrong about honour and Hal is, as
usual, precisely correct. He kills Hotspur in battle and acquires his honour,
which in time becomes the honour of the king and the kingdom he rules.

The prince's bent is essentially political, and his attitudes towards the
exercise of power and the rights of succession are remarkably uncomplicated
and practical. When the old king on his deathbed tries to explain that the
agonizing complexities resulting from his illegal seizure of the throne may

continue to haunt his heir, Hal is rather surprised. His right to the crown
is, he feels, absolute, and he intends to allow no questioning of that right:

> My gracious liege,
> You won it, wore it, kept it, gave it me;
> Then plain and right must my possession be;
> Which I with more than with a common pain
> 'Gainst all the world will rightfully maintain. (Part II, IV. v. 221–5)

This modern view of succession and power, as direct and practical as Hal's
view of honour, is a world away from that mystical theory of legitimacy and
the king's sacred involvement with God and the order of the cosmos which
Richard took for granted.

A great production sets the style and the interpretation of a play for a
generation, and the ruling version of *Henry V* in our time has been the
Laurence Olivier film with its hearts-of-oak and roast-beef-of-old-England
tone. It is the story of bluff and hearty King Hal, swaggering his way across
France, wooing in good four-square English words the shy, but delighted,
Princess of France, twirling his crown and tossing it on the back of his
throne, roaring defiance to the gift of tennis balls from the degenerate French
Dauphin, giving great battlefield speeches about St Crispin's Day and ex-
horting the troops to close up the breaches in the wall with their English
dead. It is the great swish of the arrows from the longbows of the sturdy
English yeomanry – the first national army – which scythe down the
gorgeously caparisoned but clumsy chivalry of France – the last feudal army
– charging across the field at Agincourt. It is England becoming Britain as
the hero king unites his people and draws into his order the Welshman
Fluellen, the Irishman Macmorris and the Scot Captain Jamy, the violent
and cantankerous representatives of those savage borderlands where earlier
English kings fought so many battles. It is the story of a land united as one
man which marshals a democratic modern army to attack and defeat France,
roots out traitors with almost miraculous knowledge of their treason, hangs
thieves and looters without hesitation. The new kingdom is, as Canterbury
describes it in an epic simile drawn from the *Aeneid*, like the beehive where
the 'singing masons' build 'roofs of gold' and justice delivers 'o'er to execu-
tors pale The lazy yawning drone' (I. ii. 198–204). Such rebellious elements
as remain – traitorous peers and a gang of cut-throats and thieves from the
Boar's Head – the king handles with remarkable ease.

Henry V has the public virtues of a great king – magnanimity, courage,
resourcefulness, energy, efficiency and a commanding presence. At the same

time, certain private traits seen in him earlier – flat practicality and hard objectivity, a lack of complexity amounting almost to insensitivity, a certain coldness of heart – persist, and, while contributing much to his political efficiency, raise serious questions about him as a man. As *Henry V* opens, the Bishop of Ely and the Archbishop of Canterbury tell us that Parliament has proposed to expropriate church lands, but the king has not yet committed himself on the issue. Canterbury has offered a deal: if Henry will block the bill, the clergy will provide him with a great deal of money to support his proposed expedition to France. Rather than giving a direct answer, Henry asked the archbishop what he thought about the English king's rights to the throne of France. Taking up the hint, the church is now here to interpret 'the severals and unhidden passages' of Henry's French title for him. Before the archbishop begins to speak, Henry charges him most solemnly to speak nothing but certain truth, for a war between great nations and the deaths of many men hang upon his words. For Canterbury, however, Hal's title to the throne of France is happily 'as clear as is the summer's sun', but the proof he offers is a somewhat darker jumble of ancient geography, the customs of the primitive Germans, the workings of something called the Salic Law prohibiting females from ruling in western Europe, and other obscure pedantries. The king, still not clear about his title, or wishing to exonerate himself again, asks plainly, 'May I with right and conscience make this claim?' When reassured once more, all doubt dies, and Henry determines to seize France or obliterate it: 'Now are we well resolv'd; . . . France being ours, we'll bend it to our awe, Or break it all to pieces' (I. ii. 222–5). Nothing more is heard about the expropriation of church lands. It would be most interesting to hear either Falstaff or Hotspur comment on these speeches and events, but their voices are no longer heard in Henry V's England. Whether Hal believes Canterbury's argument it is impossible to say – his motives are always as obscure as his father's – but it is equally impossible to forget the dying Henry IV's advice to his son, 'to busy giddy minds With foreign quarrels' (IV. v. 214–15).

This is not the only occasion on which there is something puzzling about Hal's motives, on which it is possible to see him acting as both the hero king and as a subtle politician. In III. iii he has brought his army across the sea to the walls of Harfleur. The town at first resists siege, but the citizens then decide that there is no hope and ask for a parley. As the parley begins, Hal turns on the citizens and storms at them for defending their town so long and putting themselves and their dependants in such danger. Furthermore, if the town continues to resist he will batter it to pieces and burn it to ashes; his inflamed soldiers will break loose 'with conscience wide as hell' to murder, rape and pillage. 'What is it to me' the King demands again and again, if these dreadful things happen? The repeated rhetorical question, 'What is it to me?' with its implicit answer, 'nothing', sounds very strange in this context. Considering the brutalities that he is describing, it should be a great deal, and who was it who assembled such cut-throats as Pistol and Nym and brought them to France 'to suck, to suck, the very blood to suck?' The very question by which the king disclaims responsibility forces a more profound consideration of the matter. I offer one more example, from among many, of this kind of thing. Shortly after the terrified Harfleur surrenders, the king rides by his army, and Fluellen tells him that no one has been lost in the recent battle except a man executed for looting a church, 'one Bardolph, if your Majesty know the man; his face is all bubukles, and whelks, and knobs, and flames o' fire; and his lips blows at his nose, and it is like a coal of fire, sometimes plue and sometimes red'. This same Bardolph is the only one of Falstaff's gang who has lived in all three *Henry* plays, and Hal has enjoyed with Falstaff and Poins many a joke about that great red nose in which the fire is at last out. But the king's only response is, 'We would have all such offenders so cut off'. He then goes on to use the occasion to issue general orders to the army prohibiting looting, 'for when lenity and cruelty play for a kingdom the gentler gamester is the soonest winner' (III. vi. 107–20).

Whether Henry's reaction expresses indifference, forgetfulness or an all-demanding sense of duty, it is impossible to say. His motives again escape us; but we can see that while there seems to be a thinness of personal feeling, there is at the same time a sure political sense of what is required of a king and the leader of a great army engaged in the conquest of a kingdom. This ambivalence emerges again and again, to reach full statement at last on the night before the battle of Agincourt. The king puts aside his public role and, covering himself with a dark cloak, walks in the night among the army. He comes to the campfire, flickering in the darkness like Richard's candle in Pomfret dungeon, of three ordinary English soldiers, John Bates, Alexander Court and Michael Williams. On the eve of the battle, the soldiers are face to face with those tragic questions which so many others have met in the *Henriad*, and they voice these questions in a most simple way – a way which contrasts powerfully with the pedantic language of the Archbishop of Canterbury which launched this army on the French adventure, and with the heroic rhetoric which exhorts the army to spring once more into the breach. The soldiers are frightened of dying and worried about their families and their own souls. Is the cause for which they fight a just one? If it is not, what happens to the soul of a man who dies hating and killing other men? How can a man reconcile his duty to his king and his duty as a Christian?

> . . . if the cause be not good, the King himself hath a heavy reckoning to make when all those legs and arms and heads, chopp'd off in a battle, shall join together at the latter day and cry all 'We died at such a place' – some swearing, some crying for a surgeon, some upon their wives left poor behind them, some upon the debts they owe, some upon their children rawly left. I am afeard there are few die well that die in a battle; for how can they charitably dispose of anything when blood is their argument? Now, if these men do not die well, it will be a black matter for the King that led them to it; who to disobey were against all proportion of subjection. (IV. i. 133–45)

Harry Plantagenet responds as authority must respond: the king's cause *is* just, and therefore the men are absolved of any responsibility before God for shedding blood. But, almost as if in doubt, he goes on to argue that 'the King is not bound to answer the particular endings of his soldiers', because he did not intend their deaths when he brought them to France. Here again, as before Harfleur, he is raising the questions he intends to solve: whether he intended death or not, he did bring his subjects to France, where they will kill and die, and surely he bears some responsibility. But he continues to avoid the full question of responsibility by arguing that many of the soldiers carry mortal sins upon their souls and that therefore if they die in battle the king bears no responsibility for their damnation: 'Every subject's duty is the King's; but every subject's soul is his own.' But this really does not answer Williams's objection that every man who dies in battle dies in sin trying to murder his fellow men, and he is doing so because his king has brought him to this place and ordered him to fight. It is impossible to forget in this discussion of the justice of the cause the doubtful way in which the French war began. In this brief scene in the middle of darkness on the edge of a great battle, Michael Williams has faced for himself and his king the most fundamental moral questions about his responsibility as ruler and as man. But Henry does not answer the questions, either because he does not fully understand them or because no ruler of a state can ever answer such questions. Pressed by Williams, he becomes angry, leaves the campfire and returns to his own tent.

The actions and the speeches of King Henry V produce a curious ambiguity. On one hand he is the hero king, the restorer of England's glory and the efficient manager of the realm; but he is at the same time, it would appear, a cunning Machiavel, a cynical politician, a man lacking in moral depth, perhaps even a limited intelligence. Our difficulties in understanding the king are intensified by the almost total absence from the play of speeches in which Henry speaks as a private man, directly revealing his own feelings. He lives in the full glare of public life, and even those usually private activities such as wooing a wife are carried out on the great stage of the world. Nor does his language yield insights into the depths of self of the kind found in the language of Richard II, Falstaff or Hotspur. Instead, Henry uses a political and heroic rhetoric whose brightly polished surface allows no penetration.

Faced with the absence of motives, critics have resolved the problem by judging Henry according to their particular moral bias and concluding that he is either a good and efficient ruler who sacrifices himself for the good of the state, or a hypocritical and cunning politician who relentlessly seizes every opportunity to extend and consolidate his power. We must, however, take Henry as Shakespeare gives him to us: a man who has no private personal self but only a public character, a character which is supremely, unerringly political, which chooses without hesitation that course of action which will make the kingdom function efficiently, balance the divisive powers within and strengthen the ruler's grasp on the body politic. This type of man is not unknown to Shakespeare's or our own time. Historians have been guessing for centuries about Elizabeth I's motives for not marrying – hatred of men because of her father's treatment of her mother? ingrown virginity? pelvic malformation? unhappy love affair in youth? – but whatever Elizabeth's reasons, her constant hesitation was a political masterpiece. To have married a Protestant would have caused her Catholic subjects to despair and set Catholic Europe against her. To have married a Catholic would have driven her Protestant subjects to rebellion and alienated England from the growing Protestant powers in Europe. So long as she remained unmarried, but always considering marriage, she could prevent, even among the proud lords in her own court, that polarization of power which would have meant civil and world war. Our own age also shares with Shakespeare some understanding of political man, and the following description of an American politician is at once a remarkable description, even down to the small details, of Henry V:

> He is a totally political man, clever but not thoughtful, calculating more than reflective. He appears at once sentimental and ruthless, thin-

skinned and imperious, remarkably attuned to public moods and utterly expert at the 'game' of political manœuver. He is all of a piece, seemingly monolithic, not only completely *in* but totally *of* politics. Upon the devices and costs of political manipulation he is capable of looking with some irony, but toward the idea of the manipulation itself and the kind of life it entails he shows no irony whatever.[1]

No one would agree more completely than Henry V that political man 'is the role', that 'the person [is] the function'.[2] As he turns away from the bitter encounter with his soldiers around the campfire, draws back from the tragic place where Richard, Hotspur, Falstaff and Henry IV looked and died, Henry pauses alone in the darkness and asks himself the question Richard had so long ago answered so confidently: 'what is a king?' Even at this moment most closely approaching vision, his speech is still rhetoric rather than poetry, and, rather than revealing a self, it is as if some vague memory of a real self were contemplating with self-pity its final disappearance into a role, into ceremony:

> No, thou proud dream,
> That play'st so subtly with a king's repose.
> I am a king that find thee; and I know
> 'Tis not the balm, the sceptre, and the ball,
> The sword, the mace, the crown imperial,
> The intertissued robe of gold and pearl,
> The farced title running fore the king,
> The throne he sits on, nor the tide of pomp
> That beats upon the high shore of this world –
> No, not all these, thrice gorgeous ceremony,
> Not all these, laid in bed majestical,
> Can sleep so soundly as the wretched slave
> Who, with a body fill'd and vacant mind,
> Gets him to rest, cramm'd with distressful bread. . . . (IV. i. 274–87)

But having seen the person fade into the political function, the king turns away from tragic knowledge and returns to his tent and to his role of the conqueror of France, the greatest of the Lancastrian kings, the husband of Katherine and the father of Henry VI.

Henry reverses the path taken by Richard II, who believed that kingship

---

[1] Irving Howe, 'I'd rather be wrong', *New York Review of Books* (17 June 1965), p. 3.
[2] Howe, op. cit., p. 3.

and rule were his reality but discovered under the battering of circumstance the mortal man beneath the public role:

> you have but mistook me all this while.
> I live with bread like you, feel want,
> Taste grief, need friends; subjected thus,
> How can you say to me I am a king? (III. ii. 174–7)

At the other end of the cycle, the king who has known from the beginning that he is a man playing king – 'yet herein will I imitate the sun' – discovers, however briefly, the claims of his humanity, only to turn away and lock himself for ever into the role. The *Henriad* traces in its kings a great paradox: necessity forces man out of role into the reality of self – necessity forces man back out of reality of self into role. The movement is much like that of the *Aeneid*, where the establishment of New Troy and, eventually, Augustan order require the absorption of the man Aeneas into the role of the founder of Rome, and the destruction of such turbulent energies as Dido and Turnus. In both the Roman and English epics the even balance of loss and gain creates finally a tone of great sadness inextricably mixed with great triumph.

The world of Henry V with its state rituals and ceremony looks much like a restoration of the English Eden, ordered, prosperous and united under a hero king. But under the surface all is changed. In Richard's feudal kingdom, society was ideally organized and life lived in accordance with the great unchanging patterns of order, mutual support and hierarchy, which were believed to govern all the created world. In Henry's national state, life is shifting and fluid, and action is taken not because it is morally, unchangeably right, but because it will bring about the desired result. Identity is now no longer God-given but only a role within which an individual is imprisoned by political necessity. The restored English garden, the beehive state, is superimposed on the ruined garden of France, a weed-filled, untilled wilderness (*Henry V*, V. ii. 36–60). Man no longer confidently expects the future to repeat the past but stands on the edge of great vistas of time and lives in the historical process of endless change. What was small and coherent by nature is now vast and tends to fragmentation, what was unchanging is now in ceaseless flux, what was real is now acted and what was external and certain is now internalized and ambiguous.

The *Henriad* is a brief history of the reigns of Richard II, Henry IV and Henry V, which traces the great psychological, social and political shifts from the medieval to the modern world. Even below the level of these great cultural shifts, however, a still more fundamental plot exists: in the begin-

ning there is a king, Richard II, and a society which with the 'oceanic feeling'
of the child believes, that the world is all of a piece, from the clod of earth
up to God Himself. Man is at the centre of this rich and brilliant universe,
and he trusts the authorities and traditions that he has inherited and assumes
that nothing will ever change from the way it is. Then, the knowledge of
death, the conflicting pressures of reality and the more violent passions –
hate, blood lust, the will to power – erupt and break up the old certainties.
When the earthly king calls for help to the heavenly King there is not even
the whisper of an answer. Feelings of isolation in great darkness grow.
Certainty of identity is lost and the vastnesses of eternity and infinity are
glimpsed. Man is driven inwards upon himself, becomes self-conscious and
is forced to realize that there is a world 'out there' which does not conform
to his will or imagination. Confused, the old innocence dies with Richard II.
Life fragments, energies are released and many previously forbidden powers
are freed: amoral pleasure, magic, the lust for death. The individual is
no longer limited to 'what he is' but is free to experiment and act out many
parts. Prince Hal – shrewd and reality-oriented – now replaces Richard as
the central figure in the psychic journey. At first he rejects the authority
figures – the king, the father, the law – to live a life of pleasure and self-
indulgence in the tavern, taking Falstaff as a father temporarily. He turns
from the flesh to the spirit and seeks to find himself on the battlefield and
in the search for honour and fame. In both tavern and battlefield, however,
he avoids total involvement with these ultimately unrealistic extremes, both
of which have death implicit in them. In the end, the prince kills wild idealism, Hotspur, and banishes unlimited pleasure, Falstaff, to return to his
true father in spirit and person. With the death of that father, the prince
assumes the burdens of rule and takes up the adult role of trying to 'make the
world work'. In the process of becoming a ruler his personal self, some
essential 'I', is lost for ever as the man disappears into the role his work
demands.

3 'Jack shall have Jill': Elizabethan comedy

(i) Knight and clown: the two comic views

Although the Renaissance critics argued that the primary function of comedy was moral:

> Comedy is an imitation of the common errors of our life, which [the poet] representeth in the most ridiculous and scornefull sort that may be; so as it is impossible that any beholder can be content to be such a one,[1]

the earlier Elizabethan comedy, while it protected itself with occasional statement of the highest moral principles, was in fact an almost unlimited expression of playfulness and a realization of freedom from the restraints of the authority of the probable. In this marvellous comic world the quest and the far journey lead to mysterious crossroads and strange lands where witches cast evil spells, where idols and oracles speak baffling prophecies, where aged magicians hold beautiful maidens in thrall and where men undergo strange transformations from youth to age, from ugliness to beauty. The journey of knight and princess into this fairytale world is shared by some very English figures. The errant knight may well be a London 'prentice in dis-

[1] Sir Philip Sidney, 'An Apology for Poetry', in G. Gregory Smith (ed.), *Elizabethan Critical Essays* (Oxford, 1904), I, 176–7.

guise, and his squire may combine the rant of Herod and the bragging of the *miles gloriosus* with the accents of a soldier home from the wars in the Low Countries. Within the dark woods these questers are as likely to encounter firecracker-throwing devils as dragons, milkmaids as maidens in distress and pratfalls as magical spells. Elements from romance, popular low comedy and Plautus and Terence mix happily with routines from the enduring subworld of protocomedy – tumbling and juggling acts, the spiel of the medicine man, ballad singing, jigs and rural festivals – to produce a not very refined but powerful sense of the world as wide, marvellous, filled with delightful variety and ultimately beneficent to the man who is lucky, good-hearted and sensible enough to take and enjoy the pleasure, sex and money that this strange world throws his way after many trials. Helen Gardner has described the essence of this type of romantic or 'pure comedy':

> The great symbol of pure comedy is marriage by which the world is renewed; and its endings are always instinct with a sense of fresh beginnings. Its rhythm is the rhythm of the life of mankind, which goes on and renews itself as the life of nature does. . . . A comedy, which contrives an end which is not implicit in its beginning, and which is, in itself, a fresh beginning, is an image of the flow of human life. The young wed, so that they may become in turn the older generation, whose children will wed, and so on, as long as the world lasts. Comedy pictures what Rosalind calls 'the full stream of the world'.[1]

The journey of the comic questers, whether the knights of romance or the apprentices of London, is an almost unlimited realization of that urgent journey towards freedom and the realms of the imagination which is the central impulse of the new theatre. But knight and maiden are accompanied on their journey by some strange figures who while contributing at first to the merriment still cast a shadow over the enterprise: the intriguing Vice with his cackling laugh and wooden dagger, the clown with his tabor and jig, the fool in motley carrying his wooden sceptre, and later, the melancholy satirist. As the age progresses, these parody figures will come increasingly to dominate the comic stage. But at first there are only hints of their ultimate meaning. Jacob Burckhardt perhaps goes too far in his *The Civilization of the Renaissance in Italy* (Volume II, chapter 4, 'Modern wit and satire') in claiming that the age developed a new and particularly savage sense of humour based on perception of the incurable folly of man as a counterbalance to the extravagant

---

[1] 'As You Like It', in John Garrett (ed.), *More Talking of Shakespeare* (London and New York, 1959), p. 21.

claims of the perfected individual that 'Men can do all things if they will'. But Harry Levin is certainly correct in his statement:

> Across Europe, along the drift from Renaissance to Reformation, from Italy to Germany, stride two gigantic protagonists, the rogue and the fool. In the conflicts of humanistic learning and empirical experience, the war between theology and science, a literature is evolved which has the expansiveness of the picaresque and the inclusiveness of satire. It is the age of Erasmus, Brandt, Rabelais, and Cervantes. It is the time to cry 'Ducdame' and call all fools into a circle.[1]

Interest in fools, dwarfs and jesters has a long history.[2] In actual life these grotesques seem to have been used in a Freudian way as objects of laughter and the basis for feelings of superiority by more normal folk. But the writers of the Renaissance, and particularly the English dramatists, contrived a number of pointed demonstrations that the joke might well work in reverse, that from a more detached point of view Puck might be quite right in exclaiming, 'Lord, what fools these mortals be!'

There are thus two opposing, though perhaps not finally unrelated, comic senses of life at work in Renaissance English comedy, and the history of comedy in this period is, in the largest terms, a shift of emphasis from the one to the other. The way is plotted by three great comic writers: John Lyly, who perfected and formalized romantic comedy; William Shakespeare, who while maintaining the dominance of romantic comedy mixed and questioned it with the comedy of human folly; and Ben Jonson, who in his plays, though not in his masques and poetry, focused almost entirely, as the English theatre was to do after him, on the folly and grotesqueness of humankind. But in the earlier years, comedies – which exceed tragedies by at least three to one in the period 1576–1613 – were predominantly of the romantic variety, and the first distinct group of new dramatists, with perhaps the exception of Nashe, made their reputations largely as authors of romantic comedy. The University Wits, Thomas Lodge (1557–1635), Thomas Nashe (1567–1601), Robert Greene (1558–92) and George Peele (1557–96), arrived in London in the late 1570s and early 1580s, fresh from Oxford or Cambridge, self-conscious of their classical learning, and prepared to make their fame and fortune as professional writers. Familiarity with the classics and the general effects of a humanistic education perhaps did something to curb native exuberance, but on the whole the comedies written and sold by the University Wits, though

---

[1] *Ben Jonson, Selected Works* (New York, 1938), p. 12.
[2] See Enid Welsford, *The Fool, His Social and Literary History* (London, 1935; New York, 1961).

advertised as being in the latest fashion, improved little on the usual jumble of romance and horseplay. Greene's *Friar Bacon and Friar Bungay* (*c.* 1589) is a mad mixture of the marvellous exploits of the magician Friar Bacon – including a patriotic magic contest with an upstart German necromancer – and the love story of Margaret, the fair maid of Fressingfield, loved by the courtier Lacy. Lacy has been sent to woo Margaret by Prince Edward, who has been smitten with her beauty but finds that both dignity and shyness prevent open avowal of his love. All turns out well: Bacon repents and gives up his dark powers, while the legitimate magical powers of love produce a happy ending for Margaret and Lacy, who are forgiven and blessed by Prince Edward.

George Peele's *Old Wives Tale* (*c.* 1590) is an even more incredible galli-maufry, which may have been intended as a parody of popular romantic comedy. The play is framed by the adventures of three serving men who are lost in a dark forest and rescued by Clunch the smith and his dog. Clunch takes them home and feeds them, and the night is passed in the telling of a tale by Madge, the smith's old wife. As she begins her tale, its characters come to life and act out the story of Sacrapant, an old Thessalian wizard, who uses his art to make himself appear young and to steal away the fair maiden Delia, whom he keeps in a trance in his cave deep in the woods. The plot centres, in so far as it has a centre, on various searches for Delia: by her two brothers, by the knight Eumenides and his bumpkin servant Corebus, and by the parody knight, the boaster Huanebango. Along the way to the magician's cell the questers encounter a prophet at the crossroads, a beautiful young shrew and her homely but agreeable sister, a magical well from which a head emerges to speak riddles, a group of countrymen arguing over the burial of the parish drunk and an extremely jovial and helpful ghost named Jack. After various adventures the questers reach the centre of the woods, and there Eumenides, with the aid of Jack, destroys the source of Sacrapant's power, a glass with a flame in its centre, which is buried under the turf. The women and the men of the story are then paired off, the tale ends and as daylight breaks Madge offers her guests a cup of ale before they depart. In both its romantic and its domesticated forms this kind of comedy remained the staple of theatre for many years, despite the intense scorn of later, more sophisticated dramatists such as John Marston, Ben Jonson and Beaumont and Fletcher (see Plate 13), whose *Knight of the Burning Pestle* (1607) is a delightful parody of domesticated romantic comedy.

The University Wits as a group found very little fame and even less for-tune, dying in straitened circumstances and forgotten by the public for which they had provided such pleasant fare. Greene's death – from a surfeit of eels and Rhenish – was the most sensational, and before he died he wrote with much bitterness of the theatre and the players, particularly one 'upstart crow' who thought himself the only 'Shake-scene' in the country. The works and lives of these playwright-poets and their chief successors in comedy, Thomas Dekker (1572?–1632?) and Thomas Heywood (1570–1641), were closer to the norm than those of the giants of the age, Marlowe, Jonson and Shakespeare. Despite their proud hopes for fame they became writers of 'entertainments'; pressed by poverty and the endless need of the repertory companies for new plays and new fashions they turned their hands to any subject likely to attract interest; the sons of the new middle class, they thought to find London a new Rome and themselves new Virgils and Horaces, but instead they became hacks and ended their lives poor and forgotten.

(ii) 'The cornucopia of the mind':[1] the plays of John Lyly

John Lyly (1554–1606), the descendant of a family long identified with humanistic scholarship, came to London from an Oxford education in 1576, the year in which the first public theatre was built. But from the beginning Lyly's eyes were turned away from the public theatre towards the court, and his writing was primarily a means to display wit and learning in order to win favour in high places. He may have served the Earl of Oxford as a secretary, and in 1583–4 the two were involved in the lease of a small private theatre in the old monastery of Blackfriars, where a group of boy choristers performed plays. The Oxford Boys, as this group is termed, performed before the queen and her court at the Christmas festivities in 1583–4, presenting Lyly's first plays, *Campaspe* and *Sapho and Phao*. The elegance and highly stylized playing of the boys must have suited Lyly, for in the late 1580s and early 1590s he wrote six plays for the boys of the choir school of St Paul's, who were at that time performing for the public and, upon invitation, for the court at festival seasons. During this time Lyly tried desperately to obtain from the queen the post of Master of the Revels, the official responsible for providing court entertainment and censoring plays, but though he was, he thought, promised much, nothing ever came of it, and like most of the public dramatists he ended his days in the country, sick and financially pressed.

His first literary works were the prose narratives, *Euphues, The Anatomy of Wit* (1578) and its sequel *Euphues and his England* (1580), which recount

---

[1] Jocelyn Powell, 'John Lyly and the language of play', in J. R. Brown and Bernard Harris (eds.), *Elizabethan Theatre*, Stratford-Upon-Avon Studies 9 (London, 1966; New York, 1967), p. 167.

the adventures and moral education of a young student from Athens in his travels to Naples and London. There is nothing remarkable in the subject matter of these books, but the highly mannered style, Euphuism, in which they are written took the fashionable world by storm. Lyly continued to use this style in his plays, and an address to Cynthia from *Endymion* reveals its chief features:

> I am none of those wolves that bark most when thou shinest brightest, but that fish (thy fish, Cynthia, in the flood Araris) which at thy waxing is as white as the driven snow, and at thy waning as black as deepest darkness. I am that Endymion, sweet Cynthia, that have carried my thoughts in equal balance with my actions, being always as free from imagining ill as enterprising; that Endymion whose eyes never esteemed anything fair but thy face, whose tongue termed nothing rare but thy virtues, and whose heart imagined nothing miraculous but thy government. (II. i. 41–53)

The characteristics of this style are easily analysed: clauses and other parts carefully balanced by repetition of elements of equal length; duplication of sound and grammatical patterns; heavy use of quasi-rhymes and alliteration; elaborate comparisons drawn chiefly from 'unnatural natural' history; catalogues of proverbs; and extended use of rhetorical questions. Every kind of word game imaginable, every possibility of playing with words, every verbal ingenuity and combination of linguistic patterns is used, as Jocelyn Powell points out, 'not only to exercise the faculties of the soul, but also to liberate them from the limitations of fact. The power of the games of the mind is that they give mind the power over matter.'[1] Euphuism, in and of itself, without reference to its content, is another implementation of that desire for freedom which lies behind the drama of the age and finds more earnest expression in Doctor Faustus's magic or Richard III's politics. It should be noted that the pleasure of the Euphuistic style comes not only from the playful elaboration of fantastic verbal patterns, the cornucopia of the mind, but also from the careful structuring and artful arrangement of the parts. Every surprising image and every flowery phrase is neatly balanced with its equal, poised against an opposite, or run into a series of similars; the dizzying reaches of fancy are interlocked like the parts of a crossword puzzle. The Elizabethan mind apparently sought its freedom and found its pleasure not in anarchy but in the creation of intricate new structures.

The balance of opposites and the unity of variety achieved in a rhetorical manner by the Euphuistic style are also the governing principles of Lyly's

[1] Powell, op. cit., p. 165.

dramaturgy. In his most popular play, *Endymion* (1588), the simple story turns around the love of the hero Endymion for the moon, Cynthia, and the jealousy of Tellus, whom Endymion formerly loved. Cynthia is the name given to a great many loosely associated similarities. She is the moon, but she is also the imagination, Queen Elizabeth, ideal or platonic love, the reality which is ever changing but ever constant, the realm of purity, and the absolute. Tellus, on the other hand, is the earth, the realm of the senses, fleshly love with all its jealousies and hatreds, and even, perhaps, Mary Queen of Scots. Between these opposites, balanced like the elements of Lyly's prose, stands Endymion, the man torn between the desire of his senses and the desire of his mind, longing for the ideal but entrapped in the actual, and silently hoping – like the courtier John Lyly – for the favour of the queen. The symmetry of this central group is further extended outwardly and inwardly: outwardly by characters who represent additional variations of attitude towards the questions phrased by the inner group; inwardly by the internalization in the characters of the struggle between Cynthia and Tellus.

The plot progresses, like the Euphuistic paragraph, through a series of external and internal debates – betweeen love and friendship, base love and the higher love, love and hate, love and duty – to a triumph of unity and order containing all variety and balancing all oppositions. Endymion's high but unvoiced love for Cynthia leads him to abandon Tellus, whom he once loved. Seeking revenge to implement a hate grown as great as her love once was, Tellus has a witch cast a spell on Endymion, and he lapses into a sleep for forty years. His friend Eumenides undertakes a quest to a magical fountain, where because of the purity of his love he is granted one wish, and after struggling with his desire to wish for love of the haughty maiden Semele, he chooses friendship instead and asks to know what will release Endymion from his sleep. The answer is that Endymion will wake if Cynthia kiss him but once. She does, he wakes with his youth restored, and all the men and women are paired off in the usual manner of comedy, except Endymion, who vows to worship chastely and eternally from a distance the beauty of Cynthia. The play can be and has been given many interpretations, ranging from an intrigue in Elizabeth's court, through a dramatization of humanistic ethics, to a theory of epistemology. These are all possible readings of Lyly's central myth of the man who longs for the high moon but is lost for ever in a deep sleep of earth; but beyond any particular meaning that the play may contain, its main power derives from its almost abstract representation of the delightful and comic freedom of the human mind ranging over all creation, selecting, playing with and ordering its parts into new and surprising possibilities.

4 'Ducdame': Shakespearian comedy to *Twelfth Night*

(i) The songs of the cuckoo and the owl: the first comedies

Shakespeare made his comedy out of the traditional plots and symbols of romance but expanded and explained their meaning by linking them to familiar psychic and social events. The magical changes wrought by wizards became the miraculous transformation of Kate the shrew into a loving wife, while metamorphosis becomes the violent shifts in affection of the lovers in the wood outside Athens. Disguise becomes a revelation of the problems of sexual differentiation, and the mystery of twinness opens up the question of alternative and hidden selves. The magician-enchanter holding young people in his spell becomes the authority figures of king and father, or the power of old law. The perilous quest and the far journey become the succession of generations and the movement of innocence through experience to adulthood. The dark woods become the emblems of mental confusion and loss of bearings. The powers of magic become love, generosity, good sense and pity.

It would be wrong, however, to think of Shakespeare's comedy as the triumph of realism, for it is at least as much the reverse. The vision of romance imparts to the events of ordinary life a sense of the mysterious and strange, just as the realism interprets the romance elements by tying them to the day-to-day world. The Shakespearian play is always located exactly on the narrow line between romance and realism, symbol and imitation, the strange and the familiar, poesis and mimesis. The characteristic Shakespearian comic plot extends this perpetual hesitation between dream and thought into action. As the play progresses, the characters move, in response to their own psychic urgencies and the great powers that flow through their worlds, from familiar, well-lighted places and states of mind, into strange, unfamiliar dim places and experiences, only to return after a period of confusion, surprise and revelation to their place of origin. The movement is, to use Shakespeare's most persistent symbols, from city to wood and back to city again. Noting the frequent references in the comedies to various games and festival occasions – Feasts of Misrule, May Day, Midsummer's Eve, Harvest Homes, Twelfth Night – C. L. Barber in *Shakespeare's Festive Comedy* has traced the ways in which the three-part movement of Shakespeare's comic plot parallels and merges at points with a similar pattern in many Elizabethan festivities: from everyday to holiday and back to everyday, from the restraints of society and order to release and freedom and then, renewed, back to work and sobriety. This festival pattern adjusts nicely with Northrop Frye's application of the pattern of classical comedy to Shakespeare. The movement in classical comedy is from an old society which has become repressive, tyrannous and life-destroying to a revolutionary explosion, usually undertaken by youth in the name of freedom and vitality, leading to a second period of disorder and excess. This phase gives way in turn to the third period of the formation of a new society, which, while including all within its feasts and celebrations, is centred on youth and the new generation.[1]

Each of the three phases of Shakespearian comedy is identified during the course of the plays with a great many social and psychic conditions, and the plot movement can therefore be described in a great variety of other ways, such as the loss and rediscovery of identity, the movement from appearance to reality, or the alternation of nurture and nature. But, whatever terms are used, the three-part movement is built not on a simple opposition of two opposed values but on a complex interaction of two basic realities, seemingly antithetical but ultimately mutually supporting. At the beginning reason grows too rational and law becomes too legal, which forces an excessive reaction in the opposite direction of absolute freedom and excessive playfulness, which finally exhausts or thwarts itself and returns, with a sense of relief but renewed, from fresh contact with the springs of life and the powers of nature

[1] 'The argument of comedy', *English Institute Essays 1948*, ed. D. A. Robertson (New York, 1949), pp. 58–73.

to the man-ordered, rationally organized world. The process usually ends with dancing, feasting and multiple marriage.

Shakespeare's comedies in the years approximately 1590–1600 show the way he characteristically developed an artistic form. The first period is one of experimentation with popular dramatic fashions during which the conventional materials are shaped to the standard Shakespearian plot pattern, shaded and modified, and their dramatic possibilities explored. But during this experimental period the form remains relatively unfixed and the potential meanings, though glimpsed briefly here and there, remain for the most part locked within a variety of symbolic patterns and situations. The four earliest comedies, dated rather inexactly between 1588 and 1595, have all the obvious trademarks of Shakespearian comedy, the romantic settings, the mingling of the high and low perspectives in the interaction of courtly lovers and rustic clowns, and the three-part plot (with constantly varying emphasis on the different parts). But the main thrust in each of these plays seems to be an attempt to identify and find suitable terms for some primal energy, some strange but fundamental power in life – sometimes psychological, sometimes physical, usually both – which is the motive power of the comic world. *The Comedy of Errors* (*c*. 1588–93), an imitation of Plautus, centres on a standard comic device, the confusion of twins, but Shakespeare doubles the sets of twins, emphasizes domestication on the one hand and wandering on the other, and in general makes of this device an encounter of the self, sudden and unexpected, with the other self, the double, the person we might have been had we been raised in Ephesus rather than Syracuse, had we drifted away from the shipwreck with the mother rather than the father, had we been slave rather than master.

The confident sense of the familiar self in an immutable world is destroyed in a less violent but more thorough way in *Love's Labour's Lost* (*c*. 1588–94). The young men of the court of Navarre who begin by forswearing love, food, sleep and all natural pleasures in order to spend all their time in study soon find themselves entangled and brought down from their high design by sudden love for four very attractive ladies; by an education in language which forces them to forswear 'Taffeta phrases, silken terms precise, Three-pil'd hyperboles' for 'russet yeas, and honest kersey noes' (V. ii. 406–13); and by the constant parody of themselves by the braggart traveller and linguist Don Armado, the pedant Holofernes and the clown Costard. The final instruction in reality comes in an encounter with death when the messenger Marcade enters to announce the death of the king of France, father to one of the young ladies involved in the love game. The news immediately breaks off the comic progression towards marriage, and the lovers are sent into a year of mourning where they must contemplate in hermitage and hospital, in isolation and amid sickness and suffering, whether their love be real or only the fancy of a wilful moment. The perspective of the play, and of all the comedies, is contained in the closing songs of the cuckoo and the owl, summer and winter, pleasure and wisdom. In both songs the foreground is a familiar world acceptable to men: a summer world of meadows covered with flowers, a shepherd playing his pipe, the birds singing in the trees, the white dresses bleaching in the sun; a winter world inside the house before a burning fire, crab apples hissing in the pot, frozen pails of milk, and the kitchenmaid scouring the pans. But from just outside the range of sight comes the song of a bird, the idiotic repetitive cry of the cuckoo in the summer, and the 'Tu-whit, Tu-who' of the 'staring owl' in the winter. Both songs reduce all the gay, vivid language of the play to a sound emerging from the very heart of nature, telling in the cry of the cuckoo of an amoral sexual appetite at the basis of things, in the cry of the owl of the inevitability of death. These are 'words of fear', unpleasing not only to the 'married ear' but to the ear of self-assured mankind, certain of his own identity and his mastery of himself and reality. It is the presence of the unknown and ignored power at the root of things which is the distinguishing mark of Shakespearian comedy.

Love and sex are the usual locomotives of romantic comedy, and they are central to Shakespearian comedy, but he uses them not only as the basis of the plot but also as entry-ways into the usually hidden, further reaches of self and nature. In *The Two Gentlemen of Verona* (1593–5), a love-friendship comedy in the manner of Lyly, the young lover Proteus, whose name suggests his potentialities, turns from a true lover and a faithful friend to a man who falls violently in love with his friend Valentine's beloved, treacherously betrays his own love and his friend in order to have the lady, and when she denies his advances follows her to the forest and plans to rape her. The violence latent in the gentle passion sometimes takes open form as antagonism and hatred for the opposing sex. In *The Taming of the Shrew* (1593–4) Kate the shrew's incredible violence of will, astounding perversity and rage at all she encounters, whether it threatens or tries to placate her, suggest a demonic will to power rather than any inclination towards love. Petruchio, the realist who frankly comes to wive it wealthily in Padua, understands the demon he has to deal with and sets out to tame Kate as one would a wild animal. He becomes more perverse, more irrational, more furious than she; denies her rest, food and comfort; until, exhausted and overmanned by an energy greater than her own, she capitulates and jumps through the hoops

Petruchio holds out for her. Whether she finds satisfaction in this relationship, or whether she simply plays the game with tongue in cheek, certain of her own ultimate domination, or whether she has discovered – though Petruchio has not – the miraculous power of love, the play does not absolutely tell us. But it does tell us in several ways that the conflict of violent, headstrong, self-seeking personalities fought out by Kate and Petruchio is a part of what the world so confidently calls love. The other lovers of the piece simply gloss over the reality with fine words and refuse to recognize that they are engaged in the same war which the shrew and her tamer fight openly.

(ii) From the city to the woods: *A Midsummer Night's Dream*

The second stage in the Shakespearian progress towards mastery of a form comes with the production of a masterpiece which gathers together the essential elements of earlier experiments, and adjusts them to one another in a way which makes clear the full meaning of what has gone before. *A Midsummer Night's Dream* (1594–6) is the fulfilment of Shakespeare's first comic period, and in it we see clearly for the first time the complete rhythm of human experience which is the essence of Shakespearian comedy.

As is usual in comedy, the characters are not highly individualized. Instead they fall into four well-defined groups. First, there is Theseus, king of Athens, and his queen-to-be, Hippolyta, queen of the Amazons, who has been subdued in battle and in love by Theseus. Second, there is the group of young lovers: Hermia and Lysander who are in love, Demetrius who once loved Helena but now loves Hermia and is favoured by her father, and Helena who still hopelessly loves Demetrius. Next, there is a group of rude mechanicals of Athens, Bottom, Quince, Flute, Starveling, Snout and Snug, who have joined to produce a play for Theseus's wedding, hoping that he will reward them with a pension. Finally, inhabiting the woods just outside Athens, there are the fairies: Oberon the king and his chief minister Puck or Robin Goodfellow, and Titania the queen with her attendant train of Peaseblossom, Cobweb, Moth and Mustardseed.

The first and last groups, the rulers of the city and the rulers of the woods, are geniuses of their respective places. When first seen, Theseus is awaiting impatiently his nuptial day and somewhat reluctantly telling the headstrong Hermia that she must either accept her father's choice of Demetrius as a husband or, in accordance with the old laws of Athens, either retire to a nunnery or be executed. Theseus, the legendary destroyer of wildness and disorder, the creator of civilization and law, is the appropriate voice of the city, law, authority and tradition. Hippolyta is also presented as the embodiment of law, for she restrains Theseus's impetuous desire with a firm reminder that they cannot be married until the four prescribed days of waiting have passed. But the other half of the Theseus–Hippolyta legend is not forgotten altogether – though the king and queen conveniently forget their past – and we are reminded briefly that Theseus once made a career of seducing and then abandoning young maidens, while Hippolyta was once the queen of those ferocious Amazons whose life was devoted to battle with men. In their past, then, Theseus and Hippolyta were representatives of the most primitive, lawless drives of the sexes, the seducer and the man-hater, the fanatical male and female, the radical left and right of the sexual spectrum. But the wildness of their earlier years has passed, and in one of the many 'concords of these discords' which the play develops they have agreed to enter into wedlock and have become the sedate and solemn champions of law, society and the city.

The earlier lives of Theseus and Hippolyta were closely related to the fairies of the woods. As if the woods were some kind of mirror image of the human world, the female principle of Titania encouraged and protected the militant maleness of Theseus during his days as ravisher, while the male Oberon was the protector of Hippolyta in her days as man-killer. These unexpected alliances suggest that at the place of basic reality things may be the opposite of what they seem to be in the familiar human world. In the woods, radical femaleness simply seeks pleasure and procreation without concern for such human moral niceties as good faith and responsibility, while radical maleness is nothing more complicated than the battle-spirit, to which the all-important human distinctions between male and female are unimportant.

The fairies are essentially fertility figures associated with a rich and burgeoning nature, the 'bank where the wild thyme blows . . . over-canopied with lucious woodbine, With sweet musk-roses, and with eglantine' (II. i. 249–52). The range of their world is as vast as its parts are rich, and they move in a flash from the Indian continent across the reaches of ocean to the woods of Warwickshire. The scale of this world is given in Oberon's command to Puck to be gone and here again 'ere the leviathan can swim a league' (II. i. 174). Though profuse and vast, the fairy world is at the same time so remarkably fine and delicate in detail that the wings of painted butterflies are used to fan moonbeams from the eyes of a sleeper.

These are not dark and killing spirits who wander abroad only at night, returning to their wormy beds at the first ray of the sun, but, as Oberon remarks, 'spirits of another sort' who while they cannot live in the full blaze of noon can and do sport abroad in the early dawn:

> I with the Morning's love have oft made sport;
> And, like a forester, the groves may tread
> Even till the eastern gate, all fiery red,
> Opening on Neptune with fair blessed beams,
> Turns into yellow gold his salt green streams. (III. ii. 389–93)

Dawn is exactly the right setting for these nature spirits, for on the one hand they participate in and guide the generous, delicate and ever-renewing benisons of a fertile nature, but on the other hand they have touches of a dark and destructive nature as well. Their sinister qualities come out most strongly in the quarrel between Titania and Oberon over the little Indian boy, the child of a votaress of Titania who 'being mortal, of that boy did die' (II. i. 135), as the fairy queen rather indifferently puts it. So imperious are the wills of the fairy king and queen that each is determined to have the boy, and out of their quarrel have come contagious fogs, floods, rotting crops, sick animals and general disorders of nature. Like the nature of Darwin's evolution, their elemental drive is to have their way, not to nourish and procreate. At the same time that they are wilful to the point of destruction, they are also inefficient and random in their workings, as their use of the plant 'Love-in-idleness' makes clear. When a drop of its essence is placed upon the eyes of a sleeper, he loves on sight the object he first sees when he wakes. The dangers for humans of this urgent plant appear in its hilarious and terrifying effects on the young Athenian lovers lost in the wood, but its full powers become clear only in its use on Titania who will, Oberon rightly predicts, love passionately anything she first sees on waking, 'Be it on lion, bear, or wolf, or bull, On meddling monkey, or on busy ape' (II. i. 180–1). Vital and beautiful as these spirits and the lushness of this nature may be, they are still to the human mind a frightening energy which pursues its ends without regard for its instruments, which does not discriminate between its objects and which seeks its ends in an imperious manner without regard for consequences.

In its more benign and amusing aspects, the random lawlessness of the fairy world is represented by that familiar figure of English folklore, the Puck, or Robin Goodfellow, who jests to Oberon. The spirit of the unexpected and the lapses in what human beings take to be the 'laws' of nature, Puck is present when the stool on which the old woman intends to sit is suddenly not there, when milk will not turn to butter in the churn nor ale ferment, when the 'fat and bean-fed horse' is aroused thinking he hears the neighing of a 'filly foal', when the roasted apple floating in the cup of ale bobs crazily and causes the drinker to spill the drink down his front. Puck sums up his own nature and points to a quality close to the centre of Shakespearian comedy when he remarks, 'And those things do best please me That befall prepost'rously' (III. ii. 120–1).

As is usual in his comedies, Shakespeare in *A Midsummer Night's Dream* creates two related but distinct places, each with its resident deities. On one hand there is the city, the man-made world of daylight, reason, law and tradition, governed by Theseus and Hippolyta. On the other hand, there is the wood outside Athens, the natural world of darkness and early light, of emotion, will, fertility, randomness, governed by the fairy king and queen. The rulers of each of these places venture only once into the other domain, Theseus to hunt on the edge of the woods in the morning, and Oberon and Titania to bless the inhabitants of the palace on the night of their wedding. But the other two groups, the lovers and the artisans, journey from the city to the wood and then back again to the city, like the villagers who left their town on Midsummer's Eve to spend a night of release in the woods before returning the next day to the town to take up once again the obligations of civil life. Behind the lovers is a time of childhood innocence when Hermia and Helena could sit side by side, singing one song in one key, and working the same flower in the same sampler, 'Like to a double cherry, seeming parted, But yet an union in partition' (III. ii. 209–10). But with the coming of adulthood – which occurs as always in Shakespeare at the point of sexual maturity – the inevitable separation into two individuals also comes. Now, at the play's opening, Demetrius and Lysander have inexplicably chosen to love Hermia, and while Hermia has decided on Lysander, her father Egeus has for some reason decided that she will marry Demetrius. The phonetic similarity of the lovers' names – Hermia and Helena, Demetrius and Lysander – stresses the fact that they are, except in height – Hermia is short, while Helena is tall – so alike in beauty and fortune as to make it impossible to find any reason for their singular and absolute preferences in love. There is about love, even love in the city, something random, inexplicable, woodlike and Puckish, and something like Oberon and Titania in the strength of will with which the lovers insist on having their way. Any interference with their choices is unbearable, and so when the rigid laws of Athens are applied to them to force their wills to yield to the controls of society, Hermia and Lysander defy king and father and flee to the woods. Love generates in Helena equally wild and woodlike passions, and hoping to gain favour with Demetrius who once loved her but has now for no reason abandoned her to pursue Hermia, she betrays her trust and tells him of the lovers' flight. Still seeking to impose his will on Hermia, Demetrius follows into the woods, and, longing for his love, Helena follows him.

As the lovers progress deeper into the woods, deeper into total commitment to passion, love reveals even more surprising qualities. Demetrius once loved Helena but now he hates her, and as she dogs his steps he comes to loathe her more and more, brutally insults her and finally threatens to rape and murder her. Each brutality only intensifies Helena's love, and she takes an absolute pleasure from his cruelty, remarking at one point that she will 'make a heaven of hell, To die upon the hand I love so well' (II. i. 243–4). All this is lightly, even laughingly, done, but the language and actions of the lovers suggest the perverse turns that love takes when left entirely to its own direction.

Love comes even closer to abnormal psychology when the fairies intervene to aid in what is after all their chief business, fertility and procreation. Seeing the sterile opposition of Demetrius and Helena, Oberon orders Puck to anoint the eyes of the sleeping Demetrius with that magical flower, Love-in-idleness – 'idle' not only in the modern sense but also with the older meaning of 'waste', 'wild', 'uncultivated' – which will cause him to love the object on which his eyes first open, hopefully Helena. Puck carries out his orders, but in typical confusion also anoints the eyes of Lysander, and both start up, no longer in love with Hermia, but now desperate for Helena. As Demetrius and Lysander scorn Hermia, whom they loved only a moment before, and adore Helena, whom they hated only a moment earlier, it becomes ever clearer that love freely following its own direction in idleness is likely to make radical and irrational changes in its objects. As this wild process continues, and the lovers become more and more lost in the forest, they also become more and more entangled in the labyrinth of passion. Helena, startled by this sudden love for her, becomes suspicious and concludes that the two young men and Hermia are playing an elaborate joke on her. The more the young men in-sist on their love, the more Helena believes they are mocking her, and the more she hates them and Hermia. Hermia, knowing that she is fair as ever, can only conclude that Helena has practised witchcraft to steal her lovers, and so she turns on her childhood friend and tries to scratch her eyes out. Paranoia, despair, thoughts of murder and suicide follow. The end is a night-mare chase through the darkness of the forest, torn by briars, stumbling over logs, hearing, always just ahead, the taunting voice of the antagonist. They run and slash out at air until they fall at last exhausted and drop off into a deep sleep, each lying isolated a few feet from the others. Love-in-idleness is a useful power within the world of nature, but, while it is necessary for human life, it is too potent in its purity for human beings. Four young people who were once close friends have by following passion to its uttermost limits become, paradoxically, violent enemies, and find not sweetness and satisfaction but hatred and unsatisfied desire.

Love is not the only way into the dark, unexplored world of the woods, into that unfamiliar reality which lies just behind the familiar surface of everyday life. Like the clowns playing with Faustus's magic, the artisans, who have nothing more in mind when they plan a play than pleasing their ruler and getting a small pension for themselves, go to the woods to rehearse their play and unsuspectingly project themselves into that strange world lying within the tragic legend of Pyramus and Thisby and within the theatre. The woods have the same effect on Bottom and company as on the lovers, translating that which was latent and metaphorical into fact and action, and Bottom is transformed into the ass he so supremely is. But he is also introduced into a marvellous world which, completely lacking imagination, he has never seen, a world where an ass may be loved by the queen of the fairies, may be attended by such gaieties as Peaseblossom and Cobweb and may be allowed to see wonders of richness and delicacy never before known to such a simple, practical man: the profusion of swelling nature, apricots, dewberries, purple grapes, green figs and mulberries; the microscopic elegancies of life, bags of honey bees, tapers made of the waxen thighs of bees and lighted 'at the fiery glowworm's eyes'; the unbelievably fine movements of the world beyond the literal eye.

But the stay in the wood, the vision of a further world opened up by love and by the theatre, can be endured by mortals for only a short time, and by the end of Act III night fades, dawn comes and the sleepers begin to wake back into the familiar daylight world. It is May Day – even as it is also the morning after Midsummer's Eve – and like the villagers returning from the wood after experiencing again the fullness of nature in all its renewed generosity and its amoral ferocity, Bottom and the lovers make their way back to Athens and civilized life. Oberon has decreed that these mortals will remember the events of the night as no more than 'the fierce vexation of a dream', and it is in this fashion that the brushes with a further reality are understood. For Bottom it was a 'most rare vision', surpassing the wit of man to interpret, and 'because it hath no bottom' he decrees that it shall be called Bottom's Dream and sung in ballads. For Demetrius looking back, the events of the night 'seem small and undistinguishable, Like far-off mountains turned into clouds', and Hermia sees the night as 'with parted eye, When everything seems double' (IV. i. 191–4). For the lovers the events of the night have at least some reality, though they have become far away, insubstantial and out of focus; but for Theseus, the tale of the lovers is only lunacy or the product of overheated imaginations:

> I never may believe
> These antique fables, nor these fairy toys.
> Lovers and madmen have such seething brains,
> Such shaping fantasies, that apprehend
> More than cool reason ever comprehends.
> The lunatic, the lover, and the poet,
> Are of imagination all compact.
> One sees more devils than vast hell can hold;
> That is the madman. The lover, all as frantic,
> Sees Helen's beauty in a brow of Egypt.
> The poet's eye, in a fine frenzy rolling,
> Doth glance from heaven to earth, from earth to heaven;
> And as imagination bodies forth
> The forms of things unknown, the poet's pen
> Turns them to shapes, and gives to airy nothing
> A local habitation and a name.
> Such tricks hath strong imagination
> That, if it would but apprehend some joy,
> It comprehends some bringer of that joy. (V. i. 2–20)

It is right for Theseus – the governor of the daylight, rational world of the city – to hold such views, for the city must exclude most of the world that imagination perceives. The flight to the woods was necessary to break the over-restrictive control of laws grown cruel and unnatural, and it is in the woods that the couples are finally sorted out and the lovers' competition eliminated; but it is only in Athens, where they duly return to be married in a great celebration of the rituals of civilized life, that the needs for orderliness can be adjusted to natural impulses to provide a satisfactory *human* life. To achieve this order and rule of law requires, however, the blanking out of the world perceived by the imagination of lover and poet in favour of a world almost exclusively rational. And so Theseus is right in one way in denying apprehension in favour of comprehension – just as he has necessarily forgotten his own wild past – but in so doing he and the civil world he represents place themselves in a most ironic position. The man who denies the truth of the process by which poets body forth airy nothings giving them a local habitation and a name, even as he speaks is himself no more than the imagined idea of government and reason given, in legend and play, the name of Theseus and the habitation of Athens.

Shakespeare continues to call our attention to the ironic condition of the characters and their world throughout Act V, where Theseus and Hippolyta and the young lovers, safely paired off, married and recovered from the fierce vexation of their collective dream, pass the hours before bedtime watching a play, 'A tedious brief scene of young Pyramus And his love Thisby; very tragical mirth'. Bottom and the other artisans are completely out of their depth in trying to deal with the magic of the imagination which resides within both the love story and the theatre, and their clumsy realism, doggerel verse and extravagant action are quite bad enough to deserve all the amused and superior comments made from the side by Theseus and his aristocratic friends. But their position as spectators at a play calls attention to the fact that they, so sure and certain of themselves and their reality, are themselves only players in a play. And just as they laugh at Bottom and company for their lack of sophistication in the conventions of the theatre and their complete inability to understand the love and sorrow of Pyramus and Thisby, so we laugh at them for taking their own reality so seriously and for closing off as mere dream those further ranges of reality in the dark woods where they once encountered the strange forces at work in themselves and their world.

As the play of Pyramus and Thisby ends and the mechanicals depart for their homes in the city, the wedded couples rise and take their way to bed thinking that the play is over and reality reigns again. But as they depart and the stage darkens, Titania, Oberon and Puck move into the light of the dying fire to bless the house and the bridal beds. The effect is startling. Just when the characters thought the play was over, another group of characters, whose existence is denied by the rational world, come on stage to continue the play, to make it clear that the scene is much larger than these mortals think it is, and to show that these powers lying outside the range of the reasoning eye are, though strange, ultimately beneficent and life-nourishing.

This is the characteristic Shakespearian comic perspective. Life is like a series of plays within plays, or a series of concentric circles with the last having no outer boundaries. Each group of characters, beginning with the artisans, inhabits one of these circles, and each group takes its own circle as all reality and laughs at the inhabitants of a smaller circle for their blindness. But outside each circle there is another and larger one, and it is only in dream, the dream of the lunatic, the lover and the poet, only under the extreme psychic urgencies of love, desire and will, only through the brush of the painter

or the door that opens on to the stage of the theatre and the world of 'let's pretend', that the further ranges of reality become visible and audible. The plot of the comedies – and to a considerable extent that of the tragedies – is a journey, usually motivated by love and the desire for freedom, from one of the inner circles to one of the outer circles. What the traveller finds there is both immensely attractive and frightening, and having glimpsed the depths of his own nature and the forces that power the world he returns for safety and fulfilment to his own construction, the city, where daylight, government and reason prevail, forgetting what he has seen and known.

(iii) The return to the city: the later comedies and *Twelfth Night*

The third stage in the Shakespearian mastery of a form comes when, to use his terms, apprehension is followed by comprehension. Having located the central issue and developed the type of plot and structural arrangements which focus and illuminate it, he proceeds while maintaining the essential pattern to play variations on it and to give his work a remarkable regularity of design. At the same time he and his characters come to be able to verbalize, to phrase directly, the meaning of those experiences which were before often only felt and lived. Much of the mystery is gone from *The Merchant of Venice* (1596–7), *Much Ado About Nothing* (1598–1600) and *As You Like It* (1599–1600), plays structured in an almost over-regular way. The caskets at Belmont containing the secret of love are three in number, one of gold, one of silver and one of lead. The generosity of Antonio is balanced by the miserliness of Shylock; Venice is poised against Belmont, mercy against law, love against duty. In *Much Ado* the paradox of love is neatly displayed in the antagonism of Beatrice and Benedick which turns to love, while the love of Hero and Claudio turns to hate. In *As You Like It* group follows group on the mandatory journey to the Forest of Arden to escape the cruelty of the usurping duke, and when assembled in the forest they comprise a spectrum of love, ranging from the pastoral lovers, Phebe and Silvius, through the paired lovers of romance, Orlando and Rosalind, Oliver and Celia, to the 'country copulatives' Touchstone and Audrey. There is even a satirist, Jaques, who rounds out the views on life by denying the possibility of love or any other good in the dismal scene of life.

Except for occasional brief glimpses of the deeper powers of life – such as Shylock's 'If you prick us, do we not bleed?' – the journey in these plays does not go into very deep woods or very tangled forests. Everything, or almost everything, is understood and said by those rather brassy females – Portia,

Beatrice, Rosalind – who dominate their plays. Women always occupy a special place in the Shakespearian world, and the virtuous woman, usually sitting 'like Patience on a monument' – Desdemona, Cordelia, Hermione – is often the carrier of all the grains of goodness that sweeten this dungy earth; while perversion of femaleness – Lady Macbeth's willingness to tear a child from her breast and dash its head against the wall – endangers all human and natural values. But what was said of Cordelia, 'Her voice was ever soft, Gentle, and low', cannot be said of any of these comic heroines. Their high, clear voices telling us that 'the quality of mercy is not strain'd', and that 'men have died from time to time, and worms have eaten them, but not for love', ring through their worlds. Their wit penetrates all obscurities, and their disguises as boys signal their participation in the mysteries of both sexes. They exhort, explain, instruct, and, standing at the centre of all the intrigues, by their skill, courage and cleverness manage to balance extremes and bring their comedies to happy conclusions. Only in their love for men, who are so much inferior to them, are these women at all surprising, and they submit to this love as some curious but functional part of their beings.

Following the period of almost excessive clarity and rationality comes the fourth stage of the Shakespearian progress in the development of a form. What was earlier treated explicitly and at length is now presented in symbolic form and with the utmost economy, leaving the playwright free to elaborate on and explore in great depth those elements which have now become the essence of his vision. *Twelfth Night* (1600–1) represents this fourth stage in the development of Shakespeare's comedy.

The comedies all begin in the human world of the city, but its civil traditions and institutions have got out of hand, grown tyrannical, developed by their own fatal logic into the destroyer rather than the preserver of the values they were designed to serve. In *Love's Labour's Lost* the desire for fame and knowledge lead to the academy and its strict vows to forswear all natural needs, such as food, sleep or sex. In *A Midsummer Night's Dream*, the law, the rule by father and by king, becomes excessive, and a young girl is threatened with death or enforced chastity if she does not obey the cruel statute which denies her own will. In Belmont the dead father locks his daughter's possibility of marriage in three caskets, and in Venice the law allows a usurer to cut a pound of flesh from a living man. In *Twelfth Night*, though there are cruel laws which threaten death, nature is thwarted in the first instance by an overdevelopment of civil and civilizing instincts of so basic a kind as to make clear the origin of the force that in earlier comedies made law and society intolerably repressive.

As the play opens, we hear the voice of Orsino, the Duke of Illyria, speaking of his sad and hopeless love for the Lady Olivia:

> If music be the food of love, play on,
> Give me excess of it, that surfeiting,
> The appetite may sicken and so die.
> That strain again! It had a dying fall;
> O, it came o'er my ear like the sweet sound
> That breathes upon a bank of violets,
> Stealing and giving odour! Enough, no more;
> 'Tis not so sweet now as it was before.
> O spirit of love, how quick and fresh art thou!
> That, notwithstanding thy capacity
> Receiveth as the sea, nought enters there,
> Of what validity and pitch soe'er,
> But falls into abatement and low price
> Even in a minute. So full of shapes is fancy,
> That it alone is high fantastical. (I. i. 1–15)

Orsino is not so much in love with the Lady Olivia as he is with love itself, or, perhaps more properly, with the idea of himself in love. He is unable, unwilling, to arise from his couch and move beyond the range of those soft sad strains of music to press his own suit vigorously. The most active gesture he can manage is to send a proxy to tell the lady of his love. The duke is an adept in the art of passive loving, an expert in the cultivation and analysis of his own refined feelings, with little interest in any vigorous or vital act. The Lady Olivia shows the perversion through excess of another peculiarly human virtue, sorrow for the death of a beloved kinsman. Because of the death of a brother, she has vowed to wear a veil, cry each day, shut herself away from the world and avoid the company of men for seven years. Authority over her household has appropriately passed into the hands of the puritanical and utterly self-centred Malvolio, and the over-repressed primal appetites, instead of being controlled and ordered, explode into the misrule and riot of those two carousing idiots, the drunken Sir Toby Belch and the dancing gull, Sir Andrew Aguecheek. This turning inward of love, the perversion of the natural urgencies of sex and pleasure by the over-refinement of human feelings, defines and interprets the way in which in the earlier comedies such humane forces as the love for learning or the need for law turn in upon and feed themselves rather than functioning to enable man to realize fully and humanely his complex nature.

In Shakespeare's comedies, the excesses of civility and the narcissism of civilization do not succeed in thwarting life, as they threaten to do at the beginning of each play. Somehow man is always forced to realize that 'what is yours to bestow is not yours to reserve', as Viola tells Olivia (I. v. 201–2). In *Love's Labour's Lost* the witty and attractive ladies arrive almost as soon as the foolish philosophers have made their vows; in *A Midsummer Night's Dream*, the lovers' desire for their own choice causes them to flee Athens; and in *As You Like It* the cruelty of human society drives the duke and all of his followers out into the Forest of Arden. In *Twelfth Night* there is no journey into a wild forest and no encounter with nature's spirits such as Oberon and Titania. Instead, the society of the self-indulgent land people is invaded by a group of sea people who have already been exposed to nature in its most violent and threatening form. The quality of the sea people is apparent in the bold Antonio, the sea captain who has survived so many violent fights and storms at sea. He gives of himself without reserve, and finding a friend in Sebastian he follows him, at the risk of his life, only to serve him. When Sebastian expresses a wish to see the town, Antonio without hesitation gives him his purse. Sebastian is himself of the same outgoing kind. Bold and direct in friendship and anger, his loving is as forthright and active as Orsino's is convoluted and passive. When Olivia mistakes him for his sister, the disguised Viola, and proposes marriage, Sebastian is puzzled, but seeing here a lady both beautiful and rich who wishes to marry him, he without hesitation accompanies her to church.

The nature of the sea people is developed in depth in Viola, who by the end of the play has released Olivia from her living death and Orsino from the wallows of self-indulgence. Cast ashore by the storm, Viola assumes the dress of a young page and seeks service with Orsino. She combines in herself the sea-tempered masculine and feminine virtues. On the masculine side she shows the same forthrightness and moral courage of the men who have survived the sea, and her feminine virtues are similarly strengthened. Though Orsino thinks that no one can love as he loves, or suffer as he suffers, Viola loves him more deeply and more profoundly than he loves Olivia. Where his love for Olivia takes the form of stroking his own feelings, Viola's love for him takes the form of self-denying service. This love is shown in her actual service to Orsino as a page, and its absoluteness is realized in Viola's willingness to serve as Orsino's emissary to Olivia to plead his case in a most effective way. By her service she instructs Orsino in the true nature of love, and by her person and her speeches she instructs Olivia in the necessity of giving one's self to life rather than to death. Viola seems to describe herself and her love perfectly in her little fiction, told to Orsino, of a sister who hopelessly loved a man. When Orsino asks – pausing for the first time to regard something other than himself – what happened to the girl, Viola replies:

> A blank, my lord. She never told her love,
> But let concealment, like a worm i' th' bud,
> Feed on her damask cheek. She pin'd in thought;
> And with a green and yellow melancholy
> She sat like Patience on a monument,
> Smiling at grief. Was not this love indeed? (II. iv. 113–18)

Tempered by their encounter with the realities of nature in storm and shipwreck, the sea people have not lost their humanity but have rather strengthened it by having been exposed to the world in which humanity must exist. This is, of course, exactly what happens in the testing scenes in *Love's Labour's Lost*, in the Forest of Arden and in that strange haunted forest outside Athens. And just as the characters in the earlier comedies return from the wild places, where they brush against the reality in which man lives, strengthened and renewed by the experience, so the sea people in this play revivify a humanity grown oversensitive and over-refined. Patience, courage, boldness, common sense and service to others and to life are the sea virtues which renew and make useful once again the ingrown land virtues of Orsino and Olivia.

All of the comedies are fantastic in their plot arrangements, but none more strange and complicated than *Twelfth Night*. A pair of identical twins, a boy and a girl, separated by shipwreck at sea, each not knowing that the other is alive, land in a city where the young girl decides to dress herself as a boy, and takes employment with the duke. As his page, she woos a lady for him, while herself loving the duke; but the lady falls in love with the page, and then by a happy mistake encounters the twin brother and marries him in a flash, leaving the girl free to marry a duke overwhelmed by her love and faithfulness. Herschel Baker remarks that 'the convolutions of the plot provide diversion of a sort, but they also bind the characters in a web of interwoven error, and thus they underscore the meaning of the play: that most men never know, and maybe never have a chance to know, the truth about themselves'.[1]

---

[1] 'Introduction', *Twelfth Night*, The Signet Shakespeare, gen. ed. Sylvan Barnet (New York, 1965), p. xxviii.

This is, I think, exactly right. But even beyond this the strange complexities and turns of Shakespeare's romantic plots consistently suggest not only how little man knows of himself but also how little he understands of the strange and miraculous events that make his destiny. He dances always in the comedies the dance of the world, while remaining at the same time sure and certain that he knows perfectly well who he is and that he controls his own destiny. Thus the validity of those marvellous fools who populate these plays – Costard the rational hind, Bottom, Touchstone and Feste – who stand in the plays almost like footnotes. Their function in the plot is always negligible, but their function in the theme is paramount. By their mere presence on stage they seem constantly to be saying what the plot also says – what lucky fools these mortals be. But since the mortals are unaware of how foolish they are, and since the world is beneficent, Jack always gets Jill and everyone congratulates himself on his sagacity and humanity.

The last fool, Feste – whose name suggests that he summarizes the festival spirit – seems to be aware that in their wanderings in strange places the mortals of this play, who have now happily trooped off to bed leaving the fool behind, have walked unsuspectingly by some dark mysteries which cannot quite be contained within the comic form. The Shakespearian range is always a bit too large for comedy, and the unreconciled anger of Malvolio at the end of *Twelfth Night* brings to mind other undigested events such as the sudden news of the death of the king of France, the views of the satirist Jaques who does not return to the city again with the revellers, and the mother of the little Indian boy who, being mortal, died at his birth leaving the king and queen of the fairies a trifle to fight over. Not all escape from the shipwreck at sea, and not all come home from the Forest of Arden; and to understand this is to understand the necessity for the onward movement of the dramatists, the more sombre comedy of Ben Jonson, and on beyond this into the desperate world of Jacobean tragedy. Feste, the clown, understands, and sings about it:

When that I was and a little tiny boy,
    With hey, ho, the wind and the rain,
A foolish thing was but a toy,
    For the rain it raineth every day.

But when I came to man's estate,
    With hey, ho, the wind and the rain,
'Gainst knaves and thieves men shut their gate,
    For the rain it raineth every day.

But when I came, alas! to wive,
   With hey, ho, the wind and the rain,
By swaggering could I never thrive,
   For the rain it raineth every day.

But when I came unto my beds,
   With hey, ho, the wind and the rain,
With toss-pots still had drunken heads,
   For the rain it raineth every day.

A great while ago the world begun,
   With hey, ho, the wind and the rain,
But that's all one, our play is done,
   And we'll strive to please you every day. (V. i. 398–417)

5 Alchemy and acting: the plays of Ben Jonson[1]

Where Shakespeare blended the comedy of romance and the comedy of folly, deriving man's folly from his failure to perceive the wonders which are romance, Jonson worked exclusively in and refined the classical comedy with its urban setting, middle-class characters and satiric emphasis on vanity and idiocy. The Jonsonian perspective is contained in brief in one of the remarks which so distressed William Drummond: 'S[ir] P[hilip] Sidney was no pleasant man in Countenance, his face being spoilled with Pimples' (*Conversations with Drummond*, 230-1). The same satiric vision appears in longer perspective in *Volpone*, II, ii, where the noble *magnifico* Volpone appears in the public square disguised as a mountebank, steps up on his trestle stage and delivers a marvellous spiel on the virtues of his medicinal oil, *oglio del Scoto*. He is followed by his zany, the dwarf Nano, who stands behind him during the performance, a shadow figure like the clown of innumerable comic routines who cautiously tries the step of the dancers only to fall flat on his face, tries to sing like the singers only to produce an out-of-tune squeak, tries the juggling act only to drop objects all over the stage. The zany is a

[1] Portions of this chapter and the final chapter on *Bartholomew Fair* appeared as an article, 'Alchemy and acting: the major plays of Ben Jonson', in *Studies in the Literary Imagination*, VI (April 1973), pp. 1-22.

living form of the satiric and comic visions of man as, despite all his fine pretences, inescapably clumsy and grotesque. The magnifico reduced to the mountebank, the mountebank reduced in turn to the misshapen dwarf: this is the paradigm of Jonson's comic world where all life moves unknowingly towards a revelation of its own zaniness.

In his person, Jonson was a mixture of contraries. Boisterous, energetic, witty, fond of drink, competitive to the point of hating all rivals and violent enough to kill, he was at the same time a meticulous scholar, a classicist and a literary and moral authoritarian. His life seems built on oppositions. In the late 1590s while in prison, Jonson became a Catholic and remained one during the years of most stringent repression, and then when the climate grew more tolerant he returned to the official church. He criticized Shakespeare's dramaturgy frequently and severely, and yet when he came to write the eulogy which prefaces the 1623 folio of Shakespeare's plays, Jonson reveals that he alone realized that 'the tother youth' (*Epicene*, II. ii. 118) was the 'Soule of the Age', and, even beyond this, 'not of an age, but for all time!'

Born in 1572, the posthumous son of a minister, Jonson (see Plate 16) was educated at Westminster School under Camden, but did not attend a university. He was apprenticed to a bricklayer, but continued his studies and in time became a great scholar. He served with the English army in the Low Countries, where, according to his story, he killed an enemy in single combat. At some time in the late 1590s he became associated with the theatre, where he worked as an actor – a bad one by malicious report – and as one of Henslowe's hacks. One of his early collaborations, *The Isle of Dogs*, written with Thomas Nashe, sent him to prison for the first of many times. He fought a duel with and killed a fellow actor and may have been one of the last men to save his life by reading his 'neck-verse'. Separated from his wife and children, he entered fully into the wild and disorderly world of the late Elizabethan theatre where philosophers like Chapman, raw hacks like Anthony Munday, simple city poets like Thomas Dekker and grammar-school geniuses like Shakespeare searched for reputation and riches by writing to satisfy the need of the great repertory companies for more and more plays. What was needed by an aspiring playwright was popular, sensational subject matter; and when Jonson broke into the theatre as an author in 1598 with *Every Man in his Humour* the fads, humours and satire were most suitable to his temperament.[1]

[1] *A Tale of A Tub* and *The Case is Altered* may have been written by 1598, but Jonson did not include either in the 1616 edition of his works, and only *A Tale of A Tub* was included in the second volume of 1640, perhaps not by Jonson's intent.

In three more plays written in quick succession, *Every Man out of his Humour* (1599), *Cynthia's Revels* (1601) and *Poetaster* (1601), Jonson purveyed dramatic portraits of a wide number of idiotic humours or obsessions.

Not removed to the study, but in the midst of the hurly-burly of the Elizabethan theatre, Jonson in these early plays took up the standards of realism and classicism, and by means of prologues, discussions of literature by his characters and the introduction of literary critics into his plays he hammered away at the barbarism of the Elizabethan stage. Its poets are, he claims, not poets by nature but by need, its language indecorous rant, its verse lame, its scenes and characters cribbed or the projections of mad minds, its scenes without order. All sense, he charges, is defied on a stage where wounds heal in the course of a few minutes, and in two hours a young child grows to an old man; where great battles are fought with 'three rustie swords' and some very long words; where the scene moves from one side of the world to another in an instant; and where the emphasis is on spectacle, tricky machines and loud sound effects.

By way of contrast, Jonson offers himself and his plays as models of what poets and drama should be. He is, he says, no slavish follower of the rules limiting time and place, but he does restrict his scene to reasonable spaces of time and shifts of locale. His language is seemly and decorous. He does not set his scene in the faraway places of romance but in the city streets, and his characters are not the wild projections of an overheated brain but imitations of men and manners one might well encounter in London. He avoids spectacular effects and ingenious machinery, concentrating instead on 'deedes, and language, such as men doe use' to 'shew an Image of the times'.[1] Above all, Jonson thunders again and again, his writings satisfy the prime requirement of poetry: they are moral in purpose and effect, teaching right conduct by ridiculing bad. As the years passed and Jonson grew famous, he became even more certain of his divine mission as the reformer of English poetry. Following the ancients he argues in *Discoveries*, one of his surviving critical writings, that the true poet like himself is in direct contact with the ultimate forces of creation and that his poetry 'utters somewhat above a mortall mouth' (2421–2). Though plays were not yet considered true literature, he published in 1616 a carefully revised and edited folio of his plays, titled it, rather grandly, 'Workes', and underscored his place in the great tradition of comedy

---

[1] The clearest, most concise statement of Jonson's critical principles is the 'Prologue' of the revised 'Englished' version of *Every Man in his Humour*, first published in 1616 but perhaps written about 1610–11. See also the 'Induction' to *Every Man out of his Humour* and the 'Epistle' to *Volpone*.

by using the format of the first printed editions of Aristophanes, Plautus and Terence.

There is no question that Jonson was a self-conscious writer who worked diligently on his plays, but his own criticism, stressing clarity, seemliness, proportion and order, does not provide an accurate index to the dramatic world of a poet who 'consumed a whole night in lying looking to his great toe, about which he hath seen tartars & turks Romans and Cathaginions feight in his imagination' (*Conversations*, 322–4). The most striking quality of the Jonsonian dramatic world is not its order but its swirling profusion, its density, its noisiness and busyness. Large numbers of people are involved. A cast of twenty is usual, sometimes rising to thirty or forty, and this number is swelled by the addition of messengers, servants, officers, passers-by and often a crowd or mob. In a characteristic Jonson scene, a great many people will be coming and going busily; talking, talking, talking; posing, looking at things, handling a variety of objects. Then the stage will suddenly clear, and a new group, announced by drums and trumpets, accompanied by barking dogs and preceded by a host of servants, will arrive wearing their outrageous fashions and trying to manage their unwieldy furnishings. *Bartholomew Fair* offers the most complete realization of this Jonsonian scene. The set is the great fair at Smithfield, with its endless, restless flow of humanity of all kinds up and down before the laden stalls of the toy vendor and the ginger-bread woman; into and out of Ursula's tent where pig and ale and punk are sold indiscriminately; in front of the stocks which grimly recall the attempts of authority to impose some restraint on all this hubbub.

Behind this multitudinous, various world of men and objects, a denser even more cluttered world is evoked by means of language. A passage from *Epicene*, in which Truewit explains to Morose what it means to be married to a lady with social aspirations, inventories a large section of English life, so deeply piled with people and things that no order can exist in it and no light be seen through it:

> shee must have that rich goune for such a great day; a new one for the next; a richer for the third; bee serv'd in silver; have the chamber fill'd with a succession of groomes, foot-men, ushers, and other messengers; besides embroyderers, jewellers, tyre-women, sempsters, fether-men, perfumers; while shee feeles not how the land drops away; nor the acres melt; nor forsees the change, when the mercer has your woods for her velvets; never weighes what her pride costs, sir: so shee may kisse a page, or a smoth chinne, that has the despaire of a beard; bee a stateswoman,

know all the news, what was done at *Salisbury*, what at the *Bath*,
what at court, what in progresse; or, so shee may censure *poets*, and
authors, and stiles, and compare 'hem, DANIEL with SPENSER, IONSON
with the tother youth, and so foorth; or, be thought cunning in con-
troversies, or the very knots of divinitie; and have, often in her mouth,
the state of the question: and then skip to the Mathematiques, and
demonstration and answere, in religion to one; in state, to another, in
baud'ry to a third. (II. ii. 104–23)

At times the perspective lengthens and the language brings into view
'worlds of other strange *ingredients*, Would burst a man to name', which
swirl in primal chaos at the bottom of Jonson's world:

> your broths, your *menstrues*, and *materialls*,
> Of pisse, and egge-shells, womens termes, mans bloud,
> Haire o' the head, burnt clouts, chalke, merdes, and clay,
> Poulder of bones, scalings of iron, glasse. . . .
>
> (*The Alchemist*, II. iii. 193–6)

The sense of a world crammed with people and things, tending towards
reduction and fragmentation, is intensified and universalized by Jonson's
verbal and dramatic style. His characters speak, most often, in a variety of
the Senecan or curt style, stringing together long series of disjunct elements,
leaping from one subject to another, stopping and starting abruptly rather
than flowing smoothly, piling up details which eddy about a central idea. (It
is ironic that the poet who championed decorum and order in language should
have had his greatest successes as a creator of characters who speak in-
decorously and confusedly. Only in the poems and masques do we find un-
interrupted instances of the clarity and seemliness Jonson prized so highly.)
The qualities of the verbal style extend into the episodic scenic arrangement,
with the parts held together only very loosely by a central story or plot. Jonson, contrary to the usual practice of the playwrights of the time, did not
build his plays around single stories drawn from other sources, but wove
together a variety of themes, images and stories to construct a large number
of scenes related in a thematic rather than an obviously causal or chronological pattern. The order, even the inevitability, are there, ultimately, but the
immediate world is a tumultuous mass of things, people and sounds, too
numerous and various to take meaningful shape, too discordant to achieve

harmony. This is the darker side of that spacious, rich world Tamburlaine and the Renaissance saw from the heights of the imagination.

Jonson's view of man is as gloomy as his view of the world. He writes in *Discoveries*, 'a man cannot imagine that thing so foolish, or rude, but will find, and enjoy an Admirer' (608–9), which indicates only a certain cynicism; but in his plays he goes beyond the Puckish perception of 'what fools these mortals be' to a vision of an *ur*-stupidity, ignorance of epic proportions, coupled with a capacity for self-deception so great as to be demonic, all joined with fantastic vanity and boundless energy. The choice of 'humours' – the theory that a character is governed by one particular longing or obsession – as a basis for characterization suggests Jonson's belief that the majority of men are mere machines, wound up by an appetite and moving automatically towards a single goal. But the humours take such bizarre, perverse forms that the possibility arises that the great majority of men may be insane. On the surface, Jonson's fools have all the usual harmless comic affectations – ludicrous desires for strange fashions, for gold, for love, for honour, for reputation – but even the least of them can suddenly open up surprising depths, such as the neighbour in *The Alchemist* who remarks that he heard one night a doleful cry from Lovewit's house, 'As I sate up, a mending my wives stocking' (V. i. 34).

The full enormity of man comes into view in the actions of the strange knight of *Every Man out of his Humour*, Puntarvolo, who is announced by a flourish of horns and trumpets each time he returns to his house. On this signal a waiting woman comes to the balcony and asks Puntarvolo, standing in the courtyard below, what he wishes. He replies that he is a knight-errant who has by magical means found his way to this castle, and wonders who is the owner of the house and what are his qualities. Is he handsome? Is he courteous? Is he magnanimous? Is he learned? To each question the well-trained maid replies positively. Upon learning that the owner is not at home, Puntarvolo asks for the lady of the house, and, when she appears on the balcony, addresses several lines of abominable love poetry to her and requests that she descend to him. This the lady does, but because of the presence of visitors we are denied the remainder of the ritual. This is Puntarvolo's humour, and the elaborate contrivance used to instrument some strange desire for romance and self-glorification reveals both the ingenuity and the fatuity of which the human mind is at once capable. The game of 'vapours' in *Bartholomew Fair* is even more revealing. The participants – any number can play – sit in a circle, drinking, and the point of the game is no more and no less than to contradict anything said by the man before you. Points are lost when a player agrees even in the slightest with what has just been said; points are gained when what has been said, no matter how sensible, is contradicted in the most violent, vulgar and idiotic way possible. The ideal player of the game of vapours is Humphrey Wasp, who displays his skill in a particularly fine retort to the statement that 'he must have reason': 'I have no reason, nor I will heare of no reason, nor I will looke for no reason, and he is an Asse, that either knowes any, or lookes for 't from me' (IV. iv. 42–4). To which the equally masterly (vapourly) reply is, 'Yes, in some sense you may have reason, Sir.'

Many strange varieties of folly take life in these plays, and Jonson has a reputation, in part deserved, for simply offering dramatic portrait galleries of idiocy. But in all their variety the Jonsonian characters are consistently trying to do the same thing, and this shared motive of folly was eventually focused and defined by Jonson as alchemy. The plot of *The Alchemist* (1610) is complex in its parts, but quite simple in its function. A well-to-do citizen, Lovewit, has fled London in fear of the plague and left his house in the care of his butler, Jeremy, who has transformed himself into Captain Face and confederated with a con man, Subtle, and a whore, Dol Common, to set up a number of swindles operating from Lovewit's house. To them, seeking fame and wealth, comes a cross-section of the London middle class: Drugger the tobacconist who wants to become a merchant prince, Dapper the lawyer's clerk who wants to become a great gambler, Kastril the country squire who wants to become a duellist, the Puritans Ananias and Tribulation Wholesome who want to make lots of money and buy political power for their sect, and Sir Epicure Mammon who wants to turn the whole world into gold. A city of plague, a house abandoned by its owner (Wit), usurped by impudence and pretence (Face), cunning (Subtle) and slatternliness (Dol Common), who pander to and cheat man's lust for power and wealth. The alchemists, Face and Subtle, are masters of a very large number of rewarding con games. They teach the latest fashions in quarrelling to a young bully, prepare love philtres, fence stolen goods, read palms, engage in counterfeiting and clipping, run a lonely-hearts club, prepare horoscopes, dabble in black and white magic, provide charms, teach cheating at cards and dice, serve as pimps and even try their hands at what is now known as 'merchandising engineering' when they design advertising and store layout for the tobacconist Drugger. Impudence and cunning, Face and Subtle, are at the centre of every petty cheat of the time, but they express themselves most fully and grandly in alchemy, which comprehends and summarizes all their other swindles.

By means of alchemy and magic the characters all hope to transform a leaden world to gold, but they are also trying to transmute their own base natures into something rich and strange. Using his marvellous ability to concentrate a whole way of life and an entire social setting in a few lines, Jonson inserts at various points of the play brief sketches of the fools and rogues which locate them very low on any scale of being. Dapper, the lawyer's clerk, desires of Doctor Subtle a charm which will permit him to gamble with such infallibility that all the wealth of England will at last become his; but the stuff out of which this king of gamblers is to be made is no more than a pitiful creature who can write a fair hand, keep accounts, read Ovid and knows something of the law. All the social aspirations and hopes of this class are gathered up in Face's ringing assertion that Dapper 'consorts with the small poets of the time' (I. ii. 52). Kastril, the country squire, wants to become a roaring boy, a duellist, a prince of cats like Tybalt, elegant, formal and sleekly dangerous; but the truth of him is that he is no more than a rustic bully who has come to town, 'To learne to quarrell, and to live by his wits, And will goe downe againe, and dye i' the countrey' (II. vi. 61–2). Abel Drugger, the tobacconist, wants to be a great merchant adventurer, but his true height is taken easily and quickly by Subtle: 'A miserable rogue, and lives with cheese, And has the wormes' (II. vi. 81–2). Each of the characters of the play has the same kind of grand aspiration, and the same gap between his reality and his desires. The learned alchemist Doctor Subtle is no more than a petty cheat and pickpocket, the noble Captain Face is no more than a butler, the Queen of Faery is no more than the whore Dol Common, the Lord's Elect, the pious Brethren, are no more than power-hungry knaves.

It is, however, in the person of Sir Epicure Mammon that the desire for alchemical transformation reaches truly heroic proportions, and in him the relation of Jonson's comic overreachers to Marlowe's tragic figures attempting to transform imagination into reality becomes apparent. Each of the petty fools of *The Alchemist* mirrors in a grotesque way the historical aspirations of some segment of Renaissance English society – the merchant, the squire, the professional man, the left-wing Protestant and the classless adventurer – but Sir Epicure, while he has English roots, is an archetypal figure who rises above place and time. His superheated dream is the eternal dream of mankind, the ultimate alchemy which transforms all that is low and heavy into dazzling light, the art that reforms nature instantly and the technology which creates *Novo Orbe*, the new age of gold, the everlasting great society. Mammon wants a world that takes his shape instantly – 'beds, blowne up; not stuft:

Downe is too hard' – a world which reflects his own image from all perspectives:

> my glasses,
>   Cut in more subtill angles, to disperse,
>   And multiply the figures, as I walke
>   Naked between my *succubae*. (II. ii. 45–8)

All women will be his, and he will have a back that will enable him to bed fifty a night. All competitors will be castrated, all mothers and fathers turned to procurers. Divines will be kept to flatter, grave statesmen to amuse and poets to sing the praises of Mammon. Mists of perfume will waft through his rooms, his baths will be as big as pools, he will roll himself dry in gossamer and rose petals, and no dish will be too rare for his table:

> My meat, shall all come in, in *Indian* shells,
>   Dishes of agate, set in gold, and studded,
>   With emeralds, saphyres, hiacynths, and rubies.
>   The tongues of carpes, dormise, and camels heeles,
>   Boil'd i' the spirit of SOL, the dissolu'd pearle,
>   (APICIUS diet, 'gainst the *epilepsie*)
>   And I will eate these broaths, with spoones of amber,
>   Headed with diamant, and carbuncle.
>   My foot-boy shall eate phesants, caluerd salmons,
>   Knots, godwits, lamprey's: I my selfe will haue
>   The beards of barbels, seru'd, in stead of sallades;
>   Oild mushromes; and the swelling vnctuous paps
>   Of a fat pregnant sow, newly cut off,
>   Drest with an exquisite, and poynant sauce;
>   For which, Ile say vnto my cooke, there's gold,
>   Goe forth, and be a knight. (II. ii. 72–87)

There is a certain amount of self-centredness in all this, but Sir Epicure has his magnanimous side too. He is the prophet of wealth and pleasure who brings glad tidings to the world, 'Be rich!' In *Novo Orbe* the 'sonnes of *sword*, and *hazard*' shall no longer drink and gamble in the tavern, riot in the brothel, or enlist in the army to satisfy their thirst for satin and velvet. Now they 'shall start up yong vice-royes', and each shall have his 'punques and punquettees'. When Sir Epicure possesses the stone and the elixir, the magical drug will flow through the water system, like fluoride, to destroy plague and all forms of sickness. As in that magic world created by modern advertising, so similar to that which Jonson's great fools dream, old age will disappear, sexual vigour will be eternal and children will become young giants. In the ultimate terms towards which all advertising copywriters still strive, nature will at last be 'naturiz'd 'gainst all infections'.

The symbol of alchemy focuses not only what it is that all the characters in *The Alchemist* are attempting to do but defines as well the leading motive of all the Jonsonian fools: to transmute base metal into gold, to overleap nature. The ladies who paint, the pedants who spout the names of poets and books, the fops who cover themselves with feathers and lace, the bumpkins who try to become courtiers, the hungry appetites who disguise themselves as per-secuted saints, the numskulls who set up for political and economic prophets, all are attempting the great projection which will change their miserable selves into godlike creatures and transform life to endless pleasure. Each of these types has, like the alchemist, his own special apparatus: instead of mortars, furnaces and alembics, they use cosmetics, feathers, swords, books and ruffs. Each has, also like the alchemist, his own special vocabulary, for in this drama words are the true and ultimate alchemical tools. One of Jonson's most remarkable powers was his ability to extract and refine for dramatic purposes the cant and technical jargon of a large number of callings. The spiel of the mountebank, the sporting terms of the bear pits, the pedantries of poetaster and scholar, the mysteries of milady's toilette, the legalese of the lawyers and the scripture-spouting of the Puritans, all attempt by means of words which have little sense but great incantatory power to transform the idiots who use them into magicians and saints, wits and beauties, courtiers and scholars.

Jonson's alchemists are satiric images of Elizabethan and Jacobean England with all its vigour, aspirations and confidence; and these figures in turn are representative of the Renaissance with its belief in the power of man by his mind and art to break the shackles of things as they are and make man and world over into the forms that imagination conceives. Nature becomes a kind of plaything, something like 'silly putty', infinitely plastic and capable of taking any shape or impression. No doubt Ben Jonson shared this opti-mism to some degree – his characters do, despite their folly, give it most powerful and zestful statement – but he was also of a most realistic and conser-vative cast of mind. Attempts have been made to identify Jonson's conserva-tism with particular philosophical and social systems – with the guild system, medieval economics and feudal order[1] – but it was in practice much more profound. It was, rather, of the kind which finds expression in *Job* or

[1] See L. C. Knights, *Drama and Society in the Age of Jonson* (London, 1937).

Ecclesiastes, a deep-rooted pessimism about the possibility of change and the potentialities of man. With writers like Swift and T. S. Eliot, with philosophers like Hobbes and Freud, who also looked long and hard at 'deedes, and language, such as men doe use', it shares an understanding of the difficulty of changing anything very much, and the consequent sad necessity for compromise, adjustment and the scaling down of ambition. It knows that perpetual motion machines and alchemy are never really going to work; that disease, suffering and death will never be banished from the earth; that pretending something is so will not make it so; that the ways of man and nature recorded by history are very likely to be the ways of the future also; that engineering and technology will never really change what is fundamental in human life; and that any true progress will come, if at all, only painfully and slowly through the endless mistakes of history and gradual ethical, not material, evolution. When seen against these beliefs, Tamburlaine becomes Sir Epicure Mammon and Faustus becomes Volpone.

Jonson's plays are the meeting place of his strongly conservative views about the resistance to improvement of a world tending towards chaos, and the boundless optimism of his characters that anything can be changed and will be bettered by change. Jonson the creator was frightened by his creations, and so great was his fear of chaos and the human ignorance which moves so busily and stupidly towards it that, like Pope and Swift whom he resembles in so many ways, his rigid classicism, moral authoritarianism and stout insistence upon form and realism seem as much desperate defences raised against disaster as rational critical positions freely chosen. Jonson's fear is most evident in the violence with which order and sense are imposed on folly in his earlier plays, up to *Poetaster*, where the moral lesson is imposed in a satiric and legal manner. Each of these plays contains some censor of morals and manners who, like the satyr-satirist in Elizabethan formal verse satire, stands slightly to the side of the main action. As the fools troop across the stage he encourages them to display their idiocy, and in a series of asides anatomizes and denounces them. In time, when folly has ripened to the point of bursting, the fools are assembled before some bar of justice where they are whipped, purged, punished, shamed and driven out of their humour. Jonson's fools seldom have any illumination which causes a radical change in their thinking; rather, some external power drives them out of their humour and compels them by shame or force to conform to more sensible modes of behaviour. *Every Man out of his Humour* remains until the end the basic Jonsonian plot, but, as time passed, the methods by which correction is administered changed, not because Jonson mellowed, but because his awed respect for the powers of folly increased, and his belief in the ability of law and society to restrain its demonic energy diminished correspondingly.

The change appears clearly in 1603 in Jonson's first tragedy, *Sejanus*, where in the Rome of Tiberius idiocy grows vicious, folly ripens to crime and virtue becomes helpless. The good and evil characters are still as easily identifiable as in earlier plays. On the one hand, there are the noble friends of Agrippina, who ceaselessly lament the disappearance from their world of those sturdy republican virtues exemplified by Cato and Brutus. They make numerous satiric attacks on the sycophants, parasites and politicians of Tiberius's court, and they seize any occasion to praise virtue directly. They are the moral legitimists to whom inaction is preferable to staining their virtue: 'A good man should and must Sit rather downe with losse then rise unjust' (IV. 165–6). The wicked are equally obvious. The devious Tiberius retires from Rome to practise his unnatural vices, Livia is unfaithful to her husband Drusus and engineers his death, Sejanus flatters and kills for power. The amorality and self-centredness of the court are perfectly rendered in the opening scene of Act II where Eudemus the physician panders for Sejanus to Livia, while she at the same time persuades him to administer a poison to her husband, and all the while she worries about her make-up and he deftly touches up her face with his cosmetic kit.

Moral virtue and dramatic effectiveness do not square, however. When the good men of the play appear on stage, they plant their feet like opera singers and deliver long, rhetorical speeches, plentifully sprinkled with *sententiae*, on the virtues of the past and the wickedness of the present. Behind them the villain Sejanus enters and moves across the stage, dispatching one piece of business after another as he goes – giving, denying, persuading – and shaping the future. The speeches become shorter and more staccato, the words more direct and forceful, and wit replaces sententiousness. The good men are no more effective in controlling the plot than they are in managing a scene. They make speeches praising virtue and deliver satires denouncing vice, but their fumbling attempts at action scarcely get under way before Sejanus's counter-mine blows them up. When trapped, they either go passively off to execution or die nobly by their own hand. The satirist Arruntius speaks truthfully when he calls himself and his virtuous friends 'the good – dull – noble lookers on', whose only function in the senate is 'to keepe the marble warme' (III. 16–17). Sejanus, with all his cleverness and energy, succeeds, however, only in shaping his own death. Desperate to keep his footing on the slippery ice of the court, he goes too far and by his efforts to climb makes Tiberius nervous. Tiberius selects a new favourite, Macro, and arranges to have Sejanus thrown to the mob, which tears him apart, and, with the parts which they have ripped from him still warm in their hands, then regret his death.

Neither Arruntius's virtue nor Sejanus's villainy is able to survive in the world of that shadowy sphinx, Tiberius. Utterly cynical and utterly depraved, his tastes are for the forbidden and the unnatural. He moves and constructs his engines from the distance of Capri and from behind a mask of piety and service to Rome, humility before its senators and concern for the multitude. He is a master of suggesting something without seeming to do so, and it is impossible ever to pin responsibility on him. His masterpiece is the letter to the Senate in which he suggests – or does he? – that if the senators decide that Sejanus is a traitor, though Tiberius knows not what to think, they should, perhaps, punish him, but they should be extremely careful to be just. Sensitive only to challenges to his absolute authority, Tiberius's life centres on a single maxim: 'Yet, then a throne, 'tis cheaper give a grave' (II. 271). The deified emperor Tiberius is the true god of Rome and the first great image of that dark power which lies below and behind all the petty forms of folly, vanity and greed in Jonson's dramatic world.

The failure of virtue and moral authority to deal with the baffling Tiberius marks a profound change in Jonson's dramaturgy. The censors and satirists disappear from the plays, the authority figures are now treated mockingly and the purer forms of virtue become both helpless and slightly ridiculous. The fools are driven out of their humours no longer by scourging satirists and wise judges but by a fatal irony inherent in their own appetites. They dream of alchemy and the transformation of themselves into gods, but each attempt to realize their dreams has the opposite effect. Let a Jonson character handle a golden idea and he immediately reduces it to lead. As they speak of beauty they transform it into cosmetics, hair styles, jewels and elaborate costumes; in their hands, learning becomes a mangled catalogue of poets' names, books, jargon and pedantry; religion is reduced to folded hands, tags from scripture and pious faces. What they do to ideas they do also to themselves, and each attempt at personal alchemy, at making themselves into saints, geniuses, gods, only succeeds in manifesting what invincible dunces they actually are, just as their attempts at literal alchemy bring them not to riches but to poverty.

The opening scene of *Volpone* (1606) provides the clearest instance of this counter-alchemy, which now becomes the basis of the Jonsonian plot. Volpone, the great Venetian merchant, rises to greet the new day and substitutes for the sun a great round gold coin, which now becomes 'the worlds soule'. In this gold-centred universe, money is the measure of all things – 'Who can get thee, He shall be noble, valiant, honest, wise –' (I. i. 26–7). Beauty can find no greater praise than to be styled, 'Bright as your gold! and lovely, as your gold!' (I. v. 114). Applying the golden test, chastity is discredited since gold itself loses nothing by being touched by many. Health and learning can be bought, ugliness transformed and salvation achieved by means of 'the thing Makes all the world her grace, her youth, her beauty' (V. ii. 104–5). As prophets of this new religion, Volpone and his parasite, Mosca, immediately set out to 'convert' their world: Volpone pretends to be dying in order to extract rich gifts from the great citizens of Venice, each of whom hopes to be named his heir. They rush to Volpone's house, bringing jewels, gold and plate; and as the competition quickens among them they part with more precious possessions: Lady Wouldbe offers her body; Corbaccio disinherits his son, Bonario, and names Volpone his heir; Corvino delivers his wife, the beautiful Celia, to Volpone's bed; and Voltore, the lawyer, sells justice and his professional honour.

As is usual in Jonson, the master cheats of *Volpone* share the desires and motives of the minor fools but amplify them until their meaning becomes fully audible. Where the lesser idiots desire gold because it is gold, Volpone and Mosca analyse their own motives and conclude that gold is only the counter in a game whose joy originates in the pleasure of tricking others, outwitting fools, demonstrating cleverness and superiority. Volpone glories 'More in the cunning purchase of my wealth, Then in the glad possession' (I. i. 31–2), and 'glad possession' means not the miserly storing up of treasure in some dark place but enjoying all the rare, rich things which money can buy:

> The heads of parrats, tongues of nightingales,
> The braines of peacoks, and of estriches
> Shall be our food: and, could we get the phoenix,
> (Though nature lost her kind) shee were our dish. . . .
> Thy bathes shall be the iuyce of iuly-flowres,
> Spirit of roses, and of violets,
> The milke of vnicornes, and panthers breath
> Gather'd in bagges, and mixt with *cretan* wines. (III. vii. 202–16)

The method by which Volpone and Mosca achieve their ends is a variant of alchemy: acting. Volpone plays again and again a sick and dying man in various stages of decay, and he leaves his bed only to play other roles: a mountebank in the public square and a clownish sergeant of the court. Mosca is an equally adept actor, particularly good at quick changes. Able to 'change a visor, swifter, then a thought' (III. i. 29), he can at one moment be a humble servant, fawning and anxious to be of help, and then in a flash become a smiling pander, an injured friend of virtue, or a sober, stern *magnifico*.

Under the persistent pressure of this theatrical conception of life, the play declares itself openly from time to time as a play and the scene becomes a theatre. Volpone's antic fools troop on stage to perform interludes, the merchant plays the mountebank on a trestle stage in the square, a 'cortaine' is strung across the stage and Volpone watches from behind it while Mosca sits before it pretending to be the heir, inventorying his goods, and putting each of the fools out of his humour as they rush in to demand what is coming to them. Volpone's great bed with its curtain which is drawn and closed at appropriate times is a small theatre in which the great pretender, made up to look like a dying man, acts out his scenes of sickness.

For Volpone and Mosca the art of acting and the ability to turn any place into a theatre are something more, finally, than the means to coin the fools of Venice into profit. Acting is for them, as for Pico, the expression of man's essential genius and the power which can make man a god. Mosca feels he can skip out of his skin, rise and fall like an arrow, shoot through the air like a star and, ultimately, 'be here, And there, and here, and yonder, all at once' (III. i. 26–7). Volpone is no less exuberant than his larcenous Ariel. 'In varying figures', he tells Celia, he 'would have contended With the blue Proteus' (III. vii. 152–3) to win her love. And that love itself, rather than suffering the limitations and satiation of mortal love, is to be raised and kept at Jovian heights by the divine power of acting:

> ... we [shall] in changed shapes, act OVIDS tales,
> Thou, like EVROPA now, and I like IOVE,
> Then I like MARS, and thou like ERYCINE,
> So, of the rest, till we have quite run through
> And weary'd all the fables of the gods.
> Then will I haue thee in more moderne formes,
> Attired like some sprightly dame of *France*,
> Brave *Tuscan* lady, or proud *Spanish* beauty;
> Sometimes, vnto the *Persian Sophies* wife;
> Or the grand-*Signiors* mistresse; and, for change,
> To one of our most art-full courtizans,
> Or some quick *Negro*, or cold *Russian*;
> And I will meet thee, in as many shapes:
> Where we may, so, trans-fuse our wandring soules,

Out at our lippes, and score up summes of pleasures,
> *That the curious shall not know*
> *How to tell them, as they flow;*
> *And the enuious, when they find*
> *What their number is, be pind.* (III. vii. 221–39)

There are some very good actors and some very poor ones in *Volpone*, but most of the characters are pretenders using their histrionic ability to cheat others and raise themselves. But pretence reveals truth when Volpone plays the mountebank, or when the lawyer Voltore recants and pretends that he has been possessed by an evil spirit 'In shape of a blew toad, with a battes wings' (V. xii. 31). The ironic pattern in which each disguise becomes a revelation, each attempt to rise a fall, is worked out most specifically in the stages of degeneration through which Volpone passes in his simulated sickness, gradually stripping himself of all human attributes. His understanding and higher faculties disappear in the opening scene where he elevates the coin and chooses literal gold over all other virtues and values. Soon his memory is gone:

> He knowes no man,
> No face or friend, nor name of any seruant,
> Who 't was that fed him last, or gaue him drinke:
> Not those, he hath begotten, or brought vp
> Can he remember. (I. v. 39–43)

His senses go next. Sight, the highest of the senses in the Aristotelian scale, goes first, and shortly afterwards he is left with only touch, the lowest of the senses. Corvino must place the pearl he has brought into Volpone's hand because ''tis onely there He apprehends: he has his feeling, yet' (I. v. 18–20). Reproductive faculties disappear next, and Mosca assures Corvino that there is no danger in giving Celia to Volpone because 'A long forgetfulnesse hath seiz'd that part' (II. vi. 66). The nutritive faculties soon disappear in this 'old, decrepit wretch',

> That ha's no sense, no sinew; takes his meate
> With others fingers; onely knowes to gape,
> When you doe scald his gummes; a voice; a shadow . . . (III. vii. 43–5)

Death inevitably follows, and by Act V, Scene ii, Volpone is pretending to be dead, a corrupted carcass that Mosca has to bury hastily. Each of these diseases is, of course, a mere pretence used by a physically vital Volpone to implement his great swindle. But they speak a truth of another order. On the spiritual plane he is indeed blind and unable to apprehend anything which he cannot touch; he has forgotten the meaning of friend or child, and his spirit is unable to nurture itself or reproduce its light in the world. Volpone has with great cunning made himself his own zany in a most systematic manner, and the skill at acting which was to have made him a god has, at last literally and figuratively, reduced him to nothing.

The surface of Jonson's plays is bright, bubbling, lively. The characters are great optimists who share with Tamburlaine and the Renaissance a heightened sense of human potential and view with joy a wide, rich world ripe for exploitation and enjoyment by the man who has the wit and the will to force it to yield the pleasures of the table, the bedroom, the treasure house and the palace. But latent in this same world is a nightmare of disorder and death, a 'zany' version of meaningful life, into which the characters tumble by their very efforts to transcend it. In *Volpone* the nightmare is a scene in which the sun is replaced by a great gold coin, dully glittering over a landscape in which carrion birds circle a dying fox, while the flesh-fly buzzes about. The great household is reduced to a master thief, his fawning parasite and a group of grotesques – a dwarf, a eunuch and a hermaphrodite – begotten by the owner in drunkenness on street beggars and kept only for entertainment. Here a decrepit father, himself on the verge of death, disinherits his son in order to be named the heir of a younger man; an insanely jealous husband calls his wife a whore because she refuses to get into the bed of a loathsome dying man; a lawyer changes his lies from moment to moment, and a court frees the guilty and condemns the innocent for the crimes committed against them. The greatest of men becomes a gasping, groaning, blind wretch, greedily seizing paste jewels. The great scene of life becomes no more than a theatre, and men reduce themselves to shadowy actors.

At the end of *Volpone* all the Proteans are permanently locked into the zany forms they have created in mockery of their own humanity through the exercise of their genius. Mosca is sent as a slave to the galleys for life, Volpone is sent to prison to be shackled like a wild animal, Voltore is disbarred and sent into perpetual exile, Corvino is turned into a civic joke by being made to wear ass's ears and sit in the pillory, while Corbaccio is confined to a monastery and treated as a moral incurable. In *Discoveries* Jonson describes the process as it applies to all men: 'I have considered our whole life is like a play; wherin every man, forgetfull of himselfe, is in travaile with expression of another. Nay, wee so insist in imitating others, as wee cannot (when it is necessary) returne to our selves . . .' (597).

It is not, however, the power of virtue or society which finally locks these creatures in their debased forms. Virtue is as helpless before cleverness as are the senators before Sejanus. Celia and Bonario, the two virtuous people of the play, are in fact bundled off to jail for the very crimes that were committed against them, and when they are finally freed they are not allowed to marry and fulfil the expectations of comedy. Celia is returned, with her dowry, to her father's house, and we hear nothing more of Bonario. The institutions of society are no more effective in restraining the great impostors: law is a cover under which villainy operates, marriage becomes another form of ownership, and the courts are completely taken in by plausibility. Only when roguery outreaches itself, when the master thieves begin to fall out over the distribution of the loot, do things begin to go badly for them. Mosca decides that, since Volpone has pretended to be dead and has made him his heir, there is no reason to change this very satisfactory situation, and despite Volpone's earnest pleas to be allowed to return to life, Mosca refuses. Controlled by the greed he had always thought he controlled, Volpone decides that punishment and revenge are preferable to poverty, and so he exposes the entire swindle to the court, which, when presented with evidence which even its stupidity cannot ignore, is properly scandalized and administers justice.

By the time of *Epicene* (1609), Jonson's views about imposing order and justice on the folly and wickedness of the world had been so modified that the figure who attempts to do so becomes the comic butt. *Epicene* offers the usual array of fashionable idiocy, particularly as it manifests itself in 'noise'. The many sounds of the London streets – vendors' cries, the pewterer's hammer, crash of hoof and wheels, blare of trumpets and rattle of drums – blend with incessant talk of fashions, food, books and amusements to create a new Babel of a city in which Sir Jack Daw is the genius of the place. All this noise is not simply the braying of the human ass – though that sound is frequently heard – but is in part at least the sound of the busyness of life going on its way earning a living and amusing itself. To still this world would be to destroy life, and this is what Morose attempts to do. Unable to endure any sound except his own voice, he retreats within a soundproof house, seeks a wife who speaks quietly and infrequently, and ends sitting on a rafter in the attic, his ears packed with wool, his nightcap pulled tightly down over his head. Moral authority and control of the plot shift from this absolutist to the more tolerant and pragmatic Truewit. Truewit describes the fools in terms which probably sum up Jonson's most optimistic views of mankind:

> all their actions are gouerned by crude opinion, without reason or cause; they know not why they doe any thing: but as they are inform'd,

> beleeue, iudge, praise, condemne, loue, hate, and in æmulation one of
> another, doe all these things alike. Onely, they haue a naturall inclination
> swayes 'hem generally to the worst, when they are left to themselues.
> (IV. vi. 64–70)

But while Truewit may intrigue to achieve wealth and pleasure, and even
administers a few kicks to the more outstanding idiots, he sees no sense in
trying to reform the world. He advises Morose and his friend Dauphine,
who has an incipient authoritarian attitude, derived from too much retirement
to his chamber and reading of books, that the main thing in life is to keep
your eye fixed on the ends of pleasure and good sense. Why condemn cosmetics, he argues, when by this means women give pleasure to themselves
and to men by becoming more attractive? Why condemn flattery when by
this means men make women happy, rescue them from fools and achieve
pleasure for all? In short, why try to stop all noise and all life? Live with it,
know it for what it is and make the best of it. In the end Truewit's view pre-
vails, the fools are restrained and the young hero gets his rich old uncle's
money.

In *The Alchemist* (1610) several forces combine to bring the plot to a comic
rather than satiric conclusion. The ironic pattern in which idiocy defeats
itself operates to drive the fools out of their humours: each attempt at alchemy has the opposite of the intended effect, impoverishing the gulls and
making them even more foolish than nature made them. But Face, Subtle
and Dol Common do very nearly bring off the alchemical trick by turning
the base metal of their clients, their gullibility and crude appetites, into good
solid treasure, neatly packed up in Lovewit's cellar, ready for the getaway.
These rogues are about to decamp, when by good luck – the traditional comic
deus ex machina which manifests comedy's belief that nature is self-righting –
the master of the house, Lovewit, returns unexpectedly. Without fully understanding what has happened, he has the good sense to realize and the lack
of scrupulousness to take advantage of his opportunity. Knowing that the
rogues cannot protest and the fools will be too ashamed to press hard their
claims for the goods and money they have given the alchemists, Lovewit
decides to keep all the gold in his cellar and to marry the rich widow, who is
by now a part of the booty. Reference is made in the play to the ancient
belief that the successful alchemist must be *homo frugi*, 'a pious, holy, and
religious man, One free from mortall sinne, a very virgin' (II. ii. 98–9). No
inhabitant of Jonson's dramatic world quite fits these specifications, but wit,
i.e. good sense, while it may not quite transform lead to gold, does at least

achieve what is possible for a limited creature in a limited world. At the very least, wit avoids that excessiveness which leads Sir Epicure Mammon when disappointed in his hopes for *Novo Orbe* to swing to the other extreme and 'goe mount a turnep-cart, and preach The end o' the world' (V. v. 81–2).

After a disastrous return to tragedy in *Catiline* (1611), Jonson brought his growing doubt in the effectiveness of authority and satiric indignation, and his growing awareness that folly and disorder are somehow the inescapable stuff of life, to a triumphant conclusion in *Bartholomew Fair* (1614). Consideration of this play will be reserved for the last chapter, where it will be treated as one of the summary plays of the age, presenting and making its peace with all the conflicting and contradictory elements out of which this drama was constructed.

6 The entrance to hell: the new tragedy

(i) The shape of fear

Isolation and inevitable death, chaos and darkness, confinement and mean-inglessness, helplessness and pain, these are the universal terrors which find expression in tragedy and seek in it some knowledge – even if it be only an understanding of what has killed – which will make the terror bearable. From their predecessors, Christian and pagan, the Elizabethan dramatists inherited a vast iconography of fear: the dark landscape of hell, the dance of death, the sufferings and crucifixion of Christ, the figure of Satan, the tortures of the martyrs, the ceaseless turn of Fortune's wheel, the stone of Sisyphus, the agonies of Tantalus and the revolution of Ixion's wheel. The dramatists also inherited and used two perennial tragic structures: the Job pattern of in-explicable, helpless suffering, which took shape in the middle ages as *de casibus* tragedy in which great men are hurled from prosperity to misery by the mechanical operations of Fortune or the working of some mysterious malevolence; and the Promethean pattern of tragic choice, which had been Christianized as the tragedy of the inevitable fall of sinful man, fatally flawed by original sin but still paradoxically responsible for his actions.

These ancient tragic patterns and the traditional images of fear did not dis-appear in the new drama – though they were refined, complicated and given more realistic forms – but became the fates and the landscape of the heroic impulses towards freedom and change. The archetypal heroes of the new values and the histrionic sensibility soon found that their way led also to the old bafflements and terrors. Doctor Faustus, the great magician and scholar, 'the insatiable speculator', the man who will pay any price for the knowledge and power to remake his world, is forced to follow to its awful conclusion the full meaning of his Promethean choice. Titus Andronicus, the personification of the civic virtue, the Stoic courage and the will to world-control which the Renaissance found in an idealized Rome and pagan antiquity, is forced for a time to endure like Job, or the heroes of Senecan tragedy, the agony of helpless suffering and an outraged sense of justice.

(ii) The magician's circle: Marlowe's *Doctor Faustus*

The modern world has been called the Faustian Age, and no myth has been quite so useful or so intriguing to the modern era of science and progress as that of the magician-scientist of Wittenberg. The manner in which Georg Faust, an itinerant conjuror and petty cheat who travelled about Germany in the early years of the sixteenth century, was transformed into 'the insatiable speculator' and an image of the Renaissance imagination is one of the most remarkable instances in literary history of the way in which myth absorbs and transforms fact. Within fifty years, the trickster of the early legends somehow became the Renaissance dream of the universal man, comprehending the learning of such polymaths as Leonardo and Paracelsus, the political curiosity and daring of Machiavelli's Prince, the inquiring science of Copernicus and Galileo and the Protestant spirit of Luther and Calvin, which dared to look at God plain, without the intervention of authority.

Faustus is the typical Marlovian overreaching hero. Poorly born, he becomes by the power of his mind the most distinguished scholar in Germany, whose *sic probo* rings through the halls of Wittenberg, bearing down all opponents. But his accomplishments bore him, and as the play opens Faustus is in his study scanning all forms of conventional knowledge and rejecting them as too limited to serve his limitless desires. Philosophy offers 'no greater miracle' than to dispute well, medicine has as its end no more than the health of the body, and law is 'nothing but external trash; Too servile and illiberal'. Divinity is no more attractive. Opening his *Vulgate*, Faustus's eye lights on *Romans*, vi. 23, 'The wages of sin is death', and then *The Epistles of John*, i. 8, 'If we say that we have no sin, we deceive ourselves, and the truth is not in us.' Neglecting to take into account the contexts of these passages, which speak of God's love for man and the forgiveness which will save the penitent man from eternal death, Faustus reasons that since man is inevitably sinful, and since the punishment of sin is death, therefore man must die: 'What will be, shall be!' Philosophy, medicine, law, divinity, all posit limits on man's capabilities and stress the consequent need for compromise and adjustment to a complex reality.

But Faustus longs for absolute powers to match and instrument his limitless imagination. Medicine would satisfy only if it enabled him to restore the dead to life or create eternal life. But magic is the only art which 'Stretcheth as far as doth the mind of man', and so Faustus takes up the 'necromantic books' with their 'Lines, circles, scenes, letters',[1] which offer him what he must have:

> O what a world of profit and delight,
> Of power, of honour, and omnipotence,
> Is promised to the studious artizan!
> All things that move between the quiet poles
> Shall be at my command: emperors and kings
> Are but obey'd in their several provinces,
> Nor can they raise the wind, or rend the clouds;
> But his dominion that exceeds in this,
> Stretcheth as far as doth the mind of man;
> A sound magician is a demi-god:
> Here, tire my brains to get a deity! (I. i. 54–64)

'Glutted with conceit' of limitless power, Faustus moves on to the magician's circle – that magical enclosed man-made space in which the imagination can be realized – where he breaks up and anagrammatizes Jehovah's name into the names of those older and newer gods, fire, air and water. The vision from Faustus's circle is at first awesome:

> the gloomy shadow of the night,
> Longing to view Orion's drizzling look,
> Leaps from th' antarctic world unto the sky,
> And dims the welkin with her pitchy breath, (I. iii. 1–4)

and the devils, obedient and pliant, arrive at once to draw up a bargain promising Faustus all that he wills for twenty-four years in exchange for his soul. But the bargain is almost from the beginning unsatisfactory. It turns out that it was not Faustus's magic which brought the devils, for Mephisto-

---

[1] This line is quoted from the 1604 text. The 1616 text omits the word 'scenes', which Boas calls 'unintelligible'.

philis says that he 'came now hither of mine own accord', and explains that devils in hopes of garnering a human soul always fly to that place where they hear the name of God abjured. Towards the end of the play (V. ii. 96–100) Mephistophilis boasts that it was in fact he who led the eye of Faustus to those particular passages in Scripture which caused him to turn away from religion to magic. The scene is from the beginning larger than Faustus's circle, and there are powers at work superior to the human mind. And while he may shrug off the hints that he is only one small counter in a cosmic struggle between God and Satan, he rapidly discovers that even in his own person he is not entirely free. He opens a vein to get the blood to sign the devilish bargain, but the blood will not at first flow. When the bargain is sealed, he immediately discovers a hitherto unknown part of himself that is terrified of the bargain and longs for a return to that safe world where God orders and protects man. Throughout the play, in his own speech and in argument between his good and evil angels, Faustus wavers between a hardened determination to pursue his own will and a newly discovered need for forgiveness and return. Each time he wavers, however, he finds himself unable to return to God because even in despair his pride and sense of his own greatness persist in the form of belief that his sins are too large and terrible to be forgiven even by God. Man the sinner is still greater than God the forgiver.

Man's ability to sustain freedom is seriously questioned by discoveries of counter-tendencies in his own nature, and the powers he gains from freedom become equally doubtful. Faustus does achieve knowledge and power, but both turn out in actuality to be unsatisfactory, though our knowledge of the extent to which Marlowe undercut Faustus's magic is complicated by the confused state of the text. The play was not printed until 1604, at least eleven years after it was written, and a different version appeared again in 1616. Both of these texts present problems, and most bibliographers have argued that they were corrupted by the methods of transmission and that they contain a good deal of material, particularly the comic subplot and some of the more grotesque scenes of magic, added by the actors in the playhouse or by other hands. In the absence of any certainty about whether the entire play is authentic Marlowe, we must, I believe, accept the full text as we have it, and we may take comfort from the fact that even the most tedious mirth in the play supports meanings discernible in the parts where the style is unquestionably Marlowe's.

One of Faustus's first desires is to know the manner in which the universe works, but Mephistophilis provides only a confused Ptolemaic explanation, which carries no real conviction or excitement even for Faustus, though he seems to be unaware of the new Copernican astronomy. The exercise of the magical powers is even more anticlimactic. The brave dreams of the magician-scientist to build a bridge between Europe and Africa, wall Germany in brass and dress the scholars all in silk come down in practice to orbiting the earth in a dragon-powered cart, hitting the Pope over the head and stealing his meat, putting horns on an insolent courtier and providing grapes out of season for a pregnant duchess. As the play progresses, Faustus descends to even lower forms of clownage, such as eating a cart of hay, selling a horse that disappears when ridden into a river and terrifying the peasantry by allowing a false head and a stage leg to be cut off. The bathos of the descent of the 'demi-god', whose dominion 'stretcheth as far as doth the mind of man', to the parlour magician is carried to a *reductio ad absurdum* in the doubtful subplot where Faustus's servant Wagner and the clown Robin use magic for such ludicrous ends as stealing cups and avoiding tavern bills, and parody Faustus's struggles with his conscience by fleeing in fear before some firecracker-throwing devils whom they have invoked.

Boredom and ennui overcome Faustus as he discovers the disappointing effects of his magic and finds that even the most striking manifestations of his power, his achievements as historian or playwright, are unsatisfactory. He calls to the stage images of the glory of the conqueror Alexander and of the incredible beauty of Helen of Troy, only to find them shadows who suck the soul away with a kiss, who cannot speak or live. The dream of omnipotence ends in the shows of a trickster whose 'artful sport drives all sad thoughts away'. And then in a moment of wild terror, swifter than could have been thought, the date of the bargain arrives, and screaming with fear, overwhelmed with despair, and chattering promises to burn his book, Faustus is dragged down to hell to pay in eternal torment for the trivialities for which he has sold his soul.

At one level *Doctor Faustus* is a crude morality play filled with literal devils from hell, bargains with Lucifer signed in blood, the spells and charms of black magic, debates between good and evil angels over a soul, a dance of the Seven Deadly Sins, the Prince of Darkness himself, and a painted hell-mouth into which a great sinner is dragged by devils to endure perpetual boiling in lead and 'ten thousand tortures that more horrid be'. The moral lesson of this play is as crude as its theology and its stagecraft:

> Faustus is gone: regard his hellish fall,
> Whose fiendful fortune may exhort the wise,

Only to wonder at unlawful things,
Whose deepness doth entice such forward wits,
To practise more than heavenly power permits. (Epilogue, 4–8)

But there is another play just behind the morality play, and the world-weary sophisticated Mephistophilis provides the bridge between the two. He indulges Faustus in his games and plays the fire-breathing, barb-tailed devil when necessary; but whenever Faustus will listen, Mephistophilis tries to tell him that the drama of salvation and damnation is not played out in the theatre of dancing devils and the material fires of hell, but in the mind of man. When Faustus wants to know where the devils are damned, Mephistophilis replies, 'In hell'. And when Faustus then wants to know 'How comes it then that thou art out of hell?', Mephistophilis explains that to be trapped in the self is hell:

Why this is hell, nor am I out of it:
Think'st thou that I, that saw the face of God,
And tasted the eternal joys of heaven,
Am not tormented with ten thousand hells,
In being depriv'd of everlasting bliss? (I. iii. 78–82)

But Faustus is unconvinced, and later he returns to the question, wanting to know the exact longitude and latitude of hell. Mephistophilis gets very specific:

Within the bowels of these elements,
Where we are tortur'd and remain for ever:
Hell hath no limits, nor is circumscrib'd
In one self place; but where we are is hell,
And where hell is, there must we ever be:
And, to be short, when all the world dissolves,
And every creature shall be purified,
All places shall be hell that is not heaven.
FAUSTUS: I think hell's a fable.
MEPHISTOPHILIS: Ay, think so still, till experience change thy mind.
(II. i. 120–9)

Mephistophilis agrees with Faustus that a literal hell is an 'old wives' tale', a ludicrous attempt to represent in material form the psychic reality of life lived without God in the isolated self; but hell is real, and Faustus's experience proves the point. Faustian man chooses power over the material world, rejecting authority and tradition, but that power, because it cannot ever match the forms of the imagination, leads to ennui and absurdity. Faustian man chooses self and freedom only to discover that this is indeed a bargain written in blood because both by nature and condition he requires a power outside himself to justify him and save him from the terrors of an existence he cannot finally control. Faustus has intimations of this need throughout the play in the debates between his good and evil angels and in his sudden surges of repentance, but full understanding comes only at the moment of his death when, facing the existential facts of the meaninglessness of the single life and the eternity of death, he calls for the mercy of God:

> The stars move still, time runs, the clock will strike,
> The devil will come, and Faustus must be damn'd.
> O, I'll leap up to my God! – Who pulls me down? –
> See, see, where Christ's blood streams in the firmament!
> One drop would save my soul, half a drop: ah, my Christ! –
> Ah, rend not my heart for naming of my Christ!
> Yet will I call on him: O, spare me, Lucifer! – (V. ii. 147–53)

But the God of mercy disappears into the wrathful God of the Old Testament, and Faustus is dragged screaming down to hell. Some surprise has been expressed that the vengeful old theology should dominate the end of the play, but its terms do fit better the tragic psychology which develops through the action. At one point where repentance and return to God are urged by the Good Angel, the Bad Angel remarks to Faustus, 'Thou art a spirit; God cannot pity thee' (II. ii. 13). The line catches the tragic irreversibility of Faustian man's psychological choice of the imagination, the self and power over the world as the only realities. There is no reneging on this bargain when it turns out to have been a bad one: the sense of human greatness and power either destroy God or give man's sins an importance that outweighs God's mercy: 'Faustus' offence can ne'er be pardoned: the serpent that tempted Eve may be saved, but not Faustus' (V. ii. 41–3). The magic circle which at first promises power and safety becomes a trap, and the choice of the self which at first confers freedom and knowledge becomes a hell of tedium and despair. This is the path travelled by the Marlovian overreacher – Tamburlaine facing the inevitable fact of death and the endlessness of worlds to conquer, Barabas dropped into the boiling pot by his own ingenious mechanism, and Faustus dragged down into hell by his own bargain – but he ends not as the sad object lesson of the dangers of sin and disobedience but the heroic explorer voyaging into the dark world of the self and discovering the fatal gap between what man wants and what is, the abyss over which the tragedy of the age was built.

The epigraph to the play, *Terminat hora diem; Terminat Author opus*, with its equation of Doctor Faustus the magician and Christopher Marlowe the playwright, has a weird appropriateness. Marlowe the free-thinker, brawler and hard liver was soon to die in a squalid tavern brawl ostensibly over paying the bill, 'a great reckoning in a little room' (*As You Like It*, III. iii. 15). But the magician and the playwright shared more than the immediacy of death, for the dramatist is another form of the overreacher who also rejected the crude didacticism, the halting verse and the timid morality of the older theatre to present his heroic images of man threatening the world in high astounding terms and striving by means of war, oratory, politics, knowledge and magic to achieve the sweet fruition of an earthly crown. The dominions of both the magician and the playwright stretch as far as doth the mind of man, and both are free to create, one in the circle of magic and the other in the circle of the theatre, whatever the imagination can conceive. If the parallel suggested by the epigraph is carried to its logical conclusion, however, it would seem that the playwright also found his magic a disappointment, found that the images he created, as Faustus creates Alexander and Helen, are but shadows which ravish with their beauty but are not real; found that, as the magician can only express himself in such crude parlour tricks as eating a cart of hay and producing grapes out of season, so the playwright can only express his dreams in such crude theatrical effects as prancing devils, exploding firecrackers and flame-belching hellmouths. 'The painter's brush consumes his dreams' in a more frightening way than Yeats thought. Whether in the end Christopher Marlowe felt that like his magician hero he had sold his soul for his art is a question about which we can only speculate. But another great playwright of the age did express unequivocally the feeling that there were soul-destroying dangers in writing for the public theatre:

O, for my sake do you with Fortune chide,
The guilty goddess of my harmful deeds,
That did not better for my life provide
Than public means which public manners breeds.
Thence comes it that my name receives a brand,
And almost thence my nature is subdu'd
To what it works in, like the dyer's hand.
Pity me then, and wish I were renew'd. . . . (Shakespeare, Sonnet 111)

(iii) 'A wilderness of tigers': *Titus Andronicus*

Written in the early 1590s when revenge tragedy in the manner of Seneca and Kyd was popular, *Titus Andronicus* is less a realistic treatment of human suffering than a catalogue of the imagery of fear and loss. As the play opens, the general Andronicus returns to Rome in triumph with two barbaric enemies, Tamora the queen of the Goths and Aaron the black Moor. One of Tamora's children is sacrificed, and a new emperor, Saturninus, whose name suggests coldness and malignancy, is chosen. Saturninus marries Tamora, and the two, along with Aaron who remains Tamora's lover, proceed to use the law as the instrument of the ruler's whim and turn Rome into a place of tyranny. Patriotism becomes a matter for laughter, and the brave Andronicus, who has given a lifetime and more than twenty sons in the service of the state, is rejected and cast aside. Two of his remaining sons are killed, and his daughter Lavinia is raped by Tamora's sons, her hands cut off and her tongue torn out to prevent her from identifying her ravishers. Andronicus goes mad when he is denied justice for these crimes and follows Hieronimo down the path of revenge to a Thyestean banquet in which Tamora is fed her own children, and to a wild mêlée in which Andronicus kills Lavinia, to erase her shame, and then stabs Tamora. Saturninus in turn kills Andronicus, only to be killed by Lucius, the last son of Titus. The sweetness of life has turned to acid: father kills child and brother murders brother; love turns to lust, rape and adultery; children are murdered, tongues torn out, hands cut off, traps are set for men; mutilation, torture and at last cannibalism become the realities of life. Existence is one long agony, and humanity expresses itself in screams in a world shaped by lust, hatred, fear, sadism, power-hunger and inexplicable malevolence. Even the countryside is involved in this change, and the briefly glimpsed fragrant fields and green woods are soon transformed into the tragic setting of 'a barren detested vale':

> The trees, though summer, yet forlorn and lean,
> Overcome with moss and baleful mistletoe;
> Here never shines the sun; here nothing breeds,
> Unless the nightly owl or fatal raven. (II. iii. 94–7)

There are suggestions of human responsibility for this suffering: Andronicus, deaf to pleas for mercy, sacrifices Tamora's son on the altars of Rome – thus prefiguring the slaughter of his own children and the deafness of the city to his own pleas for compassion and justice; by his martial conquests he brings the instruments of his destruction, Tamora and Aaron, into the city:

and he chooses Saturninus as emperor. But the emphasis is not on respon-sibility so much as it is on some malevolent, ineradicable and inexplicable evil which, to use the imagery supplied by the play, hunts life down to tear the throat and spill the blood out of sheer savagery. Hearing the horns of the hunters and the baying of the dogs in the distance, Tamora remarks that it is 'as if a double hunt were heard at once' (II. iii. 19), and while she literally means no more than to call attention to the echo, the words suggest that, even as men think they are tracking animal nature to the kill, animality is simul-taneously tracking humanity to the place of death. Such a meaning fits well the events of a play where motivation always seems thin, contrived and in-adequate to explain the characters' raw delight in causing pain or their incredible violence in seeking their pleasures. Evil and destruction have no real causes here, and they therefore take almost abstract forms: the ruler Saturninus, the Gothic queen from the cold north, and the black savage from the hot south.

But the focus is finally less sharply on the forces which create this 'wilder-ness of tigers' than it is on the condition of being locked in the centre of tragic existence and the ways in which man tries to escape. Shakespeare places behind his action a series of references to the more brutal pagan myths, drawn largely from Ovid, and emphasizes the story of Philomela, whose rape and mutilation resemble closely the suffering of Lavinia. In the *Metamorphoses* Philomela's story is but one instance of the general theme of the inevitability of change. The heavens, the gods, nature and particularly man hold one shape for only an instant and then pass swiftly on into other forms. Ovid's stories about men concentrate on events of great suffering, unendurable pain and titanic emotions, which rise to an unbearable intensity, and then at the moment of crisis the sufferers change into some object in nature, a stone, tree, reed or animal. The point is, as one critic puts it, that 'In the moments of greatest emotional stress Ovid's characters seem to lose not only individuality but even humanity as if sheer intensity of feeling made them indistinguishable from other forms of life'.[1]

Because of his persistent use of nature imagery, the constant comparisons of things human and things natural, Shakespeare's characters are always close to metamorphosis. But where in Ovid nature tends to swallow man, in Shakespeare man and nature ideally parallel and mutually sustain one another, as in the typical plot of the comedies where men move from the city to the woods and to close involvement in nature, and then, renewed, back to

[1] Eugene Waith, 'The metamorphosis of violence in *Titus Andronicus*', *Shakespeare Survey 10* (1957), p. 42.

the city again. This delicate balance and interaction of man and nature appear in metaphorical form in a passage at the end of *Titus Andronicus* where the tragic experience first reduces men to helpless objects in nature – wildfowl driven by a storm – and then transforms them into sheaves of grain – still related to nature, but a nature cultivated and shaped by man:

> You sad-fac'd men, people and sons of Rome,
> By uproars sever'd, as a flight of fowl
> Scatter'd by winds and high tempestuous gusts,
> O, let me teach you how to knit again
> This scattered corn into one mutual sheaf,
> These broken limbs again into one body. (V. iii. 67–72)

Whenever man is seriously threatened with submergence in nature, as in Gloucester's vision of man as 'a worm' or Lear's sudden sight of 'unaccommodated man . . . a poor, bare, forked animal', then fundamental disorder threatens the Shakespearian world.

Where the Ovidian experience centres on that pinnacle of emotion where humanity flashes into nature, Shakespearian tragedy centres on the effort to retain humanity under the pressure of violent emotion and terrible suffering. Violence, suffering and horror push the characters of *Titus* to the Ovidian edge of reduction to mere thing and strip them of the most characteristically human appendages, the hands and the tongue, the instruments of speaking and doing by which man expresses his humanity. Lavinia has her tongue torn out and her hands cut off, the two sons of Tamora are gagged and bound before Titus cuts their throats, Aaron is buried up to the neck in earth, and Titus chops off one of his own hands in a vain attempt to save his son. These are the physical representations of a condition presented most explicitly in Titus' image of what it feels like to sustain in utter helplessness violence upon violence:

> For now I stand as one upon a rock,
> Environ'd with a wilderness of sea,
> Who marks the waxing tide grow wave by wave,
> Expecting ever when some envious surge
> Will in his brinish bowels swallow him. (III. i. 93–7)

But the sea does not swallow Titus, as it would in Ovid. Instead, Titus begins to cast about for responses to his agony which will save his humanity from the threatened obliteration. Act III opens on a street along which passes a procession of judges and senators, taking to execution for a murder they did not commit two sons of Titus. In the foreground stands Titus alone, and as the procession passes he calls out for mercy to his city, invoking past service, age and common humanity:

> Hear me, grave fathers; noble Tribunes, stay!
> For pity of mine age, whose youth was spent
> In dangerous wars whilst you securely slept;
> For all my blood in Rome's great quarrel shed,
> For all the frosty nights that I have watch'd,
> And for these bitter tears, which now you see
> Filling the aged wrinkles in my cheeks,
> Be pitiful to my condemned sons . . . (III. i. 1–8)

But there is no answer from the Tribunes, and in a last desperate attempt to signal their humanity, Titus lies down in the street, '*and the Judges pass by him*'. Denied by the state and his fellow men, Titus turns to nature and tries to bribe the earth with promise of an eternal springtime if it will 'refuse to drink my dear sons' blood'. Where Tamburlaine commanded the world to share his joy and sorrow, the tragic Titus can only plead with the stones to receive his tears and 'seem' to weep with him. The pathetic fallacy he is trying to enact is the exact opposite of the Ovidian metamorphosis, but nature remains as silent as the world of man to Titus's attempt to salvage some remnants of his humanity by finding pity and sympathy in something outside himself.

The sons die, and the full extent of human misery becomes clear when the ravished and mutilated Lavinia enters. As his heart continues to 'beat with outrageous beating', and the question 'What shall we do?' throbs in his brain, Titus, unable simply to accept his agony, thinks of self-mutilation, chopping off those hands which have served Rome so well, to manifest his hatred. At this point Lavinia, who has already pleaded in the woods with man and nature and failed, begins to cry, and Titus, not understanding, as Lear will, that tears are one possible way of preserving humanity, searches wildly about for other ways to make something external respond to and sympathize with internal suffering:

> Gentle Lavinia, let me kiss thy lips,
> Or make some sign how I may do thee ease.
> Shall thy good uncle and thy brother Lucius
> And thou and I sit round about some fountain,
> Looking all downwards to behold our cheeks

> How they are stain'd, like meadows yet not dry
> With miry slime left on them by a flood?
> And in the fountain shall we gaze so long,
> Till the fresh taste be taken from that clearness,
> And made a brine-pit with our bitter tears?
> Or shall we cut away our hands like thine?
> Or shall we bite our tongues, and in dumb shows
> Pass the remainder of our hateful days?
> What shall we do? Let us that have our tongues
> Plot some device of further misery
> To make us wonder'd at in time to come. (III. i. 120–35)

Cry long and bitterly enough and the waters will be forced to turn to salt and the world weep with man! Cut off so many hands and tear out so many tongues – like Hieronimo – that the world cannot avoid seeing and understanding! Increase agony and mutilation to the point that it becomes a scandal which the future, if not the present, will know and pity. But future justification is not sure enough to assuage present suffering, and Titus turns away from the tribunal of the future to his last court of appeal, the heavens and the gods. He kneels to find out 'If any power pities wretched tears', and prays in hope that 'heaven shall hear'. But if the gods pity man they do not let him know it, for when Aaron proposes that Titus save the lives of his two sons by chopping off his own hand, and Titus does so gladly, he is sent in return only the bloody heads of his children.

Like Richard II trying to 'hammer it out', and like the Marlovian over-reacher trying to press human feelings on the world by force and magic, Titus's whole attempt is to get some part of the larger world outside himself to answer back to his demands for justice and conform to his own Job-like desolation. As a counterpoint to his violence, the helpless Lavinia takes the path of resignation and submission, which so many of Shakespeare's tragic heroines follow. Tears, kneeling and a few gestures of sympathy are the only responses left to her, tongueless and handless, to deal with her misery. For a time Titus learns the lesson she teaches. He kneels, cries, and becomes for Lavinia that reality which embayed humanity – like Faustus when his date comes due – so desperately needs: a register outside the self which responds sensitively and sympathetically to the suffering within the self:

> Speechless complainer, I will learn thy thought;
> In thy dumb action will I be as perfect
> As begging hermits in their holy prayers.

Thou shalt not sigh, nor hold thy stumps to heaven,
Nor wink, nor nod, nor kneel, nor make a sign,
But I of these will wrest an alphabet,
And by still practice learn to know thy meaning. (III. ii. 39–45)

In this mood Titus identifies with even the lowliest of creatures, and when his brother kills a buzzing fly, Titus, his eyes 'cloy'd with view of tyranny', protests the murder, feels the suffering of the fly's parents and enters into sympathy with the insect who 'Came here to make us merry!' (III. ii. 65).

But the resignation of Job is ultimately unendurable for the Roman Titus, and when told that the fly is as black as Aaron, his thoughts turn to the only action that can really satisfy him, revenge. As he stares at the heads of his two sons, he has 'not another tear to shed', his sanity breaks and he feels that peace can never be found again until 'all these mischiefs be return'd again, Even in their throats that have committed them' (III. i. 274–5). Madness and revenge are his ultimate efforts, his last resources, to escape – externally and internally – injustice, isolation and helplessness. He now no longer petitions the gods but ties Tamburlainish commands to arrows and fires them at the heavens, and in a final attempt to escape the Promethean pain, 'To ease the gnawing vulture of [the] mind' (V. ii. 31), he serves Tamora a stew made of her sons, and then dies in a scene of wild fury and uncontained savagery.

It is possible to see in this final self-destruction a moral judgement on revenge, but such a reading seems oblique. Shakespeare remade the Senecan revenge pattern neither as an occasion for moral and political instruction nor as an excuse to present a chamber of horrors, but as an essential image of tragic life and human response. The Senecan horrors are accumulated and intensified to create for Titus and his family a condition of absolute suffering which violates the most basic principles of justice, destroys the most sacred values of family and person, takes from the sufferers nearly all possibilities of recourse and thus threatens to obliterate their very humanity. Helplessly isolated on a rock and threatened by the sea with engulfment, pursued like an animal by a pack of dogs, faced by the silence of an indifferent society and universe, the sufferers are brought to the great tragic question, 'What shall we do?' What they do is not morally or practically satisfactory. They act, they increase the misery of themselves and others and they die in a fearful mess; but they do avoid the Ovidian fate of loss of humanity and disappearance into the great sea of nature.

Titus Andronicus and *Doctor Faustus* between them define the range and chart the landscape of the Elizabethan and Jacobean tragic world. *Doctor*

Faustus is chiefly a tragedy of human aspiration, of the death-marked greatness of the mind of man. Faustus rejects all limits, all authority and all tradition so that he may exercise absolute freedom and raise humanity to the level of the gods. When his achievements become insipid and meaningless, when he discovers that neither life nor death is tolerable for man without belief in some greater power outside the self, then he is terrified of his bargain. But the discovery comes too late, and no pity is possible for a man who has made his choice of freedom. He arrives at last at that total isolation in self which, as Mephistophilis tried to tell him, is hell. In *Titus Andronicus* isolation and the loneliness of the individual are not chosen by an unknowing act but are forced on man by dark, killing energies over which he seems to have no power. There is something vicious in life, something which hunts down other life as a pack of dogs does a rabbit, something like Tamora and Aaron the Moor, something which seeks out rape, murder, torture, something which moves inevitably towards the cannibal feast where men each other eat. Such a power isolates man from his own kind and interrupts his ties with nature as surely and inevitably as does the intellectual choice made by the magician of Wittenberg. Mephistophilis, who has once seen the face of God but must now live for ever in banishment, and Titus, standing 'as one upon a rock, Environ'd with a wilderness of sea', find their separate ways to the same place, the place to which from many directions the great tragic heroes of humanism all come in the drama which is to follow.

7 'I will not go from Troy':[1] the first phase of Shakespearian tragedy

(i) 'The mind is its own place': *Romeo*, *Caesar* and *Troilus*

The energy which created and found its satisfaction in the new drama was the Romantic desire for limitlessness, but the very power which made the new drama was from the beginning feared by its heroes and playwrights: the grandeur of Tamburlaine becomes the ugliness of Richard III, Faustus's magic brings him to a hellish isolation in the self, the brave Andronicus finds himself helpless in a wilderness of tigers, Bolingbroke sees the vast expanse of endless change stretching for ever into the future, and the greatest of playwrights often found their theatrical magic limited, unsatisfactory, a shabby attempt to cheat reality. Some of the characters turned away from the hard truths and fears, as, on the eve of the battle of Agincourt, Henry V turns away from tragic realities to take refuge in his role of hero king; but Shakespearian drama followed to its roots the conflict between the human imagination and the realities in which it must live and seek its expression.

In a series of tragedies – *Romeo and Juliet* (1595), *Julius Caesar* (1599), *Hamlet* (1601) and *Troilus and Cressida* (1602) – the idealistic energies which

[1] Tear my bright hair, and scratch my praised cheeks,
Crack my clear voice with sobs and break my heart,
With sounding 'Troilus'. I will not go from Troy. (*Troilus*, IV. ii. 113–15)

drive man towards the fullest realization of his humanity seek to create in poetry and in action a second world, a heterocosm, in which things are as man can imagine them to be. In *Romeo* the tragic energy is love of an incredibly pure and ideal variety. Where all the other characters take a utilitarian view of love as a useful passion which can be made the instrument of other more practical ends – sexual pleasure (Mercutio), economic improvement (the Capulets), civic concord (Friar Lawrence) – Romeo and Juliet alone insist upon a love which expresses and finds itself entirely in love. In the traditional manner of courtly love these lovers create a religion of love, with Eros as god, in the sonnet they share at the dance in the Capulet household; and in the garden immediately afterwards they go on to create the cosmos and society of love. The voice of Mercutio proclaiming that love is no more than sex fades away, and the lovers are left alone in the darkness, lit only by the moon, the traditional symbol of the imagination, isolated in a garden and protected by high walls from the workaday world of Verona. The realities of that world are immediately thrust aside, and, by means of metaphor, Romeo proceeds to construct love's world in which Juliet's bedroom becomes the orient, her beauty the rising sun lighting the world, her shining eyes the twinkling stars that 'through the airy region stream so bright' and her presence 'a winged messenger of heaven' sailing 'upon the bosom of the air'. Within the new cosmology of love, Juliet now proceeds to create love's society in which such accidents as name and family history are stripped from men, in which even the flesh – hand, foot, arm, face – disappears, to leave only the essential reality, that 'dear perfection' perceived by love, freed for ever from such crudities as Capulet, Romeo, Verona, feud and sex. Having constructed this imaginative world, the lovers then take it for the real world and seek to marry, as if the blood feud, the hot sun that beats down on Verona in the dog days and the violent anger of a Tybalt were unreal.

In *Julius Caesar* the ruling energy is Caesarism, a complex form of idealism combining loyalty to abstract political and ethical values with an absolute belief that reality is perceived truly and controlled entirely by the mind, particularly the rational faculties. Each of the major characters of the play is certain that his ideas and his abstract image of himself take priority over any crude physical reality such as pain, blood, evidence of the senses, or political fact. Portia, the wife of Brutus and daughter of Cato, cuts herself with a razor simply to demonstrate her worthiness, though a female, to be a part of this great Stoic tradition; and the rather extravagant manner in which she dies, swallowing live coals, suggests a carefully arranged demonstration of the superiority of mind over matter. Cassius, that radical republican who had rather be dead than 'live to be In awe of such a thing as I myself' (I. ii. 95–6), is only slightly less hysterical in his determination to prove that

> Nor stony tower, nor walls of beaten brass,
> Nor airless dungeon, nor strong links of iron,
> Can be retentive to the strength of spirit. . . . (I. iii. 93–5)

Such a man scorns another man sick with fever who groans, allows his eyes to dim and asks for water; and such a man flings himself fully armoured into the raging Tiber simply on a dare. The certainty in self and the determination to impose mind upon matter of such characters seems carved from the same granite and marble as the busts of those tough, hard, determined faces from the late Republic and early Empire which show so nakedly the qualities it took to stay alive in and rule the Roman state.

The full power of the mind, the supremacy of the rational will and the determination of the ego appear most clearly in Caesar and Brutus. On the surface the two men seem quite different, the iron-hard politician and the revolutionary idealist – Danton and Robespierre, Lenin and Trotsky – but both worship and die for an unchanging image of themselves. 'When Caesar says "Do this", it is perform'd' (I. ii. 10), and for him his will and history are identical. All other things in the world shift and change, he says in the Senate the moment before his death,

> But I am constant as the northern star,
> Of whose true-fix'd and resting quality
> There is no fellow in the firmament.
> The skies are painted with unnumb'red sparks,
> They are all fire, and every one doth shine;
> But there's but one in all doth hold his place.
> So in the world: 'tis furnish'd well with men,
> And men are flesh and blood, and apprehensive;
> Yet in the number I do know but one
> That unassailáble holds on his rank,
> Unshak'd of motion . . . (III. i. 60–70)

Brutus's idealism is more complex, more highly rationalized, than Caesar's will to power. An immensely proud aristocrat descended from a long line of king-killers and defenders of liberty, he is utterly self-contained, cool, controlled, speculative and courteous. He wants nothing for himself, but his disinterested search for freedom for Rome and his lofty reasoning lead him to some curious conclusions. Reflecting upon the necessity for Caesar's death, he admits that Caesar has given no evidence of being a tyrant, but in his mind theory takes precedence always over fact, and the theory that absolute power corrupts absolutely dooms Caesar to death. But the assassination is to be an abstraction, tyrannicide, not the brute fact of murder:

> Let's be sacrificers, but not butchers, Caius.
> We all stand up against the spirit of Caesar,
> And in the spirit of men there is no blood.
> O that we then could come by Caesar's spirit,
> And not dismember Caesar! But, alas,
> Caesar must bleed for it! (II. i. 166–71)

The position Brutus occupies in III. ii, the oration scene, where he ascends the rostrum high above the body, and speaks to the crowd in formal prose of justice and reason, is a physical realization of the way of thought which always elevates idea over fact. Out of principle he allows Antony to speak to the mob, hears the news of his wife's death with remarkable equanimity – 'Why, farewell, Portia' (IV. iii. 190) – does battle with the enemy on unfavourable ground and in the end kills himself rather than be taken. Perhaps no line reveals more clearly his certainty that 'the mind is its own place' (*Paradise Lost*, I. 254) than his flat reaction to the ghost of the murdered Caesar trying to frighten him with predictions of meeting him at Philippi: 'Why, I will see thee at Philippi, then' (IV. iii. 287). Reaction to ghosts is regularly in Shakespeare an index to crucial qualities of mind.

The full range of human idealism is displayed in *Troilus*. Man's great, eternal dream of government, order, harmony and community is embodied in Ulysses's famous speech on 'degree, priority, and place, Insisture, course, proportion, season, form' (I. iii. 86–7). The noble dream of honour takes archetypal form as the heroes of the Trojan War, Achilles, Diomedes, Hector and Troilus. The image of beauty and love blazes brightly in Paris and Helen, Troilus and Cressida. In Troy, that *locus classicus* of the Western imagination, the basic energy which lies behind all attempts to replace the world of everyday with the world that imagination conceives is openly discussed and debated. The occasion is the council scene, II. ii, in Priam's palace. The Greeks have offered to end the war, forgetting all losses of time, money and men, if only Helen is surrendered. Hector argues that Helen is not in and of herself worth all the suffering she has caused, and since the 'moral laws Of nature and of nations' (184–5) also clearly decree her return, then she must be given up to the Greeks. 'Value', he insists,

dwells not in particular will:
It holds his estimate and dignity
As well wherein 'tis precious of itself
As in the prizer. 'Tis mad idolatry
To make the service greater than the god . . . (53-7)

Though he does not overestimate Helen's intrinsic worth, Troilus, idealistic
and subjective, still goes on to argue that the honour of all Troy is involved
with keeping Helen and that men confer value on anything by the valuation
they place upon it, by the honour and courage with which they defend it:
'What's aught but as 'tis valued?' (52)

Shakespearian tragedy of this period grows from this heroic idolatry of
self-conceived images and the violent determination to maintain them as real.
But though the tragic heroes are treated with full sympathy and understanding of what they are trying to do, in the Shakespearian world view, as
in Hector's, 'Value dwells not in particular will' alone. The heroes are always
placed in a world where 'Each thing melts In mere oppugnancy' (*Troilus*,
I. iii. 110-11), where the will and the world are exactly at odds. Romeo and
Juliet are born into and must love in a world of hate. The imaginative world
of love constructed in the isolated garden must confront 'fair Verona, where
we lay our scene', with its public square, its cemetery, its great households,
its kitchens, its churches and the hot, burning sun which bears down on the
inhabitants and drives them to fury. Detail by small detail, Shakespeare
builds behind his lovers a solid reality which has little to do with idealism and
love but much to do with the heavy day-to-day immediacies of existence in
time: a feud so ancient that all have forgotten its origins, the crude sex and
appetite for trouble of servingmen like Sampson and Gregory, the anger of a
Tybalt. This is a world where meals have to be cooked, tables cleared and
dishes washed; a world where teeth decay and fall out; a world in which
great ladies have corns caused by tight shoes rubbing the foot; a world where
the children of the rich die as suddenly as Susan, the Nurse's child; a world
in which weaning comes inevitably and the child one day finds wormwood on
the dug; a world in which careful parents must plan marriages based not on
romantic love but on money and social station; a world where all men grow
old and cease to dance.

The *Caesar* world is equally oppugnant to the will of its major characters.
The power of the rational mind to understand and the iron will to order all
of life is persistently questioned. Caesar is deaf in one ear and subject to
epileptic seizures, Calpurnia is barren, Portia forgets to tell a messenger his

errand, Brutus forgets where he put his book. The surface of what is taken for reality gives way frequently to reveal powers outside the rational range. Soothsayers call out warnings about the Ides of March; there are strange, prophetic dreams of statues spouting blood in which the citizens wash themselves; ghosts walk; auguries disclose the absence of hearts in animals; eagles descend to perch on the standards of armies; lions walk the streets of Rome and the graves give up their dead; strange visions appear in the heavens of struggling armies in the clouds, and rains of blood fall to the earth. Nothing is stranger to rationality than the Roman mob, on which all designs of power and government ultimately rest. Having cheered Pompey, they now cheer Caesar, who has defeated Pompey. Their language is as unstable as their politics, and in the opening scene of the play they infuriate two tribunes by their insolent puns on words like 'sole', 'cobbler' and 'mend'. Led only by their emotions, they respond to Brutus's explanation – that he killed Caesar lest he become a dictator – with cries of 'Let him be Caesar' (III. ii. 56); to Antony's skilful manipulation of their pity and greed with shouts of 'Seek! Burn! Fire! Kill! Slay!' (III. ii. 208–9). The mob's full savagery and absolute lack of rationality comes out in the scene in which they catch Cinna the Poet and, despite his protests that he is not Cinna the conspirator, tear him to pieces, screaming, 'It is no matter, his name's Cinna; pluck but his name out of his heart' (III. iii. 37–8). The central opposition of the rational and irrational is staged perfectly in the scene in which the great roars of the mob, offering a crown to Caesar, sound from within the arena, while outside, disdaining to mingle, stand Brutus and Cassius talking of their love of liberty and honour, and their indifference to death if it comes in the struggle for freedom and equality.

The Trojan War, with its flash of weapons in the sun, the knee bent in the dust and the pervasive smell of the corpse fires, is the Western imagination's image of the many endless wars begun for doubtful causes which become ever more vague and meaningless through long years of struggle. From Homer onward, our poets have made Priam's Troy at least as real as any place we have actually seen. We know the features of the Trojan plain, the names of the rivers that flowed from the mountains to the sea; the gates of the city are named and numbered; and we have visited the islands and the palaces from which the Greek warriors came. We know Achilles in his pride, Ajax in his stubbornness, Odysseus in his cunning, Hector in his nobility and Priam in his greatness. And yet nothing is more far away and desolate than the place which is now only a mound of rubble in Asia Minor, where Priam's Troy is but one of the layers of cities buried under cities. Troy and the

Trojan War are an important part of the furniture of the Western mind, but the image is complex: at once very real and unreal, bright and dim, immediate and utterly lost. This same dual perspective of myth and history governs the world of *Troilus and Cressida*, where man's heroic efforts to make his values real take place against a historical consciousness that

> every action that hath gone before,
> Whereof we have record, trial did draw
> Bias and thwart, not answering the aim,
> And that unbodied figure of the thought
> That gave 't surmised shape. (I. iii. 13–17)

What is true of every action that hath gone before is equally true of the actions of the play when they are exposed to experience and time. Love, honour, reputation and all else that men value relentlessly fade into nothingness. Great deeds become, in Ulysses's image, 'like a gallant horse fall'n in first rank' to be 'o'er-run and trampled on' by those who follow behind (III. iii. 161–3). All the wisdom in government and political efforts of Nestor and Ulysses to restore order, hierarchy and effectiveness to the Greek army result only in more desperate confusion: they use Ajax to draw Achilles out of his tent, but Ajax then goes off to sulk in *his* tent. The great heroes in quest of honour on the battlefield become bumblers and savage animals hunting one another down in bestial fashion. The golden couple, Helen and Paris, are revealed as a pair of amorous triflers. After vowing eternal faithfulness, Cressida is sent in an exchange to the Greek camp, where she is soon flirting with the generals, and soon after, frightened and lonely as well as incurably romantic, she accepts Diomedes's aristocratically self-assured advances and gives him the sleeve which Troilus gave to her as token of his love. The fall of Troy itself, though not yet an accomplished fact, is already known to her defenders, as if they had read the same stories we have. When Ulysses tells Hector of the inevitable day when the towers of that city 'Must kiss their own feet', the Trojan accepts the truth of the prediction even while knowing he must deny it:

> I must not believe you.
> There [the walls] stand yet; and modestly I think
> The fall of every Phrygian stone will cost
> A drop of Grecian blood. The end crowns all;
> And that old common arbitrator, Time,
> Will one day end it. (IV. v. 221–6)

The plots of these three early tragedies are built around the attempts of the heroes to maintain, like Titus, their imagined worlds against the opposition of the solid given world and the unknown realities of the self. In *Romeo and Juliet* the conflict is best dramatized in a specific reversal of the earlier garden scene where the lovers constructed their own world. After their first and only night together they are wakened by the rising sun, which signals the beginning of Romeo's banishment from Verona. Juliet at first refuses to accept the world's time and insists that it is the voice of the nightingale they hear, not the lark. But as they talk, it grows more and more light, and the fear of death becomes increasingly real, until at last the lovers are forced to accept the fact that their poetry cannot transform the world or stay 'day's path and Titan's fiery wheels' (II. iii. 4). The struggle and defeat portrayed in III. v are but the climax of a long series of losses which begins in self-betrayal even in the moment of love's perfection, the balcony scene. No sooner does Juliet admit her love than she begins to wonder whether Romeo may not think her too forward, and besides, he may not be true, for old stories tell of lovers' deceits and their fickleness. The fear and uncertainty which qualify love are bred into her bones, absorbed from the stories told her in childhood, and so she can 'have no joy of this contract tonight; It is too rash, too unadvised, too sudden' (II. ii. 117–18). Frightened, she begins to bargain: 'If that thy bent of love be honourable, Thy purpose marriage . . .' (II. ii. 143–4). No doubt this is a measure of Juliet's practicality, but such practicality belongs to the world of Verona with its contracts and legal ceremonies, not in a declaration of idealized love which recognizes no authority outside itself. Because of his nature, Romeo too is unable to remain in the world of dream. When he first enters the garden, supreme happiness would be only to know that Juliet loves him, but in a few moments he is sighing, 'O, wilt thou leave me so unsatisfied?' Juliet understands him perfectly: 'What satisfaction canst thou have to-night?' (II. ii. 125–6). Even ideal lovers have bodies, and spiritual union can only seek completion in sexual union. Perhaps the saddest moment comes in Juliet's Keatsian awareness that love's perfection exists at only that fleeting instant before it is realized: she has given her love instantly and freely: 'And yet I would it were to give again' (II. ii. 128).

Towards the end of the balcony scene, the Nurse begins insistently calling from within, 'Madam!', voicing the claims of the practical real world on the lovers, claims which continue through the remainder of the play. Each of the typical lover's boasts is challenged. In the garden, names and the social realities they represent mean nothing, for 'a rose By any other name would smell as sweet', but in the square a few hours later names mean everything,

and the fact that Romeo is a Montague causes the deaths of Mercutio and
Tybalt, and leads to Romeo's banishment. The lover who has boasted in the
moonlight that 'stony limits cannot hold love out' finds that the walls of
Verona are too high and hard for him, banished from within them under pain
of death, to 'o'erperch with love's light wings'; and he goes tamely off to
Mantua. The lover who has vowed that he would adventure 'as far As that
vast shore wash'd with the farthest sea' for his love, finds it impossible to
cover the few miles separating Mantua from Verona. The lady says that her

> bounty is as boundless as the sea,
> My love as deep: the more I give to thee,
> The more I have, for both are infinite. (II. ii. 133–5)

But only a few hours later, when she discovers that her husband Romeo has
killed her kinsman Tybalt, infinite love turns in a flash to hatred, and even
when she recovers, love and hate remain surprisingly mixed.

In *Julius Caesar* the confrontation of hero and world is complicated by the
fact that, though the evidence is strikingly clear, Caesar, Cassius and Brutus –
like Marat sitting in his bath, writing, in the middle of an insane asylum –
refuse to recognize the inadequacies of their reason and the limits imposed by
the world on their wills. Even as Caesar compares himself to the unchanging
North Star, the daggers enter his body; as Brutus reasons lucidly the
necessity for Caesar's death, he encounters the actuality of conspiracy in the
shadowy assassins with their hats 'pluck'd about their ears And half their
faces buried in their cloaks' (II. i. 73–4); as the murderers move through
the city crying the abstract, bloodless words, 'Peace, freedom, and liberty'
(III. i. 110), their arms and swords raised above their heads are smeared with
Caesar's blood. Brutus is as blind to his own inability to live up to his self-
imposed ideal as he is to see that philosophic ideas are not reality. Cassius's
flattery has more than a little to do with persuading Brutus to join the conspiracy; he is too fine to wring the gold needed to maintain his army from the
wretched peasants, but he is furious with Cassius, who presumably must get
money by the same means, for not sending the requested funds; he pretends
that he has not heard earlier of Portia's death and uses the occasion to display
great fortitude; he declares that it is cowardly to commit suicide and then in
the moment of crisis kills himself. The failure of any of the characters, particularly Brutus, to accept any of the proffered scenes of tragic recognition
accounts in large degree for the truncated, unfulfilled quality of the play.

Though they are romantic lovers like Romeo and Juliet, Troilus and
Cressida are more than half certain that their love even in the moment of its

flowering is doomed. Their bright eyes seem to shine above dark shadows and a slight nervousness to play on the edge of their smiles. The conventional lover's boasts of service and faith spoken so unselfconsciously in the Capulet garden now are known as 'monstrous . . . undertakings', laughable vows 'to weep seas, live in fire, eat rocks, tame tigers; thinking it harder for our mistress to devise imposition enough than for us to undergo any difficulty imposed' (III. ii. 82–7). Cressida well understands the difference between reputation and honesty, and despite her love for Troilus, she is reluctant to give herself because she knows that 'Men prize the thing ungain'd more than it is', but 'Things won are done' (I. ii. 313–15). Troilus, like a sensual adept, knows that expectation and 'imaginary relish' are limitlessly sweet, but the senses are too crude and in the act will 'lose distinction' of the overwhelming joys (III. ii. 20–8). It is no wonder that an intermediary, Pandarus, is needed to bring these sophisticates together, and even as they are about to declare their love they spar, cautiously delay the moment of declaration, fear that the other will play the tyrant and at last feel dismay when they realize they have committed themselves. But for all their knowledge that beauty decays and love dies, they finally give themselves totally, and their protestations of the truth and durability of their love are as absolute as those of Romeo and Juliet:

> I have forgot my father;
> I know no touch of consanguinity,
> No kin, no love, no blood, no soul so near me
> As the sweet Troilus. O you gods divine,
> Make Cressid's name the very crown of falsehood,
> If ever she leave Troilus! Time, force, and death,
> Do to this body what extremes you can,
> But the strong base and building of my love
> Is as the very centre of the earth,
> Drawing all things to it. (IV. ii. 102–11)

But even as her heroic cry, 'I will not go from Troy', lingers in the air, she is transported to the Greek camp, where the warriors, anticipating the future, pass her around, kissing her in turn. The lovers' worst fears are realized in a few hours when Troilus stands looking at Cressida outside her tent dallying with Diomedes. Cressida's motives remain a mystery. We can take the view of Ulysses that she is simply a slut, or we can agree with the satirist Thersites's estimate of the scene as but another incident in this endless, ridiculous argument over a cuckold and a whore, or we can read the scene with more kindness and sympathy for a frightened girl torn from familiar surroundings, in need of a protector and desperately aware that she is betraying herself. But whatever the motive – and perhaps it is not terribly important – here, as in all of Shakespeare's tragedies, the reality, including the reality of self, is finally incapable of supporting man's great images of himself and his world.

In their encounters with the necessities of themselves and their worlds, Shakespeare's idealists are not in these early tragedies particularly successful. Caesar's blood drowns his words of pride, and Brutus dies on his own sword and his own certainty that he sees all there is to see, knows all there is to know. Troilus similarly refuses to recognize that the act of valuation cannot confer value, and he saves his dream only by positing two Cressidas, the one he knew and loved in Troy and the one his eyes and ears now reveal to him paltering with Diomedes: 'this is, and is not, Cressid' (V. ii. 146). The ideal and the reality no longer square, and all that is most dear trails away into a nothingness over which we hear only the sound of Troilus's flat words, 'But, march away; Hector is dead; there is no more to say' (V. x. 21–2).

In some ways the most innocent of Shakespeare's overreachers, Romeo and Juliet, are the most successful, despite early reverses, in imposing their will upon reality. True, they end dead by their own hands in the Capulet tomb as a result of a series of ghastly errors which might have been avoided had they been less sudden and impetuous. But as is usual in Shakespearian tragedy the causes of their loss are at once the sources of their greatness, and the energies which bring them to death also enable them partially and in unexpected ways to fulfil their earlier boasts. Romeo in his innocence had insisted in the garden that stony limits cannot hold love out, and now he shoulders aside the stone slab of the tomb to be with Juliet. Finding her apparently dead he does indeed adventure 'as far As that vast shore wash'd with the farthest sea' and joins her in death. When Juliet awakens to find his still warm body, she immediately kills herself and makes good her earlier claim of the infiniteness of her love. Once again love's poetry transforms the world, and Juliet's beauty makes the place of death 'a feasting presence full of light' (V. iii. 86). The 'continuance of their parents' rage', the Prologue tells us, 'but their children's end, nought could remove', and the death of these saints of love brings at long last an end to the feud. Youth dies to restore life to an ageing world, and lovers die to ensure that love does not die in a world of hate. But the survivors of Shakespearian tragedy never fully understand what they have seen and experienced, and even as the hands of Capulet and Montague join over the bodies of their dead children, they vow to erect the most unsuitable monument possible: huge golden statues of the lovers. As Friar Lawrence hears Juliet in the distance, rushing eagerly up the steps and down the corridors of the church on the way to marriage with Romeo, his joy in her and fear for her find expression in an image which catches perfectly the Shakespearian tragic world and provides the true monument for the lovers: the stone step worn and polished by the passage of many generations of love's worshippers:

> Here comes the lady. O, so light a foot
> Will ne'er wear out the everlasting flint. (II. vi. 16–17)

(ii) 'The desire is boundless, and the act a slave to limit': *Hamlet*

'This is the monstruosity in love, lady, that the will is infinite, and the execution confin'd; that the desire is boundless, and the act a slave to limit' (*Troilus*, III. ii. 87–90). In *Hamlet* 'this' is not only the monstruosity in love but in all things, and the limits and confinement take the solid shape of Elsinore, that constricted world lying between the sea which roars against the castle foundations on one side and the graveyard on the other, landward side. Bounded by mystery and darkness, the action moves from a battlement where men are shaken 'With thoughts beyond the reaches of [their] souls' (I. iv. 56) to a battlement where 'the rest is silence'. All places other than Elsinore – Norway, England, Paris, Poland, Wittenberg – are very far away and not quite real; even the kingdom of Denmark, where Hamlet, it is said, is much loved by the citizens, can advance no further than the gates of the castle. Travellers to these far places return, with few exceptions, to Elsinore, usually to die. The only final exit is through the graveyard, and even there there is no rest, for the bones of the dead are thrown away to make way for the bones of other dead and turn at last to dust blown about the world.

Bounded in this nutshell, man is forced to endure 'the thousand natural shocks That flesh is heir to' (III. i. 62–3): the death of a king and a father, Old Hamlet; the discovery that a mother, Gertrude, is a creature of pronounced and undiscriminating sexual appetite; the revelation that friendship, in the shapes of Rosencrantz and Guildenstern, is unlikely to endure the pressures of age and self-interest; the disappointment of love, in Ophelia, which can bear it out only to the edge of a father's command not 'to give words or talk with the Lord Hamlet' (I. iii. 134). King, father, mother, friend, lover, these are the places where, as Othello later puts it, man garners up his heart (IV. ii. 57), and the discovery that they inevitably change, corrupt and die leads onwards to other shocks such as the realization that authority is both foolish and vile, that reason cannot find truth, that honour is both sham and glory, that nothing is what it seems to be and that a man cannot finally even count on the purity of his own motives or the steadiness of his own will.

The king of this place of tragic reality is plausible enough, if the fact that he is an usurper can be forgotten, as it easily is by most. A trifle vulgar and self-satisfied, but solidly practical, efficient and long on common sense. A strong ruler, he handles difficult business with dispatch and reasons with his troublesome subjects in a sensible and even kindly manner. His rhetoric, polished, ordered, perhaps a bit repetitious and glib, dominates the public scenes in Elsinore, recommending sensible compromise – 'With mirth in funeral, and with dirge in marriage' (I. ii. 12) – and acceptance of those 'common' things like 'death of fathers' which the world has always said 'must be so' (I. ii. 106). But in his words, so seemingly sensible and reasonable, death lies for all who listen and believe. This is the 'bloat' king, the 'king of shreds and patches', the poisoner of the rapier and the chalice, the fleshly creature whose words 'fly up' but whose 'thoughts remain below' (III. iii. 97). He is instrumental to all the shocks to which flesh is heir: he kills the old king-father, seduces the mother, corrupts the friends and, present in the reasoning of his agent Polonius, forces the girl to deny her love and lend herself to deceit. Whatever ideal he touches dies – Laertes's honour, Fortinbras's piety, Gertrude's virtue – and those who do his work find unexpected death in strange places: behind the arras of a bedroom, on a Polish battlefield too small to bury those who die on it, asleep in an orchard of an afternoon, on a faraway English shore and in a cup of wine poisoned with an 'union'.

With surprising aptness, Rosencrantz characterizes himself and his inter-changeable friend as 'the indifferent children of the earth' (II. ii. 231), and the term illuminates brilliantly the nature of those many inhabitants of Elsinore who 'freely [go] With this affair along' (I. ii. 15–16). Like the queen who cannot see the ghost, yet believes 'all that is I see' (III. iv. 132), these creatures couple remarkable self-assurance with an ability to see only the obvious and the familiar. This 'dumbness' is there when those sponges Rosencrantz and Guildenstern, sweating with earnestness, speak to the frightened Claudius after *The Mousetrap* of the 'religious fear' that keeps 'those many many bodies safe That live and feed upon your majesty (III. iii. 8–10); when the idiotic courtier Osric, that 'water-fly', carries, with bows and flourishes, the ornate challenge to Hamlet to fence with Laertes, without the slightest suspicion that this is an invitation to death; when Laertes, faced with a sincere apology from Hamlet for the death of Polonius, continues to 'stand aloof' until he can consult 'some elder masters of known honour' (V. ii. 259) to find if he can accept the apology without harm to his honour. The range of these 'indifferent children of the earth' is defined by the Polonius family, so hopeful in prospect but so fated for disaster. Polonius, the father, the aged counsellor of the king, is never at a loss for something to say or do, proud of his learning and his ability to 'by indirections find directions out' (II. i. 66), but in the event so stupid and so helpless. He stands before reality and understands it no more than he understands drama – 'tragedy, comedy, history, pastoral' – or madness: 'for, to define true madness, What is't but to be nothing else but mad' (II. ii. 93–4). He categorizes learnedly and quotes many authorities, but his reasoning goes in circles, and he can conceive of no more meaningful life than to be the trusted servant of the king, any king. His son Laertes, a man of fashion and of honour, is more up-to-date but equally a slave to custom and authority. Where his father follows the old patterns of known statecraft and academic authority, Laertes thinks and lives in the patterns dictated by the codes of courtier and gentleman. Ophelia is more touching than her father and brother because more capable of genuine feeling, but the family habit of unthinking obedience to tradition and authority is equally strong. She bows her head in obedience to the commands of her father and her brother, denies her love for Hamlet, allows herself to be used to trap him and passes on to the madness and suicide latent in her choice. Even the best of these people cannot think outside the simple patterns of accustomed thought – Gertrude, vaguely aware that she may have remarried a little hastily but completely unable to see what has happened in Denmark and in whose bed she sleeps; Fortinbras, the energetic soldier who resembles Old Hamlet in so many ways, arriving on the scene of carnage at the conclusion of the play and deciding that Hamlet *might* have been a great man if only he had had a chance to be a soldier or a king like Fortinbras: 'he was likely, had he been put on, To have prov'd most royal' (V. ii. 408–9). Little blame attaches to these people; they do terrible things, but out of blindness rather than malice, and they suffer so fearsomely. Hamlet sums up rather coolly the natures and the fates of most of these children who have 'only got the tune of the time and outward habit of encounter – a kind of yesty collection, which carries them through and through the most fann'd and winnowed opinions; and do but blow them to their trial, the bubbles are out' (V. ii. 197–202).

The queen speaks for all these indifferent children of the earth who accept what must be because it is all they have ever known when, speaking of the death of Old Hamlet, she remarks with eminent good sense to her melancholy son that death is 'common – all that lives must die, Passing through nature to eternity' (I. ii. 72–3). This is true enough but not acceptable to the

Prince of Denmark – 'Ay, madam, it is common' – who contains all the boundless desires of the earlier dramatic heroes and embodies all the optimism of Renaissance humanism. Much of his hope and his greatness is but memory when the play opens, but the memory is powerful enough to reveal still a scholar who had been a student at Wittenberg like Faustus, a romantic lover like Romeo who had written tender letters and poetry to his mistress, the son of a great king and the heir to a throne like Richard II; a man of all accomplishments prized by his age:

> The courtier's, soldier's, scholar's, eye, tongue, sword;
> Th' expectancy and rose of the fair state,
> The glass of fashion and the mould of form,
> Th' observ'd of all observers. . . . (III. i. 159–62)

The overreacher's dream of the greatness of man and the beauty of the world still lingers amid the ruins of his present despair:

> it goes so heavily with my disposition that this goodly frame, the earth, seems to me a sterile promontory; this most excellent canopy the air, look you, this brave o'erhanging firmament, this majestical roof fretted with golden fire – why, it appeareth no other thing to me than a foul and pestilent congregation of vapours. What a piece of work is a man! How noble in reason! how infinite in faculties! in form and moving, how express and admirable! in action, how like an angel! in apprehension, how like a god! the beauty of the world! the paragon of animals! And yet, to me, what is this quintessence of dust? Man delights not me.
> . . . (II. ii. 309–23)

Even in the melancholy resulting from the death of his father and the hasty remarriage of his mother, Hamlet retains a remarkable gentility, sensitivity and delicacy of feeling; but his chief energy is what Claudius rightly calls 'his brains still beating' (III. i. 182). Hamlet is essentially mind or thought, never-ceasing mentality. The power of that mind is obsessive, outside the control of the will, determined to remember and grapple with what the man would forget:

> Must I remember? Why, she would hang on him
> As if increase of appetite had grown
> By what it fed on; and yet, within a month –
> Let me not think on 't. Frailty, thy name is woman! –
> A little month, or ere those shoes were old. . . . (I. ii. 143–7)

The thought racing on through all barriers is matched with an analytical imagination which leaves no perception, however painful, vague or abstract: the thought of his mother's marriage to Claudius is focused precisely on the new shoes moving along behind the bier of Old Hamlet and then, still new, following the next husband; the pain of life is directly felt as a grunting, sweating labour under a burden of fardels; even the marriage bed of his mother and uncle refuses to remain at a decent distance and flashes into vivid presence: 'the rank sweat of an enseamed bed' (III. iv. 92). No possibility escapes this mind: to think of one thing is to think of its opposite: 'to be or not to be'. No question is avoided: 'What should such fellows as I do crawling between earth and heaven?' (III. i. 130–1). Every observation leads quickly outward to its universal implications: 'Alexander died, Alexander was buried, Alexander returneth to dust; the dust is earth; of earth we make loam; and why of that loam whereto he was converted might they not stop a beer-barrel?' (V. i. 231–5).

For a mind of such range the past is always a part of the present, and the sight of a skull in a graveyard brings Adam and Eve, Cain and Abel, Caesar and Alexander to join in death with yesterday's rich lawyer and great lady. To a mind so aware of history, the ghosts of the dead appear and speak. The first act of the play is filled with the voices of fathers and father-surrogates – Claudius, Gertrude, Laertes, Polonius – advising caution, restraint and acceptance of what must be. But then comes the voice of another father from another world, from the realm of spirit; the voice of a great king speaking terrible truths which allow no paltering or temporizing; the voice of a true father speaking to a son, as fathers always seem to sons to speak, of a simple, uncomplicated ethic, of courage, steadfastness, honesty, simple piety, high honour and all the other noble virtues that gather around the idealized memories of Old Hamlet. This is the voice of the heroic past which always calls out to those who can hear it, 'adieu! Remember me', which is always present to the 'mind's eye' of such minds as Hamlet's, and which always lays fearful duties on those to whom it speaks, demanding revenge for its murder.

Claudius and Hamlet, politician and philosopher, rhetorician and poet, sense and imagination, body and mind, that which moves to death and that which seeks eternal life, these are the 'mighty opposites' whose conflict is the plot of the play. But that plot twists and turns away from the central conflict to follow out hundreds of seemingly false leads; the action rises to moments of such intensity as to promise immediate resolution, only to fall abruptly to moments of extraordinary stillness; confrontations dwindle into philosophic discussions, and a passing encounter rises in an instant to a shouting crisis. Almost anything and everything is discussed, the shape of the clouds, the nature of women, the art of playing, the values of stoicism, the management of the duello, the fate of the soul. If the chief character enters in confidence, he leaves in despair; whatever mood he is in when he exits will almost certainly not be his mood when he next appears; if bent on revenge at one moment he seems utterly to have forgotten it the next. Issues are raised only to lead to a blank wall of unanswered questions: is it a true or false ghost? did Ophelia love Hamlet and he her? does Gertrude know of the murder of her first husband? Though criticism has spent a great deal of time trying to find the answers to these questions, they are as impossible to resolve as are the more difficult moral and metaphysical problems raised by the play: 'to be or not to be', the validity of the ethic of revenge, the nature and existence of the afterworld, the value of thought, the nature of madness.

Baffling multiplicity, disjunction and absence of absolute truth are not the products of poor dramatic craftsmanship, but are rather the objective correlatives of the mysterious, tragic world of Elsinore, of the indirectness and deviousness with which its usurping king thinks and moves, and of the range and darting complexity of the hero's mind. But the plot moves gradually towards its own clarification and finally summarizes itself in the last scene, the duel in the throne-room. Like so many other occasions in *Hamlet*, the duel is presented as a perfectly ordinary event, a harmless game; but underneath, as both Hamlet and Claudius know, it is in deadly earnest. At the forward edge of the stage stand the two duellists, Hamlet and Laertes. This is exactly right, for Claudius's habitual way of working is never to engage Hamlet directly but to approach him through one of the indifferent children of the earth, most often one of the Polonius family, and now he is using the last of them. Horatio stands in his characteristic relationship to Hamlet, serving as his second – 'one, in suff'ring all, that suffers nothing' (III. ii. 71) – understanding but not acting, on the edge of the action, not at the hot centre where the hero must choose and die alone. Osric, the parody figure of all those who serve the king, serves as referee. Upstage, seated on their thrones, regarding the action, are the king, acting as always the benign ruler, and the queen, as little knowing as she is elsewhere. Gathered around are the courtiers, 'the mutes' or 'audience' to the event, unaware that all is not as it seems to be. On stage are two symbols, religious and sexual, of the values at stake in this struggle: the cup of wine and the rapier, both poisoned by a king who has already used this method literally to kill his brother and figuratively to corrupt the court and blast the most vital human relationships.

The fencing match recapitulates exactly the basic plot of the play. The rapid thrust and parry of the foils, the dextrous feint, the swift lunge and the quick guard make visible the continuing attempts of Hamlet and Claudius to penetrate one another's guard. The flickering weapons, almost invisible, but deadly, visualize precisely the quality of the earlier struggles. And here as before, Hamlet despite his disadvantages does a great deal better than expected and proves more than a match for the last of Claudius's agents. Chance plays a crucial part in the plot of the play – the fortuitous discovery that the voyage to England was a voyage to death, and the subsequent lucky encounter with the pirates – and it reappears in the scuffle where the poisoned rapier is dropped, accidentally picked up by Hamlet, and used unknowingly to give Laertes his death wound. Pleased with her son's showing, Gertrude drinks to him and dies from the poison concealed in the 'union'. The ignorance and limitation of understanding which before killed the spirit now kill the body as well. No pretences, no agents, no doubts now stand between Claudius and Hamlet, and the prince advances on his uncle-father to stab him with the poisoned foil, force him to drink the cup he has prepared and reveal him at last for what he is: 'thou incestuous, murd'rous, damned Dane' (V. ii. 317). Hamlet's death is as inevitable as the others, and the death wound he receives from the poisoned foil in the match is but the last of those poisonous wounds, the thousand natural shocks that flesh is heir to, which cannot be avoided in Elsinore.

This last scene is a great theatrical *tour de force*, a play within a play which contains in short form its container; and as such it reminds us that the theatre itself is the chief metaphor for life in *Hamlet* and the key to whatever meaning it will finally yield. Locked in their own preoccupations – sorrow, love, fear – the characters of the play never question their own reality, but the surface of that reality is constantly breaking apart to reveal the theatrical qualities of life in Elsinore. The possibility that men are actors and their world a play is constantly suggested by words like act, shape, play, perform, stage, counterfeit, paint, shadow, mirror, plot, show, part, put on, trappings, motive, cue, prologue, audience and scene. The light suggestions of these words become explicit when the play becomes a play within the play, as in the long speech from *The Murder of Priam* or the presentation of *The Murder of Gonzago*. These internal plays and the theatrical imagery force awareness that there are few moments in the play which are not a play within the play. When Claudius and Polonius arrange a scene in which Ophelia pretends to pray in order to draw Hamlet out, while they stand like an audience behind the arras; when Polonius sends a messenger to his son in

Paris, advising the man to pretend that he does not know Laertes while asking leading questions about his way of life; when Hamlet leaps into Ophelia's open grave, mouthing high heroic sorrow, to show a Laertes as yet un-accustomed to death the ridiculousness of excessive, melodramatic expres-sions of grief; when Claudius stages the fencing match – in these and many other places the 'play' quality of life is apparent. It is equally present, though more muted, in the pretences of Rosencrantz and Guildenstern to be faithful friends, of Claudius to be a kind and gentle king and of Hamlet to be mad.

Hamlet begins by disliking intensely all forms of playing and pretence. When we first encounter him in the throne-room of Elsinore, his mother is quizzing him about his unrelenting sorrow for the death of his father. Since death is to be expected, she argues, 'Why seems it so particular with thee?' To which Hamlet replies:

> Seems, madam! Nay, it is; I know not seems.
> 'Tis not alone my inky cloak, good mother,
> Nor customary suits of solemn black,
> Nor windy suspiration of forc'd breath,
> No, nor the fruitful river in the eye,
> Nor the dejected haviour of the visage,
> Together with all forms, moods, shapes of grief,
> That can denote me truly. These, indeed, seem;
> For they are actions that a man might play;
> But I have that within which passes show –
> These but the trappings and the suits of woe. (I. ii. 76–86)

This is an expression of the idealist's belief that the reality within exceeds any of the outward forms in which it must be expressed, and the suspicion of 'seems' is intensified by the knowledge that the actor's and costumer's arts can be used to conceal rather than reveal the truth. Such a suspicion is in-evitable in Elsinore where nothing is quite what it seems to be and where everything changes from moment to moment. The queen who had once seemed so virtuous a wife and mother is now revealed as a woman of pro-nounced sexual appetites, Ophelia who had once seemed another Juliet is only a timid daughter, the trusted friends of childhood are betrayers and the man who had once been a most hopeful prince is now an object of mockery in his own palace, a disappointed cynic and an ineffective melancholic. If what seems most sure can change so to its opposite, then Hamlet can only conclude that the original image of virtue was only a seeming, hiding the truth of human beastliness.

But the man who despises playing is forced almost at once to 'put an antic disposition on' and pretend madness in order to protect himself from the suspicions of the king. Not to play in a world of players is dangerous. But to begin playing is to commit yourself to a power with hitherto unsuspected consequences. Almost at once it reveals an undesired truth – that there *is* a taint of madness in Hamlet's violent reactions to his world – and it serves as a means for discovering further truth. Wearing his madness Hamlet exposes the folly of the court, as he does in III. ii, where Polonius sagely agrees that a cloud looks like a camel, then like a weasel and then a whale. By the time he has finished nodding and smiling – 'By th' mass, and 'tis like a camel indeed' (395–6) – the old councillor stands nakedly revealed as a man with no mind of his own, who will agree to anything, no matter how contrary to sense, that authority and the interests of the moment suggest. But playing can reveal deeper truths. When the travelling company of players arrives in Elsinore, the leading tragedian delivers at Hamlet's request a speech from an old play about the death of Priam. The situation in Troy has marked similarities to that in Elsinore, for in both places a great king has been killed and a queen has sorrowed. But the heroic manner of death and sorrow in Troy, and the attention of the universe itself to those events, contrast greatly with the shabby reality of the way in which Old Hamlet was poisoned and Gertrude hastily married the murderer, and nothing seems changed. Playing can, then, present the idealized life which actuality falls so far short of; but it can do even more, for the player who is only pretending – 'What's Hecuba to him or he to Hecuba' (II. ii. 585) – expresses fully and powerfully the appropriate feelings of anger and sorrow, while Hamlet, who has actually had a father killed and a mother stained, can only 'peak, Like John-a-dreams, unpregnant of [his] cause, And can say nothing' (594–6). Far from concealing truth, playing may be the only means of holding 'the mirror up to nature; to show virtue her own feature, scorn her own image, and the very age and body of the time his form and pressure' (III. ii. 22–6). The proof of this comes in an instant when a play, *The Mousetrap* or *The Murder of Gonzago*, catches 'the conscience of the king' by re-enacting his crime before him, revealing the truth to him and to others. The same method works again with the queen when Hamlet shows her the pictures of Old Hamlet and Claudius side by side and forces her to see for the first time what she has actually done. The same point is made in another more indirect way shortly afterwards when Hamlet encounters the army of Fortinbras on the way to fight and die in Poland – 'Even for an eggshell' (IV. iv. 53) – and understands that, while this war has neither sufficient cause nor reward to justify it, it is still an act of great courage which makes real man's dream of glory and honour by means of a pretence.

Man pretends in order to be real; only in disguise can truth be found; seeming alone can mirror being: in some such paradoxical form the truth slowly emerges. In relation to Hamlet's most immediate problem, however, this truth can best be stated: to act – in the sense of doing – is to act – in the sense of playing. From the beginning his problem has been to move from despair, passivity and the complexities of his own thought into the realm of action. His defects are, of course, equally his virtues, and only those qualities of mind which make it so difficult for him to act make him sensitive enough to recognize his enemy and clever enough to avoid being led from his true self and used like those other young men, Laertes and Fortinbras, who have also lost fathers and seek revenge. Only by playing can he further the desired revenge and express that within which, he once thought, 'passes show'. And only by understanding reality as pretence, the world as play, can he finally see what life truly is. The revelation comes in the graveyard where Hamlet meets, in undisguised form, the grinning skull, the antagonist – death, decay, mutability – with whom he has really been struggling in various disguised forms from the outset. All will end in the vast kingdom of death: the great lady with her fine clothes and cosmetics, the lawyer with all his skills and arguments, the rich landowner with his deeds and charters, the conquerors like Caesar and Alexander. And since all will at last end as a bare skull, a heap of bones and ultimately as a handful of dust, life is only a pretence, a role of the moment, which will end in the enduring reality of earth. This perception is coupled with the realization that life is also like a play in that the plot is not controlled by the players but by an unknown, distant author. This 'dramatic' understanding comes to Hamlet on his sea voyage where he escapes Claudius's plot to have him executed in England, not by his own will or cunning but by the merest good chance. On his return to Denmark he is a greatly changed man – calmer, more serene, more willing to accept his world in all its bewildering complexity – who can at last face the fact of death without being overwhelmed by it. He now accepts his player's status – 'There's a divinity that shapes our ends, Rough-hew them how we will' (V. ii. 10–11) – and places his trust in the author who, however mysterious, is still sensed as beneficent:

there is a special providence in the fall of a sparrow. If it be now, 'tis not to come; if it be not to come, it will be now; if it be not now, yet it will come – the readiness is all. Since no man owes of aught he leaves, what is 't to leave betimes? Let be. (V. ii. 230–6)

This is not resignation but acceptance – a willingness to do what must be done in circumstances beyond control – and the trust in 'divinity' and 'providence' is not misplaced. Even as Hamlet gives over his long-continued attempts to contrive the revenge, it takes shape. Claudius arranges the occasion which will at last betray him, providence manifests itself not in the fall of a sparrow but of a poisoned rapier, and Hamlet, once the great idealist, is ready for his assigned role.

One of the most remarkable features of Shakespearian drama is that the *dramatis personae* are curious about and determined to find answers to exactly the same questions that inevitably occur to readers and critics. The most obvious instance of this occurs regularly at the end of the tragedies where the survivors gather to ask, usually without much success, what really happened? why did it happen? what did it mean? The questions which critics have put to *Hamlet* – is it a true ghost? is Hamlet actually mad? should he act or not act? does he think too much? is revenge an acceptable ethic? – are exactly the questions with which the characters are obsessed and to which they too demand absolute answers. No answers are forthcoming, and in the end Hamlet, though not his critics, accepts the mystery of existence and the darkness of fate, realizes that the world does not give the kind of certainty, truth and judgement which the educated and sensitive mind naturally desires. The play does not finally offer factual, moral, ethical and metaphysical truths, but shows life from a longer perspective in which man stands, questioning, analysing, categorizing, reasoning, suffering, acting, before the mysteries of his own nature and the baffling complexities of human existence. Shakespearian tragedy offers us not answers but the spectacle of men seeking answers and never finding quite what they seek. Such a view of life is implicit in the dramatic mode itself, and the constant linking of Hamlet's understanding of life and his understanding of the art of playing enforces the view that the play, far from being an unnatural artistic contrivance, is in fact a scheme of the human condition. What man seems to be at one moment, he is not at the next; and life may therefore correctly be imaged as an actor playing a series of parts. Since life is never entirely within man's control, he is thus accurately figured as an actor who thinks at any moment that he is making the plot while he is in fact only the creature of some distant author who has already laid down the inescapable order of events. Because absolute truth cannot be found, the world is like a play in which there can be no certainty, only the various views of different characters. 'What happens', the plot, alone finally provides such meaning as this most ironic of modes will yield. It is not finally the contents of a play, the subject matter, but the dramatic mode itself which holds 'the mirror up to nature; to show virtue her own feature, scorn her own image, and the very age and body of the time his form and pressure' (III. ii. 22–6). But in a most remarkable way, subject and form are identical in *Hamlet*, and from deep within the world of the theatre comes the voice of the Player King speaking the only truth which Hamlet will find *and* revealing the vision of reality which is at the basis of drama:

> Our wills and fates do so contrary run
> That our devices still are overthrown;
> Our thoughts are ours, their ends none of our own. (III. ii. 221–3)

8 'Banisht!':[1] the dark world of Jacobean tragedy

(i) The Italian palace

Sin there appearing in her sluttish shape,
Would soon grow loathsome, even to blushes' sense;
Surfeit would choke intemperate appetite,
Make the soul scent the rotten breath of lust.
When in an Italian lascivious palace,
A lady guardianless,
Left to the push of all allurement,
The strongest incitements to immodesty,
To have her bound, incens'd with wanton sweets,
Her veins fill'd high with heating delicates,
Soft rest, sweet music, amorous masquers,
Lascivious banquets, sin itself gilt o'er,
Strong fantasy tricking up strange delights,
Presenting it dress'd pleasing to sense,
Sense leading it unto the soul, confirm'd
With potent examples impudent custom,

---

[1] The famous opening word of John Webster's *The White Devil*.

Entic'd by that great bawd, opportunity;
Thus being prepar'd, clap to her easy ear
Youth in good clothes, well-shap'd, rich,
Fair-spoken, promising, noble, ardent, blood-full,
Witty, flattering, – Ulysses absent,
O Ithaca, can chastest Penelope hold out?

(*The Malcontent*, III. i. 186–207)

Throughout the sixteenth century the English poets elaborated a symbolic conflict between court and country, which passed into the drama in a variety of forms such as the journey from the city to the country and back to the city of Shakespearian comedy. But towards the end of the century the earlier balanced interaction of court and country, civilization and nature, art and feeling, began to break up. With increasing frequency the world of nature and the country were excluded from the drama, or appeared only as a memory of an older, better way of life, a lost golden world. The scene narrowed to the setting of a corrupt court: the Danish court of *Hamlet*, the French court of Chapman's plays, the court of imperial Rome – as described by Tacitus – in *Sejanus* and, most often, the Italian ducal palace as it had been described nearly a century before in Guicciardini's *Storia d'Italia*. Life is lived in the Italian palace with the greatest intensity and in the full flush of power and desire. Torchlight turns the darkness for an instant to an artificial noon, golden spurs put all life to a gallop, there is gunpowder in the court, wildfire flashes at midnight, wrath burns like flaming wax, and the delicious lip and sparkling eye invite. This is the place of 'three-piled flesh', and its corridors lead man to the extremes of his own being where he finds and loses himself in murder, madness, dream, violent sexuality, terror, death, torture and mirrors of his own self.

Here in the Italian palace the most humane impulses take their perverse forms. The Faustian dream of learning becomes the pedantry of the scholar who studies himself nearly blind to determine how many knots there were on Hercules's club, the shape of Caesar's nose and whether Hector had the tooth-ache. Medicine becomes a mad doctor beating his mad patient with urinals filled with rosewater. Religion becomes a melancholy cardinal denouncing his sister, whom he is trying to murder, for never having had her children christened. Morality is reduced to sententiae, the mere form of moral discourse, memorized in childhood and pronounced without conviction on any appropriate occasion. Service becomes pandering, law the tool of power, beauty the cosmetics covering ugliness, government the cynical exercise of the will of the ruler, and politics the employment of policy and Machiavellian intrigue. The world and man are now seen as corrupt and beastly:

> Think this: – this earth is the only grave and Golgotha wherein all things that live must rot; 'tis but the draught wherein the heavenly bodies discharge their corruption; the very muck-hill on which the sublunary orbs cast their excrements: man is the slime of this dung-pit, and princes are the governors of these men. . . . (*The Malcontent*, IV. ii. 141–7)

Nature no longer moves towards any sensible end, but works blindly and randomly, an enormous process of wastage:

> Now shall we see that Nature hath no end
> In her great works responsive to their worths;
> That she, that makes so many eyes and souls
> To see and foresee, is stark blind herself;
> And as illiterate men say Latin prayers
> By rote of heart and daily iteration,
> Not knowing what they say, so Nature lays
> A deal of stuff together, and by use,
> Or by the mere necessity of matter,
> Ends such a work, fills it, or leaves it empty
> Of strength or virtue, error or clear truth,
> Not knowing what she does. . . . (*Bussy d'Ambois*, V. ii. 1–12)

A great many explanations of various kinds have been offered for the intense pessimism of this drama. It is said by some to reflect the troubles and fears attendant on the last years of Elizabeth's reign and the transfer of power to James I,[1] while others have seen it as an expression of the Counter-Renaissance, the more general darkening of the hopes of Renaissance humanism expressed by Machiavelli, Montaigne and Hobbes.[2] Or the creation of this dark world with its cynical view of man and nature is said to be the work of a special group of coterie dramatists who wrote not for the public theatres with their broad representative audiences but for the private indoor theatres and the boys' companies with their small fashionable and intellectual audiences interested in advanced ideas and curious speculation.[3] All of these factors no

[1] This view is presented fully by P. N. Siegel, *Shakespearean Tragedy and the Elizabethan Compromise* (New York, 1957).

[2] Hiram Haydn, *The Counter-Renaissance* (New York, 1950); and Theodore Spencer, *Shakespeare and the Nature of Man* (New York, 1942).

[3] Alfred Harbage, *Shakespeare and the Rival Traditions* (New York, 1952).

doubt contributed to the popularity of the Italian palace as a dramatic setting, but it seems likely that the drama might have arrived at this crisis point by the pressure of its own internal logic.

The transition from Elizabethan to Jacobean is not an abrupt shift from the green Forest of Arden and the jolly Boar's Head tavern to the sinister palaces at Rome and Amalfi, but the gradual intensification of fears present from the beginning, in Tamburlaine's dream of empire, Faustus's magic, Hieronimo's revenge and Romeo's love. In the earlier drama, the fear remained slightly to one side of the action, like Revenge and Andrea watching *The Spanish Tragedy* unfold; was forgotten as a dream with the return of daylight, like the strange experiences in the forest outside Athens; or was ignored by a resumption of authority, like the unanswered questions put by the soldiers to Henry V. But the fears that man is fatally flawed, that his greatness and destruction are inextricably intertwined, that he and his world are at exact odds would not away, and at last found full, undisguised statement in that hell, figured by the Italian palace, where the hopes of man, carried in strange forms by the tortured successors of Tamburlaine, Romeo and Brutus, now seek their realization.

(ii) 'Virtue in labour with eternal chaos': the plays of Chapman, Marston and Tourneur

George Chapman (1559?–1634), soldier, philosopher, translator, poet and playwright, considered his great translation of Homer 'the work that I was born to do', and his reputation still rests more firmly on it than on his plays or such poems as *The Shadow of Night* (1594), the continuation of Marlowe's *Hero and Leander* (1598), or *The Tears of Peace* (1609). He began writing for the theatre in the mid-1590s and first produced a series of witty comedies, such as *All Fools* (1599) and *The Gentleman Usher* (1602), which neatly blended romance and humour; but between 1604 and 1612 he concentrated on tragedy: *The Tragedy of Bussy d'Ambois* (1604), the two-part *Conspiracy and Tragedy of Charles Duke of Byron* (1608), *The Revenge of Bussy d'Ambois* (1610), *The Tragedy of Chabot* (1612?) and *Caesar and Pompey* (1612?).

The most openly philosophical and political of the playwrights of his age, Chapman set his tragedies for the most part in the French court of the preceding century. The plays are ambivalent on such matters as the divine right of kings, but the court is treated unequivocally as a place of intrigue, corruption and 'policy', where great individual heroes struggle desperately to maintain their freedom and nobility of nature. Chapman was more gifted as a thinker and lyric poet than as a dramatist, and the background of the court is seldom a living reality – only a scheme of ideas – while the plot is most often an embarrassing piece of melodrama. What live in these tragedies are Chapman's great heroes, the 'Senecal Men', those tortured and agonized versions of the Marlovian overreacher who must strive to assert their virtues in a corrupt and confusing world:

> A heap 'tis of digested villainy;
> Virtue in labour with eternal chaos
> Press'd to a living death, and rack'd beneath it,
> Her throes unpitied, every worthy man
> Limb by limb sawn out of her virgin womb,
> To live here piecemeal tortur'd. . . . (*Caesar*, V. ii. 80–5)

No great order of nature or any universal plan supports these heroes in their struggles with society, and their own lives are as transient as a torch carried in the wind. They come to the court from some prelapsarian kingless green world and bring with them the 'native noblesse' of unfallen man, which expresses itself not so much as moral or ethical virtue as an energy, like the fire or the ocean (two of Chapman's most frequent images), seeking some transcendent unnameable fulfilment:

> 'Tis immortality to die aspiring,
> As if a man were taken quick to heaven;
> What will not hold perfection, let it burst;
> What force hath any cannon, not being charg'd,
> Or being not discharg'd? To have stuff and form,
> And to lie idle, fearful, and unus'd,
> Nor form nor stuff shows; happy Semele,
> That died compress'd with glory! Happiness
> Denies comparison of less or more,
> And not at most, is nothing. . . . (*Byron's Conspiracy*, I. ii. 31–40)

But as soon as this explosive 'virtù' enters the court – and the theatre with its demands for action and sensational event – it entangles itself with its own strength, loses its purity and moves inevitably towards its own destruction. Bussy, the greatest of Chapman's Senecal heroes, though he is said to be the guardian of virtue in the court, becomes the murderer of several men to avenge a slight to his honour, the surreptitious lover of the adulterous wife of one of the courtiers and, in general, something of a braggart and bully. Shot down ignobly from ambush by the hirelings of the jealous husband, he pulls himself painfully to his feet and, supported by his sword, attempts to recover his greatness in the only place in which it seems to be able to exist, great imaginative poetry:

My sun is turn'd to blood, in whose red beams
Pindus and Ossa (hid in drifts of snow,
Laid on my heart and liver) from their veins
Melt like two hungry torrents, eating rocks,
Into the ocean of all human life,
And make it bitter, only with my blood.
O frail condition of strength, valour, virtue,
In me (like warning fire upon the top
Of some steep beacon, on a steeper hill)
Made to express it: like a falling star
Silently glanc'd, that like a thunderbolt
Look'd to have stuck and shook the firmament. (V. iv. 135–46)

Charles, Duke of Byron, is filled with the same energies and natural noblesse as Bussy, but his fate is more openly ironic. His titanic sense of his worth and power blind him to the realities of himself and his situation, and he is an easy mark for politicians who flatter him outrageously, mock him to his face and use him for their own purposes. He seeks out chaos, willing to tear down the world in order to have the pleasure of re-creating it, and intrigues against a king, who though absolute is both wise and good, to gain the crown he believes nature entitles him to. Forgiven once for his treason, he returns to it again, and is at last executed, pretending a martyrdom to which the play does not entitle him.

The playwright seems at times as confused as his heroes by the failure of virtù to square with morality, and the heroes of his later tragedies retire more and more from the world of practical politics and the corrupt court in an attempt to preserve their own truth and goodness. Clermont d'Ambois, brother to Bussy, believes that ' 'tis better To live with little, and to keep within A man's own strength still' (III. iv. 52–4). Placing his trust in a universal design beyond human understanding, he looks from a distance on the confusions and corruptions of the court and nourishes his own philosophical virtues of moderation, quietness and self-discipline. Even this Stoic philosopher does not escape the world, however, and against his will he is forced by the ghost of Bussy to undertake a revenge which leads to the usual melodramatic murders and intrigues and ends with Clermont's suicide. Chabot is a just judge who believes the law to be above all personal interest and even the will of the absolute monarch, but when his judgement brings him into the conflict with the king, he tries to maintain both the power of the law and his allegiance to his ruler. In the end the king has his way, and Chabot dies of a broken heart. Pompey, the last of Chapman's heroes, accepts defeat by Caesar and the loss of worldly power as meaningless events, and turns inwards to create in himself the only satisfactory truth man can find in a corrupt world:

> I'll build all inward; not a light shall ope
> The common outway; no expense, no art,
> No ornament, no door will I use there,
> But raise all plain and rudely, like a rampier
> Against the false society of men
> That still batters
> All reason piecemeal, and, for earthy greatness,
> All heavenly comforts rarefies to air.
> I'll therefore live in dark, and all my light,
> Like ancient temples, let in at my top. (V. i. 206–15)

With the death of Chapman's patron, Prince Henry, in 1612, Chapman too seems to have withdrawn into himself and published little from this time until his death.

John Marston (1576–1635) brought both his subject matter and his hero to the stage from his verse satires, *Pygmalion's Image and Certain Satires* (1598) and *The Scourge of Villainy* (1598–9), with which he began his literary career. Before going to prison in 1608 and taking orders in 1609, Marston wrote a number of plays for the Paul's Boys and the Children of the Chapel – *Antonio and Mellida* (1600), *Antonio's Revenge* (1601), *The Malcontent* (1604), *The Fawn* (1605) and *Sophonisba* (1606) – in which he transferred the characteristic fools and villains of verse satire – the luxury-loving lord, the lying traveller, the wastrel squire, the lascivious wife – to the stage and to the setting of the corrupt ducal palace.[1] This transformation of English folly to Italian vice was accompanied by the dramatization of that 'Tamburlaine of Vice', the satyr-satirist, a composite of Old Testament prophet, Stoic philosopher, Calvinist zealot and sadistic, lecherous satyr, developed in the late sixteenth century as the appropriate persona for speaking 'satyre'.

---

[1] The transfer of the materials of verse satire to the stage and the development of the dramatic satirist are the subjects of Alvin Kernan, *The Cankered Muse, Satire of the English Renaissance* (New Haven, 1959).

Vicious, harsh, lascivious and utterly merciless, the satirist attacks others partly out of moral outrage and a desire to correct and partly out of the pleasure to be derived from whipping. Guilty of many sins of his own, he is blind to his own weaknesses but absolutely intolerant of those of other men. Pessimistic about the possibility of change, he none the less continues to use violent means to effect a cure. He concentrates his attention in an obsessive way on the shocking, the lurid and the sexual; seeks out unerringly the scandalous, the abnormal, the rotting; and denounces these in a 'stuttering style', mixing the crude and the sublime, now as vulgar as a fishwife, now as lofty as Cicero.

This strange combination of heroic scourge of vice and peeping Tom was an appropriate defender of virtue in a drama of disillusion, and the satirist appears in a number of plays of the time: Jaques in *As You Like It*, Macilente in *Every Man out of his Humour*, Thersites in *Troilus and Cressida*, Malevole in *The Malcontent*, Flamineo in *The White Devil*. Traces of him are present in such characters as Hamlet and Lear, who become satirists during their mad periods, before passing on to tragic acceptance of their own inescapable involvement in the complexities of what cannot be changed. While Marston's poetry and plays provide the clearest history of the development of the satyr-satirist, this figure appears in his most interesting form in Tourneur's *The Revenger's Tragedy*.

We are not certain when Cyril Tourneur was born, probably about 1580, but we do know that he sailed in 1625 with the expedition against Cadiz and that he died in Ireland on 28 February 1626 as a result of illness contracted during the voyage. His widow, Mary, was left 'destitute of all means of livelihood' as a result of her husband's death. From 1613 onwards Tourneur was connected with government business, which at one point provided him with a pension, at another led to his arrest, and towards the end of his life brought him to serve as secretary to the Council of War. His literary career began in 1600 with the publication of a satirical poem, *The Transformed Metamorphosis*. Several other occasional and satiric poems are associated with him, and in 1611 a play, *The Atheist's Tragedy*, was published with his name on the title page. This heavy-handed morality play, which proves the evil of atheism, Machiavellianism, lust and naturalism, would not alone have recommended Tourneur very strongly to posterity, but in the year 1607 an anonymous play, *The Revenger's Tragedy*, was published, and in 1656, in a list of plays attached to Edward Archer's *The Old Law*, *The Revenger's Tragedy* is attributed to Tourneur. This attribution has been endlessly questioned in our own century, and a number of critics have argued very plausibly that the play was in fact written by Thomas Middleton. At the present time no one, not even those who have thrown themselves into the controversy, knows with any certainty who did write the play. My own preference is for Tourneur, and I shall speak of him as the author.

The setting of the play is the usual Italian ducal palace, ruled by a lecherous, senile duke who still lusts after young bodies. His legitimate son and heir, Lussurioso, is merely an ambulant appetite eternally in search of new objects of pleasure; the bastard son Spurio loathes his father for begetting him out of wedlock and gets revenge by allowing himself to be seduced by his stepmother, the present duchess. She, along with her three vicious children, Ambitioso, Supervacuo and the unnamed younger son, Junior, are proud, vain, lustful and utterly empty-headed. The play opens with these seven deadly dukes passing silently across the stage carrying torches, and as they live their brief theatrical moment, a disembodied voice comments upon them:

> Duke: royall letcher; goe, gray hayrde adultery,
> And thou his sonne, as impious steept as hee:
> And thou his bastard true-begott in evill:
> And thou his Dutchesse that will doe with Divill. . . . (I. i. 1–4)

The voice is that of Vindici, a melancholic country gentleman whose family and fortunes have been blasted by the ducal powers. In his hand he carries the skull of his betrothed, Gloriana, who was poisoned by the duke after she refused to submit to him, and that 'terror to fat folkes' is the touchstone by which Vindici tests all life. Against its truth all life becomes meaningless busyness and ridiculous vanity:

> Do's the Silke-worme expend her yellow labours
> For thee? for thee dos she undoe herselfe?
> Are Lord-ships sold to maintaine Lady-ships
> For the poore benefit of a bewitching minute?
> Why dos yon fellow falsify hie-waies
> And put his life betweene the Judges lippes,
> To refine such a thing, keepes horse and men
> To beate their valours for her?
> Surely wee're all mad people. . . . (III. v. 75–83)

Vindici is the ultimate satirist who tries all life against the only reality of death, and throughout the play his cynicism pierces the brilliant surface of

court life to the reality of a dark world of decay and death which lies beneath
the pretences of nobility, virtue and love:

> Now tis full sea a bed over the world;
> Theres iugling of all sides; some that were Maides
> E'en at Sun set are now perhaps ith Toale-booke;
> This woman in immodest thin apparell
> Lets in her friend by water, here a Dame
> Cunning, nayles lether-hindges to a dore,
> To avoid proclamation.
> Now Cuckolds are a quoyning, apace, apace, apace, apace.
> And carefull sisters spinne that thread ith night,
> That does maintaine them and their bawdes ith daie! (II. ii. 152–61)

His function as satirist revealing sin finds its active expression in the role of
revenger, and each step in repaying this 'nest of dukes' for the wrongs done
his family is at the same time a satiric exposure of men's viciousness. Disguised as the pander Piato, he works his way into Lussurioso's favour and
reveals the venality of womankind by persuading his own mother to 'thinke
upon the pleasure of the Pallace' and earn the rewards of 'secured ease and
state' by prostituting her daughter to the young heir's lust. Operating as a
scrambling intriguer within the court, Vindici-Piato sets the ducal family at
odds and reveals them for what they are by arranging scenes in which the
old duke sees his wife as the whore she is, in which Lussurioso thinks to find
Spurio in the duchess's bed and in which Lussurioso threatens his father's life.
The masterpiece of the satirist-revenger is the assignation he arranges for the
old duke, who has asked Piato to procure a lusty young wench for him. To
fulfil his commission, Piato dresses the skull of Gloriana in rich robes and
smears its mouth with poison. The resulting scene in which the duke comes to
the gloomy meeting place, embraces and hungrily kisses the skull and then
dies in torture is at once an implementation of Vindici's revenge and a demonstration of the satirist's view that lust is the meeting of skulls and the embrace-
ment of poison and death.

You can, Vindici says, 'deceive men, but cannot deceive wormes', but he
thinks of himself as free of the depravity and stupidity which it is his heroic
mission to scourge. But virtue is an impossibility in the world of the Italian
palace, and even heroic and moral impulses take strange, perverse forms,
turning at last into their opposites. Both as satirist and revenger, Vindici is
unstable and excessive. As satirist, he is fascinated with the corruption he
anatomizes, seeks it out and encourages it where it exists only as a possibility,

and scourges more for the delight of scourging than for moral reformation. As revenger he delights in fiendish ingenuity and unnecessary cruelty. He nails down the tongue of the old duke with a dagger, threatens to tear open his eyelids 'and make his eyes like Comets shine through bloud'. He exclaims with savage excitement – and poor critical judgement – 'When the bad bleedes, then is the Tragedie good' (III. v. 216). When Hippolito is recommending his brother, Vindici, to Lussurioso as a pander, he praises him by saying, 'This our age swims within him' (I. iii. 27), and this is true, for in this *danse macabre* Vindici has become but one skeleton leading other skeletons to the grave. At the end of the play, when Vindici and Hippolito fall upon Lussurioso, they seem in their savagery and ferocity to be determined to beat life into the death which they consider the ultimate reality. After this carnage, when the new duke, Antonio, wonders at the mysterious fashion in which the old duke was murdered, Vindici and Hippolito admit that the crime was theirs and add, with the pride of craftsmen, 'Twas some-what witty carried tho we say it'. Reasoning that if they found it so easy and so delightful to kill one duke, they might find it equally pleasant to kill another, Antonio has the brothers hauled away to swift execution.

In the end Vindici is trapped in an ironic, reflexive action which seems to be the fundamental pattern of Tourneur's world. A man reaches for what he feels he must have, only to grasp his own destruction. Lussurioso seeks a pander to instrument his desires and brings Vindici into the palace; Ambitioso and Supervacuo race to the prison with the duke's signet to order the immediate execution of Lussurioso, the brother who stands between them and power, and succeed only in ordering the execution of the younger brother, Junior, whom they had planned to save; the old duke arranges an assignation where he anticipates new pleasures, only to find himself embracing the 'bony lady'. The surprise of Lussurioso, who goes to his stepmother's bedroom to expose the incestuous Spurio and finds himself jailed for threatening his own father, is no greater than the surprise of Vindici who revenges his family and exterminates the nest of dukes, only to find that he is himself as depraved as anything he has destroyed, and that 'Tis time to die, when we are our selves our foes' (V. iii. 154).

(iii) 'Short sillables must stand for periods': the plays of John Webster

John Webster (1580?–1630?) may have studied law, but he apparently made his living as a playwright, usually working in collaboration. Only three plays attributed solely to him have survived: *The White Devil* (1612), *The Duchess of Malfi* (1614) and *The Devil's Law Case* (1616?), but these are enough to place Webster in the front rank of the English dramatists. Of the playwrights considered in this chapter, Webster alone manages to link his characters fully and meaningfully to his sensational settings and plots, and he alone manages, in two very different ways, to salvage from his strange and violent characters some belief in the grandeur, goodness and ultimate value of life lived in the darkest of worlds.

The setting of Webster's plays is the usual corrupt Italian palace filled with all the most sensational varieties of intrigue, hatred and lust, while the plots are melodramatic collections of violent incidents of murder, revenge, torture and madness. The bizarre settings and events are, however, made acceptable, even inevitable, by a style which creates and keeps constantly before us the deep perverse energies of the mind. True life is lived at great depths where restless currents stir until they surge to the surface in sudden, violent, bizarre words and actions. Normal acts, and even normal vices, are performed in a curious offhand way – like the cardinal who keeps a mistress and gambles only because these vices are expected of him. A still portrait of a courtier eating at this patron's table reveals both the placid surface and the turbulent depths:

> I have seene some,
> Feed in a Lords dish, halfe asleepe, not seeming
> To listen to any talke: and yet these Rogues
> Have cut his throat in a dreame. . . . (*Duchess of Malfi*, I. i. 308–11)

Such moments of quiescence are rare, however, and ordinarily the dream is struggling for release and realization: breaking through the metre in quick, nervous offbeat rhythms; racing outward in a rush of ideas which disrupt logic and grammar; exploding in expletives and brief, fragmented sentences; carrying to the surface a flood of images so strange that they could only come from the depths of a mind concerned scarcely at all with the aptness of the comparison but obsessed with the odd shapes forming within: a red eye to a needle used for stitching wounds, malice to a glass hammer, a mirror to the congealed blood of witches, a courtier in white satin to a black-nosed maggot, obtaining a woman's forgiveness to lighting a 'bonefire' at the bottom of the sea. 'Short sillables, Must stand for periods' (*Malfi*, III. ii. 214–15), says one of Webster's characters, and the line catches perfectly the breathless, staccato rhythms of Webster's verse and plot. Entrances and exits are abrupt, unexpected actions explode in the midst of moments of quiet, life flares up in brief intense spasms, there seems little continuity between events, and the speed of passage is breathtaking. In *The White Devil* the Duke of Brachiano looks at the beautiful Vittoria, and in a moment he is 'Quite lost'. Almost instantaneously we are watching the murder of Brachiano's duchess and Vittoria's husband, and even as they die, the duchess's brothers, Francisco de Medici and the Cardinal Monticelso, are trying Vittoria before a public tribunal and condemning her to a house for penitent whores. In a moment more she has escaped to Brachiano's palace, where Francisco's revenge at last contrives the savage extermination of herself, her lover and her family. The play is plentifully sprinkled with moral speeches and ethical judgements, but its power lies not in a demonstration of moral truth but in the force with which it presents the dark energies of the self uncoiling and striking whatever opposes them. 'My greatest sinne lay in my blood,' says Vittoria, 'Now my blood paies for't' (V. vi. 240–1). This is the reality *The White Devil* dramatizes, and to prate about it, as Flamineo says, were idle. Thunder, not flattering bells, is the fitting funeral sound for those who have sought 'paine by paine' and died in a mist.

In Webster's finest play, *The Duchess of Malfi*, the setting is again an Italian ducal palace with its intrigues, its struggles for favour on the slippery ice of court, its savage appetites, its desperate political and moral cynicism, its demented minds and its perversions of all social values and traditional humane professions. Daniel Bosola was once a scholar at Padua who studied himself melancholy without gaining advancement. Seeking to make his way in the world, he committed several murders for the Cardinal and was condemned to a number of years as a galley slave. Arriving at the palace at Amalfi as the play opens, he presses his claims on the Cardinal and is rewarded, covertly, with the job of master of the stables and made a spy in the household of the Cardinal's sister, the Duchess of Malfi. There is still enough honesty in Bosola to recognize the baseness of spying, and enough virtue to hesitate to do some of the foul jobs he is put to, but his suffering in the galleys has so coloured his view of life that he can laugh at himself for any hesitations of virtue or impulses to honesty. This world, he knows, is no more than one huge hospital 'where this mans head lies at that mans foote, and so lower, and lower' (I. i. 68–9); all appearances of love are no more than the masks of appetite; a man's face is no more to be credited than a sick man's urine; an offer of gold immediately raises the question 'whose throat must I cut?'; and everyone grows and prospers like the master of the stables, 'out of horse-doong'. In such a world a poor and powerless man can only hang like a leech on the ears of the great until he is filled with blood, and then drop off; but

Bosola hangs on too long, and dies in a confused scuffle, trying, ironically, for once to do good.

In the animal imagery of the play, the Duchess's brother, the Cardinal, is the snake, cold, coiled, impassive, deadly. He dances, courts ladies, fights duels and wagers fortunes on a tennis match, but 'such flashes' only 'super-ficially hang on him, for forme' (I. i. 157), and beneath this surface of anima-tion there is something flat and dead, passionless. When his own nature surprisingly rebels against his cruelty, he is only bored – 'How tedious is a guilty conscience!' (V. v. 4) – and he is more bemused than terrified when, from below the depths of ennui, some strange threatening form comes sliding to the surface:

> When I looke into the Fish-ponds, in my Garden,
> Me thinkes I see a thing, arm'd with a Rake
> That seemes to strike at me. . . . (V. v. 5–7)

Ferdinand, Duke of Calabria and brother to the Cardinal and the Duchess, is as violent as his brother is cold; and there is truth in his boast:

> He that can compasse me, and know my drifts,
> May say he hath put a girdle 'bout the world,
> And sounded all her quick-sands. (III. i. 104–6)

He is the Machiavellian tyrant, ingenious, imperious, sudden and savagely cruel. His courtiers may not laugh unless he does, and his laughter is the fore-runner of death, 'a deadly Cannon, That lightens ere it smoakes' (III. iii. 66–7). But it is his strange relationship to his sister, the Duchess, that sounds the quicksands of his being. As the play opens, Ferdinand and the Cardinal are taking their leaves of their recently widowed sister and warning her not to remarry lest she dishonour the name of her dead husband and adulterate the family blood. If a trifle strict, their admonitions seem at first reasonable enough, but the opposition to marriage is carried on at such length, with such vehemence and with such extravagance of phrase and curiosity of image that some unspoken motive, not entirely within the control of the men it is driving, begins to appear. It becomes more obvious when, upon learning later that the Duchess has had a child, Ferdinand's imagination carries him into her bedroom to watch her in the act with 'some strong-thigh'd Barge-man' or with 'some lovely Squire That carries coles up, to her privy lodgings'. He longs to make a sponge of her heart to wipe the memory from his brain, imagines himself a tempest tearing down her palace and laying waste to her kingdom, dreams of making a stew of the child to feed to its parents, and plans to wrap the adulterous couple in sheets of pitch and sulphur and light them like a match. His actual revenge is little less terrible than those imagined. He meets the Duchess in the dark and, pretending amity, gives her a dead man's hand, drives her from her palace and separates her from her husband and children, tries to drive her to despair by telling her of the death of her family and forcing her to endure a vision of a mad world and, at last, orders the death by strangulation of herself, her maid and her infant children. Ferdinand enters to regard the body in a curiously flat, unemotional manner, as if all passion had been spent: 'Cover her face: Mine eyes dazell: she di'd yong' (IV. ii. 281). But then revulsion overwhelms him, he reveals the unknown fact that the Duchess was his twin, turns on the murderer and blames him for her death, and at last goes mad, turning into a werewolf stalking the night, scratching open graves and carrying pieces of dismembered bodies. In his lycanthropia he still suffers an agony of guilt and cries out to the watch which apprehends him to kill his wolfish part. Unrealized incestuous desires seem the obvious explanation, but Ferdinand believes that he pursued his sister to her death only to inherit her possessions, and the play leaves his motivation a mystery about which many guesses but no certainties are possible.

In order to emphasize the inexplicable and inescapable involvement of life and death, good and evil, love and hatred, the drama of this period frequently makes members of the same family represent radically different values – Lear's three daughters, for example, or Old Hamlet and Claudius. In *The Duchess of Malfi* the murderous, death-directed brethren have a sister who resembles them in absoluteness and suddenness, but who moves always towards delight, love and life. The Duchess is one of the great romantic heroines of English drama, impulsive, impatient of social proprieties, straightforward, warm, sensual and elegantly feminine. She listens to her kinsmen warning of the dangers of hasty remarriage while already having made an appointment with the man she loves, her steward Antonio. Impatient of his conventional attitudes, she directly proposes marriage to him rather than waiting for his slow avowals. She considers private vows of love between them more binding than the ceremonies of the church; and once married she becomes pregnant immediately and produces children, whom she loves most dearly, with unladylike speed. Frankly sensual and honest, the Duchess is never gross or vulgar, and the private scenes with Antonio in her bedroom – the greatest scenes of intimacy in Renaissance drama – are wonderful mixtures of vanity and love, coquettishness and frankness, sexuality and delicacy.

One of the distinctive features of the Renaissance drama is its persistent, easy maintenance of a double focus. On the one hand, it has a distinct impulse towards social and psychological realism, which is balanced, on the other, by an equally strong impulse towards symbolism and myth. In Webster, realism and symbolism blend indistinguishably, for the pathological feelings and extreme actions which are the basis of his realism are so extravagant and outsized that they assume symbolic proportions. Even while the characters invite us by their strange words and actions to psychoanalyse them and search for their motives, that strangeness suggests that they are more symbols than representations of real men, and forces us to view them and their world from a long-range perspective. Looked at from the distance required for a symbolic reading, the palace at Amalfi loses its specificity and becomes a generalized world of torture, pain, disease, darkness and death. Ferdinand, Bosola and the Cardinal lose their individuality and become death spirits perverting and interrupting pleasure and life. They forbid and ruin marriage, they imprison and torture, they murder women and children and at last they run mad like animals and stab one another blindly in a bestial scramble on the floor among the rushes in the darkness.

Seen in this long perspective, the generous and sensual Duchess expands into a spirit of life and growth. The private world she creates around her is one of light, pleasure, laughter, marriage and fertility. Whatever she touches she nourishes; scorning social distinctions she reaches down to raise her servant up to her; scoffing at the rites and ceremonies of the church she is a part of the 'eternal church' of nature itself; joined in love she increases and multiplies with all the generosity of nature itself. Her images are the fertile palm, the harmonious spheres and the heavenly power of music. Her favours are not broadcast like those of the primitive goddess, all belly, breasts and buttocks; her love is not cruel like that of the poised and indifferent Aphrodite; and her gaze is not fixed on the next world like a pale and virginal madonna rapt in a vision of God: the Duchess is the Eros figure of Renaissance humanism, fertile but faithful, sensual but delicate, generous but civilized.

The plot of the play is ultimately a conflict between the two primal forces in the universe, the powers of destruction and the powers which nourish life. This struggle reaches its climax in Act IV where the Duchess's family has been broken apart and she is forced to endure the tortures contrived by her mad brother Ferdinand. Imprisoned and isolated from those she loves, the Duchess sits silent and brooding for hours together. Then, after Ferdinand has pressed the icy print of a dead hand on her heart and after she has seen the tableau of the dead bodies of her husband and children, she arrives at despair:

> There is not betweene heaven, and earth one wish
> I stay for after this: it wastes me more,
> Then were't my picture, fashion'd out of wax,
> Stucke with a magicall needle, and then buried
> In some fowle dung-hill. . . . (IV. i. 72–6)

Everywhere she turns, the Duchess meets only evidence of death and hatred, and so, like Lear on the heath, she threatens to curse the three smiling seasons of the year into an endless winter, to curse the world itself to chaos and to curse the stars themselves. The great medieval and Renaissance dream of a universe sympathetic with man and moving parallel to his moral laws comes crashing down in Bosola's flat observation of the ineffectiveness of her curse: 'Looke you, the Starres shine still' (IV. i. 120). Denied support by the heavens, she seeks it from the world but encounters only four madmen – an astrologer, a lawyer, a priest and a doctor – who are loosed to dance frantically and to sing of darkness, of animals, of despair and of a longing for death. The scene of human life which they offer is vile, petty and miserable. The great powers of nature, the force of love, the relationship of man with God, the operations of natural and human law, the benefits of the earth are reduced to trivia and mangled into a monstrous junk heap, something like the witches' cauldron in *Macbeth*. When they have finished their song of death, Bosola enters disguised as an old man, a tomb-maker, and summarizes the view of life implicit in all the death-dealing powers of the play. To the Duchess's shaken question, reminiscent of Lear, 'Who am I?' Bosola replies:

> Thou art a box of worme-seede, at best, but a salvatory of greene mummey: what's this flesh? a little cruded milke, phantasticall puffe-paste: our bodies are weaker than those paper prisons boyes use to keepe flies in: more contemptible: since ours is to preserve earth-wormes: didst thou ever see a Larke in a cage? such is the soule in the body: this world is like her little turfe of grasse, and the Heaven ore our heades, like her looking glasse, onely gives us a miserable knowledge of the small compasse of our prison. (IV. ii. 123–31)

But then comes the great serene answer of the play, all the more powerful for its brevity: 'I am Duchesse of *Malfy* still.' At this point the title, *Duchess of Malfi*, gathers into itself and focuses all those noble, generous and bene-ficent powers, that gay confidence in self and humankind, which have been established throughout the play as the life-nourishing forces. Where the lady's confidence derives from at the crucial moment, from what ultimate place that calm statement, 'I am Duchesse of *Malfy* still', wells up, we do not know; but the surety is suddenly there and it is never lost again. When the maid Cariola, realizing that she has arrived at the place of death, breaks in terror and begins to scream for her mistress to call for help, the Duchess's response is one of utter awareness of the situation and utter calmness: 'To whom, to our next neighbours? they are mad-folkes' (IV. ii. 200). The Duchess then dies by strangulation with absolute courage, still concerned for her children, still confident that there is 'excellent company' to be met in the next world and still loving that husband whose courage and intelligence fall so far short of hers. Even at the point of death her delicacy and care for her own person are not forgotten, and while she gives her life to the executioner she requests that her body be given to her women to be modestly prepared for burial.

Webster deprives his tragic hero of all support from outside the self for any belief in the goodness or meaning of life. The universe looks indifferently on human death; to any cry for help from the law, from medicine or from theology, there is only the mad babbling of the lawyer, the doctor and the priest; man's body informs him only of his weakness and the inevitability of corruption; his remembered life speaks only of continual uneasiness and sorrow; those he has loved and borne are dead before him; and his brothers are his murderers. The great world itself is nothing more than a dance of madmen, life is nothing more than death disguised, and death a desired release:

> Hearke, now every thing is still –
> The Schritch-Owle, and the whistler shrill,
> Call upon our Dame, aloud,
> And bid her quickly don her shrowd:
> Much you had of Land and rent,
> Your length in clay's now competent.
> A long war disturb'd your minde,
> Here your perfect peace is sign'd –
> Of what is't fooles make such vaine keeping?
> Sin their conception, their birth, weeping:
> Their life, a generall mist of error,
> Their death, a hideous storme of terror –
> Strew your haire, with powders sweete:

Don cleane linnen, bath your feete,
And (the foule feend more to checke)
A crucifixe let blesse your necke,
'Tis now full tide, 'tweene night, and day,
End your groane, and come away. (IV. ii. 180–97)

And yet in the midst of this terror the sound that lingers is one clear small voice, 'I am Duchess of *Malfy* still.'

From a moral point of view the difference between the Duchess of Malfi and Marlowe's old conqueror, Tamburlaine, is absolute; but the voice which threatened the kingdom of the gods and the voice which chatted so gaily in the bedroom at Amalfi, the hands that held the fates bound fast in iron chains and the arms which went around Antonio to create a circumference of love, these are all manifestations of the same power, the same belief in the ability of the human mind, the human voice and the human hand to re-create the world in the human image. But between 1588 and 1614 humanistic optimism found its way to some strange places and confronted some unexpected facts of its own nature. It had disappeared into hell with the despairing cry 'I'll burn my book'; it had stumbled through the wood outside Athens ever pursuing love and ever pursued by it; it had heard the words of a ghost on the battlements of Elsinore and found itself unable to execute the commanded revenge or comprehend the reason why it could not; it had found its coffers empty and seen its own idiocy in the workshop of a London alchemist; it had looked at Cressida toying with Diomed; and it had seen the face of Cordelia dead on the battlefield. And still its essential voice, that poetry which ranged from heaven to hell, unified all times and all things and transformed the world into the colours and shapes of the human imagination, continued to sound. In *The Duchess of Malfi*, the voice which once reached to the battlements of the gods is not quite stilled, but it is reduced to a single, simple line, 'I am Duchesse of *Malfy* still.'

Watching the Cardinal and Ferdinand laugh and plot the death of the Duchess, Delio refers to their speech as 'a deformed silence' (III. iii. 70), and this cryptic phrase suggests the ultimate fear that the human voice is no more than some strange sport of nature, some odd malformation of the true condition of things: total and endless silence. It is to this silence of interstellar space that the death-seeking figures go, after blindly stabbing one another to death on the floor in the darkness. The Cardinal goes back into that silence out of which he came: 'And now, I pray, let me Be layd by, and never thought of' (V. v. 112–13). For Bosola, all of them are 'onely like dead wals, or vaulted graves, That ruin'd, yeildes no eccho' (V. v. 121–2). The ultimate image of passage from silence to silence is provided by Delio looking down at the bodies strewing the rushes:

These wretched eminent things
Leave no more fame behind 'em, then should one
Fall in a frost, and leave his print in snow –
As soone as the sun shines, it ever melts,
Both forme, and matter. (V. v. 138–42)

'The rest is silence', says Hamlet at the end of his play, and in *The Duchess of Malfi* the silence seems to come when the Duchess dies at the end of the fourth act. But even death does not entirely still her voice. Ignorant of his wife's death, Antonio wanders about Milan, irredeemably innocent in his hope that he can be reconciled with Ferdinand and the Cardinal, and passes by the ruins of an ancient abbey. He pauses for a moment to reflect upon the vanity of human wishes and to remember sadly that here once lived good men who had thought that their works would endure for ever. But even in the visible ruins of hope, the silence is not total, for the old, broken walls give

the best Eccho, that you ever heard;
So hollow, and so dismall, and withall
So plaine in the destinction of our words,
That many have supposde it is a Spirit
That answeres. (V. iii. 5–9)

Then, echoing Antonio's words, out of the ruins comes the voice of the Duchess of Malfi, speaking of death and sorrow, warning of traps and dangers, and putting the final stamp on the absolute fact of death: 'never see her more'. Here is, as I understand it, the only affirmation that Webster is willing to provide to support the humanistic values his Duchess has embodied. All human things pass on to ruin, man and what he builds are mortal; but greatness of spirit, the values which construct and cherish, live and echo on in history. There is nothing at all supernatural about it, only the obvious fact that certain kinds of works and certain kinds of life speak out of the past into the present. Antonio's ability to reconstruct from the ruined forms of the abbey the goodness and the hopes of the men who once lived and built there, his own capability for sharing those same feelings, creates that echo-like dialogue between the past and the present which alone can comfort in an age where the universe has gone silent and the voice of society is no more than the babble of madmen.

9 The sight of the spider: Shakespeare's major tragedies

There may be in the cup
A spider steep'd, and one may drink, depart,
And yet partake no venom, for his knowledge
Is not infected; but if one present
Th' abhorr'd ingredient to his eye, make known
How he hath drunk, he cracks his gorge, his sides,
With violent hefts. I have drunk, and seen the spider.

(*The Winter's Tale*, II. i. 39–45)

(i) The tragic formula

Despite the swirling complexities of their worlds and the inability of their heroes to find any but the most provisional answers to the tragic questions, *Hamlet* and *Troilus*, along with the 'dark comedy' *Measure for Measure*, written about the same time, apparently led to a clarification and stabilization of the basic tragic situation for Shakespeare. In his next three tragedies, *Othello* (1604), *King Lear* (1605) and *Macbeth* (1606), the plot becomes much more direct: causes lead directly to effects, incident follows incident in a logical manner, a central issue is pursued from a beginning, through a middle, to an end. The clarity of the plot is supported internally by a pervasive orderliness of parts: the temptation of Othello is paralleled by the temptations of Roderigo, Brabantio and Cassio; the story of Lear and his daughters is balanced and substantiated by the story of Gloucester and his sons; as Macbeth kills the tremblings of conscience and hardens into unemotional acceptance of the necessity of murder to consolidate power, his wife moves in exactly the opposite direction, changing from a cynical realist into a guilt-ridden, terrified woman.

A standard character grouping appears, with the heroes occupying a central position between the two flanking groups, to both of which they are related by familial and social ties. Othello stands between his wife Desdemona and his officer Iago, Lear between his daughter Cordelia and his other daughters Goneril and Regan, Macbeth between his king, Duncan, on one side, and the witches and his wife on the other. These flanking groups represent relatively uncomplicated value systems. On the one side there are the self-seeking, destructive, anti-order figures, Iago, Goneril and Regan, Edmund, the witches, Lady Macbeth. Their strength comes with their certainty in themselves and their sure sense that they alone truly understand things as they are. Practical, pragmatic, rational, tough-minded, cynical, anti-traditional, realistic – no word seems quite to cover that deadly realism contained in Iago's certainty that Desdemona is only human and can be tempted like other women: 'Blest fig's end! The wine she drinks is made of grapes' (II. i. 257–8); in Regan's sensible advice to her angry but powerless father: 'being weak, seem so' (II. iv. 204); and in Lady Macbeth's easy assurance that the blood of the king is easily removed from the murderers' hands: 'A little water clears us of this deed' (II. ii. 67). Edmund is the philosopher of this group. His scorn for law and tradition, and his redefinition of nature (*Lear*, I. ii. 1–22) as a process of struggle in which the strongest, the smartest, the most attractive and the most ruthless survive and prosper, binds this group to the politics of Machiavelli and the views of the Marlovian overreacher, and anticipates the nature of Darwin and the society of Marx.

On the other side of the heroes are the order figures who are the exact opposite in their values. In them feeling takes precedence over thought, service over self-advancement, tradition over revolution, gentleness over strength, order over chaos, hope over cynicism, pity over antagonism. Love and concern for others are as natural and as necessary to health, Desdemona believes, as wearing gloves, keeping warm or feeding on nourishing dishes; and yet this humble, easy power admits no impediments and unites, in a world filled with seemingly irreconcilable opposites, the greatest of differences: black and white, old and young, delicate lady and grizzled soldier, sophisticated daughter of one of the first families of Venice and the stranger from unknown lands. Perhaps a trifle stiff-necked in her virtue at the beginning of the play, Cordelia becomes the source of all the healing powers – sleep, a change of garments, music, forgiveness and the unbreakable unity of man with man – which transform the old king and save him, for an instant at least, from madness and despair. Duncan, king of Scotland, is the fountain of generosity, the source of order and meaning in life, the embodiment of tradition and law.

The tragic heroes, standing like Everyman between his good and evil angels, are men of great power, great courage and great endurance, capable of registering the titanic forces which rage through themselves and their world, able to stand the course and follow their suffering to its uttermost limits where it can be forced to yield some meaning. They begin as the chief defenders of the old order against the attacks of the destructive powers: Othello is the governor of the Christian outpost of Cyprus beleaguered by the Turk, Lear is hereditary king of Britain, and Macbeth is the chief soldier of his king, protecting him from the onslaught of treason and barbarian invaders. But their natures are not simple, and they are related in a variety of ways to the powers which threaten the order they give their loyalty to. Othello was born a pagan and raised in savage lands, two of Lear's daughters are vicious, and Macbeth is married to Lady Macbeth. Inwardly, too, these heroes are drawn in opposite directions. No longer star-crossed like Romeo and Juliet, or born to set things right like Hamlet, the heroes freely choose between the opposites in their natures and their kingdoms. Inevitably, unerringly, they choose not wrongly but tragically and ensure their own destruction. Othello dismisses Cassio and makes Iago his lieutenant, believes Iago and kills Desdemona; Lear disowns Cordelia and gives his kingdom to Goneril and Regan; Macbeth listens to the witches and to his wife and murders his king. These choices immediately become the psychological, social and natural reality of their dramatic worlds, and the heroes find themselves condemned to endure states of mind, live in kingdoms and face a nature in which the principles represented by Desdemona, Cordelia and Duncan have been usurped by the principles of Iago, Edmund and Lady Macbeth. But while the life-nourishing forces are at first terribly vulnerable, they turn out to be ultimately indestructible; and, while the anti-order figures move towards the self-destruction inherent in their principles, the forces of order gradually gather strength. In the end there is a recovery of sorts, and life does not entirely disappear into chaos, beastliness and meaninglessness. But the price of the original choice is never remitted in the slightest, and the heroes come at last to the death which is latent in their fatal decisions.

The use of this basic pattern in three successive tragedies suggests that the poet had defined to his own satisfaction the fundamentals of tragedy and found the form in which to dramatize them. But despite the sureness of the outlines which seem to guarantee man's responsibility for his suffering, pinpoint the nature of the tragic choice, trace its consequences and prove its irreversibility, within the tragedies all certainty disappears, sharp objects blur into their opposites, and 'nothing is but what is not'. Troubled by the prophecies of the witches, Macbeth questions them directly:

> Say from whence
> You owe this strange intelligence, or why
> Upon this blasted heath you stop our way
> With such prophetic greeting? Speak, I charge you. (I. iii. 75–8)

The witches' answer is to vanish, as if the mere asking of a factual question of this kind shifted the frame of reference to one in which witches cannot exist, or as if man's life were influenced by a mystery which will never answer human questions. Every direct question in Shakespeare's tragic world encounters the same response. Rather than eliciting an answer, the question itself becomes inadequate or meaningless. No sooner are we certain of the heroes' responsibility for their fates than the very word 'responsibility' begins to blur. Othello does kill Desdemona, but he is seduced by Iago, misled by a series of probabilities and betrayed by fears and doubts over which he seems to have no control. Lear is indeed guilty, but guilty of what? A desire for retirement from public life after many years of struggle, a need for a public display of duty and affection from his daughters, a violent temper and a habit of command. If these be sins, 'who shall scape whipping?' And the consequences which follow from these failings are so disproportionate to their causes – such an *amplificatio ad absurdum* – as to make any theory of crime and punishment, of 'tragic flaw', unacceptable, no matter how logical. Macbeth does and persists in doing what he himself knows to be a crime against nature – his hand holds the dagger – but the workings of the witches, the urgings of Lady Macbeth and the obsessive, independent life of the crime within his mind all combine to suggest the pervasive existence of some order-killing, chaos-seeking power in the world of which Macbeth is only the agent, as much victim as Duncan.

(ii) *Othello*

The tragic sense of life in *Othello* is focused in a scenic arrangement in which small areas of varying brightness and order are surrounded by vast expanses of darkness and chaos. Again and again the scene is 'torchlit': on the balcony of Brabantio's house where he receives news that his daughter has married the Moor; outside the Sagittary where Othello encounters Brabantio and his followers wild for revenge; in the Venetian senate where news of Turkish raids and stolen daughters comes in from the darkness beyond; at the court of guard on Cyprus where the watch against the Turk is kept; on the dark streets of Cyprus where a flickering light reveals the bodies of two Venetians who have wounded one another in the night; and in that small circle of light around Desdemona's bed, which flares for a moment until the 'flaming minister', the 'Promethean heat', is at last put out. The larger world, the geography of the play, is arranged in the same Rembrandtian way. Beyond the sea walls of Venice – an island of rationality, manners and commerce, the defender of Christendom against the Turk – is the 'enchafed flood' which in its fury 'Seems to cast water on the burning Bear, And quench the guards of th' ever-fired pole' (II. i. 14–15). Beyond the raging sea are strange and violent lands, 'antres vast and deserts idle, Rough quarries, rocks, and hills whose heads touch heaven' (I. iii. 140–1), inhabited by 'Cannibals that each other eat, The Anthropophagi, and men whose heads Do grow beneath their shoulders' (I. iii. 143–5). Prowling this wilderness of water and rock, never seen but always there, are the Turks, the general enemy. Far out in the midst of this terror lies the island fortress of Cyprus, the outermost bastion of Venice and Christendom, governed by the converted Moorish general, Othello, and his Venetian bride, Desdemona.

Human character is structured in the same way as the *Othello* world. On the surface each of the characters seems to be a model of wisdom, rationality, honesty, kindness, self-control; but these small, easily extinguished areas of light in the minds and hearts of man are surrounded with vast darknesses, surging with primitive fears and energies. 'Where's that palace', says Iago, 'whereinto foul things Sometimes intrude not?' (III. iii. 137–8), and the plot of the play is made up of such intrusions. We watch one as the play opens. Brabantio, ordinarily a wise senator and a kind father, is awakened by the 'terrible summons' of voices calling out theft and rape. He enters above and stands on his balcony, secure in his beliefs that this is the civilized city of Venice, not a remote farm, and that he is one of its rulers. But out of the darkness below, where Iago and Roderigo stand unseen, come voices speaking of an old black ram tupping his white ewe, a Barbary horse covering his daughter, a Moor making the beast with two backs with the gentle Desdemona. 'Even now, now, very now' (I. i. 88) brings the act of coupling before his eyes and beats its climactic rhythm in his blood. 'This accident is not unlike my dream', says Brabantio and, terrified, he calls 'Light, I say; light!' But the fears and the hatreds which have surged up through dream and from the disembodied voices below are not dispelled by the light, and the grave and wise man who had once welcomed Othello in his house as a guest gathers his retainers and races through the streets to arrest the seducer and speak to him of 'foul charms' and black magic used to force a 'maid so tender, fair, and happy' to run 'to the sooty bosom Of such a thing as thou – to fear, not to delight' (I. ii. 66–71). On Cyprus it is wine rather than dream which looses the dark unknown. Cassio has always seemed to himself and others a gentlemanly and scholarly sort, but after one drink, urged upon him by Iago, he reveals inordinate pride – 'the Lieutenant is to be saved before the Ancient' – violent anger and a willingness to kill if crossed. The demons enter the mind through many passages – dream, wine, sex, money, pride, fear – but, with the one major exception of Desdemona, there is in this play no 'breast so pure But some uncleanly apprehension Keep leets and law-days, and in sessions sit With meditations lawful' (III. iii. 138–41). The simpleton Roderigo is easily persuaded that his money and his rank will bring him to the bed of Desdemona, who never even knows that he is alive; and the honest, sensible Emilia suddenly reveals that, though she would not give her virtue away for a trifle, it could be bought if the price were high enough.

Othello's temptation reveals most completely the power of the dark destructive powers which, like 'the gutter'd rocks, and congregated sands', below the surface of the sea, thrust up 'to enclog the guiltless keel' (II. i. 69–70). The Moor is, as Iago admits, 'of a constant, loving, noble nature' (II. i. 298), and possesses himself with enormous calm. He stood unmoved when his brother was killed beside him in battle; he stands before the Sagittary and quells a violent mob with the magnificent words, 'Keep up your bright swords, for the dew will rust them' (I. ii. 59). He explains with grand simplicity to the senate how he and Desdemona came to love – 'She lov'd me for the dangers I had pass'd; And I lov'd her that she did pity them' (I. iii. 167–8) – quiets with a few direct and powerful words the mad riot on the battlements of Cyprus. His rhetoric ennobles all that it touches; his sense of his own worth and dignity are seemingly unshakeable; his love for Desdemona is high, heroic and filled with a 'content' so great that it stops his heart with 'too much of joy' (II. i. 199). But then, a few words from Iago suggesting a relationship between Cassio and Desdemona, a few comparisons of Othello's blackness and ugliness to Desdemona's beauty and sophistication, a few flimsy pieces of evidence – a lost handkerchief, a plea from his wife for his dismissed lieutenant, the sight of Cassio laughing about the pretensions of his whore Bianca – and the work is done. Some of the foulest sexual images in literature bubble to the surface: the place of love becomes a 'corner' kept for the uses of others, a dark cistern crammed with copulating toads; women become flies born in the offal of the slaughterhouse and breeding instantly on birth; cuckolding, 'this forked plague', is every man's fate. Fury makes despair bearable: 'I will chop her into messes. Cuckold me!' (IV. i. 210). Frenzy, incoherence and uncontrollable anger lead to a seizure and unconsciousness. Othello strikes his wife publicly, pretends their bedroom is a brothel and finally kills her.

'Is this the noble Moor whom our full Senate Call all in all sufficient?' (IV. i. 275–6). The play provides no sure answer to Lodovico's wonder at the unbelievable change. Othello's words and actions suggest a great number of motives – an excess of emotion over intellect, the uneasiness of the outsider in an alien world, the fear of an old man with a young wife, a deep-founded sense of unworthiness, and so on, and so on – but these motives are no more certain than those many rationalizations provided by Iago for his actions. At the end of the play, while Desdemona's still warm body lies on the bed, Othello, as bewildered as we are by what has happened, looks at Iago, hoping to see the cloven hoof of the devil: 'I look down towards his feet – but that's a fable' (V. ii. 286). Denied a metaphysical answer, Othello seeks a more ordinary explanation, a motive: 'demand that demi-devil Why he hath thus ensnar'd my soul and body?' Iago's response does not illuminate the mystery: 'Demand me nothing. What you know, you know. From this time forth I never will speak word' (V. ii. 306–7). Though he will go on to offer many explanations of his own motives – 'not wisely, but too well', 'being wrought, Perplexed in the extreme' – Othello approves Iago's silence: 'Well, thou dost best.' He glimpses here, and accepts as impenetrable, that vast darkness of primitive energies – fear, hatred, lust, pride, of persistent animalism (goats, baboons, monkeys, flies, toads), of ceaseless random sexuality, of fire and storm, of Turks and cannibals, which surround life, responding to no rational questions about motive, perplexing every attempt to understand why.

For Iago, a practical man rather than a 'bookish theoric', this dark world is the only reality. Love, kindness, nobility, self-sacrifice, justice, honour, order – all the virtues on which civilized life is built – are only pretences covering the jungle appetites by which man really lives. The play offers considerable evidence to support this view, particularly in the all-important matter of sex. All the world, with one exception, is tainted. Brabantio is strangely moved by thoughts of his daughter in bed with the Moor, Roderigo will kill to satisfy his lust, the noble Cassio keeps a whore and laughs at her pretensions to marriage, the unhappy Bianca is 'A huswife that by selling her desires Buys herself bread and clothes' (IV. i. 94–5), and even Emilia, an honest woman despite the charges of adultery Iago lays on her, can remark that while she would not sell for a few trifles or geegaws, she would if the price were only high enough, and so would every woman. When Bianca protests that she is 'no strumpet, but of life as honest As you that thus abuse me' (V. i. 122–3), there is something to what she says.

It is Iago's function, in both speech and action, to introduce the darkness into the small areas of light. His language debases all that it touches, changing men to animals, the noble Moor to a stupid and lecherous barbarian, the gentle Desdemona to a Venetian sophisticate, jaded with familiar pleasure and seeking the exotic. His words become actions as by cunning suggestion, carefully planted barbs of doubt and skilful stage setting he releases those 'uncleanly apprehensions' lurking in the minds of these honourable ladies and gentlemen, allowing them to reveal themselves for what Iago knows them truly to be, fools, savages, murderers, whores. The city, the image of the human community, is similarly reduced by Iago's schemes to scenes of chaos, riot, ambush, murder and civil strife. But the great irony, unperceived by Iago, though he calls our attention to the fact, is that it is the power of men's virtues which make them vulnerable to his suggestions and their own darker energies. It is because man is a complex creature – both human *and* animal, both love *and* lust – not because he is a hypocrite, that he falls into the opposite of what he longs to be. Iago's method of temptation reveals the paradox:

> So will I turn [Desdemona's] virtue into pitch:
> And out of her own goodness make the net
> That shall enmesh them all. (II. iii. 366–8)

This is exactly what happens. Desdemona becomes his victim because of her sympathy and concern for other human beings: her intercession for the dismissed Cassio lays her open to the suspicions of her husband. The Moor's generous and noble nature makes him childishly easy to manipulate, and his sense of honour and the intensity of his love make tragedy inevitable once he believes that he has been deceived. Cassio's humility and willingness to admit his fault lead him to petition Desdemona for help, while his shame prevents him from going directly to Othello. Even Roderigo and Brabantio would not become Iago's dupes if they did not in their strange ways love Desdemona. Man's virtues are as necessary as his vices to Shakespearian tragedy.

There is terror in the perception that, were man worse than he is, he would suffer less and do less frightful things; but this tragic fact contains also whatever hope is to be found. Othello's ability to rationalize his murder of Desdemona as the execution of justice – 'It is the cause, it is the cause, my soul' (V. ii. 1) – is grotesque, but the fact that he cannot kill, even in near madness, without believing that he is acting justly keeps the concept of justice alive and makes its achievement on earth at least still possible. As he leans over the sleeping Desdemona, Othello weeps and says: 'This sorrow's heavenly; It strikes where it doth love' (V. ii. 21–2), and the words combine the ultimate depravity, a sentimental pleasure in murder, with an ineradicable sorrow at killing. Even as he kills, he cannot escape knowing what it is he kills:

> but once put out thy light,
> Thou cunning'st pattern of excelling nature,
> I know not where is that Promethean heat
> That can thy light relume. When I have pluck'd thy rose,
> I cannot give it vital growth again;
> It needs must wither. I'll smell thee on the tree.
> *He kisses her.* (V. ii. 10–15)

If it is Iago's function to release the dark powers latent in the mind and the world, so it is Desdemona's function to elicit feelings of love, kindness and generosity, and to encourage harmony and union. Her effect on others is at times almost mystical, and Cassio seems to divine her powers in the moment she steps on shore at Cyprus, where Aphrodite had also disembarked long before:

> O, behold,
> The riches of the ship is come ashore!
> Ye men of Cyprus, let her have your knees.
> Hail to thee, lady! and the grace of heaven,
> Before, behind thee, and on every hand,
> Enwheel thee round! (II. i. 82–7)

The love of this tender young lady for an old, war-toughened black soldier is so astounding that her father requires magic to explain it; and for Othello their embraces are moments of 'content so absolute' as to be akin to death. But what the men of the play find sublime, the lady finds most natural and simple. While hearing the tales of adventure which first subdued her heart to Othello in her father's house, Desdemona is constantly interrupted and forced to leave to tend to 'house affairs', and in her woman's world love is always involved with such practical realities as the kitchen and the nursery, not lived exclusively in the great operatic scenes which Othello imagines alone appropriate to life and love. Her love is as generous as it is natural, and to her it seems not at all difficult – though it baffles the men of the play – that she should continue to love her father in one way while loving her husband in another. It never occurs to her that the sympathy and concern she feels for an old friend in trouble, the disgraced Cassio, might be misinterpreted by men with more suspicious minds and more exclusive views of love. She encounters everyone with gentleness and sympathy, but she reserves for Othello a specially deep and intense love – 'to his honours and his valiant parts Did I my soul and fortunes consecrate' (I. iii. 253–4) – and as she lies dying on her bed, murdered by the husband she loved and trusted, she hears the question, 'O, who hath done this deed?', and responds with words which make life and future possible:

> Nobody. I myself. Farewell.
> Commend me to my kind lord. O, farewell! (V. ii. 124–5)

Desdemona has fulfilled her nature and made good her values at the ultimate place. It now remains for Othello to do the same. Some critics have never forgiven him for not accepting his guilt in Christian humility[1] – as does, say, Leontes in *The Winter's Tale*. But the old warrior looking at the body on the bed – 'Cold, cold, my girl!' – realizing that this is his 'journey's end', the 'very sea-mark' of his 'utmost sail', loses not even now his heroic sense of himself and the world in which he lives. Even his crimes can never be mean and petty, and his punishments must take place in a landscape as large as his own imagination:

> Whip me, ye devils,
> From the possession of this heavenly sight.
> Blow me about in winds, roast me in sulphur,
> Wash me in steep-down gulfs of liquid fire. (V. ii. 277–80)

For a moment he attempts to hide from what he has done behind the image of what he once was – 'I have done the state some service, and they know't' (V. ii. 339) – but only for a moment – 'No more of that'. He goes on to explain explicitly what he has done and what it means, and then does the only thing that a soldier can do to make restitution:

> When you shall these unlucky deeds relate,
> Speak of me as I am; nothing extenuate,
> Nor set down aught in malice. Then must you speak
> Of one that lov'd not wisely, but too well;
> Of one not easily jealous, but, being wrought,
> Perplexed in the extreme; of one whose hand,

[1] Most notably, T. S. Eliot, 'Shakespeare and the Stoicism of Seneca', *Selected Essays* (London, New York, 1932).

> Like the base Indian, threw a pearl away
> Richer than all his tribe; of one whose subdu'd eyes,
> Albeit unused to the melting mood.
> Drops tears as fast as the Arabian trees
> Their med'cinable gum. Set you down this:
> And say besides that in Aleppo once,
> Where a malignant and a turban'd Turk
> Beat a Venetian and traduc'd the state,
> I took by th' throat the circumcised dog,
> And smote him – thus. *He stabs himself.* (V. ii. 344)

He then dies kissing the woman he has killed.

There may be an outsized grandeur in this, even something still of bombast, but there is no shirking fact. He knows what he has done, he knows the value of what he has thrown away, his sorrow is absolute and he does not excuse himself. The dagger blow which manifests his high sense of the justice and the duty he owes himself and Desdemona, identifies him at one and the same time as the Turk, the general enemy of mankind, and as the destroyer of the Turk.

Iago was wrong. He was partly right, but ultimately he was wrong. His view of mankind as motivated finally by nothing more than appetite and self-interest cannot comprehend or account for the nobility of an Othello or the love of a Desdemona. There is some comfort in the fact that Iago was wrong – he might after all have been right – but the question persists, 'Why did such greatness have to suffer so much?' The play offers a number of partial answers, but we are brought at last to the edge of a mystery: there is in this world something mean and destructive, something that undercuts man's dreams of himself and of nature and laughs at what he thinks to be his possibilities; something to be found everywhere, in the desert and in the sea, in the wasteland and in the city, in the brute world and buried deep in the mind of man. Greatness of spirit and imagination which tries to transform this world by either rhetoric or love places itself at the mercy of the destructive forces, and can in the end assert its values and establish them only in dying.

Throughout the play Desdemona and Othello are identified with forces in and beyond nature, with the rose and the Arabian tree dropping its med'cinable gum, with devils and angels, with Adam and Eve and with Mars and Venus. They are thus archetypes, primal symbols of great forces working through all life in all places and at all times. But at the same time that they are

17a The hall screen at Hampton Court Palace (*c*. 1535)

17b Design by Robert Smythson for the hall screen at Worksop Manor (*c*. 1585)

A Platte
· at ·

For A Screene
· worsoPe ·

To bee Builte
Manner

A Screen at Worsop Manner by Smithson

18a The hall screen at the Middle Temple, London (1574)
18b The hall screen at the Charterhouse, London (1571)

universal powers, they are also highly personalized individuals brought into close human focus. The woman who is the Promethean heat and light of life is at the same time the young girl who badgers her husband for a favour, unpins her dress while singing a sad song, wants her deathbed made up with her wedding sheets, and when told she must die pleads for only a few more moments of life. Here, in Shakespeare's dramatic method, we catch something of the tragic paradox of life which is at once universal and immediate, godlike and human. And while the principle may be maintained, the Promethean light relumed, it feeds upon the individual lives which carry it. The individuals must suffer as individuals; for them there is no glimpse of the future they have transmitted.

(iii) *King Lear*

In *King Lear* the tragic situation takes a primarily temporal rather than spatial form. The terror comes from the breakneck speed and the incredible thoroughness with which actions grow into their strict logical consequences; the abruptness with which all that has seemed most certain – identity, relationships, order, law, nature, the gods – breaks up; the suddenness with which the familiar and comfortable landscape is transformed into a bleak and unknown place without landmarks; the swiftness with which power becomes helplessness and life becomes death. The plot is visualized in the metaphor Lear uses when Kent attempts to dissuade him from disinheriting Cordelia: 'The bow is bent and drawn; make from the shaft' (I. i. 145). Lear's will is the bow, drawn by his anger, and the arrow speeding on its way is the progression of events which carry Lear – helpless once the shaft is loosed – in an unbelievably swift, unerringly straight line from the palace of a great king, through the heath, to a battlefield where all his children lie dead before him.

Nowhere in Shakespeare is the iron law of dramatic logic, the relentless working of poetic justice (in the structural, not the moral, sense of that term), followed so unwaveringly to its absolute conclusion as in *King Lear*. Each event of the play is the necessary consequence of what has gone before, the elaboration and extension of what is implicit in the original acts of Lear and Gloucester. Both older men disinherit and banish the children who love them and give power to those children who seek only their own profit and advancement. Lear turns Cordelia away because she will not state publicly that she loves him boundlessly and totally, and gives his kingdom to the quietly vicious Regan, the icy, poised, ambitious, sadistic and lustful Goneril

and their husbands, the savage Cornwall and the ineffectual Albany. Gloucester, blinded by accusations that his true son Edgar has plotted against his life,
proclaims him an outlaw and makes his bastard son, the rational, cool, self-
possessed and treacherous Edmund, his heir. The kingdom immediately
begins to take its shape from the new rulers: their natures become its laws,
their power drives its motive principles. The results are catastrophic for
individual men and for society as a whole. The faithful and honest servant
Kent is driven into disguise, and service is represented by Oswald, who serves
only power and seeks only profit; the king-father becomes only a querulous
and difficult old man, an annoyance in a well-run household, who is at last
turned out to rage and run mad in the midst of a great storm; the honest,
gullible son wanders the land with a price on his head, forced to hide in
hovels, dress in rags and disguise himself as a mad beggar; power and will
grow absolute, answering to no laws except the whims of the ruler; the king's
messenger is stocked like a criminal by the duke who does not like his
message or his manners; the eyes of an old man are torn out because he has
sheltered another old man from the storm; libido breaks the bonds of marriage, and sister poisons sister to win a sexual competition. The poetry extends
this jungle world beyond the events of the plot to a vision of the universal
misery and suffering of all mankind, wandering nameless over the land,
raging helplessly at or submitting dumbly to injustice, sheltering in warrens
from the indifferent elements, eating foul things to stay alive, beaten, tortured, poor, frightened, mad, lost. When seen with the opened 'eye of
anguish' (IV. iv. 15), man appears as monstrous, tyrannical and luxurious in
prosperity as he is pitiful in adversity. The 'bloody hand' is the emblem of
this world of uncontrolled power where the beadle lashes the whore he lusts
after, where authority whips, stocks and imprisons the helpless beggar and
madman, while 'Robes and furr'd gowns' hide all sins. Sex suffuses everything: 'But to the girdle do the gods inherit, Beneath is all the fiend's'
(IV. vi. 128–9); man and animal cease to be distinguishable: 'hog in sloth,
fox in stealth, wolf in greediness, dog in madness, lion in prey' (III. iv. 95–7);
the odour of death and decay is everywhere, even on the living hand: 'Let me
wipe it first; it smells of mortality' (IV. vi. 136). Nature shares in the general
catastrophe, and the scene changes from the palace of a great king and a
prosperous kingdom – 'shadowy forest and with champains rich'd, With
plenteous rivers and wide-skirted meads' (I. i. 65–6) – to a bleak heath, barren
and ravaged by titanic powers, and on to a grey, featureless battlefield on
which father and children lie dead.

These disasters are not only the logical consequences of the literal transfer

of power, but are also the extensions, a series of glosses on the meaning, of the
original acts of Lear and Gloucester. What Gloucester did, Edmund is; and
what Lear does, his daughters and his world become. A sudden surge of
passion, a moment's indiscretion in the bedroom, and in an instant, fully
fleshed out, the consequence and the meaning of the act, lithe, virile, quick
and amoral, stand beside Gloucester in the person of Edmund, the bastard
son. In another instant the act finds expression in a philosophy which rejects
all law and 'plague of custom' and declares that the only realities are strength,
intelligence, beauty and power: 'Thou, Nature, art my goddess; to thy law
My services are bound' (I. ii. 1–2). A moment more, and that naturalistic law
which states that 'The younger rises, when the old doth fall' (III. iii. 26) requires betrayal of a brother to banishment and a father to the torturer in
order to satisfy the appetite for wealth, title and power.

Gloucester is the sensual man, both in his original act and in the suffering
(blindness) which comes from it. Lear's mistake and suffering (madness) are
mental, but his errors are as thoroughly human as Gloucester's sexual desire.
Tired after a long reign, he wants to resign his kingship and spend a few years
in peace before death; and as he gives his kingdom away he asks in return that
his daughters declare publicly their love and gratitude. With that volubility
and glibness which evil always has in Shakespeare, Goneril and Regan respond in a very satisfactory way; but Cordelia, with the reticence, the un-
willingness to be forced, which frequently accompanies untested virtue in
Shakespearian tragedy, speaks somewhat grudgingly of a gratitude in proportion to debt and of a sharing of love between father and husband. Unable
to bear thwarting, the old king explodes, and in an instant he has cursed and
disinherited his daughter, and banished the honest councillor who tries to
intervene. The future is contained in the curse which begins it:

> Here I disclaim all my paternal care,
> Propinquity and property of blood,
> And as a stranger to my heart and me
> Hold thee from this for ever. The barbarous Scythian,
> Or he that makes his generation messes
> To gorge his appetite, shall to my bosom
> Be as well neighbour'd, pitied, and believ'd,
> As thou my sometime daughter. (I. i. 115–22)

Figure of speech immediately becomes fact, for it is to cannibals and bar-
barians that Lear gives himself and his kingdom by his renunciation of kingship and fatherhood. Having cancelled at will the sacred bonds which link

parent to child and king to subject, Lear is now forced to live in a world from which Cordelia's love is banished and where the old systems of kinship and authority on which civilized life was built cease to operate. Taking their cue from him, his daughters cease to think of him as a king and father, and see him as only a difficult and powerless old fool who must be managed and instructed: 'being weak, seem so' (II. iv. 204). When he persists in his now meaningless claims to honour, gratitude and duty, exasperation grows into anger, and the old man is at last turned out of the house – 'This house is little: the old man and's people Cannot be well bestow'd' (II. iv. 291–2) – to endure the storm, the darkness and the heath, which are the full-scale revelation of the world implicit in the denial of Cordelia.

If *Tamburlaine* is the supreme statement in the drama of the age of the beauty and spaciousness of the world and man's power to shape it to his will, the heath in *King Lear* is the central statement of the fear that man is only a helpless sufferer in a small dark place racked by titanic, morally indifferent forces. But Tamburlaine's sense of the power of human imagination and will is still present in the violent, wilful old king who rages at the great storm, commanding it to punish the wicked and destroy a world in which he has been so foully mistreated:

> Strives in his little world of man to outscorn
> The to-and-fro conflicting wind and rain. (III. i. 10–11)

But the thunder does not cease at his bidding, the 'night pities neither wise men nor fools' (III. ii. 13) and the great storm 'tears his white hair . . . with eyeless rage', making 'nothing' of him (III. i. 7–9). The world of man is equally violent and amoral. The one human construction in the landscape is Gloucester's castle on the edge of the heath. The old man and his followers have been turned away from this shelter and the doors slammed close by usurping powers – Cornwall, Regan, Goneril, Edmund – as implacably cruel as nature. Within, during the night, a son betrays his father, and an old man's eyes are ripped out and stamped on by power gone wild, 'which men May blame, but not control' (III. vii. 26–7).

Castle and heath, society and nature, are now the images of that horror latent in Lear's and Gloucester's original acts. Locked within this nightmare, the weak, the old and the helpless are driven like animals, frightened and terrified, to seek shelter in hovels, to bed in filthy straw, and

> To take the basest and most poorest shape
> That ever penury in contempt of man
> Brought near to beast. (II. iii. 7–9)

Their humanity diminishes to grotesque shapes – fool, madman, beggar, fugitive – and as the mad old king looks at the huddled beggar before him, gibbering in terror about fiends and devils, man disappears at last into animal, into mere object:

> Is man no more than this? Consider him well. Thou ow'st the worm no silk, the beast no hide, the sheep no wool, the cat no perfume. Ha! here's three on's are sophisticated! Thou art the thing itself: unaccommodated man is no more but such a poor, bare, forked animal as thou art. Off, off, you lendings! Come, unbutton here. [*Tearing off his clothes.*
>
> (III. iv. 107–14)

But at that moment when man is in danger of disappearing into 'nothing' – the word which echoes threateningly through the play – a spontaneous gesture out of the depths of being stops the flight into nothingness and manifests an indestructible, irreducible humanity. The fool, whose common sense can no longer deal with the terrors he is now encountering, cries out for help when frightened by the sight of Tom o' Bedlam, and Kent, close behind him, responds instantly with 'Give me thy hand' (III. iv. 41). The clasping of hands in an attempt to guide, to help, to comfort, takes place many times in the last three acts, and each time re-establishes physically 'the holy cords . . . too intrinse t' unloose' (II. ii. 80–1), which were at the beginning of the play taken for granted. The same sympathy emerges suddenly in Lear's pity for another sufferer – 'Poor fool and knave, I have one part in my heart That's sorry yet for thee' (III. ii. 72–3) – and this flicker of feeling grows into perception of and universal pity for the boundless suffering of mankind:

> Poor naked wretches, wheresoe'er you are,
> That bide the pelting of this pitiless storm,
> How shall your houseless heads and unfed sides,
> Your loop'd and window'd raggedness, defend you
> From seasons such as these? (III. iv. 28–32)

As the awareness of human wretchedness grows, so does the sense of responsibility for justice, which can no longer be left to the gods:

> O, I have ta'en
> Too little care of this! Take physic, pomp;
> Expose thyself to feel what wretches feel,
> That thou mayst shake the superflux to them,
> And show the heavens more just. (III. iv. 32–6)

The hope contained in such actions and feelings finds expression in Edgar's tears for the suffering Lear, tears which threaten to 'mar' Edgar's 'counterfeiting' (III. vi. 64), to wash away the disguise of mad beggar which has been forced upon him and thus restore him to his rightful state of man. The changes in the individual heart continue to grow and, without anyone being aware of it, begin to bring about changes in the world. Gloucester finally ceases to temporize and risks his life by going out into the storm to aid Lear. One of Cornwall's servants, revolted by the torture of Gloucester, attacks his master and gives up his life in a vain attempt to save Gloucester's sight. As if the sympathy generated by the shock of such violent suffering were radiating outward through the world, Cordelia reappears in Britain with an army to save her father.

Even Lear yields at last. As his suffering intensifies, and as he comes to see through that suffering the suffering of other men, he steadfastly refuses to accept, to give in, to weep. Instead, tied to his own Promethean self-righteousness – 'I am a man More sinn'd against than sinning' (III. ii. 59–60) – he continues to threaten, to denounce, and since, because he has no power, his threats and denunciations have no effect, goes mad. In Act IV he is still raging, still determined to force his will upon the world – 'kill, kill, kill, kill, kill, kill' – or loose universal anarchy. But even in madness he cannot turn his eyes away from the world which has maddened him, the world where the great lady is as lustful as the gilded fly, the gods inherit but to a woman's waist, the justice is but a thief dressed in robes of office, the beadle longs for the whore he whips, the 'usurer hangs the cozener'. When the blind Gloucester asks to kiss his hand, Lear rejects the saving clasp of fellowship – 'Let me wipe it first; it smells of mortality' (IV. vi. 136) – and runs wild in the fields like an animal. 'Bound Upon a wheel of fire', where his own tears 'do scald like molten lead' (IV. vii. 46–8), the mad old king is at last captured and brought to the camp of his daughter Cordelia. Here sleep closes the eyes of anguish, and to the sound of music Lear awakes to find himself in fresh garments and in the presence of Cordelia's forgiveness and love. The first reaction is bewilderment, but this gives way to recognition of Cordelia as his daughter and himself as her father. Indignation and agony gone, the tortured, twisted language of the earlier scenes gives way to a remarkable simplicity and directness: 'as I am a man, I think this lady To be my child Cordelia' – 'And so I am, I am' (IV. vii. 69–70). Lear's humanity is, he knows, dependent on his acceptance of Cordelia as his true child and her acceptance of him, despite all wrongs, as her father. The embrace of father and daughter, their full acceptance of the 'holy cords' of their relationship, makes explicit the

Shakespearian view of human nature. Man is man only because he is capable of sympathy, of feeling and acknowledging, as Theseus accepts Oedipus at Colonos as true man and offers him sanctuary near Athens, that Lear is the father and Cordelia the true child, because the bond is unbreakable. All else can be and is stripped away – clothes, power, sanity, name, knowledge, courage, thought – but this remains, and because it does man is, though no longer the cynosure of the universe, at least something more than animal or mere object.

Gloucester's path is again the same. The last sight he saw was the fingers of another man reaching to tear out his eyes, and he wanders out of Act III in despair: 'As flies to wanton boys are we to th' gods – They kill us for their sport' (IV. i. 38–9). Unable to oppose the diabolic powers he believes to govern life, Gloucester desires only to die, and he moves towards Dover Cliff and suicide. But now his banished child, Edgar, appears, takes him by the hand, protects him and at last arranges a 'miracle' to restore at least enough faith to make it possible for Gloucester to endure life. In one way, the 'miraculous' survival of the supposed leap from the cliff is a shabby trick played on a man of middling intellect to persuade him to accept the conventional belief that life is always worth living; but seen in another way, the leap into the void is a dramatization – in the literal terms needed by a man like Gloucester – of the plunge downward from the heights of sure prosperity into the depths of nothingness endured by the characters of the play, and of their miraculous survival on the heath where they discover the foundations of their humanity. Saved in this manner, Gloucester wavers on between hope and despair as his fortunes shift, until at last he too is reunited with his lost child, Edgar, and in a moment of mixed joy and sorrow his heart at last 'burst[s] smilingly'. Act IV of *Lear* is built around these two parallel scenes of regeneration. In both a child arranges for his despairing father to *feel*, not understand, once again that man is finally something more than a forked animal or a fly tortured by whimsical gods; and because he is so, life is endurable, sanity is bearable. In both cases this new faith is not merely an imposition on men too broken and exhausted to resist it, but rather a demonstration, an extension into dramatic form, of a saving reality which Lear and Gloucester have already discovered 'feelingly' at the point that their humanity verged on disappearance into 'nothing'.

'This would have seem'd a period To such as love not sorrow' (V. iii. 204–5). Edgar's words phrase perfectly the sense of the play's characters, and of generations of readers, that the reunion of the old men with their lost children is the proper completion of a rhythm of mistake, separation, suffering, learning and regeneration. Doctor Johnson's inability to bear rereading the fifth act, the ingenious attempts of many critics to prove that Cordelia is alive at the end, and the continuance on stage for nearly 150 years of Nahum Tate's adaptation in which Cordelia is saved to marry Edgar, while Lear retires to the countryside, are re-enactments of Lear's own inability to believe that, after what he has suffered and learned, Cordelia must nonetheless die: 'Look, her lips. Look there, look there!' (V. iii. 310–11). But the rhythm of man's psychic life, his imagined pattern of loss and renewal, is not the rhythm of the tragic world. Once released, the arrow goes to *its* target; once started, the journey goes to *its* end. Again and again the characters think because they have made some concession to life – learned something, suffered something, admitted something – they have arrived at the 'promised end'. If Goneril is unkind to Lear, he need only leave her house for Regan's and all will be well. If fifty of his knights are stripped away, he believes that he can retain the other fifty. Reunited with Cordelia, he goes off to do battle with the wicked, expecting to win. Captured by the enemy, he refuses to be downcast and believes that he and Cordelia can retire from the busy world – 'We two alone will sing like birds i' th' cage' (V. iii. 9) – sufficient to themselves in their new-found understanding of one another.

But the knights are reduced to twenty-five, ten, five, one, none. Cordelia's French army is defeated. Even as Lear boasts of the happy life he and Cordelia will live in prison, Edmund is motioning to the soldier who will kill Cordelia. Again and again the travellers refuse to journey further: Lear cries out in his madness for an end, 'Pull off my boots. Harder, harder – so' (IV. vi. 174); and Gloucester, urged after the defeat of Cordelia's army to get up and move on to another unknown place, refuses, 'No further, sir; a man may rot even here' (V. ii. 8). But 'the beaten drum' (IV. vi. 292) is always heard far off, and the characters always move wearily towards it. Edgar perceives the rhythm of the plot when he emerges from the heath and finds the needed courage for living in the belief that, since he has already experienced the worst that can be imagined, whatever happens in the future can only be improvement. But even as he speaks, his blinded father is led on stage, and Edgar is forced to realize that so long as breath is in body, so long as man still bothers to raise his head and utter words, 'worse . . . may be yet. The worst is not So long as we can say "This is the worst" ' (IV. i. 29–30).

The play tests all philosophies and all defences against despair as relentlessly and thoroughly as it tests its characters and their hopes. Shakespeare never read Aeschylus's lines, 'Zeus, who guided men to think, / . . . has laid it down that wisdom / comes alone through suffering',[1] but *King Lear* traces the same process. As men suffer, they begin to understand 'feelingly', emotionally, and then, being human, they attempt to understand rationally and phrase what they have discovered in their hearts. But where in Aeschylus this process leads to the growth of the rational mind and the triumph of thought in the establishment of justice through law, in *Lear*, thought, though a crucial aspect of man's humanity, becomes strangely irrelevant. Contrary evidence and the ceaseless flow of events break down each conscious defence, each understanding and each theory with which the characters attempt to shore up their ruins. Lear's refusal to weep and his defiance of the world are shattered again and again by renewed evidence of his helplessness, Gloucester's stoicism – 'Henceforth I'll bear Affliction till it do cry out itself "Enough, enough" and die' (IV. vi. 75–7) – though frequently reiterated is always swept away again by some new unendurable disaster. The Fool's common sense – 'He that has and a little tiny wit . . . Must make content with his fortunes fit' (III. ii. 74–6) – is useful for a time but becomes meaningless in the face of the demonic powers loosed on the heath, and the Fool simply disappears from the play. The Duke of Albany tries to see the workings of heavenly justice in the affairs of men. Told that Cornwall has been killed by a servant while ripping out Gloucester's eye, he exclaims: 'This shows you are above, You justicers, that these our nether crimes So speedily can venge!' (IV. ii. 78–80); but the reality of justice fades before the limitlessness of suffering: 'But, O poor Gloucester! Lost he his other eye?'

Even Kent, who makes no pretentions to philosophy, feels compelled to try to explain the mystery of evil and suffering, why it should be that one daughter should be so kind, while two others from the same parents should be so cruel: 'It is the stars, The stars above us, govern our conditions' (IV. iii. 34–5). But the play, while it does not explain evil, does tend to support Edmund's scornful response to such suggestions that fate controls human life: 'This is the excellent foppery of the world, that, when we are sick in fortune, often the surfeits of our own behaviour, we make guilty of our disasters the sun, the moon, and stars' (I. ii. 129–33). Edgar agrees, and as he looks at the dying Edmund, he sees the straight line that leads from Edmund's begetting out of wedlock to the blinding of Gloucester:

> The gods are just, and of our pleasant vices
> Make instruments to plague us:
> The dark and vicious place where thee he got
> Cost him his eyes. (V. iii. 169–72)

---

[1] *Agamemnon*, ll. 176–8, trans. Richard Lattimore, *Aeschylus I* (Chicago, 1953).

Though the more humane characters of the play habitually refer to super-natural powers, the gods are not needed here or elsewhere to explain what happens. Man causes his own suffering, as we have already seen, and justice exists in the hands of a servant who breaks the habits of a lifetime and gives his life to try to prevent his master from blinding a helpless old man, in the hands of a king who exposes himself 'to feel what wretches feel' in order to 'shake the superflux to them, And show the heavens more just'.

But even as the play establishes human freedom and responsibility, it questions them. What human sense does it make to say that man is responsible when his most trivial acts have the most fatal consequences, when crime and punishment are linked logically but are so fiendishly disproportionate, when man's nature – his 'pleasant vices' – makes error unavoidable, when a change of heart and submission cannot halt or even modify the mechanical process set in motion so unknowingly?

The central experience of *Lear*, the plot which is its soul, can only be *understood*, if at all, as a series of ever-coiling paradoxes: freedom which is fate, wisdom which is folly, sanity which is madness, helplessness which is power, loss that is gain, justice that is injustice. Reverse these paradoxes, 'And that's true too' (V. ii. 11). The only formulations which contain any-thing like the fullness of experience are those in which opposing attitudes are in precise balance. Lear's 'When we are born, we cry that we are come To this great stage of fools' (IV. vi. 186–7) holds in those tears – which express both sorrow and pity – the probable terror and the possible hope of life. Edgar's 'Men must endure Their going hence, even as their coming hither: Ripeness is all' (V. ii. 9–11) promises that death will not come before fruition, but also threatens that man's life is no more than growing, becoming heavy, dropping from the tree and rotting into the ground. The moments of the greatest emotional truth in the play are those in which the characters ex-perience this precise mixture of hope and despair. In 'sunshine and rain . . . smiles and tears' (IV. iii. 20) Cordelia hears of her father's agonies and plans his relief; ''Twixt two extremes of passion, joy and grief' (V. iii. 198), Gloucester, reunited with the son he thought lost for ever, arrived at the moment of 'ripeness' when his heart 'burst smilingly'. But Gloucester's re-sponse to the philosophy of 'ripeness' – 'And that's true too' – expresses the view that the play will finally enforce: no human feeling, no thought, no words, even when they include opposites, are ever going to be quite adequate to experience.

Life in this play has an incredible tenacity, a perdurable toughness, an ability to endure almost anything – banishment, torture, blindness, madness, isolation, despair, grinding poverty, injustice, the indifference of the universe, the death of the gods – and still keep on coming, still hoping for the future, still preserving some essential shreds of humanity. Edgar finds wonder in this strange love affair between man and life: 'O our lives' sweetness, That we the pain of death would hourly die Rather than die at once' (V. iii. 184–6). And for a moment at the beginning of the last act it looks as if the mere ability to keep coming had won through. Edgar, changed from the virtuous but gullible youth who fled his father's house into exile without a struggle, now enters as an armed champion and kills his bastard brother. Albany, another of the ineffective virtuous, has grown from a disapproving bystander into a hard, stern judge and ruler, who can even manage a little tough-minded wit about his adulterous wife being 'subcontracted' to Edmund. As virtue gains strength from its sufferings, evil in its prosperity begins, as predicted, to 'prey on itself, Like monsters of the deep' (IV. ii. 49–50). Goneril poisons her sister Regan to prevent her from having Edmund and then, after refusing, like Iago, to speak – 'Ask me not what I know' (V. iii. 160) – kills herself. As if to demonstrate – like Claudius at his prayers in *Hamlet* – the universality of sympathy and love in the human heart, Edmund looks at the bodies of the two sisters and remarks with grotesque satisfaction: 'Yet Edmund was belov'd' (V. iii. 239). And before he dies he attempts to save Cordelia, though still believing apparently that such an act is a violation of his goddess nature: 'Some good I mean to do, Despite of mine own nature' (V. iii. 243–4).

But Shakespeare is out to test both man's endurance and his hope to the uttermost, against the worst that can be: the absolute, final, irrevocable death of innocence: '*Enter Lear with Cordelia dead in his arms.*'

> Howl, howl, howl, howl! O, you are men of stones!
> Had I your tongues and eyes, I'd use them so
> That heaven's vault should crack. She's gone for ever. (V. iii. 257–9)

Each of the hopes and answers which have sustained life to this point are now tried against the fact of the dead Cordelia and found wanting. Justice after the fact, the death of those who have caused so much suffering, Edmund, Goneril and Regan, is found to be 'but a trifle here'. The revelation of service faithful to death, Kent's announcement of his true identity to his master, elicits only the flat response, 'You are welcome hither' (289). Lear's revenge – 'I kill'd the slave that was a-hanging thee' (274) – and the memory of past glory – 'I have seen the day, with my good biting falchion, I would have made them skip' (276–7) – trail off into hopelessness. Albany's brave attempt at equity – 'All friends shall taste The wages of their virtue, and all foes The cup of their deservings' (302–4) – breaks down when his eyes fall on the body: 'O, see, see!' Not even the restoration of the kingdom to the rule of the wise and virtuous, the note of hope usually sounded at the end of Shakespearian tragedy, provides any answer to Lear's question or any relief from the full, irremediable fact of death:

> And my poor fool is hang'd! No, no, no life!
> Why should a dog, a horse, a rat have life,
> And thou no breath at all? Thou'lt come no more,
> Never, never, never, never, never. (305–8)

Before this fact, life which has endured all else fails, and the old king at last dies. Edgar tries to revive him with the words used successfully so long ago with Gloucester at the bottom of the cliff, 'Look up, my lord' (312), but life is at last gone and any attempt to rouse it again is cruelty: 'He hates him That would upon the rack of this tough world Stretch him out longer' (312–14). All voices now still, and Edgar, his former optimism gone, counsels the spectators, on stage and in the audience, to 'Speak what we feel, not what we ought to say' (324). We have heard before of the necessity of seeing things feelingly if we are to see them truthfully, but what Edgar feels is hard to know:

> The oldest hath borne most; we that are young
> Shall never see so much, nor live so long. (325–6)

Is this simply a flat formula for computing suffering, which says that the man who lives the longest suffers the most? Or is it one last whisper of hope that says because those before us have suffered to the very bottom of things we who come after will never have to suffer as they did, because experience and knowledge are passed from one generation to the next? Is man irrelevant and his sufferings meaningless, or is it possible that a new world can be built on what has been discovered in the centre of disaster? Both possibilities are there, though no answer, and so the journey goes on into the future, carrying its dead, marching to its appropriate music: '*Exeunt with a dead march.*' The play finally refuses to provide that ending which its characters and audience so desperately desire. Life cannot finally be contained even in the greatest art.

(iv) *Macbeth*

The centre of Shakespearian tragedy does not lie in the problem of why great and good men betray themselves or are betrayed to suffering. Suffering and loss are givens in Shakespeare's tragic world, and any combination of man and circumstance – Hamlet and Elsinore, Othello and Iago – leads inevitably to disaster. The question which the tragedies probe is whether, in the midst of the worst that can occur, there remains any principle of goodness, any saving power, any value on which humanity and civilization can be rebuilt. Seen in this light, *Macbeth*, where the Shakespearian tragic figure for the first time knowingly does wrong, is not a radical departure from the tragedies which precede it but only a different way of exploring the same central question. The question is now posed in the terms of what a man finds deep in his own heart and mind when he willingly enters the strange dark places which lie beneath the bright, familiar world of ordinary time and action.

The depths of the psychic underworld are entered not through disinheriting a beloved child in a fit of rage, or through the bad luck of being born in Elsinore, but through a criminal act, done with malice aforethought: the murder of a man, a man whose claim on the murder's humanity is intensified in the usual Shakespearian manner by making him a king, a benefactor, a guest and a kinsman. The world is filled with forces seeking the death of Duncan, king of Scotland: the barbarian hordes from the Western Isles and from Norway, the treasonous and 'merciless Macdonwald', Lady Macbeth who to realize her ambition would dash her own child's head against a stone, and the croaking witches. The play opens with a terrible battle, another 'Golgotha', in which Macbeth, in defence of his king, turns into a raging fury, sword smoking, covered with blood, chopping men open from nave to chaps. This release of destructive powers opens a breach through which the witches enter the world of man to speak to Macbeth of the possibility of kingship, and their appearance in turn frees thoughts in his mind which move from 'horrible imaginings' to the pronunciation of the word 'murder' (I. iii. 127–42). Ambition and murder, once released into consciousness, begin to have a life of their own, pre-empting Macbeth's mind and leading him, like the 'air-drawn dagger' which 'marshals' him to Duncan's bedroom, to the fatal act. The desire to kill the king is attended by a variety of related psychic events. The hitherto sharp outlines of right and wrong begin to blur and then run together in a murky mixture: 'This supernatural soliciting Cannot be ill; cannot be good' (I. iii. 130–1). All which was unified – 'my single state of man' (I. iii. 140) – now becomes dispersed and double, like the atmosphere in which the witches appear – 'So foul and fair a day' (I. iii. 38) – and the spells these 'imperfect speakers' pronounce: 'Fair is foul, and foul is fair' (I. i. 11), and 'Double, double, toil and trouble' (IV. i. 35). 'Confusion now hath made his masterpiece' (II. iii. 71), says Macduff after seeing the body of the murdered king, and that death, the thought of which has already broken down distinction and order in Macbeth's mind, surges outward to create a chaotic world in which service is 'twice done, and then done double' (I. vi. 15); where the poison of guts, venom of toad, flickering tongue of snake, tooth of wolf, stomach of shark, blood of baboon and 'finger of birth-strangled babe Ditch-deliver'd by a drab' (IV. i. 30–1) are mixed together by the witches in a great hurly-burly where nothing has shape, form or meaning. But the summary image of meaningless, indistinct chaos arrives in Macbeth's final vision of life: 'it is a tale Told by an idiot, full of sound and fury, Signifying nothing' (V. v. 26–8).

The breakdown of distinction between opposites – fair and foul, good and ill, losing and winning – which follows the thought of Duncan's murder is a part of a more general withdrawal from objectivity into subjectivity:

>   Present fears
> Are less than horrible imaginings.
> My thought, whose murder yet is but fantastical,
> Shakes so my single state of man
> That function is smother'd in surmise,
> And nothing is but what is not. (I. iii. 137–42)

The thoughts here are new, surprising, only on the edge of consciousness, but as the play proceeds they grow, first occupying Macbeth's mind totally and then informing the senses. Inner thought becomes outer reality when the dagger of the mind takes shape before the eyes, when the ghost of Banquo seats himself at the feast and when Lady Macbeth finds the blood of Duncan for ever on her hands. Nature ceases to have any independent existence, and the very colour of the sea is transformed by thought:

> Will all great Neptune's ocean wash this blood
> Clean from my hand? No; this my hand will rather
> The multitudinous seas incarnadine,
> Making the green one red. (II. ii. 60–3)

The murder of authority, of the king, is thus not merely a political and moral but also a psychological crime, which breaks man's ties with a solid, objective ordered, well-defined world outside the self and confines him within the self.

The crime is identical with Faustus's, who rejected God and all authority over the self; and the results are much the same, though Shakespeare's psychology is far more complex and detailed than Marlowe's. The act which first promises freedom and power gradually becomes a trap. The murderers 'on the torture of the mind . . . lie in restless ecstasy' (III. ii. 21–2). Night brings no release, for the mind, now the only reality, never ceases working, and sleep is either impossible or is tormented by 'the affliction of these terrible dreams That shake us nightly' (III. ii. 18–19). In Shakespeare's tragic world *cogito ergo sum* has a fearsome meaning, and Lady Macbeth, once so sure and certain of herself, lives out its full terror in nightmare after nightmare, until she at last escapes from the prison of the head by suicide.

Macbeth seeks release from this 'torture of the mind' by intensifying his efforts to make the whole world exactly like this mind: 'Strange things I have in head that will to hand' (III. iv. 139); 'The very firstlings of my heart shall be The firstlings of my hand' (IV. i. 147–8). He looses his thoughts on Scotland and turns the kingdom into an image of his mind, a place of murder, tyranny, confusion, flight and fear. This stifles the visions and relieves the fear, but leads only to a living death. Shortly after the murder of Duncan, Macbeth exclaims in pretended horror:

> from this instant,
> There's nothing serious in mortality –
> All is but toys; renown and grace is dead;
> The wine of life is drawn, and the mere lees
> Is left this vault to brag of. (II. iii. 97–101)

The lines predict a future in which all becomes 'but toys', where murder and treachery cease to be fearsome heartpoundings and become only boring necessities: 'I am in blood Stepp'd in so far that, should I wade no more, Returning were as tedious as go o'er' (III. iv. 136–8). Having destroyed the 'other' by making the world an image of the mind, by killing all sympathy with creatures who are not himself and by denying any authority outside the self, Macbeth's life falls 'into the sear, the yellow leaf' (V. iii. 23). He begins 'to be aweary of the sun' (V. v. 49). To the news that the woman who has shared so much with him is dead, he merely responds: 'She should have died hereafter' (V. v. 17). The mind which once seethed with conflict and terror becomes a vast empty feelinglessness. All time, all space, all life are slow, trivial, flat, meaningless, coming from nowhere and going nowhere, no more real than a scene in a theatre:

> To-morrow, and to-morrow, and to-morrow,
> Creeps in this petty pace from day to day
> To the last syllable of recorded time,

And all our yesterdays have lighted fools
The way to dusty death. Out, out, brief candle!
Life's but a walking shadow, a poor player,
That struts and frets his hour upon the stage,
And then is heard no more; it is a tale
Told by an idiot, full of sound and fury,
Signifying nothing. (V. v. 19–28)

The play proves negatively what *Lear* proved positively; that there is such a thing as 'human nature', that man is different from animal in feeling inalienable ties with something outside the self, in being capable of 'good pity'. Under the pressures of suffering and loss this innate humanity appears in *Lear* and is the source of whatever hope that play has. Denial of this humane interest in and concern for the other leads in *Macbeth* to emptiness and death. Freud and Shakespeare found very different forces in the depths of the human mind, but they agree on the dynamics of that mind. For both analyst and playwright, impulses which lie at the core of the self take perverse forms, find revenge and lead to madness if repressed and denied outlet; if totally denied and buried deep, the man dies with them. In both systems the self can only avoid madness and death by going out to and living with an 'other' reality. Having proved these truths, it is not surprising that Macbeth understands in such a modern way the sick and suffering mind:

Canst thou not minister to a mind diseas'd,
Pluck from the memory a rooted sorrow,
Raze out the written troubles of the brain,
And with some sweet oblivious antidote,
Cleanse the stuff'd bosom of that perilous stuff
Which weighs upon the heart? (V. iii. 40–5)

The answer of Macbeth's doctor, 'Therein the patient Must minister to himself', is as grimly tragic as Freud's, and Macbeth turns away from it – 'Throw physic to the dogs' – roars for his armour, and goes forth to fight till the flesh be hacked from his bones.

The man has destroyed himself, surely, unerringly, by killing the king; and yet, in another sense, he has saved himself by murdering authority and thus discovering the full depths of his being. The wages of sin is death, but it is also complete knowledge of self. How thin, wooden and typed the other characters seem alongside the Macbeths; how innocent and incompletely human does Malcolm seem when he confidently reveals what he believes to be his true nature to Macduff:

> I am yet
> Unknown to woman, never was forsworn,
> Scarcely have coveted what was mine own,
> At no time broke my faith, would not betray
> The devil to his fellow, and delight
> No less in truth than life. (IV. iii. 125–30)

One can only hope that that delight in truth will last.

Macbeth has been understood in many ways: as an elaborate compliment to James I, who was greatly interested in demonology and witchcraft; as a lesson in government proving the disasters following on the murder of a rightful king; as a Shakespearian *Crime and Punishment* showing the prohibition of murder to be not just a peculiarity of Western society but an expression of the most basic human instinct. But the way in which both the crime and the consequences are defined force a consideration of the murder of Duncan not as the abnormal, unnatural action of a strange, violent man, but rather as the dramatically intensified expression of a critical but normative event in the life of every man and every society. Duncan is the authority figure, the king-father, who embodies the past and guards the future. Obedience to him and restraint of the dark destructive energies guarantee order, clarity, ultimate fruitfulness and an identification with a larger reality than the self. But the moment comes when 'nothing is but what is not', when the urgent need for freedom and self-sovereignty forces the murder of the king and the rejection of all tradition and authority. This act of defiance was of particular interest to the Renaissance, an age in which authority in all areas – politics, religion, philosophy, science, law – was being questioned and rejected, and the consequences of king-killing for Macbeth outline the intellectual history of the modern world following on the king-killing of the Renaissance: isolation from nature, ever-intensifying relativism, the subjective–objective puzzle, increasing solipsism, a fear that history and man are meaningless in the vast reaches of time and space, an enervating tedium and an intense and painful preoccupation with the mind and the self.

Though Shakespeare seems to have understood fully the psychological condition that seems to us characteristically 'modern', he retained at the same time a most unmodern conception of the power and inevitable onward movement of a world outside the self. Macbeth and his lady cut themselves off from this outer world and end isolated, marooned, static, locked in a single place and a single time, 'cabin'd, cribb'd, confin'd' (III. iv. 24). Here all places are the same place, all times the same time, 'To-morrow, and to-morrow, and to-morrow'. Lady Macbeth, childless and unsexed, lives over and over again the murder of the king, unable to go backwards or forwards from it, unable to wash the blood from her hand. But the 'seeds of time' (I. iii. 58) cannot be killed, and 'Come what come may, Time and the hour runs through the roughest day' (I. iii. 146–7). The simplest processes of life compose the natural order – the alternation of day and night and wake and sleep, the growth of the seed from planting to harvest, the succession of service and reward, and the ongoingness of the generations of man – and despite their familiar ordinariness, these vitalities relentlessly press on to create the future. Their pressure is felt even in the individual speeches, sweeping away impediments, leaving behind, isolated on the unstable sands of the moment the man who tries to dam the flow of life:

> If it were done when 'tis done, then 'twere well
> It were done quickly. If th' assassination
> Could trammel up the consequence, and catch,
> With his surcease, success; that but this blow
> Might be the be-all and the end-all here –
> But here upon this bank and shoal of time –
> We'd jump the life to come. But in these cases
> We still have judgment here, that we but teach
> Bloody instructions, which being taught return
> To plague th' inventor. . . .
> And pity, like a naked new-born babe,
> Striding the blast, or heaven's cherubin hors'd
> Upon the sightless couriers of the air,
> Shall blow the horrid deed in every eye,
> That tears shall drown the wind. (I. vii. 1–25)

Each of the successive 'dones' is at once a doing of the desired deed and an attempt to 'trammel up the consequence'. But, like the river and the wind, the consequences break through rhetorical and rhythmic impediments to move on to a future of further rebellion, the suffering of outraged conscience, and pity for the murder of Duncan spreading through the world.

The rhythms, syntax, imagery and rhetorical patterns of this speech manifest in little the plot of the play. Again and again Macbeth tries to prevent the consequences of his crime, tries to destroy the future; but each time it escapes. Duncan is killed, but his sons Malcolm and Donalbain flee. Banquo is murdered but Fleance escapes in the confusion. Usually it is the children who escape, but sometimes the natural order is perverted: Macduff survives while his wife and children die. But such perversions of natural order cannot interrupt the 'line' that 'stretch[es] out to th' crack of doom' (IV. i. 117), the generations of men and the succession of Scottish kings derived from Banquo and eventuating in James I of England, who may have sat in the audience at the first performance. The third apparition which the witches show Macbeth, 'a Child Crowned, with a tree in his hand' (IV. i. 87), is the emblem of this triumphant ongoingness of life, whose ordinary and miraculous nature is again revealed in the instruments of Macbeth's destruction. It seems impossible that the tyrant should be killed by a man not born of woman on a day when the wood of Birnam moves to Dunsinane castle. And yet how simple it all turns out to be: Macduff was removed from his mother by Caesarean operation, and the soldiers attacking Macbeth camouflage their movements with the leafy branches of the forest. These devices are more obvious than the usual Shakespearian seamless weld of symbolism and realism; but their very obviousness shows how crucial in the play, and in the poet's mind, is the concept of life in movement, flowing into the future, escaping all efforts to prevent the continuation of the great cycles of growth from seed to flower to fruit, of the succession of the seasons and the years, parent and child, king and heir. 'The time is free' (V. viii. 55), says Macduff, holding the head of the tyrant in his hand, and the river of life rushes on beyond that bank and shoal of time into a world where, in the words of the new king, all 'needful' things will be performed 'in measure, time, and place'.

The end is more triumphant than is usual in Shakespearian tragedy, but above the scene hangs the severed head of Macbeth, which has known the fullness of the human mind. It seems to look mockingly out on all the brave hopes for the future and to say that order and prosperity and peace can only be achieved by cutting off the head, by turning away from the full complexity of human existence, by avoiding tragedy.

10 'The full stream of the world'

(i) *Timon of Athens* and *Coriolanus*

By the years 1607–8 Shakespeare was not yet done with tragedy, and two plays, *Timon of Athens* (1607) and *Coriolanus* (1608), show the world and man wrenched apart by irreconcilable opposites. *Timon* opens in the city of Athens where the rich lord Timon moves in a golden world of feasting, generosity, kindness and civility. But riches are not inexhaustible, the very excessiveness of his beneficence undoes itself, and his friends drop away in the moment of need. Maddened by their ingratitude, Timon becomes a misanthrope, withdraws from the city into the desert where nature seems as cruel as it once seemed kind, bends all his efforts to hurting and revealing man for the beast he truly seems and at last, loathing man and the world, kills himself.

The same patterns of one excessive virtue generating its opposite, of city becoming wasteland, of implacable enmity growing between man and man, take more realistic shape in the grey, bloodstained world of the Rome of *Coriolanus*. No trees or flowers grow in the great stone squares of the city, where only one butterfly ever found its way. Outside the walls there are only dusty trampled battlefields separating cities waiting for an attack or a chance to attack. The sounds which rise above this bleak landscape are harsh and strident: battle cries, the roar of the mob in the streets, the clash of shields and clang of sword on sword, the blare of trumpets, the shouts of triumph and defeat, all culminating in the scream of the conspirators at the end of the play: 'Kill, kill, kill, kill, kill him!' The plebeians and the aristocrats hate and fear one another, the Romans and the Volscians have been at war for ever and will continue so until one or the other is destroyed, Coriolanus and Aufidius live only for the other's death. Even their dreams are filled with murder at close quarters: 'down together in . . . sleep, Unbuckling helms, fisting each other's throat –' (IV. v. 130–1). Just as class is set against class, city against city and man against man, so is man set against himself, and his virtues become his vices in changed contexts. Coriolanus's pride and courage make him the saviour of Rome in battle, but they lead him to betray Rome when insulted by its citizens. He lives only for martial honour, but he cannot bear to hear his exploits praised. He proudly believes that the aristocrats are the proper leaders of the city, but his pride will not allow him to make those political gestures which would ensure oligarchic rule. 'Anger's my meat,' says Volumnia, the mother of Coriolanus, 'I sup upon myself, And so shall starve with feeding' (IV. ii. 50–1), and the words catch the self-cannibalism of these incredibly proud and violent people.

Both Coriolanus and Timon act 'like a thing Made by some other deity than Nature, That shapes man better' (*Coriolanus*, IV. vi. 90–2). They are absolute in their judgements and utterly inflexible in their virtues. Their rigidity, their unchanging adoration of their images of themselves, their excessiveness, lead them to meaningless death in a world where no single truth is adequate to the complexities of reality, where life is constantly shifting and changing shape, where 'the full stream of the world' (*As You Like It*, III. ii. 439) flows on by the bank and shoal of time where men stand hoping to have done with mutability. All of the Shakesperian tragic heroes want permanence, solidity, order and clarity. Troilus wants Cressida to remain exclusively his for ever; Hamlet wants king, mother, friend, beloved and self to be always as he imagined them; Othello wishes to be always the brave, honourable and reasonable man, unshaken by the most terrible of events; Lear thinks always to be king and father, able to impose his will upon the world and enjoy its unquenchable love for him; Macbeth hopes to trammel up the consequences of his murder of Duncan and 'catch with his surcease success'. But 'this world is not for aye', and Cressida becomes the toy of Diomed, Claudius becomes King of Denmark, Othello becomes the ignorant savage who throws away a pearl richer than all his tribe, Lear becomes a wandering madman, helpless as a child, Macbeth finds himself cut off from the flow of life on into the future.

Some of the tragic heroes – Brutus, Troilus, Macbeth, Timon and Corio-lanus – refuse to enter the world of flux, accept change in themselves and others, modify their own absolute beliefs. Others – Hamlet, Lear, Othello – without ever entirely giving up their original values, move, however reluc-tantly, with the stream of the world, changing, suffering, pondering the meaning of their experiences, enduring the unwilled journey. The end of the journey is death in every case, but those who move and change with the world, finally accepting readiness or ripeness as all, find at least some gain to balance their losses. As the tragedies proceed, certain beneficent powers gain strength and effectiveness. Hamlet's resignation of himself to 'divinity' or 'providence' grows into the unshakeable love of Desdemona and the high sense of justice and truth which Othello manifests in his execution of himself. These isolated figures of love and courage in turn grow into a community of fellowship and pity in *Lear*, and in *Macbeth* the great orders of nature and society become an irresistible flow carrying life on into the future.

(ii) Antony and Cleopatra

Both man's desire for permanence and the ceaseless change of the world are fully realized in *Antony and Cleopatra* (1607). After the narrow, constricted world of the tragedies, the scene opens to 'Whate'er the ocean pales or sky inclips' (II. vii. 74). There are over forty changes of scene in this play where the action shifts swiftly from Alexandria to Rome, to Sicily, to Parthia, to Athens, to Actium and to Egypt again. The language takes us further out along the 'wide arch Of the rang'd empire' (I. i. 33–4) to distant exotic lands, Cyprus, Lydia, Media, Mesopotamia, Sardinia, Scythia, Syria, Cappadocia, Paphlagonia and Arabia. This world, as bounteous as it is large, throbs with life and pulses with vitality. As the Nile spreads its rich mud over the fields, the sower merely drops his seeds and plenty springs up. Where one thing dies another grows immediately out of the rot. The world is heavy with produce, flesh, wine and food.

The condition of this fecundity is rapid and constant change, symbolized by the rise and fall of the floods of the Nile, bringing the ooze out of which animals and plants spring up. Nothing keeps its shape for more than an instant. The clouds change form even as they assume it:

> That which is now a horse, even with a thought
> The rack dislimns, and makes it indistinct,
> As water is in water. (IV. xix. 9–11)

The ocean moves ceaselessly, and all things that ride upon its changes ultimately die into it. Life

> Like to a vagabond flag upon the stream
> Goes to and back, lackeying the varying tide,
> To rot itself with motion. (I. iv. 45–7)

As it is with nature, so is it with men. The 'slippery people' (I. ii. 192) are only constant in their fickleness, loving now Pompey, now Caesar, now Antony. Human nature cannot endure sameness: 'quietness, grown sick of rest, would purge By any desperate change' (I. iii. 53–4). Man longs only for that which is not until it is: hearing of the long desired death of his wife Fulvia, Antony finds himself wishing she were again alive:

> What our contempts doth often hurl from us
> We wish it ours again; the present pleasure,
> By revolution low'ring, does become
> The opposite of itself. She's good, being gone;
> The hand could pluck her back that shov'd her on. (I. ii. 126–30)

Messenger follows messenger bringing 'news' of changes in a political world which turns with giddy speed. At the beginning of Act II Pompey and his generals in Sicily, deciding to challenge the triumvirs, Antony, Caesar and Lepidus, count on success because Antony is in Egypt with his army. Even as they talk, news is brought that Antony is already in Rome, and in a few lines more the opponents confront one another, a deal is made and Pompey is feasting everyone on his ship. Shortly afterwards Antony marries Caesar's sister, Octavia, and leaves Rome for Athens, apparently never to see Egypt or Cleopatra again. In Rome, Caesar and Lepidus are in power, but they at once turn on Pompey, destroy his army and shortly murder him. Pompey out of the way, Lepidus is imprisoned. Octavia returns to Rome to make peace between her brother and her husband, but before she arrives Antony has left Greece for Alexandria, held ceremonies in which Cleopatra appeared as his queen and made their illegitimate children rulers of various parts of the Roman Empire. Almost at once Caesar's fleet is at Actium, where Antony is put to flight. In a moment more the armies are engaged outside Alexandria, Caesar wins, and Antony, who was so shortly before one of the rulers of the world, is a powerless fugitive. He escapes into death and Cleopatra follows him.

When counselled to be patient and await the gifts of the gods in their due time, Pompey reveals a profound insight into a world in which everything that man seeks disappears even as he seeks it: 'Whiles we are suitors to their throne, decays The thing we sue for' (II. i. 4–5). The great process of change, the flux and fluidity of the world, is literally danced out on one occasion, the banquet on Pompey's ship, where the 'triple pillars' celebrate the signing of an eternal treaty. The cup is passed many times, until all, even Caesar, are drunk enough to be out of themselves. Trumpets, drums and flutes sound, and these great men all join hands to dance the Egyptian bacchanal. Forming a circle, they go round and round, roaring out a song to one of the gods who drives their world about:

> Come, thou monarch of the vine,
> Plumpy Bacchus with pink eyne!
> In thy fats our cares be drown'd,
> With thy grapes our hairs be crown'd.
> Cup us till the world go round,
> Cup us till the world go round! (II. vii. 120–5)

In the midst of the vastness and flux of the world of *Antony and Cleopatra*, there are two distinct geographical places, two distinct states of mind, Rome and Egypt. The two are juxtaposed at the opening of the play in Alexandria. On stage stand two Roman soldiers, stern, severe and hard as the battledress they wear. One of them speaks:

> Nay, but this dotage of our general's
> O'erflows the measure. Those his goodly eyes,
> That o'er the files and musters of the war
> Have glow'd like plated Mars, now bend, now turn,
> The office and devotion of their view
> Upon a tawny front. His captain's heart
> Which in the scuffles of great fights hath burst
> The buckles on his breast, reneges all temper,
> And is become the bellows and the fan
> To cool a gipsy's lust. (I. i. 1–10)

For these Romans what matters is control ('measure' and 'temper'), battle spirit and close attention to the business of war and state. As Philo's scornful words die away, Egypt appears on stage: '*Flourish, Enter* Antony, Cleopatra, *her* Ladies, the *Train, with* Eunuchs *fanning her.*' The talk immediately turns to the chief business of Egypt – love. Antony is caught up within a woman's world, surrounded by Cleopatra and her ladies. The only men in this Egyptian world, other than the enchanted Antony, are, significantly enough, eunuchs.

With a few words and a few simple stage effects, Shakespeare has sketched in his opening lines the contrasting worlds of Egypt and Rome. One is feminine, the other is masculine; one is gay and luxurious, the other stern and moderate; one takes love for its chief business, the other war and statecraft; one is self-indulgent, the other self-denying; one is gay and witty, the other ponderous and sober; one is emotional and passionate, the other rational and logical.

Each of these worlds has its genius of the place, Octavius Caesar in Rome and Cleopatra in Egypt. The tough-minded, practical politician does not fare very well in Shakespeare – Richard III, Henry IV, Henry V, Claudius – but Caesar is no villain from melodrama. A cold, calculating administrator and man of affairs, he is innately fastidious, disliking the smell of sweat and the confusion of wine. He cannot tolerate disorder and imprecision, and he has the aristocrat's sense of caste and complete disdain for the mob. He kills when it is politic to do so, murdering Pompey at the opportune moment; he is cynical about the necessity for explaining the operations of power, dismissing the harmless Lepidus with the remarkable explanation that he had grown too cruel; he lies when necessary; and he never loses sight of his main purpose, the exercise and enlargement of political power. But most often he is neither treacherous nor bloody, only careful, skilful and efficient. He believes in history and understands the price it exacts:

> Be you not troubled with the time, which drives
> O'er your content these strong necessities,
> But let determin'd things to destiny
> Hold unbewail'd their way. (III. vi. 82–5)

This unemotional acceptance of history is made more easy by his belief that it moves to make him emperor of Rome and ruler of the world; and, believing that his desires are one with destiny, he hunts all competitors down implacably and destroys, one by one, all those volcanic energies which are the source of disorder in his world. In his person, and in his actions, Caesar is directly opposed to the physicality and flux of the great world, and his mission is to bring order and rule to the ceaseless to-and-fro movement in which all things rot themselves with motion.

Cleopatra is the very opposite: emotional, self-indulgent, idle, vain, senselessly cruel, passionate, cunning, stupid, overwhelmingly physical and above all unstable. The method by which she keeps Antony in thrall reveals her nature perfectly: 'If you find him sad, Say I am dancing; if in mirth, report That I am sudden sick' (I. iii. 3–5). Like the land over which she rules, the river which flows through it and the serpent which is its symbol, Cleopatra is unpredictable, constantly changing, excessive in all she does, mobile, always assuming new shapes. This is all very bad by Roman standards, but Cleopatra's feminine changeability transcends moral and political judgements to become godlike:

> Age cannot wither her, nor custom stale
> Her infinite variety. Other women cloy
> The appetites they feed, but she makes hungry
> Where most she satisfies. . . . (II. ii. 240–3)

The character grouping in the play is that of the major tragedies: the hero, Antony, is placed between Caesar and Cleopatra, Rome and Egypt, participating in the natures of both and attracted alternately to both. At one time he is the most Roman of Romans, leading his troops across the frozen Alps, drinking the urine of horses and feeding on the flesh of men without revealing any despair or weakness. At another time he is the most Egyptian of Egyptians, playing in Cleopatra's bed, banqueting and drinking to surfeit, revelling in the streets and sitting like a god on a throne of gold. Now Cleopatra is his entire world; now Octavia, the demure Roman matron, is what he most longs for. But the drift of his nature is towards Egypt, and his life is ultimately tied to Cleopatra. But even here there is no stability, for at one moment he loves her beyond all bounds and cannot have enough of her caresses, but at the next he loathes her like a Roman and curses her as a foul Egyptian strumpet. The very things which make her enchanting to him at one instant make her utterly vile the next.

The great rhythms of the world – the ebb and flow of the tides, the rise and fall of the Nile, the ever-shifting shape of the clouds, the continuous process of growth, death and new growth out of death – are, for all the difference in the two characters, the rhythms of the personal lives of Antony and Cleopatra. They are in tune with their world, where Caesar in his fastidious person and his Roman politics is at odds with it. And just as this 'extravagant and wheeling' world is finally acceptable because of its fecundity and generosity, so Antony and Cleopatra in their restless variousness are redeemed by their vitality and a quality which the Renaissance aptly labelled magnificence, the virtue of princes, which expressed itself in grandness of thought, large-scale life style and generosity in all things. When Antony sends a great pearl to Cleopatra, he scorns the rich jewel as no more than the 'treasure of an oyster' and promises in the future 'to mend the petty present' by placing kingdoms at the foot of her 'opulent throne' (I. v. 44–6). In the same extravagant spirit

Cleopatra sends messenger after messenger to Antony and boasts that he 'shall have every day a several greeting, Or I'll unpeople Egypt' (I. v. 77–8). When Enobarbus, the Roman soldier who is the embodiment of Roman practicality and good sense, decides against the tug of his heart that Antony by his folly has lost for ever any possibility of rule, he defects to Caesar. Upon hearing the news of this loss, Antony is deeply touched and knows that his day is indeed dimming, but there are no recriminations and no speeches about betrayal and loyalty. Instead, Antony dispatches after Enobarbus all the treasures that he has collected in Antony's service. The results are catastrophic for Enobarbus, for he discovers that even a man of his rocklike practicality can be torn between two values, and so he kills himself in a Roman way, but with most un-Roman sorrow, to expiate his betrayal of such generosity.

Magnificence, it would seem, is a virtue which may have at least as strong a claim on the heart as logic has on the mind, and it appears in its full grandeur in the palace of Alexandria where Antony sits, having left the battle of Actium like a coward to follow the sails of the fleeing Cleopatra. He knows with full loathing of himself what he has done and what he has lost. In his despair he is near madness, raging and cursing himself and his fate, tortured by the thought that he, who 'with half the bulk o' th' world play'd as I pleas'd' (III. xi. 64), must now humble himself before the 'young man' Caesar. Cleopatra is rightly afraid to approach him, but gradually moves close enough to lay her hands upon him, and, after a few more convulsions of spirit, Antony responds to her weeping with a generosity that is only godlike:

> Fall not a tear, I say; one of them rates
> All that is won and lost. Give me a kiss;
> Even this repays me. (III. xi. 69–71)

Cleopatra memorializes this transcendence of all human pettiness in imagery which pictures Antony participating in his world but rising out of it:

> His face was as the heav'ns, and therein stuck
> A sun and moon, which kept their course and lighted
> The little O, the earth. . . .
> His legs bestrid the ocean; his rear'd arm
> Crested the world. His voice was propertied
> As all the tuned spheres, and that to friends;
> But when he meant to quail and shake the orb,
> He was as rattling thunder. For his bounty,
> There was no winter in't; an autumn 'twas

That grew the more by reaping. His delights
Were dolphin-like: they show'd his back above
The element they liv'd in. In his livery
Walk'd crowns and crownets; realms and islands were
As plates dropp'd from his pocket. (V. ii. 79–92)

But even as she deifies Antony, Cleopatra momentarily doubts whether such a creature ever existed or whether he was only the dream that all men dream, the hope that man somehow rises out of the element he lives in. She turns to Dolabella, and questions him: 'Think you there was or might be such a man As this I dreamt of?' Dolabella's sad reply, 'Gentle madam, no', confirms the unbridgeable gap between imagination and reality, but then Cleopatra suddenly intuits a union, at some far remove, between imagination and nature, towards which Shakespearian tragedy has been moving:

You lie, up to the hearing of the gods.
But if there be nor ever were one such,
It's past the size of dreaming. Nature wants stuff
To vie strange forms with fancy; yet t' imagine
An Antony were nature's piece 'gainst fancy,
Condemning shadows quite. (V. ii. 95–100)

The passage is crucial for an understanding of Shakespeare and the drama of which his works were the centre. From the beginning, as we have seen, the great conflict has been between imagination and reality, man's dreams and the given facts of existence. But now Cleopatra, in the moment of her loss, perceives that while ordinarily nature falls short of what man imagines, on rare occasions it creates things 'past the size of dreaming . . . Condemning shadows quite'. Such a perception does not invalidate the imagination but rather supports it by suggesting some ultimate identification between man's seemingly hopeless dreams and the strange workings of nature. Man is not absurd; there are powers in the universe which answer back to and even outgo his desires. The 'naturalness' and the greatness of Antony and Cleopatra, their complete involvement in nature and transcendence of it, give dramatic form to this philosophical perception, and the lives and fates of the two lovers make clear its meaning.

As different as the ways of Rome and Egypt are, one in opposition to and one in agreement with nature, both still share the characteristic human desire for that permanence which nature denies:

To do that thing that ends all other deeds,
Which shackles accidents and bolts up change,
Which sleeps, and never palates more the dung,[1]
The beggar's nurse and Caesar's. (V. ii. 5–8)

For Octavius Caesar the desire to shackle accident and bolt up change seeks its satisfaction in the establishment of the Roman Empire and the *Pax Romana*. He senses his historical mission on the eve of the last great battle with Mark Antony and remarks that 'the time of universal peace is near' (IV. vi. 5). But Shakespeare seems to agree with Tacitus's view of Roman peace: 'They make a desert and call it peace.'[2] 'Feed and sleep' (V. ii. 187) is the advice that the 'universal landlord', the 'sole sir o' th' world', offers Cleopatra after Antony's death, and the words open on a world as efficient and prosperous, but as lifeless, as Caesar. Such a well-run state has no place for Antony and Cleopatra, the personifications of discord and instability, and as Cleopatra looks upon the body of her dead lover, her gaze goes on beyond him to a landscape from which Antony is gone. 'Shall I abide,' she asks,

In this dull world, which in thy absence is
No better than a sty? O, see, my women,
The crown o' th' earth doth melt. My lord!
O, wither'd is the garland of the war,
The soldier's pole is fall'n! Young boys and girls
Are level now with men. The odds is gone,
And there is nothing left remarkable
Beneath the visiting moon. (IV. xv. 61–8)

The world of Caesar is very orderly, but its order is that of death. All odds are gone and only evens are left, the soldier's pole (symbol of the violence of both war and sex) is levelled in the dust, there is no difference between youth and maturity, the garlands of the war and the crowns of the earth are melted into a flat landscape where nothing is different from anything else, and no life moves beneath the cold, pale eye of the moon.

The immortal longings of Antony and Cleopatra are more complex than those of Caesar. The lovers share Caesar's dreams of a world of permanence, as they share his disdain for the petty present and the paltriness of ordinary life. And yet for them life is, in Cleopatra's phrase, a 'knot intrinsicate', for

---

[1] So the Folio reads.
[2] '. . . ubi solitudinem faciunt, pacem appellant' (*Agricola*, 30, 1. 22).

they are immersed, inextricably involved with the ever-shifting world of the senses. In the lovers, as Antony sees, 'very force entangles Itself with strength' (IV. xiv. 48–9), and they live and view life not from the distance from which Caesar looks on, but from within the inferno of existence itself, suffering the hammer blows of being while longing to escape, forced to realize that they are themselves in part what they seek to escape from. Every attempt to achieve an existence more permanent and more shapely than that provided by the natural world entangles them more deeply in that world. Cleopatra's only method for keeping Antony's love unchanging is to change constantly. In an attempt to preserve his honour inviolate, Antony falls on his own sword, but he bungles the job and gives himself an immediately painful, though ultimately fatal, wound. Cleopatra's 'immortal longings' pause only an instant in the realm of the abstract before becoming sensual fact: 'no more The juice of Egypt's grape shall moist this lip' (V. ii. 283–4). Death is 'a lover's pinch, Which hurts and is desir'd' (V. ii. 298–9). When her maid Iras dies before her, Cleopatra hurries her own death lest Iras should encounter the 'curled Antony' and that incurably amorous gallant give her the first otherworldly kiss. Inescapably tied to the pulse of living things, these frivolous Egyptians transform dying itself into an excited preparation for another great assignation: as her mistress slumps in death, Charmian notes that her appearance is no longer perfection: 'Your crown's awry; I'll mend it and then play –' (V. ii. 321–2).

The lives of this grizzled Romeo and his ageing Juliet, 'with Phoebus' amorous pinches black, And wrinkled deep in time' (I. v. 28–9), have wandered like the trail of the snake through the mud of Nile. Their fortunes, their feelings and their attitudes have shifted constantly as Antony moved between Rome and Egypt, and Cleopatra, the great actress, has changed as rapidly as the colours of the rainbow on 'the varying shore o' th' world'. But in all the infinite variety of life and fortune, they have returned always to one another, and so in the midst of change they have found permanence. Caesar's Rome, which seems so stable and durable, will ultimately crumble: ''Tis paltry to be Caesar: Not being Fortune, he's but Fortune's knave' (V. ii. 2–3). But the lovers pass through nature, leaving behind the dungy earth and the everchanging sea in which life rots itself with motion, for a transcendent world of fire and air, of song and legend, where they are 'marble-constant'.

The play leaves us with two summary forms of the experience which Antony and Cleopatra have lived. The first reveals them as they will appear to the moral eyes of Rome on the platform stage of some Roman version of the Globe Theatre:

> the quick comedians
> Extemporally will stage us, and present
> Our Alexandrian revels; Antony
> Shall be brought drunken forth, and I shall see
> Some squeaking Cleopatra boy my greatness
> I' th' posture of a whore. (V. ii. 216–21)

The second summation is more complex. Looking at the body of Cleopatra and trying, like detectives, to discover the cause of death, Caesar and his generals note the tiny dots of blood and slight swelling on Cleopatra's breast. On the floor there are some marks:

> This is an aspic's trail; and these fig-leaves
> Have slime upon them, such as th' aspic leaves
> Upon the caves of Nile. (V. ii. 354–6)

The passage reaches back through the entire play to gather some of its images into a symbol of the lives of Antony and Cleopatra: the sacred snake of Egypt, often identified with its sinuous river and its subtle queen; the figs which the witty Egyptian ladies, concerned only with the immediate present, once said they valued equally with long life; the oozy liquidity of Egypt and the 'slimy jaws' of 'tawny-finn'd fishes' (II. v. 12–13), which the queen caught in the river, thinking 'every one an Antony'; the ever-flooding Nile bringing its rich mud to Egypt. At the same time, the conjunction of snake, slime and cave emphasize the essential sexuality of the lovers and their fecund world, always rising and falling, bearing and dying. Even beyond this, the presence of serpent and fig leaves identifies this as another version, more pagan than Christian in its implications, of the departure from innocence and Eden into the flux of experience.

It is all here, attractive and loathsome, mysterious and obvious, crooked and straight, foul and beautiful. The trail is there and the slime of passage, but the strange creatures are gone, and our attempts at Roman definition are likely to get no further than Lepidus's efforts to understand another of the wondrous beasts of Nile:

ANTONY: It is shaped, sir, like itself, and it is as broad as it hath breadth; it is just so high as it is, and moves with it own organs. It lives by that which nourisheth it, and the elements once out of it, it transmigrates.

LEPIDUS: What colour is it of?

ANTONY: Of its own colour too.

LEPIDUS: 'Tis a strange serpent.

ANTONY: 'Tis so. And the tears of it are wet. (II. vii. 47–55)

(iii) The late romances

With Shakespeare, as we have already seen, a new perception leads to a new dramatic form which is experimented with for a time, then stabilized and exploited to the fullest, until it leads in turn to new ideas and forms. Nothing is left behind in the process of development, and, in his last phase, Shakespeare did not forget the knowledge that tragedy is inevitable, that 'Our natures do pursue, Like rats that ravin down their proper bane, A thirsty evil; and when we drink we die' (*Measure for Measure*, I. ii. 132–4). But tragic knowledge now becomes but a part of a larger vision which includes a power, sometimes known in *Macbeth* and *Antony and Cleopatra* as 'time' or 'nature', operating in ways not understood by or even acceptable to man, over long reaches of time and vast reaches of space, to preserve and nourish life. This power, which appears in such symbolic forms as the crowned child with the tree in his hand and the ebbing and flooding Nile, becomes the shaping force in Shakespeare's last plays, *Pericles* (1608), *Cymbeline* (1609), *The Winter's Tale* (1610), *The Tempest* (1611) and *Henry VIII* (1613), the latter usually said to be only partly by Shakespeare. Each of the plays tells, with varying emphasis, the same simple romance story in which a savage act, frequently involving some perversion of the sexual instincts, disrupts a family and a society. Some member of the family, usually a child, is banished or lost in an alien land where birthright and identity are obliterated. The exile involves a long journey, usually a sea voyage, a great storm and wreckage on a desolate shore. After the passage of long periods of time, during which certain healing processes take place and the younger generation grows to maturity, reunion and restoration miraculously take place. Father and child – usually a father and daughter – husband and wife are reunited, and the sins of the past are forgiven. The romance or fairy-tale pattern dominates the realistic detail, and the overall effect is to suggest the workings of the miraculous and the strange in human life. *Henry VIII*, where the erring parent is England and the lost child found Elizabeth, extends this romance pattern into history.

(iv) *The Winter's Tale*

The Winter's Tale is the best play in which to see the use that Shakespeare made of the romance plot, for it contains the full cycle from sad beginning to happy ending, and it makes clear the complex meanings assigned to each of the parts. The title is explained by the young Prince Mamillius who, when asked by his mother to tell her a story, replies, 'A sad tale's best for winter.

19a A Flemish booth stage (Peter Breughel the Elder), *c.* 1560

19b A booth stage in a market square of Louvain, 1594

20a A booth stage in Holland, 1618

20b A booth stage in a market square, 1660

I have one Of sprites and goblins.' He begins: 'There was a man . . . Dwelt by a churchyard –' (II. i. 25–30). Shakespeare's play is also of sprites and goblins, of the strange powers at work in the human mind, and it too begins by a churchyard, the place of death and burial. In the court of Sicilia, the king, Leontes, is overwhelmed with a sudden suspicion that his queen, Hermione, has betrayed him with his guest and lifelong friend, the king of Bohemia, Polixenes. Wild with jealousy, Leontes attempts to murder his friend, but Polixenes is warned by one of Leontes's nobles, Camillo, and the two escape to Bohemia. In his fury Leontes then imprisons Hermione, accuses her publicly of adultery and causes her child born in prison, Perdita, to be exposed in a barren land to die. Sickening with the disgrace of his mother, Leontes's heir, the older child Mamillius, dies soon after. The queen is pronounced chaste and faithful by the oracle of Apollo, but, griefstruck, Hermione apparently dies. Leontes, overwhelmed by his sin, vows to spend the remainder of his life in prayer and repentance. The child exposed to the elements is luckily saved by two shepherds and raised by them in Bohemia. Sixteen years pass, and Perdita has grown into a young shepherdess of enchanting beauty, beloved by prince Florizel, the son of Polixenes, who discovers the love of his son for the shepherdess and forbids their marriage. The lovers take ship and flee to Sicilia, where they meet Leontes; but they are pursued by Polixenes, accompanied by the two shepherds who originally saved Perdita. In Sicilia the truth is at last made known, that Perdita is the lost daughter of Leontes, and her marriage to Florizel is then blessed. The two kings, Leontes and Polixenes, embrace and reaffirm their former love for one another. Then, in the greatest miracle of all, it develops that Hermione, Leontes's queen, did not die but retired instead to a secluded house, where she has waited all these years, sorrowing over her lost children. She is now introduced as a statue, stony cold and immobile. Her lost daughter appears before her and weeps, and as her husband speaks of former sins and of years of repentance, the statue comes to life, Hermione embraces her daughter and her husband and the promised end is arrived at: that which was lost has been found.

By means of poetry Shakespeare manages to make this charming but simple story carry an extraordinary set of complex, interlocking meanings, which are best understood as a group of duplicating plots, each nestled inside and conforming to the others. By means of imagery and references to agricultural festivals such as sheepshearings and harvest homes, the story of loss, death and miraculous restoration is also made the cycle of the seasons from the frozen immobility of winter through the rebirth of spring and the fruition of summer to the harvest of autumn. This natural cycle is at the same time one with the life of man in which childhood grows through maturity to old age, and even as it seems to die gives place to a new generation, born free of the old crimes, unencumbered by the old memories and sorrows. Ideally the transition from season to season and generation to generation would be a smooth and easy succession, but in these plays it is, though ultimately as inevitable as the happy ending of the fairy tale, interrupted and threatened with the cracking of nature's moulds and the destruction of all 'germens'. Winter seems to kill all life, and there seems to be an uncompromising antagonism between old and young. Leontes kills and exiles his children, and the old shepherd wishes that 'there were no age between ten and three and twenty . . . for there is nothing in the between but getting wenches with child, wronging the ancientry, stealing, fighting' (III. iii. 59–63). The younger generation, Perdita and Florizel, will allow no interference with their wills, believe only in the goodness of nature and the power of their own beauty and love and accept no advice from their elders.

As it is with the seasons and the generations, so is it with society; and at this level the play begins to offer explanations of why life follows the pattern it does. The movement is from Sicilia to Bohemia and back to Sicilia again. Sicilia is the world of art and civilization, the world that man makes. The scenes are set indoors, particularly in those places where civil values find their most pronounced expression: the palace of a king, a council chamber, a court of law, a prison and, finally, an art gallery. Here at first appearance the potential of human life, made possible by man's arts, is fully realized. Here is the flowering of friendship between man and man, Polixenes and Leontes, between nation and nation, Sicilia and Bohemia. The rich setting, the courtly manners, the prosperity of all are a fulfilment of the possible generosity of life. Marriage, the rich love and faithfulness of Hermione, the kindness of her husband and the clear imprint of the father's features on the face of the child bring the anarchic energies of sex to controlled satisfaction and completion. But even as we watch the triumph of civilization it begins to sour. Art becomes too artful, ceases to be an instrument for furthering nature and becomes instead a way of perverting it, like cosmetics used not to heighten natural beauty but to distort and destroy it. Friendship, courtesy and the kindness of host to guest in a foreign land become overripe and fall into their opposite, as Leontes presses Polixenes unmercifully to extend his stay in Sicilia, until his hospitality becomes 'a whip'. Marriage ripens swiftly into a possessiveness so complete that the wife's every glance of friendship is seen by the husband as an invitation to adultery. Decay increases swiftly as the play proceeds. The civilized virtues of loyalty and obedience to a legal superior are converted into the means for murder as the king commands the subject to poison the guest. The greatest of human arts, the ordered society founded on justice and law, becomes the instrument of tyranny as Leontes turns into a tyrant who curses and mocks his faithful counsellors, and uses the law unjustly to imprison, try and condemn Hermione to death. Winter and death overwhelm Sicilia as Hermione and her children die and Leontes is bound in sorrow to a life of perpetual chastity, fasting and penitence.

As Sicilia darkens with death, life flees to Bohemia, the pastoral or shepherd kingdom, the world that nature makes. The scenes here are out-of-doors, the inhabitants, milkmaids, shepherds, countrymen, farmers and itinerant pedlars. The great occasions are agricultural festivals. Clothes are plain, manners direct, speech simple. Human virtues – attraction, love, pity, mercy, cherishing the young – are direct and spontaneous. But the excesses of civilization expose man to the excesses of nature, and the first glimpse of Bohemia shows not a pastoral but a wasteland torn by uncontrolled energy – the great storm at sea which destroys the ship and all its crew – and ruled by savage appetite – the bear who seizes Antigonus and, indifferent to his cries for pity, tears him apart and eats the pieces. A gentler nature immediately comes into play, however, with the appearance of the shepherds who, partly out of pity and partly out of delight in the treasure left with her, rescue the abandoned infant, Perdita, and carry her out of the desert to their rural home. Sixteen years pass, and Perdita grows into a beautiful young shepherdess, now in love with Florizel, the son of King Polixenes. Nature has once again healed: the new generation has regained the innocence, vitality and hope which the older generation had lost, and winter has once more given way to spring. But even in this new Eden freedom of instinct and natural action are already moving towards their excessive forms, licence and wilfulness. A dance of the twelve satyrs, charming as it is, suggests the lust and brutality lying just below the surface of nature; the gay songs and joyfulness of the pedlar Autolycus, the primal thief, scarcely conceal an anarchic energy which takes whatever is seen and liked; the simple delight of the countryfolk in marvellous stories and the trinkets from Autolycus's pack verges on mere mindlessness; and honesty about sex moves towards greasiness and sluttishness. Just as the shepherds' feast needs a few exotic spices – saffron, mace, dates, nutmeg, ginger – to give savour to the food, so could their world be improved by a few touches of art and civility.

It is, however, in the love of Perdita and Florizel that the dangers of the natural state are explored in depth. They loved at first sight, and they now refuse to allow any difference of social station to interfere with that love. Though they plan to marry and intend no sexual relations until they are married, they reject any other impediments to their will. When Polixenes in disguise suggests that they ask the blessing of Florizel's father for quite 'natural' reasons – 'The father – all whose joy is nothing else But fair posterity – should hold some counsel In such a business' (IV. iv. 418–20) – the lovers adamantly refuse. And when Polixenes reveals himself and divorces the lovers, they choose to flee 'to unpath'd waters, undream'd shores, most certain To miseries enough' (IV. iv. 577–8), rather than submit. When Camillo attempts to dissuade them, pointing out the disasters and changes to which love is subject – 'Prosperity's the very bond of love, Whose fresh complexion and whose heart together Affliction alters' – Perdita responds confidently: 'I think affliction may subdue the cheek, But not take in the mind.' Camillo's dry response, 'Yea, say you so?', contains sad knowledge of what happens to love supported by nothing but natural desire when beauty dies and adversity comes on. The absolute trust of the lovers in their own natural instincts and wills emerges in a discussion of flowers and gardening by Perdita, which focuses the art-nature conflict at the centre of the play. She refuses to have in her garden any hybrids – carnations or gillyvors – because 'there is an art which in their piedness shares With great creating nature' (IV. iv. 87–8). Polixenes's response explains the ideal relationship between art and nature and makes clear that, just as imagination and nature are not ultimately opposed in *Antony and Cleopatra*, so the higher arts are not the opposite of nature but its 'natural' extensions:

> nature is made better by no mean
> But nature makes that mean; so over that art,
> Which you say adds to nature, is an art
> That nature makes. You see, sweet maid, we marry
> A gentler scion to the wildest stock,
> And make conceive a bark of baser kind
> By bud of nobler race. This is an art
> Which does mend nature – change it rather; but
> The art itself is nature (IV. iv. 89–97)

Perdita understands but is not convinced: 'I'll not put The dibble in earth to set one slip of them.' And so, following their nature, the lovers adventure out into the wild world to go where chance may lead them, and take ship for unknown shores. The ship carries them, by Camillo's plan, back to the civil world of Sicilia, and here even as nature had once preserved life which an over-refined civilization was about to destroy, civilization now preserves the life and love which an undirected nature threatens with a lifetime of wandering and suffering. Perdita is recognized and her identity as the daughter of a king and heir to a kingdom established. Her marriage with Florizel is blessed and their future prosperity assured. Children and parents, friend and friend, are reunited. At the same time that art and civilization bring nature to fulfilment, nature reinvigorates civilization, and the return of the lost daughter, the appearance of the next generation with its promise for the future, frees Leontes from his living death of sorrow and changes Hermione from a statue to a living woman.

The plot rhythm, which governs the succession of seasons and generations and the historical shifts of a culture between the man-made world and that of nature, also controls the life, both external and psychic, of individual man. The romance plot of the play views life from far off, from the perspective of great spaces and long periods of time; but the individual life is seen, in the character of Leontes, from a tragic perspective, close up, focused on feelings so intense that only the thought of the immediate experienced moment is real. The resultant mixture of tragic realism and fairytale plot creates the remarkable blend, so characteristic of Shakespeare's late plays, of real and unreal, the single moment and the eternal, the particular and the universal, the objective and the symbolic.

As the play opens, Leontes is already in the summer of his life, a king, husband and father. Childhood, when he and Polixenes 'were as twinn'd lambs that did frisk i' th' sun' (I. ii. 67), when time and change had no meaning and they thought only 'to be boy eternal', when they 'knew not The doctrine of ill-doing, nor dream'd That any did' – this condition of springtime innocence is far behind. Polixenes remarks that as children they would have 'answer'd heaven Boldly "Not guilty", the imposition clear'd Hereditary ours' (I. ii. 73–5); but they do not escape the imposed guilt. 'Hereditary ours' suggests the 'imposition' to be original sin, but this theological abstraction is dramatically translated into the existential fact of sex. (Sexual awareness is regularly in Shakespeare the dividing line between innocence and experience, and in the tragedies sexual disgust, a sense of a world overwhelmed with random ceaseless sexuality, is the extreme metaphor for the despair felt by Hamlet, Troilus, Othello and Lear.) The court of Sicilia is intensely sexual, though the sexuality is submerged, often in puns, beneath the surface of civil life. But suddenly, without realistic motive, Leontes looks at his wife and friend in mannerly exchange of courtesy and sees 'paddling palms and

pinching fingers' (I. ii. 115). In an instant more suspicion grows into a Lear-
like certainty that all the world is corrupt:

> It is a bawdy planet, that will strike
> Where 'tis predominant; and 'tis pow'rful, think it,
> From east, west, north, and south. Be it concluded,
> No barricado for a belly. Know't,
> It will let in and out the enemy
> With bag and baggage. (I. ii. 201–6)

Although the specific cause of sexual nausea may be unidentifiable, the
means by which this obsession is loosed is another instance of a civilized
virtue or art, in this case mind – observation, analysis, self-consciousness –
developing to the point where it becomes a danger to the life it should serve.
Leontes's first suspicions are delivered in an aside, while behind him, now
stilled, the gracious and innocent activity of his court continues. His voice
and his mind swiftly become the only reality:

> Affection! thy intention stabs the centre.
> Thou dost make possible things not so held,
> Communicat'st with dreams – how can this be? –
> With what's unreal thou coactive art,
> And fellow'st nothing. Then 'tis very credent
> Thou mayst co-join with something; and thou dost –
> And that beyond commission; and I find it . . . (I. ii. 138–44)

The lines, sometimes said to be corrupt because of their difficulty, render
perfectly a mind turning, Macbeth-fashion, in upon itself, making thought
the measure of all things. Solipsism soon takes the form of paranoia –
'They're here with me already; whisp'ring, rounding, "Sicilia is a so-forth"'
(I. ii. 217–18) – every harmless word, e.g., 'satisfy', takes on sinister meanings.
Fury seizes him when anyone argues that things are not as he sees them, and
sleeplessness comes to the still-beating mind that finds 'Nor night nor day no
rest!' Again like Macbeth, Leontes seeks release from the pain of thought by
forcing the world to conform to his mind, and so he becomes the tyrant,
forcing the court to agree sycophantically with him, banishing all that argue
with him and proclaiming Hermione an adulteress.

   But the world resists this tyranny, and Hermione is proved chaste. Like
all tragic figures when they arrive at their tragic moment, Leontes believes
that what has been done can be undone: 'I'll reconcile me to Polixenes, New
woo my queen, recall the good Camillo' (III. ii. 156–7). But the queen is

gone, the friends fled beyond recall, the young prince dead, the new daughter lost. The trap closes to lock Leontes into the memory of what he has done, into the mind which he has made the only reality:

> Prithee, bring me
> To the dead bodies of my queen and son.
> One grave shall be for both. Upon them shall
> The causes of their death appear, unto
> Our shame perpetual. Once a day I'll visit
> The chapel where they lie; and tears shed there
> Shall be my recreation. So long as nature
> Will bear up with this exercise, so long
> I daily vow to use it. Come, and lead me
> To these sorrows. (III. ii. 235–44)

Having passed through spring and summer, the man now comes to his winter, isolate, barren, tied to the memory of past wrongs and sorrows, daily doing ritual penance for what cannot be changed. Even after sixteen years pass, he is still unable to forgive himself or to remarry and enter again the full stream of the world. For many, Hermione is now forgotten, and her beauty and the cruel events of long ago are only a winter's tale, but the individual cannot forget, and the brilliant eyes of the living are only 'dead coals' compared to the 'Stars, stars' (V. i. 67–8) of the dead woman. This condition of death in life, of fixedness, of thought without heat, is the realistic form of the statue state of Hermione. But then at the moment when all seemed frozen in death, spring arrives, the younger generation thought lost for ever returns, old friendships are renewed, wife forgives husband and death gives way once more to life. The miraculous nature of the restoration and its meaning is conveyed by the language with which Paulina brings the statue of Hermione to life:

> Music, awake her: strike. [*Music.*
> 'Tis time; descend; be stone no more; approach;
> Strike all that look upon with marvel. Come;
> I'll fill your grave up. Stir; nay, come away.
> Bequeath to death your numbness, for from him
> Dear life redeems you. (V. iii. 98–103)

The play is hopeful in its promise of some restoration for even the individual man in the course of things. Suspicion, jealousy, subjectivity and tragedy are inevitable, as inevitable as the change from summer to winter;

but penitence, the durability of love, the growth of new generations bring about some release in old age before death finally arrives. The romance plot, though it controls the flow of events, does not entirely overwhelm, however, the mind and the individual's knowledge that what has been lost will not quite ever be found again. Hermione returns to life, but her face is aged and wrinkled; in her joy at the return of Perdita, Paulina remembers that her husband Antigonus died in saving the child; Mamillius still lies in the grave, a delicate flower of early spring that died before it could 'behold Bright Phoebus in his strength' (IV. iv. 123–4). At the moment of revelation, the characters 'look'd as they had heard of a world ransom'd, or one destroyed' (V. ii. 16–17), that familiar mixture of tears and smiles with which life in the Shakespearian world is felt in the moments when it is experienced fully and truly.

The sense of life as ongoingness and ceaseless change which is so central to the Shakespearian world is offered in *The Winter's Tale* as an endless pulsation between winter and summer, death and life, civil and natural life, art and nature, age and youth, joy and sorrow, mind and feeling, subjectivity and objectivity: the dualities around which most of Renaissance and modern thought turns. In Shakespeare's plays an ideal balance of these mutually supporting qualities is impossible to maintain because of a tendency in man and his world to hypertrophy. Like the overreaching heroes of the drama, each virtue seeks its own absolute expression and ends by destroying that with which it would ideally interact to further the whole of life. This in turn forces life towards a radical opposite, and the same process of growth and overdevelopment again takes place. This natural, historical and psychological rhythm is personified in this play as Time:

> I, that please some, try all, both joy and terror
> Of good and bad, that makes and unfolds error,
> . . . .
>   it is in my pow'r
> To o'erthrow law, and in one self-born hour
> To plant and o'erwhelm custom. Let me pass
> The same I am, ere ancient'st order was
> Or what is now receiv'd. I witness to
> The times that brought them in; so shall I do
> To th' freshest things now reigning, and make stale
> The glistering of this present, as my tale
> Now seems to it. (IV. i. 1–15)

Where in the tragedies the characters caught up in this process are denied all but the briefest glimpses of its potential benefits or any sense that at some far remove great powers are at work sustaining life, here in the last plays the saving forces are visible and audible. Hermione, like Desdemona, is chaste and pure, but proof of her faith does not rest, as she believes, on her own testimony alone. The oracle of Apollo declares her innocence in clear, direct terms, and by doing so guarantees that at some great distance from the fevers and hatreds of life there is a presence, a serenity, which knows the truth of things in this world and will speak, when questioned, to make the truth known. That Apollo is the god of the civil arts, of learning, healing and poetry, of the lyre rather than the flute, suggests that the arts – plays like *The Winter's Tale* and statues like that in which Hermione is preserved during her seeming death – may also be the oracles which preserve life and declare truth. But the oracle of the god and the work of art are only two of the many forces interacting and working for the preservation of life. Where in the tragedies the world was sufficiently ambiguous to give at least the appearance of total corruption – any belief in goodness in man and life was dependent on faith – here in *The Winter's Tale* the corruption is located entirely in the mind of the perceiver, and even during the winter of Leontes's rage there are numerous forces of life, some natural, some social, stirring and preparing for the future. Camillo accepts exile rather than poison the king who has trusted his life to him; even as Mamillius dies, deep in the prison another child is born; Paulina risks her life to take the child out of prison and present her to Leontes as his own child; Antigonus dies to save the child from certain death and provide her with at least the possibility of life; Leontes even in his fury cannot entirely ignore law and justice, and he arranges a trial for Hermione which leads to her exoneration; the old shepherd is moved by pity for the exposed child to take her up and raise her; and Leontes, on learning of his error, punishes himself for his guilt with a life of penitence, which makes his ultimate reunion with his wife possible. Such is the inclusiveness of the Shakespearian vision of the persistence of life, the constant interaction of art and nature, that even what are ordinarily accounted vices, shrewishness, greed, wilfulness and theft, contribute to the saving of the child and the establishment of her true identity as a princess.

11 The great fair of the world and the ocean island: *Bartholomew Fair* and *The Tempest*

(i) Jonson and Shakespeare

The English drama of the Renaissance turned around the opposition of two great forces, man's Faustian drive towards autonomy and absolute power, and a stubborn world which seems directly to oppose human desire. The conflict between man and world, dream and reality, is, of course, central to Western thought and not peculiar to the Renaissance, but the English playwrights apparently felt it with unusual intensity, felt that the forces involved were equally imperative, equally titanic and equally real. Its implications extended to include nearly every crucial duality, art and nature, imagination and reason, mind and body, ideal and actual, permanence and change, myth and history, freedom and fate. Their medium itself was closely involved, and the theatre – which frees man to assume identities at will and create imaginative worlds, and at the same time reduces man to a transient shadow acting in a plot beyond his control – was both the means of presenting and the most comprehensive image of the great conflict.

By and large, the drama of the period 1576–1613 was unable to resolve the subjective–objective, man–world opposition. Man locks himself in the dreadful isolation of his mind, like Faustus dragged screaming down to hell; is paralysed like Troilus before a division of reality which cannot be closed;

'This is, and is not, Cressid'; stands defying a reality he will not accept but cannot control, like Bussy or Vittoria Corombona; imposes his will upon the world, like Tamburlaine and Octavius Caesar; is swept away into history, like the Duchess of Malfi; or accepts a world which he cannot understand but must trust, like Hamlet. As time passed, the drama tended more and more to avoid the fundamental issue altogether and escaped into romance, sensationalism, cynical displays of folly, fashionable pastoralism, exquisite and extended debates on the priorities of love and honour, and an emphasis on spectacular scenic effects and song and dance.

Only two poet-playwrights travelled the full path traced earlier by Sophocles from Thebes to Colonos, by Dante from hell through purgatory to paradise. Only Ben Jonson and William Shakespeare continued through their long careers to face the central issues directly, to progress steadily towards greater understanding of the problem through continuing experiments in dramatic form and subject matter, and at last, still doggedly refusing to accept a final incompatibility of man and world, to succeed in writing plays in which the opposing forces appear not as absolute antagonists but as parts of a complex whole. Neither *Bartholomew Fair* (1614) nor *The Tempest* (1611) was the last play of its author – Shakespeare was to have at least a hand in writing *Henry VIII* in 1613, and Jonson continued to write, with ever-decreasing success, for another fifteen years – but both plays are the completion of an arc of thought and dramatic art which built steadily throughout the authors' working lives in the theatre. Both give perfect form to the two playwrights' characteristic visions of the world and its energies. The 'realistic' Jonson offers the world as the great annual fair at Smithfield, while the 'romantic' Shakespeare makes his summary image a mysterious island in a faraway sea.

Wo do not know what Shakespeare thought of Jonson, but Jonson was always intensely, nervously aware of his great competitor. He 'lov'd the man' and honoured 'his memory (on this side Idolatry)' (*Discoveries*, 654–5), but he could never resist criticizing his work, and in the Induction to *Bartholomew Fair* he glances scornfully at the fairytale quality of *The Winter's Tale* and *The Tempest*:

> If there bee never a *Servant-monster* i'the *Fayre*; who can helpe it? [the author] says: nor a nest of *Antiques*? Hee is loth to make Nature afraid in his *Playes*, like those that beget *Tales*, *Tempests*, and such like *Drolleries*. . . . (127–30)

Later in the play, the very realistic tapster who works in the pig booth is referred to as 'Mooncalf', a title also given to Caliban,

Despite Jonson's belief that *Bartholomew Fair* and *The Tempest* are very different kinds of plays, the two resemble one another, *mutatis mutandis*, in many ways. In both, a group of travellers progress to the centre of a strange enchanting place, and the journey provides regenerative insights into the self. The ultimate mysteries of both the fair and the island are located at their centres and tended by a genius of the place. The centre of the fair is a pig booth, presided over by Ursula the pigwoman, attended by thieves, whores and quarrellers. The ocean island centres on Prospero's cell, ruled by the great magician, attended by those two emblems of the contrary impulses in human nature, Ariel and Caliban, and by his daughter Miranda. Both of these places are ultimately transformed into theatres and their mysteries presented as a play within a play. The difference in these internal plays is exactly the difference in the two authors' views of humanity. In Jonson's play, the satirist and writer of realistic comedy presents as his ultimate image of reality a grotesque puppet show; while Shakespeare, whose view of human nature was always more generous than Jonson's, offers a great masque celebrating the beauty and beneficence of nature, the interaction of man and the gods, and the triumph of social life through the civil institution of marriage. After their experiences in the fair and on the island, the travellers, greatly changed, return from the worlds of play and magic to the realities of daily life, to Justice Overdo's house for a feast, and to Milan to resume the duties of rule and government.

(ii) *Bartholomew Fair*

Beginning about 1604 and continuing through many years, Jonson, in collaboration with the architect and scene designer Inigo Jones, wrote an annual masque for the Stuart court. These beautiful spectacles featured songs and elaborate dances – the dancers were usually the more prominent courtiers – ingenious scenic effects and gorgeous costumes. In Jonson's hands the masque was built around a conflict of opposites – nature and alchemy, blackness and light, opinion and truth, order and chaos, the sphinx and love, the age of gold and the age of iron. The destructive powers usually appear first, singing and dancing out wild threats to order and authority, but this grotesqueness is then banished in an instant by the appearance of some superior power, and the main masque begins with serene songs and stately measures. At the end, the dancers blend with the remainder of the court, and, led by the king, the entire assembly moves out of the theatre. In a few masques, such as *Pleasure Reconciled to Virtue*, there is a fusion of the vigour of the antimasque with the control of the masque proper; but most often the grotesques are simply removed from the stage – frequently in one of Inigo Jones's marvellous machines – by the command of a god, who represents not only the power of truth but also the power of the king, who sat in the audience as the chief spectator.

Besides being elaborate compliments to the king, Jonson's masques are celebrations of the miraculous power of civil and moral authority to control and order the energies of chaos and destruction. But removed from the noble setting of the Banqueting Hall at Whitehall to the Hope Theatre, where plays were presented between bear-baitings, and the smell of the animals lingered on during theatrical performances,[1] the forces of disorder and order looked and sounded very differently. Even the gorgeous spectacles and wonderful machinery of the masques, which contributed so much to a sense of the power of art to order the world, could seem from the perspective of the public theatre no more than children's toys, and the great world no more than a fair or carnival:

> *What* petty things they are, wee wonder at? like children, that esteeme every trifle; and preferre a *Fairing* before their Fathers: what difference is betweene us, and them? but that we are dearer Fooles, Cockscombes, at a higher rate? They are pleas'd with Cockleshels, Whistles, Hobby-horses, and such like: we with Statues, marble Pillars, Pictures, guilded Roofes, where under-neath is Lath, and Lyme; perhaps Lome. Yet, we take pleasure in the lye, and are glad, wee can cousen our selves. (*Discoveries*, 1437–45)

It was in the Hope, on 31 October 1614, that *Bartholomew Fair* was first presented. Like the dancers in the masques, the characters of the play are divided into two distinct groups; those who earn their living at the fair, and those who visit it. The first group is a strange assortment of common clay: corncutters and mousetrap vendors, whores and pimps, bullies and gamesters; Lantern Leatherhead, a seller of toys and master of a puppet show; Joan Trash, the gingerbread woman; Ezekiel Edgworth, the civil cutpurse; Nightingale, the ballad singer; Jordan Knockem, the horsetrader and fighter; and Ursula, who sells roast pig and bottled ale. Food, drink, toys, sex, horses, money and entertainment are the basic commodities of the fair, and the people who deal in them are as basic as their wares. At the centre of the stage is the summary symbol of the fair, Ursula's pig booth, where pigs are roasted

---

[1] The bears also linger on in the name of one of the leading characters, Ursula, or Urs'la, as Jonson spells it.

over the hot smoky fire and where the ale froths. Here everyone comes to eat pork, to drink, to buy and sell women, to relieve themselves, to quarrel and fight, to lend and borrow, to share the loot. Ursula is 'the good race-*Bawd* o' Smithfield' (II. v. 171–2), and Zeal-of-the-Land Busy perceives that she is the very essence of the fair:

> But the fleshly woman (which you call *Ursla*) is above all to be avoyded, having the marks upon her, of the three enemies of Man, the World, as being in the *Faire*; the Devill, as being in the fire; and the Flesh, as being her selfe. (III. vi. 33–7)

Busy's rhetorical progression from World, through Devil, to Flesh is accurate, for meat and flesh are the primary stuff of the fair, and Ursula's booth is heavy with carnality. She is so enormously fat that she sweats grease, the drippings from the roasting pigs crackle and hiss, the smell of cooked meat fills the air. Here, too, whores like Punk Alice gather to sell another equally basic kind of flesh. But, for all its greasiness and disorder, this temple of the flesh is not unattractive compared to Jonson's earlier symbols for the basic energies of the world, such as the gold coin in *Volpone*, or Tiberius the deified emperor of Rome.

To the fair come a number of middle-class visitors, amused or scandalized by its crudeness and vulgarity, certain of their own moral and aesthetic superiority. Many of these visitors are authorities, members of the establishment whose function it is to supervise, license and control the busy, bustling disorder of the world. But the visitors' true motives for going to the fair, however much they may be disguised under a mask of gravity or condescension, are little different from the cruder appetites which make the fair go round. Win-the-fight Littlewit goes to see the curious sights and satisfy her desire, strengthened by pregnancy, for roast pig; her husband, the clerk of the court John Littlewit, goes to satisfy his vanity as author of the play he has written for Leatherhead's puppets. Bartholomew Cokes, the country squire, who delightedly points out that it is *his* fair since it bears his name, goes to see all the sights and buy all the toys and gingerbread. Quarlous and Winwife, two fashionable young wits, go to laugh at the fools and search for a rich wife. Zeal-of-the-Land Busy and Dame Purecraft, male and female Puritans, go, so they say, to reprehend the abominations of this modern Babylon, but, in reality, to indulge their appetite for roast pig, and those even more basic appetites, the public display of self-righteousness and the delight in attacking anything they dislike.

The fair serves as a touchstone or a funhouse mirror which reveals the truth about these superior folk, and the play involves them, as the day of heat and dust and noise wears on, in situations which reveal their close kinship with that primal world they think themselves so far above. The fine ladies soon find themselves under pressure of what delicately but accurately used to be termed 'a call of nature', and are delighted to make use of the bottom of a broken bottle in the back of the pig booth, that place of reality which reduces all humanity to its basics as surely as Lear's heath or the magical wood outside Athens. The reduction proceeds more grimly when Win and Mistress Overdo, those two models of middle-class virtue, drunk with ale and delighted with the promise of coaches, fine clothes and a succession of new gallants for lovers, agree to a business proposition by Captain Whit, who finds himself short of a commodity of whores at this crucial time. Perhaps the best instance of the way in which the fair involves and exposes all visitors occurs when Quarlous stands laughing outside the circle of the game of vapours. Only a cross word or two is needed to draw him into the circle and reveal him as the contentious creature which his name suggests he is under all his fine manners.

The edge of Jonson's comedy cuts deeper to expose those who come not merely to laugh at the fair but to rule it. Zeal-of-the-Land Busy, the sanctified saint from Banbury, arrives to eat pig 'with a reformed mouth, with *sobriety*, and humblenesse' (I. vi. 73–4). But a meal of roast pork and several bottles of ale stir up a prophetic fury, and he girds up his loins to strip the masks from the faces of offence and cast down the tents of the wicked. Before he is through, the fair reveals him not only as a notable glutton but as a consummate idiot. His measure is best taken before the toy stall where he calls down the wrath of the Old Testament God on a drum and a doll:

> the broken belly of the Beast . . . the opening of the merchandise of *Babylon* againe, & the peeping of *Popery* upon the stals, here, here, in the high places. See you not *Goldylocks*, the purple strumpet, there? in her yellow gowne and greene sleeves? the prophane pipes, the tinckling timbrells? A shop of reliques! (III. vi. 67–97)

Worked to a fever pitch by his own rhetoric, he hurls the stall and toys to the ground and creates the riot his nature lusts after. As a mirror for magistrates, Humphrey Wasp, the luckless guardian of Bartholomew Cokes, is even more of a disaster. Like the insect he is named for, he buzzes angrily at everyone he meets, engages in endless quarrels, is robbed of the marriage licence which has been entrusted to him and loses his charge.

The chief questions about not only the ability but the right of authority to govern are asked through the person of Justice Adam Overdo, the magistrate of the court of Pie-Powders, which has jurisdiction over the fair. In one of those disguises which reveal, Overdo enters the fair dressed as a local mad-man, to search out and punish such enormities as short measures and theft. In accents which combine several traditional authorities – the jurist, the Puritan reformer, the Juvenalian satirist and the Old Testament prophet – he denounces such abominations as bottle ale and tobacco, quarrelling and whoring, cheating and taking of purses. But Overdo's motives are suspect. The Dogberrian constabulary, Haggis, Bristle and Poacher (the watch that is so busy gawking at the sights of the fair that it never knows what time it is, always arrives late at the scene of the crime and always arrests the wrong person), know very well that Overdo is 'a very parantory person', who 'will be angry too, when him list, . . . and when hee is angry, be it right or wrong; hee has the Law on's side, ever' (IV. i. 79–81). The exercise of power, not the search for justice, is Overdo's main spring, and his actions are as muddled as his motives. He mistakes the cutpurse for the victim and succeeds at every turn in furthering the crime and riot which he seeks to control. With rare justice, he and his fellow authorities, Wasp and Busy, are soundly beaten and put in the stocks for the trouble they cause and the interference they offer to the happy life of the fair.

Jonson goes considerably further, however, in his questioning of authority than merely showing how inept and hypocritical it is. Through the fair rambles a madman known as Troubleall, once a minor official in Overdo's court, but now dismissed and crazed by disappointment. Troubleall asks everyone the plaintive question, 'What's your warrant for it?' He will himself do nothing without a warrant, neither shift his shirt nor make water, and for him only Justice Overdo's warrant is valid. The continuing question of this learned philosopher verbalizes the issue the play dramatizes: which man and what authority have the right and the wisdom to control the great fair of the world? Are revelation and the words of the Old Testament a sufficient warrant for the zeal and violence of the Puritans against all pleasure? Are the robes of the magistrate and the traditions of the law sufficient warrant for the stocks and other heavy restraints that society lays upon individuals? By what right does civil authority make girls and children – Grace and Cokes – the wards of others, or pre-empt the power to license marriages – and plays? Jonson, the great literary and moral authoritarian, opens through Trouble-all's question a vision of the great abyss of nothingness and chaos which lies below the surface of familiar day-to-day life. He goes on to explore it in the puppet show with which the play ends.

The puppet show stands to the world of the fair as the fair stands in turn to the larger scene of Renaissance England and the total scene of human life. And just as the fair, like all of Jonson's satiric images, is a reduction – a low burlesque – of humanity, so the puppet show is a reduction of the life of the fair to a point where humanity nearly disappears. As presented in the puppet show, men are mere automata manipulated by a foolish puppet-master, Leatherhead, playing in a 'motion' written by a vain idiot, Littlewit. This is the ultimate version of the play Jonson wrote again and again in which sense-less humours characters are manipulated by some more cunning fool like Volpone or Face. Here too, as in the other Jonsonian motions, life is a parody of an ideal. The characters of the puppet show, Damon and Pythias, Hero and Leander, bear heroic names associated with two primary Renaissance ideals, friendship and love. But in the puppet show Damon and Pythias become a pair of drunken London brawlers, Hero a whore and a fishwife, and Leander a lecherous, quarrelsome dyer's son. Friendship turns to bragging and brawling, love to drinking and whoring, and heroic speech to doggerel rant.

But even this ultimate reduction of life is defended against the attempts of authority to abolish it. When Busy bursts into the puppet tent with mouth wide open, gaping like an oyster for the destruction of theatres and playing, Puritan folly in attacking the theatres is made clear by the contrast between the trivial things he attacks and the outsize prophetic tones and Old Testament language in which the attack is delivered. In his overblown rhetoric, he first denounces playing for being profane and 'no lawful calling'. When the puppet Dionysius – who seems to be both the tyrant of Syracuse who later became a schoolmaster, and the god who presided over the far ranges of the human spirit and the theatre – outshouts and confutes Busy, the Puritan goes on to his chief point: 'my maine argument against you, is, that you are an *abomination*: for the Male, among you, putteth on the apparell of the *Female*, and the *Female* of the *Male*' (V. v. 98–100). To this charge of trans-vestism, warranted by *Deuteronomy*, Dionysius's answer is a simple one: he pulls up his clothing and reveals that puppets are sexless. To a blockhead like Busy such literal proof is overwhelming, and he immediately reforms and agrees to let the play go on, becoming a 'beholder' with the rest, ceasing to interfere any longer with the free play of life. But the strategic placement of this event suggests that something more important than Busy understands is going on here. *Bartholomew Fair* consists of a series of images, each of which, like a box within boxes, is a reduction of its larger predecessor. The great world is reduced to the fair, the fair to the pig booth, the booth to the puppet show. Within the puppet play, the final reduction, the drawing of the last curtain, is the lifting of the puppet's costume to reveal – nothing. Even sex, which is at the basis of so much activity in the great fair, finally has no reality. This is the same point at which Troubleall's question, 'What's your warrant?' finally arrived. And against such a vision of nothing, what warrant can be valid finally? What authority dare impose itself in what name on life?

None of the characters is aware of the abyss that lies beneath, but each is forced to recognize that his warrant is somehow suspect and his authority therefore limited. As Busy falls back into the audience to become participator rather than legislator, Justice Overdo steps forward with the awesome words, 'looke upon mee, O *London*! and see me, O *Smithfield*; The *example of Justice*, and *Mirror of Magistrates*: the true top of formality, and scourge of enormity' (V. vi. 33–6). Where Busy had sought to impose revealed authority, Overdo prepares to impose civil authority, but the results are equally catastrophic. In a short time Overdo is made to know all his fumbling mistakes which have brought about the very opposite of the results he intended. A moment later his wife, who has become a 'bird o' th' game' and is sitting drunkenly asleep in the audience, wakes up and is sick. Quarlous drives the lesson home: 'remember you are but *Adam*, Flesh, and blood! You have your frailty, forget your other name of *Overdoo*, and invite us all to supper' (96–8). Somewhat dampened by the knowledge that they are all Adam, the visitors troop off for a feast at Overdo's house where, as Cokes remarks somewhat more wisely than he knows, 'wee'll ha' the rest o' the *Play* at home'.

The only answer to the vision of ultimate emptiness is the provisional one of accepting your own limitations and realizing that no warrant confers very much authority. Perhaps, in the long run, good sense and natural instinct are the surest and only warrants the world provides. When the young gallants Quarlous and Winwife desire to marry the heiress Grace Wellborn, they simply steal the licence already issued by the court for her marriage to the idiot Cokes, erase his name and substitute another. When Troubleall refuses to drink with Jordan Knockem unless he have Justice Overdo's warrant, Knockem simply calls for pen and paper, writes out a warrant and signs Overdo's name. This satisfies Troubleall, and he drinks, wipes his lips and goes on his way refreshed. Even in the theatre life gets its business done and satisfies its needs by a reasonable adjustment of interests, and in the Induction to *Bartholomew Fair* the dramatist who had for so long used his warrants of moral and classical authority to thunder at his audience and scourge his fools now settles for an agreement with his auditors in which he undertakes to endure their just censures and provide them with pleasure and wholesome entertainment for two hours in return for their sixpences and the exercise of reasonable restraint and good judgement.

(iii) *The Tempest*

Through the workings of some great passion or by suffering one of the thousand natural shocks that flesh is heir to, Shakespeare's characters are regularly brought to a strange place – the wood outside Athens, the graveyard of Elsinore, Lear's heath – where, as in the theatre itself, all bearings are lost, where no man knows who he is and where all warrants come into question. In *The Tempest* this place of strangeness is an unidentified island far out in the ocean sea. Real enough in some ways, furnished with springs and brine pits, berries and trees, fish and birds, pignuts and filberts, it is also a mysterious enchanted place,

> full of noises,
> Sounds, and sweet airs, that give delight, and hurt not,
> Sometimes a thousand twangling instruments
> Will hum about mine ears; and sometime voices,
> That, if I then had wak'd after long sleep,
> Will make me sleep again; and then, in dreaming,
> The clouds methought would open and show riches
> Ready to drop upon me, that, when I wak'd
> I cried to dream again. (III. ii. 144–52)

It is a place of joy and terror, of beauty and ugliness, where the 'printless foot' flies across yellow sands bordering on flats of oozy mud; animal howls sound suddenly, wild fire flashes, and strange visions appear and disappear. Around its edges the deep ocean rises and subsides, revealing and covering again, like the stream of Nile, the muddy shallows; and beneath the dark blue waters the bones of drowned men slowly change to coral, and rich pearls glitter from the eye-sockets of the scattered skulls.

To this island every man must come, wrecked by great sea storms or helplessly adrift in the broad ocean. Many years before the action begins, Prospero is the great Duke of Milan who, in order to devote more time to his studies, gives over rule of his kingdom to his brother, Antonio, who stages a palace revolution and sets his brother and niece, the infant Miranda, adrift on the ocean in an unseaworthy boat. Fortunate winds blow them to the island, where they find the strange creatures Ariel and Caliban, and here they live, isolated and castaway, for many years. For the other characters of the play, loss comes more abruptly with a great storm which drives their ship aground on the island, hurls them into the waters and at last washes them up on the desolate beach. These natural catastrophes are associated with a series of psychic events of the kind which in earlier plays precipitated man into alien surroundings where all life seemed drained of meaning and hope. Prospero engages in deep study and endures a brother's betrayal; Alonso, king of Naples, is wrecked while returning from marrying a daughter, whom he never expects to see again, in the faraway kingdom of Tunis, and he believes that his other child, his heir Ferdinand, is drowned in the wreck; Ferdinand, separated from the rest of the party, sits despairing on the beach believing that his father is dead. But rather than emphasizing and exploring the tragic events which cast men up on this island, the play simply offers them in passing – often concentrating in a single line or two the complex experiences which earlier had occupied entire plays – and moves on to trace in a variety of forms a symbolic journey from the beach to Prospero's cave at the centre of the island, from fear and despair to regeneration and reunion.

There are many ways of undertaking and understanding this journey, and the characters discover what they are capable of finding in this strange place: an opportunity to plunder an unguarded land or to create the utopia of man's dreams, a chance to kill or the possibility of forgiveness for old crimes, loss or salvation, nothing or everything. For some the journey is taken only by proxy: the sailors who man the ship remain asleep until the end of the play, when they are conducted to Prospero's cell to share in the great reunion. Others make the journey but experience the mysteries of the island like the drunks or blind men of the comedy routine who run along high cliffs and over narrow bridges without being aware that anything unusual is happening. For the servants Stephano and Trinculo, drink is the portal to the island – Stephano rides ashore on a wine cask – and once their fear of the island and its strange creatures is overcome with drunkenness, they, like travellers to the other new worlds being discovered in the sixteenth and seventeenth centuries, see only oddities which can be captured and displayed in a zoo for profit, and find in their freedom only a chance to murder, pillage and tyrannize. Appropriately, the creature they encounter on landing is the bestial Caliban, and led by him singing, 'Freedom, high-day! high-day, freedom! freedom, high-day, freedom!' (II. ii. 190–1), they advance towards Prospero's cell to cut his throat, rape Miranda and seize the island. Before they can execute their gory plans, they find some gaily coloured clothes and bright fripperies, which Ariel has placed in their way, and they stop excitedly to put on a bright coat, attach a sword, try on a plumed hat. Prospero then contrives their final disgrace and makes manifest their animality. A pack of hunting dogs comes yelping through the woods to chase these vicious fools through brambles and briars and drive them at last into a foul and stagnant pond where they are mired up to their chins in mud and rotting matter. Their situation in the pool dramatizes their reality, but it is extremely doubtful that any of them learn very much about themselves, though Stephano at the final reunion does mumble something which suggests that he has somehow, in some way, participated in some part of the lesson which the others have learned: 'Every man shift for all the rest, and let no man take care for himself; for all is but fortune' (V. i. 256–8).

Of all who are 'sea-swallowed' and then cast up, Ferdinand, the young prince of Naples, travelling alone, moves to the centre of the island most swiftly and directly. As he sits, unmoving, on the beach, paralysed by the loss of his father and the world he has always known, the island begins to sing to him:

> Sitting on a bank,
> Weeping again the King my father's wreck,
> This music crept by me upon the waters,
> Allaying both their fury and my passion
> With its sweet air; thence I have follow'd it,
> Or it hath drawn me rather. But 'tis gone.
> No, it begins again.

> *Ariel's Song*
> Full fathom five thy father lies;
>   Of his bones are coral made;
> Those are pearls that were his eyes;
>   Nothing of him that doth fade
> But doth suffer a sea-change
> Into something rich and strange. (I. ii. 389–401)

The song's promise of the transformation of loss to gain is immediately fulfilled as Ferdinand follows the music and sees before him the beauty of Miranda, already in love with him. Their love would be consummated at once, but Prospero appears and by his magic forces Ferdinand to undergo a series of trials which teach certain necessary lessons. He is first taught human helplessness by being frozen with his sword uplifted. Next he is put to the humiliating work of dragging in heavy logs in order that he may understand the hard manual labour necessary to keep the fires of the world burning, and the fact that the full enjoyment of anything requires that it be earned. During the time that Ferdinand is learning these sea lessons, Miranda is also being instructed by her father: and then, their initiations passed, the young lovers are at last brought together at the magical centre of the island, where they are shown a vision and put to playing a game of chess. The intricate game is a model for that artful ordering of nature, the containment of freedom within mutually agreed on and understood boundaries and rules, which it has been Prospero's purpose to teach these young people.

The next group which journeys to the magic circle in the centre of the island is made up of mature men of established authority: Alonso, king of Naples; Gonzalo, the old counsellor and friend to Prospero; Antonio, Prospero's usurping brother; and Sebastian, the brother of Alonso. Burdened by old guilts, hardened in familiar modes of thought, or weakened in hope, these older men move slowly, painfully and indirectly to the centre. For the good old romantic Gonzalo this strange place is an opportunity for a new start, a world where man can create for himself a new Eden in which nature will pour forth its plenty 'without sweat or endeavour', where 'sword, pike, knife, gun, or need of any engine' (II. i. 160–1) will not be known. His impossible dream is balanced by the equally extravagant cynicism of Antonio and Sebastian, for whom the island is a heart of darkness where, freed from all law and restraint, these conquistadors can kill the king and seize power for themselves. Debating, intriguing, unable to escape despair, these travellers wander, hungry and thirsty, 'through forth-rights and meanders' (III. iii. 3), as in a maze, until, at the point that lostness seems eternal, Ariel appears with attendant spirits to offer a vision of a rich banquet. But even as they move towards the banquet, Ariel changes into a harpy and the vision disappears. The vision of the banquet of life suggests the potential beneficence and plenty of the world, and its disappearance suggests that it can be fouled and replaced by poverty and emptiness. Ariel now proceeds to explain that this is what Alonso, Antonio and Sebastian did when they joined many years ago to supplant Prospero and set him and his child adrift. Those old injuries are now revenged by the sea, and the travellers' only hope to escape the wrath of the just powers 'is nothing but heart's sorrow, And a clear life ensuing' (III. iii. 81–2). Like other unrepentant Shakespearian villains, Sebastian and Antonio react to the knowledge of their guilt with fury, and, determined to hew their way out or die with harness on their backs, draw their swords and rush wildly about the island striking blindly at whatever they encounter. Alonso, the sorrowing king, feels for the first time the great wrong he has done and repents, but acceptance of his sin – 'O, it is monstrous, monstrous!'

– carries with it the belief that it is unforgivable, and he determines to follow his dead son into the sea 'deeper than e'er plummet sounded, And with him there lie mudded' (III. iii. 101–2). In this condition, 'spell-stopp'd', the travellers are brought by Ariel to the centre of the island where '*They all enter the circle which Prospero had made, and there stand charm'd*' (stage direction, V. i. 57), until Prospero forgives them for the harms they did him long ago and reveals to Alonso that Ferdinand is alive and engaged to Miranda. Alonso then begs Prospero's forgiveness and restores Milan to him.

The pattern of loss leading through sorrow and despair to penitence and miraculous restitution which is basic to the late romances has here been accomplished not over the long periods of time of *The Winter's Tale* but within the space of four hours or less (I. ii. 239–41). Transformation is not only the slow work of time but the result of the incredible magical instant separating the life lived half awake and half aware from 'sea-change Into something rich and strange' and the startled recognition that finding lies on the other side of losing:

> Was Milan thrust from Milan, that his issue
> Should become King of Naples? O, rejoice
> Beyond a common joy, and set it down
> With gold on lasting pillars: in one voyage
> Did Claribel her husband find at Tunis;
> And Ferdinand, her brother, found a wife
> Where he himself was lost; Prospero his dukedom
> In a poor isle; and all of us ourselves
> When no man was his own. (V. i. 205–13)

As real and painful as the experiences of the characters are to them, the causes of their sorrows are finally only illusions. The ship which seemed to split on the rocks rides safe in a calm anchorage, neither father nor son dies in the storm, and even the garments of the castaways, though 'drench'd in the sea, hold, notwithstanding, their freshness and glosses, being rather newdy'd, than stain'd with salt water' (II. i. 62–4). The point is the same as that made in all the late Shakespearian romances by the use of the fairytale story to contain realistic human feeling and thought: the world is stranger than man thinks and the experiences of the moment, no matter how intense, lose their reality in the miraculous process of change and transformation through which all life passes. But in *The Tempest* the illusions are all the products of the magical arts of Prospero.

This great period of English drama is guarded at its beginning and its ending by two magicians, Faustus and Prospero, both of whom lose themselves in their passion for study and knowledge, use their art to shape their world to their desire, discover themselves in the exercise of their magic and in the end abjure their art to return to the reality it has revealed to them: in one case the eternal hell of a life without God, in the other the practical affairs of government and the working world of Milan. Both magicians are archetypes of Renaissance man and the overreaching heroes of the drama who sought to impose their minds upon the world; and both are images of the poet-playwrights who also turned the leaden world to gold, conferred eternal life on their creatures and made real the dreams of man. The identification of magician and poet contained in the cliché 'the magic of poetry' is made explicit in *The Tempest* where Prospero's magic expresses itself in games, song, dance, story, music, tableaux and, above all, short plays. This poet-magician is made, not born, and his art was acquired not by the sale of his soul but by a long and arduous education which began with a thirst for knowledge that caused him to bury himself in the study to master the learning of the past, exposed him to human betrayal in a brother's willingness to kill to satisfy his lust for power, took him out in an open boat to experience the power of nature in the open sea and at last isolated him, except for the small child, on the strange island where he discovers and at last masters those hitherto neglected and unknown aspects of himself, Caliban and Ariel. These two odd creatures, roughly analogous to the appetites and the fancy, come from a primitive past in which bruteness ruled the world, and the fancy, undirected by mind or reason, was lost in dreams of fear and terror. When Prospero arrived on these shores he found Caliban in possession of the island left to him by his mother, the witch Sycorax, and her strange god Setebos, while Ariel, groaning continuously, was imprisoned in a cleft tree. These creatures are never easy with one another or with Prospero, but despite their continuous longing for liberty, he harnesses them to his moral and rational purposes, using Caliban to gather food and keep the fire, and sending Ariel out to

> tread the ooze
> Of the salt deep,
> To run upon the sharp wind of the north,
> To do me business in the veins o' th' earth
> When it is bak'd with frost. (I. ii. 252–6)

The relationship with Caliban is particularly difficult, and while at first each found the other fascinating, and taught the other many things, Caliban soon attempts to rape Miranda, and, frightened of this amoral power, Prospero rules him tyrannically from that time forward by means of fear and pain. Whatever long process of mental evolution and psychomachy may be figured in the relations of Prospero with Caliban and Ariel, the outcome is an understanding and uneasy mastery of primal energies.

Knowledge of the past gained through study, knowledge of the extremities to which man may be exposed gained through betrayal and experience of the open sea, and knowledge of the self gained through isolation are the sources of Prospero's magic both figuratively and literally, for Prospero now uses his art to dramatize and teach what he has himself previously experienced. Miranda, at the divide between childhood and womanhood, is given a glimpse by means of storytelling of 'the dark backward and abysm of time' (I. ii. 50), her origins and the voyage which brought her to this place, and the continuing dangers of Caliban. Ferdinand is led from despair back into life by a song which sings of loss, fear and transformation; taught helplessness by being frozen, Pyrrhus-like, with his sword in mid-air; and made to know Caliban by doing his work of hauling logs. The proper relationship of lovers, in which art orders feeling, is demonstrated when Prospero the stagekeeper pulls aside the curtain and reveals Ferdinand and Miranda playing chess. Stephano and Trinculo are revealed as quarrellers and cowards when Ariel imitates their voices, saying aloud what they think but dare not say; as children delighting in gaudy trinkets when they dress themselves in the finery Ariel places in their way; as frightened animals running wildly before a pack of imagined dogs; and, finally, as creatures immersed in the base stuff of the world when they are left mired up to their chins in a stinking pond. For Alonso and his companions, Prospero saves some of his most powerful arts: the sound of fierce animal roarings, strange dreams, briefly heard harmonies and snatches of song and the great spectacle of the rich banquet which disappears when approached.

The ultimate revelation of Prospero's art, the greatest of his plays presenting all his wisdom, is the masque of Juno and Ceres, shown to Ferdinand and Miranda as a wedding entertainment. Iris, goddess of the rainbow, as gorgeous and as transient as a dream or a play, appears first to invoke Ceres, goddess of plenty, by means of a vision of the vastness, foison and variety of the world: 'rich leas Of wheat, rye, barley, vetches, oats, and pease . . . turfy mountains . . . nibbling sheep . . . flat meads', the fresh streams, the 'pole-clipt vineyard' and the 'sea-marge, sterile and rocky-hard . . .' (IV. i. 60–9). Juno, goddess of civil values, then arrives to celebrate the union of human fruitfulness with that of nature – 'honour, riches, marriage-blessing, Long continuance, and increasing' – and Ceres lays before the young couple a world winterless and heavy with produce:

> Earth's increase, foison plenty,
> Barns and garners never empty;
> Vines with clust'ring bunches growing,
> Plants with goodly burden bowing;
> Spring come to you at the farthest,
> In the very end of harvest! (IV. i. 110–15)

To round out this 'most majestic vision' a number of nymphs and sicklemen, the minor deities of spring and harvest, appear to dance out the union of the great energies flowing through this world; the sower and the reaper, the water and the land, the spring and the fall, the male and the female, the beginning and the end.

But then this vision of plenty created out of the harmonious interaction of opposites, of ultimate unity in the midst of infinite variety, is interrupted, as it so regularly is in Shakespearian drama, by the approach of an antithetical reality, the drunken Caliban, Stephano and Trinculo. The spell broken by this intrusion of the 'real', the view lengthens, and the masque and the transcendent vision of life it contains are seen once again, as so often before in this drama, as mere pretence, nothing more than theatrical makebelieve:

> Our revels now are ended. These our actors,
> As I foretold you, were all spirits, and
> Are melted into air, into thin air;
> And, like the baseless fabric of this vision,
> The cloud-capp'd towers, the gorgeous palaces,
> The solemn temples, the great globe itself,
> Yea, all which it inherit, shall dissolve
> And, like this insubstantial pageant faded,
> Leave not a rack behind. We are such stuff
> As dreams are made on; and our little life
> Is rounded with a sleep. (IV. i. 148–58)

Not only man's plays and dreams but all of life and the world in which it lives shall perish into some ultimate nothingness, without even a wisp of cloud to mark where it once was. For old Hieronimo looking at the play to which his life has been reduced, for the Player King sadly knowing 'our thoughts are ours, their ends none of our own', for the terrified woman looking at the dance of the madmen and insisting 'I am Duchess of *Malfy* still' and for the audience gaping at the puppet show in Smithfield and watching Dionysius pull up his skirts to reveal nothing, the realization that life is no more real than a play and man no more real than a role is disillusioning and terrifying. But now, though the possibility of the meaninglessness of drama and of life is fully accepted, the magician-dramatist counsels his audience 'be cheerful', for, though man may be only the dream of some great sleeper dreaming us, or life only an instant of dreaming in the midst of an everlasting undisturbed sleep, in dream, and in play, we glimpse not the unreal but that which is ultimately real and true. Man's imagination and the art which embodies it, though subject to disruption by 'realism', are ultimately the only valid modes of perception. All the great dreamers of the Elizabethan and Jacobean drama – Tamburlaine, Romeo, Hamlet, Troilus – and the playwrights who created them to express their dreams, were, though tangled in and limited by the realities of life and the theatre in which they had to work, perceivers of and strugglers for those ultimate humane realities of love, honour, freedom, forgiveness, justice and art. And it is art, says *The Tempest*, which brings man to a vision and fulfilment of these truths, just as the travellers are brought by Prospero's harmless magic to the truth of themselves by suffering tempest, shipwreck, isolation and, ultimately, repentance, forgiveness and sea change into something rich and strange.

Whether William Shakespeare, about to retire from his professional life as an actor and playwright on the magical island of the London stage to spend the remainder of his life in Stratford with his wife and two daughters, saw an image of himself in Prospero abjuring his 'rough magic' and returning to Milan is impossible to prove. Nor can we be at all certain that the justification of art and dreaming which *The Tempest* provides satisfied the playwright who may have long felt, like so many of his fellows, the shame of having

> gone here and there
> And made myself a motley to the view,
> Gor'd mine own thoughts, sold cheap what is most dear,
> Made old offences of affections new.
> Most true it is that I have look'd on truth
> Askance and strangely . . . (Sonnet 110)

An absolute identification of Shakespeare with Prospero would lead to some strange conclusions, for in the process of using his art the magician discovers his own full humanity as surely as do those on whom he works. His original motives for the exercise of his art are vengeance and profit: he first uses his magic to stage shipwrecks and tempests to revenge himself upon the world, regain his fortunes and make others feel what he has suffered. But in the course of his punitive actions, his fancy (Ariel) allows him to see and feel the sufferings of others and by means of this sympathy brings him at last to know and forgive: 'the rarer action is In virtue than in vengeance' (V. i. 27–8).

Whatever the relationship of Prospero and Shakespeare, there can be no better description of that marvellous world created in the late sixteenth and early seventeenth centuries by Shakespeare and his fellows in the London theatres than Prospero's summation of his art at the moment he abandons it:

> Ye elves of hills, brooks, standing lakes, and groves;
> And ye that on the sands with printless foot
> Do chase the ebbing Neptune, and do fly him
> When he comes back; you demi-puppets that
> By moonshine do the green sour ringlets make,
> Whereof the ewe not bites; and you whose pastime
> Is to make the midnight mushrooms, that rejoice
> To hear the solemn curfew; by whose aid –
> Weak masters though ye be – I have bedimm'd
> The noontide sun, call'd forth the mutinous winds,
> And 'twixt the green sea and the azur'd vault
> Set roaring war. To the dread rattling thunder
> Have I given fire, and rifted Jove's stout oak
> With his own bolt; and the strong-bas'd promontory
> Have I made shake, and by the spurs pluck'd up
> The pine and cedar. Graves at my command
> Have wak'd their sleepers, op'd, and let 'em forth,
> By my so potent art. But this rough magic
> I here abjure; and, when I have requir'd
> Some heavenly music – which even now I do –
> To work mine end upon their senses that
> This airy charm is for, I'll break my staff,
> Bury it certain fathoms in the earth,
> And deeper than did ever plummet sound
> I'll drown my book.   [*Solemn music.*

Bibliography

Abbreviations

DNB	*Dictionary of National Biography* (ed. L. Stephen and S. Lee, London, 1882–1931)
ELH	*Journal of English Literary History*
ES	*English Studies*
JEGP	*Journal of English and Germanic Philology*
MLR	*Modern Language Review*
MSC	*Malone Society Collections*
N & Q	*Notes and Queries*
PMLA	*Publications of the Modern Language Association of America*
REL	*Review of English Literature*
RES	*Review of English Studies*
SEL	*Studies in English Literature, 1500–1900*
STC	*Short Title Catalogue of Books Printed . . . 1475–1640* (ed. A. W. Pollard and G. R. Redgrave, London, 1946)
TLS	*Times Literary Supplement*

I The social and literary context

Many specifically historical studies of the late Elizabethan and early Jacobean period exist. Studies taking the rulers as their centre are J. E. Neale's *Queen Elizabeth* (London, 1934), J. B. Black's *The Reign of Elizabeth* (Oxford, 1956), and G. Davies's *The Early Stuarts* (Oxford, 1937). W. Gordon Zeefeld, in *The Foundation of Tudor Policy* (Cambridge, Mass., 1948), is concerned with political principles and practice, while A. L. Rowse's *The England of Elizabeth : the Structure of Society* (London, 1951) and Lawrence Stone's *The Crisis of the Aristocracy, 1558–1641* (Oxford, 1965) deal with interrelated issues of politics and social structure.

The relevant part of G. M. Trevelyan's *English Social History* (New York, 1942; London, 1944) covers a great deal of ground in small compass, and relates life to literature in a stimulating way: the illustrated edition is recommended. Another well-illustrated survey of life in the period is *Shakespeare's England* (ed. Sidney Lee and C. T. Onions, 2 vols, Oxford, 1916): its subtitle is 'an Account of the Life and Manners of his Age', and its thirty chapters are the first place to which to go for information about religion, the court, the armed forces, exploration abroad and travel at home, education and scholarship, commerce, farming and gardening, medicine and other sciences and pseudo-sciences (like alchemy), law and order, town life, low life, home life, popular superstitions, the arts, costume, heraldry, sports and pastimes, etc.; a number of the chapters bear on specially literary-social topics, such as authorship and patronage, printing and publishing, acting and the theatre. See also *Shakespeare Survey 17* (1964) for more recent information. J. Dover Wilson's *Life in Shakespeare's England* (London, 1911; repr. Harmondsworth, 1968) similarly takes the reader through many of these fields by means of extracts from contemporary writings.

Besides these general surveys and reference books, there are special studies of certain aspects of Elizabethan and Jacobean social and intellectual matters. Edward E. Rich discusses 'The population of Elizabethan England', *Economic History Review*, 2nd series, II (1950). Wages and the cost of living are the theme of William Beveridge's *Prices and Wages in England from the Twelfth to the Nineteenth Century* (London, 1939), Y. S. Brenner's 'The inflation of prices in England, 1551–1650', *Economic History Review*, 2nd series, XV (1962); Albert E. Feavearyear's *The Pound Sterling, a History of English Money* (Oxford, 1931; revised by E. Victor Morgan, Oxford and New York, 1963), and Charles W. C. Oman's *The Coinage of England* (Oxford, 1931), may also be consulted. See also Mildred L. Campbell's *The*

English Yeoman under Elizabeth and the Early Stuarts (New Haven, Conn., 1942).

Some disagreeable aspects of Elizabethan life were the dangers of plague and the prevalence of vagrancy. The medical history of plague, and its effects upon society, are discussed in Charles F. Mullett's book *The Bubonic Plague in England: an essay in the history of preventive medicine* (Lexington, Ky., 1956) and in his two papers 'Some neglected aspects of plague medicine in sixteenth century England', *Scientific Monthly*, XLIV (1937), and 'The plague of 1603 in England', *Annals of Medical History*, IX (1937); see also F. P. Wilson's *The Plague in Shakespeare's London* (Oxford, 1927), and 'Plague orders for London, 1583', ed. E. K. Chambers and W. W. Greg, *Malone Society Collections*, I (Oxford, 1908–9). Vagrancy is the theme of Frank Aydelotte's *Elizabethan Rogues and Vagabonds* (Oxford, 1913) and of A. V. Judges's *The Elizabethan Underworld* (London, 1930). It is suggested by William Ingram, ' "Neere the Play Howse": the Swan Theater and community blight', *Renaissance Drama*, IV (1971), that the presence of a theatre was felt to reduce the value of adjacent property.

The more picturesque side of Elizabethan life is represented by two collections of contemporary accounts of royal occasions by John Nichols, *The Progression and Public Processions of Queen Elizabeth*, 3 vols (London, 1798–1805), and *The Progresses, Processions, and Magnificent Festivities of King James the First*, 4 vols (London, 1828), and in more inclusive books on *English Pageantry* by Robert Withington, 2 vols (Cambridge, Mass., and London, 1918–20) and *English Civic Pageantry 1558–1642* by David M. Bergeron (London, 1971).

The basic study of the ideas and beliefs of the time, and of its medieval heritage, is E. M. W. Tillyard's *The Elizabethan World Picture* (London, 1943); Hardin Craig's *The Enchanted Glass: the Elizabethan mind in literature* (New York, 1936), Hiram Haydn's *The Counter-Renaissance* (New York, 1950), and J. M. Bamborough's *The Little World of Man* (London, 1952), enlarge and modify Tillyard's work. Particular influences are considered by Fritz Caspari, *Humanism and the Social Order in Tudor England* (Chicago, 1954), and William Haller, *The Rise of Puritanism: the way to the New Jerusalem as set forth in pulpit and press from Thomas Cartwright to John Lilburne and John Milton, 1570–1643* (New York, 1938); for another side of religious activity, see A. C. Southern's *Elizabethan Recusant Prose, 1559–1582* (London, 1950).

Louis B. Wright is the author of two important studies, *Middle-Class Culture in Elizabethan England* (Chapel Hill, NC, 1953) and (in collaboration with Virginia A. Lamar) *Life and Letters in Tudor and Stuart England* (Ithaca, NY, 1962).

At this point it will be useful to give a list of primary historical sources to which reference has been made in compiling this section of Volume III. *A Guide to Research Facilities in History in the Universities of Great Britain and Ireland* has been compiled by G. Kitson Clark and Geoffrey R. Elton (Cambridge and New York, 1963). John R. Dasent and others edited *The Acts of the Privy Council of England, 1452–1628* (32 vols, London, 1890–1907); Robert Lemon and Mary A. Green the *Calendar of State Papers, Domestic, 1547–1526* (12 vols, London, 1856–72); J. H. Collingridge and others the *Calendar of the Patent Rolls, Elizabeth I, 1558–72* (4 vols, London, 1939–66); Paul L. Hughes and James F. Larkin, *Tudor Royal Proclamations* [1485–1603] (3 vols, New Haven, Conn., 1964–9), and *Stuart Royal Proclamations*, I [1603–25] (Oxford, 1973). The MS Journals of the Corporation of London (vols XVI–XXII, 1550–1605) are kept at the Corporation of London Records Office, Guildhall, London. R. H. Tawney and Eileen Power edited *Tudor Economic Documents: being select documents illustrating the economic and social history of Tudor England* (3 vols, London, 1924). John Stow's *The Annales of England, continued to 1614 by Edmund Howes* (*STC* 23338, London, 1614) gives the history of the age as seen through contemporary eyes.

The standard reference work on the subject of acting, acting conditions, various aspects of governmental control, and indeed on all matters theatrical, including the original circumstances of performance and publication where these are known, is E. K. Chambers's *The Elizabethan Stage* (4 vols, Oxford, 1923: an additional *Index* to this work and to the same author's *William Shakespeare* was compiled by Beatrice White, Oxford, 1934). The history is continued with similar completeness by G. E. Bentley, *The Jacobean and Caroline Stage* (7 vols, Oxford, 1941–68).

Documents relating to the Office of the Revels in the Time of Queen Elizabeth are edited by A. Feuillerat as vol. XXI of W. Bang's (general ed.) *Materialien zur Kunde des älteren Englischen Dramas* (Louvain, 1908), and see also E. K. Chambers, *Notes on the History of the Revels Office under the Tudors* (Oxford, 1906), and A. Edinburgh, 'The early Tudor Revels Office', *Shakespeare Quarterly*, II (1951). F. B. Benger's *A Calendar of References to Sir Thomas Benger, Master of the Revels and Masques to Queen Elizabeth, 1560–72* (privately printed, 1946) collects the relevant information. J. Q. Adams has edited *The Dramatic Records of Sir Henry Herbert* (New Haven, Conn., 1917). For drama at court see also F. P. Wilson's 'Court payments for plays, 1610–11, 1612–13, 1616–17', *Bodleian Library Record*, IV (1955). Giles Dawson edited 'Records of plays and players in Kent, 1450–1642' in *Malone Society Collections*, VII (Oxford, 1965). *Henslowe's Diary* has been edited by W. W. Greg (2 vols, London, 1904–8), with the supplementary *Henslowe Papers* (London, 1907), and more recently by R. A. Foakes and R. T. Rickert (Cambridge, 1961).

On the subject of publication, the primary material is *A Short-Title Catalogue of Books Printed in England, Scotland and Ireland, and of English Books Printed Abroad, 1475–1640*, ed. A. W. Pollard and G. R. Redgrave (London, 1946); an *Index of Printers, Publishers and Booksellers* in this catalogue is edited by Paul G. Morrison (Bibliographical Society of the University of Virginia, 1950). Edward Arber edited *A Transcript of the Register of the Company of Stationers of London, 1554–1640* (London and Birmingham, 1875–94); see also W. W. Greg, *A Companion to Arber* (Oxford, 1967), a calendar of the documents contained therein. W. W. Greg also edited the standard list of all editions and issues of plays of the period in *A Bibliography of the English Printed Drama to the Restoration* (4 vols, London, 1939–59), and, with Eleanor Boswell, *Records of the Court of the Stationers' Company, 1576–1602* (London, 1930); the history is continued, under the same title, from *1602 to 1640*, by W. A. Jackson (London, 1957). *The Stationers' Company: a History, 1403–1959*, by Cyprian Blagden (Cambridge, Mass., 1960) is a lucid survey. The best guide on how to approach all this material remains R. B. McKerrow's *An Introduction to Bibliography for Literary Students* (Oxford, 1927); under such guidance the reader can proceed to many other studies by W. W. Greg and others (which are too numerous to be listed here) dealing with the details of publication and the transmission of dramatic texts.

II The companies and actors

(i) COMPANIES

The standard source of information on Elizabethan companies and actors is E. K. Chambers, *The Elizabethan Stage*, 4 vols (Oxford, 1923; repr. 1961), particularly vol. II. More detailed information, especially about provincial companies, will be found in John Tucker Murray, *English Dramatic Companies 1558–1642*, 2 vols (London, 1910; repr. New York, 1963); and there is a convenient index of the major companies, with their dates of operation and other information, in Alfred Harbage, *Annals of English Drama 975–1700*, revised by S. Schoenbaum (London, 1964), 297–302.

There have been two notable studies of the Chamberlain's–King's company: T. W. Baldwin, *The Organization and Personnel of the Shakespearean Company* (Princeton, NJ, 1927; repr. New York, 1961), contains many useful facts as well as much fanciful speculation; Bernard Beckerman's *Shakespeare at the Globe, 1599–1609* (New York, 1962) is a more modest and sober work which may also be recommended for its account of Elizabethan theatrical procedure in general. The most comprehensive study of the boys' companies is H. N. Hillebrand, *The Child Actors* (Urbana, Ill., 1926; repr. New York, 1964). R. A. Foakes, 'Tragedy at the children's theatres after 1600: a challenge to the adult stage', *The Elizabethan Theatre 2*, ed. David Galloway (Toronto, 1970), gives a concise account of this final phase in the development of the child actors, and the influence of their repertoire on the adult stage. The repertoires of the adult and children's companies are compared in Alfred Harbage's influential *Shakespeare and the Rival Traditions* (New York, 1952; repr. Bloomington, Ind., 1970). His general conclusions are not unreasonable, but his partisan zeal for the public theatres and against the private ones leads him to drastic oversimplifications on points of detail.

(ii) PRODUCTION

The studies of Baldwin and Beckerman, mentioned above, consider Elizabethan procedures for putting on a play. Evidence for the author's involvement is collected by David Klein, 'Did Shakespeare produce his own plays?', *Modern Language Review*, LVII (1962). Evidence about backstage procedures may be found in W. W. Greg, *Dramatic Documents from the Elizabethan Playhouses*, 2 vols (Oxford, 1931; repr. 1969). The size of the company, and the effect of this on casting, are discussed by William A. Ringler, Jr, 'The number of actors in Shakespeare's early plays', *The Seventeenth Century Stage*, ed. Gerald Eades Bentley (Chicago, 1968); though his insistence that there were twelve men but only four boys available leads him to conclusions that some readers will find strange. (Unlike the other articles in Bentley's useful collection, Ringler's is printed there for the first time.) See also Scott McMillin, 'Casting for Pembroke's Men', *Shakespeare Quarterly*, XXIII (1972).

(iii) ACTORS

Contemporary references to Elizabethan actors are conveniently collected by Edwin Nungezer, *A Dictionary of Actors and of Other Personages Associated with the Public Presentation of Plays in England before 1642* (New

Haven, Conn., 1929; repr. New York, 1968). M. C. Bradbrook, *The Rise of the Common Player* (London and Cambridge, Mass., 1962), traces the development of the acting profession, with special reference to its changing social status. The paucity of evidence has prevented satisfactory book-length studies of individual performers, but some articles may be recommended, among them Percy Simpson's 'Actors and acting' in *Shakespeare's England* (London, 1916). William A. Armstrong, 'Shakespeare and the acting of Edward Alleyn', *Shakespeare Survey 7* (1954), considers the question of Alleyn's acting as compared with Burbage's; see also Andrew Gurr, 'Who strutted and bellowed?', *Shakespeare Survey 16* (1963); Austin K. Gray, 'Robert Armine, the Foole', *PMLA*, XLII (1927), offers some interesting speculations on Kempe and Armin. Allison Gaw has written on 'Actors' names in basic Shakespearean texts', *PMLA*, XL (1925), and 'John Sincklo as one of Shakespeare's actors', *Anglia*, XLIX (1926).

(iv) ACTING STYLE

The development of Elizabethan acting is surveyed by William A. Armstrong, 'Actors and theatres', *Shakespeare Survey 17* (1964), and Daniel Seltzer, 'The actors and staging', *A New Companion to Shakespeare Studies*, ed. Kenneth Muir and S. Schoenbaum (Cambridge, 1971). Both are useful for the reader who would like a general account without becoming too embroiled in the controversy and special pleading that have affected this subject. However, a reader who enjoys being so embroiled might well start with B. L. Joseph, *Elizabethan Acting* (Oxford, 1951), where Elizabethan theories of rhetoric and oratory are applied to acting. The second edition (Oxford, 1964), so thoroughly rewritten as to be virtually a different book, contains less in the way of technical detail, more from the author's own experience of production, and a more explicit insistence that Elizabethan acting was 'natural' in its reproduction of observable human behaviour.

The most extreme statements of the position that Elizabethan acting was 'formal' (in other words, dependent on predictable conventions) are found in Alfred Harbage, 'Elizabethan acting', *PMLA*, LIV (1939), reprinted in his *A Theatre for Shakespeare* (Toronto, 1955), and M. C. Bradbrook, *Themes and Conventions of Elizabethan Tragedy* (Cambridge, 1935; repr. 1960). A more moderate statement is that of S. L. Bethell, 'Shakespeare's actors', *Review of English Studies*, n.s., I (1950), where it is argued that Elizabethan acting was essentially formal, with touches of naturalism. This view is reversed by John Russell Brown, 'On the acting of Shakespeare's plays', *The Quarterly Journal of Speech*, XXXIV (1953), reprinted in Bentley, *Seventeenth Century Stage*. Brown argues that an older style of formal acting was probably present in Shakespeare's time, but was rapidly being replaced by a more naturalistic style aiming at the imitation of life. The 'naturalist' case is supported by Marvin Rosenberg, 'Elizabethan actors: men or marionettes?', *PMLA*, XLIX (1954); reprinted in Bentley, *Seventeenth Century Stage*. Alan S. Downer, 'Prolegomenon to a study of Elizabethan acting', *Maske und Kothurn*, X (1964), considers the debate and pronounces it meaningless, arguing for a complex style that combined formality and naturalism.

Andrew Gurr, 'Elizabethan action', *Studies in Philology*, LXIII (1966), stresses the importance of character portrayal. R. A. Foakes connects the Elizabethans' acting with their psychological theory in 'The player's passion: some notes on Elizabethan psychology and acting', *Essays and Studies*, n.s., VII (London, 1954). The importance of fitness and decorum is argued by Lise-Lone Marker, 'Nature and decorum in the theory of Elizabethan acting', *The Elizabethan Theatre 2*, ed. David Galloway (Toronto, 1970). The special problem of what the boy actors were like is surveyed by Michael Jamieson, 'Shakespeare's celibate stage', *Papers Mainly Shakespearian*, ed. G. I. Duthie (Edinburgh, 1964; repr. in Bentley, *Seventeenth Century Stage*), and W. Robertson Davies's book *Shakespeare's Boy Actors* (London, 1939) is still serviceable. The most balanced account of acting style in the boys' companies is Michael Shapiro, 'Children's troupes: dramatic illusion and acting style', *Comparative Drama*, III (1969).

III The playhouses

Basic information about playhouses and the stage is collected by E. K. Chambers in *The Elizabethan Stage* (Oxford, 1923) and G. E. Bentley in *The Jacobean and Caroline Stage* (Oxford, 1941–68). A good book-length survey of the subject is provided by Andrew Gurr, *The Shakespearean Stage, 1574–1642* (Cambridge, 1970). Shorter surveys, each stressing a particular aspect of the subject, are available in W. F. Rothwell, 'Was there a typical Elizabethan stage?', *Shakespeare Survey 12* (1959); Richard Hosley, 'The playhouses and the stage', in *A New Companion to Shakespeare Studies*, ed. K. Muir and S. Schoenbaum (Cambridge, 1971); T. J. King, 'The stage in the time of Shakespeare: a survey of major scholarship', *Renaissance Drama*, IV (1971); D. F. Rowan, 'The English playhouse, 1595–1630', ibid.; and

Michael Jamieson, 'Shakespeare in the theatre', in *Shakespeare*, ed. S. Wells (Select Bibliographical Guides, Oxford, 1973).

Older general studies still of value are T. Fairman Ordish, *Early London Theatres in the Fields* (London, 1894); George F. Reynolds, 'Some principles of Elizabethan staging', *Modern Philology*, II (1904–5), III (1905–6); Ashley H. Thorndike, *Shakespeare's Theater* (New York, 1916); Joseph Quincy Adams, *Shakespearean Playhouses* (Boston, 1917); and Thornton S. Graves, *The Court and the London Theatres during the Reign of Elizabeth* (Menasha, Wis., 1913). Recent general studies of value are A. M. Nagler, *Shakespeare's Stage* (New Haven, 1958); Glynne Wickham, *Early English Stages, 1300 to 1600*, vols I (London, 1959), II.i (1963), II.ii (1972); and T. J. King, *Shakespearean Staging, 1599–1642* (Cambridge, Mass., 1971). Good studies of the audience are provided by Alfred Harbage, *Shakespeare's Audience* (New York, 1941), and William A. Armstrong, 'The audience of the Elizabethan private theatres', *Review of English Studies*, X (1959). Important background studies are Richard Southern's *Staging of Plays before Shakespeare* (London, 1973) and George R. Kernodle, *From Art to Theatre: form and convention in the Renaissance* (Chicago, 1944). The essential type of the Elizabethan stage is defined by Richard Southern in *The Open Stage* (London, 1953). In *Theatre for Shakespeare* (Toronto, 1955) Alfred Harbage criticizes modern Shakespearian production styles.

Pictorial sources of information about both public and private playhouses are catalogued and discussed by Ida Darlington and James Howgego in *Printed Maps of London circa 1553–1850* (London, 1964) and by Arthur M. Hind in *Wenceslaus Hollar and his Views of London and Windsor in the Seventeenth Century* (London, 1922). A good analysis of pictorial evidence for the public playhouses is provided by I. A. Shapiro in 'The Bankside theatres: early engravings', *Shakespeare Survey 1* (1948).

The theories that the Elizabethan tiring-house originated in the screens passage of the Tudor great hall and the amphitheatrical frame of the public playhouses in the Bankside animal-baiting houses are elaborated by Richard Hosley in 'The origins of the Shakespearian playhouse', *Shakespeare Quarterly*, XV (1964). Additional information on the Tudor hall screen is presented by Richard Southern in *The Staging of Plays before Shakespeare* (London, 1973) and by Richard Hosley in 'Three Renaissance English indoor playhouses', *English Literary Renaissance*, III (1973). Giles E. Dawson has published a contemporary description of one of the Bankside baiting-houses: 'London's bull-baiting and bear-baiting arena in 1562', *Shakespeare Quarterly*, XV (1964). Production in inn yards is discussed by W. J. Lawrence in 'The inn-yard playing places: their uprise and characteristics', in *Pre-Restoration Stage Studies* (Cambridge, Mass., 1927), in which also he supports the theory that the form of the public playhouse originated in the inn yard. An inn-yard playhouse, the Boar's Head, is studied in detail by C. J. Sisson in *The Boar's Head Theatre: an inn-yard theatre of the Elizabethan age*, ed. S. Wells (London, 1972), and by Herbert Berry in 'The playhouse in the Boar's Head Inn, Whitechapel', in *The Elizabethan Theatre 1*, ed. D. Galloway (Toronto, 1969), and other articles.

There are a number of general studies of particular aspects of the public playhouses. W. J. Lawrence treats 'Early systems of admission' in *The Elizabethan Playhouse*, 2nd ser. (Stratford-upon-Avon, 1913). F. P. Wilson discusses William Lambarde's description of an admission system in 'Lambarde, the Bel Savage, and the Theatre', *Notes and Queries*, CCVIII (1963). Lawrence has useful studies of the trap door and the Lords' room: 'Stage traps in the early English theatre', in *Pre-Restoration Stage Studies* (Cambridge, Mass., 1927), and 'The situation of the Lords' room', in *The Elizabethan Playhouse*, 1st ser. (Stratford-upon-Avon, 1912). The Lords' room in its relation to an upper performance-area is treated by Richard Hosley in 'The gallery over the stage in the public playhouse of Shakespeare's time', *Shakespeare Quarterly*, VIII (1957). R. C. Bald proposes a theory of two general entrances to the public playhouse in 'The entrance to the Elizabethan theater', ibid., III (1952). An important reconstruction of a generalized Elizabethan public playhouse based mainly on the Swan Drawing has been put forward by Richard Southern in 'On reconstructing a practicable Elizabethan public playhouse', *Shakespeare Survey 12* (1959).

The Swan Playhouse is of special importance because of its depiction in the so-called De Witt Drawing, discovered and first published by Karl Theodor Gaedertz in *Zur Kenntnis der altenglischen Bühne* (Bremen, 1888). The Swan has been reconstructed by Richard Hosley in 'Reconstitution du théâtre du Swan', in *Le Lieu théâtral à la Renaissance*, ed. J. Jacquot (Paris, 1964). Particular aspects of the De Witt Drawing or of the Swan Playhouse are discussed by Thornton S. Graves, 'A note on the Swan Theatre', *Modern Philology*, IX (1911–12), on hangings at the Swan in 1602; Andrew Gurr, 'De Witt's sketch of the Swan', *Notes and Queries*, CCV (1960), suggesting that the vertical lines drawn under the stage may represent openings in hangings; C. Walter Hodges, 'De Witt again', *Theatre Notebook*, V (1950–1), suggesting that the man shown in the hut doorway is not necessarily blowing a trumpet; Martin Holmes, 'A new theory about the Swan Drawing', ibid., X (1955–6), suggesting that De Witt depicted a rehearsal; D. F. Rowan,

'The Swan revisited', *Research Opportunities in Renaissance Drama*, X (1967), including discussion of the staging of Middleton's *Chaste Maid in Cheapside*; and William Ingram, ' "Neere the Playe Howse": the Swan Theater and community blight', *Renaissance Drama*, IV (1971).

The once doubtful site of the Globe was established by W. W. Braines in *The Site of the Globe Playhouse, Southwark* (London, 1921). An important reconstruction of the First Globe by J. H. Farrar and G. Topham Forrest was published as an appendix to Braines's book: 'The architecture of the First Globe Theatre'. The best reconstruction of the First Globe is by C. Walter Hodges: *The Globe Restored: a study of the Elizabethan theatre* (London, 1953; 2nd ed., 1968). The reconstruction by John Cranford Adams, *The Globe Playhouse: its design and equipment* (Cambridge, Mass., 1942; 2nd ed., 1961), neglects vital external evidence, accepts inappropriate internal evidence, and bases its arguments on fantastic theories of Elizabethan staging. Criticism of Adams's reconstruction and his staging theories is provided by George F. Reynolds in 'Was there a "tarras" in Shakespeare's Globe?', *Shakespeare Survey 4* (1951), and by Richard Hosley in 'Shakespeare's use of a gallery over the stage', *Shakespeare Survey 10* (1957), 'Was there a music-room in Shakespeare's Globe?', ibid., 13 (1960), and 'The origins of the so-called Elizabethan multiple stage', *The Drama Review*, XII (1967–8). Bernard Beckerman has a good general study of the Globe based largely on the evidence of the plays: *Shakespeare at the Globe, 1599–1609* (New York, 1962). Richard Hosley deals with particular components of the Globe tiring-house in his article on the music-room cited above and in 'The discovery-space in Shakespeare's Globe', *Shakespeare Survey 12* (1959). Other aspects of the Globe are discussed by Charlotte Carmichael Stopes, 'The Burbages and the transportation of "The Theatre" ', *Athenaeum*, 16 October 1909, suggesting that the timbers of the Theatre were carried across the Thames by water in order to avoid wheelage and passage dues on London Bridge; Irwin Smith, 'Theatre into Globe', *Shakespeare Quarterly*, III (1952), suggesting that the timbers of the Theatre bore carpenter's marks making possible reassembly in their original relationships; and Ernest Schanzer, 'Thomas Platter's observations on the Elizabethan stage', *Notes and Queries*, CCI (1956), correcting earlier mistranslations of the Swiss traveller's description of a performance at the Globe in 1599.

The Second Globe, constructed in 1614 after the destruction of the First Globe by fire the previous year, is not treated in the present book. However, some reference is desirable here because of the relationship of the Second Globe to the First and because of the general importance of Hollar's depiction of the Second Globe in his Long Bird's-Eye view of London (1647). Hollar's manuscript sketch for that view was published by I. A. Shapiro in 'An original drawing of the Globe Theatre', *Shakespeare Survey 2* (1949). And C. Walter Hodges has devoted a book to the subject: *Shakespeare's Second Globe: the missing monument* (London, 1973). Hodges also discusses the problems of building a full-scale replica in 'The arguments for and against attempting a full-scale reconstruction of an Elizabethan playhouse, and the uses such a building might (or might not) have', *Shakespeare 1971*, ed. C. Leech and J. M. R. Margeson (Toronto, 1972).

Rather less material is available on other public playhouses. A reconstruction of the First Fortune by Walter H. Godfrey and William Archer was published by Godfrey in 'An Elizabethan theatre', *Architectural Review*, XXIII (1908). There is an excellent study of the Red Bull by George F. Reynolds, based largely on evidence of the plays: *The Staging of Elizabethan Plays at the Red Bull Theater, 1605–25* (New York, 1940). An illustration depicting the Curtain was discovered and published by Leslie Hotson: ' "This Wooden O": Shakespeare's Curtain Theatre identified', *The Times*, 26 March 1954. Sidney Fisher, however, in *The Theatre, the Curtain, and the Globe* (Montreal, 1964), suggests that both the Curtain and the Theatre (rather than the Curtain only) are depicted in this illustration.

William A. Armstrong has written a good general study of the private playhouses: *The Elizabethan Private Theatres: facts and problems* (The Society for Theatre Research, London, 1958). W. J. Lawrence has a shorter discussion of the subject in 'The Elizabethan private playhouse', in *Those Nut-Cracking Elizabethans* (London, 1935). Information about the early private playhouses (Paul's and the First Blackfriars) may be found in Harold Newcomb Hillebrand, *The Child Actors: a chapter in Elizabethan stage history* (Urbana, Ill., 1926). Robert K. Sarlos treats 'Development and operation of the First Blackfriars Theatre' in *Studies in the Elizabethan Theatre*, ed. C. T. Prouty (Hamden, Conn., 1961). The basic records relating to both the First and Second Blackfriars are printed by Albert Feuillerat in *Blackfriars Records* (*Malone Society Collections*, II.i, Oxford, 1913). The sites of the two Blackfriars playhouses, together with various buildings of the Dominican Priory of London, are discussed by Alfred W. Clapham, 'On the topography of the Dominican Priory of London', *Archaeologia*, LXIII (1911–12), and Joseph Quincy Adams, 'The conventual buildings of Blackfriars, London, and the playhouses constructed therein', *Studies in Philology*, XIV (1917). Charles William Wallace treats the Second Blackfriars in considerable detail but falls short of advancing a reconstruction:

The Children of the Chapel at Blackfriars (Lincoln, Neb., 1908). Reconstructions are proposed by J. H. Farrar and G. Topham Forrest in 'Blackfriars Theatre: conjectural reconstruction', *The Times*, 21 November 1921; Irwin Smith, *Shakespeare's Blackfriars Playhouse* (New York, 1964); and Richard Hosley, 'A reconstruction of the Second Blackfriars', in *The Elizabethan Theatre 1*, ed. D. Galloway (Toronto, 1969). Interesting but questionable theories about particular aspects of the Second Blackfriars are proposed by Herbert Berry, 'The stage and boxes at Blackfriars', *Studies in Philology*, LXIII (1966), and by Robert M. Wren, 'The five-entry stage at Blackfriars', *Theatre Research*, VIII (1967).

Records relating to production at court are published by Albert Feuillerat, *Documents relating to the Office of the Revels in the Time of Queen Elizabeth* (Louvain, 1908). A careful study of these records has been made by Morton Paterson, 'The stagecraft of the Revels Office during the reign of Elizabeth', in *Studies in the Elizabethan Theatre*, ed. C. T. Prouty (Hamden, Conn., 1961). Court production is discussed by Thornton S. Graves in *The Court and the London Theatres during the Reign of Elizabeth* (Menasha, Wis., 1913). Richard Hosley proposes a reconstruction of the playhouse in the Great Hall of Hampton Court Palace in 'Three Renaissance English indoor playhouses', *English Literary Renaissance*, III (1973). The production of masques at court is treated by Allardyce Nicoll in *Stuart Masques and the Renaissance Stage* (London, 1937) and by Richard Southern in *Changeable Scenery: its origin and development in the British theatre* (London, 1952). Evidence for masque scenery is collected by Percy Simpson and C. F. Bell in *Designs by Inigo Jones for Masques and Plays at Court* (London, 1924) and by Stephen Orgel and Roy Strong in *Inigo Jones: the theatre of the Stuart court* (London, 1973).

IV The plays and the playwrights

PART I GENERAL

Bibliography: An annual bibliography of studies in English Renaissance literature, including drama, was published until 1968 by *Studies in Philology*. An annual review article of critical writings on Elizabethan and Jacobean drama appears in *Studies in English Literature 1500–1900*. Helpful portable bibliographies are Irving Ribner's *Tudor and Stuart Drama* (Goldentree Bibliographies, gen. ed. O. B. Hardison, New York, 1966) and *Shakespeare* and *English Drama* (Select Bibliographical Guides, gen. ed. Stanley Wells, Oxford, 1973, 1974).

For a listing of the dramatic texts, years and conditions of publication, the standard work is W. W. Greg, *A Bibliography of the English Printed Drama to the Restoration*, 4 vols (London, 1939–59). A shorter and in many ways more handy work in tabular form is Alfred Harbage, *Annals of English Drama, 975–1700*, rev. Samuel Schoenbaum (London and Philadelphia, 1964).

On all matters of fact about plays, playwrights, theatres, etc., the first and often the most valuable sources of information are E. K. Chambers, *The Elizabethan Stage*, 4 vols (Oxford, 1923), and the continuation, G. E. Bentley, *The Jacobean and Caroline Stage*, 7 vols (Oxford, 1941–68).

Critical histories: Although not planned for this purpose, the best history of the drama of this period is made up by four volumes of the Stratford-upon-Avon Studies (London and New York), ed. J. R. Brown and Bernard Harris: *Elizabethan Theatre* (1966), *Early Shakespeare* (1961), *Later Shakespeare* (1966), and *Jacobean Theatre* (1960). A good general history is *English Drama to 1710*, ed. Christopher Ricks, vol. III of the *Sphere History of Literature in the English Language* (London, 1971). Shorter histories made up by collecting and arranging individual articles are *Shakespeare's Contemporaries*, eds. Max Bluestone and Norman Rabkin, 2nd ed. (Englewood Cliffs, NJ, 1970); and *Elizabethan Drama, Modern Essays in Criticism*, ed. Ralph J. Kaufman (New York and Oxford, 1961). A good single-volume history with discussion of historical and social background is *The Age of Shakespeare*, vol. II of *A Guide to English Literature*, ed. Boris Ford (Harmondsworth and Baltimore, 1955). F. P. Wilson, *Elizabethan and Jacobean* (Oxford, 1945), provides a good short view of the crucial transition between the two ages and the two styles. A good treatment of the later period is that of Una Ellis-Fermor, *The Jacobean Drama* (London, 1936; repr. 1953). See also R. Hosley (ed.), *Essays on Shakespeare and Elizabethan Drama in Honor of Hardin Craig* (Columbia, Mo., and London, 1962).

Dramaturgy: The basic critical theory and its relation to the practice of the dramatists is the subject of Madeleine Doran, *Endeavors of Art: a study of form in Elizabethan drama* (Madison, Wis., 1954) and M. C. Bradbrook, *English Dramatic Form: A History of Its Development* (New York, 1965). The effect of the playing company on the plays is traced by David Bevington, *From 'Mankind' to Marlowe: growth of structure in the popular drama of Tudor England* (Cambridge, Mass., 1962). The conventions of the drama are the subject of M. C. Bradbrook, *Themes and Conventions of Elizabethan Tragedy* (Cambridge, 1935). See also R. A. Foakes, 'The profession of playwright', in *Early Shakespeare*, ed. J. R. Brown and B. Harris (London, 1961). Alfred Hart, 'Play abridgement' in his *Shakespeare and the Homilies* (Melbourne, 1934) deals with length, time of representation and acting versions of Elizabethan and Jacobean plays. Special aspects of dramatic form are discussed by Thelma N. Greenfield, *The Induction of Elizabethan Drama* (Eugene, Ore., 1969) by Dieter Mehl, *The Elizabethan Dumb-Show* (London, 1965) and by Richard Levin, *The Multiple Plot in English Renaissance Drama* (Chicago, 1971). A very special view of the problem is T. B. Stroup, *Microcosmos: the Shape of the Elizabethan Play* (Lexington, Ky., 1965).

The history play : Growth and development of the history play are the subject of Irving Ribner, *The English History Play in the Age of Shakespeare* (Princeton, NJ, 1957; rev. ed. London, 1965). For the basic political theories underlying the history plays see M. M. Reese, *The Cease of Majesty* (London, 1961). Two recent studies should be consulted by anyone interested in the exact relationship of Elizabethan drama to actual events and to current theoretical views of history: David Bevington, *Tudor Drama and Politics* (Cambridge, Mass., 1968); and Wilbur Sanders, *The Dramatist and the Received Idea* (Cambridge, 1968).

Comedy : The background is provided by M. C. Bradbrook, *The Growth and Structure of Elizabethan Comedy* (London, 1955; Berkeley and Los Angeles, Calif., 1956). Background theory is to be found in Marvin T. Herrick, *Comic Theory in the Sixteenth Century* (Urbana, Ill., 1960). Enid Welsford, *The Fool, His Social and Literary History* (London, 1935; London and New York, 1961), should be consulted on the history and function of this most important figure. Among the several general theories of comedy which throw light on Elizabethan practice, the following are particularly helpful: Northrop Frye, 'The Mythos of spring: comedy', *Anatomy of Criticism* (Princeton, 1957), and Suzanne Langer, 'The great dramatic forms: the comic rhythm', *Feeling and Form* (New York, 1953).

Tragedy : The necessary general background is provided by Willard Farnham, *The Medieval Heritage of Elizabethan Tragedy* (Berkeley, Calif., 1936; rev. ed. Oxford, 1950). See also Marvin T. Herrick, *Italian Tragedy in the Renaissance* (Urbana, Ill., 1965). A good introduction to Seneca and his influence on Elizabethan tragedy is Clarence Mendell, *Our Seneca* (New Haven, Conn., 1941). See also T. S. Eliot, 'Seneca in Elizabethan translations' and 'Shakespeare and the Stoicism of Seneca' in *Selected Essays* (new ed., London, New York, 1950); and F. L. Lucas, *Seneca and Elizabethan Tragedy* (Cambridge, 1922). The best treatment of the basic components of this tragedy is in M. C. Bradbrook, *Themes and Conventions of Elizabethan Tragedy* (Cambridge, 1935); while language and verbal style are dealt with by Moody E. Prior, *The Language of Tragedy* (New York, 1947) and by Wolfgang Clemen, *English Tragedy before Shakespeare: the development of dramatic speech* (trans. T. S. Dorsch, London, 1961). Among the many works dealing with the tragedy of the period the following are particularly helpful as introductions and guides: Helen Gardner, 'Milton's Satan and the theme of damnation in Elizabethan tragedy', *English Studies 1948*, n.s., I (1949); Robert Ornstein, *The Moral Vision of Jacobean Tragedy* (Madison, Wis., 1960); and T. B. Tomlinson, *A Study of Elizabethan and Jacobean Tragedy* (Cambridge, 1964).

PART II THE INDIVIDUAL PLAYWRIGHTS AND THEIR WORKS

George Chapman

Editions: The standard edition is that of T. M. Parrott, *The Plays and Poems of George Chapman*, 2 vols (London, *Tragedies* 1910, *Comedies* 1914; New York, 4 vols, 1961). The first volume, *The Comedies*, of a new, more bibliographically elaborate edition, *The Plays of George Chapman*, gen. ed. Allan Holaday (Urbana, Ill.) appeared in 1969. The translations of Homer were edited by Allardyce Nicoll, *Chapman's Homer*, 2 vols (New York, 1956).

Life and works: Millar MacLure, *George Chapman, A Critical Study* (Toronto, 1966) has provided a most useful coherent view of Chapman's entire career as poet and playwright, as has J. Jacquot, *George Chapman: sa vie, sa poésie, son théâtre, sa pensée* (Paris, 1951).

Criticism: On the comedies see chapter 3 of MacLure. The tragedies have received more attention and several excellent treatments are available: Edwin Muir, '"Royal Man": notes on the tragedies of George Chapman', *Essays on Literature and Society* (London, 1949); Robert Ornstein, 'George Chapman', *The Moral Vision of Jacobean Tragedy* (Madison, Wis., 1960), chapter 2; and Peter Ure, 'Chapman's tragedies', *Jacobean Theatre*, Stratford-upon-Avon Studies I, ed. J. R. Brown and Bernard Harris (London, 1960; New York, 1961). For more extensive treatment see Ennis Rees, *The Tra-*

gedies of George Chapman: Renaissance Ethics in Action (Cambridge, Mass., 1954). More general treatments of Chapman's philosophic position are: Roy W. Battenhouse, 'Chapman and the nature of man', *ELH*, XII (1945), and Michael H. Higgins, 'The development of "Senecal man": Chapman's *Bussy d'Ambois* and some precursors', *RES*, XXIII (1947). Among the tragedies, *Bussy* has attracted most interest, and the problems of that play are well treated by C. L. Barber, 'The ambivalence of *Bussy d'Ambois*', *REL*, II (1961); by Eugene M. Waith, 'Chapman', in *The Herculean Hero* (London and New York, 1962), chapter 4, and by N. Brooke in his introductory essay to his edition (The Revels Plays, London, 1964).

Thomas Dekker

Editions: The standard edition is that of Fredson Bowers, *The Dramatic Works of Thomas Dekker*, 4 vols (Cambridge, 1953–61).

Biography and criticism: The most complete study of Dekker is T. M. Jones-Davies, *Un Peintre de la Vie Londonienne: Thomas Dekker*, 2 vols (Paris, 1967). Good discussions are to be found in M. C. Bradbrook, *The Growth and Structure of Elizabethan Comedy*, and Arthur Brown, 'Citizen comedy and domestic drama', *Jacobean Theatre*, Stratford-upon-Avon Studies I, ed. J. R. Brown and Bernard Harris (London, 1960, and New York, 1961).

Robert Greene

Editions: The standard collected edition is *The Plays and Poems of Robert Greene*, ed. John Churton Collins, 2 vols (Oxford, 1905). See, however, the editions of *James the Fourth* by J. A. Lavin (New Mermaids, London, 1967) and N. Sanders (The Revels Plays, London, 1970), in both of which a necessary rearrangement of text is made.

Biography and criticism: Kenneth Muir, 'Robert Greene as dramatist', *Essays on Shakespeare and Elizabethan Drama in Honor of Hardin Craig*, ed. Richard Hosley (Columbia, Mo., and London, 1962). Norman Sanders, 'The comedy of Greene and Shakespeare', *Early Shakespeare*, Stratford-upon-Avon Studies III, ed. J. R. Brown and Bernard Harris (London, 1961; New York, 1962).

Ben Jonson

Editions: The standard text is one of the great editions of Renaissance drama, *Ben Jonson*, ed. C. H. Herford and Percy and Evelyn Simpson, 11 vols

(Oxford, 1925–52). Reliable modern-spelling editions of the major plays are available in the Yale Ben Jonson and The Revels Plays.

Biography: The necessary materials are in Herford and Simpson, vols I and II, *Ben Jonson: the man and his work.* A more popular biography is that of Marchette Chute, *Ben Jonson of Westminster* (New York, 1953).

Criticism, general: The best introduction is through two fine general essays, Harry Levin, 'Introduction', *Ben Jonson, Selected Works* (New York, 1938); and L. C. Knights, 'Ben Jonson, dramatist', *The Age of Shakespeare*, *Vol. II of A Guide to English Literature*, ed. Boris Ford (Harmondsworth and Baltimore, 1955), pp. 302–17. A good collection of essays on Jonson is *Ben Jonson, A Collection of Critical Essays*, ed. Jonas Barish, Twentieth Century Views (Englewood Cliffs, NJ, 1963). Several widely differing but interesting books on Jonson's drama are J. J. Enck, *Jonson and the Comic Truth* (Madison, Wis., 1957); Edward B. Partridge, *The Broken Compass, A Study of the Major Comedies of Ben Jonson* (New York and London, 1958); and C. G. Thayer, *Ben Jonson, Studies in the Plays* (Norman, Okla., 1963).

Jonson's poetics: G. B. Jackson, *Vision and Judgment in Ben Jonson's Drama* (New Haven, Conn., 1968).

Style and dramaturgy: W. A. Armstrong, 'Ben Jonson and Jacobean stage-craft', in *Jacobean Theatre*, Stratford-upon-Avon Studies I (London, 1960; New York, 1961); Jonas Barish, *Ben Jonson and the Language of Prose Comedy* (Cambridge, Mass., 1960); Ray L. Heffner, Jr, 'Unifying symbols in the comedy of Ben Jonson', *English Stage Comedy*, ed. W. K. Wimsatt, Jr, *English Institute Essays 1954* (New York, 1955); Jonas Barish, 'Feasting and Judging in Jonsonian Comedy', *Renaissance Drama*, V (1972).

The masques: Stephen Orgel, *The Jonsonian Masque* (Cambridge, Mass., 1965). Orgel has also edited a modern edition, *Jonson: The Complete Masques*, Yale Ben Jonson, gen. eds R. B. Young and A. Kernan (New Haven, Conn., 1969). See also, Steven Orgel and Roy Strong, *Inigo Jones, The Theatre of the Stuart Court*, 2 vols (London, 1973).

The tragedies: Robert Ornstein, *The Moral Vision of Jacobean Tragedy* (Madison, Wis. Press, 1960), chapters 1 and 2.

Volpone: Jonas Barish, 'The double plot in *Volpone*', *Modern Philology*, LI (1953). Alvin Kernan, *The Plot of Satire* (New Haven, Conn., 1965), chapter 9. Ian Donaldson, '*Volpone*: quick and dead', *Essays in Criticism*, XXI (April 1971).

The Alchemist: Ian Donaldson, 'Language, noise and nonsense', *Seventeenth-Century Imagery*, ed. Earl Miner (Los Angeles, Calif., 1971). Alvin Kernan, 'Introduction', *The Alchemist*, Yale Ben Jonson (New Haven, Conn.,

1974). F. H. Mares, 'Introduction', *The Alchemist*, The Revels Plays (London and Cambridge, Mass., 1967).

Bartholomew Fair: Jackson I. Cope, '*Bartholomew Fair* as blasphemy', *Renaissance Drama*, VIII (1965); E. A. Horsman, 'Introduction', *Bartholomew Fair*, The Revels Plays (London, Cambridge, Mass., 1960); E. M. Waith, 'The staging of *Bartholomew Fair*', *SEL*, II (1962).

Thomas Kyd

Editions: The standard edition remains that of F. S. Boas, *The Works of Thomas Kyd* (Oxford, 1901, 1955). A very good edition of *The Spanish Tragedy* has been produced by Philip Edwards, The Revels Plays (London, 1959).

Biography and bibliography: The many problems connected with Kyd's life and canon have now been summarized and treated with great skill by Arthur Freeman, *Thomas Kyd, Facts and Problems* (Oxford, 1967).

Criticism: Jonas A. Barish, '*The Spanish Tragedy*, or the pleasures and perils of rhetoric', *Elizabethan Theatre*, Stratford-upon-Avon Studies IX, ed. J. R. Brown and B. Harris (London, 1966; New York, 1967), treats Kyd's style and its meaning with great perception. More general articles on the play are: G. K. Hunter, 'Ironies of justice in *The Spanish Tragedy*', *Renaissance Drama*, VIII (1965); William Empson, '*The Spanish Tragedy*', *Nimbus*, III (summer 1956). P. B. Murray, *Thomas Kyd* (New York, 1969) is wholly concerned with *The Spanish Tragedy*, which he analyses in detail. There is also a good short introduction to Kyd and his contemporaries by P. Edwards, *Thomas Kyd and Early Elizabethan Tragedy* (Writers and their Work, London, 1966). On the revenge ethic see Fredson Bowers, *Elizabethan Revenge Tragedy* (Princeton, NJ, 1940), and Michael H. Levin, ' "Vindicta Mihi!" Meaning, morality and motivation in *The Spanish Tragedy*', *SEL*, IV (1964). On Kyd's use of imagery of the theatre see: Ejner J. Jensen, 'Kyd's *Spanish Tragedy*: the play explains itself', *JEGP*, LXIV (1966). See also two studies in *Essays on Shakespeare and Elizabethan Drama in Honor of Hardin Craig*, ed. R. Hosley (Columbia, Mo., and London, 1962): A. Harbage, 'Intrigue in Elizabethan tragedy', and S. F. Johnson, '*The Spanish Tragedy*, or Babylon revisited'.

John Lyly

Editions: The standard edition remains *The Complete Works of John Lyly*, ed. R. Warwick Bond, 3 vols (Oxford, 1902). A new edition by G. K. Hunter is in preparation.

Biography: A fine study of both the life and works in their relationship to the intellectual currents of the time is G. K. Hunter, *John Lyly, The Humanist as Courtier* (London and Cambridge, Mass., 1962).

Criticism: For a brief view of Lyly's achievement see G. Wilson Knight, 'Lyly', *RES*, XV (1939). The style is analysed by Jonas A. Barish, 'The prose style of John Lyly', *ELH*, XXIII (1956), and a most interesting treatment of Lyly's style and dramaturgy as 'game' is Jocelyn Powell, 'John Lyly and the language of play', *Elizabethan Theatre*, Stratford-upon-Avon Studies IX, ed. J. R. Brown and Bernard Harris (London, 1966; New York, 1967). Peter Saccio, *The Court Comedies of John Lyly, A Study in Allegorical Dramaturgy* (Princeton, NJ, 1969), investigates the function of allegory in Lyly's works. See also John Dover Wilson, *John Lyly* (Cambridge, 1905).

Christopher Marlowe

Editions: The standard edition is *The Works and Life of Christopher Marlowe*, gen. ed. R. H. Case, 6 vols (London, 1930–3): Life and *Dido*, ed. C. F. Tucker Brooke, 1930; *Tamburlaine*, ed. U. M. Ellis-Fermor, 1930; *The Jew of Malta* and *The Massacre at Paris*, ed. H. S. Bennett, 1931; *Poems*, ed. L. C. Martin, 1931; *Doctor Faustus*, ed. F. S. Boas, 1932; *Edward II*, ed. H. B. Charlton and R. D. Waller, 1933 (rev. F. N. Lees, 1955). An old-spelling edition in one volume was made by C. F. Tucker Brooke (Oxford, 1910); another by Fredson Bowers is published in two volumes (Cambridge, 1973). Two well-edited single-volume editions are those of Irving Ribner, *The Complete Plays of Christopher Marlowe* (New York, 1963), and J. B. Steane, *Christopher Marlowe: The Complete Plays* (Harmondsworth and Baltimore, 1969). The Revels Plays editions of single plays are highly recommended: *Dido, Queen of Carthage and The Massacre at Paris*, ed. H. J. Oliver, 1968; *Doctor Faustus*, ed. J. D. Jump, 1962. The difficult textual problem of *Doctor Faustus* has been explicated and dealt with in the best possible way in *Marlowe's Doctor Faustus 1604–1616: Parallel Texts*, ed. W. W. Greg (Oxford, 1950), and in *The Tragical History of the Life and Death of Doctor Faustus: A Conjectural Reconstruction*, ed. W. W. Greg (Oxford, 1950).

Biography and bibliography: The strange facts relating to Marlowe's death were discovered by Leslie Hotson, *The Death of Christopher Marlowe* (London, 1925). Extensive biographies relating Marlowe and his plays to his times are: John Bakeless, *The Tragical History of Christopher Marlowe*, 2 vols (Cambridge, Mass., 1942); Paul H. Kocher, *Christopher Marlowe, A Study of His Thought, Learning and Character* (Chapel Hill, NC, 1946).

Criticism: Three excellent collections of the most important Marlowe criticism exist: *Marlowe, A Collection of Critical Essays*, ed. Clifford Leech, Twentieth Century Views (Englewood Cliffs, NJ, 1964); *Christopher Marlowe's 'Dr Faustus', Text and Major Criticism*, ed. Irving Ribner (New York, 1966); and *Twentieth-Century Interpretations of 'Doctor Faustus' : a collection of critical essays*, ed. W. Farnham, Twentieth Century Interpretations (Englewood Cliffs, NJ, 1969). The most useful books dealing with all the plays are: Una Ellis-Fermor, *Christopher Marlowe* (London, 1927); Harry Levin, *The Overreacher: a study of Christopher Marlowe* (Cambridge, Mass., 1952); F. P. Wilson, *Marlowe and the Early Shakespeare* (Oxford, 1953); and J. B. Steane, *Marlowe: a critical study* (Cambridge, 1964). A study comparing Marlowe's achievement with Shakespeare's is Wilbur Sanders, *The Dramatist and the Received Idea: studies in the plays of Marlowe and Shakespeare* (Cambridge, 1968), esp. chapters 2, 3, 7, 11 and 12. Among the many excellent articles on Marlowe, the following will be found particularly helpful at the beginning of study: C. L. Barber, 'The form of *Faustus*' fortunes good or bad', *Tulane Drama Review*, VIII (1964); T. S. Eliot, 'Christopher Marlowe', *Selected Essays* (London and New York, 1932); Clifford Leech, 'The structure of *Tamburlaine*', *Tulane Drama Review*, VIII (1964); Robert Ornstein, 'The comic synthesis in *Doctor Faustus*', *ELH*, XXII (1955); Hallett Smith, '*Tamburlaine* and the Renaissance', *Elizabethan Studies and Other Essays: in honor of George F. Reynolds* (Boulder, Colo., 1945); Eugene Waith, '*Edward II*: the shadow of action', *Tulane Drama Review*, VIII (1964); Clifford Leech, 'Marlowe's *Edward II*: power and suffering', *Critical Quarterly*, I (1959).

John Marston

Editions: The standard edition remains that of A. H. Bullen, *The Plays of John Marston*, 3 vols (London, 1887). This edition has the advantage of line numbers over the later and in some ways more complete edition of H. Harvey Wood, *The Plays of John Marston*, 3 vols (Edinburgh, 1934–9).

Life and background: A recent book assembles the relevant material and provides a consistent view of Marston, his works, and his times: Philip J. Finkelpearl, *John Marston of the Middle Temple, An Elizabethan Dramatist in his Social Setting* (Cambridge, Mass., 1969).

Criticism: The best full-length study is Anthony Caputi, *John Marston, Satirist* (Ithaca, NY, 1961). Articles of particular interest are G. K. Hunter, 'English folly and Italian vice: the moral landscape of John Marston', *Jacobean Theatre*, Stratford-upon-Avon Studies I, ed. J. R. Brown and Bernard Harris (London, 1960; New York, 1961); John Peter, 'John

Marston's plays', *Scrutiny*, 18 (1950). For a discussion of Marston's place in the Elizabethan satiric tradition see Alvin Kernan, *The Cankered Muse, Satire of the English Renaissance* (New Haven, Conn., 1959).

George Peele

Editions : An old-spelling edition is *The Life and Works of George Peele*, gen. ed. C. T. Prouty (London and New Haven, Conn., 1952–70). Vol. I, *The Life and Minor Works of George Peele*, by David Horne, provides the best discussion available of Peele's life and dramatic career. Vol. II contains *Edward I*, ed. Frank S. Hook, and *The Battle of Alcazar*, ed. John Yokla-vich. Vol. III contains *The Araygnement of Paris*, ed. R. Mark Benbow, *David and Bethsabe*, ed. Elmer M. Blistein, and *The Old Wives Tale*, ed. Frank S. Hook.

   Criticism : M. C. Bradbrook, 'Peele's *Old Wives Tale*: a play of enchant-ment', *ES*, XLIII (1962), and I. S. Ewbank, 'The house of David in Renaissance drama', *Renaissance Drama* (1965).

William Shakespeare

The vast number of works on Shakespeare and his plays makes it impossible to do more than list a few writings which will provide good, clear introductions to particular plays and themes, and a few collections of material which will, in turn, provide the necessary information for further study. The plays are dealt with in groups – e.g., 'histories', 'tragedies', etc. – and each group begins with a number of general works on the plays under that heading.

   Editions : Many excellent editions of Shakespeare's plays exist, but atten-tion should be called to the following specialized editions: *The New Arden Shakespeare*, ed. U. Ellis-Fermor, H. F. Brooks, H. Jenkins *et al.* (London, 1951–   ; Cambridge, Mass., 1951–   ), single-volume editions with complete textual apparatus and full glosses of difficult words and passages. *A New Variorum Edition of the Works of Shakespeare*, gen. eds H. H. Furness and H. H. Furness, Jr, *et al.* (Philadelphia and London, 1871–   ), a continuing project to print the old-spelling text and accumulated commentary. *The Norton Shakespeare, The First Folio of Shakespeare*, ed. Charlton Hinman (New York, 1968), a 'corrected' edition of the 1623 Folio assembled by collating numerous copies of the first edition and printing as one volume both the cleanest pages and those which were reset after being proof-read and corrected.

   Text : No better introduction to the very difficult problems surrounding the transmission and printing of Shakespeare's plays can be found than the two volumes by Sir Walter Greg: *The Editorial Problem in Shakespeare* (Oxford, 1942, 1954); and *The Shakespeare First Folio : its bibliographical and textual history* (Oxford, 1955). See also E. A. J. Honigmann, *The Stability of Shakespeare's Text* (Lincoln, Neb., 1965).

Concordances: The standard concordance has long been that of John Bartlett (London, 1894), which is keyed to The Globe Edition of *The Works of William Shakespeare*, ed. W. G. Clark and W. A. Wright (London, 1864). A new concordance is now complete, computerized and edited by Marvin Spevack, *A Complete and Systematic Concordance to the Works of Shakespeare*, 6 vols (Hildesheim, 1968–70), and the one volume *Harvard Concordance to Shakespeare*; both are keyed to *The Riverside Shakespeare*, text edited by G. Blakemore Evans, general introduction by Harry Levin, introduction by Herschel Baker *et al.* (Boston, 1974).

Reference and surveys of criticism : A most useful compendium of information and bibliography is *The Reader's Encyclopedia of Shakespeare*, ed. O. J. Campbell and E. G. Quinn (New York, 1966); another is *A New Companion to Shakespeare Studies*, ed. K. Muir and S. Schoenbaum (Cambridge, 1971). Annual articles on 'Critical studies', 'Shakespeare's life, time, and stage' and 'Textual studies' appear in *Shakespeare Survey*, and a complete annual bibliography appears in *Shakespeare Quarterly*. A good guide to the development of work on the plays is Arthur M. Eastman, *A Short History of Shakespearean Criticism* (New York, 1968). Several comprehensive bibliographies exist: W. Ebisch and L. L. Schücking, *A Shakespeare Bibliography* (Oxford, 1931, Supplement 1930–5, 1937); G. R. Smith, *A Classified Shakespeare Bibliography, 1936–1958* (University Park, Pa., 1963); Ronald Berman, *A Reader's Guide to Shakespeare's Plays : A Discursive bibliography* (Glenview, Ill., 1965); Stanley Wells (ed.), *Shakespeare* (Select Bibliographical Guides, Oxford, 1973).

Biography : The basic materials are collected by E. K. Chambers, *William Shakespeare: a study of facts and problems*, 2 vols (Oxford, 1930). T. W. Baldwin, *William Shakespeare's Small Latine and Less Greeke*, 2 vols (Urbana, Ill., 1944), reconstructs the education Shakespeare would have received in grammar school. G. E. Bentley, *Shakespeare, A Biographical Handbook* (New Haven, Conn., 1961), staying close to surviving documents, provides a brief clear description of the life and work in the theatre. The development of Shakespearian biography and scholarship is wonderfully chronicled in Samuel Schoenbaum, *Shakespeare's Lives* (Oxford, 1970).

General studies of the plays : Useful for a general introduction to the works are: Derek Traversi, *An Approach to Shakespeare* (London, 1938; 2nd rev.

498   Bibliography

ed., New York, 1956), Harold Goddard, *The Meaning of Shakespeare* (Chicago, Ill., 1951), and Peter Alexander, *Shakespeare's Life and Art* (London, 1939; repr., New York, 1967).

Sources: A collection of major sources and analogues, with discussion of Shakespeare's use of this material, is Geoffrey Bullough, *Narrative and Dramatic Sources of Shakespeare*, 8 vols (London and New York, 1957–   ).

Intellectual background: The most useful and comprehensive study of the world view against which the plays were written remains Theodore Spencer, *Shakespeare and the Nature of Man* (New York, 1942); but see also Geoffrey Bush, *Shakespeare and the Natural Condition* (Cambridge, Mass., 1956); and John Danby, *Shakespeare's Doctrine of Nature: a study of 'King Lear'* (London, 1949). However, the relation of the plays to contemporary views is most problematical, and readers should consult two other books – Norman Rabkin, *Shakespeare and the Commun Understanding* (New York and London, 1967); and Wilbur Sanders, *The Dramatist and the Received Idea, Studies in the Plays of Marlowe and Shakespeare* (Cambridge, 1968) – which open up the full complexity of the plays' relationship to contemporary ideas.

Use of the stage: The fact that Shakespeare was a dramatist writing for theatrical production, and that his plays can often be best understood by seeing what happens on stage, not in reading, was first systematically developed by H. Granville-Barker, *Prefaces to Shakespeare* (reprinted in 2 vols, Princeton, NJ, 1946–7). His ideas have been extended and given historical dimension by J. R. Brown, *Shakespeare's Plays in Performance* (London, 1966; New York, 1967; repr. with additions, Harmondsworth, 1969). An extremely interesting variant view is G. Wilson Knight, *Principles of Shakespearean Production, with Especial Reference to the Tragedies* (London, 1936; rev. and enlarged, London and Evanston, Ill., 1964). For the effect of actual theatrical conditions on the plays see Bernard Beckerman, *Shakespeare at the Globe, 1599–1609* (New York, 1962). For the use of stage productions as a technique of criticism see Carol Jones Carlisle, *Shakespeare from the Greenroom, Actors' Criticisms of Four Major Tragedies* (Chapel Hill, NC, 1969).

Dramaturgy: For easily understandable reasons we have as yet no single book which describes Shakespeare's 'dramatics'. A posthumous collection of essays by Una Ellis-Fermor, *Shakespeare the Dramatist*, ed. Kenneth Muir (London and New York, 1961) indicates the direction such a study should take; and Madeleine Doran, *Endeavors of Art: a study of form in Elizabethan drama* (Madison, Wis., 1954), provides the necessary historical understanding of contemporary critical views. But for an application of modern critical theory to the play structure we are dependent on a series of penetrating but brief insights such as Alan S. Downer, 'The life of our design: the function of imagery in poetic drama', *The Hudson Review*, II (summer 1949); Harry Levin, 'The Shakespeare overplot', *Renaissance Drama*, VIII (1965). S. L. Bethell, *Shakespeare and the Popular Dramatic Tradition* (London and Durham, NC, 1944); and Hereward T. Price, 'Mirror-scenes in Shakespeare', *Joseph Quincy Adams Memorial Studies*, ed. McManaway, Dawson, and Willoughby (Washington, DC, 1948). See also Emrys Jones, *Scenic Form in Shakespeare* (Oxford, 1971), and Mark Rose, *Shakespearean Design* (Cambridge, Mass., 1972).

Language and verbal style: Here again we lack a competent comprehensive work, but verbal style has received more attention than dramaturgy, and there are a large number of examinations of various aspects of Shakespeare's poetry. Perhaps the best general essay on the style and the causes for change is Patrick Crutwell, *The Shakespearean Moment and Its Place in the Poetry of the Seventeenth Century* (London, 1954; New York, 1960); see especially chapter 1. Study of the imagery has developed chiefly through three books: Caroline Spurgeon, *Shakespeare's Imagery and What It Tells Us* (Cambridge, 1935); Donald Stauffer, *Shakespeare's World of Images: the development of his moral ideas* (New York, 1949); and Wolfgang Clemen, *The Development of Shakespeare's Imagery* (London and Cambridge, Mass., 1951; a revision of *Shakespeares Bilder. Ihre Entwicklung und Ihre Funktionen im Dramatischen Werk*, Bonn, 1936). Puns are dealt with by M. M. Mahood, *Shakespeare's Wordplay* (London and New York, 1957); Helge Kökeritz, *Shakespeare's Pronunciation* (New Haven, Conn., 1953) should be consulted for puns based on Elizabethan pronunciations. Shakespeare's sexual allusions are explicated in glossary form in Eric Partridge, *Shakespeare's Bawdy* (London, 1948; rev. ed. New York, 1969). Though dominated by the doubtful thesis that Shakespeare wrote almost exclusively in the iambic pentameter line, with only a very few variations, the metrical question is most thoroughly presented by Dorothy L. Sipe, *Shakespeare's Metrics*, Yale Studies in English 166 (New Haven, Conn., 1968). The use of the formal devices of rhetoric is detailed in Sister Miriam Joseph, *Shakespeare's Use of the Arts of Language* (New York, 1947). On punctuation see Peter Alexander, *Shakespeare's Punctuation* (London, 1945). The prose is analysed by Milton Crane, *Shakespeare's Prose* (Chicago, Ill., 1951) and by Brian Vickers, *Shakespeare's Prose* (Cambridge, 1971). For more general studies see F. E. Halliday, *The Poetry of Shakespeare's Plays* (London, 1954); and Paul A. Jorgensen, *Redeeming Shakespeare's Words* (Berkeley and Los Angeles, Calif., 1962).

Treatment of characters: The range of possible points of view is nicely illustrated by three works: (1) unrealistic characters created for maximum theatrical effect, E. E. Stoll, *Shakespeare and Other Masters* (Cambridge, Mass., 1940); (2) characters not psychologically improbable if a sufficiently complex psychology is used, J. I. M. Stewart, *Character and Motive in Shakespeare: some recent appraisals examined* (London, 1949); and (3) characters not realistic imitations but parts of a central vision broken up by the dramatic prism, Arthur Sewell, *Character and Society in Shakespeare* (Oxford, 1951).

Shakespeare and religion: A systematic treatment of this question is Roland M. Frye, *Shakespeare and Christian Doctrine* (Princeton, NJ, 1963); a study of a different kind is Honor Matthews, *Character and Symbol in Shakespeare's Plays: a study of certain Christian and pre-Christian elements in their structure and imagery* (Cambridge, 1962).

Psychoanalytic criticism: This difficult question has been examined with great perception, and a solution proposed by Norman Holland, *Psychoanalysis and Shakespeare* (New York, 1966). The middle section of this book is a summary, play by play, of the various major psychoanalytic explanations of the plays, with complete bibliography. Perhaps the most famous single example of this approach is Ernest Jones, *Hamlet and Oedipus* (London, 1949).

Music: The most authoritative modern books are F. W. Sternfeld, *Music in Shakespearean Tragedy* (London and New York, 1963), Peter J. Seng, *The Vocal Songs in the Plays of Shakespeare* (Cambridge, Mass., 1967), and John H. Long, *Shakespeare's Use of Music: A Study of the Music and its Performance in the Original Production of Seven Comedies* and *Shakespeare's Use of Music: The Final Comedies* (Gainesville, Fla., 1961). For a more theoretical discussion of the view of music, see John Hollander, *The Untuning of the Sky: ideas of music in English poetry 1500–1700* (Princeton, NJ, 1961), and for an idiosyncratic one, see W. H. Auden, 'Music in Shakespeare', *Encounter*, IX (1957). See also R. Noble, *Shakespeare's Use of Song, with the Text of the Principal Songs* (London, 1923).

Shakespeare's English history plays

General: An excellent collection of articles on the history plays is provided by R. J. Dorius, *Discussions of Shakespeare's Histories: 'Richard II' to 'Henry V'* (Boston, 1964). A major study summing up the extensive work on these plays in recent years is Moody E. Prior, *The Drama of Power, Studies in Shakespeare's History Plays* (Evanston, Ill., 1973). See also Eugene M. Waith, *Shakespeare The Histories, A Collection of Critical Essays*, Twentieth Century

Views (Englewood Cliffs, NJ, 1965). For a view of Renaissance theories of history and Shakespeare as conservative defender of the old order see E. M. W. Tillyard, *Shakespeare's History Plays* (London, 1944; New York, 1946). For a view of the meaning of the plays as more ambiguous see the close readings of Derek Traversi, *Shakespeare from 'Richard II' to 'Henry V'* (Stanford, Calif., 1957), and the historically based study of Henry A. Kelly, *Divine Providence in the England of Shakespeare's Histories* (Cambridge, Mass., 1970).

1, 2, and *3 Henry VI*: J. P. Brockbank, 'The frame of disorder – *Henry VI*', *Early Shakespeare*, Stratford-upon-Avon Studies III, ed. J. R. Brown and Bernard Harris (London, 1961; New York, 1962: repr. in Waith).

Richard III: A. P. Rossiter, 'The unity of *Richard III*', *Angel with Horns* (London and New York, 1961: repr. in Waith); N. Brooke, *Shakespeare's Early Tragedies* (London, 1968).

Richard II: R. J. Dorius, 'Prudence and excess in *Richard II* and the histories', *Shakespeare Quarterly*, XI (winter 1960). A. R. Humphreys, *Shakespeare: Richard II*, Studies in English Literature (London, 1967).

1 Henry IV: C. L. Barber, 'From ritual to comedy: an examination of *Henry IV*', *English Stage Comedy*, in *English Institute Essays 1954*, ed. W. K. Wimsatt Jr (New York, 1954); J. Dover Wilson, *The Fortunes of Falstaff* (Cambridge, 1943). A. R. Humphreys, 'Introduction', New Arden Shakespeare, *Henry IV Part I* (London and Cambridge, Mass., 1960).

2 Henry IV: Harold Jenkins, *The Structural Problem in Shakespeare's 'Henry the Fourth'* (London, 1956; repr. in Dorius); Clifford Leech, 'The unity of *2 Henry IV*', *Shakespeare Survey 6* (1953: repr. in Dorius); James Winny, *The Player King* (London, 1968).

Henry V: J. H. Walter, 'Introduction', New Arden Shakespeare: *'King Henry V'* (London and Cambridge, Mass., 1954); Ernst Kris, 'Prince Hal's conflict', chapter 12 in *Psychoanalytic Explorations in Art* (New York, 1952).

Two long pieces attempt to synthesize the structure and meaning of Shakespeare's second tetralogy: Sigurd Burckhard, ' "Swoll'n with Some Other Grief": Shakespeare's Prince Hal trilogy', in *Shakespearean Meanings*

(Princeton, NJ, 1968); and Alvin B. Kernan, 'The *Henriad*: Shakespeare's major history plays', *Yale Review*, LXI (fall 1964).

Early Comedy

General: A good introduction and survey is *Shakespeare, the comedies*, ed. Kenneth Muir, Twentieth Century Views (Englewood Cliffs, NJ, 1965). The relation of the comedies to Elizabethan festivals is detailed by C. L. Barber, *Shakespeare's Festive Comedy, A Study of Dramatic Form and Its Relation to Social Custom* (Princeton, NJ, 1959). A purely critical organization of Shakespeare's comic world is Northrop Frye, *A Natural Perspective: the development of Shakespearean comedy and romance* (New York, 1965), and Ralph Berry, *Shakespeare's Comedies: explorations in form* (Princeton, NJ, 1972) provides readings of the individual works, as does Alexander Leggatt, *Shakespeare's Comedy of Love* (London, 1974).

The Comedy of Errors: Harry Levin, 'Introduction', *The Comedy of Errors*, Signet Shakespeare (New York, 1965).

The Taming of the Shrew: Maynard Mack, 'Engagement and detachment in Shakespeare's plays', *Essays on Shakespeare and Elizabethan Drama in Honor of Hardin Craig*, ed. R. Hosley (Columbia, Mo., 1962).

The Two Gentlemen of Verona: John F. Danby, 'Shakespeare criticism and *Two Gentlemen of Verona*', *Critical Quarterly*, II (1960); Clifford Leech, 'Introduction', New Arden Shakespeare, *Two Gentlemen of Verona* (London and Cambridge, Mass., 1969); H. F. Brooks, 'Two clowns in a comedy (to say nothing of the dog); Speed, Launce (and Crab) in *The Two Gentlemen of Verona*', *Essays and Studies* (1963).

Love's Labour's Lost: Richard David, 'Introduction', New Arden Shakespeare, *Love's Labour's Lost* (London, 1951); Alfred Harbage, '*Love's Labour's Lost* and the early Shakespeare', *Philological Quarterly*, XLI (1962); F. A. Yates, *A Study of 'Love's Labour's Lost'* (Cambridge, 1936); Bobbyann Roesen, '*Love's Labour's Lost*', *Shakespeare Quarterly*, IV (1953).

A Midsummer Night's Dream: Ernest Schanzer, 'The moon and the fairies in *A Midsummer Night's Dream*', *University of Toronto Quarterly*, XXIV (1955); David P. Young, *Something of Great Constancy: the art of 'A Midsummer Night's Dream'* (New Haven, Conn., 1966).

The Merchant of Venice: J. R. Brown, *Shakespeare's Plays in Performance* (London, 1966; New York, 1967), chapter 6; M.C. Bradbrook, *Shakespeare and Elizabethan Poetry* (London, 1951).

Much Ado About Nothing: Paul A. Jorgensen, '*Much Ado About Nothing*', *Shakespeare Quarterly*, V (1954); A. P. Rossiter, *Angel with Horns* (London, 1961).

As You Like It: Helen Gardner, '*As You Like It*', *More Talking of Shakespeare*, ed. John W. P. Garrett (London and New York, 1959); David P. Young, *The Heart's Forest: a study of Shakespeare's pastoral plays* (New Haven, Conn., 1972), chapters 1, 2.

Twelfth Night: John Hollander, '*Twelfth Night* and the morality of indulgence', *Sewanee Review*, LXI (1959); Clifford Leech, '*Twelfth Night*' *and Shakespearean Comedy* (Toronto, 1965); L. G. Salingar, 'The design of *Twelfth Night*', *Shakespeare Quarterly*, IX (1958); J. Summers, 'The masks of *Twelfth Night*', *University of Kansas City Review*, XXII (1955); J. R. Brown, *Shakespeare's Plays in Performance* (London, 1966; Harmondsworth, 1969).

Measure for Measure: J. W. Bennett, '*Measure for Measure*' *as Royal Entertainment* (New York, 1966); R. W. Chambers, '*Measure for Measure*', in *Man's Unconquerable Mind* (London, 1939, repr. 1952); G. Wilson Knight, '*Measure for Measure* and the gospels' in *The Wheel of Fire* (Oxford, 1930; New York, rev. ed., 1957); J. W. Lever, 'Introduction', New Arden Shakespeare, *Measure for Measure* (London and Cambridge, Mass., 1965).

Shakespeare's tragedies

General: In the midst of the extraordinary number of works dealing with Shakespearian tragedy, the general reader will find it most helpful to begin with two collections: *Shakespeare, The Tragedies, A Collection of Critical Essays*, ed. Alfred Harbage, Twentieth Century Views (Englewood Cliffs, NJ, 1964); and *Shakespeare's Tragedies, an Anthology of Modern Criticism*, ed. Laurence Lerner (Harmondsworth and Baltimore, 1963). The place to begin serious study remains A. C. Bradley, *Shakespearean Tragedy* (London, 1904); but this should be supplemented with the following works offering coherent views of widely differing kinds: Northrop Frye, *Fools of Time: studies in Shakespearean tragedy* (Toronto, 1967); John Holloway, *The Story of the*

Night: studies in Shakespeare's major tragedies (London, 1961); G. Wilson Knight, *The Wheel of Fire, Interpretations of Shakespearean Tragedy* (Oxford, 1930; New York, rev. ed., 1957); Maynard Mack, 'The Jacobean Shakespeare: some observations on the constructions of the tragedies', *Jacobean Theatre*, Stratford-upon-Avon Studies I, eds J. R. Brown and Bernard Harris (London, 1960; New York, 1961). The most helpful study of the intellectual setting out of which the tragedies grew is Patrick Crutwell, *The Shakespearean Moment and its Place in the Poetry of the Seventeenth Century* (London, 1954; New York, 1960).

Titus Andronicus: James L. Calderwood, '*Titus Andronicus*: word, act, authority', *Shakespearean Metadrama* (Minneapolis, Minn., 1971); Alan Sommers, '"Wilderness of tigers": structure and symbolism in *Titus Andronicus*', *Essays in Criticism*, X (1960).

Romeo and Juliet: Nicholas Brooke, *Shakespeare's Early Tragedies* (London, 1968); John Lawlor, '*Romeo and Juliet*', *Early Shakespeare*, Stratford-upon-Avon Studies III, eds J. R. Brown and Bernard Harris (London and New York, 1961); Harry Levin, 'Form and formality in *Romeo and Juliet*', *Shakespeare Quarterly*, XI (1960).

Julius Caesar: Allan Bloom, 'The morality of the pagan hero: *Julius Caesar*', *Shakespeare's Politics* (London and New York, 1964); Adrien Bonjour, *The Structure of 'Julius Caesar'* (Liverpool, 1958); Maurice Charney, *Shakespeare's Roman Plays, The Function of Imagery in the Drama* (Cambridge, Mass., 1961); R. A. Foakes, 'An approach to *Julius Caesar*', *Shakespeare Quarterly*, V (1954).

Hamlet: The essential problems, though not the answers, are laid out with great clarity in J. Dover Wilson, *What Happens in 'Hamlet'* (Cambridge, 1935). This book should be read in conjunction with an essay which argues that there are no answers to the questions which the play inevitably raises, Maynard Mack, 'The world of *Hamlet*', *Yale Review*, XLI (1952). There are numerous collections of the extensive *Hamlet* criticism, and among the most useful is *Hamlet*, Stratford-upon-Avon Studies V, eds J. R. Brown and Bernard Harris (London and New York, 1964). *Hamlet* criticism to 1955 is discussed by Clifford Leech, 'Studies in *Hamlet*, 1901–1955' in *Shakespeare Survey 9* (1956). The psychological discussion which has grown up around the play is reviewed and sifted in Norman Holland, *Psychoanalysis and*

Shakespeare (New York, 1966), pp. 163–206. Every student of *Hamlet* should be familiar with G. Wilson Knight's famous attack on Hamlet as a death-bringer, 'The embassy of death: an essay on *Hamlet*', *The Wheel of Fire* (see above) and the later modification, '*Hamlet* reconsidered' (1947), appearing in the 4th and 5th rev. eds. No better single-volume treatment of the play can be found than Harry Levin, *The Question of Hamlet* (Oxford, 1959).

Troilus and Cressida : Una Ellis-Fermor, 'Discord in the spheres: the universe of *Troilus and Cressida*', *The Frontiers of Drama* (London, 1945); R. A. Foakes, '*Troilus and Cressida* reconsidered', *University of Toronto Quarterly*, XXXII (1963); I. A. Richards, '*Troilus and Cressida* and Plato', *Hudson Review*, I (1948); Winifred Nowottny, ' "Opinion" and "Value" in *Troilus and Cressida*', *Essays in Criticism*, IV (1954).

Othello : The most elaborate study of the networks of meaning and structure is Robert B. Heilman, *Magic in the Web: action and language in 'Othello'* (Lexington, Ky., 1956). A useful history of stage productions is Marvin Rosenberg, *The Masks of Othello: the search for the identity of Othello, Iago, and Desdemona by three centuries of actors and critics* (Berkeley and Los Angeles, Calif., 1961). Useful single articles are G. Wilson Knight, 'The *Othello* music', *The Wheel of Fire* (Oxford, 1930; New York, rev. ed., 1957); Winifred T. Nowottny, 'Justice and love in *Othello*', *University of Toronto Quarterly*, XXI (1952).

King Lear : The Shakespearean concept of Nature, particularly as it applies to *Lear*, is treated by John F. Danby, *Shakespeare's Doctrine of Nature: a study of 'King Lear'* (London, 1949). The philosophical and artistic traditions from which the play draws its 'iconology' are explored in Russell A. Fraser, *Shakespeare's Poetics in Relation to 'King Lear'* (London, 1962; Nashville, Tenn., 1964). Among the many excellent works on *Lear*, the following complete treatments of the play will lead the reader to other more special studies: Nicholas Brooke, *Shakespeare: King Lear*, Studies in English Literature (London, 1963); W. R. Elton, *King Lear and the Gods* (San Marino, Calif., 1965); Robert B. Heilman, *This Great Stage: image and structure in 'King Lear'* (Baton Rouge, La., 1948); G. Wilson Knight's two *Lear* chapters in *The Wheel of Fire*, 'The *Lear* universe' and '*King Lear* and the comedy of the grotesque'; Paul A. Jorgensen, *Lear's Self-Discovery* (Berkeley and Los Angeles, Calif., 1967); and Maynard Mack, '*King Lear*' in Our Time (Berkeley and Los Angeles, Calif., 1965).

Macbeth: An interesting and useful attempt to recreate the context of the first performance, particularly James I's interest in demonology, is Henry N. Paul, *The Royal Play of 'Macbeth'* (New York, 1950). A famous controversy over critical method centred on a reading of *Macbeth*: Cleanth Brooks, 'The naked babe and the cloak of manliness', *The Well Wrought Urn* (New York, 1947), and O. J. Campbell, 'Shakespeare and the "new critics"', *Joseph Quincy Adams: Memorial Studies*, ed. J. G. McManaway *et al.* (Washington, DC, 1948). See also Francis Fergusson, '*Macbeth* as the imitation of an action', *English Institute Essays 1951* (New York, 1952); and Roy Walker, *The Time is Free: a study of 'Macbeth'* (London, 1949).

Timon of Athens: Una Ellis-Fermor, '*Timon of Athens*: an unfinished play', *RES*, XVIII (1942); David Cook, '*Timon of Athens*', *Shakespeare Survey 16* (1963). The place of this play in the tradition of Elizabethan satire is discussed by O. J. Campbell, *Shakespeare's Satire* (New York, 1943), and Alvin Kernan, *The Cankered Muse, Satire of the English Renaissance* (New Haven, Conn., 1959).

Coriolanus: Maurice Charney, *Shakespeare's Roman Plays, The Function of Imagery in the Drama* (Cambridge, Mass., 1961); D. J. Enwright, '*Coriolanus*: tragedy or debate', *Essays in Criticism*, IV (1954); Eugene Waith, *The Herculean Hero* (London and New York, 1962).

Antony and Cleopatra: John F. Danby, *Poets on Fortune's Hill, Studies in Sidney, Shakespeare, Beaumont and Fletcher* (London, 1952), chapter 5 (republished 1964 as *Elizabethan and Jacobean Poets*); John Holloway, *The Story of the Night: studies in Shakespeare's major tragedies* (London, 1961), chapter 6; Robert Ornstein, 'The ethic of the imagination: love and art in *Antony and Cleopatra*', Stratford-upon-Avon Studies, *Later Shakespeare*, eds J. R. Brown and Bernard Harris (London, 1966; New York, 1967).

The late romances

The most useful general theory of romance is that of Northrop Frye, 'The mythos of summer: romance', *Anatomy of Criticism* (Princeton, NJ, 1957); Frye's theory is applied to Shakespeare in *A Natural Perspective, The Development of Shakespearean Comedy and Romance* (New York and London, 1965). Excellent background material is supplied by E. C. Pettet, *Shakespeare and the Romance Tradition* (London, 1949). *Shakespeare Survey 2* (1958) is devoted to a variety of articles on the romances. The basic pattern of the last plays is isolated and developed in E. M. W. Tillyard, *Shakespeare's Last*

Plays (London, 1938), and a closer analysis is provided by Derek Traversi, *Shakespeare: the last phase* (New York, 1955; London, 1954). Three recent studies of the romance pattern are Howard Felperin, *Shakespearean Romance* (Princeton, NJ, 1972), Hallett Smith, *Shakespeare's Romances* (San Marino, Calif., 1972), and David P. Young, *The Heart's Forest: a study of Shakespeare's plays* (New Haven, Conn., 1972).

Pericles: John Arthos, '*Pericles, Prince of Tyre*: a study in the dramatic use of romantic narrative', *Shakespeare Quarterly*, IV (1953); G. Wilson Knight, '*Pericles*', *The Crown of Life: interpretations of Shakespeare's final plays* (Oxford, 1947).

Cymbeline: Bernard Harris, ' "What's past is prologue": *Cymbeline* and *Henry VIII*', *Later Shakespeare*, Stratford-upon-Avon Studies VIII, eds J. R. Brown and Bernard Harris (London, 1966; New York, 1967).

The Winter's Tale: S. L. Bethell, '*The Winter's Tale*: *A Study* (London, 1947); Northrop Frye, 'Recognition in *The Winter's Tale*', *Essays on Shakespeare and Elizabethan Drama in Honor of Hardin Craig* (Columbia, Mo., 1962); F. D. Hoeniger, 'The meaning of *The Winter's Tale*', *University of Toronto Quarterly*, XX (1950); Ernest Schanzer, 'The structural pattern of *The Winter's Tale*', *REL*, V (2), (1964).

The Tempest: W. H. Auden, 'The sea and the mirror: a commentary on Shakespeare's *The Tempest*', *For the Time Being* (New York, 1945); Reuben A. Brower, 'The mirror of analogy: *The Tempest*', *The Fields of Light* (New York, 1951); Frank Kermode, 'Introduction', New Arden Shakespeare, *The Tempest* (London and Cambridge, Mass., 1954); Bernard Knox, '*The Tempest* and the ancient comic tradition', *English Stage Comedy*, *English Institute Essays, 1954*, ed. W. K. Wimsatt, Jr (New York, 1955); 'Introduction', New Penguin Shakespeare: *The Tempest*, ed. Anne Righter (Harmondsworth and Baltimore, 1968).

Cyril Tourneur

Editions: The standard text is that edited by Allardyce Nicoll, *The Works of Cyril Tourneur* (London, 1930; New York, 1963). The Revels editions of the plays are, however, more useful in many ways, particularly for introductions and notes: *The Revenger's Tragedy*, ed. R. A. Foakes (London and Cambridge, Mass., 1966); *The Atheist's Tragedy*, ed. Irving Ribner (London and Cambridge, Mass., 1964).

Bibliography: There has been a great deal of discussion of the authorship of *The Revenger's Tragedy*, and an interested reader will find a full bibliography and coherent treatment of the question in Peter B. Murray, *A Study of Cyril Tourneur* (Philadelphia, 1964).

Criticism: Murray's book is most helpful, but there are several excellent essays which should be read: T. S. Eliot, 'Cyril Tourneur', *Selected Essays 1917–1932* (London and New York, 1932); Una Ellis-Fermor, *The Jacobean Drama* (London, 1936; 3rd rev. ed., 1953); Peter Lisca, '*The Revenger's Tragedy*: a study in irony', *Philological Quarterly*, XXXVIII (1959); L. G. Salingar, '*The Revenger's Tragedy* and the morality tradition', *Scrutiny*, XI (1938); T. B. Tomlinson, 'The morality of revenge: Tourneur's critics', *Essays in Criticism*, X (1960).

John Webster

Editions: The four-volume old-spelling edition of *The Works of John Webster*, ed. F. L. Lucas (London, 1927; reproduced by University Microfilms, Ann Arbor, Mich., 1966) is one of the masterpieces of Elizabethan dramatic editing. Its apparatus is as fascinating as its text is reliable, and it remains the place to begin a study of Webster. There is an excellent edition of *The Duchess of Malfi*, ed. J. R. Brown, The Revels Plays (London and Cambridge, Mass., 1964), and one of *The White Devil* by the same editor in the same series (1960).

Sources: Because of the vast extent and nature of his borrowing, the sources of Webster's plays constitute a special problem and prove an interesting insight into the way in which the dramatist used other materials. The necessary information is gathered in R. W. Dent, *John Webster's Borrowing* (Berkeley and Los Angeles, Calif., 1960). For thorough studies of the ways the borrowings were used see Gunnar Boklund, *The Sources of 'The White Devil'* (Uppsala and Cambridge, Mass., 1957); and Gunnar Boklund, '*The Duchess of Malfi'*: *sources, themes, characters* (Cambridge, Mass., 1962).

Criticism: The Webster bibliography is extensive, particularly on the two major plays, but a good introduction to the playwright and his works is Clifford Leech, *John Webster, A Critical Study* (London, 1951). Bibliography and criticism have been conveniently collected in *Twentieth Century Interpretations of 'The Duchess of Malfi'*, ed. Norman Rabkin (Englewood Cliffs, NJ, 1968). See also, Travis Bogard, *The Tragic Satire of John Webster* (Berkeley, Calif., 1955); Clifford Leech, *Webster: 'The Duchess of Malfi'* (London, 1965); and J. R. Mulryne, '*The White Devil* and *The Duchess of Malfi*', *Jacobean Theatre*, Stratford-upon-Avon Studies I, eds J. R. Brown and Bernard Harris (London, 1960; New York, 1961).

Index

Abraham and Lot, 65
Abraham's Sacrifice, 56
Abuses, 89
act divisions, 230–1
    in Globe plays, 191
action above,
    at First Globe, 188–90
    at Second Blackfriars, 222–4, 226
    at Swan and Second Blackfriars, 232–3
actors,
    companies of, *see also under individual*
        companies
      and statutes against retainers, 8–10
      and statutes against vagabonds, 9
    and dramatists, 113
    and guild system, 30
    parts assigned to, 97
    problems of, 28–40, 114
    regulation of, by City of London, 32–3
    style of, 114–17
Adelphe, 94
admission, prices of, 48–9
Admiral's Men, 101–4
    decline of, 104

    and Edward Alleyn, 102–3
    decline of, 104
Aeneas and Dido, 89
Agamemnon, 57
Agamemnon and Ulysses, 58
Ajax, 88
Alba or Vertumnus, 88
Alchemist, The, 93, 330, 331, 332–6, 344–5
    plot of, 332–6
Alexander and Lodowick, 80, 81, 82, 83
Alexandrian Tragedy, The, 90
All Fools, 88, 387
    discovery avoided in, 218
    at Second Blackfriars, 218
All for Money, 56
Alleyn, Edward, 26, 103, 241, Pl. 6
    and Admiral's Men, 102–3
    and Burbage, 103
    roles played by, 98, 112
All's Well That Ends Well,
    at First Globe, 181
    music station in, 190
    no discovery in, 182
Almanac, The, 92

Alucius, 56
Amynta's Pastoral, 60
Antonio and Mellida, 86, 390
Antonio's Revenge, 86, 390
Antonius, 63, 76
Antony and Cleopatra, 436–45, 446
   action above in, 189
   doors required in, 182
   at First Globe, 182
   music station in, 191
   no discovery in, 182, 183
   'other world' in, 247
   suspension gear in, 192–3, 196
   and *The Winter's Tale*, 450
   understage area in, 195
Antony and Vallia, 70, 73, 74
Antigone, 57
Arden of Faversham, 63, 85
Ariodante and Genevora, 58
Armin, Robert, 107
   roles played by, 98
   successor to Tarlton, 101, 107
Arraignment of Paris, The, 58
   in Chapel Royal repertoire, 110
As You Like It, 319, 322, 353
   at First Globe, 181
   no discovery in, 182
   and satire, 391
Atheist's Tragedy, The, 92, 391
audience, 47
   assessment of, 47–8
   of plays performed by scholars, 47–8
   prices paid by, 48–9
   social structure of, 48, 123

Bad Beginning Makes a Good Ending, A, 93
baiting-houses, 125–6, 127
   and shape of playhouses, 131
Bankside, 125–6, 127, 136
Bartholomew Fair, 101, 113, 329, 331, 345, 457–65
Beaumont, Francis, 104, 303, Pl. 13
Bel Sauvage, 160
Belin Dun, 65, 66, 67, 68, 79, 81, 82, 83
Benger, Sir Thomas
   death of, 20
   as Master of the Revels, 15, 19
     appointment of, 20–1
Bernado and Fiammetta, 74, 75, 76, 77
Betterton, Thomas, 108

Bindo and Ricardo, 61, 62
Blackfriars, liberty of the, acting in, 33, *see also* First Blackfriars *and* Second Blackfriars
Blagrave, Thomas, and office of Master of the Revels, 20
Blind Beggar of Alexandria, 77, 78, 79, 80, 81, 84
Blurt Master-Constable, 86
Boar's Head inn, permanent playhouse in, 128
Book of Common Prayer, 41
Booke called the Owle, A, 87
books, censorship of, 44–5
booth stage, 124–5, Pl. 19a, 19b, 20a, 20b
boxes,
   at Swan, 169
   used for discovery and action above, 233–4
     at First Globe, 195
     at Second Blackfriars, 215–16
boy actors, 108
boys' companies, 109–12
   and dramatists, 113
   styles in, 116
   traditions of, 98–9
Brandimer, 61, 62
Brazen Age, The, 94
Bridgewater, Earl of, actors of, 10
Bryan, George, 25
Buc, Sir George, Master of the Revels, 27
Buckingham, 64, 65
Burbage, Cuthbert,
   and First Globe, 175
   and Second Blackfriars, 204
Burbage, James, 23, 241
   and Chamberlain's Men, 104
   and Edward Alleyn, 103
   and design of Theatre, 131–2
   and indoor performances, 112
   in Lord Hunsdon's company, 25
   popularity of, 101
   roles played by, 98, 105–6, 114
   and Second Blackfriars, 105, 197
     conversion of, 204, 207
     purchase of, 203–4
   style of, 115, 117
   and writ for pulling down playhouses, 40
Burbage, Richard, Pl. 5
   and First Globe, 175
   and Second Blackfriars, 204

Burghley, Lord (William Cecil), 23, 26, Pl. 1
  as Lord Treasurer, 21
  and riots, 39
  and Sunday plays, 24
Bussy d'Ambois, 90, 386, 387, 388–90
  in repertoire of Paul's Boys, 110

Caesar and Pompey, 68, 69, 70, 71, 73
Caesar and Pompey (Chapman), 387, 388, 390
Caesar's Revenge, 89
Calvin, Jean, 260
Cambyses, 264
Campaspe, 58, 60, 304
Canterbury, Archbishop of,
  and censorship, 42
  intercedes with Tilney, 37
Captain, The, 93
Captain Thomas Stukeley, 79, 80, 81, 82, 83, 88
Cardenio, 93, 94
Carey, George, *see* Hunsdon, 2nd Lord
Carey, Henry, *see* Hunsdon, 1st Lord
Case is Altered, The, 91, 327
Cataline, 92, 345
Cawarden, Sir Thomas, 15
  appointment of, as Master of the Revels, 20–1
  appointment of, as Master of the Revels, 20–1
Cecil, William, *see* Burghley, Lord
censorship, 41–6
  and Book of Common Prayer, 41
  of books, 44–5
  in City of London, 33, 42
  and historical plays, 264–5
  of religious and political matters, 42
Chamber Accounts, and Revels Accounts, 54–5
Chamber, Treasurer of, 54
Chamberlain, John, and burning of First Globe, 158, 168
Chamberlain's Men (later King's Men *q.v.*), 104–8
  and Admiral's Men, 102
  at court, 104
  at First Globe, 176
Chapel Boys (otherwise Children of the Queen's Chapel and later Children

of the Queen's Revels *q.v.*), 109, 111–12, Pl. 8b
  at court, 50, 51
  plays by, 217–18
  at Second Blackfriars, 204
Chapel Royal, boys' group from, *see* Chapel Boys
Chapel Royal, Windsor, boys' group from
  at court, 50, 51
Chapman, George, 110, 327
  and Admiral's Men, 102
  imprisonment of, 111
  plays of, 387–90
  and Prince Henry, 390
1 Charles Duke of Byron, 91, 387, 388, 389
  discovery avoided in, 218
  doors required for, 218
  at Second Blackfriars, 218
2 Charles Duke of Byron, 91, 387, 388, 389
  music station in, 224
  at Second Blackfriars, 218
Charterhouse, Pl. 18b
Chaste Maid in Cheapside, A, 137, 172
  music in, 231
  and Swan, 172–4
Chaucer, Geoffrey, view of, of honour, 291
Chief Promises of God, The, 56
Children at Blackfriars, *see* Children of the Queen's Revels
Children of the King's Revels, 113
Children of the Queen's Chapel, *see* Chapel Boys
Children of the Queen's Revels,
  at court, 50, 51
  performances by, 111–12
  plays by, 217–18
  renamed as, 111
  at Second Blackfriars, 134, 204
Children of the Revels, *see* Children of the Queen's Revels
children's companies, *see also under individual companies*
  at court, 22
Chinon of England, 76, 77, 78, 79
Chloris and Orgasto, 61
choir schools, 48
Christian Turned Turk, A, 93
City of London,
  attempted bribery of Tilney by, 36, 37
  attitude of nobility towards, 31
  censorship by, 42

City of London – *Contd.*
  and players, 24, 28–40
  prohibition of plays in inns by, 126–7
  and Queen's Men, 25
  regulation of players by, 32–3
  and suburbs, 31–2
  support for plays in, 48–9
Claudius Tiberius Nero, 89
Cleopatra, 76, 84, 85, 86, 88, 90, 92
Clerk Comptroller of the Revels, proposed, 17
Clinton, Edward, *see* Lincoln, 1st Earl of
Clyomon and Clamydes, 85
Cobbler's Prophecy, The, 69
Cobham, Lord (William Brooke), appointed Lord Chamberlain, 27
comedy,
  Elizabethan, 300–6
  Shakespearian, 307–25
Comedy of Beauty and Housewifery, A, 57
Comedy Called Delight, A, 57
Comedy of Cosmo, The, 63, 64
Comedy of Errors, The, 87, 266, 309
Comedy or Moral devised on a Game of the Cards, A, 57
Common Conditions, 55
Conflict of Conscience, 57
Conspiracy and Tragedy of Charles ⌊Duke of Byron, The, see 1 and 2 Charles Duke of Byron
Constantine, 61
Contention between Liberality and Prodigality, 86, 87
1 Converted Courtesan, The, 87
2 Converted Courtesan, The, 91
Cooke, John, 109
copyright, 53
Coriolanus,
  action above in, 190
  and censorship, 46
  doors required in, 182
  at First Globe, 182
  no discovery in, 182, 183
  and *Timon of Athens*, 434–6
Cornelia, 69, 76, 258
counter-Renaissance, and Jacobean tragedy, 386
Countess of Pembroke's Ivychurch, The, 60
court,
  audience for plays at, 47
  Chamberlain's Men at, 104

  dates of revelry at, 15–16
  and Lent, 36
  table of performances at, 49–52
Coxcomb, The, 93
Crack me this Nut, 73, 74, 75, 76, 77, 78
craft cycles, 29
craft guilds, 8
criticism, dramatic, 97
Croesus, 87, 90
Cundall, Henry, 107
Cupid's Revenge, 93, 94
Cupid's Whirligig, 90, 93, 113
Curtain (playhouse), 44, 122, 132, 228
  petition for demolishing of, 39–40
  stage superstructure at, 171
  stair-tower at, 160
Cutlack, 65, 66, 67
Cymbeline, 446
Cynthia's Revels, 86, 328
  at Second Blackfriars, 217
  trapwork in, 225
Cynthia's Revenge, 94

Daniel, Samuel, before Privy Council, 111
Darius, 56, 88, 90
Davenant, Sir William, and *Henry VIII*, 107
David, John, 30
Day, John, 111
De Witt, 136, 146, 147, 148, 150, 154, 155, Pl. 11
  and capacity of the Swan, 143
  and entrances to theatres, 160, 161
  and galleries of the Swan, 156
Death of Robert, Earl of Huntingdon, The, 86
Dekker, Thomas, 104, 110, 169, 304, 327
Derby, Earl of, company of actors of, 22
  at court, 50, 51
Devil's Charter, The, 89, 90
  act divisions in, 191
  action above in, 189
  discovery in, 185–6, 187
  doors required in, 182
  at First Globe, 182
  music station in, 191
  post in, 193
  trap door in, 194–5
Devil's Law Case, The, 395
Dido, 58, 250
Diocletian, 68, 69

discovery,
  and 'inner stage', 234–5
  in plays at First Globe, 182–8
  in plays at Second Blackfriars, 218–22,
    226
  space for, in Swan and Second Black-
    friars, 233–4
Disguises, 74
Doctor Faustus, 68, 69, 70, 71, 72, 73, 77,
    78, 79, 80, 83, 87, 91, 92, 250,
    347–53
  Alleyn in, 103
  'other world' in, 247
  popularity of, 102
  textual problems of, 349
  and *Titus Andronicus*, 359–60
doors,
  at First Globe, 182
  at Second Blackfriars, 218
*Downfall of Robert, Earl of Huntingdon,
    The*, 86
dramatists, and actors, 113
Drayton, Michael, on Marlowe, 252–3
Duchess of Malfi, The, 106, 107, 395, 396–
    403
  image of world in, 249, 396
Dudley, Ambrose, *see* Warwick, Earl of
Dudley, Robert, *see* Leicester, Earl of
Duke of Guise, 64
Dumb Knight, The, 91
Dutch Courtesan, The, 88, 94
  action above in, 222
  curtain in, 220
  discovery avoided in, 218
  doors avoided in, 218
Dutton, Lawrence, 11, 12, 13

Earl of Lincoln's Men, 11
  a t court, 13, 50, 51
  and Earl of Warwick, 13
  in the provinces, 13
Earl of Pembroke's Men, 44
  at court, 50
  and Privy Council, 102
Earl of Sussex's Men, at court, 4, 10, 11,
    14, 50, 51
Earl of Warwick's Men, 12
  at court, 13, 14
  and Earl of Lincoln's Men, 13
Eastwood Ho, 88, 111
  actions above in, 223–4

discoveries in, 221
doors required in, 218
at Second Blackfriars, 218
Edward I, 64, 85
Edward II, 64, 84, 94, 250, 264
Edward III, 80, 85
Edward IV, 84, 86, 88, 94
Eliot, T. S., 336, 413
Elizabeth I,
  and Henry V, 296
  las t years of, 386
Elizabeth's Men, *see* Lady Elizabeth's
    Men
Endymion, 59, 60, 305, 306
Englishmen for my Money . . ., 86
  and Admiral's Men, 102
Enterlude called Bonos Nochios, An, 91
*Enterlude called, Craft uppon Subtiltyes
    backe, An*, 91
entrances to theatres, 158–63
  at First Globe, 177
Epicene, 111, 112, 327, 329, 343–4
Essex, Earl of, reference to in *Philotas*, 111
Essex, Lady, company of, 51
Eton, 47
  acting group from at court, 50
Euphues and his England, 304
Euphues, The Anatomy of Wit, 304
Euphuism, 305
Evans, Henry, and Second Blackfriars, 204
Evelyn, company of, at court, 51
Every Man in his Humour, 86, 88, 327, 328
  and Chamberlain's Men, 105
Every Man out of his Humour, 85, 328, 331,
    336
  act division in, 191
  action above in, 188
  and Chamberlain's Men, 105, 181
  no discovery in, 182, 184
  satire in, 391
  and theatre design, 168, 177
Every Woman in her Humour, 91

Fair Em, 64
Fair Maid of Bristow, The, 88
  doors required in, 182
  at First Globe, 181
  no discovery in, 182
Fair Maid of Italy, The, 65
Fair Maid of the Exchange, 90
Faithful Shepherdess, The, 92

Falstaff, in *Henry IV*, 278–81, 286, 287–9, 290–1
Family of Love, The, 90
Famous Chronicle of Henry the First, The, 70, 75
famous history called Valentine and Orsson, A, 85
Famous History of John of Gaunt, The, 70
Famous Victories of Henry V, The, 84
Farrant, Richard, 109
    and First Blackfriars, 133
Fawn, The, 89, 390
    actions above in, 223, 231
    discoveries avoided in, 218
    inter-act music in, 224
    at Second Blackfriars, 218
Fedele and Fortunio, 58, 59
Felix and Philiomena, 58
Ferrar, 58
Field, Nathan, 112
First Blackfriars, 122, 228
    design of, 133
    site of, 197
    stage in, 229
First Fortune, 43, 122, 227
    and Admiral's Men, 103
    capacity of, 143
    contract for, 136
        and First Globe, 176
        floor-joists in, 151
        gentlemen's rooms in, 154
        rooms in, 154–5
        stage in, 165
        stairs in, 157
        tiring-house in, 165, 167, 169
    dimensions of, 148–50
    ground plan of, 141–2
    height of, 144
    and Second Blackfriars, 208, 209, 212
    shape of, 123, 131, 143
    tiring-house in, 228
First Globe, 32, 104, 105, 122, 175–96
    burning of, 158, 160, 175–6, 177
    construction of, 175, 195–6
    design of, 176–81
    evidence for, 134–5, 227
    galleries of, 180
    gathering of admission fees at, 163, 180
    pictures of, 176
    plays at, 92, 181–96
    roof of, 180

site of, 175
    and Swan, 176, 180
First Part of the Contention of the Two Famous Houses of York and Lancaster, The, 69, 86
First Part of the Famous History of Chinon of England, The, 80
First Part of Jeronimo, The, 88
First Part of the Tragical Reign of Selimus, The, 70
First Part . . . of Sir John Oldcastle, The, 85
Five Plays in One, 58, 81, 82, 83
Fleer, The, 89, 92
    discoveries in, 221
    doors required in, 218
    at Second Blackfriars, 218
Fleetwood, William, 23, 39
Fletcher, John, 104, 303, Pl. 13
1 Fortunatus, 76, 77, 78
Fortune (playhouse), *see* First Fortune
Fountain of Self-Love, The, 86, *see* also *Cynthia's Revels*
Four Plays in One, 61
Four Sons of Fabius, The, 57
Frederick and Basilea, 82, 83
French Comedy, The, 71, 72, 73, 82, 83
French Doctor, The, 68, 70, 71, 72, 73, 78, 79
Freud, Sigmund, and Ben Jonson, 336
Friar Bacon, 60, 61, 62, 63, 64, 65
Friar Bacon and Friar Bungay, 69, 303
    and Admiral's Men, 102
Friar Francis, 64, 65
Friar Spendleton, 83

Galathea, 59, 63
Galioso, 66, 67, 68
galleries, at Second Blackfriars, 211–13
gallery stairs, 157–8
    at First Globe, 177
Game at Chess, 143
Gentleman Usher, The, 89, 387
    actions above in, 222
    discovery avoided in, 218
    inter-act music in, 224
    at Second Blackfriars, 217
gentlemen's rooms in theatres, 154, 162, 163
George a Green, 64, 65, 84
Globe (playhouse), *see* First Globe

God Speed the Plough, 64, 86
2 *Godfrey of Bulloigne*, 66, 67, 68, 70, 72, 73
Golden Age, The, 92
Gorboduc, 60, 264
blank verse in, 242
Gosson, Stephen, 30
Gray's Inn, company of, at court, 51
Grecian Comedy, The, 69, 70, 71, 72, 74
Greene, Robert, 99, 102, 103, 114, 302, 303
attack of, on Shakespeare, 265, 304
death of, 303–4
Greene, Thomas, 108–9
Greene's Tu Quoque, 92, 93, 109, 114
Groatsworth of Wit, attack on Shakespeare in, 265
Guicciardini, Francesco, 385
Guido, 81, 82
guild system, and actors, 30
Gull's Hornbook, The, and theatre design, 169
Gyve a man luck and throwe him into the Sea, 85

Hamlet, 87, 92, 242, 361, 372–83, 436
'cleaning-up' of language in, 43
at First Globe, 181
image of world in, 249
and major Shakespearian tragedies, 404
no discovery in, 182, 184, 233–4
'other world' in, 247
subplot in, 246
trap door in, 193–4
understage area in, 195
Hampton Court Palace, 208, Pl. 17a
Hardicanute, 83
Harry of Cornwall, 61, 62
Harry the Fifth, 75, 76, 77, 78, 79
Haughton, William, and Admiral's Men, 102
hierarchical view, 262–5
Heminges, John, 107
roles played by, 98
Hengist, 83
Henriad, 269–99, *see also under constituent plays*
historical necessity in, 285
identity in, 273–6, 278
'worlds' in, 277–9
Henry I, 82, 83

1 Henry IV, 84, 85, 88, 91, 93, 94, 269, 277–92
2 Henry IV, 85, 269, 277–92
Henry V, 85, 87, 269, 273, 288, 290–9
action above in, 188
concept of honour in, 291–2
and Elizabeth I, 294
at First Globe, 181
Laurence Olivier film of, 292
no discovery in, 182
'other world' in, 247
and theatre design, 177, 182
Henry VI, 61, 62, 63, 64, 75, 243, 264, 266
Henry VIII, 107, 446, 457
Henry, Prince of Wales, death of, and Chapman, 390
Henslowe, Philip,
and Admiral's Men, 102
and Jonson, 327
payments by, to actors, 48
payments by, to Tilney, 37–8
playhouse of, 102
receipts of,
and capacity of Rose, 143
and structure of Rose, 158
as source of information on performances, 53–4, 55, 102
1 Hercules, 72, 73, 74, 75, 76
2 Hercules, 72, 73, 74, 75
Hercules Furens, 57
Hercules Oetaeus, 57
Hero and Leander, 250
continued by Chapman, 387
Hertford, Earl of, players of, 26
Hester and Ahasuerus 65
Heywood, Thomas, 114, 115, 304
and Queen Anne's Men, 108
Hippolytus, 60
Historie of the Collier, The, 55
History of the Cruelty of a Stepmother, An, 56
History of the Cynocephali, The, 56
History of the Duke of Milan and the Marquess of Mantua, A, 56
History of Error, The, 56
History of Murderous Michael, The, 56
History of Mutius Scaevola, The, 56
history plays, 262–99
History of Sir John Oldcastle, 85
History of the Solitary Knight, The 56
History of Titus and Gisippus, The, 56

Histriomastix, 92
Hobbes, Thomas, 260, 386
　and Jonson, 336
Hog Hath Lost his Pearl, The, 94
Hollar, Wenzel,
　and entrances, 161
　and Second Blackfriars, 198–201, Pl. 12a,
　　12b
　and Second Globe, 177, Pl. 12a, 12b
　and stair-towers, 164
holy days, regulation of plays upon, 38
Honest Whore, The, 104
1 Honest Whore, 87, 88
2 Honest Whore, 91
honour, concept of, in *Henry V*, 291
Hope (playhouse), Pl. 12a, 12b
　and *Bartholomew Fair*, 459
　contract for, 136, 145
　　bressumers specified in, 144, 150
　　entrances of, 161
　　gentlemen's rooms in, 154
　　roof specified in, 150
　　rooms in, 154–5, 162
　　stair-towers in, 164
　　stairs in, 157, 158, 160
　　structural members specified in, 150–4
　pictures of, 137, 143–4, Pl. 12a, 12b
　and Swan, 144
Hotspur, in *Henry IV*, 281–2, 284, 286,
　287, 288–9, 291
*How a Man may Choose a Good Wife from
　a Bad*, 87, 88, 91
How to Learn of a Woman to Woo, 87
Howard of Effingham, 1st Lord, 3–4, 14
Howard of Effingham, 2nd Lord, 14
　becomes Lord Admiral, 23–4, 25
　as Lord Chamberlain, 23
　players of, 14, 25, 26, 27, 70
　at court, 50, 51, 52
Humour out of Breath, 90
Humorous Day's Mirth, An, 82, 83, 85
Hunsdon, 1st Lord (Henry Carey),
　appointed Lord Chamberlain, 24, 25
　company of actors of, 23, 25
　　at court, 50, 51, 52
　and office of Lord Chamberlain, 23
Hunsdon, 2nd Lord (George Carey),
　appointed Lord Chamberlain, 26
　players of, 26
　　at court, 50, 51, 52
Hunting of Cupid, 60

Huon of Bordeaux, 64, 65
Hymenaei, 89
Hymenaeus, 56
Hymen's Holiday, 93
Hyppolytus, 57

identity, problems of,
　in *Henry IV*, 278
　in *Richard II*, 273–6
If It Be Not Good the Devil is in It, 93
1 If You Know Not Me You Know Nobody,
　88, 89, 91, 92, 94
2 If You Know Not Me You Know Nobody,
　89, 91
Il Fidele, 59
Il Pastor Fido, 86
ingressus, see entrances
'inner stage', 234–5
inns, as temporary playhouses, 126–8
Insatiable Countess, The, 94
inter-act music,
　in First Globe plays, 191–2
　in Second Blackfriars plays, 224–5, 226
Interlude of Valentyne and Orsson, An, 75
Irish Knight, The, 56
Irish Masque, The, 94
Isle of Dogs, The, 327
　and Privy Council, 102
Isle of Gulls, The, 89, 111
　at Second Blackfriars, 218

Jack Drum's Entertainment, 86
　in repertoire of Paul's Boys, 110
Jack Straw, 64, 88, 264
James I and VI,
　accession of, and drama, 386
　and *Macbeth*, 431, 433
　unfavourably depicted at Blackfriars,
　　111
James IV, 84
Jealous Comedy, The, 63
Jerusalem, 61, 62
Jew of Malta, 61, 62, 63, 64, 65, 66, 67, 68,
　69, 70, 76, 77, 78, 250
　Alleyn in, 103
　'other world' in, 247
jigs, 101, 107
　suppression of, 43–4
Jocasta, 59
John a Kent and John a Cumber, 102
Jones, Inigo, and Jonson, 458

Jonson, Ben, 105, 113, 168, 180, 302, 303, 304, Pl. 16
  arrest of, 44
  and *Bartholomew Fair*, 345, 457–65
  conservatism of, 336
  Conversations of, 329
  Discoveries of, 328, 331, 342
  and *Epicene*, 343–4
  imprisonment of, 111
  and Inigo Jones, 458
  life of, 327–9
  plays of, 326–45, 457–65
  and *Sejanus*, 191, 337–8
  and Shakespeare, 456–8
  and Shakespearian comedy, 324, 326
  staging by, 231–2
  and Tarlton, 101
  and *Volpone*, 338–43
Julian the Apostate, 77, 78
Julius Caesar, 90, 93, 361, 362–4, 365–6, 369, 371
  action above in, 188
  at First Globe, 181
  music in, 190
  no discovery in, 182

Kempe, William, 25, 241, Pl. 8a
  and Queen Anne's Men, 108
  roles played by, 98, 106–7
  successor to Tarlton, 101
Kenilworth Castle, Great Hall of, and Upper Frater, 201–3
'king, killing of', 264–5
  and *Henriad*, 283
  and *Macbeth*, 431
  and *Richard III*, 265–9
King Lear, 89, 90, 415–25, 436
  and censorship, 45
  doors required in, 182
  at First Globe, 182
  music station in, 190
  no discovery in, 182, 183
  and other major Shakespearian tragedies, 404–7, 430
  subplot in, 246
King Leir, 65, 88
King Lud, 65
King and No King, A, 92, 93
King's Men (formerly Chamberlain's Men *q.v.*), 33, 112
  at court, 50, 51

  and Second Blackfriars, 105, 123, 134, 204
  and inter-act music, 231
Knack to Know a Knave, A, 63, 64, 69
  and Alleyn, 102–3
  and Kempe, 106
Knack to Know an Honest Man, A, 68, 69, 70, 71, 72, 73, 76, 77, 79, 80
Knaves, The, 94
Knight in the Burning Rock, The, 56
Knight of the Burning Pestle, The, 94, 303
  action above in, 224
  discovery in, 221
  at Second Blackfriars, 218
Knot of Fools, A, 93
Kyd, Thomas, 102, 252, 257–61
  and Marlowe, 257
  and pessimism, 259–61
  and Pirandello, 260
  style of, 258

Lady Elizabeth's Men,
  at court, 51
  incorporate Children of the Chapel, 111
Laelia, 70
Lane, Sir Robert,
  company of, at court, 50, 51
  as patron, 12
Langley, Francis,
  and Swan, 136
  tiring-house at, 207
Larum for London, A, 86
  action above in, 188–9
  at First Globe, 181
  no discovery in, 182
  post in, 193
  suspension gear in, 192
  trap door in, 193
Law Tricks, 90
  discoveries in, 221
  at Second Blackfriars, 217
Leicester, Earl of (Robert Dudley), 4, Pl. 4
  company of actors of, *see* Leicester's Men
  created Absolute Governor of the United Provinces, 25
  and Earl of Sussex, 11
  political and matrimonial plans of, 10–11
  in Privy Council, 19
  and statute against retainers, 10
  and Tilney, 22

Leicester's Men,
  at court, 4, 10, 11, 14, 25, 50, 51
  and Leicester's ambitions, 10–11
  and Queen's Men, 24, 25
  and statutes against retainers, 8, 10
Lent,
  and court performances, 36
  performances in, banned, 35, 36
  performances in, in Blackfriars, 33
'liberties', plays in, 33
libido dominandi, 254–5, 262
licensing of plays, and bribery, 38
Life and Death of Heliogabalus, 70
Like Will to Like, 59
Lincoln, 1st Earl of (Edward Clinton), 11,
  12, Pl. 3
  company of, *see* Earl of Lincoln's Men
Lingua, 89
Locrine, 75
Lodge, Thomas, 302
London, *see* City of London
London, Prodigal The, 88
  and Chamberlain's Men, 104, 181
  no discovery in, 182
Long Meg of Westminister, 71, 72, 73, 74,
  79, 80
Longshanks, 73, 74, 75, 76, 77, 78, 79
Look About You, 85
Looking Glass for London and England, A,
  61, 62, 69, 84, 87
Lord Chamberlain,
  appoints Blagrave Master of the Revels, 20
  hiatus in office of, 23
  office of, 3
  and proposals for reform of Office of the
    Revels, 18, 19
Lord Mayor (of London),
  and actors, 28
  attitude of, towards nobility, 31
  and censorship, 42
  installation of, 29
  jurisdiction of, 31–2
  letter to, from Earl of Warwick, 30
  petition of, for demolishing Theatre and
    Curtain, 39–40
  and plays in Lent, 35
Lord Treasurer, and Office of the Revels,
  21, 22
Lords' Masque, The, 94, Pl. 9b
Love of an English Lady, The, 67, 68
Love and Fortune, 57

Love Freed from Ignorance and Folly, 92
Love of a Grecian Lady, The, 68
*Love of King David and Fair Bathsheba,
  The*, 84
Love's Labour's Lost, 80, 84, 88, 309–10,
  320, 322, 323
Love's Metamorphosis, 86
Lowin, John, 107
Loyalty and Beauty, 56
Lyly, John, 304–6
  and boys' companies, 304
  and comedy, 302
  and Mastership of the Revels, 304
  and *The Two Gentlemen of Verona*, 310

Macbeth, 404, 426–33, 436, 446
  acted after supposed Elizabethan style,
    115
  at First Globe, 182
  images in, 248
  music station in, 191
  no discovery in, 182, 183
  and other major Shakespearian tragedies,
    404–7
  trap door in, 194
Machiavelli, 61, 62
Machiavelli, Nicolò, 245, 260, 284, 386
Machiavellus, 80
Mack, The, 71
Mad World My Masters, A, 91
Maid's Metamorphosis, The, 85
Maid's Tragedy, The, 93, 134
Malcontent, The, 384–5, 386, 390
  action above in, 222
  doors required in, 218
  inter-act music in, 224, 230
  produced by King's (Chamberlain's)
    Men, 99, 105
  satire in, 391
  at Second Blackfriars, 218
  and stage area, 228
Marlowe, Christopher, 250–7, 304
  and Admiral's Company, 102
  death of, 251, 353
  and *Doctor Faustus*, 347–53
  Drayton on, 252–3
  and *2 Henry IV*, 287
  and style of acting, 115
  stylistic devices of, 255–7
  and *Tamburlaine*, 251–7
  and Tarlton, 101

and *Titus Andronicus*, 358–60
Marprelate controversy, 110
Marriage of Mind and Measure, The, 56
Marshal Osric, 81
Martin Swarte, 83
Masque of Beauty, The, 90
Masque of Blackness, The, 88, 90, Pl. 9c
Masque at Lord Haddington's Marriage, The, 90
Masque at Lord Hay's Marriage, 89
Masque of the Inner Temple and Gray's Inn, The, 94
Masque for Lord Montacute, 59
Masque of the Middle Temple and Lincoln's Inn, The, 94
Masque of Oberon, The, 92, Pl. 10
Masque of Queens, The, 91
masques, 458–9
Massacre at Paris, The, 64, 66, 67, 70, 250
Master of the Revels, 15
    appointments to, 20–1
    bribery of, 36–8
    and Lyly, 304
    proposals for reform of office of, 17–20
    qualities required of, 20
Marston, John, 110, 303, 390–1
    flight of, 111
May Day, 92
Measure for Measure, 87, 446
    Armin in, 107
    doors required in, 182
    at First Globe, 181
    no discovery in, 182
    and major tragedies, 404
Medea, 57
Menaechmi, 75
Merchant of Emden, The, 66
Merchant Taylors, refusal of to pay annuity to Tilney, 36
Merchant Taylors' school, 47
    group from, at court, 50, 51
Merchant of Venice, The, 85, 88, 319
Merry Devil of Edmonton, The, 90, 93, 94
    and Chamberlain's Men, 104
    discovery in, 185
    at First Globe, 181
    and theatre design, 177
Merry Wives of Windsor, The, 86, 87
    discovery in, 184, 187
    at First Globe, 181
Michaelmas Term, 90

Midas, 60, 63
Middle Temple, 208, Pl. 18a
Middlesex, suppression of jigs in, 43–4
Middleton, Thomas, 104, 110, 137, 143
    and acting style, 115
    and *The Revenger's Tragedy*, 392
Midsummer Night's Dream, A, 85, 311–19, 320, 322
    business in, 114
Milton, John, 287
Mingo, 56
Miseries of Enforced Marriage, The, 90, 93
    action above in, 189–90
    and Chamberlain's Men, 104, 182
    no discoveries in, 182
    and post on stage, 193
Misfortune of Arthur, The, 59, 264
Mahommed, 67, 68, 69, 71
Monarchic Tragedies, The, 87, 90
Monsieur D'Olive, 89
    action above in, 222–3
    at Second Blackfriars, 218
Montaigne, Michel Eyquem de, 245, 386
Morall of Clothe Breeches and velvet hose, A, 85
Most Virtuous and Godly Susanna, The, 56
Mother Bombie, 69, 84
Mousetrap, The, 373, 378, 380
Mucedorus, 84, 89, 92, 94
    and Chamberlain's Men, 104
Much Ado About Nothing, 85, 93, 319
Muly Mollocco, 60, 61, 62, 63, 64
Munday, Anthony, 102, 327
Murder of Gonzago, The, see The Mousetrap
Murder of Priam, The, 378
music station,
    in First Globe plays, 190–2
    in First Globe and Second Blackfriars, 230–2
    in Second Blackfriars plays, 224, 226
Mustapha, 91

Nashe, Thomas, 116, 250, 302, 327
Nebuchadnezzar, 79, 80, 81
Nero, 87
New Way to Pay Old Debts, A, 244
New World's Tragedy, The, 73, 74, 75, 76, 77
Nobleman, The, 93
Nobody and Somebody, 89

Northward Ho, 90
  in repertoire of Paul's Boys, 110
Nottingham, Earl of, *see* Howard of
    Effingham, 2nd Lord

Octavia, 57
Oedipus, 57
Office of the Revels, 14–27
  accounts of, 26, 53, 54–5
  concept of, 47
  difficulties of, 16–17, 20
  and Earl of Sussex's Men, 4
  and Lord Chamberlain, 3
  partition of, 15, 16
  proposals for reform of, 17–20
  under Tilney, 21–3
  and visit of party representing King of
    France, 10
Office of the Tents, 15, 21
Office of the Toils, 15, 21
Old Fortunatus, 84, 85
Old Wives Tale, The, 75, 303
Olympio and Eugenio, 71, 72, 73, 74, 75,
    77
order, myth of, in *Richard II*, 272–3
Orlando Furioso, 60, 69, 85, 99, 114
  Alleyn in, 103
Othello, 87, 93, 407–15
  action above in, 189
  at First Globe, 182
  music station in, 190
  no discovery in, 182, 183
  and other major Shakespearian tragedies,
    404–7
  and post on stage, 193
Ovid, source for *Titus Andronicus*, 355–7,
    359
Oxford, Earl of, patronage of, of boys'
    companies, 109

pageants, attitude of City of London to,
    30
Painter's Daughter, The, 55
Palamon and Arcite, 67, 68
Paradox, The, 78
Paris Garden (playhouse), 160
  collapse of, 24
Pastoral of Phillyda and Choryn, A, 58
Pastorall or History of a Greek Maid, A, 56
pathetic fallacy, and Marlowe, 256
Patient Grissel, 87

Paul's Boys,
  at court, 50, 51
  dissolution of, 110
  performances by, 109, 110–11
  Playhouse, 122, 228
    design of, 132–3
    stage in, 229
  reappearance of, 110
  second dissolution of, 111
Pavey, Salomon, 111
Peddler's Prophecy, The, 75
Peele, George, 99, 110, 302, 303
Perambulation of Kent, The, 160
Periander, 90
Pericles Prince of Tyre, 91, 93, 446
  discovery in, 186–7
  doors required in, 182
  at First Globe, 182
  suspension gear in, 193
Philaster, 93
  and stage area, 228
Phillipo and Hippolito, 66, 67, 68
Philomathes, 90
Philomathes' Dream, 58
Philomathes' Second Dream, 59
Philomela, 89
Philotas, 87, 88, 90, 92
  and Privy Council, 111
  at Second Blackfriars, 218
Philotus, 87, 94
Phoenix, The, 90
Pico, Giovanni, 245
Pilgrimage to Parnassus, 89
Pirandello, Luigi, and Thomas Kyd, 260
plague,
  and attitude of City of London to
    players, 32, 34–6
  effects of, on performances, 34–6
  and bribery, 37
  and performances in 1581, 22, 34
  and performances in 1582, 23, 34
  and performances in 1583, 24, 34
Platter, Thomas, description of theatres by,
    163
Plautus, 301
Play of Cutwell, The, 56
playhouses, 121–235, *see also under names
    of individual houses*
  external evidence for, 133–5
  general account of, 121–2
  internal evidence for, 134–5

public and private, 122–4, 130–3
temporary, 124–30
  baiting houses, 125–6, 127
  booth stage, 124–5
  indoors, 128–30
  inns, 126–8
Pleasant Comedy of Robin Hood and Little John, The, 70
Pleasure Reconciled to Virtue, 458
Poetaster, 328, 336
  action above in, 222
  at Second Blackfriars, 217
  trapwork in, 225
Pompey, 57
  in repertoire of Paul's Boys, 110
Pope, Alexander, and Jonson, 336
Pope Joan, 61
Pope, Thomas, 25
Portio and Demorantes, 57
Prince's company, at court, 50, 51
printing, licensing of, 44–5
private playhouses, 122–4
  music in, 230–2
  stage sizes in, 228, 229, 230
Privy Council,
  ban of, on playing in Lent, 35
  and censorship, 44, 111
  and closure of playhouses, 39, 40
  control by, of players in time of plague, 34
  and Office of Revels, 17–18, 19
    under Tilney, 22, 42
  petition of actors to, 22
  and *Philotas,* 111
  request of, to Lord Mayor concerning players, 24
  and Second Blackfriars, 204
  and Sunday playing, 39
  and *The Isle of Dogs,* 102
Promos and Cassandra, 56
Proteus, image of, 245
  and Falstaff, 278
  and *Richard III,* 269
  in *The Two Gentlemen of Verona,* 310
Proud Maid's Tragedy, The, 93
public playhouses, 122–4, *and see also* playhouses
  music in, 230–2
  stage sizes in, 228, 229
Puritan, The, 90
Puritans, 30

Pygmalion's Image and Certain Satires, 390
Pythagoras, 76, 77, 78, 79

Queen Anne's Men, 108–9
  at court, 50, 51
Queen's Arcadia, The, 89, 90, 92
Queen's Men (Elizabeth I),
  City licence for, 35
  at court, 50, 51
  decline of, 26, 27, 101
  formation of, 24–5, 99
  status of, 25, 99–100
  and writ for pulling down playhouses, 40

Radcliffe, Thomas, *see* Sussex, Earl of
Ralegh, Sir Walter, 248
Ram Alley, 92
Ranger's Comedy, The, 65, 66, 67, 68, 70
Rape of Lucrece, 91, 93
Rape of the Second Helen, The, 56
Rare Triumphs of Love and Fortune, The, 60
Raymond Duke of Lyons, 94
Red Bull (playhouse), 99, 122, 227–8
  and Queen Anne's Men, 108
  staging at, 231–2
  tiring-house at, 228
Red Knight, The, 55
retainers, statutes against, 5–8
  and companies of players, 8–10
Return from Parnassus, The, 89
  Kempe in, 106–7, 115
Revels, Master of, *see* Master of the Revels
Revenge of Bussy d'Ambois, The, 94, 387
Revenger's Tragedy, The, 90, 391–4
  act divisions in, 191
  discovery in, 185, 187
  at First Globe, 182
Richard II, 84, 91, 269, 270–8, 283
Richard II (not Shakespeare's), 92
Richard III, 84, 87, 88, 94, 266
  and 'killing the king', 265–9
Richard the Confessor, 64, 65
Richard Whittington, 88
Rivales, 58
Roaring Girl, The, 92, 104
rock festivals, 29
role-playing, 243–50
Romeo and Juliet, 84, 85, 91, 361–2, 368–9, 371–2

Rose (playhouse), 32, 122, 132, 228
  and Admiral's Men, 102
  capacity of, 143
  plays at, 60-3, 63-4, 64-9, 70-5, 76-80,
    80-3
  stairs in, 158

Saint Paul's Cathedral, boys from, *see*
    Paul's Boys
Sappho and Phao, 58, 60, 304
Sarpedon, 57
Satire of the Three Estates, A, 87, 88
Satiromastix, 86
  discovery in, 184, 187
  at First Globe, 181
  and theatre design, 169, 182
Saturnalia, 89
satyr-satirist, 390-4
Scipio Africanus, 57
  in repertoire of Paul's Boys, 110
Scourge of Villainy, The, 390
Scyros, 94
Second Blackfriars, 197-226, Pl. 12a, 12b
  boys' acting group from at court, 50, 51
  and boys' companies, 109-11
  and Chamberlain's Men, 204
  closure of, 110
  design of, 133
  dimensions of, 206-17
  evidence for, 134
  galleries at, 211-13
    and galleries at Fortune, 212
  and King's Men, 105
  pit at, 213-14
  pictures of, 198-201
  plays performed at, 217-18
    action above in, 222-4, 226
    discoveries in, 218-22, 226
    doors required in, 218
    music stations in, 224, 226
    suspension gear in, 225, 226
    trapwork in, 225, 226
  and Privy Council, 204
  public and private performances at, 124
  reconstruction of, 205-17
  site of, 197-9, 204-5
  stage of, 209-11, 228
    and Fortune, 209
    spectators on, 215-16
    and Swan, 228
  suspension gear at, 216

tiring-house of, 207-9, 228-9
  and Fortune, 208
  and Swan, 228-9, 232-4
unfavourable depiction of James I at, 111
verbal evidence of, 197-8
Second Globe, 176, Pl. 12a, 12b
  capacity of, 143
  entrances to, 161
  pictures of, 137, 143-4, 176
  stairs in, 157-8, 160
  stair-towers in, 164
Sejanus, 88, 337-8
  and Chamberlain's Men, 105, 181
  inter-act music in, 191
  no discovery in, 182, 184
  plot of, 337
  and theatre design, 177
self, Renaissance concept of, 244-50
Seneca,
  and Chapman, 388
  revenge tragedy of, 354, 359
Seneca his Ten Tragedies, 57
Sergeant of the Revels, proposed, 17
Serpent of Division, 60
Set at Mawe, A, 69, 70, 71
Seven Days of the Week, 72, 73, 74, 75, 76,
    77, 79, 80
Shadow of Night, The, 387
Shakespeare, William, 25, 265, 304, 327,
    Pl. 15, *see also under plays by*
  as actor, 108
  attack on by Greene, 265
  and Chamberlain's Men, 104
  and comedy, 302, 307-25
    descriptions of, 308-9
  and *Hamlet*, 372-83
  and *Henriad*, 269-99
  historical plays of, 264, 265-99
  instructions of, for playing *Henry VIII*,
    107-8
  and Jonson, 456-8
  and Jonsonian comedy, 324, 326
  and Kempe, 107
  and 'killing of king', 265-9
  late romances of, 446-74
  major tragedies of, 404-33
  parts in plays by, 112
  and Prospero, 473-4
  retirement of, 242
  and *Richard III*, 265-9
  and style of acting, 115, 116, 117

and *The Tempest*, 465–74
and *Titus Andronicus*, 354–60
tragedies of, 354–60, 361–83, 434–45
Sharpham, Edward, 113, 114
Shaw, Robert, arrest of, 44
Shoemaker's Holiday, The, 85, 92
Sidney, Sir Philip, 300, 326
Siege of London, The, 69, 70, 71, 73, 76, 78
Silver Age, The, 93, 94
Sir Gyles Goosecap, 89
  discovery in, 220
  doors required in, 218
  at Second Blackfriars, 217
Sir John Mandeville, 60, 61, 62, 63, 64
Sir Thomas More, censorship of, by Tilney, 45–6
Sir Thomas Wyatt, 90, 94
Sly, William, roles played by, 98
Soliman and Perseda, 63, 85, 258
Sophonisba, 89, 390
  discovery avoided in, 218, 219–20
  doors required in, 218
  inter-act music in, 224–5
  music station in, 224, 231
  at Second Blackfriars, 218
  trapwork in, 225
Southwark, as site for playhouses, 32
Spanish Armada, 25
Spanish Comedy, The, 60, 61, 62, 63, 83, 85
Spanish Maze, The, 88
Spanish Tragedy, The, 61, 62, 63, 64, 70, 80, 81, 82, 87, 92, 99, 258–61
  and Admiral's Men, 102
  and Chamberlain's Men, 105
  discovery in, 233
  and Jacobean tragedy, 387
Spencer, Gabriel, arrest of, 44
stage,
  of First Globe, 181
  in private playhouses, 229–30
  of Second Blackfriars, 209–11, 229–30
    spectators on, 211, 215–16
  of Swan, 165, 229–30
stage superstructure,
  of First Globe, 181, 195–6
  of Swan, 170–2
Stationers, Company of,
  and censorship, 44–5
  registration by, 53
Stationers' Register, 53

Strange, Lord (Ferdinando Stanley), 26
  players of, 26, 64
  and Admiral's Men, 101
  at court, 50, 51
Storia d'Italia, 385
Stubbes, Phillip, 30
suburbs, of London,
  players in, 31–2
  and censorship, 42
  theatres in, 32, 33, 123
  and riots, 39
Sultan and the Duke of ——, The, 57
Summer's Last Will and Testament, 85
  comments in, on style, 116
Sundays, regulation of plays on, 31, 32, 33, 38
  and bribery, 37
Supposes, 58
suspension gear,
  in Globe plays, 192–3
  in Second Blackfriars plays, 225, 226
  at Swan and Second Blackfriars, 232
Sussex, 3rd Earl of (Thomas Radcliffe), Pl. 2
  appointed Lord Chamberlain, 4, 21
  company of actors of, *see* Earl of Sussex's Men
  death of, 14, 23, 24
  and Earl of Leicester, 11
  and Office of the Revels, 21, 22
  in Privy Council, 19
  and statutes against retainers, 10
Sussex, 4th Earl of, players of, at court, 26
Swan (playhouse), 122, 136–74, Pl. 11
  A Chaste Maid in Cheapside at, 172–4
  capacity of, 143
  De Witt's drawing of, 146–8
  design of, influences on, 132
    evidence for, 134–5
  dimensions of, 144
  entrances in, 158–64
  and First Globe, 176
  galleries in, 155–6
  gentlemen's rooms at, 154
  ground plan of, 141–4
  horizontal dimensions of, 148–9
  pictures of, 136–40, 141
  roof of, 150
  rooms at, 154
  shape of, 137–48

Swan (playhouse) – *Contd.*
  stage area of, 165, 228
  stage superstructure in, 170-2
  stairs in, 157, 158, 162, 163
  tiring-house in, 164-70, 172-3, 207, 209,
    228-9, 232-4
Swift, Jonathan, and Jonson, 336

Tamar Cam (*1 & 2 Tamar Cam*), 62, 63,
    64, 77, 78, 79,
1 Tamburlaine, 64, 73, 74, 79, 84, 88, 101
2 Tamburlaine, 64, 69, 70, 71, 72, 74, 74,
    84, 88, 257
Tamburlaine (*1 & 2 Tamburlaine*), 60, 64,
    67, 68, 69, 71, 72, 250-7, 263-4
  and Alleyn, 103
  and *Henriad*, 287
  and 'killing the king', 265
  other world in, 247
  popularity of, 102
Taming of a Shrew, The, 65, 69, 80, 90
Taming of the Shrew, The, 310-11
  comments in, on acting, 115
Tancred and Gismund, 60
Tanner of Denmark, The, 62
Tarlton, Richard, 100-1, 241, Pl. 7
  and Armin, 107
*Tartarian Crippell Emperor of Constanti-
    nople, The*, 85
Tasso's Melancholy, 67, 68, 69, 70, 71, 72
Tears of Peace, The, 387
Telomo, 58
Tempest, The, 92, 93, 446, 457, 465-74
  and Jonson, 457, 458
  'other world' in, 247
Tents, Office of the, *see* Office of the
    Tents
Terence, 301
Tethys' Festival, 91, 92
That will be shall be, 80, 81, 82, 83
Theatre (playhouse), 33, 122, 228
  design of, 131-2
  petition for demolishing of, 39-40
  stage superstructure at, 171
  stair-tower at, 160
theatrical activity, upsurges in, 241-2
Thebais, 57
Thomas Lord Cromwell, 86, 94
  discovery in, 185, 187
  at First Globe, 181
Three Ladies of London, The, 58, 63

*Three Lords and Three Ladies of London,
    The*, 60
Three Plays in One, 58
Three Sisters of Mantua, The, 56
Thyestes, 57
Tide Tarrieth No Man, The, 55, 242
Tilney, Sir Edmund,
  bribery of, by Henslowe, 37-8
  censorship by, 42-3
    of *Sir Thomas More*, 45-6
  and City of London, 36-7
  control of acting standards by, 23
  death of, 27
  intercession of Archbishop of Canter-
    bury with, 37
  powers of, 21-2, 23, 24, 38, 43
  receives royal patent as Master of the
    Revels, 21
  suggested bribery of, by City, 36, 37
Time's Triumph and Fortune, 81
Timon of Athens,
  action above in, 190
  and *Coriolanus*, 434-6
  doors required in, 182
  at First Globe, 182
  no discovery in, 182, 183
Tinker of Totnes, The, 79
tiring-house,
  in booth stage, 125
  doors in, 228-9
  evidence for, 133-5
  of First Globe, 181, 195-6, 228-9
  in halls, 129, 130
  permanent, 131
  in private playhouses, 132, 228
  of Second Blackfriars, 207-9, 228
  of Swan, 147, 164-70, 172-3, 207, 228-9
Titus Andronicus, 65, 69, 86, 92, 266,
    354-60, Pl. 9a
  plot of, 354-60
  and *Tamburlaine*, 358-9
Titus and Vespasian, 61, 62, 63, 64
Toils, Office of the, *see* Office of the Toils
Toolie, 55
Tourneur, Cyril, 391-4
  life of, 391
  and *The Revenger's Tragedy*, 391-4
Toy to Please Chaste Ladies, A, 74, 75, 76,
    77, 78, 79
*Tragedie of Ninus and Semiramis, the First
    Monarchs of the World, The*, 75

tragedy,
  Jacobean, 384–403
  Shakespearian, 354–83, 404–33
Tragedy of Chabot, The, 387
Tragedy of Cleopatra, The, 70
Tragedy of Darius, The, 87
Tragedy of Dido, The, 70
Tragedy of the Guise, The, 64, 65
Tragedy of Mariam, The, 94
Tragedy of Phocas, The, 78, 79
Tragick Comedy of Celestina, The, 84
Transformed Metamorphosis, The, 391
trap door,
  in First Globe plays, 193–5
  in Second Blackfriars plays, 225, 226
  at Swan and Second Blackfriars, 232
Travels of the Three English Brothers, The,
    90
  Kempe in, 106
Trial of Chivalry, The, 88
Trick to Catch the Olde One, A, 91
Troas, 57
Troilus and Cressida, 91, 361, 364–5, 366–7,
    369–71
  Armin in, 107
  discovery in, 185
  doors required in, 182
  at First Globe, 181
  hierarchical concept in, 263
  and the major Shakespearian tragedies,
    404
  music station in, 190
  and satire, 391
Troublesome Reign of King John, The, 60,
    92, 264
Troy, 78, 79
True historye of George Scanderbarge, The,
    86
*True Tragedy of Richard Duke of York,
    The*, 75, 86
True Tragedy of Richard the Third, The, 69
*True Tragicall Histories of Kinge Rufus the
    First with the Life and Death of
    Belyn Dun, The*, 75
Turk, The, 92
Twelfth Night, 320–5
  doors required in, 182
  at First Globe, 181
  no discovery in, 182
Twins' Tragedy, The, 93
Two Angry Women of Abingdon, The, 85

Two Gentlemen of Verona, The, 100, 266,
    310
Two Lamentable Tragedies, 86
Two Maids of Moreclacke, The, 91, 107
Two Noble Kinsmen, The, 134

Ulysses Redux, 60
University Wits, 302–4
Upper Frater, 197–205
  appearance of, 198–201
  conversion of, by Burbage, 204
  dimensions of, 201–3
  purchase of, by Burbage, 203–4
  stairs at, 205–6
ur-Hamlet, 65, 258
Uther Pendragon, 82, 83

vagabonds, statutes against, 9
Van Buchell, 158, 160, 161
Venetian Comedy, The, 67, 68, 69, 71, 72
Vertumnus sive Annus Recurrens, 88
Vice-Chamberlain, 18
  office of, 23
Virtuous Octavia, The, 84
Vision of the Twelve Goddesses, The, 87
Vives, Juan Luis, 245
Volpone, 90, 244, 326–7, 328, 338–43
  act divisions in, 191
  action above in, 189
  discovery in, 185, 187
  at First Globe, 182
  'other world' in, 247
Vortigern, 79, 80, 81

Walsingham, Sir Francis, founds Queen's
    Men, 99
Warlamchester, 69, 72, 73
Warning for Fair Women, A, 84
Wars of Cyrus, The, 70
Warwick, Earl of (Ambrose Dudley), 12
  company of, at court, 50, 51
  in Privy Council, 19
  writes to Lord Mayor, 30–1
Weakest Goeth to the Wall, The, 85
Webster, John, 99, 110
  and acting styles, 115
  plays of, 394–403
Welshman, The, 75
Westcott, Sebastian, 132
Westminster School, boys' group from, at
    court, 50

Westward Ho, 89
   in repertoire of Paul's Boys, 110
What Mischief Worketh in the Mind of Man, 56
What You Will, 90
When You See Me You Know Me, 88, 94
White Devil, The, 93, 395, 396
   failure of at Red Bull, 99
   and satire, 391
Whitefriars, liberty of, 33
   boys' acting group from, at court, 51
   Children of the Revels at, 111
   playhouse at, 94, 122, 228
Widows' Tears, The, 93, 94
   discoveries in, 220–1
   at Second Blackfriars, 217
   suspension gear in, 225
Wiley Beguiled, 89
Wilson, Robert, 24, 101
Winter's Tale, The, 92, 93, 413, 446–55
   and Jonson, 457
   plot of, 447
   and *The Tempest*, 469
Wisdom of Doctor Dodypoll, The, 85
Wiseman of Westchester, The, 69, 70, 71, 72, 73, 74, 75, 76, 77, 78, 79, 83

   and Admiral's Men, 102
Wit of a Woman, The, 87
Witch of Islington, The, 83
Woman Hard to Please, A, 81, 82
Woman-Hater, The, 90
Woman Killed with Kindness, A, 90, 115
Woman in the Moon, The, 84
Woman is a Weathercock, A, 93
Woman will have her Will, A, 86
Whore of Babylon, The, 89
Worcester, Earl of, company of (Queen Anne's Men), 108–9
Worksop Manor, Pl. 17b
Wonder of a Woman, A, 74, 75, 76, 77
Wounds of Civil War, The, 69, 264
William the Conqueror, 64

York, Duke of, company of, at court, 51
Yorkshire Tragedy, A, 91
   at First Globe, 182
   no discovery in, 182, 183
Your Five Gallants, 90
   discovery avoided in, 218
   at Second Blackfriars, 218

Zenobia, 61